CORBA 3

CORBA 3

Reaz Hoque

IDG Books Worldwide, Inc.
An International Data Group Company

Foster City, CA ◆ Chicago, IL ◆ Indianapolis, IN ◆ New York, NY

CORBA 3 Developer's Guide

Published by
IDG Books Worldwide, Inc.
An International Data Group Company
919 E. Hillsdale Blvd., Suite 400
Foster City, CA 94404
www.idgbooks.com **(IDG Books Worldwide Web site)**

Library of Congress Catalog Card No.: 98-070261

ISBN: 0-7645-3200-6

Printed in the United States of America

10 9 8 7 6 5 4 3 2 1

1B/RT/QV/ZY/FC

Distributed in the United States by IDG Books Worldwide, Inc.

Distributed by Macmillan Canada for Canada; by Transworld Publishers Limited in the United Kingdom; by IDG Norge Books for Norway; by IDG Sweden Books for Sweden; by Woodslane Pty. Ltd. for Australia; by Woodslane (NZ) Ltd. for New Zealand; by Addison Wesley Longman Singapore Pte Ltd. for Singapore, Malaysia, Thailand, Indonesia, and Korea; by Norma Comunicaciones S.A. for Colombia; by Intersoft for South Africa; by International Thomson Publishing for Germany, Austria, and Switzerland; by Toppan Company Ltd. for Japan; by Distribuidora Cuspide for Argentina; by Livraria Cultura for Brazil; by Ediciencia S.A. for Ecuador; by Ediciones ZETA S.C.R. Ltda. for Peru; by WS Computer Publishing Corporation, Inc., for the Philippines; by Unalis Corporation for Taiwan; by Contemporanea de Ediciones for Venezuela; by Computer Book & Magazine Store for Puerto Rico; by Express Computer Distributors for the Caribbean and West Indies. Authorized Sales Agent: Anthony Rudkin Associates for the Middle East and North Africa.

For general information on IDG Books Worldwide's books in the U.S., please call our Consumer Customer Service department at 800-762-2974. For reseller information, including discounts and premium sales, please call our Reseller Customer Service department at 800-434-3422.

For information on where to purchase IDG Books Worldwide's books outside the U.S., please contact our International Sales department at 650-655-3200 or fax 650-655-3297.

For information on foreign language translations, please contact our Foreign & Subsidiary Rights department at 650-655-3021 or fax 650-655-3281.

For sales inquiries and special prices for bulk quantities, please contact our Sales department at 650-655-3200 or write to the address above.

For information on using IDG Books Worldwide's books in the classroom or for ordering examination copies, please contact our Educational Sales department at 800-434-2086.

For press review copies, author interviews, or other publicity information, please contact our Public Relations department at 650-655-3000 or fax 650-655-3299.

For authorization to photocopy items for corporate, personal, or educational use, please contact Copyright Clearance Center, 222 Rosewood Drive, Danvers, MA 01923, or fax 978-750-4470.

is a trademark under exclusive license to IDG Books Worldwide, Inc., from International Data Group, Inc.

ABOUT IDG BOOKS WORLDWIDE

Welcome to the world of IDG Books Worldwide.

IDG Books Worldwide, Inc., is a subsidiary of International Data Group, the world's largest publisher of computer-related information and the leading global provider of information services on information technology. IDG was founded more than 25 years ago and now employs more than 8,500 people worldwide. IDG publishes more than 275 computer publications in over 75 countries (see listing below). More than 60 million people read one or more IDG publications each month.

Launched in 1990, IDG Books Worldwide is today the #1 publisher of best-selling computer books in the United States. We are proud to have received eight awards from the Computer Press Association in recognition of editorial excellence and three from *Computer Currents'* First Annual Readers' Choice Awards. Our best-selling *...For Dummies®* series has more than 30 million copies in print with translations in 30 languages. IDG Books Worldwide, through a joint venture with IDG's Hi-Tech Beijing, became the first U.S. publisher to publish a computer book in the People's Republic of China. In record time, IDG Books Worldwide has become the first choice for millions of readers around the world who want to learn how to better manage their businesses.

Our mission is simple: Every one of our books is designed to bring extra value and skill-building instructions to the reader. Our books are written by experts who understand and care about our readers. The knowledge base of our editorial staff comes from years of experience in publishing, education, and journalism — experience we use to produce books for the '90s. In short, we care about books, so we attract the best people. We devote special attention to details such as audience, interior design, use of icons, and illustrations. And because we use an efficient process of authoring, editing, and desktop publishing our books electronically, we can spend more time ensuring superior content and spend less time on the technicalities of making books.

You can count on our commitment to deliver high-quality books at competitive prices on topics you want to read about. At IDG Books Worldwide, we continue in the IDG tradition of delivering quality for more than 25 years. You'll find no better book on a subject than one from IDG Books Worldwide.

John Kilcullen
CEO
IDG Books Worldwide, Inc.

Steven Berkowitz
President and Publisher
IDG Books Worldwide, Inc.

Eighth Annual Computer Press Awards ≥1992

Ninth Annual Computer Press Awards ≥1993

Tenth Annual Computer Press Awards ≥1994

Eleventh Annual Computer Press Awards ≥1995

IDG Books Worldwide, Inc., is a subsidiary of International Data Group, the world's largest publisher of computer-related information and the leading global provider of information services on information technology. International Data Group publishes over 275 computer publications in over 75 countries. Sixty million people read one or more International Data Group publications each month. International Data Group's publications include: **ARGENTINA:** Buyer's Guide, Computerworld Argentina, PC World Argentina; **AUSTRALIA:** Australian Macworld, Australian PC World, Australian Reseller News, Computerworld, IT Casebook, Network World, Publish, Webmaster; **AUSTRIA:** Computerwelt Osterreich, Networks Austria, PC Tip Austria; **BANGLADESH:** PC World Bangladesh; **BELARUS:** PC World Belarus; **BELGIUM:** Data News; **BRAZIL:** Annuário de Informática, Computerworld, Connections, Macworld, PC Player, PC World, Publish, Reseller News, Supergamepower; **BULGARIA:** Computerworld Bulgaria, Network World Bulgaria, PC & MacWorld Bulgaria; **CANADA:** CIO Canada, Client/Server World, ComputerWorld Canada, InfoWorld Canada, NetworkWorld Canada, WebWorld; **CHILE:** Computerworld Chile, PC World Chile; **COLOMBIA:** Computerworld Colombia, PC World Colombia; **COSTA RICA:** PC World Centro America; **THE CZECH AND SLOVAK REPUBLICS:** Computerworld Czechoslovakia, Macworld Czech Republic, PC World Czechoslovakia; **DENMARK:** Communications World Danmark, Computerworld Danmark, Macworld Danmark, PC World Danmark, Techworld Denmark; **DOMINICAN REPUBLIC:** PC World Republica Dominicana; **ECUADOR:** PC World Ecuador; **EGYPT:** Computerworld Middle East, PC World Middle East; **EL SALVADOR:** PC World Centro America; **FINLAND:** MikroPC, Tietoverkko, Tietoviikko; **FRANCE:** Distributique, Hebdo, Info PC, Le Monde Informatique, Macworld, Reseaux & Telecoms, WebMaster France; **GERMANY:** Computer Partner, Computerwoche, Computerwoche Extra, Computerwoche FOCUS, Global Online, Macwelt, PC Welt; **GREECE:** Amiga Computing, GamePro Greece, Multimedia World; **GUATEMALA:** PC World Centro America; **HONDURAS:** PC World Centro America; **HONG KONG:** Computerworld Hong Kong, PC World Hong Kong, Publish in Asia; **HUNGARY:** ABCD CD-ROM, Computerworld Szamitastechnika, Internetto online Magazine, PC World Hungary, PC-X Magazin Hungary; **ICELAND:** Tolvuheimur PC World Island; **INDIA:** Information Communications World, Information Systems Computerworld, PC World India, Publish in Asia; **INDONESIA:** InfoKomputer PC World, Komputek Computerworld, Publish in Asia; **IRELAND:** ComputerScope, PC Live!; **ISRAEL:** Macworld Israel, People & Computers/Computerworld; **ITALY:** Computerworld Italia, Macworld Italia, Networking Italia, PC World Italia; **JAPAN:** DTP World, Macworld Japan, Nikkei Personal Computing, OS/2 World Japan, SunWorld Japan, Windows NT World, Windows World Japan; **KENYA:** PC World East African; **KOREA:** Hi-Tech Information, Macworld Korea, PC World Korea; **MACEDONIA:** PC World Macedonia; **MALAYSIA:** Computerworld Malaysia, PC World Malaysia, Publish in Asia; **MALTA:** PC World Malta; **MEXICO:** Computerworld Mexico, PC World Mexico; **MYANMAR:** PC World Myanmar; **NETHERLANDS:** Computer! Totaal, LAN Internetworking Magazine, LAN World Buyers Guide, Macworld Netherlands, Net, WebWereld; **NEW ZEALAND:** Absolute Beginners Guide and Plain & Simple Series, Computer Buyer, Computer Industry Directory, Computerworld New Zealand, MTB, Network World, PC World New Zealand; **NICARAGUA:** PC World Centro America; **NORWAY:** Computerworld Norge, CW Rapport, Datamagasinet, Financial Rapport, Kursguide Norge, Macworld Norge, Multimediaworld Norge, PC World Ekspress Norge, PC World Nettverk, PC World Norge, PC World ProduktGuide Norge; **PAKISTAN:** Computerworld Pakistan; **PANAMA:** PC World Panama; **PEOPLE'S REPUBLIC OF CHINA:** China Computer Users, China Computerworld, China InfoWorld, China Telecom World Weekly, Computer & Communication, Electronic Design China, Electronics Today, Electronics Weekly, Game Software, PC World China, Popular Computer Week, Software Weekly, Software World, Telecom World; **PERU:** Computerworld Peru, PC World Profesional Peru, PC World SoHo Peru; **PHILIPPINES:** Click!, Computerworld Philippines, PC World Philippines, Publish in Asia; **POLAND:** Computerworld Poland, Computerworld Special Report Poland, Cyber, Macworld Poland, Networld Poland, PC World Komputer; **PORTUGAL:** Cerebro/PC World, Computerworld/Correio Informático, Dealer World Portugal, Mac*In/PC*In Portugal, Multimedia World; **PUERTO RICO:** PC World Puerto Rico; **ROMANIA:** Computerworld Romania, PC World Romania, Telecom Romania; **RUSSIA:** Computerworld Russia, Mir PK, Publish, Seti; **SINGAPORE:** Computerworld Singapore, PC World Singapore, Publish in Asia; **SLOVENIA:** Monitor; **SOUTH AFRICA:** Computing SA, Network World SA, Software World SA; **SPAIN:** Communicaciones World España, Computerworld España, Dealer World España, Macworld España, PC World España; **SRI LANKA:** Infolink PC World; **SWEDEN:** CAP&Design, Computer Sweden, Corporate Computing Sweden, Internetworld Sweden, it.branschen, Macworld Sweden, MaxiData Sweden, MikroDatorn, Nätverk & Kommunikation, PC World Sweden, PCaktiv, Windows World Sweden; **SWITZERLAND:** Computerworld Schweiz, Macworld Schweiz, PCtip; **TAIWAN:** Computerworld Taiwan, Macworld Taiwan, NEW ViSiON/Publish, PC World Taiwan, Windows World Taiwan; **THAILAND:** Publish in Asia, Thai Computerworld; **TURKEY:** Computerworld Turkiye, Macworld Turkiye, Network World Turkiye, PC World Turkiye; **UKRAINE:** Computerworld Kiev, Multimedia World Ukraine, PC World Ukraine; **UNITED KINGDOM:** Acorn User UK, Amiga Action UK, Amiga Computing UK, Apple Talk UK, Computing, Macworld, Parents and Computers UK, PC Advisor, PC Home, PSX Pro, The WEB; **UNITED STATES:** Cable in the Classroom, CIO Magazine, Computerworld, DOS World, Federal Computer Week, GamePro Magazine, InfoWorld, I-Way, Macworld, Network World, PC Games, PC World, Publish, Video Event, THE WEB Magazine, and WebMaster; online webzines: JavaWorld, NetscapeWorld, and SunWorld Online; **URUGUAY:** InfoWorld Uruguay; **VENEZUELA:** Computerworld Venezuela, PC World Venezuela; and **VIETNAM:** PC World Vietnam.
3/24/97

Credits

ACQUISITIONS EDITOR
John Osborn

DEVELOPMENT EDITORS
Jeff Cogswell
Barbra Guerra

TECHNICAL EDITOR
Jeff Cogswell

COPY EDITOR
Marcia Baker

PROJECT COORDINATOR
Tom Debolski

BOOK DESIGNER
Jim Donohue

COVER DESIGN
© mike parsons design

GRAPHICS AND
PRODUCTION SPECIALISTS
Renee Dunn
Stephanie Hollier
Jude Levinson
Dina Quan

QUALITY CONTROL SPECIALISTS
Mick Arellano
Mark Schumann

GRAPHICS TECHNICIANS
Linda Marousek
Hector Mendoza

ILLUSTRATOR
Jesse Coleman

PROOFREADER
Arielle Carole Mennelle

INDEXER
Rebecca Plunkett

Cover image was created with support to Space Telescope Science Institute, operated by the Association of Universities for Research in Astronomy, Inc., from NASA contract NAS5-26555 and is reproduced here with permission from AURA/STScl.

About the Author

Reaz Hoque is an author, lecturer, and software developer who works closely with Netscape Communications Corporation. He contributes Web-related articles for online and print magazines around the world. Some of Reaz's articles have appeared in *Netscape DevEdge Site, Developer.com, ZD Internet Magazine, Web Techniques, Internet World,* and *NetscapeWorld*. His previous books include *Practical JavaScript Programming, Programming Web Components,* and *JavaBeans 1.1 Handbook*. Reaz recently spoke at Netscape's DevCon, Software Development, Web Design, and Object Expo.

About the Contributing Authors

Vishal Anand is a software engineer and object-oriented design consultant who specializes in NT and C++ programming. He maintains a developer's forum on the Internet where he answers questions on C++, MFC/SDK, and NT-related issues. Anand studied both engineering and computer science at Delhi Institute of Technology. He enjoys reading humor and going for long drives with his wife.

Ken Cartwright is a software engineer with a master's degree in software systems engineering from George Mason University. He has been developing complex software systems for many years and has spent the past four years developing object-oriented distributed systems using CORBA in combination with object-oriented databases, 3D graphics, C++, and, most recently, Java.

Sukanta Ganguly has been in the computing profession for the past eight years. He has been involved with distributed computing for the past three years. Ganguly's passions are compilers, interpreters, and programming languages. He has spent long hours studying the different types of distributed development environments and platforms. Ganguly also has a strong interest in operating systems and databases. He is lucky enough to have a supportive wife and the blessings of his parents.

James Grady is a software engineer for MRJ Technology Solutions, a high-tech engineering and software development firm in Virginia. Grady graduated with a bachelor of science degree in mathematics from the College of William and Mary; he has spent most of his career working on war-game simulation software. Grady has developed object-oriented simulation software for more than seven years, with more recent emphasis on C++, MFC, and CORBA. He is currently leading an effort to integrate an existing CORBA-based application with the newest Web technologies. Grady would like to thank Victor Lena and MRJ Technology Solutions for their support, and Lori Causa for her constant help throughout this project. His work on this book is dedicated to Thomas and Robin Grady.

John Kohler is a systems architect at MRJ Technology Solutions. He has a bachelor of science degree in electrical engineering from Drexel University and has spent several years in graduate school studying laser physics. Kohler has more than ten years experience in simulation software development and systems/network administration. He has written simulation systems ranging from modeling laser cavities to networks to war-game systems. Kohler has spent the past four years designing and developing distributed object-oriented systems. He is fluent in C/C++, lex, yacc, perl, and (sigh) even Fortran. Kohler is currently leading a team in the design and development of a distributed object-oriented simulation support tool using CORBA, MFC, and an embedded GIS. John thanks his wife, Valerie, for her love and support, and their son, Devon, for the smiles only he can bring.

First I would like to dedicate this book to my mother for loving me and believing in me. She is an unbelievable mother and has made countless sacrifices to make her family happy. I also dedicate this book to Vishal Anand, Ken Cartwright, Sukanta Ganguly, James Grady, John Kohler, Jeff Cogswell, and David Huntley, some of the most dedicated and talented people in the industry.

Preface

If you are an enterprise developer, you may have already heard the buzz word CORBA: Common Object Request Broker Architecture. This technology has been creating a lot of noise in the industry lately, which may be why you are holding this book. Regardless of whether you are a Web developer or a client-server programmer, a network is where your applications must run today. These applications are not concerned with which computer you are using, where the other pieces of the applications exist, or in what languages the pieces of applications are created. This is where CORBA plays a big role. CORBA distributes applications over the network, regardless of the language and platform.

CORBA is not new. CORBA has been around for a while, but today this technology is ready for mission-critical applications. This is why the noise about CORBA is louder than ever. But is CORBA only a dream? Is it just a theory? Many books present CORBA vaguely, but never show you what can actually be done with it. But this is an application-based book. Not only do you learn what CORBA is all about, you also get hands-on techniques on how to create both Web applications and client-server applications using this technology. This book shows you exactly what you need to service this ever-changing software industry. Hop in — you may enjoy the ride!

What to Expect from This Book

The book is divided into four parts.

In Part I, we discuss the fundamentals of CORBA. We cover CORBA services, interface design, and IDL. The chapters in this part have considerable architectural and programming basics so developers can get ready for the next two parts of the book. The chapters in Part I appeal to those of you who don't have much time, but who want to learn enough to begin.

In Part II, we show developers how to create client/server applications using CORBA. We developed examples readers can reuse on a regular basis. These tutorial-based chapters show developers how to tackle dynamic invocation, multi-threading, interface repository, and so forth. Each chapter explains how to develop the architecture (road map) of the application, write essential code, and, finally, how to put together the whole application.

In Part III, we show how to use CORBA to create Web applications. Here, we discuss the architecture involved in creating Web applications with CORBA. Then we give examples of Java and ODBMS working with CORBA.

In Part IV, we cover the future of CORBA or, more specifically, CORBA 3.0.

Who Should Read This Book?

This book is not for everyone. It requires prior knowledge of object orientation, C++, or Java. If you are unfamiliar with these technologies, pick up a copy of a book on C++ or Java before you read this book. The chapter on OODBMS and CORBA requires you know something about object-oriented databases. Serious software developers will find this book most helpful.

This book is for you if you are:

◆ An Internet/intranet/extranet application developer who wants to create mission-critical cross-platform applications.

◆ Someone learning how distributed objects work.

◆ A software developer who wants to get exposed to CORBA in relation to OODBMS, Java, and threads.

◆ A student and/or researcher who wants to keep up with the cutting-edge object technology.

Icons Used in the Book

Three icons are used to get your attention throughout the text.

 To point out information so you remember it. The text accompanied by the note icon requires your full attention.

 To give you suggestions on certain topics. The tip is to make sure you can follow the suggestion easily.

 To warn you about certain issues. Make sure you take the warnings seriously. They may save you time and effort, and keep you from getting into trouble.

Acknowledgments

First, I would like to thank my publisher who has done a great job of making this book a success. I, especially thank my editors, John Osborn and Barbra Guerra, for their constant help and feedback.

David Huntley and I spent hours creating an outline that would make this book interesting. I thank David for his help on this project and wish him all the best.

Next I want to thank the team I have worked with during the long process of writing this book. Without Vishal Anand, Ken Cartwright, Sukanta Ganguly, James Grady, and John Kohler providing their help, this book would not have been possible. They put hours into listening to all my ideas — and complaints — and offered endless support. I really can't express how grateful I am for their help.

Thank you also to Jeff Cogswell for providing an expert technical review of the book and for taking this project so seriously.

I would like to extend my thanks to those who gave me permission to include software on the CD-ROM. Sheila Richardson, Bill Reichle, and Terry McElroy at IBM were a great help. Thanks to Sarah Lima at IONA Technologies for helping me get the OrbixWeb and Orbix 2 software.

Thanks to my family and friends who were my constant support. My parents, Faisal Hoque and his wife Christine will always have a special place in my heart. Thanks to my friend Tarun Shamra for his sincere help and encouragement. Also thanks to Pieter R. Humphrey and Terrence Curley for helping me with the CD-ROM.

I know I am a very lucky person to be able to do all the things I am doing today. I do understand they are happening because of God's mercy, and I offer thanks for all the good things that have been happening in my life lately.

Contents at a Glance

Contents

Appendixes

Part I

CORBA Essentials

Chapter 1

Distributed Objects and CORBA

IN THIS CHAPTER

If builders build buildings the way programmers write programs, the first wood-pecker will destroy this civilization. – Anonymous

- ◆ What are distributed objects?

- ◆ Web and distributed objects

- ◆ What is CORBA? How CORBA fits in distributed objects technology

- ◆ Advantages of CORBA

- ◆ Limitations of CORBA

- ◆ General applications in CORBA

- ◆ Web-based applications in CORBA

- ◆ CORBA security

- ◆ Competing frameworks

- ◆ CORBA development tools

OBJECT–ORIENTED TECHNOLOGY has finally affected the way our software industry works and is seen by many as an antidote to its evils. Advocates have been promising us code reusability and higher levels of software productivity for the past 20 years. Now, it seems, objects are mainstream with an impact that is both immense and far-reaching. End users of computer systems and computer-based systems are beginning to notice the effects of object-oriented technology in the form of increasingly easy-to-use software applications and operating systems and in more flexible services provided by such industries as banking, telecommunications, and cable television. For the software engineer, object-oriented technology has led to object-oriented programming languages, object-oriented development methodologies, management of object-oriented projects, object-oriented computer hardware, and object-oriented computer-aided software engineering, among others.

Because an object encapsulates data, as well as business logic, it is extremely well-suited for creating flexible systems. Distributed Object technology allows these objects to be located anywhere within the distributed system. Objects themselves being sufficiently independent would enable the end users to plug in different objects and to try customized solutions according to their needs. The user then needn't *compile* again just because he or she added a new component.

The coming generations of systems inevitably will be built using distributed objects. With a proper technology to hold these objects together, the industry is poised for another revolution. This chapter takes you through various technologies available in the market now and describes how CORBA is going to help you sail successfully across this transition from current systems to distributed systems.

What Are Distributed Objects?

If you are familiar with object-oriented concepts, the following approach may seem a little unusual. For those who are unfamiliar with object-oriented concepts, you might refer to the appendix periodically, which contains a list of object-oriented definitions.

An *object* is an abstract entity that understands and executes a well-defined set of commands. These commands are called the *methods* of the object.

Objects can interact by sending messages to one another. Such a *message* is a request to execute a certain method of an object. To emphasize object independence, one often speaks of objects as communicating by message passing. When a message is sent to an object, the corresponding method is looked up, executed, and possibly the result is returned. This result is typically again an object. Thus, the methods of an object implement its behavior (they describe how the object will respond to the messages sent to it).

An object is an independent, self-contained entity. It contains attributes and operations and it shows a characteristic behavior. A class describes objects with similar properties. The objects in the class called *instances* provide the same attributes and share the same properties.

A *distributed computing system* can be defined as a system of multiple autonomous processors that do not share the primary memory, but that cooperate by sending messages over a communication network. This definition captures the behavior of physically separated components and logically autonomous modules communicating via messages.

A distributed system can also be defined as a system whose components have encapsulation boundaries that are opaque in both directions. That is, both client access to component resources and component access to client resources are inaccessible except through messages mediated by component interface.

Object-Oriented Definitions

Object: An abstraction of a real world entity.
Class: A set of collection of objects having common features.

Feature: A routine, activity, or attribute serving as part of the definition of an object or class.

Method: A feature performing an operation on an object.

Instance variable: An attribute feature of an object.

Execution-time creation: The dynamic or runtime creation of an object or instance of class.

Message: A protocol composed of a method or routine and an object reference or address.

Object-Oriented Development: Construction of an object-oriented system from its requirements by object-oriented analysis, design, and programming.

Object-Oriented Language: A well-defined notation that supports object-oriented properties and specifications of an object-oriented system.

Object-Oriented Programming: An object-oriented development method that leads to a software system based on the objects every system/subsystem manipulates, rather than the function it is meant to ensure.

Object-Oriented Properties

Information hiding: Separation of representation details of an object, class, or system from its application development details.
Abstraction: Separation of unnecessary details from systems requirements or specification to reduce complexities of understanding requirements or specification.

Dynamic binding: Instantiation of an identifier or variable, defined by use of an object-oriented language, with an object during the execution of the system.

Inheritance: A relationship between two classes of objects, such that one of the classes, the child, takes on all relevant features of the other class, the parent.

These components are called *distributed objects*. The primary difference between a normal C++ or a Smalltalk object and distributed objects is a traditional C++ or a Smalltalk object does what you want it to do, but in its traditional compiled language or address-space boundaries. In contrast, distributed objects are packaged as binary components accessible to remote clients by means of method invocations. In other words, when a distributed object is invoked, the object's code is executed in another address space or on another computer altogether. The distributed objects can exist anywhere on the network. Because these objects are executing on a separate computer or address space and a communications system is standing between them, the language and the compiler used to create distributed objects can be anything and are totally transparent to their clients. Clients needn't know where the distributed object resides or on what operating system it executes. It can be on the same machine or on a machine that sits across a network in another country. All they want is its name and the interface it publishes.

As the name implies, distributed objects encompass two paradigms: the notion of distribution and the notion of object orientation. These two concepts converge in what is referred to as middleware. *Middleware* can be called a region that is somewhat in-between clients and servers where a great deal of time and effort is often spent in developing applications. Middleware is a communication software that makes sure when an object on one system sends a message to an object in another system, the message actually gets there and causes a method in the other object (called the *remote object)* to execute. Middleware is to distributed objects as the telephone company is to telephones.

Moreover, as these systems have had to share data and exchange information, an entanglement of messages has evolved exacting a high cost to develop and an even higher cost to maintain. To make matters worse, mixtures of middleware ranging from sockets to RPCs to proprietary implementations are used to foster communications. The convoluted solution induced by such middleware often dwarfs the complexity of the business problem domain itself. Complex messaging among *stove-pipe systems* or *islands of automation* contradicts requirements for increased flexibility and extensibility in information systems. Businesses, which are finding themselves under increasing competitive pressure to introduce new services and to integrate with other information systems quickly and economically, are looking to Distributed Object Systems for the solution. In a properly designed Distributed Object System, enterprises have the capability to access any information by any system (or user) that has proper authorization and to do so in a uniform and consistent fashion. In an admittedly oversimplified decomposition, two things are required to do this. The first is to make everything (including legacy systems) appear object oriented and the second is to be able to access those objects across systems boundaries.

The distributed object infrastructure must make it easier for components to be more autonomous, self-managing, and collaborative. This undertaking is much more ambitious than anything attempted by competing forms of client/server middleware. The ultimate thing in a client/server components business is super-smart components that do more than just interoperate – they collaborate at the semantic level to get a job done. The catch is to get components, which have no previous knowledge of one another, to do the same. To get to this point, we need standards that set the rules of engagement for different component interaction boundaries.

Unfortunately, different companies have developed different rules. Such a lack of standards has resulted in many players with their respective technologies.

ActiveX, JavaBeans, Component Object Model (COM), Distributed Component Object Model (DCOM), Common Object Request Broker Architecture (CORBA), Internet Inter ORB Protocol (IIOP), Remote Method Invocation (RMI), and OpenDoc to name a few. They all have interfaces, which are not always compatible with one another, making Inter-Operability more difficult.

The Web and Distributed Objects

The Web was initially thought of as a two-tier system in which the client had a browser and the server stored data the client would see on his or her browser. But as more and more client interaction became important and the content became dynamic, the need for a middle tier became evident. The Web's original middle tier was made up of applications, which use Common Gateway Interface (CGI). CGI enabled Web-developers to extend a Web server to access nearly any OS-level function, using development environments as simple as a shell script and as complex as C++. Also, because CGI is portable, applications developed for an Apache server could usually run against Netscape or Microsoft servers with little or no porting. CGI programs were the first pieces of Web componentware. The most common visible application of CGI programs was forms, which can still be seen in many sites when browsing the Web. Figure 1-1 shows the relationship of the Web to distributed objects.

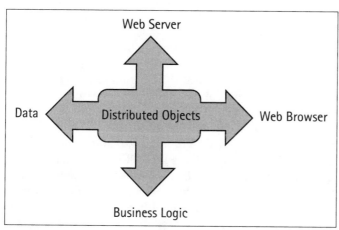

Figure 1-1: Web and Distributed Objects

Now all the client needed was a universal browser and distributing the application meant clicking a hyperlink. Advantages became obvious. Many vendors, including the database vendors, began making applications based on these criteria. Across the Web, site designers were putting forms on their Web pages, allowing for a much more dynamic approach to the Web. Whereas Web pages previously were static and something to be read and viewed, now they enabled a way for the user to interact with the computer on the Internet at the other end.

But disadvantages existed, too. CGI applications were slow. Private vendors provided solutions to give access to server internals; Microsoft and Netscape came up with server specific APIs. Microsoft came up with Internet Services API (ISAPI) and Netscape came up with Netscape Server APIs (NSAPI). These enabled speedy improvements, but they were not good enough: they were incompatible with one another.

Then there was CORBA, the Object Management Group's (OMG) answer to the need for interoperability among the rapidly increasing number of hardware and software products available today. CORBA as a specification allows applications to communicate with one another no matter where they are located or who has designed them. This is a not a specific product put out by OMG, but it is a specification the others are free to implement. CORBA 1.1 was introduced in 1991 by OMG and defined the Interface Definition Language (IDL) and the Application Programming Interfaces (API) that enable client/server object interaction within a specific implementation of an Object Request Broker (ORB). ORB provides the foundation and the underlying operation for the distributed objects and their management. It provides an infrastructure that allows objects to talk to each other, independent of the specific platforms and techniques used to implement objects. CORBA 2.0, adopted in December of 1994, defines true interoperability by specifying how ORBs from different vendors can interoperate.

Microsoft came up with ActiveX controls based on the extension of their existing technology of VBXs and OCXs, now called Distributed Component Architecture Model (DCOM). The catch was the big word *Microsoft*, thus making the objects distributed in a Microsoft way. DCOM is currently available only on Microsoft Windows NT and Microsoft Windows 95. While Microsoft is working with Software AG and Digital to port DCOM to UNIX platforms, DCOM is unlikely to become as omnipresent as CORBA, because most platform vendors are investing in CORBA. Even if DCOM is available on other platforms, it is almost a given that its center of gravity will continue to be the Microsoft Windows platform.

In parallel, Sun Microsystems came up with *Java applets,* platform-independent Web components. While not in direct competition with CORBA, Java applets were made using – what else – Java language, which is a platform-independent language. Java, like COM, provides a mechanism for components to discover each other's interfaces at runtime, but they can also run on different platforms by virtue of the Java Virtual Machine. *JavaBeans,* a further extension of applets, can also run as applets outside any container application and Java Class Loaders can download any libraries a component needs along with the component. Consequently, JavaBeans needn't be registered the way ActiveX components must, which makes them suitable for building highly dynamic systems. JavaBeans score over ActiveX in the more flexible way they can interact with application builder tools.

Who Is Object Management Group?

Object Management Group (OMG) is a consortium of software vendors, software developers, and end users. OMG provides specifications for common architectural framework for object-oriented applications. Its mission is to promote theory and practice of object technology for the development of distributed computing systems.

OMG was founded in 1989 to standardize object-oriented software to create and promote component-based software implementations and standard interfaces for Distributed Object Computing. It started with eight companies: 3Com Corporation, American Airlines, Canon Inc., Data General, Hewlett-Packard, Philips Telecommunications N.V., Sun Microsystems, and Unisys Corporation. OMG now has a strong following of more than 750 members, which includes all major names in the industry. The only notable exception is Microsoft, which is promoting its own distributed technology called Distributed Component Object Model (DCOM). The need for standards was to make a heterogeneous computing environment across all major operating systems and hardware platforms. The organization's charter includes the establishment of industry guidelines and detailed object management specifications to provide a common framework for application development. Implementations of OMG's specification can now be found in almost all major operating systems. OMG is responsible for where CORBA is today and maintains and updates standard specifications like CORBA/IIOP, Object Services, Internet Facilities, and Domain Interface specifications. These specifications are used throughout the industry to develop and implement distributed applications.

OMG works with the help of its specialized task forces and special interest groups. The task forces are chartered by the one of the three OMG technology committees to solve some particular problem or problems within a specific area for recommendation to the Technology Committee. Specifically, task forces generate Requests for Information (RFIs) or Requests for Proposals (RFPs) and evaluate the responses. They generally meet when the technical committee meets every six to eight weeks. Currently, seven domain task forces and two platform task forces exist. The domain task forces include: Business Object Task Force, Electronic Commerce Domain Task Force, Financial Domain Task Force, Manufacturing Domain Task Force, CORBAmed Task Force Telecommunications Task Force, and Transportation Domain Task Force.

The domain task forces are responsible for promoting the use of the OMG object technology in their respective domains. They identify relevant standards for the specific domains. The domain task forces are also responsible for issuing and evaluating RFI and RFPs for CORBA-based technology for the relevant industry and domain. The platform technology task forces include the Object Analysis and Design Task Force and the ORB/Object Services Task Force. The Object Analysis and Design Task Force is responsible for issuing RFIs and RFPs concerning the technology adoption process for OMG-compliant OA&D methodologies and tools. They are also responsible for giving directions to the developers to enable them to develop applications using the

(continued)

Who Is Object Management Group? *(Continued)*

Object Technology. The ORB/Object Services Task Force is responsible for giving suggestions to the OMG in areas of Object Request Broker technology and general purpose Object Services.

The Special Interest Group is formed by OMG members who share a common interest in the application of object technology to a specific vertical market or technology area. They play an important part in the OMG architecture, providing important insight into how the specifications can be changed to incorporate growing demands of new technologies. Special Interest Groups meet in conjunction with the technical committee meeting, approximately once every six to eight weeks. Meetings are from one- to two-day working sessions with an agenda and a list of specific results to accomplish. After each meeting, SIG minutes and major conclusions are distributed to all OMG members. SIG subgroups may also work between meetings on specific task areas. Currently, twelve different active OMG Special Interest Groups exist: four in the Domain Technology Committee, four in the Platform Technology Committee, and four under the Architecture Board.

The Domain Special Interest Groups include:

◆ Life Sciences Research Domain Special Group, whose mission is to improve the quality and utility of software and information systems used in Life Sciences research through the use of CORBA and the Object Management Architecture (OMA).

◆ Distributed Simulation Special Interest Group, who work hard to extend the OMG standards to include distributed simulation.

◆ CORBAsig Special Interest Group, which formed to facilitate the use of geospatial information in the distributed object environment, as defined by the OMA and instantiated in CORBA and its associated services and facilities.

◆ C4I (Command, Control, Computing, Communications, and Intelligence) A special interest group that works with OMG to support the requirements of the C4 community.

The Platform Special Interest Groups include Document Management Special Interest Group, formed to examine the role and requirements of document management, Internet Special Interest Group, responsible for making OMG and Internet Architecture interoperate by promoting standards and tools and applications over Internet-based OMGs distributed technologies, and Japan Special Interest Group, and Realtime Special Interest Group, whose primary responsibility is to augment the distributed object technology with real time systems. The Architectural Board special interest groups include End User Special Interest Group, created to improve the quality of content and speed the delivery of CORBA-complaint products to end users, Security Special Interest Group, which analyzes and reports the security requirement for end users, Metrics Special Interest Group and Test Special Interest Group.

The official Web site for OMG is http://www.omg.org.

Another distributed object technology, which also will play a major part, is JavaSoft's Java RMI (Remote Method Invocation). Java RMI is part of the Java 1.1 Development Kit and is a solution for building distributed Java-only applications. Not only are the clients and (transient) servers written in the Java language, but the Java language is also used as the IDL. Note, though, Sun is promoting CORBA/IIOP as the solution for building scalable distributed enterprise applications; it leverages Java computing, as well as promoting multilanguage heterogeneous environments.

Java applications can use RMI to call methods in components on remote machines. RMI resembles COM. If all goes according to their plans, cooperation among JavaSoft, Netscape, IBM, and others will also make it possible for JavaBeans to communicate using CORBA IIOP.

In theory, COM, CORBA IIOP, and Java RMI could all be platform-neutral component standards. But the commercial reality is different. First, while CORBA and Java are available for a variety of platforms, issues with their interoperability remain to be found and ironed out. So far, Microsoft has implemented COM only for Windows platforms (although Digital, Hewlett-Packard, and Software AG are all working on ports to other OSes).

ACTIVEX   Most of you are familiar with components through COM, which underlies the ActiveX components you can deploy from C++ and Visual Basic programs, and from Microsoft Office applications. How a COM object calls methods in another COM object depends on where they are running. If they are in the same process, they can call directly into each other's code referring to the objects by pointers in the single address space. Objects running in different processes interact via proxy objects and stubs that pack and unpack the call parameters into a standard format for transmission. Communication between components running on different machines takes place via remote procedure calls (RPCs) – the core technology inside distributed COM.

In all these cases, however, the client object's method needn't know the details of how the communication is done (location transparency). Proxies and stubs provide a static link between components, but COM also enables components to discover and call new interfaces at runtime. This is the basis of ActiveX. You can assemble an application by dragging-and-dropping components that have no prior knowledge of one another onto the same form. Automation between, say, Microsoft Word and Excel works because these Office applications make their key internal functions visible to other programs as COM objects.

In an absolute ActiveX world, clients run Active Desktop (now coming with Internet Explorer 4.0 and, as Microsoft promises, it will be an integral part of newer versions of Windows NT and Windows 95), where embedded ActiveX controls can provide a UI to remote services. These components send requests via either HTTP or COM and Microsoft's Advanced Data Connector (ADC) to a middle-tier application server. There, Active Server Pages (ASPs) may employ server-side Visual Basic scripts or JavaScripts to query an SQL database via ActiveX Data Objects (ADOs). The ADOs generate dynamic HTML pages for returning the query results to the client and call server-side ActiveX components running under Microsoft Transaction Server (MTS) that perform any application processing.

The key to this picture is MTS, which will be integrated into Microsoft Internet Information Server (IIS) 4.0. MTS provides an environment for executing distributed applications built from ActiveX components communicating with one another via the COM protocols. A programmer can write a component as a single-user ActiveX DLL and simply install it into MTS, which will run it as a secure multiuser application.

MTS handles all the management of sharing, processes, and threads. It maintains pools of threads, network sessions, and database connections, automatically recycling them when they're no longer being used. All the components that make up an application can share these resource pools. Consequently, using MTS may actually improve performance compared to stand-alone execution, in both time and memory.

CORBA   Common Object Request Broker Architecture (CORBA) is a set of specifications defining the ways software objects should work together in a distributed environment. The responsible body for these specifications is OMG, described previously, which has hundreds of members representing a major portion of the software industry. The members work together in tandem to make specifications, so as to allow software objects to be developed independently and yet work together in a harmonic fashion.

The fundamental piece of CORBA is the ORB. The ORB can be viewed like a bus carrying the objects between the clients, which are the consumers of the objects, and the servers, which are the producers of the objects. The consumers are provided with object interfaces defined using a language called the Interface Definition Language. The detailed implementation of the objects by the producers is totally shielded from the consumers.

What Is CORBA and How Does It Fit in the Distributed Object Technology?

As mentioned, CORBA is a specification for distributed objects from the OMG. The specification defines a language and platform-independent object bus called an ORB, which lets objects transparently make requests to, and receive responses from, other objects located locally or remotely. It takes care of all the ugly details involved in such a system making the process transparent to the end user.

IIOP (Internet Inter-ORB Protocol) is an ORB transport protocol, defined as part of the CORBA 2.0 specification, which enables network objects from multiple CORBA-compliant ORBs to interoperate transparently over TCP/IP.

CORBA works through software engines. Whenever one object needs to call another, it sends a message to an ORB, which handles the whole transaction on its behalf. An ORB can translate between different data formats, and other attributes, making CORBA objects processor, OS, and language-independent. CORBA makes no distinction between client-side and server-side objects: They're all objects. The basic CORBA 2 ORB specification doesn't deal with issues such as concurrency, integrity, and security, all of which must be provided as separate CORBA services. For example, transactions are handled via OTMs that work alongside an ORB.

ORB can also be called an object bus that lets the objects interoperate across address spaces, networks, operating systems, and languages. This bus also allows objects to discover each other. A CORBA ORB connects the client to the object it wishes to use. The client application needn't know whether the object resides in the same computer or on a different computer across the network. For the client, the only information required is the object's name and how to use its interface. The ORB takes care of the details of locating the object, routing the request, and returning the result. This architecture is demonstrated in Figure 1-2.

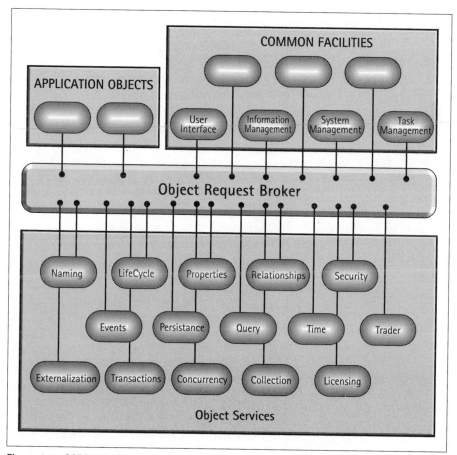

Figure 1-2: CORBA Architecture

CORBA fits the component-based and Internet-based approaches to building and using software. It defines a way to divide application logic over objects distributed over the network. CORBA also defines a way for these objects to communicate with one another and to use each other's services. It also manages how objects identify themselves, find others, learn about network events, handle object-to-object transactions, and maintain the object security. The primary services include:

Naming Service: This helps CORBA clients in locating a named CORBA object. Every CORBA object has its unique name.

Event Service: CORBA is synchronous by nature. The Event Service provides an asynchronous messaging layer to complement the synchronous nature of CORBA communications. There are event channels where the publishers and subscribers connect. The publisher sends messages to the event channel and the subscriber gets these messages asynchronously.

Transaction Service. This service is responsible for defining the transaction between objects.

Security Service: It provides security functions like encryption, authentication and authorization, controls user access to objects, and protects data in objects.

Various other services exist, which include persistence, lifecycle, query, time, collections, and so forth, which help objects communicate in the distributed system.

Advantages of CORBA

CORBA has several primary benefits over DCOM, OpenDoc, and OLE/COM, including language-, vendor-, and operating-system independence. CORBA ORBs are available on every major operating system in use today (including more Microsoft operating systems than DCOM itself!). CORBA ORBs also exist to bind to a wide variety of languages including C++, Ada, COBOL, Smalltalk, and Java. Using IIOP (Internet Inter-ORB Protocol), a CORBA ORB developed by one vendor (Visigenic, for instance) can retrieve and manipulate objects obtained from a remote ORB developed by another vendor (IONA, for instance). Java ORBs enable Java clients to be written without requiring any special software to be installed on the client. (The Java ORB classes are downloaded dynamically with the applet or are included with the browser itself.)

CORBA is currently available in many languages. It also supports mixing of languages within a single distributed application. IDL bridges programming languages, operating systems, networks, and object systems. It supports both distribution and object orientation. It provides a high degree of interoperability, thus insuring distributed objects built on top of different CORBA products can communicate. The advantage is a large company needn't mandate a single CORBA product for all development. An agreed protocol exists – IIOP – for communication between ORBs, which helps us with this high level of interoperability. IIOP interworks well with different middleware, including OLE scripting languages, such as Visual Basic, which can be used to implement interfaces. IIOP is integrated with other technologies, such as databases, reliable messaging systems, threads, user interface generation systems, and so on.

The CORBA services provide a set of optional extensions that address areas the core itself could not address (for example, transactions, naming, events, and trading.) It applies to many different vertical markets. The core level is applicable to all of these and specialized implementations can be provided in areas such as real time and embedded systems. The upper layers, both the CORBAservices and the CORBAfacilities, can be applied differently in the various vertical markets. The OMG has set up a number of active special interest groups to address these special needs. It supports both static and dynamic usage. Web-based clients and servers are allowed, in particular through Java-based implementations of CORBA. CORBA now is an industry standard. This creates competition among CORBA vendors and ensures quality implementations exist. The use of the CORBA standard also provides the developer with a certain degree of portability between implementations.

One of the most important aspects of CORBA/IIOP is its platform independence. The capability of CORBA ORBs to interoperate without regard to vendor origin makes CORBA/IIOP the truly ideal solution for the Internet, especially considering its vast size and the disparate hardware and software deployed there. This platform independence enables businesses to take advantage of the Internet without having to rebuild systems and networking hardware and software or forcing them to commit to a single vendor solution. CORBA/IIOP will allow almost every system now in operation to be incorporated with comparatively minor modifications, so a business's installed base, even if it is made up of equipment and software packages from a variety of vendors, can work together seamlessly.

Another supporting factor for the characteristic of platform independence is OMG. The only notable exception in this group is Microsoft, which is also trying to promote its own distributed object technology called Distributed Component Object Model (DCOM). But in terms of an important aspect of distributed technology, which is the ability to run on various platforms, Microsoft falls short. With the wide member base of OMG, all from different platforms and backgrounds, CORBA will never become platform dependent.

The use of CORBA as communication middleware enhances application flexibility and portability by automating many common development tasks such as object location, parameter marshalling, and object activation. CORBA is an improvement over conventional procedural RPC middleware (such as OSF DCE and ONC RPC) because it supports object-oriented language features (such as encapsulation, interface inheritance, parameterized types, and exception handling) and more flexible communication mechanisms (such as object references that support peer-to-peer communication and dynamic invocation capabilities). These features enable complex distributed and concurrent applications to be developed more rapidly and correctly. The number of free and commercially available ORBs is also growing by leaps and bounds (a number of them are described later in this chapter). With so many vendors and private developers investing their time and money in this technology, the future of CORBA looks bright.

Another advantage this technology has is the great advent of the Internet. CORBA is almost what the doctor ordered. With Java as its platform-independent language, Java ORBs are in a position to change many of the already existing applications with a truly distributed technology. These Java ORBs make it possible to write 100 percent pure Java clients and servers that run on any platform where a Java Virtual Machine is available. In contrast, ActiveX controls written in the Java language need to be wrapped by platform-specific binary code. Application developers using ActiveX, therefore, need to maintain multiple copies of each ActiveX control – at least one for each client platform they must support. It also provides a stronger security model as compared to its counterpart Microsoft's ActiveX.

DCOM, due to its heritage in compound document technology, has an unnecessarily complex API. In addition, DCOM applications are too fat to run on anything but the desktop. CORBA, on the other hand, was designed from scratch without any such restrictions. Java implementations of CORBA, due to their small footprint, can run on thin network computers, on low-end Java consumer devices and on embedded systems.

These advantages will enable CORBA/IIOP, coupled with Java technology, to assume a central role in shaping the Internet and distributed systems during the next phase of its evolution.

Limitations of CORBA

Although OMG has handled the interoperability issue well in CORBA 2.0, it has not sufficiently addressed the security aspects. The responsibility falls on the shoulders of OMG Object Security Service specification, which I discuss later. This has been a major obstacle for serious and mission-critical applications development, particularly for those who still employ legacy systems.

CORBA as a technology has been maturing rapidly and has been accepted widely across the industry. OMG technology, however, has had only slow acceptance, as OMG/CORBA technology is an object-oriented technology for distributed computing, an area where many users are not technically ready to apply and deploy in real environments. With the recent popularity of the Internet, the future of CORBA lies greatly in its use in open distributed tools and services. This depends on both the publicity efforts on the part of OMG in encouraging software and system vendors to use CORBA and on CORBA's technical merits in enabling true compatibility among different platforms and other Internet programming languages and applications.

Another notable drawback is with application architecture. Some applications want to make distributed requests, but not wait for the response. Ideally, they want to be notified when the response is available. Threads can be used to allow applications to make more than one request or to continue performing other tasks while waiting for a response, but the thread making a request is blocked until the response is available. CORBA communication is basically a synchronous request/response. This is true for all static invocations. Dynamic invocations do support a deferred request response. This means an application can issue a request and poll for the response. CORBA communication can be used to notify applications when responses associated with earlier requests are available. This can lead to more complex application architectures.

CORBA Success Stories

Regardless of the complex application architecture, it has not deterred companies of various backgrounds from adopting this technology. The strong reusable background acts as a strong point for big applications whose re-engineering cost is reduced using the object technology. Industries ranging from aerospace, defense, banking, finance, healthcare, manufacturing, telecommunication, transport and more have adopted this technology and implemented it in their applications. Here are some examples from these areas:

TELECOMMUNICATIONS   Nokia Telecommunications, is using IONA's CORBA product, called Orbix, as an ORB to develop, deploy, and manage value added services based on a common Intelligent Network (IN) architecture. Ericsson Radio Systems AB, Cellular Systems-American Standards, is using Orbix to develop its Cellular Management Operations System (CMOS) based on the Telecommunications Management Network (TMN) architecture. Bellsouth, is using Orbix to integrate their MVS systems, on which are stored much of their data and business logic, with modern client/server environments that present information to end users. Bellsouth has already produced a proof-of-concept application, code-named VIPER, which demonstrates the use of MVS in a multiplatform environment. A video-on-demand billing system, VIPER takes information from a Visual Basic video server, queues information events on an HP/UX machine, and then creates and stores invoice information on an MVS mainframe. The demo also features clients implemented in Java and Motif, which are able to access and manipulate MVS stored data. Motorola Inc., with its much acclaimed IRIDIUM project is using Orbix to build and control the system. The IRIDIUM® Global Cellular Network is one of the most ambitious telecommunications projects ever undertaken. When complete, IRIDIUM will provide global, wireless, hand-held telecommunications services including voice, facsimile, data, and paging via 66 lightweight satellites in low-earth orbit.

AEROSPACE/DEFENSE   Boeing Commercial Airplane Group, the largest manufacturer of commercial aircraft, has embraced CORBA as its technology for its IT systems for airplane design and manufacturing process. It uses the help of ORBIX as a key integration tool within the IT solution. British Aerospace Airbus is using the help of ICL, the European computer giant and their Dais Object Request Broker (ORB), for the integration of its legacy business systems and applications into a unified information infrastructure linked with new object-based applications. Allied Signal, Engines Division has spent the past two years building reusable objects based on CORBA application programming interfaces and set up CORBA to serve as the plumbing that connects components, clients, and servers.

BANKING/FINANCE   Digital Equipment Corporation with Linkvest designed a software layer called the Credit Risk Management (CRM) framework for Banque Paribas. The layer sits on top of BEA Systems, Inc.'s ObjectBroker and provides additional services for the application and BEA ObjectBroker itself. The CRM framework deals primarily with three functions important to investment banking: fault management, interface implementation management to the customer, and type of investment management. West Coast Financial Institution, also used Digital's BEA ObjectBroker to streamline customer service and other banking operations by converting from the traditional stove-pipe application structure to one that is more customer-centric in structure. Nations Bank is using CORBAplus ORB from Expertsoft to design its telephone banking software and its Web banking software. The Telephone Banking Project encompasses the Voice Response Units and Customer Services Centers. The Web Banking Project provides consumer bank customers of Nations Bank with a Web browser interface to their accounts, as well as other financial services.

MANUFACTURING   Silicon Graphics has licensed Visigenic's VisiBroker for Java and VisiBroker for C++ ORB technology to be integrated into future versions of IRIX, the Silicon Graphics multithreaded UNIX system-based 64-bit operating environment. By integrating Visigenic's VisiBroker ORBs, Silicon Graphics offers developers immediate support for CORBA and the native Internet Inter-ORB Protocol (IIOP) and the capability to deploy robust distributed applications across the IRIX operating environment. With this partnership, Silicon Graphics becomes the first major hardware manufacturer to provide integrated operating system support for IIOP and CORBA. I-DEAS Master Series, a software developed by Structural Dynamics Research Corporation, uses IONA's Orbix to develop the world's first fully CORBA-compliant industrial design solution. Master Series provides the key enabling technologies for companies developing electronic prototypes of complex vehicles and products from aerospace, electromechanical, and industrial equipment industries. Containing more than 90 integrated software modules, Master Series addresses the chief areas of mechanical product development. The Orbix CORBA technology is embedded as the underlying communications and interoperability mechanism within the Master Series design solution. This enables the customers to merge their design resources quickly with the organization's existing enterprise infrastructure.

Similar examples are available in other areas of healthcare/insurance, government, advertisement/marketing, publishing, retail, real estate, transport, and utilities. The OMG keeps tab of all these success stories and can be obtained from their Web site at http://www.corba.org.

General Applications in CORBA

Many implementations of CORBA are currently available. They vary in the degree of CORBA-compliance, quality of support, portability, and availability of additional features.

Orbix from IONA is a solid, fully compliant commercial implementation with excellent support. VisiBroker from Visigenic is also 2.0 compliant and offers interoperability with Java. ObjectBroker from Digital is 1.2 compliant. Other implementations include ObjectBroker from Digital, Expersoft's XShell, a Distributed Object Oriented Management (DOME) system, which also is CORBA compliant. HP's Distributed Smalltalk product also implements OMG CORBA 1.1 Object Request Broker. For more information on these and other CORBA products, see the CORBA Development Tools section later in this chapter.

Architecture for General Applications Using CORBA

The design of CORBA systems is based on the OMG Object Model. The system provides interoperability among objects in a heterogeneous distributed environment in such a way that it is transparent to the programmer.

The CORBA standard defines a set of components that enable client applications to invoke operations with arguments on object implementations. Object implementations can be configured to run locally as well as remotely without affecting the implementations or use. Figure 1-3 illustrates the primary components of the CORBA architecture.

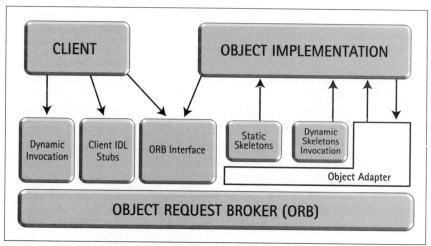

Figure 1-3: Components in CORBA Distributed Object Computing Model

The *client* is a program entity that invokes an operation on an object implementation. *Object implementation* defines operations that implement a CORBA IDL interface. Object implementations can be written using languages like C, C++, Java, Smalltalk and Ada. According to CORBA specifications, the way the client accesses the services of the object should be transparent to the caller. Ideally, it should be as simple as calling a method of an object. ORB is responsible for finding the object implementation when the client invokes an operation for an object. If required, the ORB may also pass a message to the object and return a response, if any, to the client.

To maintain the transparency between the client and the ORB, the CORBA specifications define an abstract interface for an ORB, depicted by ORB Interface here. This interface provides various functions, such as converting object references to strings and vice versa, and creating the argument list for requests made through the Dynamic Invocation Interface (DII). The DII enables the client to specify requests to objects whose definition and interface are unknown at the client's compile time. To use DII, the client has to compose a request (in a way common to all ORBs) including the object reference, the operation, and a list of parameters. These specifications of objects and the services they provide are retrieved from the Interface Repository, a database that provides persistent storage of object interface definitions. The Interface Repository also contains information about types of parameters, certain debugging information, and so forth.

IDL stubs and skeletons serve as a glue between the client and the server applications and the ORB. A CORBA IDL compiler automates the transformation between CORBA IDL definitions and the target programming language. The use of this compiler greatly reduces the potential for inconsistencies between the client and the server stubs. This IDL compilation is done when the programmer is developing the application. IDL stubs only enable RPC-style requests. DII, on the other hand, also enables clients to make nonblocking deferred synchronous (separate send and receive applications) and one-way (send-only) calls. A server side analogue to DII is the Dynamic Skeleton Interface (DSI). With the use of this interface, the operation is no longer accessed through an operation-specific skeleton, generated from an IDL interface specification. Instead, it is reached through an interface that provides access to the operation name and parameters (as in DII above the information can be retrieved from the Interface Repository). Thus DSI is a way to deliver requests from the ORB to an object implementation that does not have compile-time knowledge of the object it is implementing.

DSI is an answer to interactive software development tools based on interpreters and debuggers. It can also be used to provide inter-ORB interoperability. Object adapter assists the ORB with delivering requests to the object and with activating the object. It handles services such as generation and interpretation of object references, method invocation, security of interactions, object and implementation activation and deactivation, mapping references corresponding to object implementations, and registration of implementations. Many different special-purpose object adapters are expected to fulfill the needs of specific systems (for example, databases).

Limitations to the Architecture

The most obvious limitation lies in the use of CORBA on wide area networks. Then the performance becomes hardware specific. It falls down considerably in the absence of a strong network backbone.

Benefits of Using CORBA

The benefits are many. Being truly object-oriented, CORBA is easier to maintain. The addition of newer features and the changing of the implementation of the interfaces are also transparent to the user. Thus, changing the system depending on the rapidly changing business environments becomes easy and fast. A strong feature of CORBA is its language and platform independence, which help its distributed nature. You can even have Java applets in a Java-enabled Web browser instead of Java applications – used as clients right now – which simplifies the job for the user even more when the application is spread on the Web.

Web-Based Applications in CORBA

With CORBA being a strong distributed technology and with the growth of the Internet in a stupendous fashion, seeing a large number of resources spent on developing Web-based applications using CORBA as the underlying technology is not surprising. The supporting factor is a backing of major players like Sun Microsystems, Netscape, and Oracle, who, with the help of their resources, do not allow the pace of the technological development to slow them down.

Architecture for Web Applications Using CORBA

The Web began as a giant unidirectional medium for publishing and broadcasting static electronic documents. Basically the Web was a giant URL-based file server. In late 1995, the Web evolved into a more interactive medium with the introduction of three-tier client/server, CGI style. CGI is now known to access every known server environment.

But the Web with CGI is a slow, cumbersome, and stateless protocol. As the CGI scripts run on the sever side, for servers that take thousands of hits a day, this can really slow down the system. CGI is unsuitable for writing modern client server applications and is no match for object-oriented Java clients. It launches a new process to service each incoming client request. To get around this limitation many vendors have introduced server extensions that have, as yet, ended up being non-standard and, sometimes, platform-specific extensions.

The next generation of the Web – in its various forms of the Internet, intranet, and Extranets – must evolve into a full-blown client server medium that can run business applications. The current HTTP/CGI paradigm cannot meet these requirements. To move to this next step, the Web needs distributed objects. Figure 1-4 shows this evolution.

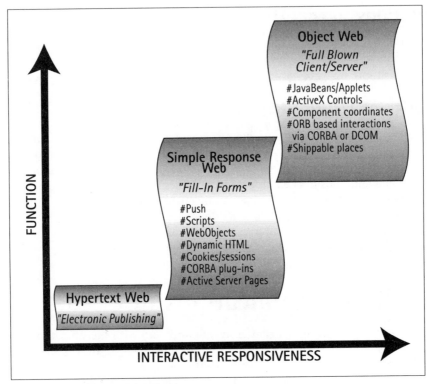

Figure 1-4: Evolution of Web Architecture

One approach to creating this kind of Web is with CORBA and Java. CORBA –
which is, in itself, a complete distributed object platform – extends the reach of
Java applications across networks, languages, component boundaries, and operating systems. Java on its part is a mobile object system and allows CORBA objects
to run on everything from mainframes to network computers to mobile phones.
Java's bytecode behavior simplifies distribution of code in large CORBA systems.
Java, with its built-in multithreading, garbage collection, and error management
makes it easier to write robust networked objects. The bottom line is both are technologies that compliment each other well. Java begins where CORBA leaves off.
CORBA deals with network transparency and Java deals with implementation
transparency.

In a typical Java/CORBA scenario, when browsing the Web, the Web browser
downloads the HTML page that includes references to embedded Java applets. The
Web browser, upon seeing the reference, downloads the Java applet from the HTTP
server. The HTTP server, in turn, retrieves the Java applet and sends it to the
browser in the form of bytecodes (generally in *class files* with a .class extension).
The Web browser, after receiving the applet, loads it. The applet is first run through
the Java security portion and then loaded into the memory. The applet then invokes

the CORBA server objects. Java can include the IDL-generated client stubs, which let it invoke the object on the ORB server. The session between the Java applet and the CORBA server applets exists until either side decides to disconnect. The server object can generate the next HTML page for this client. After preparing the next pages, the server can tell the client what URL to download next. This dynamic HTML generation on the server side is generally not needed with the object Web. A client application is packaged as a single HTML page with embedded components such as applets (or JavaBeans via the object tag). In contrast to HTTP/CGI, CORBA enables you to interact instantaneously with the server by clicking any of the components embedded in the HTML layers without switching out of the page's context to obtain the response.

The future of the Web is in object Web. All new applications on the object Web will be built and packaged as components. You can use CORBA IDL as a wrapper for any existing code, written in any language, with object interfaces. These IDLized components can then be used later in the Web-based applications or they can even help in porting the existing huge mainframe-based applications to the Web.

CORBA/JAVA OBJECT WEB AND THE CORRESPONDING CLIENT SERVER ARCHITECTURE

The object Web will bring another revolution in the client/server paradigm. The first one is from mainframe-/legacy-based systems to client/server systems. With more and more applications now being made around the Web architecture, care should be taken while moving the existing applications to the Web. The client/server architecture of the object Web will be divided in three tiers. The first tier will be the client and the second tier will include CORBA objects. They will also talk to any existing server applications in the third tier using Java's database capabilities (JDBC) or any other message-oriented middleware. The third tier will be made up of almost anything the CORBA objects can access. This includes message oriented middleware, DBMS, ODBMS, and e-mail.

As we said before, the client — the first tier of the object Web — will be made of traditional Web browsers and the new Web centric desktops. As opposed to today's static Web pages, the new content will have more of the look and feel of the real objects. You will interact with these objects via drag-and-drop and other forms of direct manipulation. HTTP will be used to download Web pages and images, and CORBA will be used for Java client-to-server and server-to-client communications.

The second tier runs on any server that can service both HTTP and CORBA clients. The CORBA/HTTP is supported on almost every server OS platform, including UNIXes, NT, OS/2, NetWare, MacOS, OS/400, MVS, and Tandem NonStop kernel. CORBA objects, which could eventually be packaged as Enterprise JavaBeans or existing C++ objects with an interface defined using IDL, act as middle tier application servers. They encapsulate the business logic. These objects interact with the client objects via CORBA/IIOP. CORBA objects on the server interact with one another using the CORBA ORB. They can also talk to any existing server applications in the third tier using JDBC, Java Database Connectivity, or any other middleware. The server side must also provide a server side component coordinator, also known as *object TP monitor*. Unlike traditional TP monitors managing remote procedures, object TP monitors manage objects. They also prestart a pool of objects, distribute, load, provide fault tolerance, and coordinate multicomponent transactions. In a CORBA/Java object Web, the second tier also acts as a store of component titles, HTML pages, and shippable places. These can be stored in shippable Java packages (called *jars*) that are managed by an ODBMS or DBMS.

The third tier can be called the *back end*. It comprises almost anything the CORBA object can access, including procedural TP monitors, message-oriented middleware, Lotus Notes, DBMSes, ODBMSes, and e-mail. This is an area where CORBA's interlanguage communication capabilities will be useful.

WAYS TO ACCESS CORBA OBJECTS FROM WEB-BASED APPLICATIONS

A number of ways exist in which CORBA objects can be accessed from Web-based applications.

Java applets are capable of directly accessing CORBA objects via IIOP. They can be downloaded directly as Web-based applications. A number of Java-based ORBs are available on the market. By introducing CORBA communication into a Java applet, arbitrary CORBA services can be accessed directly. These services can be developed in any language supported by CORBA or on top of any CORBA product that supports IIOP.

Web servers from Netscape and Oracle are beginning to support IIOP directly. This means, in addition to supporting HTTP, FTP access, and news groups access, they will be capable of accessing any CORBA object capable of supporting IIOP.

CGI Gateways let pure HTML-based applications access CORBA objects. Arbitrary and unknown CORBA objects can be accessed by a single precompiled client application via Dynamic Invocation. A precompiled application can dynamically generate HTML pages based upon results obtained from arbitrary invocation of operations. This solution has the advantage of being based only upon HTML; it is not specific to a particular Web browser.

A similar approach to the CGI CORBA gateway can allow CORBA objects to be accessed without the performance impact associated with process spawning. A plug-in can be developed for a particular browser that enables it to speak directly to any CORBA object through IIOP.

MOVING FROM HTTP TO CORBA/IIOP

For the most part, moving from HTTP to IIOP will be transparent to end users, except that with IIOP, the applications they use will become more sophisticated and have better performance. Initially, Web applications that use IIOP will most likely take the form of Java applets downloaded via HTTP. Once the applet is downloaded, it takes over communication with remote objects using IIOP. The CORBA model and tools that support it enable programmers to build this kind of application more quickly, to develop more functionality, and to make use of existing components.

As Web-related CORBA standards progress, standard URL formats for object references and requests, and for scripting languages such as JavaScript and component models such as JavaBeans, will probably have built-in support for IIOP. This step will give less sophisticated users access to powerful object-oriented services throughout the Web, regardless of the specific object technology used to build them.

CORBA and IIOP also guarantee objects can describe their interfaces at runtime. This offers powerful capabilities not available in other protocols, including HTTP. Web applications will be able to take an object reference – in the form of a URL – and ask the object to describe itself. The capability to do this in object and component models is often called *introspection*. The description takes a standard form, prescribed by the CORBA 2.0 specification. This capability enables users much more powerful browsing capabilities. Rather than just downloading documents, users can interactively discover and inquire about a wider range of more sophisticated object services.

WEB APPLICATIONS THAT USE CORBA

The Web transforms CORBA/Java from a set of standards to a set of products that fulfill our distributed object needs. The main players of this are Netscape, Oracle, JavaSoft, and IBM/Lotus Notes. Many vendors also who provide specialized ORBs, tools, components, and services.

Netscape is bundling the VisiBroker for Java ORB with every browser. Netscape is also using CORBA for its server-to-server infrastructure. Because of CORBA, this allows Netscape servers to play with other servers in the enterprise. With a wide base of Netscape browsers, we are looking at an installed base of around 45 million CORBA ORBs on the client and over a million on the server.

JavaSoft is making CORBA the foundation of distributed Java. SunSoft is building its Internet server strategy around CORBA using its NEO ORB and Solstice.

Oracle has adopted CORBA as its platform for its Network Computing Architecture. Oracle has planned to change its entire software line, including everything from the database engines to stored procedures, tools, and the Internet, which will be built on a CORBA object bus. Oracle is building most of the CORBA services on top of the Visigenic IIOP ORB. This ORB will first appear in the next release of Oracle Web Server and it will serve as the foundation for Oracle's Internet products.

IBM/Lotus with its wide installed base is building its next generation of cross-platform network computing infrastructure on CORBA/Java. IBM intends to bundle a Java runtime with all its OS platforms. The IBM VisualAge tool will target CORBA/Java objects on both clients and servers across all the IBM platforms. The IBM Component Broker is a scalable server-side component coordinator for managing middle-tier CORBA/Java objects. Finally, the next Lotus Domino is being built on an IIOP foundation.

Various others exist: Apple, HP, SunSoft, IONA, Digital, Novell, and Expersoft. The ODBMS vendors include ODI, Gemstone, and Versant. The major tool vendors are Symantec, ParcPlace, Borland, Penumbra, and Sybase.

Limitations

The most important factor hindering the efforts of vendors to shift their large Web-based applications into CORBA is a lack of strong security infrastructure. Also a lack of a common standard for the Web and the conflicts between major players like Microsoft and Sun regarding Web standards are slowing the process of distributed applications on the Web.

Benefits

With the help of the Web, CORBA is now able to use its capabilities to the fullest. Being an object-oriented technology for distributed computing, CORBA is in a position to harness the true power of the Web. The future of CORBA lies in the ability to use its open distributed tools and services. And with platform independent technologies like Java and JavaBeans, CORBA can take full advantage of its already strong technology and use it to the fullest.

How Java and CORBA Relate

Java has impacted our computing world with a bang. And all the credit is not unwarranted. The almost perfect portability of Java application and the famous Java applets is a great boon to the multiplatform world. The close integration of Java with Web browsers makes it an ideal medium for Web- and Internet-based development. Java's ease of use compared to its predecessor C++ makes it accessible to a much wider range of developers and speeds the development process measurably. But Java has its drawbacks, too.

Java lacks a client/server method invocation paradigm. Once at the client end, the applet has no mechanism for invoking remote methods back on its dispatching site or on any other distributed server object. Java lacks distribution services, as well as persistence and streamable storage (although a few third-party vendors have come up with libraries to handle such situations). Once applets are brought to a client site, the more valuable ones will need to be stored. Presumably, they will need to be stored intact with the additional HTML and other content found on the server page. They may then need to be retrieved from storage and *peeled away* from the other forms of content (for example, HTML text, JPEG or GIF images, and so forth). This requires a compound document storage facility similar to OpenDoc's Bento or OLE's streamable storage. Many of these limitations of Java are addressed by CORBA. Even though Java offers great flexibility for distributed object development and it is going to act as a building block for object Web, it lacks a client/server paradigm. Java does not have a distributed object infrastructure that is used for communication between clients and servers.

Java acts in its entirety and does not support method invocations among other Java objects. Neither does it acts in a plug-and-play fashion, which would allow different Java objects to interact with one another, pass messages, and call each other's methods. To do this, Java must be augmented with a distributed object infrastructure, which is where OMG's CORBA comes to its rescue. CORBA provides the missing link between Java's portable application environment and the distributed environment of platform, language, and network independence and the services offered by the distributed and the back-end objects. The merge of Java and CORBA object technologies is the next step in the evolution of object Web.

Java enables you to create portable objects and easily distribute them. CORBA enables you to connect them and to integrate them with rest of your computing environments – databases, legacy systems, and objects – or applications written in other languages. Java and CORBA complement each other nicely, therefore, in Web development.

JavaBeans and CORBA

JavaBeans has rapidly emerged as an important standard for component objects. JavaBeans enables developers to create reusable software components that can then be assembled using visual application builder tools from independent software developers. JavaBeans is designed as the platform-neutral, component architecture for Java. JavaBeans brings the extraordinary power of Java to component development, offering the ideal environment for a developer who wants to extend the concept of reusable component development beyond one platform and one architecture to embrace every platform and every architecture in the industry. JavaBeans is a complete component model. It supports the standard component architecture features of properties, events, methods, and persistence.

In addition, JavaBeans provides support for introspection (to allow automatic analysis of a JavaBeans component) and customization (to make it easy to configure a JavaBeans component). In contrast to OLE or OpenDoc, JavaBeans has the virtue of being hardware- and operating system-independent (albeit expressed in Java). The existing synergy between CORBA and Java would be greatly enhanced by defining a CORBA component model compatible with Java Beans. This means the information required by the JavaBeans introspection interface must be available from the CORBA component in a form the JavaBeans environment can access. A recent coalition between IBM, Netscape, Sun, and Oracle plans to do the same.

Security Considerations in CORBA

Security has always been a point of concern for client/server systems. You cannot simply trust the client operating systems on the network to protect the resources of the server. And even if we did manage to make the clients secure in any way, our network is highly prone to attacks. Information is highly unsafe in transit. Sniffer devices can easily record traffic between machines and put Trojan horses into the systems. Distributed objects inherit all these problems plus more.

In a client/server world you can typically trust the server, but not the clients. On the contrary, in distributed systems, an object can act as a client as well as a server. Objects that are both server and client come into a position where you don't know whether to trust them. Being more flexible, they can interact in more ad hoc ways.

This is a double-edged sword that can be a strength as well as a weakness. Because objects are flexible, they can easily be impersonated. This can be a dream-come true for all hackers, who can impersonate the legitimate objects and replace them with ones that could create havoc over the network. As all objects can also act as servers, managing the rights for all these servers would be a security nightmare. CORBA must be able to overcome these drawbacks and help manage the security in the tough world of distributed systems.

In the following section, we explain the security model using the specification as given by OMG. The model provides the overall framework for CORBA security. It enables us to define many different security policies that can be used to achieve the appropriate level of functionality and assurance. The security reference model functions as a guide to the security architecture of CORBA. The complete security service specification by OMG can be obtained from `http://www.omg.org/ library/corbserv.htm#sec`.

Security Reference Model

A Security Reference Model describes how and where a secure system enforces security policies. Security policies define the conditions under which active entities may access objects. An example of an active entity could be clients acting on behalf of users. What authentication of users and other principals is required to prove who they are, what they are allowed to do, and whether they can delegate their rights? A *principal* is a human user or system entity registered in and authentic to the system. Security policy is responsible for the security of communications between objects, including the trust required between them and the quality of protection of the data in transit between them.

Figure 1-5 depicts the model for CORBA-secure object systems. All object invocations are mediated by appropriate security to enforce policies, such as access controls. As defined by CORBA specifications, these functions should be tamper-proof, always be invoked when required by security policy, and must function correctly.

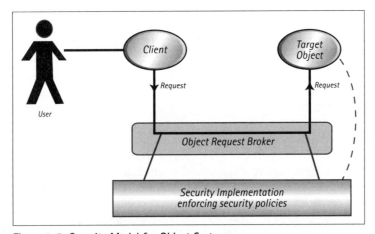

Figure 1-5: Security Model for Object Systems

Many application objects are unaware of the security policy and how it is enforced. The user can be authenticated prior to calling the application client and then security is subsequently enforced automatically during object invocations. Some applications will need to control or influence what policy is enforced by the system on their behalf, but they will not do the enforcement themselves. Some applications will need to enforce their own security, for example, to control access to their own data or audit their own security-relevant activities.

The ORB cannot be completely unaware of security as this would result in insecure systems. The ORB is assumed at least to handle requests correctly without violating security policy and to call security services as required by security policy. IONA's Orbix and Visigenic's VisiBroker are among the ones providing such security measures.

A security model normally defines a specific set of security policies. Because the OMA must support a wide variety of different security policies to meet the needs of many commercial markets, a single instance of a security model is not appropriate for the OMA. Instead, a security reference model is defined that provides a framework for building many different kinds of policies. The security reference model is a metapolicy because it is intended to encompass all possible security policies supported by the OMA.

The metapolicy defines the abstract interfaces that are provided by the security architecture defined in this document. The model enumerates the security functions that are defined as well as the information available. In this manner, the meta-policy ORB request Client Target Object Security Implementation enforcing security policies provides guidance on the permitted flexibility of the policy definition. The remaining sections describe the elements of the meta-model. We have deliberately kept the description general at this point.

Principals and Their Security Attributes

An active entity must establish its rights to access objects in the system. It must either be a principal, or a client acting on behalf of a principal.

As previously stated, a principal is a human user or system entity registered in and authentic to the system. *Initiating principals* are the ones who initiate activities. An initiating principal may be authenticated in a number of ways, the most common of which for human users is a password. For systems entities, the authentication information, such as its long-term key, needs to be associated with the object.

An initiating principal has at least one, and possibly several identities (represented in the system by attributes), which may be used as a means of:

◆ Making the principal accountable for its actions.

◆ Obtaining access to protected objects (though other privilege attributes of a principal may also be required for access control).

♦ Identifying the originator of a message.

♦ Identifying who to charge for use of the system.

Several forms of identity may be used for different purposes. For example, the *audit identity* may need to be anonymous to all but the audit administrator, but the *access identity* may need to be understood so it can be specified as an entry in an access control list. The same value of the identity can be used for several of the previous.

The principal may also have privilege attributes that can be used to decide what it can access. A variety of privilege attributes may be available depending on access policies. The privilege attributes, which a principal is permitted to take, are known by the system. At any one time, the principal may be using only a subset of these permitted attributes, either chosen by the principal (or an application running on its behalf) or by using a default set specified for the principal. Limits may be on the duration for which these privilege attributes are valid and controls may be on where and when they can be used.

Security attributes may be acquired in three ways:

♦ Some attributes may be available, without authentication, to any principal. This specification defines one such attribute, called *Public*.

♦ Some attributes are acquired through authentication. *Identity attributes* and *privilege attributes* are in this category.

♦ Some attributes are acquired through *delegation* from other principals.

When a user or other principal is authenticated, it normally supplies:

♦ Its security name.

♦ The authentication information needed by the particular authentication method used.

♦ Requested privilege attributes (although the principal may change these later).

♦ A principal's security attributes are maintained in secure CORBA systems in a credential, as shown in Figure 1-6.

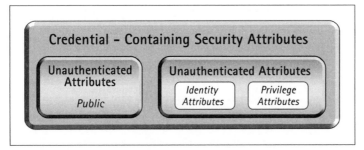

Figure 1-6: Security Attributes

Structural Model

The structural model has four major levels used during object invocation:

1. Application-level components, which may or may not be aware of security.

2. Components implementing the security services, independently of any specific underlying security technology. (This specification allows the use of an isolating interface between this level and the security technology, allowing different security technologies to be accommodated within the architecture.)

   These components are:

   ■ The ORB core and the ORB service it uses.

   ■ Security services.

   ■ Policy objects used by these to enforce the security policy.

3. Components implementing specific security technology.

4. Basic protection and communication generally provided by a combination of hardware and operating system mechanisms.

Figure 1-7 illustrates the major levels and components of the structural model, indicating the relationships between them.

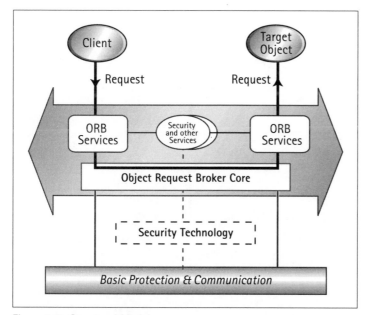

Figure 1-7: Structural Model

Application Components

Many application components are unaware of security and rely on the ORB to call the required security services during object invocation. Some applications enforce their own security and, therefore, call on security services directly. As in the OMA, the client may or may not be an object.

ORB Services

The *ORB Core* is defined in the CORBA architecture as "that part of the ORB that provides the basic representation of objects and the communication of requests." The ORB Core, therefore, supports the minimum functionality necessary to enable a client to invoke an operation on a target object, with (some of) the distribution transparencies required by the CORBA architecture.

An object request may be generated within an implicit context, which affects the way in which the ORB handles it, though not the way in which a client makes the request. The implicit context may include elements such as transaction identifiers, recovery data, and, in particular, security context. All of these are associated with elements of functionality, termed ORB Services, additional to that of the ORB Core, but from the application view, logically present in the ORB.

A client's ORB determines which ORB Services to use at the client when invoking operations on a target object. Figure 1-8 illustrates the Client's request to the target object. The target's ORB determines which ORB Services to use at the target. If one ORB does not support the full set of services required, then either the interaction cannot proceed or it can only do so with reduced facilities, which may be agreed to by a process of negotiation between ORBs.

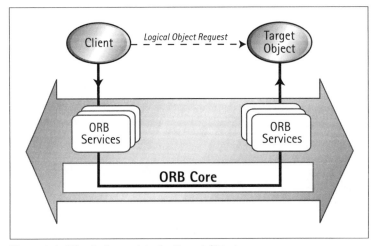

Figure 1-8: Client's Request to the Target Object

Security Services

In a secure object system, the ORB Services called will include ORB Security Services for secure invocation and access control.

ORB Security Services and applications may call on Object Security Services for authentication, access control, audit, nonrepudiation, and secure invocations. These security services form the Security Replaceability Conformance option.

These Object Security Services may, in turn, call on external security services to implement security technology.

Security Policies and Domain Objects

A *security policy domain* is the set of objects to which common security policies apply. The domain itself is not an object. A policy domain manager exists, however, for each security policy domain. This domain manager is used when finding and managing the policies that apply to the domain. The ORB and security services use these to enforce the security policies relevant to object invocation.

Security Technology

The Object Security Services previously described insulate the applications and ORBs from the security technology used. Existing security components may provide security technology. These do not have domain managers or objects. Security technology could be provided by the operating system. Distributed, heterogeneous environments are increasingly being used, however, and for these, security technology is provided by a set of distributed security services. This architecture identifies a separate layer containing those components, which actually implement the security services. Various technologies may be used to provide these and a (set of) generic security interface(s), such as the GSS-API, will be used to insulate the implementations of the security services from detailed knowledge of the underlying mechanisms. The range of services (and corresponding APIs) includes:

1. The means of creating and handling the security information required to establish security associations, including keys.

2. Message protection services providing confidentiality and integrity.

The use of standard, generic APIs for interactions with external security services not only allows interchangeability of security mechanisms, but also enables exploitation of existing, proven implementations of such mechanisms.

CORBA Competitors

Just like any other technology, CORBA has some competitors. Here are three major competitors who come close to being CORBA's enemies.

Remote Procedure Calls versus CORBA

Remote Procedure Call (RPC) was introduced by the Open Software Foundation (OSF), a consortium of companies defining and accepting standards. RPC is a part of the Distributed Computing Environment (DCE) propagated by the consortium. RPC was introduced OSF in the mid 80s. This was a bold attempt made by the OSF group to break through the legacy style of building applications. Prior to the existence of RPC, applications no doubt shared data, but they did it in a passive mode. For example, if one application wanted to share data with another application, it generated a persistent format of data in terms of data files, which the other application would read to access the data. This was acceptable in those days, as instantaneous data sharing was not a strong need. Having applications share data while they were still running and having applications share their services were not thought of in those days.

Breakthrough occurred in the technology wherein data could be shared among processes via shared memory, memory mapped files, and so forth. But application developers did not need the system to be in the process of sharing executable code. The concept of function callback did exist, but it was a rather crude way of sharing code. Because function callback was a passive approach, it cannot be considered code sharing. The needy application could not initiate it. Only if the service rich application wanted to share its services with others would it provide the service needy application a hook to call the request service. With RPC, this was one of the biggest innovations. One application, while it was executing, would share its services with other applications. This provided each application with the freedom to concentrate on their own strength. Whenever an application needed access to some other specific types of services not rendered by itself, it could easily locate other applications that excelled in performing those services. If an application issued a request to another application to perform a service, then it could perform it. (This is exactly how people react in the world. No individual is master of all existing domains. Whenever people need to make use of services with which we are unfamiliar, we approach the individual or organization that deals with those services and satisfy our needs.)

RPC functions on the principle of client-server technology. The concept of a remote procedure call is analogous to the procedure calls in the legacy programming approach. In the structured programming world, huge programming tasks are simplified by writing smaller procedures. These procedures keep the programs manageable as well as modularized. Thus, the call path of the program would have many procedures and subprocedures calling one another. The program call stack keeps the return addresses so the called procedure returns to the correct address.

These procedures are called to perform the subtasks and they return the values obtained as a result of the calling procedure. This reduces the complexities in writing large programs. When one procedure makes a call to another procedure the control of execution of transferred from the calling procedure to the called procedure. This is not thought of as an extraordinary way of program execution. The system resources are used optimally in a single machine environment.

In the world of networks, you find many different types of computers involved in the setup targeted to perform different tasks. In such an environment, you try to configure the environment in such a manner that maximum capabilities of all the available resources are used. After all, this is what computer science and computer scientists are all about. Making the most of the available resources in the most optimized manner is the goal we always try to achieve. We need to make use of all the available systems within the network so the applications work to our satisfaction. Also, this provides a feeling that our investment in all these machines and the network is being used to its fullest.

The thought of passing on the control of execution to another machine is a smart idea. The passing of control of execution could be from one application to another application. The best part being, the other application could be on the same machine or on a different machine and the application passing on the execution control would be unaware of the distance. For example, suppose you had a network of two computers and computer A was performing a task of collecting real time data from one of its communication ports. The application running on computer A needs to perform some kind of mathematical analysis on the data to acquire the results. Because B is a system with a high power computation processor, it could very well execute a remote procedure on the second computer B. B could return the results of the computation to the calling procedure from machine A. A could later perform the needful operations. RPC is an elegant way of expressing such a model.

RPC provides a high level of abstraction and hides all the complexities of dealing with the network under the hoods. RPC presents a simple and transparent solution. The model is close to the structured programming procedure-call approach in that not many changes must be done in the system to get RPC to work. It hides the internals of the network transport protocol from the application so the application remains portable from one network topology to another. RPC minimizes the amount of time an application programmer has to spend in learning the internals of the networking aspects to get the application up and running in a networked environment.

RPC allows the system to expose the methods that help other applications to make use of them when required. Such methods or procedures are called *interfaces*. These methods become the gateway for the outside world and help maintain the system's integrity. Procedures to be executed in the remote address space must be defined as an interface. The interface is defined using the Interface Definition Language. The interface is defined to generate the bridge between the client portion of the procedure call and the server portion. The interface definition is then run through an Interface Definition Language compiler which generates the client and the server stubs.

The IDL is a language in its own right, which helps to address the problems of definition of interfaces very well. A separate chapter is dedicated to the IDL, so we won't go into the detail here. The output of the IDL compiler serves specific purposes. The client stub is linked into the client application and the server stub is linked into the server application. When the client makes a procedure call that is remote (the remote procedure call looks exactly like a local procedure call and differentiating between the two calls can be difficult), the client stub takes over. The client stub takes in the parameters passed to the procedure and translates them into a standard network data representation (NDR) format for transmission over the network. It then calls the RPC client library method to send the request to the server. When the server receives the request, it calls the server stub procedure. The server stub procedure converts the passed data from the network data representation format to the format understood by the procedure. It then issues a call to the local procedure on the server. The local procedure on the server is executed and the return value, if any, is sent to the server stub. The server stub takes in the return value and translates it into the network data representation format. It then makes a call to the RPC library on the server side, which then generates a network request back to the client. When the client receives the network request, it first translates the data from the network data representation format back to the format understood by the client procedure and then returns to the calling routine from the client application.

Figure 1-9 shows an instance of a remote procedure application. The client and the server application talk to each other over the network using remote procedure calls. The client application links to the client stub, which proxies the remote procedure. The client application is also linked to the RPC client runtime library, which is called by the client stub to get the data over the network in a well-defined pattern. The server application, in turn, is linked to the server stub and the RPC server runtime library. The process seems lengthy, but RPC does the job extremely fast.

Performance was a key factor when the RPC model was designed. The process of translating data from the local format to the network data representation format and vice versa is called *marshalling*. An important part of the system, marshalling is performed with extreme caution. The conversion of data from one format to another cannot loose data. Loss of data is an irrecoverable process as the other side of the wire relies on the data passed to it. No traces are left for the other side to rectify the error caused by data loss. A remote procedure call is a synchronous call, hence, the application will block until the call actually returns. This is also analogous to the normal procedure call that is blocking. The execution at the calling procedure has to wait until the called procedure returns. In a highly parallel environment, such a blocking technique is not looked upon positively. It defeats the purpose of a parallel architecture. Various other ways exist to make such things parallel, but those approaches are more of a programming solution than a system provided feature.

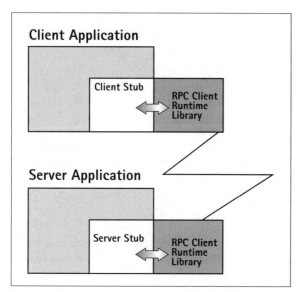

Figure 1-9: Remote Procedure Call Based Applications

The marshalling and unmarshalling of data is done in the client stub and the server stub. Those are the only two places where both the data formats are well understood (The two data formats are the parameters to the method and the network data representation format). The RPC model also defines an application configuration file (ACF) by using the interface definition file. The application configuration file is used mainly by the applications involved in the communication. This allows the application to define application-specific handles and data structure, which could be used between the client and the server applications. The application configuration files help maintain the connection context for the client and the server. The ACF format is identical to the IDL format and is also run through the interface language definition compiler. The custom data structures defined in the ACF are not passed over the network. The ACF file is not important to the RPC definition model.

You have seen that RPC is a good development framework. It can certainly be used for any complex project development work. CORBA, on the other hand, has much to offer in terms of the framework and the working services. CORBA has much more modularity built into the system and the services identified by CORBA are well separated. The horizontal sections in the service world are addressed in much more detail with CORBA. RPC is system-related and does not target its solutions toward specific application domains. The design of RPC is fairly universal and works for the basic communication tasks. A remote procedure is a higher-level communication protocol. CORBA attaches more semantics to the process.

CORBA is more of an application-level protocol, a situation that not only allows object communication, but also involves itself with object management, facilitating application development. CORBA deals with much more than just procedure remoting. It identifies the difficulties in product development in a distributed environment and offers much more semantically rich solutions to the entire domain. RPC covers a small and restricted domain in comparison to CORBA. CORBA attempts to provide a total solution. CORBA has had the privilege of having much more awareness from the industry than RPC. The OMG consortium has many people from the software industry concentrating on the overall architecture, hence, the framework has more finesse to it.

CORBA enables the application developers to query the available services and then decide on which one of the service to use during runtime. This provides a more flexible development environment. The application developer has much more control on the flow of the application. This comes at the cost of writing more code to make the application flexible.

RPC is more of a static system. It does not enable the developer to decide the type of service to use during runtime. The selection on the type of service to use is made during the code-writing phase. Because any changes to the selection of service type require a change in the application code, the application would have to be rebuilt.

CORBA allows remote calls to be synchronous, asynchronous, and deferred synchronous. This addresses a large number of performance-related-issues. RPC does not have the capability to make calls that are deferred synchronous or asynchronous. Hence, RPC-based applications are tied down to calls that block. Both frame works use the Interface Definition Language. Both frame works leave the interface definition task to IDL, which is a standard language used for definitions. A similar concept is followed in both the environments. Only CORBA allows more plug-in services to tap in to the system, such as call authentication and server object life transparency. RPC handles the remote method invocation matter in a simplistic manner, while CORBA takes further steps to identify the issues involved in the process and tries to suggest solutions. RPC was invented long before CORBA came into the picture, so competing with CORBA was not the issue. CORBA, on the other hand, picked up where RPC left off and went ahead with answering more of the issues with distributed applications.

Distributed Component Object Model versus CORBA

Distributed Component Object Model (DCOM) is a distributed object frame architecture designed by Microsoft. Microsoft initially came out with a component object model and later enhanced the architecture to be suitable in a distributed environment. DCOM provides a language neutral approach to the development environment. Distributed object frame works have historically been hurt by the development language concerns. This has plagued the enhancements to the development framework. DCOM provides a rather attractive solution. DCOM objects interoperate at the binary level. This enables developers to write applications in C or C++ or Visual Basic; these objects can interoperate with one another without the need of any intermediate interpretation.

A DCOM object is a collection of code working on some data. It provides interfaces so the outside world can coordinate with it. The DCOM object model separates the interface from the implementation. The interface is expressed using the Interface Definition Language. To provide binary compatibility, the DCOM object model provides a query interface that allows other objects to search for a particular required interface. The DCOM object functions as an entity of its own. DCOM is based on Distributed Computing Environment's Remote Procedure Call (DCE RPC) architecture. Slight alterations are done to the DCE RPC model in the terms that it is now Object-Oriented Remote Procedure Call (ORPC). The ORPC model deals with objects as addressable entities, rather than just methods. Applications understand and interpret objects. The interaction is done among objects. Hence, DCOM is also termed an application-level protocol.

DCOM deals with the distributed framework of the COM objects. The architecture hides underneath the complexities of resolving the issues involved in the distributed world. The matter gets even more complex when the distribution is done on objects as opposed to methods. Objects have affiliations and relations to other objects based on their state and any alteration of the state of an object from an outbound request could destabilize the environment. The DCOM object model presents a programming methodology that must be obeyed by the system to be DCOM-compliant. Because DCOM allows a binary interoperability among objects, few requirements must be religiously obeyed by the DCOM-based applications. Some of the requirements can be missed by a DCOM application and still function well in this environment. The limitation would be that it would not be in the position to make use of all the facilities provided by the DCOM environment. DCOM applications are flexible as far as their deployment is concerned. They are also scaleable, due to the manner in which their functionalities can be extended.

Figure 1-10 shows a simple DCOM-based application. The DCOM objects talk to one another using the DCOM protocol. The figure shows a DCOM-compliant client application which, via DCOM runtime module, locates a DCOM object server and makes use of the interfaces exposed by the object. Just as any other distributed object framework, DCOM has a common area wherein all the objects make themselves and their services known. This common area is known as the registry. The *registry* is the common repository where all the objects and their services are registered. The interface provided by a DCOM-compliant object is a collection of semantically alike methods that are exposed under a specific interface category. All these methods exposed via an interface are strongly typed.

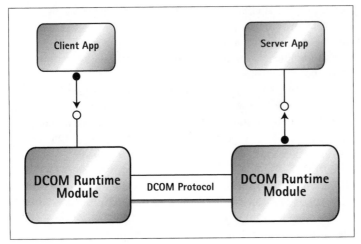

Figure 1-10: A Simple DCOM based Application

Every object class registered within a registry is uniquely identified by a 128-bit Globally Unique Identifier (GUID). The composition of the 128-bit identifier keeps this identifier unique for every class definition. The GUID identifying the object class is called the *classid*. The GUID is the same as the Universally Unique Identifier (UUID) defined by the DCE. Every interface defined within the object class is also uniquely identified by the interface identifier. The interface defines the methods supported by it. The implementation of the interface is purely up to the interface programmer responsible for the implementation. The interface does not dictate any kind of behavior. Rather, it isolates the implementation from the methods. The methods supported by an interface are arranged in terms of function pointers and the interface maintains an interface function pointer table.

In the DCOM programming model, the client is provided with an interface pointer, which is transparent and does not expose the internals of the object. After locating the object within the registry, the client queries the required interface based on the interface identifier. If the specified interface is supported by the object, then the interface pointer is returned to the client application. Because the interface identifiers are unique, the methods required by the client are available through the interface pointer.

The DCOM object model supports two basic types of object server models. The two models differ in the execution strategy. One of the object server types could be written as a Dynamic Link Library (DLL). These DLLs (also called *in-process servers*) are loaded by the client application. In-process servers cannot exist on their own and execute within the client's address space. *Local servers* are the other type of object server and they are written as executables. Local servers are stand-alone servers, can exist on their own, and can execute within their own address space. They do not need a client application explicitly to load them to start functioning.

Another object model was later derived from the two basic servers – called remote servers – which is geared more toward the distributed architecture.

Remote servers are object servers executing on a different machine than the client. In contrast to the other two object server models, which are executing on the same machine, Remote servers do not work on the same machine as the client application. Remote servers can be written as DLLs or as local servers. If remote servers are developed as DLLs, then a surrogate process is created for them on the remote machine. (Remember, DLLs cannot exist on their own. They need a process to load them.)

DCOM sets up the initial connection between the client application and the object server. Once the connection is established, the client and object server interacts directly without being routed through the DCOM runtime modules. DCOM provides location transparency. The client application communicating to the object server does not have to deal with special cases of the object server model. If the object server is an in-process server, then DCOM runtime loads the object module and returns the interface pointer to the client. If the object server is a local server, then DCOM starts the object server module. In this case, DCOM makes use of remote procedure calls to the local server to retrieve the interface pointer. Once the interface pointer is obtained, the client communicates directly with the local server. If the object server is a remote object server, DCOM manages the show under the cover. The registry stores the specific location information for the remote object server. DCOM issues remote procedure calls to the DCOM runtime module on the remote machine to start the remote object server. Once the remote object server is started by the remote DCOM runtime module, it retrieves interface pointers and returns to the calling DCOM runtime module. The DCOM runtime module on the local machine is passed on the interface pointer to the client application and from there on, it is the client application's responsibility.

DCOM provides inheritance via aggregation and inheritance via containment and delegation. Both the inheritance models are useful. The aggregation model allows the application to form composite objects whose basic job is to aggregate interfaces from different objects together in itself. Figure 1-11 shows a simple inheritance by aggregation model in DCOM. In this figure, object Object_1 has an interface called Interface O1, object Object_2 exposes the interface Interface O2 and object Object_3 exposes the interface Interface O3. For a client application to make use of all the three interface within the same application, it would have to locate all the three different objects. It must go through the DCOM protocol to connect to those objects and then make use of the interfaces. This could be a rather tedious process. To simply this, the application could form a composite object (Aggregate Object AO) that aggregates the three interfaces and exposes it through one object. Any client application that wants to make use of the interface can instantiate the composite object and work with one object to satisfy its needs. The composite object activates all the three objects under the cover. When it gets a request from the client application for a particular interface, it guides it to the right object. This is a simple application, but it assists in a big way in the development process.

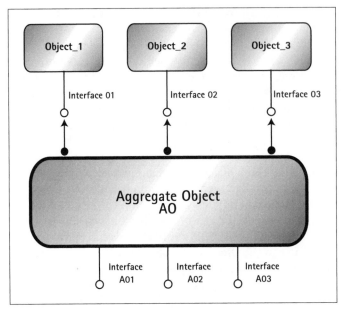

Figure 1-11: Inheritance by Aggregation

The other kind of inheritance model supported by DCOM is containment and delegation. Containment and delegation takes a step further in the aggregation model. In aggregation, you saw that the composite object exposes the interface of the other objects it aggregates within itself. These other objects and their interfaces are also available to the client objects to access directly without going through the composite object. The containment and delegation model is built especially for the outer object to contain the inner objects completely. (The containment is not real as the inner object is actually outside the outer object's domain.) The outer object can filter and validate, if necessary, the requests targeted toward the interfaces of the inner objects. Please remember, neither of the models binds the developer to use strictly one or the other. The separation of the two models is purely conceptual and a mix and match is possible.

Figure 1-12 shows a containment and delegation model. The inner object is entirely contained within the outer object. The inner object's interface is exposed only via the outer object. This serves one good purpose. If the inner object changes its interface, then due to the level of indirection, the client application does not get impacted instantaneously. This would specifically be useful when the inner object has just updated its version and the new version of the interface needs more management-related information passed into it. The outer interface could still stay the same, but the outer object could retrieve the required information to be passed to the inner object without the client being aware of the changes. This would, of course, not work if the interface changes drastically so that more information from the client is required. But, in any event, if such a drastic change in the interface occurs, you would provide a new interface to the client application to work with.

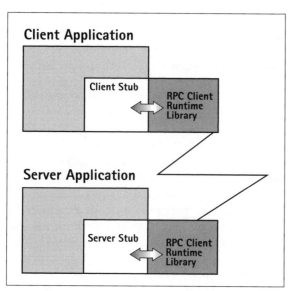

Figure 1-12: Inheritance by Containment and Delegation

DCOM does not dictate the number of interfaces the DCOM object should support. The DCOM object could support multiple interfaces. One particular interface is important for DCOM to function in the standard fashion, however. This interface is called IUnknown. Every DCOM object needs to implement IUnknown. This interface has three methods called QueryInterface, AddRef, and Release. Before going into these three methods, you should understand the importance of the IUnknown interface.

In the previous paragraphs on DCOM, you learned that when the client application identifies the object server from the registry, the client application tries to activate the object server. You then learned the DCOM runtime retrieved the interface pointer and passed it on to the client application. Which interface? The IUnknown interface pointer. This is always the first interface obtained by the client application. The IUnknown interface is the gateway to all object servers. To get to the other interfaces supported by the object, the IUnknown interface has a method called QueryInterface. The client issues a QueryInterface call using the IUnknown interface pointer. The call takes in the interface identifier for which the client is looking. If the object supports that particular interface, then the QueryInterface method returns the pointer to the interface. Using the IUnknown interface pointer, the client could walk though all the interfaces supported by the client. The IUnknown interface pointer helps the client to locate the right kind of interface needed for the job. Based on this dynamism, the client can augment the behavior of its applications based on the runtime situation, rather than having all the required services known during the compilation time.

The AddRef and Release are used for controlling the life span of the object. DCOM objects use reference counting for controlling the life span of the object. This is the classical reference counting approach, wherein the AddRef increments the reference count of the object and Release decrements it. This helps in avoiding multiple copies of an object in memory. If the reference count of the object is greater than zero, someone is referring to the object and has an active reference to the object. This object will be kept alive in memory. As soon as the reference count goes to zero, the object is removed from memory. When a client application tries to locate the DCOM object based on its classid, the DCOM runtime module locates the object and then tries to activate it. Because every DCOM object is an entity of its own, it would know how to create an instance of itself. So every DCOM object must provide an interface that would help activate itself on request. Every DCOM object, therefore, implements a IClassFactory interface. One of the methods present in the IClassFactory interface is called CreateInstance. This method provides a path for the DCOM object to create an instance of itself. The creation code is dependent on the DCOM object itself.

CORBA is a distributed object oriented framework and is highly modularized by design. CORBA acts like an object, but it brings the different object functionalities together and builds a fully functional network of objects. CORBA is object oriented in design, dealing with objects as the basic functioning unit. It also stems from the client-server world, wherein the client object and the server object come from two different address spaces. The object's implementation and the interfaces are separated.

IDL is used to capture the interfaces of the object. DCOM also uses IDL to define the interface between the client and server module. DCOM's object model proposes incremental development processes that are targeted toward the ease of application developers. Although versatility in the development process is needed in a distributed object framework, DCOM tries to approach this goal with ease of development as the prime path. The issues are kept as simple as possible. The DCOM model avoids overwhelming the application developer with too much information to handle at a particular time.

The DCOM architecture is fairly open, but restrictive in its widespread approach. The restriction shown is good to some extent, due to the number of erroneous paths it avoids. Both CORBA and DCOM provide an advanced client-server programming environment. The server object provides the service, which is used by the client object. The client and the server objects could be in two different address spaces. The framework builds the bridge needed to connect the two objects and to satisfy the needs. DCOM uses remote procedure calls as the application level communication protocol. CORBA, on the other hand, uses IIOP as the application level communication protocol. DCOM refers to the client portion of the interface as the proxy and the server portion of the interface as the stub. CORBA refers to the client portion of the interface as the *stub* and the server portion as the *skeleton*. Although the nomenclature may be slightly different, both are chartered to do similar tasks. In a distributed framework, there must be a common repository from which the objects and their interfaces could be located.

The DCOM registry serves the purpose of a repository wherein the object's references are stored. The registry helps in locating the object servers. In CORBA, dedicated services are available for object server location. These services are called the *Trader Services*. DCOM is particularly strong in its approach of incremental enhancements. Developers are often faced with the situation of incremental deployment of application objects. The deployment should be performed so it does not break the existing setup. DCOM helps in adding newer interfaces, while still supporting the existing interfaces, so the new version of the application object will work with the existing set of client applications. This kind of setup method would keep the older sets of client application working with the older interfaces being supported by the newer installed object server. At the same time, newer clients writing to the newer interfaces would also work with the same object server.

DCOM, however, does not allow versioning of interfaces. Interface versions need more information on past versions of the interfaces to be stored with every interface. The difference in versions could get difficult to manage. The benefits obtained by versioning them would not be enough to undertake the complexities involved. CORBA and DCOM support the same concept of an interface being a collection of semantically alike methods. CORBA provides different language bindings from IDL to C++, IDL to C, IDL to Java, and so forth. DCOM does not provide any language bindings. DCOM supports basic fault-tolerant mechanisms and it possesses the capability to reroute objects from one server to another without needing any input from the client at runtime. This is possible when the environment is set up for such needs. DCOM similarly performs load balancing by working closely with the operating system. Because Windows NT is the primary development platform, it leverages from the load balancing features available from the operating system. On the contrary, CORBA does not implicitly support such features. Fault tolerance is an external service that can be implemented on a CORBA-based environment. The benefit of implementing such services on CORBA is that CORBA is not bound tightly to the operating system. Also, CORBA does not specify the type of implementation and it is open in architecture. You could implement the load-balancing features or fault-tolerant features according to the needs of the actual environment.

Remote Method Invocation versus CORBA

Remote Method Invocation (RMI) was introduced by JavaSoft. RMI is JavaSoft's attempt to make Java a widespread and preferential distributed framed environment. RMI extends Java in a way that remote methods could be invoked by a Java application (or an applet). By remote methods, we mean methods within a remote Java object. RMI was introduced with JDK 1.1. The RMI API includes the new remote interfaces that must be implemented by a Java object to make the object remote. To make a Java object remote, the JDK includes an RMI compiler, which runs through the Java binary file (the .class file) to generate the client stubs and the server skeleton files. The server object, which wants to expose its interface to be accessed remotely, uses the skeleton file generated by the compiler. Any client application that wants to make use of the server object via RMI must use the client stub portion. The client stub acts as the server's proxy and helps the client make the remote call. Because the stub has the remote call defined in the client stub file, the Java compiler (javac) will not complain while compiling the client application.

To locate a remote object, a common entry point must exist where every Java application will query to locate the remote object. This common entry point is called the *rmiregistry*. The working of the rmiregistry is somewhat similar to what the other frame works provide. The registry in RMI is a nonpersistent entity. This implies the information stored in the registry is lost as soon as the registry is unloaded from the system. The registry helps in locating the objects in the network. More improvements in the registry implementation will be seen from JavaSoft in the near future.

Within a networked environment you could have one registry per machine or one registry for the entire network. When a server object wants to be accessed remotely, it will register itself with the registry. Once the server object is registered with the registry, any client querying the server object is handed by the server object reference. The client object takes the reference and tries to activate the server object from the appropriate location. Once the server object is located and activated, the client can make necessary calls to execute the methods remotely. RMI also enables dynamically downloading of the stub code if it is not present in the local machine. This is a strong feature that comes to the aid of the programmers and automates the dynamic invocation process to some extent. This helps in making sure that, at any instant, the client has the required stub code to make use of the remote object's services.

When the client makes a call to the remote method, the stub code picks up the call and, via RMI, sends the required data to the server. RMI has features that marshal the data passed from the client to the server and vice versa. RMI has made Java work with a push approach. With the previous releases of Java and the development kits, Java had introduced the concept of downloading applications from the server workstation on the clients for execution. This could be desirable or undesirable. We would often like to execute a method on to the server and obtain the result. The processing scripts could be retained on the server itself. The client application could pass the required criteria to the server. RMI makes such a wish a reality. Of course, difficulties are involved in such a programming model. The RMI-based server could be present anywhere within the network. If a client wishes to execute a method on one of the remote servers and the object is not located with the rmiregistry local to the client application, the rmiregistry local to the client would try to contact the other available rmiregistry for the server object.

We'll assume the client must go through two rmiregistry to get to the server object. While the remote method is being executed on the server, if the link between the two rmiregistry is broken due to some network error, no way exists for the client application to obtain the result of the remote method execution. This is a difficult situation and there is no documented solution to this problem. This problem is not directly related to RMI. Such complex issues are involved in a distributed framework world. (CORBA faces the problem. The solution to this problem cannot be provided entirely by the object framework. The communication protocol in close association with the base network could provide a solution.)

Java allows exception handling in its environment. RMI has extended the exception handling to remote object management. The difficulty level in handling exceptions in a distributed environment (executing services from a remote site) is much more complex than in local exception handling. While many new parameters exist to consider when managing such a show, the Java RMI system does not have a proper answer to this.

Java has a garbage-collection system built into its environment, which is based on reference counting of the objects. Any object that has a reference count greater than one will not be removed from the memory, but the ones with reference counts of zero will be removed by the garbage-collector module. Garbage collection helps in moving the common programming problem of memory leaks from the programmer's domain to the system's domain. Solving the problem from the system's point of view is much easier because the operations are simple. The intelligence built into the system will take care of the object cleaning process; hence, memory leaks are avoided.

This also introduces a new paradigm mismatch in the object-oriented programming world. The garbage collector in the Java environment operates based on a scheduling mechanism. In a classical object-oriented world, every object has a construction and a destruction point defined. The construction point is an object creation phase. After going through the construction point, two possible situations exist: either the object is created and fully initialized or the object creation failed due to some error. Likewise, after the destruction call, either the call was successful and the object was destroyed (removed from memory) or the call failed and the object was not destroyed, implying the object is still alive. This means only two states are defined in this state diagram. In the case of the garbage-collected system, after a successful call to the object's destructor, the object is lost from the application's point of view, but the object is not removed from memory. The garbage collector does the job of object clean up. So, the object is still in physical memory until the time the garbage collector wakes up.

RMI introduced remote garbage collection. When a Java object executes a method within a remote object, the remote object is loaded into the address space of the remote machine and the reference count of the object is incremented. This is a *remote reference count*. This remote link to the object is maintained by a network connection (typically a TCP/IP link). If the connection goes down, then the garbage collector on the remote machine will delete the remote object, but the local object still has a valid reference to the remote object. The remote exception (an exception on the local machine) is thrown as soon as the local object tries to access the remote object. If the connection comes back up, RMI does not do an automatic rebinding to the remote object. This brings in somewhat of an overhead on the application programmer because the application programmer must keep track of the remote exceptions to take care of such problems. Another visible thing is the garbage collector must differentiate between the objects that have local reference counts and the objects that have remote reference counts. The garbage collector must check the links of the objects having remote reference counts to determine whether they must be removed from the memory. This does add an extra amount of overhead to the garbage collector.

RMI is a pure Java-based development environment designed to keep Java as its main platform of operation. RMI needs the Java Virtual Machine at both ends to function correctly. A non-Java object cannot talk to a Java object via RMI. Such homogeneity has advantages as well as disadvantages. One advantage is because the system runs totally under Java, the application's behavior is predictable. No violation would be observed as a security system is completely enforced within the system. A disadvantage is people must convert their existing applications from a non-Java environment to a Java-based application to make use of RMI (or to provide a Java wrapper around the existing application).

Interoperability with other environments is not yet available. Generally, distributed architectures try to promote multienvironment and multilanguage interoperability. This helps the acceptance of a distributed architecture as the existing tools can be used with the new system without making major alterations to the system. Minor changes are usually required to support the new architecture. Different distributed architectures attempt to solve the problem in different manners. Some provide binary interoperability so the existing binary could plug into the new system by adding some attachments or by providing some layers on top of the existing working system while others provide language mappings. They promote mapping from the existing language to a universal language understood by the distributed framework. Many of the frameworks discussed in this chapter provide mappings to IDL, which is universally accepted as the generic language for such distributed frameworks. Such attempts, although they add some extra number of layers in the system, make the evolutionary process less painful. They do not demand a complete transfer of the existing application to the new environment.

CORBA and RMI face some similar issues that are difficult to resolve, such as remote exceptions; a proper network failure recovery mechanism, and so on. Both rely on IDL for the interface definition phase. Each is faced with the problem of when changes are made to the interface on the server, the clients are not automatically updated. The client application, instead, being bound to the previous version of the interface definition, would have to be rebuilt. RMI does enable the client to download the client stub; but it neither addresses the issue of conflicts nor provides a good reconciliation mechanism. RMI depends on a pure Java-based execution model while CORBA has no such requirements. CORBA provides a much more diverse development environment without any kind of dependencies on the operating platform. Also, due to its close ties with Java, RMI is an interpreted environment.

CORBA Development Tools

Many free, as well as commercial, ORBs are available in the market today. This list contains the more popular ones, but those not mentioned are in no way inferior.

CORBAPLUS

Expersoft's CORBAPlus is available for a 60-day trial. CORBAPlus unifies a network-computing environment by supporting multiple object models (CORBA, COM), languages (C++, Java), and platforms (Windows 95, Windows NT, and UNIX). It is available at: http://www.expersoft.com/.

FNORB

This is a CORBA ORB written in the Python language. Fnorb includes a language mapping for Python and currently requires a third-party Interface Repository to parse and store IDL definitions. Fnorb is free for noncommercial use. It is available at http://www.dstc.edu.au/AU/staff/martin-chilvers/Fnorb/.

OMNI-ORB 2

Olivetti and Oracle Research Laboratories with their joint efforts have come up with Omni-ORB 2, which is a CORBA 2-compliant ORB. It supports C++ bindings and it is freely available at http://www.orl.co.uk/omniORB/omniORB.html.

JTRADER

jTrader is not a full-blown ORB; instead, it is a Java implementation of the COS Trading Object Service, available under the terms of the GNU Public License (GPL). jTrader currently runs on top of OmniBroker 2.0b3 or VisiBroker 3.0. It is available at: http://www.intellisoft.com/~mark/.

MICO

MICO stands for Mico Is CORBA. The MICO project provides a freely available and complete CORBA 2.0 implementation under the GNU public license. The ORB is made for educational purposes and is developed in C++ using standard UNIX API. Full source code is available with the ORB It is available at: http://diamant-atm.vsb.cs.uni-frankfurt.de/~mico/.

JOE

Joe is a Sun CORBA product that works with NEO. Joe includes an Object Request Broker (ORB) that connects Java applets to remote CORBA objects running on any machine across the Internet or intranet. The Joe ORB is automatically downloaded into Web browsers along with Java applets that require its use. Joe then establishes and manages connections between local Java objects and remote CORBA objects using the industry-standard Internet Inter-ORB Protocol (IIOP). Joe 1.0 is available for free and can be downloaded from http://www.sun.com/sunsoft/neo/joe/index.html.

JYLU

Jylu is a freely available, freely distributable CORBA ORB from Stanford Digital Library Testbed Development, Department of Computer Science, Stanford University. Jylu is an implementation of Xerox PARC's ILU runtime kernel and Java language binding developed completely in the Java language. It is on-the-wire compatible with ILU 2.0 (any ILU 2.0 client can call the methods of any Jylu true object and any Jylu surrogate can call methods of any ILU 2.0 true object). As Jylu is developed completely in Java, it can run anywhere Java is supported. Julu can be obtained from `http://coho.stanford.edu/~hassan/Jylu/`.

JACORB

JacORB, developed by Gerald Brose, is a free ORB written in Java. An Object Request Broker written in Java, JacORB is a partial implementation of OMG's CORBA standard. JacORB is free and it's easy to install and use. It enables (almost) transparent method invocation across virtual machine boundaries. It's available at: `http://www.inf.fu-berlin.de/~brose/jacorb/`.

ELECTRA

Electra is a CORBA 2.0 Object Request Broker, written by Silvano Maffeis, which supports the implementation of distributed applications. It runs on communication subsystems like Horus, Ensemble, and Isis. Electra is designed so it can be easily ported to a new communication subsystem. It is available in source code form from `http://www.olsen.ch/~maffeis/electra.html`.

ILU

The Inter-Language Unification system (ILU) is a multilanguage object interface system developed at Xerox. ILU supports the many programming languages including C++, ANSI C, Python, Java, and Common Lisp. ILU runs on almost all flavors of UNIX (SunOS, Solaris, HP-UX, AIX, OSF, IRIX, FreeBSD, Linux, LynxOS, SCO UNIX, and so forth) and Microsoft Windows 3.1, Windows 95, and Windows NT. With such a wide variety of languages supported, ILU can be used to build multilingual class libraries, and with such a wide number of platforms supported, ILU can be used to implement distributed systems. ILU can also be used to define and document interfaces between the modules of nondistributed programs. ILU interfaces can be specified in either the OMG's CORBA Interface Definition Language (OMG IDL), or in ILU's Interface Specification Language (ISL). It is available from `ftp://beta.xerox.com/pub/ilu/ilu.html`.

OAK

OAK is a CORBA2-compliant ORB available from Paragon Software Inc. for a wide variety of platforms. It supports C++ and Java bindings, IIOP, DII, DSI, and plans to support naming and events. A full version of OAK is available for evaluation purposes from `http://www.paragon-software.com/oak/`.

DOME

DOME (Distributed Object Management Environment) is a C++ Object Request Broker toolkit for the implementation of Distributed Systems. DOME allows services, data, and applications to be easily and effectively distributed across heterogeneous systems, integrating old and new systems into a common enterprisewide framework. Developed by Object Oriented Technologies Ltd., DOME is available free for personal use on the C-Linux platform from http://www.realobj.demon.co.uk.

ORBIXWEB

OrbixWeb from the IONA Technologies is a full CORBA2 ORB implemented in Java and is available for download free for 60 days. It enables your Java applets and applications to be *plugged* into the CORBA infrastructure and thereby enables them to interoperate seamlessly with both Java and non-Java applications and components across the enterprise. It is available at their site at http://www.iona.com/Products/Orbix/OrbixWeb/.

CHORUS/COOL ORB

CHORUS/COOL ORB is a CORBA-compliant Object Request Broker for Distributed Real time Embedded Systems. CHORUS/COOL ORB provides a standards-based development environment combining OMG's CORBA object-oriented architecture with CHORUS componentized operating system technology. It is available on a variety of popular host systems, including Windows NT, Windows 95, Linux, Solaris, SunOS, and HP/UX. CHORUS/COOL ORB interoperates across all these platforms. With IIOP, true interoperability with other ORBs is achieved. It can be obtained from http://www.chorus.com/Products/Cool/index.html.

VISIGENIC

Visigenic has made CORBA development tools for both C++ and Java. Called VisiBroker for C++ and Java, respectively. Objects built with VisiBroker for C++ can easily be accessed by Web-based applications that communicate using CORBA's Internet-Inter-ORB protocol (IIOP). It is available at http://www.Visigenic.com/.

Summary

CORBA, or Common Object Request Broker Architecture, is a set of specifications defining the ways software objects should work together in a distributed environment. CORBA presents a strong, universal, powerful framework. This framework enables objects to talk to one another across network, platform, and language boundaries. Although many distributed architectures are available now – all with their respective benefits – CORBA is beginning to show its advantages. The advantages of CORBA over other distributed computing architectures, such as Distributed Component Object Model (DCOM), include not only its object-oriented foundation, but also its location transparency and multilanguage, multiplatform support. The advent of the Web in a major form has also helped in the growth of CORBA. The systems no longer work in their own vicinity; instead, thanks to CORBA, they are now distributed. The promise of the interworking of software objects from different vendors through CORBA has induced major players in the industry to endorse OMG's drive aggressively for such a distributed environment.

Chapter 2

CORBA: An Architectural Overview

IN THIS CHAPTER

We explore the details of CORBA in this chapter. The architecture of CORBA is based on the object Management Architecture (OMA), which was created by the Object Management Group (OMG). OMG was founded to standardize object-oriented software to create and promote component-based software implementations and standard interfaces for Distributed Object Computing. OMG does this through the help of the architectural framework of OMA. These specifications help in taking OMG to its goal of interoperable, reusable; portable software components based on open, standard, object-oriented interfaces.

- ◆ The Object Management Architecture Model
- ◆ CORBA architecture
- ◆ BOA and other object adapters
- ◆ How CORBA frameworks work
- ◆ Example of a CORBA application
- ◆ Inter-ORB architecture

The Object Management Architecture Model

OMA is the high level design of a distributed system provided by OMG. It is made up of five main components catering to three main segments of our software industry. The main components, which define the OMA, are object Request Broker, object Services, Common Facilities, Domain Interfaces, and Application Objects. OMA addresses an industry-wide solution for interoperable software by dividing it into three main segments, mainly *Application Oriented*, *System Oriented*, and *Vertical Market Oriented*. For handling the Application-Oriented systems, the OMA characterizes Interfaces and Common Facilities as solution-specific components that rest closest to the user. The object Request Brokers and object Services help in defining the System and infrastructure aspects of distributed object computing and management. The Vertical Market segment is handled by *Domain Interfaces,* which are vertical applications or domain-specific interfaces.

Of all these components, object Request Broker (ORB) is the one that constitutes the foundation of OMA and manages all communication among components. ORB is responsible for enabling different objects – lying across the network and unaware of each other's implementation methods – to interact in a heterogeneous, distributed environment. In performing its task, ORB relies on *object Services,* which are responsible for general object management, such as creating objects, access control, and keeping track of relocated objects. Common Facilities and Application Objects are the components closest to the end user and in their functions they invoke services of the system components. Figure 2-1 illustrates the overall Object Management Architecture.

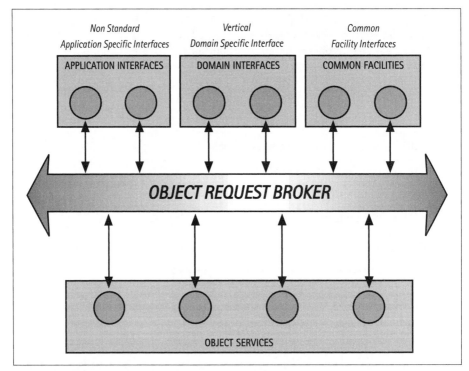

Figure 2–1: Object Management Architecture

OMA Components

The heart or the main component of the OMA is ORB, also known commercially as CORBA. ORB provides the foundation and underlying operation for the distributed objects and their management. It provides an infrastructure that enables object to talk to one another, independent of the specific platforms and techniques used to implement the objects. Compliance with the ORB standard guarantees portability and interoperability of objects over a network of heterogeneous systems.

Object Services are a collection of services that support basic functions for using and implementing objects. They help in standardizing the life-cycle management of objects. Interfaces are provided to create objects, to control access to objects, to keep track of relocated objects, and to control the relationship among styles of objects (class management). Also provided are the generic environments in which single objects can perform their tasks. object Services provide for application consistency and help to increase programmer productivity. object Services are independent of application domains; they do not tell how objects are implemented in the application.

The collection of services that many applications can share, but are not as fundamental as object Services, is called *Common Facilities*. Commercially known as *CORBAfacilities,* common facilities provide a set of generic application functions that can be configured to the specific requirements of a particular configuration. These are facilities, such as printing, document management, database, and electronic mail, that sit closer to the user. Standardization leads to uniformity in generic operations and to better options for end users for configuring their working environments. CORBAfacilities also include facilities for use over the Internet.

Application Objects constitute the uppermost layer of the reference model. They are built by independent vendors who control the interfaces of the objects. The Application Interfaces represent component-based applications performing specialized tasks for the user. As these are essentially applications developed by private vendors, they are not standardized by OMG.

Domain Interfaces represent vertical areas that provide functionality of direct interest to end users, particularly application domains. Domain interfaces may combine some common facilities and object services, but are designed to perform particular tasks for users within a certain vertical market or industry.

These components that make up OMA are standard OMA components, available to the developer at the time of development. The developer needn't develop these components to make the applications that are CORBA-complaint.

OMG'S OBJECT MODEL OMG's object model underlies the CORBA architecture and acts as a basis for developing objects in a distributed environment. The object model helps in defining concepts so an object system can define services for the client in an implementation-independent manner. The implementation-independent principle is important because it enables different object technologies to grow and define the solution in their own manner. The OMG object model provides an organized presentation of object concepts and terminology. The object Model first describes concepts that are meaningful to clients, including such concepts as object creation and identity, requests and operations, and types and signatures. It then describes concepts related to object implementations, including such concepts as methods, execution engines, and activation.

The OMG object model defines a core set of requirements defined on the basis of basic concepts of objects, methods, attributes, types, requests, creation and destruction of objects, that must be supported in any system that complies with the object model standard. While the core object model serves as a common ground for the OMG object model, extension to the core model is allowed to enable even greater commonality among different technology domains.

Common Object Request Broker Architecture

In Chapter 1, we briefly describe the architecture of CORBA. Here we cover the architecture in more detail. Because we are looking at the architecture, I mainly explore it from the perspective of the big picture, so the details of how to use the different components aren't covered. Instead, we discuss how the different components fit together.

Before beginning, though, we want to summarize the process of developing a CORBA application. This will help you understand the architecture.

To develop a CORBA application, you will create the IDL, which represents the remotely accessible object. You run this IDL through an IDL Compiler, which generates client and server (or implementation) code based on the definitions in your IDL. Because IDL contains only definitions and no code, it's your job as the programmer to expand each of these resulting code sets by inserting the desired features. For the client, you create code that accesses and uses the object. For the implementation, you provide the actual code for the object – that is, you provide the implementation.

In your client code, you have what's called a *proxy object,* which represents the remote object. When your client calls methods in this proxy object, the associated operation will take place in the remote object. The way this works is the proxy object has code that calls into the CORBA client library.

On the server end, the CORBA library handles the hard work of calling into your implementation code to create the object. It also calls into your code to perform the operations. Most of this happens automatically by the CORBA library running under a process on the server computer, but it's important for you to understand how all this works to get the most out CORBA.

CORBA represents the core of OMA, the Object Request Broker. The ORB is the middleware that establishes the client-server relationships between objects. In the architecture, the ORB, which you will typically obtain from a third-party CORBA tool, is not required to be implemented as a single component, but rather it is defined by its interfaces. With an ORB, the protocol is defined through the application interfaces via a single implementation, language-independent specification, the Interface definition language (IDL). As a result, the developer can choose the most appropriate operating system, execution environment, and even programming language to use for each component of a system under construction. Using an ORB, a client can transparently invoke a method on a server object, which can be on the same machine or across a network. The ORB intercepts the call and is responsible for finding an object that can implement the request, pass it the parameters, invoke its method, and return the results. The client needn't be aware of where the object is located, its programming language, its operating system, or any other system aspects that are not part of an object's interface. In so doing, the ORB provides inter-operability between applications on different machines in heterogeneous distributed environments and seamlessly interconnects multiple object systems.

Object Request Broker (ORB)

Figure 2-2 shows the structure of the ORB. To make a request, the client can use an OMG IDL Stub or it may dynamically connect to the remote object using an inter-face known as Dynamic Invocation Interface (DII), whereby the client can dynami-cally discover the interfaces supplied by the remote object. The client can also interact directly with the ORB by calling some of its functions.

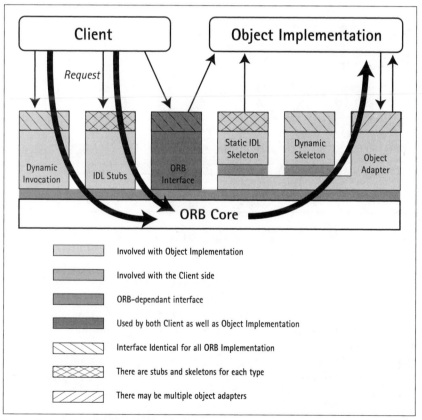

Figure 2-2: Object Request Broker Interfaces

Interfaces to objects can be defined in two ways. First, they can be defined statically using IDL. This language defines the types of objects according to the operations that may be performed on them and the parameters to those operations. Second, or in addition, interfaces can be added to an Interface Repository service, which represents the components of an interface as objects, permitting run-time access to these components. In any ORB implementation, the IDL and the Interface Repository have equivalent expressive power.

The client performs a request by having access to an object reference for an object and by knowing the type of the object and the desired operation to be performed. The client initiates the request by calling stub routines (OMG IDL stubs) specific to the object or by constructing the request dynamically (DII). The dynamic and stub interfaces for invoking a request satisfy the same request semantics, and the receiver of the message cannot tell how the request was invoked. This is illustrated in Figure 2-3.

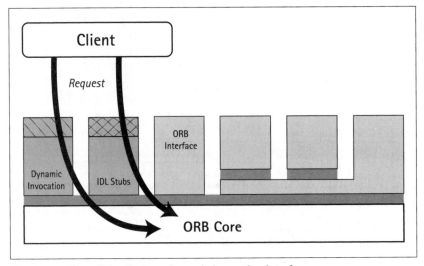

Figure 2-3: Client Using Stubs or Dynamic Invocation Interface

The ORB locates the appropriate implementation code and then transmits parameters and transfers control to the object Implementation through an IDL skeleton or a dynamic skeleton. Skeletons are specific to the interface and the object adapter. In performing the request, the object implementation may obtain some services from the ORB through the object adapter. When the request is complete, control and output values are returned to the client. The object Implementation may choose which object adapter to use. This decision is based on what kind of services the object Implementation requires. Figure 2-4 shows this.

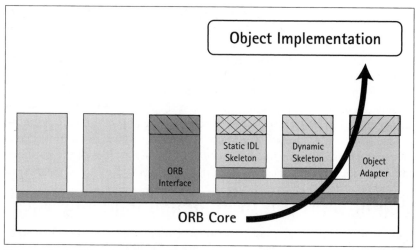

Figure 2-4: An Object Implementation Receiving a Request

OMG's Interface Definition Language

As the name suggests, the *OMG Interface definition language(OMG IDL)*, is a language used to define the types of objects by specifying the interfaces. An object interface is its window to the world and defines the object's properties. Programmatically, the interface is defined using named operations and parameters to those operations. The IDL defines the types of objects, their attributes, the methods they export, and the method parameters.

Object implementations use IDL to tell its potential clients what operations are available and how they should be invoked. IDL definitions are used to map the CORBA objects into programming languages or object systems. IDL provides a framework for describing the objects manipulated by the ORB. But it is unnecessary for IDL source code to be available for the ORB to work. As long as equivalent information is available in the form of either stub routines or run-time interface repository, an ORB may be able to function correctly. The CORBA IDL is a subset of ANSI C++ with additional constructs to support distribution. It is a purely declarative language and uses C++ syntax for constant, type, and operation definitions.

Here's a brief example of an IDL. The details of how this is used is covered later, but here's an example, so you know how an IDL looks:

```
interface ObjTimeServer {
   String getTime();
};
```

This sample IDL defines an object interface called *ObjTimeServer,* which consists of one operation, getTime, which returns a string. In the sample later in this chapter, this interface is put to use.

As you work through this book, you'll see a great deal of IDL, so this is a good chance to go through a topic regarding the interfaces. Interfaces include operations that, ultimately, become methods in a class that the client can call. Although the previous code does not have any parameters in the getTime() operation, each parameter in an operation is designated either in, out, or inout. This simply refers to the direction of the data. In an *in parameter,* the data is sent to the server object when the client calls the operation; in an *out parameter,* the data is sent from the server back to the client — that is, it's returned to the client, much like a function result. In an *inout parameter,* the data goes both ways. In other words, with an inout parameter, the client can specify a value and send it to the server; the server can then change the value, and return it back to the client.

Mapping of OMG IDL to Programming Languages

Because you're ultimately developing your CORBA-compliant application in a standard language, such as C++ or Java, you will use the CORBA tools to convert the IDL into C++ or Java skeleton code. This includes the so-called stub routines, which call into the underlying ORB library. The programmer then expands this resulting code. The question then arises, What does this skeleton code look like — that is, how is the IDL converted to C++ or Java? This is called a language mapping.

A *language mapping* includes definitions of the language specific data types and procedure interfaces access objects through the ORB. It also includes the structure of client stub interfaces for nonobject-oriented languages, DII, implementation skeleton, object adapters, and the direct ORB interface. By OMG's specification, you can be assured the Language mapping of OMG IDL to a language will be the same across different ORBs. The ORB representation of the object reference, methods, and so on, should be invisible to the client. A language mapping also defines the interaction between object invocations and the threads of control in the client or implementation.

Client

A client application accesses a remote object by maintaining a reference to the object. Using the object reference, the client is able to invoke operations on the object. An object reference is a token that may be invoked or passed as a parameter to an invocation on a different object. Invocation of an object involves specifying the object to be invoked, the operations to be performed, and parameters to be given to the operation or returned from it. A client only knows the logical structure of the object through the interfaces and accesses the properties of the object through the invocations.

The client sees objects and ORB interfaces through the perspective of a language mapping. Clients are maximally portable and should be able to work without source changes or any ORB that supports the desired language with any object instance that implements the desired language. Clients have no knowledge of the implementation of the object or which ORB is used to access it.

The ORB is responsible for managing the control transfer and data transfer to the object implementation and back to the client. Clients see objects and ORB interfaces through the perspective of language mapping. All implementations will provide language-specific data types to refer to objects. The client then passes this object reference to the stub routines to initiate an invocation.

As shown in Figure 2-5, clients access object-type-specific stubs as library routines in their program so the client program sees routines callable in the normal way in its programming language. The implementations usually provide a language-specific data type to refer to the object concerned, often an opaque pointer. To initiate invocation, the client uses the object reference to the stub routines. The stubs on their part have access to the object reference representation and interact with the ORB to perform the invocation.

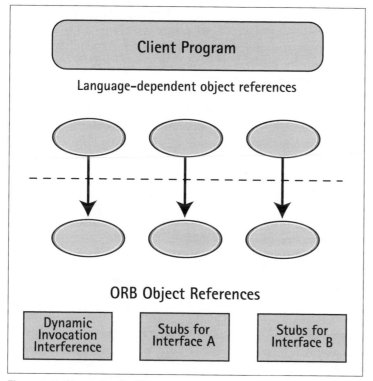

Figure 2-5: Structure of a Client

An alternative set of library code is available, which may be used to perform invocations on objects. A typical example of this is when the object was not defined for the client at compile time. In this case, the client program provides additional information to name the type of the object and the method being invoked, and performs a sequence of calls to specify the parameters and initiate the invocation.

Clients most commonly obtain object references by receiving them from invocations on other objects for which they have references. When a client is also an implementation, it receives object references on invocations to objects it implements. An object reference can also be converted to a string that can be stored in files or preserved or communicated by different means and, subsequently, turned back into an object reference by the ORB that produced the string.

Object Implementation

At the other end from the client is the actual object, known as the object implementation. The *object implementation* provides the actual state and behavior of an object, and it can be structured in a variety of ways. The object implementation defines the methods for operations of the objects and procedures for activating and deactivating objects. It defines methods to object states and ways to control access and to implement methods. The object implementation interacts with the ORB, with the help of an object adapter. The object adapter provides an interface to ORB services that is convenient for a particular style of object implementation. The object implementation interacts with the ORB to establish its identity, to create new objects, and to obtain ORB-dependent services.

When a new objects is created, the ORB may be notified, so it knows where to find the implementation of this object. Usually the implementation also registers itself as implementing objects of a particular interface and specifies how to start the implementation, if it is not already running.

When an invocation occurs, the ORB, an object adapter, and a skeleton arrange a call to be made to the appropriate method of the implementation. (Remember, you, as the programmer of the implementation, supply the code for these methods of the implementation. What is described here is handled automatically by the CORBA system.) A parameter to this method specifies the object being invoked, which the method can use to locate the data for the object. Additional parameters are supplied according to the skeleton definition. When the method is complete, it returns, causing output parameters or exception results to be transmitted back to the client. This process is shown in Figure 2-6.

Most object implementations provide their behavior using facilities in addition to the ORB and object adapter. For example, although the Basic object adapter (the standard object adapter in most CORBA systems) provides some persistent data associated with an object, that relatively small amount of data is typically used as an identifier for the actual object data stored in a storage service of the object implementation's choosing. With this structure, not only can different object implementations use the same storage service, but objects can also choose the service most appropriate for them.

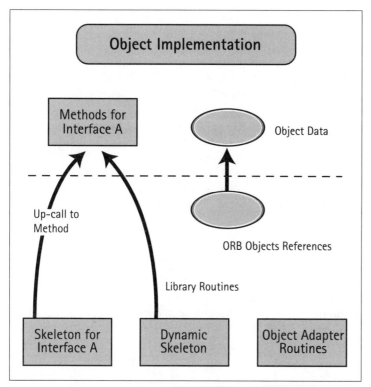

Figure 2-6: Structure of Object Implementation

Object References

As we briefly described earlier, an object reference is a unique name or identifier that provides the information needed to specify an object uniquely within a distributed ORB system. Both the client and the object implementations have an opaque notion of object references according to the language mapping and, thus, are unaffected by the actual representation of them. Two ORB implementations may differ in their choice of object reference representations. Note, the representation of an object handed to a client is valid only for the lifetime of that client.

According to standards, a program written in a particular language should be able to access an object (through an object reference) independent of the ORB. This means all the ORBs must provide the same object mapping to an object reference for a particular language. The language mapping may also provide additional ways to access object references in a typed way for the convenience of the programmer.

Client Stubs

CORBA can be used in both object-oriented languages (such as C++ and Java) and procedural languages (such as C). Object-oriented languages provide methods and interfaces that enable the user to define and access properties of the object. This is lacking in nonobject-oriented languages, which require a programming interface to the stubs for each interface type. Usually the stubs present access to the OMG IDL-defined operations on an object in a way that is easy for programmers to predict, once they are familiar with the OMG IDL and the language mapping for the particular programming language. The stubs make calls on the rest of the ORB using interfaces that are private to, and presumably optimized for, the ORB core. If more ORBs are available, then different stubs may correspond to the different ORBs. In this case, the ORB and language mapping must cooperate to associate the correct stubs with the particular object reference.

Dynamic Invocation Interface (DII)

For situations where the client would like to specify the object to be invoked and the operations to be performed, instead of specifying a particular operation for a particular object, an interface that allows the dynamic construction of object invocations is available. In such cases, the client code must supply the information about the operation performed and the types of parameters passed. This information is usually obtained from a run-time source, such as an Interface Repository. After obtaining the information at runtime, the client code makes the call dynamically using what is called the Dynamic Invocation Interface (DII).

The nature of the dynamic programming interface may vary substantially from one programming language mapping to another. Further, CORBA defines standard APIs for looking up the metadata that defines the server interface, generating the parameters, issuing the remote call, and getting back the results. Read Chapter 7 to learn more about DII.

Object Adapters

If you refer to Figure 2-2, the primary way an object implementation accesses services provided by the ORB is through an object adapter. The object adapter, which is part of a CORBA library, sits on top of the ORB's core communication services and accepts requests on behalf of the server's objects. It provides the run-time environment for instantiating server objects; passing requests to them, and assigning them object IDs. The object adapter also registers the classes it supports and their run-time instances with the Implementation Repository. CORBA specifies that each ORB must support a standard adapter called the Basic Object Adapter (BOA). A server may support more than one object adapter.

Services provided by the ORB through an object adapter often include generation and interpretation of object references, method invocation, security and interactions, object and implementation activation and deactivation, mapping object references to implementations, and registration of implementations. Through object adapters, it is possible for the ORB to target particular groups of object implementations that have similar requirements with interfaces tailored to them.

STRUCTURE OF AN OBJECT ADAPTER An object adapter is the primary means for an object implementation to access ORB services, such as object reference generation. An object adapter exports a public interface to the object implementation and a private interface to the skeleton. Built on a private ORB interface, an object adapter is responsible for various functions, including:

◆ generation and interpretation of the object reference

◆ method invocation

◆ security and interactions

◆ object and implementation activation and deactivation

◆ mapping object references to the corresponding object implementations

◆ registration of implementations

All these functions are performed with the help of ORB core and additional components if required.

You can see from Figure 2-7, the object adapter is implicitly involved in the invocation of methods. The object adapter defines most of the services from the ORB on which the object implementation can depend. With the object adapters, it is possible for an object implementation to have access to a service whether it is implemented in the ORB core. If the ORB core provides the service, then the adapter simply provides an interface to it. If not, then the adapter must implement it on top of the ORB core. Every instance of the adapter provides the same interface and service for all the ORBs on which is implemented. It is also important for the object adapters to provide the same interface. Depending on the requirement, the object adapter should be tuned for a special kind of object implementations. Then it can take the advantage of particular ORB core details to provide the most effective access to the ORB.

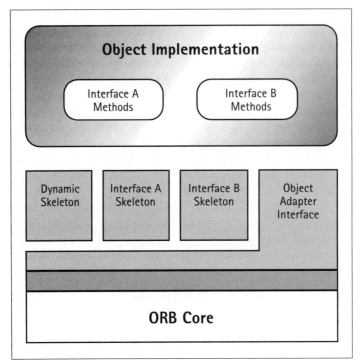

Figure 2-7: Structure of Object Adapter

Implementation Skeleton

For a particular language mapping, and possibly depending on the object adapter, there will be an interface to the methods that implement each type of object. The interface will generally be an up-call interface, in that the developer of the object implementation writes routines that conform to the interface and the ORB calls them through the skeleton.

Note, though, the existence of a skeleton does not imply the existence of a corresponding client stub. The clients can also make requests via the DII.

Also realize that some language mappings do not use skeletons. This is typically true in Smalltalk.

Dynamics Skeleton Interfaces

Dynamic Skeleton Interfaces provide a run time binding mechanism for servers that need to handle incoming method calls for objects that do not have IDL-based compiled skeletons or stubs. The dynamic skeleton looks at the parameter values in an incoming message to determine which object is being called and which method is being invoked. This is in contrast to using normal compiled skeletons, which are defined for a particular object and expect a method implementation for each IDL-defined method.

The implementation code must provide descriptions of all the operation parameters to the ORB and the ORB provides the values of any input parameters for use in performing the operation. The implementation code provides the values of any output parameters, or an exception, to the ORB after performing the operation. The nature of the dynamic skeleton interface may vary substantially from one programming language mapping or object adapter to another, but will typically be an up-call interface. Dynamic skeletons may be invoked both through client stubs and the DII. Either style of client request construction interface provides identical results.

The ORB Interface

The ORB interface is made up of few APIs to local services that are of interest to an application. This is an interface that directly goes to the ORB and is the same for all ORBs. The ORB interface does not depend on the object adapter or the object's interfaces. As most of the functionality of the ORB is provided through the object adapter, stubs, skeletons or dynamic invocations, only a few operations are common across all objects. These operations are useful to both the client and implementation of objects. The common operations include functions like get_interface and get_implementation, which work on any object reference and are used to obtain an Interface Repository object or an Implementation Repository object, respectively, which you learn about next.

Interface Repository

The Interface Repository is a service that provides IDL information in a format available at run-time. The ORB — to perform requests from clients — may use the Interface Repository information. Client programs may also use this information. Using the information available in the Interface Repository, such a program may encounter an object whose interface was unknown when the client program was compiled, yet it could determine what operations are valid on it and make one of these operations. The Interface Repository is also a common database that stores additional information associated with interfaces to ORB objects, such as object definitions, debugging information, and libraries of stubs or skeletons.

Implementation Repository

The Implementation Repository contains information that allows the ORB to locate and activate implementations of objects. It provides a run-time repository of information about the classes the server supports, the objects that are instantiated, and their IDs. Although most of the information in the Implementation Repository is specific to an ORB or operating environment, the Implementation Repository is the conventional place for recording such information. Ordinarily, installation of implementations and control of policies related to the activation and execution of object implementations are done through operations on the Implementation Repository.

In addition to its role in the functioning of the ORB, the Implementation Repository is a common place for the ORB to store additional information associated with the implementations of ORB objects, such as debugging information, administrative control, resource allocation, and security.

BOA and Other Object Adapters

An object adapter handles the task of activating objects. According to needs, the server could have a variety of object adapters. Because the object adapter is something an object implementation depends on, however, keeping only those that are practical is desirable. OMG, after all, does not want see the proliferation of object adapter types. To avoid this, the specification defines an object adapter that can be used for most ORB objects with conventional implementations. The universal adapter is called a *Basic Object Adapter (BOA).*

CORBA specifications require a BOA to be available in every ORB. Object implementations that use the basic object adapter should be able to run on any ORB that supports the required language bindings. The OMG also requires the following functions and features be provided by the BOA implementation for CORBA systems:

1. An Implementation Repository that enables programmers to install and register an object implementation. It should also enable the programmer to provide information that describes the object.

2. Ways of generating and interpreting the object references.

3. Activating and deactivating object implementations.

4. Invoking methods and passing the parameters through stubs and skeletons.

5. A security method that includes the mechanism for authenticating the client making the call. By OMG's specification, a BOA should not enforce any specific style of security. Instead, the BOA must guarantee that for every object or method invocation, it will identify the client on whose behalf the request is performed and allow the object implementation to act accordingly.

Library Object Adapters are primarily used for objects that have library implementations. They access persistent storage in files and do not support activation or deactivation, as the objects are assumed to be in the client's program. Another adapter, called the *Object-Oriented Database (OODB) Adapter,* uses a connection to the object-oriented database to provide access to the objects stored in it. Because the OODB provides the methods and persistent storage, objects may be registered implicitly and no state is required in the object adapter.

How CORBA Framework Works

CORBA is an Object Request Broker framework designed to manage objects from heterogeneous worlds. CORBA is a subset of the much bigger architecture presented by the Object Management Group (OMG), called the Object Management Architecture (OMA). As mentioned in the previous chapter, the OMG is a consortium of over 600 companies in the software industry. The OMG began with a goal to establish a standard way of writing applications for most of the available application domain. OMG, an open consortium, encouraged businesses from all the sectors of the computer world to create a design of their individual applications. The commonalties among the workings of all the applications proved a common architecture existed that most of the applications followed, which was neither documented nor designed properly. The OMA is a result of the work put forward by the consortium in capturing all the information and sorting it accordingly. The OMA is versatile in nature and has found applicability in all application domains. Rather than being simply theoretical, the OMA is real in its approach and does, indeed, help developers design new applications that will work well in the existing world.

As you have seen, objects are the unit of operation for CORBA. This is a simple principle. The objects that actually do the interoperating within the CORBA environment are far more complex. But reducing the operation unit to objects simplifies the object's management concerns. Because objects are entities, providing rules in managing such entities as a whole is easier. One such rule is this: the objects working within the environment must support interfaces through which they talk to the outside world. The Object Request Broker helps to locate objects, to build communication channels among them, and to maintain transparent relational integrity.

The ORB works like a base infrastructure on which complex applications could be built with ease. It provides the hooks needed by an application to perform tasks as smoothly as possible. The CORBA standard not only provides a base for the objects of the application to interoperate, it also tries to address the issues of the vertical, as well as the horizontal, business sector. The consortium goes to the extent of helping application domains generate rules that should be obeyed to generate applications. This helps to reduce the differences in design approaches in the software sector. This also makes interoperability a more realized task.

What Exactly Are Frameworks?

Frameworks are established working sets for a programming environment. Frameworks help developers save considerable time in project development work. In every software project development effort, a sizable amount of time is spent to set up the basic development tools together to provide a smooth development experience throughout the actual phase. Such a process has been repeated for many projects undertaken. As a result, the concept of frameworks came into existence. They provide a basic development environment that could be used to begin the development work. Such frameworks have been well-tested by the industry and are typically built and customized to address a particular application domain. The frameworks capture the basic requirements for applications within that specific domain and reduce the amount of extra cycles the developers have to go though to get the setup working. Saying such customized frameworks nowadays exist for most of the development domains would not be an exaggeration.

The development of frameworks is a massive project in itself. It involves a tremendous amount of foresight on the part of the developer of the system to visualize the needs of future developers. Most of the requirements are gathered from past experiences and many are generated as an estimation for the desired ease to be provided to the user of the framework. Because frameworks provide a proper platform for development, they have many facets. Based on the domain they are addressing, the needs satisfied by frameworks could range from providing simple development tools like integrated editors, compilers, debuggers to supporting multiple communication protocols and providing protocol independence to the applications, and integrated communication models for the environment.

Frameworks could be a visually pleasing tool for more conceptual libraries. The industry has taken a liking toward graphically rich development environments as the generic framework. The goal of all frameworks is the same: simplify the efforts required in project development work and reduce redundant work. The effort of framework development targeted toward a particular application domain is well-appreciated. The documented proof of such appreciation is clearly shown by the ratio of framework developers to framework users. In the software industry, the number of framework users is considerably more than the number of framework developers.

Figure 2-8 shows two standard applications being executed within the same machine (that is, the same physical domain). Each application has its own address space. The application "APP_1" contains an object "O_1_1" that needs to make use of a service being offered by "O_2_1" in "APP_2". These two applications require some kind of simple, effective communication mechanism. The distribution of services needs a simple and protective way of passing data around.

This data-passing mechanism should maintain the application's integrity and not expose the unwanted details to the other application or any other process. This system would probably be happy with some sort of interprocess communication mechanism.

The interprocess communication mechanism would need some support from the operating system on which it is built. While this would certainly work (and it has worked), such a proprietary method would make this system less portable.

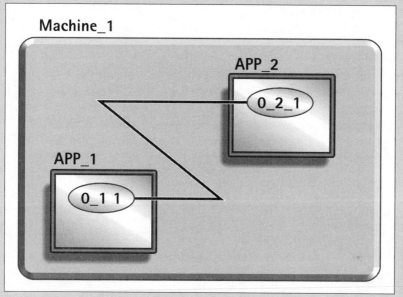

Figure 2-8: Two Applications Executing Within the Same Machine

Portability is an important concern in the software development process. We have all seen the amount of time and money spent by companies in porting applications from one operating system to another and from one environment to another. For the framework to work, therefore, it would need to provide some generic mechanism of transferring data from one process to another.

Figure 2-9 shows the same example, except this time the applications are being executed on different physical machines. This scenario would add difficulties in this sense: Along with the existing sets of issues involved with the applications executing in the same machine, now we must deal with the existing network involved in connecting the two machines. This environment would have to provide a better error-handling mechanism and some auto-correcting facilities as the number of possible failure situations has increased. Also, because the layers of communication between the applications have increased, the errors and the data transfer would be well-cascaded from the generator to the final consumer. At the same time, to be fully successful, the environment would have to provide the same interfaces to the working applications, irrespective of the network built underneath, to keep the application code transparent of the system below.

Continued

What Exactly Are Frameworks? *(Continued)*

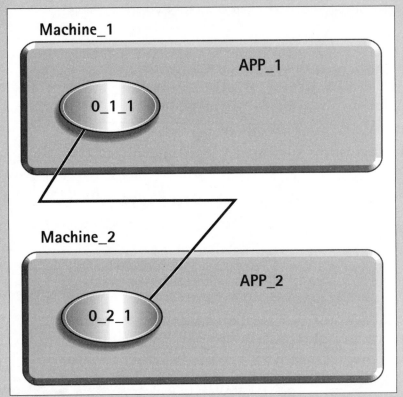

Figure 2-9: Two Applications Executing on Different Machines

It would not be a clean approach for applications to have an extra amount of code to determine whether it is running over a networked environment or within the same physical machine. Such unwanted code for checking the service locations and applying the access code would make the application heavy and slow. Ideally, the application should run on either context without needing any kind of alterations to the application itself. Further, the checks and the access to the services should be done in the lowest level possible, below the applications. These are some of the tough problems a framework helps us resolve. The difficulties involved in building such an environment and how different types of existing frameworks attempt to resolve these issues are shown in more detail in this chapter.

Many task force groups address the different vertical business application domains while remembering the CORBA principles. This provides the developers using CORBA with a huge cooperative working community. An application developer can concentrate on addressing the problem zone of the application in a focused manner. The concerns in software development not directly related to the application are no more the responsibility of the application developer. This is worked on at a much higher level in the food chain of software development.

CORBA applications work in somewhat of a client-server fashion, although the client-server model is not fully obeyed here due to the lack of proper definition and bounds of clients and servers. The client portion of the software talks to the ORB to help it satisfy a service. The client and the server communicate by passing messages between each other. Because the objects are implemented at a remote site (remote in reference to the client), CORBA must provide a way for the client application to locate the server object that would help meet the client's needs. This is performed in a number of ways, the simplest of which is via the Static Invocation Interface (SII). This is analogous to compiling and linking with the dynamic link library calls within the application. Using dynamic link libraries, the programmer develops applications that make calls to functions present in a library. Because the library is linked in dynamically at runtime, the application code is compiled and linked with a stub to the library. The stub helps the compiler understand the syntax of the function call along with the parameters and their types. The stub also helps the linker understand where the code associated with the library call would be available when required during its execution. At runtime, the operating system's loader then loads both the application and the library (if the library isn't already loaded) and connects the two so the application can call into the library.

The Static Invocation Interface allows the application static typing but dynamic binding (or runtime binding). The Static Invocation Interface requires the stub to be available to the client while building the application.

The alternate way of locating the CORBA compliant server object by a CORBA compliant client is by making use of DII. The DII does not require the client application to be aware of the server object interfaces during the compilation time. The client object takes the help of the Trader Services to locate the server object. *Trader Services,* one type of the services defined by the OMG group, is like the Yellow Pages assistance you have in real life. When you want to locate a certain business, you use the Yellow Pages provided by your local telephone company. The Yellow Pages have listings of business phone numbers and addresses.

Trader Services are a similar kind of service available within an ORB environment. Once the server object is located, the client queries the Interface Repository and the Trader Services for the services provided by the server object. When the interfaces of server object are determined, the client decides which interface to use to satisfy a particular request. This needs an extra amount of coding on behalf of the client developer because the location of the server object must be determined and then the interfaces are searched and identified. The actual call is then made to serve the request; however, this scenario offers the client the flexibility to decide on the server objects and its services at runtime. Generally speaking, such CORBA-compliant applications are meant to be run in a network environment wherein such new services are periodically added. The dynamism involved in the application helps it in such environments.

Another feature of the DII protocol is the multiple ways of invoking the server methods from the client. In the case of an application based on SII protocol (that is, it's static, IDL-based), the client application can make a call to a server method and the call is a synchronous or a blocking call from the client's side. This is to some extent a bottleneck because the client application has to wait until the call returns. The call made to the server could be blocked for various reasons and many could be unrelated to the application. Note, CORBA does provide somewhat of a work-around here. Within the IDL scripts written, one could easily make such calls one-way. This construct informs the compiler that no return value is expected from the call; hence, it could continue execution immediately after the call to the server method. This is only good for operations that do not return a value to the client, however.

DII, on the other hand, enables calls to be synchronous, as well as asynchronous. Further, DII also enables calls to be what's known as *deferred synchronous*. Many times in the application, a function call is made and the function is expected to return a value. The return value, though obtained, may not be required immediately for calculation purposes. The return value may be needed further down in the application for some calculation or evaluation. DII takes advantage of such a deferring need and states that if the return value is not needed immediately, then the client can make a call to the server method (remote method) and continue to execute within the client application domain. When the value for a calculation at the client side is actually needed, you could check for the return value for its existence. If the return value does not appear yet, then you would poll for the return value. This addresses the blocking call problem for many applications. Of course, such a sce-nario does not exist all the time. And not all the applications can benefit from the deferred synchronous calls, as they may need the return value immediately in the next statement for its calculation purposes. But think for a moment: How many times are you faced with such a scenario? I am sure you will all find this helpful. These minor features can make a CORBA-based application achieve the performance it's expected to attain and it may even exceed the required performance level.

CORBA specifies an interface called the *Interface Repository (IR)*. According to CORBA standards, every ORB has to provide an implementation of the IR. The IR performs the task, just as its name suggests, of providing a storage bin for the inter-faces of the objects accessible to the ORB. The form of storage is not specified by OMG, but the only requirement from OMG is the information must be maintained in a persistent form. The implementation depends on the implementers of the ORB.

Different ORB vendors will have different implementations of the storage for-mat. Every unit is stored as an object and objects do have inheritance hierarchy built into them. Object databases are a useful tool to store such objects as they serve the purpose well, but using object databases only is not a hard and fast rule.

One ORB may use relational databases, distributed databases, flat file systems storing the object relations, or distributed files over the network. Implementation of the storage system is immaterial, but what matters most is, when demanded, the Interface Repository should retrieve the information about the objects in a semantically correct format.

The Interface Repository is geared toward storing the information from the IDL of the interface. Everyone knows the interfaces of the remote objects are described in the IDL. This IDL is used to generate the stub and skeleton code of the CORBA-aware client and server applications. The Interface Repository takes in the interface definition from the IDL and parsers the interface components into object units. The object units consist of the interface itself, the parameters passed to the interface, the data types of the parameters, the module definition, and exception objects.

Why does this information need to be stored in the Interface Repository?. First and most important is it provides the benefits of ORB interoperability, irrespective of the ORB implementation. The Interface Repository stores only the interface elements; none of the ORB implementations are exposed. This would allow two ORBs implemented by different vendors to browse through each other's supported interfaces. Because OMG does not limit an ORB to a single Interface Repository, an ORB vendor could, if seen as necessary, develop an ORB with multiple Interface Repositories.

Different Interface Repository could be exposed to different types of client applications. Higher priority client applications could have the leisure of being exposed to more confidential interfaces provided by the ORB that may be unavailable to lower priority client applications. Because the data stored in terms of the interfaces within the Interface Repository could be identical – with only the priority restricting the number and types of interfaces – the two Interface Repositories could be implemented in so the higher priority Interface Repository stores only the confidential information. For accessing the general information, this repository could, under the covers, talk to the other Interface Repository.

Every Interface Repository has a unique identifier. The repository identifier is represented by the Universally Unique Identifier (UUID). The only rule to be observed here is: Interface Repositories represented by different repository identifiers could have similar or dissimilar interfaces, but Interface Repositories represented by similar repository identifiers (that is, having the same value) must be identical. Many combinations of mix-and-match could be performed to make the best use of the system. OMG provides a standard way of querying the Interface Repository to obtain the entire interface set provided by the ORB and you could browse through them and reconstruct the original interface definition. The Interface Repository also helps in the type-checking of the interface calls. The number of parameters the interface accepts and the types of the parameters can all be checked during runtime.

Until now, only one side of the picture has been shown. The client side of the system has been investigated, and now we'll study the server side, which is a complete ecosystem of its own. The word *server* is a loosely used word. This word has been overloaded so much its actual meaning has been lost. The basic definition of *server* is one who serves requests. This is a strong meaning and, without attaching too many strings to this definition, let us show how the server-side implementation works. This is called *server side implementation* because this is the zone that helps satisfy the client's needs (also, at the beginning of the discussion, we mention CORBA portrays a client-server type of a view).

Many of the object implementations are executable servers in their own respect. They have the complete capability of loading themselves on external requests and serving the requested functionality made from the outside world (from anything outside the server's own process). When the servers are done with the task allotted, they can shut themselves down happily. They could terminate themselves success-fully on a request issued from outside. To make it simple, the servers are entities of their own and do not have external dependencies for their working (please note, multiple executables could be put together to form a server. Their bounds would be the sum of the bounds of all the individual executables and all of them together form a unit). In this regard, such units would be called *the object server.*

The server from our perspective is the entire system that would function as a single unit from the client's view. The ORB on the server has the BOA, which acts as the guide. The BOA serves many purposes. One of its most important tasks is to perform the initial communication with the object server implementation. The BOA loads the object server when needed and helps in the generation and interpretation of the object references. From the client's perspective, the object server is always up and running because the client does not concern itself with loading the object server. When the client wants a service offered by an object server, with the help of the Trader Services, it identifies the object server and then issues a request to it. The BOA takes care of the job of loading the object server and activating the required object within the server to get the request satisfied for the client.

The BOA provides the illusion that all the object servers are constantly up and running. The servers may not actually be running, though. Because many such object servers are linked to the ORB, keeping all the object servers up and running may be impossible. This would require an enormous amount of system resources. When the request arrives from the client about a service exhibited by a specific object server, the ORB tries to locate a running instance of the object. If the ORB discovers the object is not loaded, it must create an instance of the object. First it activates the server that contains the object.

The Implementation Repository is the only connection point between the object server implementation and the BOA. For the BOA to start an object server imple-mentation, it must initiate the process through the implementation specifics pro-/vided by the object implementation. The Implementation Repository may not be the most portable layer of the system as it contains system specific information for the object server. The system proprietary information could be in terms of operat-ing system specific calls, the object server specific information for loading and unloading, and so on. Once the object server is loaded, it communicates with the BOA to let it know it is ready to accept requests. At this moment, the BOA may request activation of a particular object within the server implementation. This object activation mechanism is called the *activation policy* by the OMG and is one of the other tasks of the BOA. The activation policies are the rules the BOA should follow to activate a particular object within the object server. According to OMG, four such policies are supported by the BOA:

- ◆ A shared server policy, in which multiple active objects of a given implementation share the same server.

- ◆ Persistent server policy, in which the server is activated by something outside the BOA. The server, nonetheless, must register with the BOA to receive invocations. A persistent server policy is assumed to be shared by multiple active objects.

- ◆ An unshared server policy, in which only one object of a given implementation at a time can be active in one server.

- ◆ A server-per-method policy, in which each invocation of a method is implemented by a separate server being started, with each server terminating when the respective method completes.

Figure 2-10 illustrates the different implementation activation policies. In the figure, *A* is a shared server as it has multiple objects implemented in it and the client could request any one of the objects. BOA starts the shared server and then it registers with the BOA. *B* is a persistent server, identical in its external working, except for the fact that the BOA does not start the server. Even then, server *B* registers with the BOA. Server *C* is an unshared server. It has one object implemented within it and it is started by the BOA and after initializing itself, *C* registers with the BOA. Server *D* is an instance of server-per-method policy. Each method invocation to an object within the server-per-method would cause the server to be started by the BOA and, at the end of the method, the server terminates itself.

CORBA supports many other services, so we have included a separate chapter dedicated to CORBA services. The services provided by CORBA target the operational activities. The services are designed in such a manner that the maximum benefit could be exploited from a distributed architecture. The services make the system over all highly modular. The approach of the design is systematic and an appreciable amount of effort is provided in simplifying the entire system. The modularity, simplicity, and the interoperability are the strong points of CORBA.

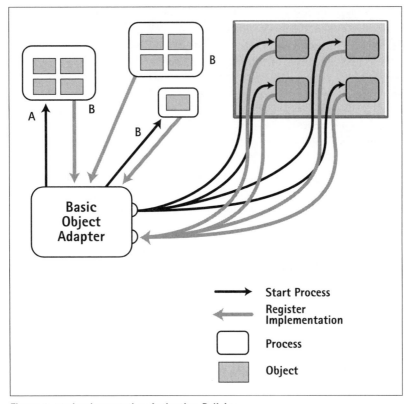

Figure 2-10: Implementation Activation Policies

A Primer on Writing a CORBA Application

Although in Chapter 5 you learn how to create your first CORBA application in greater detail, we'll explain here, with the help of a small example, what a CORBA application looks like. This is no "working of a rocket propulsion system," but it can be used as a reference for understanding the applications made using CORBA. This small distributed application simply requests the current time from a time server. The clients are Java applications. The server supports object implementation and is similarly written in Java.

The interface to our time object is called ObjTimeServer and it has a method called getTime(), which returns you the current time in a string format. The first step in writing a CORBA object is to write its interface. The interface is written using IDL. The written interface is then compiled using an IDL compiler. The IDL compiler by default comes with the ORB I am using (for example, VisiBroker). On compiling the IDL file, the compiler generates two sets of code files. These code files are in the language the particular IDL compiler generates. In this case, because the ORB we are using is a Java ORB, the code files will be in Java.

The first set of code generated by the IDL compiler is the set of proxy objects; the second set of code is the skeleton code. The client uses proxy objects for making invocations on object references of the interface types based in the IDL file. In other words, the proxy objects are the "stand-in" objects the client works with, making the remote object appear as a local object. Skeleton code is used for access to objects that support those interfaces.

The code generated implements location transparency. By location transparency, we mean it will convert an object reference into a network connection to a remote server and marshal the arguments provided to an operation on the object reference, convey them to the current method in the object denoted by our object reference, execute the method, and return the results. In other words, the client will be working with the proxy objects generated by the IDL compiler and it will seem as if it is working with a local object. It is the job of the proxy objects to communicate with the ORB, which, will in turn manage the network connections, pass parameters to the actual server functions, and then return the results, thus maintaining the transparency of how the implementation is done.

We now explain the previous process with help of pseudo code. As before, we start first with the IDL file for TestTimeServer.

```
// TestTimeServer.idl
module TestTimeServer {
      interface ObjTimeServer {
      String getTime();
      };
};
```

Compiling this IDL will generate the stub and skeleton code. Assume the compiler generates a file named ObjTimeServer_Skeleton.java, which has the skeleton code to be used on the server side. Now we must implement the object whose interface has been specified in the IDL — that is, we must write the server code or implementation. For writing the object implementation class, it must be associated with the skeleton class generated by the IDL compiler. The association can be done using either inheritance or delegation.

```
// pseudo code for the implementation class
// TestTimeServerImpl.java
import CORBA.*;
class ObjTimeServerImpl extends
 TestTimeServer.ObjTimeServer_Skeleton{
      // variable declarations
      :
      :

      // constructor
      :
      :
```

```
// method
public String getTime() throws CORBA.SystemException{
//      return "The current time is : " + current_time;
}
};
```

Now you actually implement the server. This class does the job of initialing the environment, creating the implementation object, making it available to clients, and listening for the events.

```
// pseudo code for the server object
import CORBA.*;
public class TimeServer_Server{
    public static void main(String[] args){
      try{
          // initialize ORB
          CORBA.ORB orb = CORBA.ORB.init();
          :
      // create Implementation class
      ObjTimeServerImpl time_server_obj =
            New ObjTimeServerImpl( args[0] );
      :
          }
      catch(CORBA.SystemException e){
      System.err.println(e);
      }
      }
};
```

Compiling and executing the server will return a stringified IOR, just for arguments sake:

```
IOR:0000000000123456789002338426236423....(it is a big number)
```

The client implementation is done in basically three steps. We begin by initializing the CORBA environment, which is the ORB. Initializing an ORB means obtaining the reference to an ORB pseudo-object. The ORB is called a *pseudo-object* because its methods will be provided by a library in communication with the run-time system and its pseudo-object reference cannot be passed as a parameter to CORBA interface operations. The next step involves obtaining the object reference. Object references are opaque data structures. However, an object reference can be made persistent by converting it into a string. This is known as *stringifying* an object reference. The resulting string is called a *stringified object reference*. Stringified object references are re-convertible into "live" object references. This is done using the two corresponding operations object_to_string() and string_to_object() defined on the CORBA: ORB interface. Any CORBA 2.0 compliant ORB can convert stringified interoperable object references into working object references. Narrowing down the object to its appropriate type achieves this; the operation is called *narrow*. (Note, the narrow operation is type safe, thus if an incorrect object reference is passed, it will raise an exception, specifically one called CORBA: SystemException.) After the ORB has been initialized and an object reference is obtained, CORBA programming behaves like standard object-oriented programming. A client invokes methods for objects and it appears to the client that it's working with a local object, when, in fact, it's working with a remote object.

This next code initializes the remote object and causes the remote object's main to execute.

```
// pseudo code for the above steps
// TimeServer_Client.java
import java.io.*;
public class TimeServer_Client{
      public static void main(String args[]){
      try{
      // initialize the orb
      CORBA.ORB  orb = CORBA.ORB.init();
      :
      :
      // get the object reference, assumption here is
      // stringified object reference is the 1st
      // argument to the client program
      CORBA.object myObj =
          orb.string_to_object( args[0] );
      :
      :
      // now we try to narrow down the object reference
      // to its appropriate type.
      TestTimeServer.ObjTimeServer TimeServer =
            TestTimeServer.ObjTimeServer_var.narrow(obj);

      }
      catch(SystemException exception){
      System.err.println(exception);
      }
      }
}
```

For running the application, we must use the IOR obtained by the server

```
c:\>java TimeServer_Client IOR:00000000012345678900233842..
```

The remote object, upon being executed, will start its main procedure. It will print the time obtained from the server.

```
The current time is : 11:25:50.82
```

The Inter-ORB Architecture

Even though it's rare to develop distributed applications that will use multiple ORBs, seeing CORBA's inter-ORB architecture is interesting. The OMG, in developing CORBA, a true open architecture, wants CORBA to maintain its lead in this area and has presented a specification for applications working across different ORBs. Here is what CORBA has to offer.

Figure 2-11 shows the Inter-ORB Architecture. Handling of the object requests still must be done using the CORBA IDL. Two protocols – General Inter-ORB Protocol and Environment-Specific Inter-ORB Protocol – usually do the transfer and messaging.

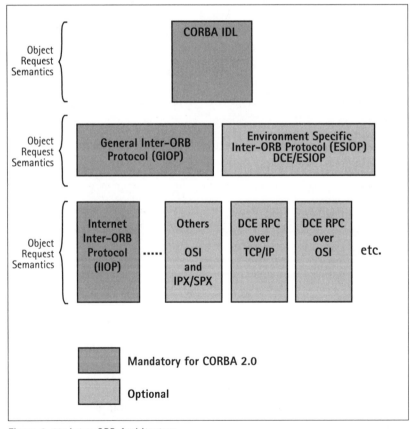

Figure 2-11: Inter-ORB Architecture

General Inter-ORB Protocol (GIOP) defines a set of message formats and common data representations for communications between ORBs. The whole idea behind GIOP was the ORB-to-ORB transactions. It is designed to operate directly over any connection-oriented transport protocol. Common Data Representation (CDR) is used for mapping the data types defined in OMG IDL into flat networked message representations. The CDR also handles the inter-platform issues such as byte ordering. GIOP defines seven message formats that cover all ORB request/reply semantics. No format negotiations are needed and, in most cases, clients can send requests almost immediately after they open a connection. GIOP also defines a format for Interoperable Object References (IORs). An ORB must create an object reference whenever an object reference is passed across ORBs. IORs associate a collection of tagged profiles with object references, which help in providing information about how to contact the object using a particular ORB's mechanism.

Environment-Specific Inter-ORB Protocols (ESIOPs), as the name suggests, is specific to certain environments. CORBA specifies DCE (Distributed Computing Environment) as the first of many optional ESIOPs (pronounced *E-SOPs*). Like GIOP, DCE/ESIOP supports IORs using the DCE tagged profiles. These environments come with their own strengths and weaknesses. They sometimes have their own ways of optimized calling procedures. DCE, for example, provides advanced features like Kerberos security, cell and global directories, distributed time, and authenticated RPC. DCE also supports multiple transport protocols and enables you to transport large numbers of data efficiently.

Internet Inter-ORB Protocol (IIOP) now has become synonymous with CORBA and is heard more commonly on the Internet whenever a reference is made to CORBA. This protocol specifies how GIOP messages are exchanged over a TCP/IP network. IIOP makes it possible to use the Internet itself as the backbone ORB through which the other ORBs can merge. To be CORBA 2.0 compatible, an ORB must support GIOP over TCP/IP. Both IIOP and DCE/ESIOP have built in mechanisms for implicitly transmitting context data associated with the transactions and security services. The ORB takes care of passing these requests without the application's involvement and the CORBA standard on its part specifies the location of this context data in an ORB-generated message.

Summary

In this chapter, we discussed the base of CORBA, the OMA model. We also discussed the different components of the OMA and how they fit in a CORBA framework. A brief introduction on the inter-ORB architecture was made to broaden the horizon before going into depth with CORBA in later chapters and a small primer was given about writing CORBA applications.

Chapter 3

Writing Your First CORBA Application

IN THIS CHAPTER

This chapter leads you through all the phases necessary to build your first CORBA application. So far, you have read a considerable information describing the OMG and its creation of CORBA, which is at the forefront of the newest object-oriented technology wave. The technology behind CORBA sounds interesting, but does it really work? And, more important, is it easy to learn, understand, and use? The answer to these questions is a resounding Yes! This chapter takes the principles you have learned and demonstrates them in a simple, easy-to-understand CORBA application.

Three main assumptions were made in writing this example. First, you should have a general understanding of object-oriented programming and a fair understanding of C++. The code is written in C++ using Microsoft's Developer Studio, with Visual C++ Version 4.2. If you are using a different compiler, the code should still work correctly, as long as all compile and link settings are equivalent. The second assumption deals with the Object Request Broker (ORB) used. Visigenic's VisiBroker 3.0 has been chosen as the ORB for this chapter, as well as the rest of the book. To learn to program in CORBA, we recommend you download an evaluation copy of the ORB and compile and run all the examples. Better yet, use the examples as a starting point to begin adding your own code extensions. The third assumption is you have e-mail and Web access. This is essential for downloading

- ◆ Object Adapters
- ◆ CORBA application architecture
- ◆ ORB downloading and description
- ◆ The eight steps to creating a CORBA application
- ◆ Writing and compiling the IDL
- ◆ Creating a server
- ◆ Creating a client and binding to the server
- ◆ Enhancing the client and server objects

the ORB.

◆ Using Exceptions to make your code more robust

◆ Using the Object Activation Daemon to save time

◆ CORBA Memory Management

Object Adapters

As you will soon see in a number of CORBA examples, our CORBA code constantly needs to communicate with the ORB and also with the Basic Object Adapter (BOA). Before we begin writing code to do this, it may be helpful to describe object adapters – specifically the BOA – and explain how the BOA provides us with some powerful communication support. As you have seen, an object adapter is one of the many building blocks defined by the OMG that combines to make CORBA work for us. The *object adapter* is the primary facility an object implementation uses to interact with the ORB. It lies between a server's implementation and the ORB, creating a public interface for a server's implementation object and a private interface for the server skeleton used internally by the server. Object adapters can be specific for a given type of object implementation, but they almost always, to some degree, provide the following functionality:

◆ Creation of object references

◆ Support for function invocations on these references

◆ Support for security concerns with these interactions

◆ Object and implementation creation (activation) and deactivation

◆ Linking of object references to their respective implementation

◆ Registration of object implementations with the ORB

When describing object adapters, the OMG realized no way exists to create an adapter definition that would work for every type of CORBA application. For instance, database applications typically have requirements not generally found in nondatabase applications, and it would be difficult to create a generic adapter that would suffice for both. The members of the OMG realized if no adapters were defined, however, the potential existed for a large number of similar adapters to end up on the market, leading to minute differences between the adapter implementations, which would quickly cause compatibility problems in the software community. To confront this problem and to keep the number of adapters to a minimum, the OMG decided to design a basic adapter that would work for most applications, which did not have unusual data and communication requirements. This is how the BOA was created.

The *BOA* is a generic adapter designed to support a wide variety of common object implementations. It provides most of the functionality previously mentioned. Figure 3-1 shows how the BOA fits into our server architecture:

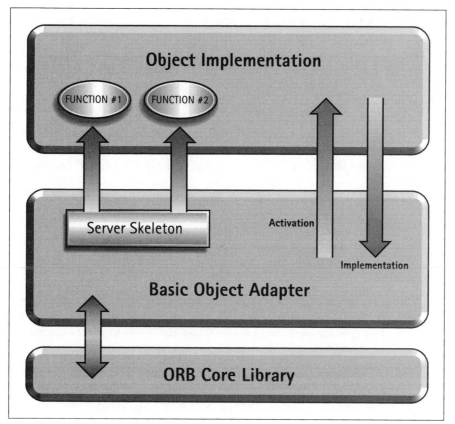

Figure 3-1: The Basic Object Adapter

As you can see, the adapter sits between the server implementation and the core ORB library. The adapter is involved in the invocation of functions on the implementation, but the direct interface is through the server skeleton. The BOA provides a direct link to functions dealing with object registration and activation, such as *obj_is_ready()* and *impl_is_ready()*, while implementation function invocations go through the skeleton. One subject is worth mentioning here: The BOA (as well as most other adapters) relies on system facilities to succeed in communication. These facilities are not part of the OMG specification, which renders the BOA nonportable. If you have written code that takes advantage of one ORB vendor's extension to the BOA implementation, you may have some small portability problems when you port that code to another ORB.

The BOA does a number of things. First, it generates object references for an implementation that can be used by clients in the system. The reference describes the object and enables the client – through its ORB library – to find and interact with the object. This is done with the help of the implementation repository, which stores location and activation information for a given server. The BOA has built-in support for the use of this object reference to invoke functions on the implementation. The BOA also provides a small amount of authentication and access control for the object. For any function invocation on an implementation, the BOA provides information on who made the request. The BOA also stores access information for a given object and decides if an invocation can take place based on these rights.

The BOA also takes care of object and implementation activation and deactivation. When a request comes in for a specific object or implementation, the BOA helps coordinate the launching and initialization of the desired entity. As you will see in upcoming examples, the BOA interacts with VisiBroker's Object Activation Daemon to provide this activation support. Four types of activation are available:

1. **Shared server** activation, where multiple objects in a given server are available to clients and are all running in the same address space on the server machine. In this case, multiple clients are all sharing a single server process.

2. **Unshared server** activation, where a single object in a server is available to each client. Each client talks to its own server, with each server running in its own address space and process. Thus, the server processes are not shared.

3. **Server-per-method** activation, which causes a new process to be created on the server machine for each method invocation on the object in the server. As you can imagine, this can be resource-intensive.

4. **Persistent server** activation, where the server process is activated by some facility not related to the BOA. This is how we usually activate servers because, in most instances, they are manually launched. The server is responsible for telling the BOA it is up and running so the BOA can route client requests to it when required.

We alluded to the final capability the BOA provides: registration of object implementations with the ORB. You will see all the examples tell the BOA a new implementation is ready for client requests. The BOA, in turn, tells the ORB he implementation is now ready for requests.

This has been an overview of the BOA. You will come in contact with other adapters, such as the TIE approach, but you will probably use the BOA for most of your applications. The BOA is a building block that provides built-in communication support for your clients and servers.

CORBA Application Architecture

The best way to learn is by example. And the best example to follow is one with which you are familiar. In these days of bulging stock market prices and high tech takeovers, almost everyone has an eye on a stock or two. Because feverish investing and profit taking is happening everywhere, a SecurityQuote example seems fitting.

The SecurityQuote example runs off *canned data,* meaning the data is present for a small number of securities, but it is static and by no means accurate. The data could provide both stock and mutual fund quotes but, for now, we have provided data for a few stocks. If you want, you can expand the code to hit real-time databases on the Web or another data source to which you may have access.

We build the application in a number of steps. The first step is the basic no-frills client/server example, much like the Hello World of stock quote applications. The architecture is then expanded to include a CORBA object called a *SecurityQuote object,* which is passed between the client and the different servers. This object has attributes you would expect, such as high price, low price, closing price, and share volume. The architecture of this expanded example calls for a main server (the SecurityQuoteServer) and a helper server (the DataQueryServer). The SecurityQuoteServer is visible to clients, and has a well-known interface with which it enables the client to interact. This server filters requests and asks the DataQueryServer for prices and data based on incoming requests. A client program makes requests for the data of a given security, based on a string symbol (such as INTC). This string is passed to the SecurityQuoteServer, which then passes it to the DataQueryServer. This server allocates a SecurityQuote object, initializes it with data, and passes it back to the DataQueryServer. Finally, the instantiated and initialized object is returned to the client, which can ask the object for its data. Figure 3-2 is a general diagram of the overall application architecture. We will show you more intricate diagrams as we build this example in different steps.

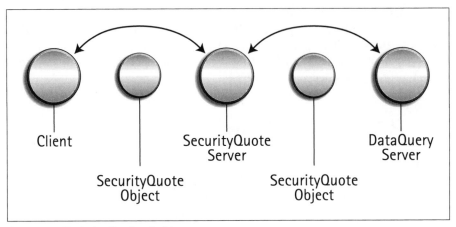

Figure 3-2: Basic Application Architecture

The DataQuery server is separated from the main server in an effort to provide data encapsulation. As mentioned, this application uses canned data. The query server can be upgraded to use real data, however, without affecting the workings of the main SecurityQuoteServer. The DataQueryServer could also be totally exchanged for a similar server with more functionality, as long as the interface contract is not broken. This is one of the great benefits of using CORBA: a CORBA server talks to interfaces with no regard for the level of functionality that exists behind the interface. The server-side implementation of an interface can be changed, improved, or totally replaced, and the client will still work correctly with no required relinking or code changes, as long as the IDL for the server does not change any existing function signatures. In other CORBA projects, we have built applications that use the same IDL for multiple server implementations. The different server implementations provide varying levels of functionality. This approach adds great strength and diversity to an application.

ORB Downloading and Description

Now that the application has been described, let's get to work. The first step in this process is obtaining an object request broker (ORB). An *ORB* is much like a CORBA telephone operator: it sits and waits for requests and attempts to satisfy each one. As a request comes in, the ORB determines where the request is headed and helps it to find its way there, if possible. If the request is invalid, or the target of the request does not exist, the ORB tells the caller that an error has been made.

As mentioned earlier, Visigenic's VisiBroker 3.0 is used in this section. Visigenic is a leader in the ORB vendor race and has put out a well-engineered and well-built ORB. Visigenic has easy-to-understand commands and a number of intuitive individual utility applications that help make the process of configuring CORBA objects more straightforward. The documentation that comes with the evaluation copy of Version 3.0 is exceptional. Do not hesitate to download and browse the programmer's manual. It covers a variety of topics in a clear, thorough fashion.

Visigenic has been kind enough to provide an evaluation of VisiBroker, readily available for download from their Web site. The evaluation period is 60 days from the date of installation, which is ample time to enable you to try our examples and gain a good understanding of CORBA. To get this ORB, point your browser to:

www.visigenic.com/store/

Click VisiBroker for C++ and follow the download instructions. You will be prompted for some personal information (remember they are loaning you an expensive piece of software) and then you can get the software. No license string is needed for Version 3.0, so once you download it, you are ready to install the ORB and all its related tools. The downloaded file is a self-extracting executable. Just double-click the file and follow the installation instructions. Once the installation is complete, find the README file that comes with the software and read about any settings you must make on your system.

When the installation is complete, you will notice the new VisiBroker bin directory contains a number of executables and batch files – some you will use and some you won't. Nonetheless, a quick explanation of all these applications helps shed some light on the software you just installed, software you'll become quite familiar with in this and coming chapters.

idl2cpp.bat – The IDL to C++ compiler, which runs from a command prompt. It takes IDL files as input and generates C++ classes for a client and server, as well as client stubs and server skeletons.

idl2ir.bat – Enables you to populate the Interface Repository with information found in a given IDL file.

irep.bat – Enables you to create and view an Interface Repository, which contains data describing the object interfaces available for use.

oad.exe – The Object Activation Daemon used to register objects. The **OAD** notifies the **OSAGENT** that a new object has been registered and works with the **OSAGENT** to help activate (launch) a given VisiBroker object when it is requested. This piece of software enables you to run your client when none of your CORBA servers are running. As these servers are required by the client, the **OAD** starts and initializes them for you. You are not required to use the **OAD**, but it can make administration of your deployed system easier and more robust.

oadutil.bat – A utility batch file that enables you to register and unregister objects with the **OAD**.

orbeline.bat – An IDL compiler command provided for backward compatibility with older versions of VisiBroker. Use the **idl2cpp** command instead.

osagent.exe – Starts the Object Services Agent, which provides CORBA object directory services and failure detection. This agent should be running whenever you plan to initiate CORBA client and server communication. On NT, start this command with the -C option to allow it to run in a DOS prompt. It can also be configured as an NT service.

osfind.exe – Helps find **OSAGENT** and **OAD** applications running across the network, as well as VisiBroker C++ objects, which are active on the local system or other systems across the network. It is also helpful for finding *zombie* objects on your system, which are CORBA objects started manually and never deactivated.

vbj.exe – The Java implementation for **idl2cpp, idl2ir, irep,** and **oadutil.** This works with JavaSoft's Java Runtime Environment (JRE), which is bundled with VisiBroker.

vbver.exe – Provides version information for the other VisiBroker files. Type the command in a DOS prompt and it gives you examples of the correct command syntax.

vregedit.exe – Provides a Windows dialog box that enables you to edit environment variables used by VisiBroker. The OSAGENT_PORT environment variable defines the port on which the Smart Agent listens. The VBROKER_ADM variable defines the directory that VisiBroker uses to store the Implementation and Interface Repositories.

If you are unsure of the syntax for these commands, try using the following syntax for a more detailed description:

```
command -?
```

Eight Steps to Creating a CORBA Application

When building distributed CORBA applications, you will find you usually must complete eight steps. These steps are universal – they are not ORB-dependent and the steps are typical for the simplest to the most complex CORBA client/server program. Understanding these general steps helps you comprehend the overall architecture of a CORBA application. We describe and provide examples of each step in the following sections:

1. **Write IDL code that defines the interface for an object.** The IDL defines the operations an object provides for its clients, describes the parameters passed to a given operation, and indicates what return value, if any, the operation provides. Attributes for an object can also be defined in the IDL specification. When the IDL is compiled, set/get functions are generated to enable clients to manipulate the attributes.

2. **Compile the IDL.** You compile the IDL by running it through an IDL compiler, which scans the IDL file and generates new files in one of a number of programming languages. (Currently, IDL compilers exist for most of the popular languages, including C, C++, Java, SmallTalk, and ADA, among others). We use an IDL-to-C++ compiler that provides us with a number of C++ files. These files define a new set of objects that enable our clients and servers to talk to each other using ORB libraries to which they both link.

   Three types of files are generated: Include files that define these new objects, client stubs that provide CORBA communication channels between a client and the ORB, and a server skeleton, which allow functions on the server to be called by the ORB. These files are generated, so you should *never* edit them. In fact, you should hardly ever have to look at them. They are quite cryptic, so viewing or debugging the files is quite a task. Because the files are generated, you are not tied to a specific ORB implementation. If you want to change ORBs, you simply have to recompile your IDL. (You also may have to update the way you communicate with the BOA, which is ORB-dependent.) Figure 3-3 illustrates the compilation of IDL.

3. **Write the code for your server.** To do this, you must first provide an implementation for the object defined in Step 1. (Remember, the implementation is the code for the actual object, which lives in the server.) This implementation file provides the functionality defined by the operations listed in your IDL file. This implementation is usually a new class you define and it is provided in its own file. When the implementation is finished, you then write a server main loop. This code is a standalone application. It does the following things, which we discuss when this step is covered in detail later in this chapter:

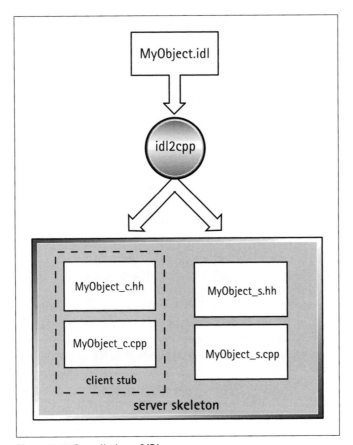

Figure 3-3: Compilation of IDL

    a.   Initializes the ORB.

    b.   Initializes the Basic Object Adapter (BOA).

    c.   Instantiates one of your newly created implementation objects.

    d.   Tells the BOA the object is ready for clients.

    e.   Tells the ORB it is ready to receive client requests.

4. **Compile your server.** To do this, you compile and link your server main loop and the implementation file for your object, as well as the server skeleton for your object. Some ORB implementations, VisiBroker included, also require you compile and link in the client stub with the server.

5. **Write the code for your client.** Your client code is also a standalone application. It should first initialize the ORB and then bind to the server. After binding, your client will have a pointer to a server object. It can then invoke any of the operations on that server previously defined in your IDL file simply by calling the functions in the proxy object. Internally, the invocations are done as simple function calls to the server. However, the calls are going from client to server via ORB libraries linked with both the client and server. The client could be calling a local server or a server on the other side of the world. Its location is of no importance to the client.

6. **Compile your client.** To do this, you will compile and link your client main loop and the client stub for the object you previously defined in the IDL. There is no mention of the inclusion of the object implementation in the compile/link process because your client has no knowledge of the implementation of the server. The only view your client has of the server is provided by the client stub. You can constantly change and upgrade the implementation on the server side without ever impacting the client, as long as you do not change the operations originally defined in the IDL. If the IDL does change for some reason, your client simply must recompile and link with the newly generated client stub.

7. **Run your server.** Before running the server, make certain you have your ORB daemon running on the server machine. With VisiBroker, this means you must first start **OSAGENT**, which provides the ORB communication between client and server. Once you launch the server, it tells **OSAGENT** it is ready to receive client requests.

8. **Run your client.** If you are not using the Object Activation Daemon (OAD), you must be sure your server is running before your client binds to the server. If the OAD is running and properly configured, it will figure out you client needs to talk to your server, and launch the server automatically. We discuss the OAD in the section titled "Using the Object Activation Daemon to Save Time." Once the client executes binds, all the functionality of your server becomes available.

This is CORBA client/server programming in a nutshell. Deviations may occur in these eight steps, based on the type of application you develop (DII applications, which are discussed in the next chapter, are one example) but, for most cases, this is the general procedure you use to develop a CORBA application.

Write Interface Definition Language Code

So far in this chapter, you have learned about the application architecture, down-loading and installing the ORB, and about object adapters and how they allow CORBA to succeed in allowing objects to communicate. Now, let's get down to the nuts and bolts of CORBA programming. In this section, we define and compile the Interface Definition Language (IDL) for the first example program and show you what the compilation process provides. *IDL* is a generic language that is one of the main building blocks for the CORBA architecture. IDL is platform independent and its generic syntax is easy-to-learn and understand. It is analogous to C++ in many ways, so if you are familiar with C++ or even Java, IDL should be an easy language to master.

As you remember, our sample application is to retrieve security quotes from a data source. The first iteration of this example is simple – we don't want to throw too many new concepts at you in the beginning. Once you create and comprehend the beginning application, we'll expand it to illustrate a few more CORBA concepts.

This first iteration features a client that talks to a CORBA server via a single function call. It is not much more intricate than the famous Hello World example, but it is slightly more interesting. The function call will use only floating point and string values. Later, we will pass complex objects between servers but, for now, the primitive types help simplify our first example.

Figure 3-4 shows an illustration of the architecture for this example.

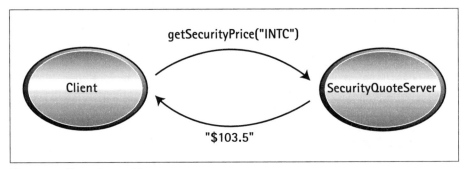

Figure 3-4: Example 1 architecture

When building CORBA applications, try to think in terms of servers. How can you break out functional sections of your application into standalone modules that provide a given set of data? Any such module can be packaged into a CORBA server. The *server* is a standalone application that waits for requests from the ORB. It services these requests and returns any desired data. This is the secret of Object-Oriented Technology and – more specifically – CORBA. Modular design promotes reuse, easy rehosting of CORBA servers, ease of code maintenance, and it improves overall system performance.

The first step to create the application is to write the IDL Interface Definition Language (IDL) that describes how a client interfaces with the server. This IDL is the interface contract between a server and its clients. When you create an IDL interface, you are saying the CORBA object described by this IDL agrees to support this interface for all clients. If the contract is broken, it may render numerous clients – both known and unknown – useless.

Take great care when changing the interface. In fact, try to always be backward-compatible, meaning any intact interfaces should always be supported. If you need to add new pieces to the interface, add them, but be extremely careful when replacing a piece of the interface on which clients may rely.

Interfaces may change over time and VisiBroker has found one solution to this problem. VisiBroker supports versioning of interfaces, which enables you to create a new version of your IDL when a large change needs to take place, while still allowing older versions to remain intact. Clients use the Interface Repository to find the correct version they need, so legacy clients can continue to use the older interface version, while newer ones are created and published.

Back to this example. Here is the IDL for the first iteration of our SecurityQuote Server interface:

```
interface SecurityQuoteServer
{
  float getSecurityPrice(in string securitySymbol);
};
```

This IDL is fairly straightforward. The interface keyword defines an interface, which is much like a C++ class definition. This interface is the only view that external applications will have into a CORBA object. It is essentially a list of functions that a client can call. The types are similar to C++ types. The string attribute maps to a char *, while float maps to its appropriate C++ data type.

The next section moves to step two: compiling.

Compiling the IDL Code

Compiling this IDL code is simple. This book's example code (in the accompanying CD-ROM) contains a file named exmak at the root level of the different examples for this chapter. This file is the template makefile for all the examples, which in turn have their own file named Makefile. The exmak file specifies settings that all the examples use, such as the IDL compiler settings. For this IDL, the command is:

```
idl2cpp -no_tie -src_suffix cpp SecurityQuoteServer.idl
```

For some unknown reason, the idl2cpp command needs the TCP/IP stack to be initialized. You must be connected via dial-up to the Internet or hooked to a valid network for the command to work properly. The following section entitled "Creating a Client and Binding to the Server" addresses this problem in more detail.

In this command, idl2cpp is the name of the VisiBroker IDL to C++ compiler. The -no_tie flag tells the compiler not to generate tie delegation classes for the object. Instead, we use the Basic Object Adapter (BOA) as we build the implementation. The -src_suffix cpp asks the compiler to generate all client stubs and server skeletons with the .cpp suffix – by default, the client stub and server skeleton suffix is .CC.

When the IDL compilation concludes, four new files exist in the directory that contains the IDL. A quick description of these files justifies their creation:

SecurityQuoteServer_c.hh contains the definitions for the client stubs defined in SecurityQuoteServer_c.cpp.

SecurityQuoteServer_s.hh contains the definitions for the server skeletons found in SecurityQuoteServer_s.cpp.

SecurityQuoteServer_c.cpp contains functions that act as a proxy for the SecurityQuoteServer object. This file also provides functionality for binding to the SecurityQuoteServer as well as marshalling functions to package requests in a form that the ORB uses to pass on the invocations to the server.

SecurityQuoteServer_s.cpp contains functions that unmarshall (unpackage) requests from the ORB. These requests are then forwarded to the future implementation class.

Creating a Server

Now that the IDL has been written and correctly compiled, it is time to build a server. The first step is creating an implementation for the object defined in the IDL. This implementation simply fills in the function definitions specified in the IDL. The IDL portrays what tasks the implementation will complete while the implementation actually completes these tasks. The next step is to provide a *main loop*, or main program, to initialize the ORB, usually initialize the Basic Object Adapter, instantiate an implementation object, and tell the ORB this object is ready for client requests.

Let's create the implementation for the object. As mentioned previously, the compilation of IDL provides a number of files, including SecurityQuoteServer_s.hh. The section of the file in Listing 3-1 helps define how we build the implementation:

Listing 3-1: SecurityQuoteServer_s.hh — the server skeleton header file

```
#include "SecurityQuoteServer_c.hh"
class _sk_SecurityQuoteServer : public SecurityQuoteServer
{
.
some code omitted here
.
// The following operations need to be implemented

virtual CORBA::Float getSecurityPrice(
const char* securitySymbol) = 0;

// Skeleton Operations implemented automatically
.
some code omitted here
.
};
```

Because the server skeleton links the object implementation and the ORB, the skeleton definition ensures implementation of all IDL-specified functions. Therefore, every function outlined in the IDL is defined as a pure virtual function in the preceding code, meaning the function must be implemented to avoid a compile-time or runtime system error. SecurityQuoteServer_s.hh is always a good starting point for defining and creating the implementation because it lists the exact functions signatures as they need to appear. We copy the signatures from this file and paste them into a new file, which will become the definition (.h) for the implementation. Place the implementation in its own file and name it in a recognizable fashion. These examples use the naming convention *InterfaceName*Impl to name classes. Using these strategies, Listing 3-2 illustrates the definition for SecurityQuoteServerImpl, the implementation for our object:

Listing 3-2: SecurityQuoteServerImpl.h — the implementation definition file

```
#include <SecurityQuoteServer_s.hh>
class SecurityQuoteServerImpl : public _sk_SecurityQuoteServer
{
public:
  SecurityQuoteServerImpl(const char *objName=NULL);
  ~SecurityQuoteServerImpl();
  virtual CORBA::Float getSecurityPrice(const char *securitySymbol);
};
```

The definition of this class is not very complicated, but there are a few important items to discuss. We have subclassed from sk_SecurityQuoteServer, a class generated when the IDL was compiled. The class _sk_SecurityQuoteServer is the SecurityQuoteServer Basic Object Adapter, which unmarshalls requests from the ORB and passes them to the implementation. Inheriting from this class almost invisibly provides a powerful communication layer between the server object and the ORB. Also, the definition of the getSecurityPrice is similar to _sk_SecurityQuoteServer, except it is no longer a pure virtual function. Listing 3-3 implements this function.

Listing 3-3: SecurityQuoteServerImpl.cpp — the implementation file

```
#include "SecurityQuoteServerImpl.h"
//
// This is the constructor for the object implementation. The
// C++ parameter list is used to invoke the same constructor in
// the parent class.
//
SecurityQuoteServerImpl::SecurityQuoteServerImpl
      (const char *objName)
      : _sk_SecurityQuoteServer(objName)
{
  cout << "Creating object named: " << objName << endl;
}
//
// Default destructor for this class
//
SecurityQuoteServerImpl::~SecurityQuoteServerImpl()
{
  cout << "In SecurityQuoteServerImpl destructor." << endl;
}
/*********************************/
//
// Following are the public CORBA functions, which are available for
// all clients to call.
//
/*********************************/
//
// This function returns a hard coded price for the input
// security, based on the symbol.
//
CORBA::Float SecurityQuoteServerImpl::getSecurityPrice
      (const char * securitySymbol)
{
  CORBA::Float price = CORBA::Float(0.0);
  cout << "Processing request for security: " << securitySymbol
   << endl;
  if (! securitySymbol, "INTC")
  {
```

```
        price = CORBA::Float(103.5);
  }
  return price;
}
```

Listing 3-3 is the entire source code for SecurityQuoteServerImpl. It provides
a class inherited from _sk_SecurityQuoteServer, which first invokes this class's
constructor with an object name via direct initialization in the constructor
declaration.

> The function getSecurityPrice uses the type CORBA::Float for CORBA com-
> pliance. We could use the simple C++ type float, but it is a good habit to use
> the CORBA-defined types (especially when dealing with short and long,
> which can be different sizes on different machines). The use of CORBA::Short
> and CORBA:: Long ensures your code will be portable to any machine and
> any ORB implementation.

The implementation of SecurityQuoteServerImpl now provides the functionality defined in the IDL. Creating a server main loop is the last step in the server-
creation process. Listing 3-4 illustrates a fairly standard CORBA main() function.
Your application can easily expand on this example to provide more application-
specific initialization of CORBA objects.

Listing 3-4: ServerMain.cpp — the server main loop

```
#include "SecurityQuoteServerImpl.h"
int main(int argc, char * const *argv)
{
  SecurityQuoteServerImpl *server;
  // Initialize the ORB
  cout << "Initializing the ORB from SecurityQuoteServer" << endl;
  CORBA::ORB_ptr orb = CORBA::ORB_init(argc, argv);
  CORBA::BOA_ptr boa = orb->BOA_init(argc, argv);
  // Create a new copy of the SecurityQuoteServer implementation
  // object. If a name has been passed in, use it for the new
  // object.
  if (argc == 2)
  {
      server = new SecurityQuoteServerImpl(argv[1]);
  }
  else
  {
      server = new SecurityQuoteServerImpl("SecurityQuoteServer");
  }
```

```
cout <<"Calling obj_is_ready in SecurityQuoteServer" << endl;
boa->obj_is_ready(server);

cout << "Calling impl_is_ready in SecurityQuoteServer" << endl;
boa->impl_is_ready();

// impl_is_ready() never returns.
cout << "Returned from impl_is_ready in SecurityQuoteServer"
 << endl;
    return(1);
}
```

The server first initializes the ORB by calling CORBA::ORB_Init(…) and then initializes the BOA with CORBA::BOA_Init(…). A local copy of the SecurityQuoteServerImpl object is created and the BOA is told that the object is now ready for client requests. Because this is a server, you usually have to enter some type of infinite loop that sits and processes requests. Rather than writing event processing code for every server, a function called impl_is_ready() provides this service. Under normal circumstances, this function call does not return (although it returns if a timeout is waiting for a client connection or an exception — see your ORB documentation for more ORB-specific details). This function asks the ORB to begin a request loop that invisibly accepts client requests for the SecurityQuoteServerImpl object and then passes the requests to the object for processing. (This is only one technique you can use for your CORBA servers. In a following chapter describing server-threading models, we depict another way to build your server main loop. In this example, we only create a single object that the server publishes to clients, but you could easily create and publish numerous object types that the server brokers out to clients.)

We check the input command line arguments to determine if there is a desired name to use when creating the server. This task facilitates the creation of multiple server instances by using different naming conventions and the discovery of a specific server by specifying the correct parameters to a client's _bind() statement. We explain how to use this functionality in a following section.

Compiling the Server

After writing the server code, the final step is to compile and link the server. All the examples have a makefile to build all executables. Every makefile includes a main makefile that defines settings and specific files to be compiled. The makefiles work with the nmake utility, which is part of the Microsoft Visual C++ software development package.

Before attempting to build, make sure you are set up correctly to use Microsoft Visual C++ (MsDev). Your path environment variable must include the bin directory for MsDev:

```
set path=%path%;c:\msdev\bin
```

Your lib environment variable must include the path to the libraries of MsDev:

```
set lib=%lib%;c:\msdev\lib
```

Listing 3-5 examines the makefile, which you can use as a starting point when building your own CORBA applications. The makefile specifies the dependencies existing between the files and how to build and clean out the executable and object files.

Listing 3-5: The makefile for this example.

```
include ../exmak
EXE = client.exe SecurityQuoteServer.exe
all: $(EXE)
clean:
  del *.obj *.ipp *.hh *_c.cpp *_s.cpp $(EXE) *.log
SecurityQuoteServer_c.cpp: SecurityQuoteServer.idl
  $(ORBCC) SecurityQuoteServer.idl
SecurityQuoteServer_s.cpp: SecurityQuoteServer.idl
  $(ORBCC) SecurityQuoteServer.idl
client.exe: SecurityQuoteServer_c.obj client.obj
  $(CC) -o client.exe client.obj SecurityQuoteServer_c.obj $(LIBORB)
  $(STDCC_LIBS)
SecurityQuoteServer.exe: SecurityQuoteServer_s.obj \
    SecurityQuoteServer_c.obj \
    SecurityQuoteServerImpl.obj ServerMain.obj
  $(CC) -o SecurityQuoteServer.exe ServerMain.obj \
    SecurityQuoteServer_s.obj \
        SecurityQuoteServerImpl.obj SecurityQuoteServer_c.obj
  $(LIBORB) \
    $(STDCC_LIBS)
```

All example makefiles use the main makefile, exmak, illustrated in Listing 3-6. This file defines compile settings for CPP and IDL files, libraries to use, and different directories needed in the compile/link process. You have to change the directory settings to allow nmake to find your ORB and MsDev libraries and include files.

Listing 3-6: The main makefile, exmak, used for all examples.

```
CC = CL -DWIN32 /GX /MT /02
DEBUG =
ORBELINEDIR = c:\Book\VisiBroker
COMPILERDIR = c:\Apps\Msdev
LIB = c:\Apps\Msdev\lib
ORBCC = idl2cpp        -no_tie -src_suffix cpp
ORBCCINH = idl2cpp -src_suffix cpp
CCINCLUDES = -I. -I$(ORBELINEDIR)\include -I$(COMPILERDIR)\include
CCFLAGS = $(CCINCLUDES) $(DEBUG)
LIBDIR = $(ORBELINEDIR)\lib
STDCC_LIBS = wsock32.lib kernel32.lib
LIBORB = $(LIBDIR)\orb.lib
.SUFFIXES: .cpp .obj .h .hh
.CPP.obj:
 $(CC) $(CCFLAGS) -c $<
```

To use the makefile, open a DOS prompt and change directories to the directory you would like to build. In this case, change directories to ex0601 and type:

```
nmake
```

The examples for this chapter can be built individually using nmake or you can build all examples in one step. A file named makeall.bat in the parent directory compiles and links all examples. A related file named cleanall.bat removes all object files, generated files, and executables. In a similar fashion, type the following command in any example directory to clean out files for a given example:

```
nmake clean
```

The server is built by compiling and linking the following files:

ServerMain.cpp

SecurityQuoteServerImpl.cpp

SecurityQuoteServer_s.cpp

SecurityQuoteServer_c.cpp

orb.lib, wsock32.lib, kernel32.lib

When these files are compiled and linked, you have an executable named SecurityQuoteServer.exe. The library orb.lib is included to provide VisiBroker's ORB functionality (if you are multithreading, the library orb_r.lib is included in its place). Interestingly, the file SecurityQuoteServer_c.cpp is the client stub file but the server is also uses it. Although most CORBA literature indicates the client only uses the client stub, but the server also needs this stub. Some ORB implementations automatically include the client stub in the server skeleton when the files are generated. Because VisiBroker does not contain this feature, we are required to link in the client stub with both the client and the server.

If you see the following error message when compiling, you probably have another ORB installed on your system and the compiler is first finding the CORBA.h file for your other ORB (CORBA.h is common to most ORBs.):

```
error C2433: 'NCistream' : 'friend' not permitted on data
declarations
```

To avoid this problem, make the VisiBroker include a higher directory in the path search list than the include directory for your other ORB. The makefiles provided with the examples will probably not display this error, but this problem may arise if you begin building new examples with a development environment such as Visual C++ and have another ORB installed.

Creating a Client and Binding to the Server

The first server is built and ready for action. Let's create a client to talk to that server and make invocations on the object that the server provides. The client needs to initialize the ORB, bind to the server, and then make requests on that server. Listing 3-7 illustrates the client code:

Listing 3-7: client.cpp — the client main loop

```
#include "SecurityQuoteServer_c.hh"
//
// This program illustrates a simplistic use of CORBA. This client
// binds to a StockQuoteServer, and asks it for a price for the
// Intel stock (INTC). The price is returned by the server.
//
int main(int argc, char * const *argv)
{
  try
  {
      CORBA::Float securityPrice;
```

```
    char *securityStr;
    // Initialize the ORB
    cout << "Initializing the ORB in client" << endl;
    CORBA::ORB_ptr orb = CORBA::ORB_init(argc, argv);
    // Allocate storage for the string to be passed.
    securityStr = CORBA::string_alloc(5);
    strcpy(securityStr, "INTC");
    // Bind to the SecurityQuoteServer
    cout << "Binding to SQS in client" << endl;
    SecurityQuoteServer_var quoteServer;
    if (argc == 2)
    {
    quoteServer = SecurityQuoteServer::_bind(argv[1]);
    cout << "Binding to SQS: " << argv[1] << endl;
    }
    else
    {
    quoteServer = SecurityQuoteServer::_bind();
    }

    // Ask the quoteServer for a quote. The price is returned
// by the function:
    securityPrice = quoteServer->getSecurityPrice(securityStr);
    // Print out the data to verify that things worked.
    cout << "Security data for : " << securityStr << endl;
    cout << " price    : " << securityPrice << endl;
    cout << endl;
    CORBA::string_free(securityStr);
    // We don't call release on the SQS pointer, since
    // it is a _var type, which does its own memory mgt.
}
catch(CORBA::SystemException& e)
{
    cout << "CORBA System Exception" << endl;
    cout << e;
    return (1);
}
return (0);
}
```

By first initializing the ORB, the client starts out much like the server. Next, the client calls _bind(), which asks the ORB to find the implementation for the SecurityQuoteServer and to return an object reference for this server. If a name is passed in via the command line (argv[1]), it is passed to the _bind() function. If a name is passed to _bind(), we ask for a specific server object implementation with the given name. If no name is specified, the client binds with the last implementation registered with the ORB. To illustrate this concept, we run the client in two ways: one that asks for any object implementation and one that asks for a specific implementation. Once the client has the reference for this server, it can use the reference to call any server-supported functions. In this case, we simply call the function *getSecurityPrice*, which takes a string security symbol (such as "INTC") and returns a floating-point value for the security's price.

TIP The _bind() function provides a client with numerous ways to find a specific server implementation. Check the VisiBroker programmer's manual for further explanations.

The use of the *CORBA::string_alloc* and the *CORBA::string_free* functions raises the issue of CORBA compliance. When you allocate strings to be passed through the ORB, you must refrain from using normal C++ allocation and deallocation. These string functions are implemented differently on different systems and rapidly cause memory management headaches. Try to conform to CORBA specifications even if a nonconforming approach works. Building good habits keeps you from running into roadblocks in the future.

Another important client aspect is the declaration of the `Security QuoteServer_var` attribute. Like the type `SecurityQuoteServer_ptr`, *SecurityQuoteServer_var* is a type automatically generated by the IDL compiler although the two types handle memory differently. The `_ptr` variable is the more primitive type, acting like any standard C++ pointer. The developer is responsible for memory management when using `_ptr` variables. The `_var` type contains built-in memory management assistance and ensures the object is released when deallocated or reassigned to a new value. In a following section on CORBA memory management, we describe the concept of reference counting and the effects of releasing an object.

Compiling the Client

The client is completed and needs to be compiled and linked. If you built the server using `nmake` and the provided makefile, then the client is already built and ready for action. If you are building the client in your work area, the following files are necessary to compile and link:

client.cpp

SecurityQuoteServer_c.cpp

orb.lib, wsock32.lib, kernel32.lib

Do not compile or link in the implementation of the `SecurityQuoteServer`. The client stub provides the information needed to communicate with the implementation.

Run the Server

Your first journey into CORBA programming is almost complete. You have built a server and a client that talks to the server. The final step is running both these programs and examining how they interact. When running the CORBA example applications, you must run the OSAGENT in the background. This process first accepts obj_is_ready() and impl_is_ready() messages from the server. When a _bind() request arrives from a client, the OSAGENT tells the desired server that a client has asked for a communication channel with the server. After setting up the communication link between client and server, the programs directly communicate via sockets (see Figure 3-5).

To run this first example, start a DOS prompt and change directories to the ex0601 directory (which contains the two recently-built executables). To start the OSAGENT from Windows95, type the following in the DOS prompt window:

```
start osagent
```

If you are running Windows NT, type:

```
start osagent -c
```

This command instructs the OSAGENT to run in a console window. (It can also be configured to run as an NT service.) If you are on a operating network, the OSAGENT should run correctly.

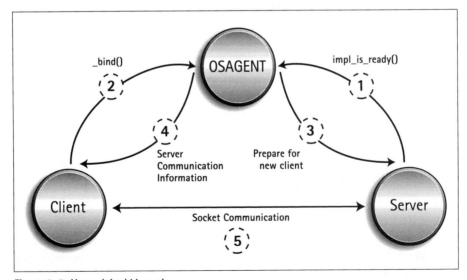

Figure 3-5: How _bind() works

Unfortunately, if you run these examples on a standalone computer, you need to connect to the Internet before the OSAGENT will run. The Internet connection activates the TCP/IP stack necessary for the agent to properly communicate. Another approach to solve this ORB-TCP/IP problem involves buying and installing an inexpensive generic network card for your stand-alone computer. After installation, use a T connector with two terminators to create a NULL network. This approach may seem a little unconventional, especially if your home computer will never see a network. This unconventional approach solves the ORB-TCP/IP problem without incurring Internet service charges.

Now start the `SecurityQuoteServer`. Unless you use the Object Activation Deamon (OAD), you need to start any servers manually before a client attempts to connect and begin communication. From the same DOS prompt, type:

```
start SecurityQuoteServer
```

This command brings up a new DOS prompt window running the server. The following messages indicate the server has initialized the ORB, registered a new object with the ORB, and finally called impl_is_ready (which indicates the server is ready to receive client requests):

```
Initializing the ORB from SecurityQuoteServer
Creating object named: SecurityQuoteServer
Calling obj_is_ready in SecurityQuoteServer
Calling impl_is_ready in SecurityQuoteServer
```

Run the Client

Start the client from the same DOS prompt: in the same directory, type:

```
client
```

The client produces the following output indicating the ORB has been correctly initialized, the server has been contacted, and a request has successfully been made on the server:

```
Initializing the ORB in client
Binding to SQS in client
Security data for : INTC
 price    : 103.5
```

Problems Running the Client and Server

Although problems can arise when running the client and server, most are simple configuration problems that can be quickly resolved. If you see the following message:

```
Initializing the ORB in client
Invoking SecurityQuoteServer in client
CORBA System Exception
Exception: CORBA::NO_IMPLEMENT
  Minor: :0
Completion Status: NO
```

then the SecurityQuoteServer is not running and the OSAGENT cannot start it automatically with the help of the OAD. If, like this chapter's examples, you are not using the OAD, remember to start the server before invoking the client:

If you see an alert panel titled:

```
Unable to locate DLL
```

then add the VisiBroker bin directory to your path environment variable. The problem arises because the operating system looks for either orb.dll or orb_r.dll, depending on the VisiBroker library linked to the client. Fix the problem with the following command, issued in the DOS prompt:

```
set path=%path%;c:\VisiBroker\bin
```

where c:\VisiBroker\bin is the bin directory in the directory tree in which you installed VisiBroker. Finally, if you see this message when running the client:

```
Initializing the ORB in client
Invoking SecurityQuoteServer in client
VisiBroker: Unable to locate agent. Will try every 15 seconds
 to locate agent
VisiBroker: Unable to locate agent. Will try every 15 seconds
 to locate agent
```

then you have not successfully started the OSAGENT. Stop the client (Ctrl-C), restart the OSAGENT, and retry the server and client.

As the client is running, a new message pops up in the server window:

```
Processing request for security: INTC
```

This message indicates a request has come from the ORB for price information for the stock "INTC." This information is then returned to the ORB, which in turn passes it back to the client.

Figure 3-6 diagrams the application:

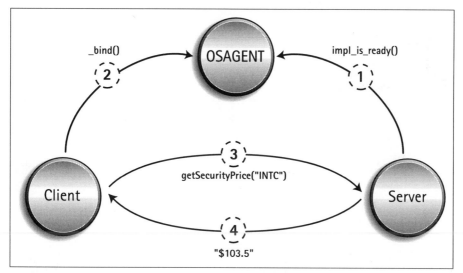

Figure 3-6: Example1 execution

The client can bind to a specific server implementation by name simply by passing the name to the _bind() function. As illustrated in preceding client and server listings, the client looks at the command line arguments to determine if there is a specific SecurityQuoteServer with which to bind and the SecurityQuoteServer uses the command line arguments to determine which name to use when registering with the ORB. Therefore, to illustrate the technique of binding to a specific server, start two SecurityQuoteServers with different names and then start the client with one of these names (see Figure 3-7). This sequence causes the client to bind and communicate with a specific server. First start the two servers with different names, which will be names of quote services in this example:

```
start SecurityQuoteServer Schwab
start SecurityQuoteServer e-trade
```

You now have 2 DOS windows ready to accept client requests: one running the Schwab server and one running the e-trade server. Start the client and instruct it to talk to the Schwab server with the following:

```
client Schwab
```

This command produces the following client output:

```
Initializing the ORB in client
Binding to SQS in client
Binding to SQS: Schwab
Security data for : INTC
 price    : 103.5
```

The window running the Schwab server shows communication information while the e-trade window does not:

```
Initializing the ORB from SecurityQuoteServer
Creating object named: Schwab
Calling obj_is_ready in SecurityQuoteServer
Calling impl_is_ready in SecurityQuoteServer
Processing request for security: INTC
```

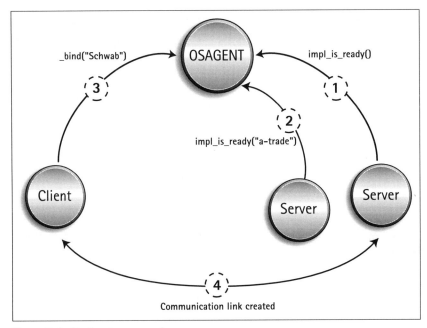

Figure 3-7: Binding to a server by name

Congratulations! You have just seen your first CORBA program work. You have ventured into the world of distributed object computing without writing any low-level communication code. This example was created on a single machine, but it could have been run across a local area network or even the Internet.

Enhancing the Client and Server Objects

This first example was fairly simple and helped illustrate the basic eight-step CORBA application framework. But, there is one outstanding issue: although CORBA facilitates distributed object computing, the first example only passed primitive types between client and server. Any object-oriented programmer knows once an object-oriented program evolves into an intricate application, the need to pass objects between functions or different applications quickly arises. Passing primitive types does not provide the necessary data transfer power.

To illustrate how to pass objects between CORBA clients and servers, we use the previous example as a starting point and build more extensions to both the client and server. In the process, we also add, define, and implement a new object called a SecurityQuote object. Lastly, we add a new server called the DataQueryServer to the existing software building blocks. The DataQueryServer allocates a SecurityQuote object, fills in its data, and passes a proxy back to the SecurityQuoteServer, which in turn passes the object proxy back to the client. The client is then free to invoke functions on this object as if the object existed in the client's process space.

ex0602 is the new example described in this section. Build this application before investigating how the example is put together. As with the first example, you can use nmake to compile all the executables in this example (this example contains 3 executables – a client and 2 servers). From a DOS prompt, type:

```
cd ex0602
nmake
```

This sequence produces three executables:

client.exe

SecurityQuoteServer.exe

DataQueryServer.exe

Figure 3-8 illustrates the architecture for this example:

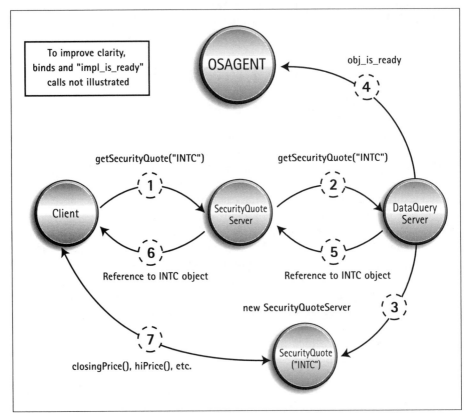

Figure 3-8: Example 2 architecture

Let's step back and examine the construction of this application. After this examination, we will run the application and inspect its output. To upgrading our existing example, first create a new object representing a *Security*, which means it contains the expected security attributes such as high price, low price, and closing price. In Listing 3-8, step one in our eight-step process defines a new object using IDL:

Listing 3-8: Security.idl — the IDL for our new Security object

```
interface Security
{
    attribute string symbol;   // INTC, GTGEX
    attribute string name;       // Intel, G.T. Europe Growth Fund
    attribute float hiPrice;   // in fractional dollars per share
    attribute float loPrice    // in fractional dollars per share
```

```
   attribute float closingPrice; // in fractional dollars per share
   attribute long volume;     // Number of shares traded today.
   string printData();
};
```

This interface is more complicated than the previous example. The object uses the primitive types string, float, and long. The object has a single function (*printData*) to be called by clients, which provides a character string with formatted information about the object. The keyword attribute defines attributes for the object, which are very similar to attributes defined in a C++ class. Attributes hidden from clients should not be defined in the IDL file; instead, declared these attributes as members of the class when the implementation for the interface is created. Clients will have access to set/get any attribute in the interface, unless it is defined as read-only, in which the client only has get privileges. Although the set/get functions are not defined in the interface, the IDL compiler automatically generates these functions (which are published for all clients) for every attribute in the interface. When you code the implementation of the object, you are required to simply fill in the logic for these functions. Listing 3-9 provides a sample of the generated functions in the client stub:

Listing 3-9: Security_s.hh — the server skeleton definition for the new Security object

```
#include "Security_c.hh"
class _sk_Security : public Security
{
.
some code omitted here
.
public:
// The following operations need to be implemented
 virtual char* symbol() = 0;
 virtual void symbol(const char* _val) = 0;
 virtual CORBA::Float loPrice() = 0;
 virtual void loPrice(CORBA::Float _val) = 0;
 virtual char* name() = 0;
 virtual void name(const char* _val) = 0;
 virtual char* printData() = 0;
 virtual CORBA::Float closingPrice() = 0;
 virtual void closingPrice(CORBA::Float _val) = 0;
 virtual CORBA::Long volume() = 0;
 virtual void volume(CORBA::Long _val) = 0;
 virtual CORBA::Float hiPrice() = 0;
 virtual void hiPrice(CORBA::Float _val) = 0;
.
some code omitted here
.
};
```

The set and get operations are now present for each attribute. Next, define and implement the Security object using the standard naming convention for this chapter. The server skeleton definition generates pure virtual function declarations that must be implemented to avoid compile-time or runtime errors. Listing 3-10 depicts the definition:

Listing 3-10: SecurityImpl.h — the implementation definition for the new Security object

```
#include "Security_s.hh"
class SecurityImpl : public _sk_Security
{
protected:
  char *m_symbol;
  char *m_name;
  CORBA::Float m_hiPrice;
  CORBA::Float m_loPrice;
  CORBA::Float m_closingPrice;
  CORBA::Long m_volume;
public:
  SecurityImpl(const char *objName=NULL);
  ~SecurityImpl();
char * symbol();
void symbol(const char * val);
char * name();
void name(const char * val);
CORBA::Float hiPrice();
void hiPrice(CORBA::Float val);
CORBA::Float loPrice();
void loPrice(CORBA::Float val);
CORBA::Float closingPrice();
void closingPrice(CORBA::Float val);
CORBA::Long volume();
void volume(CORBA::Long val);
char * printData();
};
```

This class definition has the same attributes and attribute types defined in the accompanying IDL — to remain CORBA-compliant, float and long have been replaced with CORBA::Float and CORBA::Long. As expected, all the pure virtual functions have been defined in this include file. The implementation inherits from _sk_Security, which provides the CORBA communication functionality for the class. You must create the code for these functions, as illustrated in Listing 3-11:

Listing 3-11: SecurityImpl.cpp — the implementation for the new Security object

```
#include "SecurityImpl.h"
//
// This is the constructor for the SecurityImpl class. It
// uses the initialization list to construct its parent
```

```
// (_sk_Security), as well as most of its local data members.
//
SecurityImpl::SecurityImpl(const char *objName)
              : _sk_Security(objName),
                m_loPrice((CORBA::Float)0.0),
                m_hiPrice((CORBA::Float)0.0),
                m_closingPrice((CORBA::Float)0.0),
                m_volume(0)
{
  m_name = CORBA::string_alloc(strlen(objName)+1);
  m_name = CORBA::string_dup(objName);
  m_symbol = CORBA::string_alloc(10);
  m_symbol = CORBA::string_dup("No Symbol");
  cout << "Security object created: " << objName << endl;
}
SecurityImpl::~SecurityImpl()
{
  cout << "In destructor for SecurityImpl." << endl;
}
//
// Get method for the symbol attribute.
//
char * SecurityImpl::symbol()
{
 char *tempPtr =
        CORBA::string_alloc(strlen(m_symbol)+1);
 tempPtr = CORBA::string_dup(m_symbol);
  return tempPtr;
}
//
// Set method for the symbol attribute.
//
void SecurityImpl::symbol(const char * val)
{
  if(m_symbol)
  {
      CORBA::string_free(m_symbol);
  }
  m_symbol = CORBA::string_alloc(strlen(val) + 1);
  m_symbol = CORBA::string_dup(val);
}

//
// Get method for the symbol attribute.
//
char * SecurityImpl::name()
{
  char *tempPtr =
        CORBA::string_alloc(strlen(m_name)+1);
  tempPtr = CORBA::string_dup(m_name);
  return tempPtr;
}
//
// Set method for the symbol attribute.
```

```
//
void SecurityImpl::name(const char * val)
{
  if (m_name)
  {
      CORBA::string_free(m_name);
  }
  m_name = CORBA::string_alloc(strlen(val) + 1);
  m_name = CORBA::string_dup(val);
}
//
// Get method for the symbol attribute.
//
CORBA::Float SecurityImpl::hiPrice()
{
  return m_hiPrice;
}
//
// Set method for the symbol attribute.
//
void SecurityImpl::hiPrice(CORBA::Float val)
{
  m_hiPrice = val;
}
//
// Get method for the symbol attribute.
//
CORBA::Float SecurityImpl::loPrice()
{
  return m_loPrice;
}
//
// Set method for the symbol attribute.
//
void SecurityImpl::loPrice(CORBA::Float val)
{
  m_loPrice = val;
}
//
// Get method for the symbol attribute.
//
CORBA::Float SecurityImpl::closingPrice()
{
  return m_closingPrice;
}
//
// Set method for the symbol attribute.
//
void SecurityImpl::closingPrice(CORBA::Float val)
{
  m_closingPrice = val;
}
//
```

```
// Get method for the symbol attribute.
//
CORBA::Long SecurityImpl::volume()
{
  return m_volume;
}
//
// Set method for the symbol attribute.
//
void SecurityImpl::volume(CORBA::Long val)
{
  m_volume = val;
}
char * SecurityImpl::printData()
{
  // A better allocation scheme could be used here.
  char *str = CORBA::string_alloc(500);
  char *tmpName, tmpSymbol;
  char buf[100];
  tmpSymbol = symbol();
  sprintf(str, "Security data for : %s\n", tmpSymbol);
  tmpName = name();
  sprintf(buf, " name   : %s\n", tmpName);  strcat(str, buf);
  sprintf(buf, " hi price  : %f\n", hiPrice());
  strcat(str, buf);
  sprintf(buf, " lo price  : %f\n", loPrice());
  strcat(str, buf);
  sprintf(buf, " closing price : %f\n", closingPrice());
  strcat(str, buf);
  sprintf(buf, " volume   : %d\n", volume());
  strcat(str, buf);
  cout << "Symbol: " << tmpSymbol << " Name: " << tmpName
  << endl;  CORBA::string_free(tmpSymbol);
  CORBA::string_free(tmpName);
  return str;
}
```

This implementation uses a constructor similar to the one used in the first example. The constructor first invokes the parent constructor (_sk_Security) and takes advantage of the initialization list to initialize a number of the class attributes. The constructor also uses the CORBA-compliant string functions for allocation and deallocation of string memory in the set/get functions. The printData function provides a simple way to print out formatted descriptions of the object with minimal coding.

The Security object now inherits from CORBA::Object and is ready to be passed between client and server. How do you use this object and leverage its capabilities to improve the existing system? This example introduces a new server called the DataQueryServer, which creates SecurityQuote objects, fills them with data, and passes them to clients. Listing 3-12 illustrates the IDL for this new server:

Listing 3-12: DataQueryServer.idl — the IDL for the new DataQueryServer

```
#include "Security.idl"
interface DataQueryServer
{
  Security getSecurityData(in string securitySymbol);
};
```

This new interface has a single function that takes a string security symbol as input and returns a newly created Security object with the preceding interface. You can include other IDL files in IDL files with the #include statement (as in C++). The next step defines the implementation for this DataQueryServer. Listing 3-13 illustrates the DataQueryServerImpl definition:

Listing 3-13: DataQueryServerImpl.h — the impl definition for the new DataQueryServer

```
#include <DataQueryServer_s.hh>
#include <Security_c.hh>
class DataQueryServerImpl : public _sk_DataQueryServer
{
public:
  DataQueryServerImpl(const char *objName=NULL);
  ~DataQueryServerImpl();
  Security_ptr getSecurityData(const char* securitySymbol);
};
```

This definition declares a single function — the same function defined in the IDL. This function returns a *Security_ptr*, which is a pointer to a SecurityImpl object. Listing 3-14 illustrates the accompanying implementation for this object:

Listing 3-14: DataQueryServer.cpp — the implementation for the new DataQueryServer

```
#include "DataQueryServerImpl.h"
#include "SecurityImpl.h"
.
Constructor/destructor code omitted
.
Security_ptr DataQueryServerImpl::getSecurityData
       (const char * securitySymbol)
{
  CORBA::BOA_var boa = _boa();
  SecurityImpl *securityObj = new SecurityImpl(securitySymbol);
  try
  {
      boa->obj_is_ready(securityObj);
  }
  catch (CORBA::SystemException &except)
  {
```

```
            cout << "Failed to register object named "
     << securitySymbol << endl;
            return NULL; // this is bad, but if we get here
        // we already have bad problems!
    }
    securityObj->symbol(securitySymbol);
    cout << "Processing request for security: "
    << securitySymbol << endl;if (! strcmp(securitySymbol, "INTC"))
    {
        securityObj->name("Intel Corporation");
        securityObj->hiPrice((CORBA::Float)100.25);
        securityObj->loPrice((CORBA::Float)99.75);
        securityObj->closingPrice((CORBA::Float)100.0);
        securityObj->volume(120340000);
    }
    else if (! strcmp(securitySymbol, "NSCP"))
    {
        securityObj->name("Netscape Communications Corporation");
        securityObj->hiPrice((CORBA::Float)55.5);
        securityObj->loPrice((CORBA::Float)55.25);
        securityObj->closingPrice((CORBA::Float)55.5);
        securityObj->volume(54680000);
    }
    SecurityImpl::_duplicate(securityObj);
    cout << "Refcount for obj before returning from dataserver: "
    << securityObj->_ref_count() << endl;
    return securityObj;
}
```

Although some code for this implementation has been omitted, the most important function, *getSecurityData*, illustrates how you create a new CORBA object on the fly, notify the BOA the object is ready for service, and then fill in the object and pass it through the ORB to a client. The function _boa() obtains a pointer to the BOA. This function is automatically inherited by all CORBA objects; as an object of this type, DataQueryServerImpl has access to the function. The functions that obtain pointers to the ORB and the BOA are implementation-dependent — if you change the ORB, you may have to change the functions used to obtain references to the ORB and the BOA. The SecurityImpl object is created dynamically (just as you would create any C++ class) and filled in with "canned" security data based on the given security symbol. Before the object is returned by the function, the function _duplicate() is called. CORBA objects implement *reference counting* — the object knows how many users have a valid pointer to the object. When an object's reference count goes to zero, the object is automatically deleted. When this function returns, the allocated SecurityImpl object automatically has its reference count decremented, so the _duplicate() function is needed to bump the reference count and keep the object in existence. Use the _ref_count() function, which asks an object for its current reference count, to confirm proper reference counting.

The final step in completing the DataQueryServer provides its server main loop, which acts like the server in the first example. Listing 3-15 illustrates the main loop for this server:

Listing 3-15: DataQueryServerMain.cpp — the main loop for the new DataQueryServer

```
#include "DataQueryServerImpl.h"
int main(int argc, char * const *argv)
{
  CORBA::ORB_ptr orb = CORBA::ORB_init(argc, argv);
  CORBA::BOA_ptr boa = orb->BOA_init(argc, argv);
  DataQueryServerImpl server("DataQueryServer");
  cout <<"Calling obj_is_ready in DataQueryServer" << endl;
  boa->obj_is_ready(&server);
  cout << "Calling impl_is_ready in DataQueryServer" << endl;
  boa->impl_is_ready();
  cout << "Returned from impl_is_ready" << endl;
  return(1);
}
```

Most of your servers look much like this familiar example. (There are different ways to implement your server, however, which we discuss in following chapters.) After building the new DataQueryServer, tie it in to the existing application by adding a new function to the SecurityQuoteServer interface. When implemented, the new function talks to the DataQueryServer and returns the new Security object to the client. The rest of this server's functionality remains intact, so we just highlight the new additions to the files. The new function in the SecurityQuoteServer.idl file looks similar to the operation found in the DataQueryServer.idl file:

```
Security getSecurityQuote(in string securitySymbol);
```

As defined in the updated include file, the implementation definition for this function (illustrated in Listing 3-16) also looks familiar:

Listing 3-16: SecurityQuoteServer.h, second iteration

```
#include <Security_c.hh>
class SecurityQuoteServerImpl : public _sk_SecurityQuoteServer
{
protected:
  DataQueryServer_var dataServer;
public:
  SecurityQuoteServerImpl(const char *objName=NULL);
  ~SecurityQuoteServerImpl();
  CORBA::Float getSecurityPrice(const char* securitySymbol);
  Security_ptr getSecurityQuote(const char* securitySymbol);
};
```

We added a new attribute to this class that does not exist in the associated IDL. This new attribute, DataQueryServer_var, binds to the new server. The attribute is not included in the IDL because clients do not need to see or even know about the existence of this attribute. The actual implementation of this function requires a few addition to the SecurityQuoteServer, as illustrated in Listing 3-17:

Listing 3-17: SecurityQuoteServer.cpp, second iteration

```
#include "SecurityQuoteServerImpl.h"
#include "SecurityImpl.h"
SecurityQuoteServerImpl::SecurityQuoteServerImpl
      (const char *objName)
      : _sk_SecurityQuoteServer(objName)
{
  cout << "Creating object named: " << objName << endl;
  cout << "Binding to DataQueryServer. " << endl;
  dataServer = DataQueryServer::_bind();
}
//
// Default constructor for this class
//
SecurityQuoteServerImpl::~SecurityQuoteServerImpl()
{
}
.
Some code omitted
.
//
// This is the main function added from example1. This function
// simple passes the request to the DataQueryServer (DQS) The DQS
// will fill in all the data for a new security object, pass it
// back, and then it is passed back to the client.
//
Security_ptr SecurityQuoteServerImpl::getSecurityQuote
      (const char* securitySymbol)
{
  Security_ptr secPtr;
  // Ask the dataquery server to fill in the object.
  cout << "Invoking DataQueryServer. " << endl;
  secPtr = dataServer->getSecurityData(securitySymbol);
  cout << " After invocation, refcount is: "
  << secPtr->_ref_count() << endl;
  SecurityImpl::_duplicate(secPtr);
  return (secPtr);
}
```

The constructor for this implementation immediately binds to the new **DataQueryServer** using the protected DataQueryServer_var attribute. This object reference will be used when client requests arrive that require the use of this new server. In essence, the **SecurityQuoteServer** acts as a client of the **DataQueryServer**. The function **getSecurityQuote** is a pass-through function, because it only passes the request on to the **DataQueryServer** and returns the results to the client. The reference count must be incremented before the function returns to keep the **SecurityImpl** object alive. We could allow a client to call the **DataQueryServer** directly, but the illustration of server-to-server bindings is important.

The final upgrade to this new and improved example involves the client. The client needs new logic to call this new function on the `SecurityQuoteServer` and then invoke functions on the returned `SecurityImpl` object. Listing 3-18 illustrates the upgraded client code:

Listing 3-18: client.cpp, second iteration

```cpp
#include "SecurityQuoteServer_c.hh"
int main(int argc, char * const *argv)
{
  try
  {
      Security_ptr securityObj;
      char *str;
      // Initialize the ORB
      cout << "Initializing the ORB in client" << endl;
      CORBA::ORB_ptr orb = CORBA::ORB_init(argc, argv);
      // Bind to the SecurityQuoteServer
      cout << "Binding to SQS in client" << endl;
      SecurityQuoteServer_var quoteServer;
      if (argc == 2)
      {
          quoteServer = SecurityQuoteServer::_bind(argv[1]);
          cout << "Binding to SQS: " << argv[1] << endl;
      }
      else
      {
          quoteServer = SecurityQuoteServer::_bind();
      }
.
Some code omitted
.
      //
      // This call returns a CORBA object that is filled with
// quote data.
      //
      securityObj = quoteServer->getSecurityQuote("INTC");
      cout << "refcount of securityobj: "
   << securityObj->_ref_count() << endl;
      // Get a formatted information string for the object.
      str = securityObj->printData();
      cout << str << endl;
      CORBA::string_free(str);
      //
      // Remember - if securityObj was a _var variable, release
// will crash, because the _var does its own memory
// management.
      //
      cout << "Releasing with refcount: "
   << securityObj->_ref_count() << endl;
      CORBA::release(securityObj);
```

```
.
Some code omitted
.
}
   catch(CORBA::SystemException& e)
   {
       cout << "CORBA System Exception" << endl;
       cout << e;
       return (1);
   }
   return (0);
}
```

The client obtains a pointer to a `SecurityImpl` object by invoking the `SecurityQuoteServer`'s `getSecurityQuote()` function. The object then acts just like a normal C++ object and any available functions on the object can be invoked. The client asks the object to `printData()`, which creates a formatted information string and passes it through the ORB back to the client. This sequence saves time for the client, which takes the string and sends it to `cout`. A question: "Why doesn't the `printData()` function simply print all object information to `cout` to avoid passing a string across the network?" This approach is flawed in one major way. The `SecurityImpl` object reference performs like a normal C++ pointer, but does not reference an object in the local process space. Instead, it is a proxy for an object that lives in a separate process space on the current or any other machine. If the object tries to print its data, it prints to the DOS prompt in which it runs – which does not help the client. Lastly, when finished with the object, the client calls `_release()`, which decrements the reference count for the object and indicates the object is no longer needed.

Assuming you have built the executables in ex0602, let's run the servers and the client. As always, first make sure your **OSAGENT** is running.

```
start osagent
```

If you use dial-up Internet access to supply the TCP/IP support for OSAGENT, you may run into a problem. If OSAGENT is running and your Internet connection times out, your first instinct is to restart the Internet connection. With this action, OSAGENT will continue to run but will no longer have the correct communication support. If you need to start a new Internet connection, stop and restart OSAGENT.

Next, you must start the new `DataQueryServer` from a DOS prompt with current directory ex0602.

```
start DataQueryServer
```

Then start the `SecurityQuoteServer`. The order is important because this server immediately binds to the `DataQueryServer`. If this server is not running, the bind will not work correctly (unless you are using the Object Activation Daemon, which provides automatic server start services).

```
start SecurityQuoteServer
```

Finally, start the client from the current DOS prompt and examine the output.

```
client
```

The following output should appear in the following DOS windows.
In the `DataQueryServer` DOS window:

```
Creating object named: DataQueryServer
Calling obj_is_ready in DataQueryServer
Calling impl_is_ready in DataQueryServer
Security object created: INTC
Processing request for security: INTC
Refcount for obj before returning from dataserver: 2
Symbol: INTC Name: Intel Corporation
Security object created: NSCP
Processing request for security: NSCP
Refcount for obj before returning from dataserver: 2
Symbol: NSCP Name: Netscape Communications Corporation
```

In the `SecurityQuoteServer` DOS window:

```
Initializing the ORB from SecurityQuoteServer
Creating object named: SecurityQuoteServer
Binding to DataQueryServer.
Calling obj_is_ready in SecurityQuoteServer
Calling impl_is_ready in SecurityQuoteServer
Processing request for security: INTC
Invoking DataQueryServer.
 After invocation, refcount is: 1
Invoking DataQueryServer.
 After invocation, refcount is: 1
```

In the client DOS window:

```
Initializing the ORB in client
Invoking SecurityQuoteServer in client
Security data for : INTC
 price    : 103.5
Making more detailed quote request:
refcount of securityobj: 1
Security data for : INTC
 name   : Intel Corporation
 hi price   : 100.250000
 lo price   : 99.750000
 closing price : 100.000000
 volume   : 120340000
Releasing with refcount: 1
Security data for : NSCP
 name   : Netscape Communications Corporation
 hi price   : 55.500000
 lo price   : 55.250000
 closing price : 55.500000
 volume   : 54680000
Releasing with refcount: 1
```

Congratulations again! You have just taken another step in the journey to become a CORBA programmer. This example illustrates how to define a new CORBA object, add functionality to the object, instantiate the object, and pass it around between clients and servers. Once you understand how to add highly functional objects to your system, your CORBA applications will know no bounds. One final note: time spent creating a CORBA object for your system can be passed to any CORBA client or server. This example was written completely in C++. If you write either the client or server in Java or another language with CORBA bindings, however, this new object would work effortlessly with the new program.

From this example, imagine how you would create a server that takes requests from multiple clients and dishes out new exchange objects with each request. All the clients need only know of the single server which sends these requests. This strategy is a common approach in CORBA programming.

We just illustrated how to create a new CORBA object from scratch, but CORBA is often leveraged to wrap existing legacy objects, and it may not be possible to spend the time converting all these legacy objects to true CORBA objects. In this situation, examine the TIE functionality, which enables you to associate an existing C++ object with a new skeleton CORBA object and save large amounts of rewriting time. The VisiBroker programmer's manual provides further information on the TIE approach.

Using Exceptions to Make Your Code More Robust

If you have prior experience with client/server architectures, you probably understand such applications can be complex and usually have many potential points of failure. CORBA applications exacerbate this problem; these applications usually communicate between different machines with potentially different operating systems and the client and server could be implemented using ORBs from different vendors. These variables produce an error checking nightmare. Picture running a client on your NT machine that causes an error in your server running on a UNIX workstation somewhere else on your network. How do you identify and process that error without writing tons of error checking code? Use CORBA exceptions to provide simple and efficient error handling in your application.

We bracket a large portion of the code with the conventional C++ try-catch-throw mechanism because CORBA automatically generates an elaborate set of SystemExceptions to help determine when and why an error occurs. Use the try-catch-throw functionality to your advantage whenever possible. Any communication going *across the wire* (between client and server) should be bracketed in an exception handling block. When an error occurs, your code quickly indicates the problem and makes fixing the problem a quick and easy job. Table 3-1 lists some of the common SystemExceptions encountered when building CORBA client/server programs. For the full list of exceptions, examine the VisiBroker programmer's manual, which gives detailed descriptions and possible causes of all exceptions.

TABLE 3-1 SYSTEM EXCEPTIONS

Exception	Possible Cause
CORBA::BAD_OPERATION	Thrown by server when a request is received for an operation that does not exist on the server. Usually called when client and server are not in sync with the current IDL.
CORBA::BAD_PARAM	Usually thrown during an attempt to pass a NULL string or NIL object reference.
CORBA::COMM_FAILURE	Thrown when the connection between client and server has closed.
CORBA::INITIALIZE	Thrown when the ORB_Init() and BOA_Init() functions are not called.
CORBA::MARSHALL	Can be thrown when the server receives a string of zero length.

Continued

Exception	Possible Cause
CORBA::NO_IMPLEMENT	Thrown when a bind() call fails, usually because the desired object is not registered with OSAGENT.
CORBA::OBJECT_NOT_EXIST	Thrown when an invocation is made on a nonexistent or deactivated object. Usually occurs when reference counting is done incorrectly and an object goes out of scope.
CORBA::UNKNOWN	Can be thrown when a client and server are not in sync with the IDL during the definition of a new UserException. Also thrown when a server throws a Windows runtime exception.
CORBA::UNKNOWN_USER_EXCEPTION	Thrown when a client receives a thrown UserException undefined in the linked-in client stub.

All CORBA system exceptions provide a programmer with robust error checking. The set of existing exceptions is excellent for providing graceful handing of errors that occur during client/server communications, but this set imparts little help in pinpointing errors that occur within a given server. CORBA *UserExceptions*, a CORBA class that inherits from CORBA::Exception, remedies this inadequacy by defining, throwing, and catching exceptions specific to a server's implementation. Like the preceding CORBA example objects, a UserException is defined in IDL, and CORBA generates client stubs and server skeletons to allow the exception to be passed between client and server. The UserException can have any declared attributes. Best of all, the IDL compiler generates a constructor for the exception that inputs all attributes that define the exception. This characteristic enables you to create and throw the UserException at the first indication of trouble.

Listing 3-19 illustrates how to use CORBA SystemExceptions and UserExceptions. Every client in the preceding example code uses a convention similar to the following:

Listing 3-19: Catching a SystemException

```
  try
{
.
.
Make some CORBA invocations
.
.
}
```

```
catch(CORBA::SystemException& e)
  {
      cout << "CORBA System Exception" << endl;
      cout << e;
      return (1);
  }
```

This try-catch works like any other C++ try-catch block. The caught exception is a *CORBA::SystemException*, which prints all its information to *cout* or *cerr*. Typically, we bracket the entire client in the try-catch block, which catches most thrown exceptions. Ideally, to gain utmost efficiency, bracket each individual CORBA invocation in its own try-catch block. This strategy helps you quickly recognize the exception source and decrease required debugging time.

CORBA UserExceptions work in a similar manner, but you can define the exception to operate efficiently with a given server implementation. To illustrate this concept, we revisit the SecurityQuote example and prompt one of the servers to throw a UserException caught by the client. We simply define and throw the exception. We make no effort to ensure the exception finds its way across the wire back to a client. CORBA again manages this communications nightmare without additional required code. Listing 3-20 first alters the example (ex0603) by defining a new UserException (the **DataException**) and Listings 3-21 and 3-22 indicate which interfaces throw this exception.

Listing 3-20: Exceptions.idl — definition of the DataException interface

```
exception DataException
{
  string reason;  // "Data not found", etc.
  string symbol; // F, KO, etc.
  short severity; // 1 to 10
  string quoteSource; // "Schwab, etc"
};
```

Listing 3-21: DataQueryServer.idl — the updated interface

```
#include "Security.idl"
#include "Exceptions.idl"
interface DataQueryServer
{
  Security getSecurityData(in string securitySymbol)
      raises(DataException);
};
```

Listing 3-22: SecurityQuoteServer.idl — the updated interface

```
#include "Security.idl"
#include "Exceptions.idl"
interface SecurityQuoteServer
{
  float getSecurityPrice(in string securitySymbol);
  Security getSecurityQuote(in string securitySymbol)
      raises(DataException);
};
```

The preceding code listings display all the IDL changes necessary to define and throw a UserException. Exceptions.idl defines the new exception, which has three string attributes and a short attribute. DataQueryServer.idl and SecurityQuote Server.idl have changed slightly — they simply indicate which operations raise the new DataException, which is thrown when requested data is unavailable. To implement this exception in the example, first modify the DataQueryServer to throw the exception when appropriate, as illustrated in Listing 3-23:

Listing 3-23: DataQueryServerImpl.cpp — the DQS throws a UserException

```
Security_ptr DataQueryServerImpl::getSecurityData
      (const char * securitySymbol)
{
  CORBA::BOA_var boa = _boa();
  SecurityImpl *securityObj = new SecurityImpl(securitySymbol);
  try
  {
      boa->obj_is_ready(securityObj);
  }
  catch (CORBA::SystemException &except)
  {
      cout << "Failed to register object named " << securitySymbol
  << endl;
      return NULL; // this is bad, but if we get here we already
  // have bad problems!
  }
  securityObj->symbol(securitySymbol);
  if (! strcmp(securitySymbol, "INTC"))
  {
      securityObj->name("Intel Corporation");
securityObj->hiPrice((CORBA::Float)100.25);
securityObj->loPrice((CORBA::Float)99.75);
      securityObj->closingPrice((CORBA::Float)100.0);
      securityObj->volume(120340000);
  }
  else if (! strcmp(securitySymbol, "NSCP"))
  {
```

```
            securityObj->name("Netscape Communications Corporation");
            securityObj->hiPrice((CORBA::Float)55.5);
            securityObj->loPrice((CORBA::Float)55.25);
            securityObj->closingPrice((CORBA::Float)55.5);
            securityObj->volume(54680000);
    }
    else
    {
            char *tmpSymbol = securityObj->symbol();
            char *msg1 = CORBA::string_alloc(100);
            char *msg2 = CORBA::string_alloc(100);
            char *msg3 = CORBA::string_alloc(100);
            sprintf(msg1, "Cannot find data for stock");
            sprintf(msg2, tmpSymbol);
            CORBA::string_free(tmpSymbol);
            sprintf(msg3, "Agent: Mercadante Quotes");
            CORBA::Short severity = 9;
            cout << "Throwing Data Exception in DataQueryServer."
      << endl;
            throw DataException(msg1, msg2, severity, msg3);
    }
    SecurityImpl::_duplicate(securityObj);
    cout << "Refcount for obj before returning from dataserver: "
    << securityObj->_ref_count() << endl;
    return securityObj;
}
```

This code differs little from the second example's DQS, except a DataException is created and thrown if a request is received for nonexistent security data. The exception is created by simply initializing the exception attributes and passing them to the generated class constructor. Initially, the code appears to leak memory by creating new character strings and never freeing them. However, as Listing 3-24 illustrates, the generated constructor shows the construction is completed by simple parameter assignment, so the allocated memory now belongs to the exception object:

Listing 3-24: DataException_c.cpp — the client stub for the DataException class

```
DataException(
 const char * _reason,
 const char * _symbol,
 CORBA::Short _severity,
 const char * _quoteSource) {
 reason = _reason;
 symbol = _symbol;
 severity = _severity;
 quoteSource = _quoteSource;
 }
```

After the `DataQueryServer` throws the exception, the `SecurityQuoteServer` must catch the exception and pass it back to the client. Listing 3-25 illustrates this process.

Listing 3-25: SecurityQuoteServerImpl.cpp – handling the `DataException`

```
Security_ptr SecurityQuoteServerImpl::getSecurityQuote
      (const char* securitySymbol)
{
  Security_ptr secPtr;
  // Ask the dataquery server to fill in the object.
  cout << "Invoking DataQueryServer. " << endl;
  try
  {
      secPtr = dataServer->getSecurityData(securitySymbol);
  }
  catch(DataException e)
  {
      cout << "Data Exception: " << endl;
      cout << e << endl;
      throw e;
  }
  cout << " After invocation, refcount is: " << secPtr->_ref_count()
  << endl;
  SecurityImpl::_duplicate(secPtr);
  return (secPtr);
}
```

The `SecurityQuoteServer` addition is also simple. The server brackets the `getSecurityData` function call to the `DataQueryServer` in a try-catch block. If a `DataException` is caught, it is printed and thrown in hope that the client will catch and process it. The client uses the same approach to handle the `DataException`. The following portion of the client's code works with this new exception:

```
        try
        {
            securityObj = quoteServer->getSecurityQuote("CLNX");
            //
            // Check the refcount to see what is going on.
            //
            cout << "refcount of securityobj: "
  << securityObj->_ref_count() << endl;
            //
            // Get a char string filled with formatted data for
  // printing the quote. This is done because if the
  // security object prints itself out, it will be in
  // the wrong process space, and
```

```
        // thus the wrong DOS window.
        //
        str = securityObj->printData();
        cout << str << endl;
        CORBA::string_free(str);
        //
        // Remember - if securityObj was a _var variable,
// release should not be called
    // because the _var does its own memory management.
        //
        cout << "Releasing with refcount: "
  << securityObj->_ref_count() << endl;
        securityObj->_release();
    }
    catch(DataException e)
    {
        cout << endl << "Caught a DataException: " << endl;
        cout << e << endl;
    }
```

The client asks for security information for the stock CLNX, which does not exist in the DataQueryServer's database. We run this example as we did the second example, starting the DataQueryServer, then the SecurityQuoteServer, and then finally the client. The client's new output with new exception handling code follows:

```
Initializing the ORB in client
Binding to SQS in client
Caught a DataExeption:
EXCEPTION DataException {
  reason:
Cannot find data for stock
  symbol:
CLNX
  severity:
9
  quoteSource:
Agent: Mercadante Quotes
}
```

Figure 3-9 illustrates this construction.

Using the Object Activation Daemon to Save Time

At this point, you are probably tired of starting servers at every execution of a client. In a complex CORBA application, this approach is wasteful and sometimes difficult, because you have to start all servers before running a client to ensure the server desired by the client is running and available. To solve this problem, use the Object Activation Daemon (OAD) in VisiBroker. The OAD works with the OSAGENT to provide object location and activation services. After registering an object with the OAD, a client bind to the object causes the OSAGENT to ask the OAD to find, start, and initialize the object automatically. Registering objects with the OAD and using these objects is a simple task. To illustrate this procedure, we return to the first example, which consists of a client and server. We register the SecurityQuoteServer with the OAD and use this process to launch the server automatically (with no additional effort required from the client).

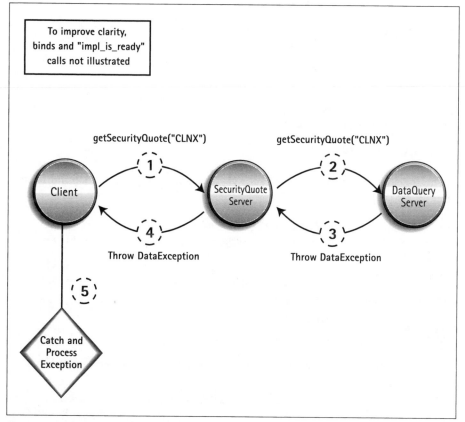

Figure 3-9: Handling exceptions

First, start the OSAGENT and the OAD:

```
start osagent
start oad
```

Next, the SecurityQuoteServer is registered with the OAD. The OAD registration process imparts the name of the implementation (the -i flag), the name of the object (-o), the full path to the executable (-cpp), and any required command line arguments for the registered server (-a). (You can also pass other available options to the OAD.) In the first example, we used two SecurityQuoteServers: Schwab and e-trade. Both are registered with the system using the oadutil program, which registers, unregisters, and lists objects in the implementation repository. First, register the Schwab SecurityQuoteServer:

```
oadutil reg -i SecurityQuoteServer -o Schwab
  -cpp c:\book\writing\examples\example1\SecurityQuoteServer.exe
  -a Schwab
```

This registration produces the following output:

```
Completed registration of repository_id  =
  IDL:SecurityQuoteServer:1.0
object_name  = Schwab
reference data =
path_name  =
  c:\book\writing\examples\example1\SecurityQuoteServer.exe
activation_policy = SHARED_SERVER
args    = (length=1)[Schwab; ]
env    = NONE
for OAD on host 207.0.141.89
```

The registration of the e-trade SecurityQuoteServer produces similar output from the OAD:

```
oadutil reg -i SecurityQuoteServer -o e-trade
  -cpp c:\book\writing\examples\example1\SecurityQuoteServer.exe
  -a e-trade
```

If you see the following error while attempting to register an object with oadutil in Windows 95:

```
Out of Environment Space
```

then you need to increase your DOS environment space. Proceed in one of two ways:

- ◆ Add /e:1024 to end of the Shell= line in your config.sys file and reboot.

- ◆ Open a DOS window and bring up the properties panel. Click the Memory tab, set the Initial Environment drop-down to at least 1024 and reboot.

To verify the registration process has worked correctly, take advantage of another VisiBroker application. osfind gives information about objects registered in the implementation repository as well as OSAGENTs and OADs running on your system.

First, type the following command to start osfind:

```
osfind
```

This command shows you the two registered versions of the SecurityQuoteServer: Schwab and e-trade.

```
osfind: Found one agent at port 14000
 HOST: pm1-9.rmaonline.net
osfind: Found 1 OADs in your domain
 HOST: pm1-9.myhost.net
osfind: Following are the list of Implementations registered with
 OADs.
 HOST: pm1-9.myhost.net
  REPOSITORY ID: IDL:SecurityQuoteServer:1.0
   OBJECT NAME: e-trade
   OBJECT NAME: Schwab
osfind: Following are the list of Implementations started manually.
 HOST: pm1-9.rmaonline.net
  REPOSITORY ID: IDL:visigenic.com/Activation/OAD:1.0
   OBJECT NAME: 1.1.1.1
```

Start the client with e-trade as the only command line argument. This command informs the OSAGENT you want to communicate with the SecurityQuoteServer named e-trade. The OSAGENT negotiates with the OAD to start and initialize this particular server. A communication link is created between the client and this server to facilitate normal communications.

```
client e-trade
Initializing the ORB in client
Binding to SQS in client
Binding to SQS: e-trade
Security data for : INTC
price    : 103.5
```

In this section, you have registered a server with the OAD, which allows this server to be started *on demand* — as soon a client on the system desires to communicate with the server. When building your CORBA application, consider using the OAD to save time and make your entire system run more efficiently.

CORBA Memory Management

Memory management is always a nagging issue in complex software projects. It is sometimes overlooked until excessive memory usage forces project managers to choose between two solutions: buy more RAM or prioritize memory leak detection. Although the second option is preferable, this decision will never come to pass if memory management considered in the initial project stages. With clients and servers running in different process spaces and usually on different machines, CORBA applications increase memory management difficulties.

An understanding of reference counting keeps you from calling RAM vendors for memory price quotes. When a CORBA object is created, it has a reference count of one. When the count goes to zero, the object is deleted from the system. Anytime an object is handed out for use, its reference count should be incremented (with the _duplicate() function). Thus, the reference count calculates the number of objects, or clients, using a given object. Reference counting is a two-way street. It is the responsibility of an object broker to increment the reference count when brokering an object, but it is also the responsibility of the client to decrement the count when the object is no longer needed. The _release() function performs the decrement. If the broker (a server in preceding examples) or the client fails to fulfill its reference counting obligation, memory leaks will squander your system resources.

You should never call delete on an object that implements reference counting — the object is automatically deleted when the reference count falls to zero. Calling delete yanks the rug out from under a client expecting a valid object pointer. If you are unsure about reference counting, take advantage of the reference count capabilities in a CORBA object's _ref_count() function.

The two new types generated by the IDL compiler, _var and _ptr types, also address memory management. These types are generated for all CORBA objects created during IDL compilation. Although both are pointers to objects that implement reference counting, but subtle and important differences exist between the two types. The _ptr type acts like any normal C++ object pointer. If a program, function, or object is given one of these types, that program must _release() the variable when it is no longer needed. The _var type is a pointer to a new class wrapped around the object pointer. This new class provides automatic memory management. When a _var type goes out of scope, _release() is automatically called. You are not obligated to call _release(), and under normal circumstances you should not call this function on _var types. Also, when a _var type is assigned to a new object, _release() is automatically called on the object that the pointer initially references.

Now it gets interesting. One of the difficult concepts of CORBA memory management passes objects between client and server as function parameters or return values. When using strings between client and server, always use the CORBA-compliant string_alloc and string_free functions – the standard malloc and free causes numerous problems. The appropriate memory management approach is directly related to the type of parameter passed; the parameter type is directly related to its IDL definition, which embodies one of three IDL types:

◆ in

◆ out and return values

◆ inout

The in type provides the simplest memory management approach. On the client side, storage is allocated for the parameter and passed to the server. The parameter is available for the entire life of the function on the server side, but is freed on the server side when the function returns. If the server needs to keep the data for later use, it needs to call _duplicate() if the parameter is an object reference – if the parameter is a string, it needs to be copied to new memory on the server side. Simple assignment of primitive types saves the value for the server.

Managing memory for out and return types is more complicated. The client must declare a pointer passed as the server function's out parameter. We recommend a _var type be passed because it provides built-in memory management. The server must initialize and allocate storage for the data. When the function returns, the newly allocated storage is deleted automatically on the server side (the data returns to the client intact). Therefore, if you work with object references and want the object to stay alive on the server side, _duplicate() must be called. If the server does not regard the object after the life of the function, _duplicate() does not need to be called – the memory will be freed when the function returns. Use a similar approach with strings. The server allocates and returns a string. If the string needs to remain on the server side, use the CORBA string_var type during the allocation and _duplicate() this pointer before returning. Data is returned via a function return type in a similar manner as the out parameters.

In the preceding examples, we illustrate how to properly manage memory passed as a return type. The DataQueryServer allocates and returns a SecurityQuote object. _duplicate() is called on this object before the return, however, because the object is managed by the DataQueryServer. The client must _release() the object when finished, which brings the object's reference count to zero.

The inout type provides new elements to CORBA memory management. First, examine passing object references. On the client side, a valid _var type must be passed and the variable must point to a valid object. If the original object reference is needed by the client after the function invocation, it should first be reassigned to a _ptr type. The client should call _duplicate() because the server will probably reassign the _var parameter. This reassignment automatically releases the original object, causing it to be deallocated. On the server side, the object reference is only valid for the life of the function. The server is free to reassign the parameter to a new value: reallocate the parameter to a new _var variable or call _release(), and then assign it to a valid _ptr type. The original _var input parameter is deallocated on the server side when the function returns. If a string (char *) is passed in, the rules are the same. The string can be reassigned by the server, but must be deleted before new memory is allocated to the input pointer (it can also be assigned to a string_var parameter, which causes the deletion of the original memory). If the string is not changed, the server memory for the string is automatically deleted when the function returns.

If you understand the three preceding memory management concepts, you can build leak-proof CORBA applications. Just remember these three simple rules:

♦ Pay attention to reference counting.

♦ Pay attention to your use of the _var and _ptr types and apply the correct memory management rules based on the type used in your code.

♦ Pay attention to the parameter type you pass to a server function, and follow the memory management rules dictated by the type.

If you follow these rules, you can spend your money on something other than unnecessary RAM!

Summary

This chapter describes the main concepts needed to become a great CORBA programmer. To expedite the CORBA programming process, you can use the Visigenic ORB utility programs. We have talked about different programming techniques that are used as the building blocks of powerful CORBA applications. In discussing different CORBA programming techniques, the chapter examines simple and advanced client/server CORBA applications while highlighting important concepts. Download the Visigenic ORB, compile and run the examples, and build your own programs — writing and running your own examples is the best way to learn. Many of the upcoming chapters provide you with more intricate and complex CORBA examples. This chapter gives you the knowledge to tackle and understand such examples.

Chapter 4

CORBA Services

IN THIS CHAPTER

One of the greatest inefficiencies in software development is "the reinvention of the wheel," a phrase most software developers have heard often. Every day, countless programmers build the same functionality for their different software projects, wasting time that could be better spent improving the internals of their individual programs. If the software development community existed in a perfect world, we would all write code specific to our application domain and then use existing building blocks as glue between our application-specific pieces. Unfortunately, our community has not reached such a level of perfection. In recent years, a large influx of software toolkits have been seen that help promote reuse of common components but, in reality, we all have a long way to go in our quest to stop the reinvention of the wheel.

This chapter discusses CORBA Services, individual software components designed to promote a greater amount of software reuse. Following a description of how and why the CORBA Services were designed, it moves into a description of all the services as defined by the Object Management Group. Because many services exist (15) and some are quite complex, our discussion will look at each service from a high-level point of view. The intention of this chapter is to give you a good understanding of the different services and how they could potentially be used in your CORBA application. While this chapter is not an exhaustive technical investigation of the services, it is a thorough description of each. Following descriptions of the services, we discuss how actively the current ORB vendors are moving to provide the implementation of services for us. This chapter ends with a CORBA Services quick reference guide. This guide gives you a quick summary of the services in an easy-to-find place. Welcome to the world of CORBA Services.

- ◆ CORBA Services in general

- ◆ Descriptions of the 15 CORBA Services

- ◆ The current status of CORBA Services

CORBA Services in General

The definition of the Common Object Request Broker Architecture (CORBA) is a huge (and ongoing) undertaking for the Object Management Group (OMG). CORBA provides us with a new middleware architecture that has taken the best qualities of existing client/server architectures and may replace client/server programming as we have come to know it. The OMG took on the project with the desire to stream-line distributed object programming. At the same time, the group worked to pro-vide us with the ability to make software reuse an attainable goal. This is where CORBA Services come into play. In defining the services, the OMG took an in-depth look at the software development process and tried to focus on common steps or pieces of functionality most programs need to implement. These common steps turned into the CORBA 2.0 Services Specification, which currently defines 15 ser-vices. Each service has been defined and engineered with two main underlying concepts:

1. The service must be generic, meaning it should be domain-independent.

2. The service should do one specific task in a thorough manner.

These services are building blocks from which our CORBA objects can inherit functionality or standalone components with which our objects interact. A quick example may help explain how this works. If you are building a CORBA banking application, you may define a CORBA object that represents a bank Account. You will define the Account object to have expected properties, such as a name and a monetary balance. Your application will pass this object from a server to a client, which will interact with the Account object. In this example, the server represents the main bank that stores all customer data. The client will probably be a branch bank that receives deposits and withdrawals from a customer and needs to post the changes to the Account object. Unfortunately, some quick roadblocks appear as you try to tie your application together. How will your client easily find the desired Account? How will you enforce security as you pass the Account object around your system? How will you track the entire transaction process and ensure a trans-action was successful? You could answer these three questions by saying "I will write code that will solve these problems." Before the invention of CORBA Services, this was the correct answer and, in most cases, the only answer. Instead of writing and maintaining the code to solve these three problems, you could simply use the functionality found in the CORBA Naming, Security, and Transaction Services. You will write the domain-specific code for your Account, client, and server objects, and let the services do the rest of the work for you.

As we discuss in the upcoming section "The Current Status of CORBA Services," the majority of ORB vendors have been somewhat slow in providing commercial implementations of the different services. This is unfortunate because once all ser-vices are available, the development life cycle of a CORBA application will be sub-stantially shortened. The good news is, with each day, more and more ORB vendors are bringing different service implementations to market. If anything is stressed in this chapter, this is: Take advantage of CORBA Services. Don't reinvent the wheel!

Some of the authors of this book have been building CORBA applications since CORBA was in its infancy. Looking back on some of these applications, we realize we wrote large amounts of code that provided us with functionality similar to what is available in some of the current CORBA Services. We have spent countless days designing, writing, maintaining, and upgrading this code. At the time, no services were implemented, so we had no choice but to implement them ourselves. You are in a much better position because many services are available for use today.

Here's some final service-related advice: As you begin your CORBA development cycle, be sure to look at the available services before designing and implementing any nondomain components. In the next section. We describe all 15 services. If you see a service that provides a capability your application needs, try to use the service to its full advantage. This will save countless days of unnecessary programming and maintenance. Also, remember services when you choose your ORB vendor. And, finally, watch for service implementations that are not compliant with the OMG specification. Once you commit to a noncompliant service, your ability to move your code to a new ORB becomes greatly impeded.

In the following sections, we provide an in-depth description and a good sense for the functionality provided by each of the current 15 CORBA Services. Some of these services are more complex than others. In many cases, the interfaces defined by a particular service are discussed. An *interface* defines the functions a service publishes for use by clients. We touch on some of the more useful interfaces for most of these services, but in no way can we show you all the available capabilities. Our hope is these service descriptions will portray which services are needed by your system. Once you decide, the vendor's documentation can be consulted for a finer level of interface detail.

Naming Service

As you saw in Chapter 3, "Writing Your First CORBA Application," one of the main steps in CORBA involves a client binding to a server. This binding process provides a direct communication link between the two processes. The Naming Service helps facilitate this process. *The Naming Service* provides the capability for CORBA objects to find other CORBA objects using an easily distinguished naming convention. With the help of the Naming Service, one object can find another through the use of an easily-recognizable name. The Naming Service also enables you to associate a logical name with an object at runtime, which provides more flexibility in how you configure your distributed object system. With the normal binding process, an object can have only one name. But the Naming Service enables you to associate more than one logical name with a single object. In the next section, this service is investigated by first looking at the definition of a CORBA object name and at some terms used to refer to this name. Then you will see some of the interfaces of the Naming Service and the functionality they provide.

CORBA Object Names

To understand the Naming Service completely, you must first understand the concept of a CORBA object name. As you would expect, a *name* is some language representation for a given object. This concept is slightly more complex than you may expect, however.

An object name is defined using a few new terms. First, a name-to-object association is called a *name binding*. If you create a Person object and you name it "Tom," you have created a name binding. The name is a structure consisting of two attributes – the identifier attribute and the kind attribute, both IDL strings. The *identifier attribute* is the object's name string and the *kind attribute* is an additional string used for descriptive purposes. Each binding exists in what is called a *naming context*, which is a container object that holds a set of unique bindings. You *resolve* a name by determining which object is associated with the name in a given context. You *bind* a name by providing a name for an object relative to a given context. Every object is named relative to a context. No absolute object names exist. Each context can itself have a name binding within a higher-level context. This process leads to a naming graph (as shown in Figure 4-1), which consists of nodes that are contexts. By traversing this graph, you can find a specific object using a compound name, which indicates the path to the desired object through its containing naming contexts. Confused? This can be hard to follow. The following illustration may help.

In this illustration, naming contexts are used to find a Person object named "Tom" in our model of a software company. This is done by using the naming context "SoftwareDevelopment," which contains other naming contexts, one being "SimulationSystems." This context contains the Person object we are looking for, having a simple name binding of "Tom." The compound name for this object, using the naming contexts, would be < SoftwareDevelopment ; SimulationSystems ;Tom>.

Naming Service Interfaces

Now that we understand the concept of a CORBA object name, let's see how the Naming Service enables us to use these compound names in our distributed systems. We will do this by looking at the different interfaces of this service. Only two interfaces are used to make this service work and both are defined in the CosNaming module. (The *Cos* portion of the name stands for *Common Object Services*.)

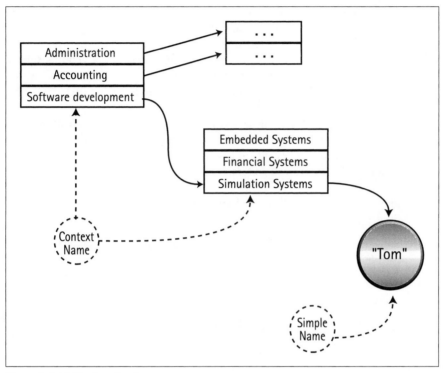

Figure 4-1: A Naming Graph

♦ The NamingContext interface contains operations for managing and manipulating object names and naming contexts. You invoke *bind()* to associate a compound or simple name with an object, relative to a naming context. *Rebind()* acts in a similar manner, but works even if the name is already bound in the context. To remove a name binding from a given naming context, use *unbind()*. The *bind_context()* operation binds a name to an existing naming context, which can be created with *new_context()*. To save time, *bind_new_context()* can be used to both create a new context and bind a name to it. The *resolve()* operation is used to find an object based on its compound name. It returns a generic object that you narrow to the correct object type. Finally, this interface provides an operation called *list()*. You use this operation to get a list of name bindings that exist in a naming context. It returns a BindingInterator object, which is described next.

♦ The *BindingIterator* interface enables clients to navigate through a set of bindings found in a naming context. You invoke *next_one()* to get the next name binding in the list. For a subset of name bindings, use *next_n()*, which returns as many bindings as you care to work with.

These are the base interfaces for the Naming Service. They provide good capabilities to create and navigate names and naming contexts. The Naming Service has already been implemented by a number of companies, many of whom have chosen to extend these base interfaces further. For instance, many vendors supply a *resolve()* operation that can be used with IIOP communications, which is invaluable for finding your CORBA objects from locations around the Internet.

In CORBA 3.0, this service will probably be enhanced with the *Interoperable Naming Service*, which is an improvement of the existing Naming Service specification. After the Naming Service arrived in the commercial marketplace, its lack of flexibility made this evident: it is impossible for clients to build uniform systems that can interoperate. The new version of this service will add improvements in the following areas:

- ◆ Independent clients will be configured at runtime to use a common, initial-naming context.

- ◆ Using stringified names interoperably among independent clients will be possible.

- ◆ A better definition of identity will exist between different CosNaming::Name components.

- ◆ Support for naming – using URL formats – will exist.

Naming Service Summary

In summary, the Naming Service can be used to assign names logically to objects in a naming context and to find these objects easily, based on their compound names. The location services can be configured at runtime and can be helpful in locating objects in complex distributed systems.

Event Service

The *Event Service* provides a decoupled communication channel between CORBA objects. Objects in a software system send and receive events, which are notifications of a change somewhere in the system. The Event Service is analogous to the event models used extensively in most user interface software, but is useful in all types of programs. In CORBA programs, a given server may be running in its own process, but could be interested in events generated by another server somewhere else in the system. For instance, an example of a CORBA application that uses the Event Service may be a computational server that does a large amount of scientific analysis on a CORBA object. This server is initiated by a client server, which is also running somewhere in the system. The client has specific tasks that must be accomplished, but only when the computational server has finished. The client does other processing while waiting for the completion of the analysis. In this case, the computational server generates an "I am finished" event. The client receives this event and is then able to finish its other tasks. The Event Service provides the capability to generate and process these requests easily and provides a few different ways to do this. To understand how the Event Service works, we discuss a few basic concepts in the next section: suppliers and consumers, the event channel, event proxies, pull and push models, and, finally, the two types of events available.

Suppliers and Consumers

The *Event Service* is built around the concept of suppliers and consumers. In this model, *suppliers* generate events and *consumers* receive and process the event data. Considering the previous example, the computational server was an event supplier and our client was the event consumer. A given event can have multiple consumers and multiple suppliers. Based on the design of your application, consumers can either request events periodically (the polling approach or the *pull model*) or they can be notified of events when they are created by registering itself as a consumer (called the *push model*). In the push model, a single event generated by a supplier is automatically broadcast to all registered consumers. A supplier usually generates events with no knowledge of who will consume the event. In a similar fashion, the consumer can receive events with no knowledge of where the event originated. In the following sections, you see how this works.

The Event Channel

The *EventChannel* is a CORBA object that resides on the ORB. This object receives and distributes event data, so it is both a consumer and a supplier of events. The Event Channel acts as a middleman in the communication process by routing multiple supplier events to multiple consumers in an asynchronous manner. The Event Service's decoupling property is provided by this object because it channels the events in a way that does not require consumer and supplier to have knowledge of each other. Figure 4-2 illustrates how the EventChannel fits into our supplier-consumer event architecture:

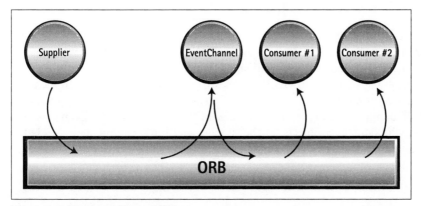

Figure 4-2: The Event Channel Object

An EventChannel is found by both consumer and supplier by binding to an EventChannel object, which can be started programmatically or manually. The binding operation returns a reference to an EventChannel object. If a name is passed in the binding process, then both supplier and consumer will talk to a specific EventChannel. This approach enables you to have multiple event channels in existence, each processing specific events. The EventChannel is defined in standard IDL and defines three operations: 1) *for_consumers()*, which enables consumers to connect to the event channel; 2) *for_suppliers()*, which enables suppliers to connect to the event channel; 3) *destroy()*, which disconnects all suppliers and consumers from the channel and destroys the channel.

The EventChannel is in charge of queuing events and providing them when required by consumers. The queuing period and length are configurable, based on your application needs. This is important for a server that may come up and down at different times, yet is still dependent on events that occurred when the server was not operational. To picture how valuable this can be, think of how you use e-mail. You probably turn you computer on and off on a frequent basis or you log in and out if you are at work. If you think of incoming e-mail as events, then you can understand how important it is for these events to be queued up and waiting for you. If, upon arrival, the events were discarded because there wasn't a current consumer, the entire system would not work.

Event Proxies

Proxy objects reside within the EventChannel and provide the decoupling property of the Event Service. A proxy object sits in place of a consumer or supplier and ensures event messaging is passed to the object associated with the proxy. An EventChannel can have multiple proxy objects for both consumer and supplier at any given time. Figure 4-3 illustrates how proxy objects channel communications between suppliers and consumers:

As you will see next, different types of proxies are created based on the event-transfer model being used.

The Push and Pull Models

Two models of event transfers exist: the push model and the pull model. In the push model, suppliers dictate the flow of event data by pushing events through the EventChannel to consumers. In the *pull model,* consumers dictate the flow of data by pulling it from the supplier. Different proxies are created for each model. In the *push model,* the EventChannel holds ProxyPushConsumer objects for the supplier, and ProxyPushSupplier objects for the consumer. In the pull model, the EventChannel holds ProxyPullConsumer objects for the supplier and ProxyPullSupplier objects for the consumer.

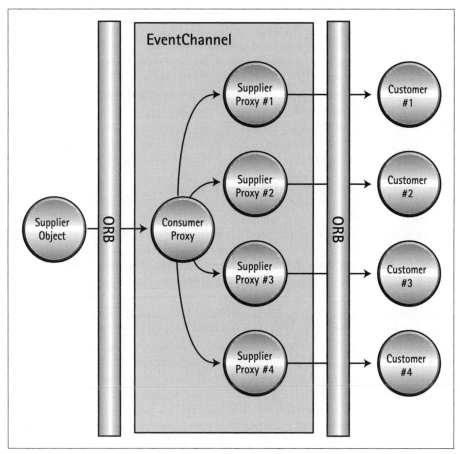

Figure 4-3: Consumer and Supplier Proxy Objects

Let's look at the client/computational server example we talked about earlier in this section, where the server is the supplier and the client is the consumer. If we use a push approach (the best approach for this example), the supplier will send data to its ProxyPushConsumer object when it has finished doing its computation. The consumer will spend most of its time checking for new data that has arrived from its ProxyPushSupplier object. The EventChannel takes care of data transfer between the ProxyPushConsumer and the ProxyPushSupplier. The push approach is usually the more common approach to take when handling events, but, based on your application design, both are important.

If we used the pull approach, things would work differently. The EventChannel periodically pulls data from the supplier, places it in a queue, and waits for pull requests for the consumer. The pull supplier spends much of its time waiting for a pull request from the EventChannel via the ProxyPullConsumer. The consumer pulls data through its ProxyPullSupplier object. The EventChannel is responsible for pulling data from the supplier to a queue and making it available when a request comes in from the ProxyPullSupplier. In the example, the supplier finishes its computation and waits for a pull request to come in. When such a request arrives, the event ("I am finished") is pulled up to the EventChannel to await client pull requests. As you probably surmised, the pull approach is slightly awkward for this example.

Generic and Typed Events

Up to this point, push and pull generic events have been discussed. A *generic event* does not understand what type of data it is passing. It simply takes a single input parameter of type *any* (a generic object). The *any* parameter can represent a variety of objects, but the representation must be well-understood by both suppliers and consumers. For instance, the *any* parameter could be a *string*, but both consumer and supplier must understand it is a *string* and what this *string* represents.

Another event propagation approach is the use of typed events. *Typed events* allow applications to define an interface using IDL that is well-understood by both suppliers and consumers. Suppliers are then able to invoke operations on consumers using the interface, as long as operations on the interface accept *in* values only and do not produce a return value. Both push and pull approaches are supported when using typed events. Suppliers and consumers exchange proxy objects, but events do not go through the EventChannel when using typed events. Instead, a supplier's responsibilities are keeping track of all its consumers and talking directly to them, via a specified IDL interface. When using this approach, consumers must keep track of all associated suppliers. As you can see, this approach has its drawbacks. It requires a large amount of bookkeeping for both supplier and consumer, and it puts the burden of queuing on the shoulders of either the consumer or supplier.

Event Service Summary

In summary, the Event Service provides the capability for your CORBA applications to send and receive events. Based on your architecture, you can decide which event-handling approach to use to fulfill your application needs.

Persistent Object Service

The Persistent Object Service (POS) tackles the tough issue of object persistence. When an object is created, its lifetime is generally that of the object or the client that created it. *Object persistence* refers to an object's ability to maintain its state outside the scope of the client or object that originally created it. This service provides the capability for an object to be saved in some type of datastore and retrieved at a later time when needed. The datastore could be one of a number of storage mechanisms, including flat files, relational databases, and object databases. This service was written in a generic fashion because the issue of object persistence is an intricate one. Clients and objects can have vastly different persistence requirements based on the type of application in which they live. With this in mind, the OS has been engineered to provide the maximum amount of flexibility for object storage from both the client and object point of view.

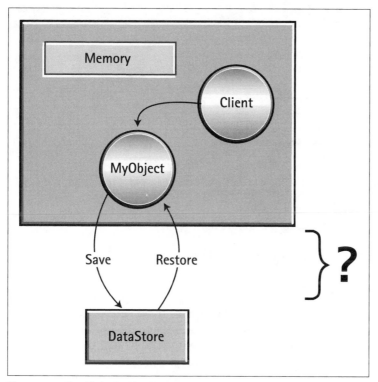

Figure 4-4: Our Main Problem

Object persistence can be a valuable asset to an application, but as you can see in Figure 4-4, the storage and retrieval of an object from a datastore can be a confusing issue. This is where the *Persistent Object Service*, as shown in Figure 4-5, steps in.

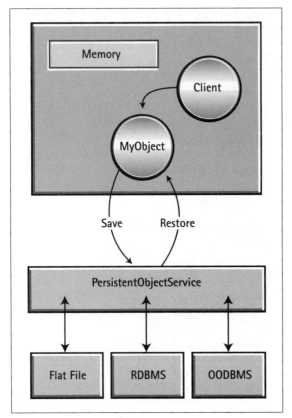

Figure 4-5: The Persistent Object Service Comes to the Rescue

As you can see, this service lives in a layer between our objects and their respective datastore, but quite a bit of hand waving seems to be here. A generic persistence model is a complicated thing. The OMG has, thankfully, broken this process into a number of major components that help ORB vendors build this service in a way that will work for all types of applications. Figure 4-6 illustrates the components and how they relate to each other:

PERSISTENT IDENTIFIER

The *Persistent Identifier (PID)* identifies one or more locations within a datastore that house the persistent data for an object. This ID is generated in a string representation and an object must have a PID to store its data. A client can create and initialize a PID, and associate it with an object to be used in a persistence model. This ID is different than a CORBA object ID (OID), which is only a reference to an object. The PID is, instead, a reference to an object's data. The PID is defined in the CosPersistencePID module, which contains an interface for naming and retrieving a PID.

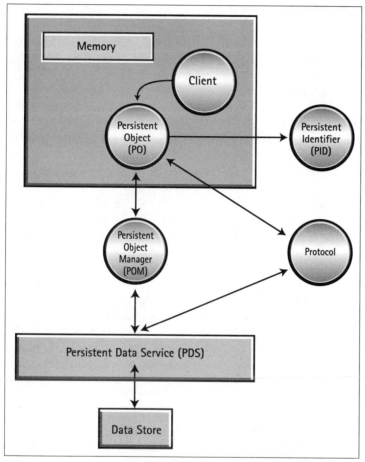

Figure 4-6: The Components of the Persistent Object Service

PERSISTENT OBJECT

Persistent objects (*PO*) are objects that can store and retrieve their own data. A given CORBA object can be made persistent by inheriting via IDL from the PO interface, which is defined in the CosPersistencePO module. This interface provides an object with operations to *connect()* to and *disconnect()* from a datastore, as well as the expected *store()*, *restore()*, and *delete()* operations. The implementation of the persistent object dictates which attributes of the object are involved in these operations. For instance, an object may have attributes that only make sense in a given scope, making it unnecessary to save these attributes to the datastore.

PERSISTENT OBJECT MANAGER

The *Persistent Object Manager* (*POM*) acts as a buffer between Persistent Objects and their respective Persistent Data Services. In essence, the POM is acting as a switchboard, routing requests from Persistent Objects to the correct datastore. The POM is defined in the CosPersistencePOM module, which defines a single interface: the POM interface. This interface has the same operations as found on the PO interface (*connect()*, *disconnect()*, *store()*, *restore()*, *delete()*). The POM uses an input PID to talk directly to the correct datastore, however, and then manipulated the actual data in this datastore. Because the POM acts as a router for a client, the client is shielded from the specific data storage and retrieval mechanism used by a given datastore.

PERSISTENT DATA SERVICE

The *Persistent Data Service* (*PDS*) acts as the intermediary between a Persistent Object and its associated datastore. The PDS interacts with the object using one of a number of protocols to get data in and out of the object. In a similar fashion, the PDS interacts with the datastore to get data in and out of the datastore. Because datastores can come in a wide variety, the approach used to accomplish PDS to datastore interaction will vary based on your datastore. For instance, data stored in flat files may use one protocol, whereas data stored in a commercial database may be better suited by the choice of a different protocol. The PDS is defined in the CosPersidtencePDS module. As before, this module once again defines the expected *connect()*, *disconnect()*, *store()*, *restore()*, and *delete()* operations. All these operations work with a PID and a PO.

PROTOCOL

As mentioned, a PDS interacts to get data in and out of an object using one of a number of protocols. Many different ways exist to initiate this transfer and a protocol defines the transfer process for a given approach. There is no standard protocol, but the OMG has attempted to cover most bases by defining three standard protocols: the Direct Attribute Protocol, the ODMG Protocol, and the Dynamic Data Object Protocol. You are not limited to these three protocols but, hopefully, they will provide the functionality that will suffice for most application architectures.

The Persistent Data Service Direct Attribute Protocol (PDS_DA) provides access to persistent data using a new Data Definition Language (DDL). This DDL is a subset of the IDL language with which we are familiar. The responsibility of a Persistent Object is to use this DDL to define the types of data objects it uses. Using this protocol, you can achieve direct access between your data storage mechanism and your persistent object. This protocol is primarily used with relational databases.

The ODMG protocol is similar to the PDS_DA protocol, except it uses the Object Definition Language (ODL) instead of the DDL. ODL provides language mappings similar to those found in IDL. As with the PDS_DA approach, this protocol enables you direct access between your data storage mechanism and your persistent object. This protocol is primarily used with object-oriented databases.

Finally, the Dynamic Data Object (DDO) protocol can be used in the interactions between the PDS and the persistent objects. The *DDO* represents an object's attributes in a datastore-neutral manner and ensures all data for a given object is available. This is a generic protocol.

DATASTORE

The final piece to the Persistent Object Service puzzle is the *datastore,* which provides operations on data possibly using one of the protocols just defined. A datastore is the actual implementation that stores and retrieves an object's data. It could be a flat file, a relational database, an object database, or any other implementation that suits your needs. A generic datastore interface is provided in the CosPersistenceDS_CLI module, which provides an interface based on the X/Open Data Management Call Level Interface. Based on the protocol you choose and the type of datastore/object interaction it provides, you may opt to use or disregard this interface.

 In CORBA 3.0, this service may fall victim to the OMG's *sunset policy,* used to phase out services that are too complex, incorrectly designed, or simply not used by the software community. It may be replaced with a new and improved service called the Persistent State Service (PSS).

The PSS is simpler for vendors to implement, easier for clients to use, and more readily address existing data storage technologies. The PSS is not required to be compatible with the older POS.

Persistent Object Service Summary

In summary, the Persistent Object Service provides the capability to store and retrieve objects from a number of datastores. This service's generic architecture ensures a wide variety of choices for how and where an object is stored.

Transaction Service

The *Transaction Service* is important because it brings a great amount of reliability to a distributed object system. CORBA enables us to build large scale distributed systems, but without transaction control and error detection, the reliability of these systems quickly comes into question. In this section, we first describe the transaction concept and then delve deeper into the components that comprise the Transaction Service. To complete the discussion of this service, we outline the interfaces upon which the Transaction Service is built.

The Definition of a Transaction

If you have ever done any database administration, you are probably familiar with the concept of a transaction. The definition provided by the OMG does not vary much from what you would expect, but we will, nonetheless, reflect on the concept of transactions in the programming world.

In a general sense, a *transaction* is a small event that monitors some work done by your application. A transaction has a clearly defined start and end point, both usually bracketing some set of instructions that are similar in function. For instance, a transaction in the database world could be defined as the operations needed to save one object's data to the database. The transaction begins when the save process is initiated and ends when the save operation is finished. If an error occurs during the life of a transaction, there is usually an error notification and some facility to recover from the error. The OMG defines a transaction in a more specific way, using a set of definitions named ACID characteristics (ACID is an acronym of the different characteristics). These four characteristics are:

- ◆ Atomic. If a transaction encounters a failure during its execution interval, there must be some way to undo all effects, usually through some rollback mechanism.

- ◆ Consistent. The effects of a given transaction provide invariant results.

- ◆ Isolated. The intermediate states of a transaction are not visible to other transactions.

- ◆ Durable. The effects of a completed transaction are always preserved, except in the case of some terrible, unusual failure.

A transaction can terminate in one of only two ways. If the transaction is successful, all changes made during the life of a transaction are committed, meaning they are saved permanently. If a failure occurs, all changes are rolled back, or undone.

Transaction Service Overview

The Transaction Service specification dictates that a Transaction Service must provide a defined set of operations. First, the service needs to control the scope and length of a transaction. It must also allow multiple objects to have involvement in an individual, atomic transaction. The service must also allow objects to associate a transaction with some change in their internal state. Finally, the Transaction Service must assist in coordination of a transaction completion.

Two transaction models are supported by this service: flat and nested transactions. A *flat transaction* is the most basic of transactions. In this model, a single transaction brackets a small set of operations. The flat transaction is not contained in any other transactions and is, therefore, called a *top-level transaction*. In a *nested transaction*, smaller sibling subtransactions are embedded within a larger, encompassing parent transaction. This nested model resembles a tree hierarchy. Each sibling in the tree is also a parent of its children. A given sibling cannot commit changes until all the siblings in its subtree have committed. If a sibling needs to rollback changes, all its siblings are automatically rolled back. Figure 4-7 illustrates a nested transaction. It depicts a simple backup of disk space, where the root directory is bracketed by a top-level transaction and each child directory backup is bracketed in its own subtransaction:

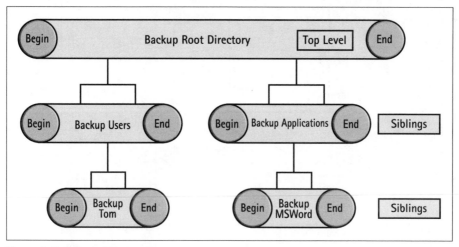

Figure 4-7: A Nested Transaction

In addition to supporting the two transaction models, the Transaction Service also supports some other valuable functionality. It provides for model interoperability, meaning that a single transaction can contain ORB and non-ORB applications and resources, such as inclusion of the X/Open Distributed Transaction Processing Model. This service also makes provisions for network interoperability, meaning a transaction can span across multiple, multivendor ORBs. This is extremely important on larger distributed systems, which must track the integrity of a transaction as it is executed across a network that uses multiple heterogeneous ORBs. The Transaction Service also supports both single and multithreaded applications. Finally, this service allows a wide spectrum of implementation choices, which allows extremely robust transaction tracking for mission-critical applications and a less restrictive, lightweight tracking mechanism where extreme degrees of checking are not required or impossible due to system resources.

Entities of the Transaction Service

In this section, we look at the entities that combine to make the Transaction Service work for our applications. We begin by first looking at a high-level diagram of this architecture, which shows how a CORBA client initiates a transaction and how that transaction is handled by both the ORB and the Transaction Service. This is shown in Figure 4-8.

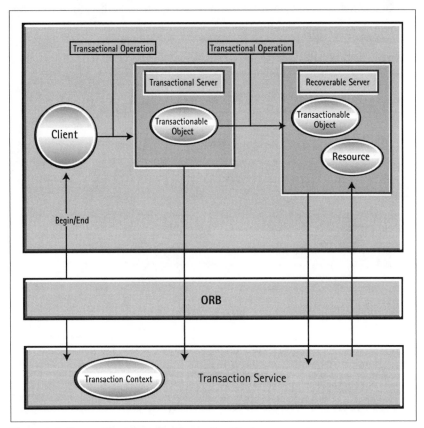

Figure 4-8: How a Client Uses the Transaction Service.

TRANSACTIONAL CLIENT

The *transactional client* (TC), which is the simple entity in Figure 4-8, represents any client in a system using the Transaction Service. This TC tells the Transaction Server when a transaction is beginning and when it has finished. During a single transaction, this client may make multiple operation invocations on one or more transactional objects. When a transaction begins, the Transaction Service creates a transaction context object that defines the scope of the transaction and that is automatically propagated to all objects involved in the transaction. The TC is shielded from the intricate operations that take place during a transaction. The TC simply starts a transaction, issues some requests on a transactional object, and then ends the request. If all goes well, the changes are committed and the transaction is a success.

TRANSACTIONAL OBJECTS

A *transactional object* (TO) is an object whose internal representation is affected by invocations during the scope of a transaction. This TO usually has different data attributes that are changed by the invocations. The TO can choose to provide transaction support for all or only some of its internal operations. This choice is left to the object designer. Any operations that do not provide transactional support will not survive a failure because they do not provide any roll back mechanism. In the previous diagram, a TO lives within a Transactional Server, which is a server that supports the Transaction Service. Operations on this object are invoked by the client. At any time, an error condition may arise, in which case a notification is sent to the Transaction Service indicating a roll back is necessary.

RECOVERABLE OBJECTS

Recoverable objects are objects that directly manage data subject to change during the life of a transaction. These objects are required to implement certain protocols required by the Transaction Service. These protocols ensure all transaction participants agree on a transaction's completion or a transaction's failure. By definition, a recoverable object is also a transactional object (it implements a set of methods defined by the Transaction Service). This object registers a resource with the Transaction Service, which issues requests on the resource during the commit process. The resource objects inherit from an interface that allow them to vote for or against a commit at the moment the commit is going to occur.

TRANSACTION SERVERS

A *transaction server* is a collection of one or more transactional objects. The behavior of these objects is affected by a transaction, but these objects do not actually possess critical data that is recoverable if the transaction fails. Instead, they rely on Recoverable Objects to recover the state of a transaction should failure occur.

RECOVERABLE SERVERS

These servers contain one or more recoverable objects whose data is changed during the course of a transaction. A recoverable object has a resource that is changed during a transaction. Such an object participates in rollback operations if an error occurs.

TRANSACTION SERVICE INTERFACES

The Transaction Service is a complicated service and, therefore, must provide a large amount of functionality in its interfaces. In this section, some of the most important aspects of the different interfaces are discussed. All the described interfaces can be found in the CosTransactions module.

- The *Current interface* provides clients with the ability to manage transactions by allowing a client to begin, end, and obtain information about a certain transaction. It provides operations such as *begin()*, *commit()*, *rollback()*, and *get_status()*.

- The *TransactionFactory interface* is provided to allow clients to create a new top-level transaction. It supports a single operation named *create()*.

- The *Control interface* allows an application to manage and propagate explicitly a given transaction's context. It has two operations. The *get_coordinator()* operation returns a Coordinator object, required by resources to help with the transaction, while *get_terminator()* returns a Terminator object, which can be used to end a transaction.

- The *Terminator interface* provides the *commit()* and *rollback()* operations used to terminate a transaction.

- The *Coordinator interface* provides operations used by participants in a transaction to coordinate with each other during the transaction. It provides *get_status()*, *get_parent_status()*, *get_top_level_status()* for finding the status of pieces of transaction. It provides operations for describing a given transaction, such as *is_same_transaction()*, *is_ancestor_transaction()*, and *is_top_level_transaction()*, among others. It also has a *create_subtransaction()* operation that allows a parent transaction to create a sibling transaction.

- The *Recovery Coordinator interface* helps lead the recovery process if a failure occurs.

- The *Resource interface* uses a two-phase commit process to end a top-level transaction for each registered resource. This interface is implemented by recoverable objects. If there is only one resource in a transaction, the two-phase commit process is disregarded. For multiple resources, however, the commit process occurs like this: First, all resources are sent a *prepare()* message that asks if each resource wants to commit. In turn, each returns a Vote value, which can be either *VoteCommit* ("Yes!"), *VoteReadOnly* ("Yes, but I wasn't changed."), or *VoteRollBack* ("No, I don't want to."). If all answers are "Yes!" or "Yes, but I wasn't changed", the *commit* takes place. Otherwise, a *rollback()* operation is invoked.

- The *SubTransactionAwareResource interface* is used by recoverable objects that are working with nested transactions. It is derived from the Resource interface and adds the operations *commit_subtransaction()* and *rollback_subtransaction()*.

- The TransactionalObject interface is an abstract interface that objects use to indicate they are transactional objects. The transaction context is automatically propagated to objects that inherit from this interface.

Transaction Service Summary

In summary, the Transaction Service provides the capability to create and execute transactions in a distributed CORBA system. The service provides a good layer of error-handling and recovery, and can be valuable in providing integrity to your system.

Concurrency Control Service

Yes, we are talking about it in the chapter dealing with CORBA allows us to build powerful distributed object systems. As these systems grow in complexity, however, they quickly run into a bookkeeping brick wall. This impediment is concurrency control, which is addressed by the Concurrency Control Service. As our systems become more complex, it becomes quite possible for multiple clients in the system to need concurrent access to a particular object. If one client is changing an object, while another is attempting to read it, or if two clients attempt to change the object at the same time, our system quickly runs into critical concurrency problems. This problem is the distributed object analogy to multithreaded synchronization, which we discuss in upcoming chapters. The Concurrency Control Service solves this problem and provides a few different approaches we can use, based on the architecture of our system. The *Concurrency Control Service* is based on the concept of clients and their interaction with shared resources. *Resources* are typically thought of as objects, but a client is in charge of defining resources and identifying potentially conflicting uses of these resources. Before we discuss this service in depth, let's first look at a diagram of a typical concurrency control problem, as shown in Figure 4-9. In this diagram, two clients are attempting to read and update the values of an object. Client *A* first reads the object. While this client is changing the object, client *B* reads the object. Client *A* then updates the object's values. The problem arises when client *B* attempts to implement its changes on the object based on the values previously read, because the object now has different values than client *B* expects. This can immediately lead to data inconsistency and corruption.

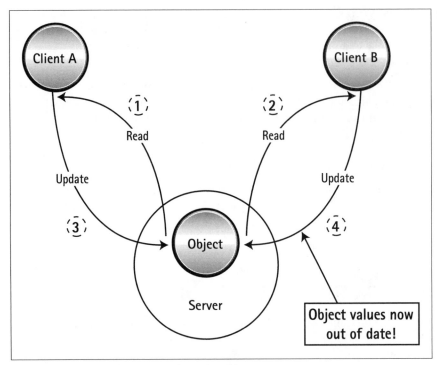

Figure 4-9: A Typical Concurrency Control Problem

In this section, we discuss the Concurrency Control Service in a few steps. First, we look at the different locking mechanisms this service supports. Then, we discuss how this service has been engineered to work well with the Transaction Service. Finally, we highlight some of the interfaces defined for the Concurrency Control Service and explain the functionality they provide.

Locking Mechanisms

This service controls concurrent client use of a shared resource with the use of locks. A *lock* is like a permission slip, associated with one client and one resource. A lock gives the client permission to access a given resource in a particular fashion. Different clients can hold simultaneous locks on a given resource, but the locks are granted in a fashion that will prevent conflict between the different clients' use of the resource. The Concurrency Control Service acts as a conflict manager by only granting locks on a resource that are compatible with each other. Different locking mechanisms, or modes, are available for a resource. These modes are read, write, intention read, intention write, and upgrade. *Read locks* can be held by multiple clients on a given resource. *Write locks* will conflict with read locks and other write locks on a resource. *Upgrade locks* are used to prevent the problem illustrated in the previous diagram. *Upgrade locks* are a type of read lock usually followed by a write lock.

Intention write and *intention read* locks are two additional modes that provide a different amount of locking granularity. The locking granularity is directly related to an application's definition of resources to be locked. A fine granularity has specific resources defined. This approach creates a higher number of locks in a system, which contributes to system overhead. A course granularity defines fewer resources, allowing less locks and lower overhead. This, in turn, provides for more potential locking conflicts. The intention write and intention read locks are used to lock at a more course level of granularity. They are used when working with hierarchies of related resources. Consider the example of a database resource that contains multiple record resources. If a client desires to change one record in the database, it would set an intention read lock on the entire database and a read lock on the desired record. Before making the change, the client would set an intention write lock on the database and set a read lock on the record. The change would then be made. The intention locks are used to ensure the overall database is not changed while the specific resource (the record) is read and written (for instance, the entire database file could not be overwritten). The intention locks, however, enable other clients to create and dispose of locks concurrently on other individual resources in the database, as long as no locking conflicts are generated.

The final component of the locking mechanism is the lock set. A *lock set* is a set of locks associated with a specific resource. The client must to allocate and associate a lock set with a protected resource.

Transactions and the Concurrency Control Service

The Concurrency Control Service provides for two types of clients: a transactional client and a nontransactional client. A transactional client is one that supports transactions defined by the Transaction Service. The definition and operation of a transaction are left to the Transaction Service, but the Concurrency Control Service is designed to support the concept of transactions. With transactional clients, the release of locks is driven by the Transaction Service as a transaction commits or aborts, while nontransactional clients are responsible for releasing locks at the appropriate time.

A few different rules are used when dealing with transactional clients, especially those that use nested transactions. Some conflicts are allowed in nested transactions, provided the conflict is between a child transaction and one of its ancestors. If a child transaction attempts to lock a resource already locked by its parent, a conflict does not occur. Instead, ownership of the lock is transferred to the child. When the child commits or aborts, the ownership is transferred back to the parent. All locks obtained during the lifetime of a transaction are automatically released when the transaction finishes. As you would probably expect, locking conflicts that occur between unrelated transactions are handled exactly as conflicts between unrelated clients are handled.

Interfaces of the Concurrency Control Service

The CosConcurrencyControl Module provides the interfaces that form the Concurrency Control Service. In this section, we outline the different interfaces provided in this module.

- ◆ The LockCoordinator Interface is provided for use by transactional clients. It provides a single operation, drop_locks(), that is called when a transaction commits or aborts. A nested transaction must make the call if it aborts, but the operation must only be invoked once for a transaction family when the transaction commits.

- ◆ The LockSet Interface enables you to acquire and release locks. The lock() operation returns a new lock on a resource. If your client cannot afford to block until a lock is available, try_lock() can be used. This operation will return immediately if the lock is unavailable. The unlock operation releases a lock. Change_mode() is used to change the mode of a single lock. If the newly desired lock mode is unavailable, this operation will block the client until the mode is available.

- ◆ The TransactionalLockSet Interface has the same operations as the LockSet interface, except each operation accepts a TransactionCoordinator reference. This allows the LockSet operations to be available for a specific transaction.

- ◆ The LockSetFactory Interface provides the capability to create lock sets. It provides the create operation for normal lock sets and the create_transactional() operation for transactional lock sets. The create_related() and create_transactional_related() operations allow the creation of new lock sets related to existing lock sets. Related lock sets release all locks at the same time.

Concurrency Control Service Summary

In summary, the Concurrency Control Service provides control over concurrent access of system resources by multiple objects. As distributed systems grow in complexity, this service becomes necessary to prevent potentially damaging resource conflicts.

Relationship Service

In a distributed object system, you rarely see objects that exist on a standalone basis. Objects in such a system almost always rely on other objects. We use distributed object systems to model real-world situations. In the real world, objects rely on other objects, so the objects in our systems are usually related to other objects. The Relationship Service provides the capability to relate one object to another or one object to multiple objects. It also provides a number of descriptive ways to define the relationship. Best of all, the Relationship Service requires no changes to the objects included in a relationship and the objects in a relationship have no knowledge they are included in a relationship. This allows immutable objects created before the Relationship Service to be eligible for inclusion in relationships.

Without the help of the Relationship Service, we can simply use object references to define a relationship between two objects, but this leaves something to be desired. Object references are one-way relationships, so an object contained by another object has no knowledge of the relationship. This deficiency makes traversal of object relationships using simple object references a difficult task. It also makes the dynamic creation of relationships impossible because the references are hard-coded at compile time. On the other hand, relationships defined with the Relationship Service have built-in traversal and navigation functionality, and they can be created dynamically as dictated by runtime conditions. The relationships are also extensible, enabling programmers to add functionality required by a specific implementation. Figure 4-10 shows the relationship.

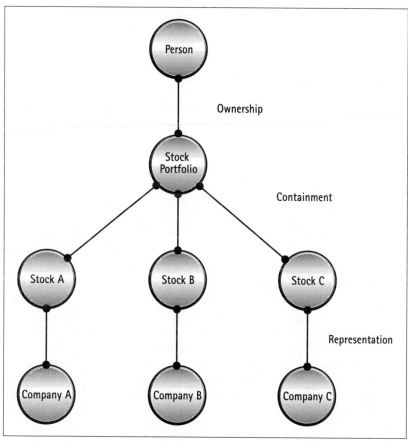

Figure 4-10: A Relationship Diagram

This figure shows a simple relationship diagram. A person has ownership of a stock portfolio, which contains some stocks, each representing a small piece of a specific company. Another way of looking at the relationships is to say a piece of each company is represented by stock, which is contained in a portfolio, which is owned by a person. Each portion of the diagram is a relationship. For instance, a stock portfolio contains one or more stocks.

The Definition of a Relationship

Each relationship has a number of built-in properties that must be discussed. Every *relationship* has a set of entities and defines roles the entities play. In the previously mentioned ownership relationship, a person plays the owner role and the stock portfolio plays the ownee role. The term degree defines how many roles a relationship has. In the example, all relationships are of degree two. *Cardinality* describes the maximum number of relationships involved with a given role. Our ownership relationship is a one-to-one relationship, while the containment relationship is one-to-many. A relationship may also have specific attributes and operations we can define. For instance, a stock symbol could be an attribute of the containment relationship and an operation would return the stock symbol when required.

Relationship Levels

The Relationship Service provides three levels of service, each having specific interfaces. The interface levels are base relationships, object relationship graphs, and specific relationships. We investigate each of these levels and explain the associated functionality.

BASE RELATIONSHIPS

The Relationship Services' base interface provides the capability to create and destroy Role and Relationship objects. The first step in creating a relationship is to create different Role objects. This is done using the RoleFactory::create() operation, which is found on the RoleFactory interface. During the creation of the Role, the minimum and maximum cardinality is indicated, which describes how many relationships with which the new Role can be associated. A Relationship is created by passing a sequence of roles to the RelationshipFactory::create() operation found on the RelationshipFactory interface. During this creation process, the Role types and cardinality are checked to ensure the Relationship can be created. The newly created Role and Relationship objects will inherit from the interface IdentifiableObject, which provides an is_identical() operation. This operation provides the capability to determine if two CORBA objects are the same instance.

Base relationships interact with two new modules. The first is the CosObjectIdentity module, which provides the previously mentioned IdentifiableObject interface. The second interface is the CosRelationships module, which provided the interfaces for Role and Relationship objects, the associated Factory interfaces for these objects, and an iteration object called the *RelationshipIterator.* This interface enables you to traverse all the Relationships with which a given Role is associated.

GRAPH RELATIONSHIPS

When multiple objects are connected using relationships, a graph of the related objects is formed. The graph is comprised of nodes and edges, where the nodes are CORBA objects in the graph and the edges are represented by the relationships that tie the objects together. This interface level defines a new module called *CosGraphs,* which provides operations to make traversing a complicated object graph simple.

These interfaces provide some great functionality for traversing an object graph. The *NodeFactory interface* creates *Nodes,* which store Role information for a given object. The *TraversalFactory interface* creates Traversal objects that enable you to begin a graph traversal starting at a node, which you pass to a Traversal object. The *TraversalCriteria interface* is supported by a call-back object you create. This object is used by the Traversal object to determine how to traverse a graph. This interaction can allow a traversal to be depth-first, breadth-first, or best-first. An *EdgeIterator interface* is also available, which enables you to iterate over the roles associated with a relationship. This iterator is obtained by invoking CosGraphs::Role::get_edges().

SPECIFIC RELATIONSHIPS

As you create new relationships between your objects, you frequently create new relationship types specific to the domain being modeled. Many object graphs also rely on two common relationship types: containment and reference relationships. With this in mind, the Relationship Service has created these two specific relationships. A *containment relationship* is a one-to-many relationship, where one object contains many other objects. On the other hand, a *reference relationship* is a many-to-many relationship, where an object can reference many objects and, at the same time, can be referenced by many objects. Two new modules, *CosContainment* and *CosReference,* define new interfaces that describe these specific relationships. These new interfaces – Containment and Reference – do not add any new types but, instead, simply inherit all their functionality from CosRelationships::Relationship.

Relationship Service Summary

In summary, the Relationship Service provides the capability to join arbitrary objects and groups of objects in relationships, with no requirement that the objects know they are contained in a relationship. These relationships can be created at runtime and add powerful capabilities to your CORBA system.

Life Cycle Service

CORBA applications rely heavily on distributed objects. As the objects are distributed around a given system, a number of bookkeeping questions quickly arise, especially when dealing with complex objects, (objects that contain other objects). The *Life Cycle Service* defines the convention used when creating, copying, deleting, and moving objects in your CORBA system. It supports these operations on graphs of related objects, such as the graphs discussed in the section titled "Relationship Service." In fact, many of the Life Cycle interfaces inherit from interfaces defined by the Relationship Service. This goes along with the idea that each service should do one specific task. The Life Cycle Service takes care of issues related to the state of objects and object graphs, but relies on the Relationship Service to provide the means to maintain the relations in a graph. Consider Figure 4-11 of a client using a Car object, which is associated with an Engine object and four Tire objects:

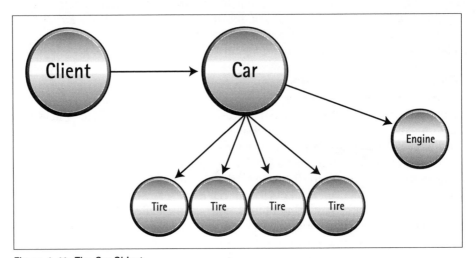

Figure 4-11: The Car Object

Before we create and use this object, a few issues must be resolved:

1. How does my client create this object?

2. If I copy or move the Car object, do the Engine and Tire objects also get copied or moved?

3. Is my client responsible for deleting the Engine and Tire objects when the Car object is deleted?

The Life Cycle Service answers all these questions. The *Life Cycle Service* uses the notion of object Factories to create objects and provides a facility for finding the correct Factory to create a given object. The Car object is created by finding a CarFactory object (created by us), which defines the specific operations needed to create and initialize the Car. A Car object is returned. This object supports the LifeCycle interface and, thus, has knowledge of how to use the copy(), move() and remove() operations correctly. A new addition to this Service is that of the *Compound Life Cycle Interface,* which interacts with graphs of objects using the Node, Role, and Relationship classes, which are derived from the same classes in the Relationship Service. This interface supports the same operations, but also adds a delete() operation. In this example, operations for our complex graph are executed using the functionality found in the Compound Life Cycle interface. Realize that when we invoke the move() operation on a Car object, we are, in essence, invoking that operation on the entire Car object graph. Finally, there is the notion of both deep and shallow moves and copies. These two levels of functionality can be important based on your application architecture.

Life Cycle Service Summary

In summary, the Life Cycle Service provides underlying functionality that takes care of complex object operations for you. It works well with the Relationship Service to support object handling and manipulation in diverse CORBA systems.

Externalization Service

The *Externalization Service* describes the convention for saving and restoring the state of an object. Two main concepts are associated with this service: externalization and internalization. *Externalization* refers to the capability to save an object's state in a stream of data. *Internalization* refers to the capability to retrieve an object's data from a stream of data. As you may know, a *stream* is an object that knows how to read and write data to a given chunk of data storage. This storage could be a place in memory or a file on disk, among other things. Externalization and internalization combine to provide a prolonged-copy functionality. The traditional copy operation, much like that defined in the Life Cycle Service, is an immediate operation. In a different manner, externalization/internalization enables you to copy an object in two steps separated by an arbitrary amount of time. For instance, an object's state can be externalized to disk on one day and then recreated via internalization when needed a few weeks later. The externalization/internalization process not only provides the capability to save an object's state, but also to export it outside the ORB environment, to a different machine, or to a different ORB. It also allows objects to be passed by value, one of the great missing pieces of current CORBA functionality. Finally, the Externalization Service's functionality can be leveraged by the POS based on the protocol being used by the POS. Take a look at Figure 4-12 for a demonstration of the Externaliziation/Internalization mode.

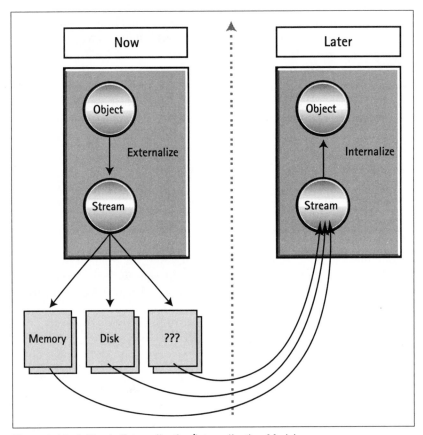

Figure 4-12: A Simple Externalization/Internalization Model

To describe this service's architecture, we review three different views of externalization: the client's view, the stream's view, and the object's view. In the process of describing each viewpoint, we discuss the specific Externalization interfaces each view must use.

The Client's View of Object Externalization

The client's view of externalization is simple. The client first obtains a reference to a Stream object using one of two methods: StreamFactory::create() returns a Stream object, while FileStreamFactory::create() returns a Stream associated with a specific flat file used for the storage. The client then invokes the externalize() operation on the stream and passes an object reference to the operation. This causes the object's data to be saved to the stream. The client is shielded from whether the object saves a simple set of data, a set of related objects, or an entire object graph. The externalize() operation takes care of all these situations for the client with one simple function call.

At times, a client may need to save more than one object to a stream. This is easily done by first calling begin_context(), issuing all externalize() requests and then calling end_context(). This causes all the objects' data to be stored in one common Stream.

If a client desires to recreate an object, it invokes internalize() on a Stream object, providing a factory finder. The Stream uses the factory finder to create an object of the correct type. The internalize() operation returns a newly created object, initialized with the data stored in the stream.

The Stream's View of Object Externalization

To get its work done, the Stream object makes the assumption any object passed to it for externalization must inherit, usually via multiple inheritance, from the Streamable interface. Once the Stream receives the externalize() request, it immediately invokes the object's externalize_to_stream() operation and passes a reference to a StreamIO object with the request. The StreamIO object is used by the object to write its data to the correct data storage location.

When a stream is asked to internalize() an object, it acts in much the same manner. It first must determine the type of object to be internalized. This is done by referencing an object type key stored in the stream's data. The key is used with a factory finder (passed to the internalize() operation) to create the correct type of object. The object is then told to internalize_from_stream(), and is passed a StreamIO object the object uses to initialize its state based on the externalized data. After the object is done recreating its state, it is passed back to the client.

The Stream also understands the begin_context() and end_context() operations. It ensures multiple objects, even those referencing one another, are externalized and internalized correctly.

The Object's View of Object Externalization

The object is the workhorse in the externalization/internalization process. As previously mentioned, every object that desires to be externalizable must inherit from the Streamable interface and must use the correct operations on the StreamIO interface. When an object receives an externalize_to_stream() request, the work begins. The object is passed a StreamIO object. This object has write_<type>() operations, where <type> can be string, char, octet, unsigned_long, unsigned_short, long, short, float, double, or boolean. For every primitive type, the object will use the appropriate operation. If the object happens to contain other object references, it will use the write_object() operation. If it contains a complex object graph, the write_graph() function will come into play. The object is responsible for writing out all data that eventually must be internalized. Note, though, it can choose to omit some of its attributes in the externalize process.

The object's internalization process is a mirror image of that used in externalization. The object receives an internalize_to_stream() request, which also contains a StreamIO object. The object being internalized reads data using similar StreamIO::read_<type>() operations. As each piece of data is read from the stream, it is used to initialize the correct object attribute.

Externalization Service Summary

In summary, the Externalization Service provides the capability to save an object's state in a wide variety of ways and restore it at a later time when needed. It takes advantage of streams to get this work done and can add great object storage and retrieval functionality to your system.

Query Service

For those of you who are not fluent in database terminology, a *query* is an inquiry for data invoked on some given collection of data. The collection of data is historically a *database,* but it can also be a collection of objects, an individual object, or any other datastore defined by your application architecture. *The Query Service* was designed in a generic fashion to provide arbitrary query operations on collections of objects. The query operations are able to specify values of object attributes and are allowed to leverage the capabilities of other CORBA Services, such as the Life Cycle, Persistent Object, and Relationship Service. The architecture of this service provides for the use of multiple nested queries, which can be useful in more complex systems. As you would expect, the Query Service must have some underlying query language that drives the query operations. In defining this service, the OMG has tried to keep it from being dependent on any specific query language. In fact, an implementation of this service can be based on one or a number of query languages. In a somewhat contradictory manner, the OMG has decided the service *must* at least support either SQL Query or the Object Query Language (OQL). This was done in the hope of facilitating interoperability across a wide variety of query systems and to provide object-level interoperability more easily.

We review this service in three steps. First, we discuss the types of queries you can use with this service. Then, we investigate how object collections relate to the service. In these first two steps, we highlight some of the interfaces that make the Query Service work. Finally, we discuss the remaining interfaces that close out the Query Service.

Types of Queries

Three general types of queries are supported by the Query Service, but the service is in no way limited to supporting only these types. These query types are:

- Queries on an individual object.

- Queries on a collection of objects.

- Queries on a native query system.

The first type of query is used when a client needs to query for information from an individual object. The second is used when a client has access to a collection of objects and needs to ask for a subset of data from the collection. The third query type occurs when a client is querying a native query system, such as a relational or object database. All three of these query types take advantage of an interface called QueryEvalutator, which is defined in the CosQuery module. This interface helps drive the query process. It has one operation, evaluate(), which takes as input a description of a query, as well as the query language that should be used with the query. The operation returns the results, packaged in a generic fashion using the type *any*.

The last two types of queries are comprised of multiple, nested QueryEvaluator objects. When a request arrives at a QueryEvaluator, the Query Service decides either to execute the request or delegate it to one or more additional, nested QueryEvaluators. The Query Service takes the results from all nested evaluators and returns the final results to the client that began the query. Figure 4-13 illustrates how the QueryEvaluator is used for all three query types:

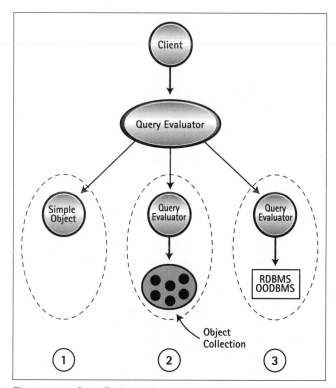

Figure 4-13: QueryEvaluator in Action

Queries and Collections

In the previous section, you learned a query returns results in the form of an *any* type variable. In actuality, the query returns an object that is a collection of objects, over which your client can iterate. The collections are defined in a new set of interfaces, which contain a subset of the functionality defined in the *Collection* Service, and that can be extended with the help of the *Collection* Service. The collections contain operations for traversal and retrieval of objects, and can contain arbitrary CORBA object types. The three interfaces providing this collection capability are defined in the CosCollection module and have these characteristics:

◆ The CollectionFactory Interface has a single operation, create(), which creates a new instance of a Collection and returns it to the caller.

◆ The Collection Interface defines a lightweight version of the Collection Service's object collection. It has the expected collection operations, such as add_element(), add_all_elements(), insert_element_at(), replace_element_at(), remove_element_at(), remove_all_elements(), and retrieve_element_at(). The Collection Interface also provides an operation named create_iterator(), which returns a new Iterator object for use in browsing the collection.

◆ The Iterator Interface facilitates easy traversal of a collection. The next() operation returns the next object in the collection. Reset() returns the iterator to the beginning of the collection and more() asks if any more objects are available for traversal.

These collections provide the capability to use and traverse simple collections of objects. If a more strictly defined collection is needed for a given query, the Collection Service can be leveraged to provide the added functionality. For instance, if your client needs results returned in a sorted collection that uses object keys to identify values, the Collection Service could be asked to provide this functionality.

Remaining Query Interfaces

So far we have discussed QueryEvaluators and Collections, and how they relate to the Query Service. In this section, we highlight some of the remaining interfaces and show how they help the Query Service work. The CosQuery module defines a number of interfaces, including the previously-mentioned QueryEvaluator. Here is a quick description of the other powerful interfaces found in this module:

◆ The Query Interface defines the representation of a query, which is comprised of a query specification, the query status, and the query results. The prepare() operation compiles a query and readies it for execution, which is achieved with the execute() operation Status can be determined with the use of get_status() and the results of the query are obtained with get_result(). In addition, this interface has a reference, usually through a QueryManager, to the queryable collection with which it is working.

♦ QueryManager is a subtype of the QueryEvaluator Interface. It allows creation of a Query object (using create()) and works hand-in-hand with the Query object to manage the processing and monitoring of a query.

♦ QueryableCollection is a subtype of both QueryEvaluator and CosQueryCollection::Collection. This inheritance approach gives a QueryableCollection a powerful capability. Such an object can act as a collection of objects that is the result of a query and also can be used to define the scope in which further queries are applied. This interface helps facilitate the nested query architecture discussed earlier.

Query Service Summary

In summary, the Query Service provides generic query functionality that can be used with a wide variety of CORBA objects and a number of different datastores, including flat files, object collections, and many types of commercial databases.

Licensing Service

You are probably familiar with current software licensing practices; without them, most of us would, essentially, be working for nothing. Software development is not an easy job and free software distribution is usually not the desired fruit of our labor. In the software development cycle of days past, licensing was a much more simplistic process. Standalone applications were built and we could easily build licensing support into our applications as they were distributed to customers. In the CORBA component world, licensing has become slightly more complicated. Instead of simple applications, we now create and sell CORBA servers and objects, and we must decide the most efficient and fair way to secure just compensation from the users of our components. The *Licensing Service* was created to solve many of the problems that arise from licensing of CORBA software components. The creation of the Licensing Service was done with the vision to provide licensing capabilities that can fit a wide range of licensing demands. This is important because our customers are different and the way in which our CORBA components will be used will vary drastically with the customers purchasing and using them. As with all the services, the Licensing Service has a wealth of functionality that should fit almost all our needs, thus enabling us to focus more time on component development instead of wasting time reinventing the Licensing Wheel.

The investigation of the Licensing Service begins with a summary of the types of licensing approaches this service supports. We then discuss the design principles implemented to ensure this service is robust enough to handle most types of licensing requirements. Finally, we discuss the interfaces provided with this service and the functionality these interfaces provide.

Licensing Approaches

Licensing is the cornerstone of the software development community because it ensures we are all compensated for our work. The licensing approach chosen must be appealing to the supplier of the software but, more importantly, it must be appealing to the consumer. If consumers are unhappy with how a product is licensed, they usually choose to find another product with more appealing licensing constraints. This is a delicately balanced relationship — we want to make money and our consumers want to save money. If the balance tips one way, we unnecessarily lose money by selling our work at far too cheap a price. If the balance tips the other way, our suppliers pay too much and we may still lose money as they shift their software use to one of our competitors. To achieve the correct balance, the correct business model must be chosen. This model must fit both supplier and consumer, and it varies according to a consumer's needs and the use of the software in question.

The approaches used in licensing have evolved with the changes in our hardware and software industry. The nodelocked license was the first approach taken. This approach provided permission for a software product to be used on a single computer. As computers became less expensive and internal company networks began to grow at an exhaustive pace, the nodelocked license quickly became obsolete. Companies with these huge networks could no longer afford to pay for software for each individual machine. This problem led to the site license, which enabled a company to pay a fixed price for unlimited use of a software product on its network. This approach quickly disrupted the supplier/consumer satisfaction balance. Suppliers felt they were being cheated because they were forced to created price models when they did not understand a company's potential use of their software. On the other hand, consumers felt they were losing because they were paying fees for usage estimates they usually did not expect to attain. Concurrent licenses helped solve this problem. This licensing approach enabled a company to purchase a set number of licenses that could be used at one time from anywhere on a network. As a company's needs expanded, it could easily expand the number of concurrent licenses they owned for a particular software product. Consumers thus felt they were paying for their software use and suppliers felt they were being compensated correctly for the use of their products. The delicate supplier/consumer balance was momentarily steady.

The sale and use of CORBA software components quickly disrupted the balance once again. These traditional approaches (nodelocked, site, and concurrent licenses) no longer worked well in a distributed component system. The Licensing Service steps in to help provide a wide range of component licensing options. This service can be configured in a number of ways and it helps keep specific licensing issues from the components you are using. A component only knows it needs to be controlled, but the Licensing Service takes care of how that licensing control is executed. This enables the supplier to configure different licensing approaches easily for different consumer needs with no changes to the components being sold.

Licensing approaches can be tailored for individual components and groups of components. They can be directed at individual users, small groups of users, or large organizations. You can choose levels of *strictness* when implementing your licensing approach. For instance, you could choose to license based on individual object use or take a more strict approach and license on individual method invocations on that object. This service can easily be used to provide evaluation periods for the components, which is always helpful when dealing with new customers. A good level of security is provided with the service, which ensures the licensing policy you choose is actually being enforced. Finally, this service provides the capability to collect and monitor component use metrics, which can be helpful in ensuring both supplier and consumer are being treated fairly.

Licensing Service Design Principles

As mentioned, the Licensing Service provides licensing functionality that should suit most business models in a way that satisfies both supplier and consumer. It also has provisions to accommodate existing shrink-wrapped applications. This is a great characteristic because this service is beneficial to existing applications, but it is not feasible to change shrink-wrapped software to make it compatible with the service's capabilities. The capability to provide such generic and wide-ranging functionality dictated the Licensing Service be designed in a thorough, robust manner. In doing the design, the OMG used four main principles. They are:

◆ **Neutrality** – This principle ensures the Licensing Service does not dictate how a supplier designs and builds software. The design of a given software component should not be constrained by the interfaces provided by the Licensing Service.

◆ **Extensibility** – The Licensing Service is built in a manner that promotes easy addition of new licensing functionality. Countless licensing approaches can be used, but as a supplier you can easily tailor a new approach that best fits your customers.

◆ **Security** – The service provides runtime authentication mechanisms that ensure components are interacting with an authentic Licensing Service. If a valid Licensing Service can easily be circumvented by an invalid pirate version, the entire licensing process fails.

◆ **Performance** – The service can be configure in a manner that best suits your consumer's performance needs. For example, if you are licensing a component based on individual method invocations, you may choose to use asynchronous communication with the Licensing Service as the method is invoked. Compromises between the level of licensing strictness and the level of component performance can easily be made.

Interfaces of the Licensing Service

The Licensing Service furnishes two interfaces that provide all the functionality necessary for your objects to adhere to your licensing approach. The interfaces are mandatory for all your object implementations that will be licensed. They enable the implementations to indicate when they are being used. Most important, the interfaces are designed in a way that the implementations know nothing of the current licensing approach being used. An object implementation simply says "I am now being used." You must decide what to do with this information. These interfaces are contained in the CosLicensing Module:

◆ The LicenseServiceManager interface defines a single operation, obtain_producer_specific_license_service(), that enables you to obtain a Licensing Service object that is specific to the calling object implementation. The term *producer* refers to the object being licensed to the consumer.

◆ ProducerSpecificLicenseService is the interface that allows an object to register use with the Licensing Service. The start_use() operation indicates the calling resource is about to be used by a consumer. The check_use() operation tells the Licensing Service an object previously registered with start_use() is still being used. Finally, the end_use() operation indicates that use of a particular object has ended. Information is passed to these functions indicating the user's runtime context. Such information is typically a user name, network address and node name, and the local time. Based on the information, the Licensing Service can choose to reject a request for use based on the licensing currently available.

Licensing Service Summary

In summary, the Licensing Service provides a highly configurable licensing capability for your distributed applications. The approach used in licensing can vary depending on your customer's needs and your compensation requirements. Most important, this service can be used to ensure proper developer compensation in the complex world of CORBA distributed programming.

Property Service

Have you ever looked at a shrink-wrapped component and said, "If that object only had an XYZ attribute, I would be in hog heaven!"? Or, worse yet, have you ever developed an object from scratch when a commercial version that suited your needs existed, but it lacked an attribute or two you had to have? If you have done either of these things, you need the Property Service in your software arsenal. The *Property Service* provides you with the ability to add named attributes (properties) dynamically to existing shrink-wrapped components with (of course!) no change to the component. The object being extended is not required to originate from the IDL type system, but if it does, it will also work well. The properties created with the Property Service have some added advantages over attributes created in the standard IDL fashion. These new properties can be created on the fly. Once created, you can name them, set and get their values, set their access modes, and delete them.

Such a property is either represented as a name-value pair or a name-value-mode tuple. The name is a simple IDL *string*. The value is stored as an IDL type *any*. The mode can be one of five mutually exclusive types:

◆ Normal means no restrictions are on the property.

◆ Readonly means a client can read and delete a property, but not change its value.

◆ Fixed_Normal means the property cannot be deleted, but its value may be changed when necessary.

◆ Fixed_Readonly means the property cannot be changed or deleted.

◆ Undefined is used when a get operation is invoked on a property that cannot be found.

Here's a simple example. Imagine you purchased a shrink-wrapped Polygon object representing an *n*-sided polygon with a list of points. You begin using the object in your system and life is good. Later in your development cycle, you realize your Polygon object needs an attribute that indicates if the Polygon's points are oriented in a clockwise or counterclockwise direction. What do you do? Use the Property Service! Figure 4-14 shows how to extend this object to have the new attribute your system requires:

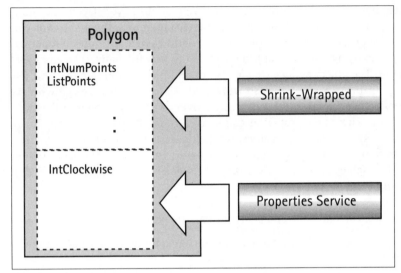

Figure 4-14: Extending a Shrink-Wrapped Object

As you see in Figure 4-14, you start out with a commercial Polygon Object. The Property Service is used to add a clockwise attribute. You can ask for this new attribute and check its value when necessary. The object now has all the functionality your system requires.

PROPERTY SERVICE INTERFACES

In this section, the interfaces that drive the Property Service are described. Six interfaces are defined in the CosPropertyService Module: Two are Factory interfaces, two are iterator interfaces, and two are the interfaces that provide the main Property functionality. These interfaces are:

- ◆ PropertySet – an interface that defines operations for defining, modifying, and deleting properties, as well as operations for working with groups of properties as a whole. The define_property() and define_properties() operations enable you to create a single or multiple properties, respectively. You can look up individual or all properties with get_all_property_names(), get_property_value(), get_properties(), and get_all_properties(). Properties are deleted with either delete_property(), delete_properties(), or delete_all_properties(). Finally, the PropertySet provides the is_property_defined() operation to indicate if a property is defined in the given PropertySet.

- ◆ PropertySetDef – a subclass of PropertySet. It inherits the operations for defining, modifying, and deleting properties, and adds the ability to manipulate property modes. This interface provides get/set operations for manipulating the mode of existing and new properties.

- PropertySetFactory – used to create a new PropertySet object. It provides the capability to construct a PropertySet or to initialize it from the start with a set of Properties.

- PropertySetDefFactory is used to create new PropertySetDef objects. It also enables constructing and initializing a PropertySetDef as it is created.

- PropertiesIterator defines an iterator that can be used to traverse sequences of properties returned by an operation invocation such as PropertySet::get_all_properties().

- PropertyNamesIterator works in a similar way. It provides an iterator for traversing a sequence of names, such as that returned by PropertySet::get_all_property_names().

Property Service Summary

In summary, the Property Service enables you to extend commercial shrink-wrapped objects dynamically. This is done by creating and manipulating new name-value-mode properties as needed and associating them with existing objects.

Time Service

The *Time Service* was created to provide support to distributed CORBA applications that need current time information with an indication of the associated level of error. The concept of time becomes quite cloudy in distributed systems because they can easily be running on computers with different sources for time and also quite possibly be running on computers in different time zones. In addition to providing current time information, this service also provides the capability to ascertain the order in which events took place, the capability to generate time-based events based on timers and alarms, and, finally, the capability to compute the interval between two events. If your CORBA system will rely on the current time or needs to dispatch operations at specified intervals, the Time Service should be used.

Many different ways currently exist to represent time in the software community and many sources exist for finding the current time. The Time Service does not try to dictate which approach you choose for using time and it is not attempting to propose a new unifying representation of time. Instead, this service exists to provide interfaces to work more easily with time in a uniform manner across your distributed environment. To help simplify matters, this service has chosen to use the Universal Time Coordinated (UTC) representation from the X/Open DCE Time Service, which most would consider a software industry standard. This representation of time can be obtained from a number of sources: One source is the WWV radio station of the National Bureau of Standards, which constantly broadcasts the time in UTC format. UTC is represented in 100 nanosecond increments since

October 15, 1582, which is the beginning of the Gregorian calendar. In the Time Service, the UTC information always refers to the Greenwich Time Zone.

This service is divided into two logical subservices, each with an associated set of interfaces. The TimeService interface provides operations for managing time-related objects. The TimerEventService interface provides operations for managing time-triggered events and event handlers. These events combine functionality provided by the Time Service with that provided by the Event Service. Now let's investigate these two interfaces and describe the functionality found in each.

TimeService Interface

Defined in the CosTime module, this interface interacts with two types of time-specific objects: Universal Time Objects (UTOs) and Time Interval Objects (TIOs), both of which are defined in their own interfaces.

The *UTO interface* defines an object that represents basic time. It represents the current UTC time and indicates an error associated with that time. The UTO object is immutable because it does not make sense to change the current time. This interface has an operation called compare_time(), which is used to compare the time represented by one UTO with the time represented by another. It also provides interval(), which returns an error time interval that brackets the UTO. The time_to_interval() operation returns a time interval object that represents the time interval between the current UTO and a UTO that is passed to the operation.

The *TIO interface* describes Time Interval Objects, which are objects with data and operations that refer to intervals of time. The time() operation returns a UTO with an error interval equal to the current TIO. The spans() operation takes as input a UTO object and the overlaps() operation takes a TIO object. Both operations return an OverlapType value, which describes how the interval described by the current TIO object and the time in the input parameter overlap. The types of overlap are shown in Figure 4-15.

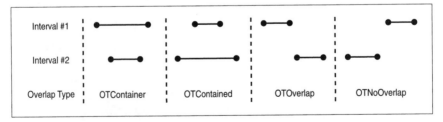

Figure 4-15: Time Interval Overlap Types

The TimeService interface provides higher level time creation operations that use the previously described UTO and TIO interfaces. Invoking universal_time() gives you a new UTO object with an associate error estimate, whereas universal_time_secure() does the same job, but ensures the UTO originated from a secure source. You can use new_universal_time() to create a new UTO with specified parameters. A new UTO can be created by passing a representation of UTC to uto_from_utc() and a new TIO can be created by passing a lower and upper interval bound to new_interval().

TimerEventService Interface

This interface enables you to create and handle events that occur at specified intervals of time. It works with the Event Service, using event channels. For timed events, only the Push model is supported. The TimerEventHandler interface contains information related to an event that will be triggered at a specified time and describes the action to be taken when the trigger initiates. You use the set_timer() operation to set the time when an event should trigger and cancel_timer() to cancel an event that has not yet triggered. The set_data() operation is used to set the data passed to an event when it is triggered.

The TimerEventService interface provides operations for registering and unregistering events. The register() operation takes as input a PushConsumer object and data associated with the event and returns a TimerEventHandler. You invoke unregister() to destroy the TimerEventHandler when it is no longer needed. To find out when an event was triggered, you can call event_time().

Time Service Summary

In summary, the Time Service provides the capability to retrieve time in a consistent manner across distributed CORBA systems. It also works with the Event Service to provide timed events throughout your system.

Security Service

Security is always a major concern in most software systems. It is a complex problem, though, and much different than the problems solved by the services discussed up to this point. The *Security Service* tackles the issue of security in a distributed CORBA system. To be successful, this service must address all aspects of security in a similar fashion because the security *chain* is only as strong as its weakest link. If a security policy is adopted that is strong in some areas and weak in other areas, a weak security policy has been adopted. People who attack our systems in malicious ways always look for the easiest way to make the attack successful. The Security Service was designed to plug all security holes that may be found by malicious intruders or by nonmalicious users using our systems in incorrect ways. The Security Service is also designed in a manner that allows objects interacting in a secure environment to have no knowledge of the security practices being used.

This is important because legacy objects can be made secure through an integration with the Security Service. Unfortunately, the burden is put on Security Service administrators, who must have an intimate knowledge of the service to configure and implement a security policy correctly.

Implementing a security policy in a successful manner can be difficult in traditional client/server environments. In a CORBA-distributed object system, the difficulty of this task increases dramatically. We refer to a security policy that contains our local domain, as well as domains potentially scattered across the world, different ORBs, countless different platforms, and miles of nonsecure network cable. This is a playground for malicious hackers. The wide scope of distributed object systems introduces countless points of attack, which must be addressed appropriately.

A multivolume book set could be written on the CORBA Security Service. Unfortunately, the time to investigate the subject in such depth is unavailable. Instead, we discuss this service from a high level in the hope of providing you with a sense of what the service does and how it can be helpful to your CORBA system. We do this in two steps. First, we cover the potential security threats associated with a distributed CORBA system; second, we discuss the key features of the Security Service that address these threats and provide protection against them.

Threats to a Distributed Object System

As we just mentioned, a distributed object system provides numerous opportunities for security breaches, both by malicious intruders and by nonmalicious users acting in incorrect ways. The Security Service has been designed to counter some of the following threats:

◆ Authorized users of your system can access data that should be hidden from them. Many systems will have levels of data that should only be accessed by certain groups of users. This service helps manage the access control granted to these different levels of data.

◆ Unauthorized users of the system can potentially enter your system masquerading as an authorized user, thus having the ability to access all information available to the user as whom the intruder is posing. All actions of the intruder are attributed to the wrong person. This type of security breach can have grave consequences.

◆ If security controls are not robust, they can easily be bypassed by an intruder or an authorized user, which quickly compromises data in your system.

◆ Because distributed systems may use nonsecure networks for communication, a great potential exists for eavesdropping on the messages passed around the system, which can easily compromise confidential data.

♦ Objects in a distributed system can be tampered with as they pass through the system. This service helps assure the integrity of objects as they move between nodes in your system.

♦ If a lack of accountability is in a distributed system, an associated security problem occurs. Without accountability of actions in the system, no way exists to determine if you have security breaches. The Security Service helps fill this void.

Key Security Service Features

The threats just outlined must be addressed to have a secure distributed object system. In this section, we discuss the key features of the Security Service and how they work to counter these threats. Here are the six main features of this service.

♦ The identification and authentication of principals. In a distributed system, a *principal* is defined as a user or an object, both having a set of access rights under which they operate. Every principal is a registered user or entity of your system and has associated security attributes. For example, a human user will have a password used for authentication purposes.

♦ Principal authorization and access control. Every principal has associated security attributes that indicate what objects in the system it is allowed to access. After a principal is authenticated in your system, any actions it initiates must be checked for correct authorization.

♦ The Security Service provides security auditing, which provides a level of accountability for all actions undertaken by principals. This auditing capability is secure in local domains, as well as across different domains and different ORBs. Object invocations that travel through multiple objects before reaching their destination preserve auditing data based on the originating principal of the invocation.

♦ Secure object communication is provided. This can be a difficult task because such communication usually takes place over nonsecure lines of communication. The task is accomplished by first establishing a security association between a principal and the object with which it is communicating. This is done by establishing a trust that both parties are who they claim to be, based on the credentials of both parties. Once the trust is established and it is determined the principal has authorization to communicate with the object, the issue of message protection must be addressed. When a message is sent to the target object, it can be protected in one of two ways. You, as the programmer developing code that uses this service, can choose simply to protect the integrity of the message and its data. This means you use security mechanisms on both ends of the wire to ensure a message sent to an object has not been changed in its travels to the object. You may also choose to protect the confidentiality of the message, which ensures a third party is not eavesdropping on the message in transit. This is accomplished with a choice of cryptographic algorithms used in the transmission process.

◆ Nonrepudiation services are available. These services provide irrefutable proof an event or action has taken place and combats false claims to the contrary. This evidence includes a time stamp, as well as a description of the action or event, and any parameters involved in the transaction. It can be stored and queried at a later time to resolve any disputes. Imagine a CORBA banking application used to wire money to clients. If no source of irrefutable transaction evidence exists, dishonest clients could claim they never received money transfers they actually did receive.

◆ Security Administration is also provided by the Security Service. As previously mentioned, the burden of this service falls on its administrators because objects in the system are typically shielded from security policies. Administrators have the ability to create and manage domains, including the users and objects in the domains. Also, they can configure the security policy used between different domains. For instance, if your local system interacts with objects in a domain owned by the XYZ Company, your administrator can negotiate with the XYZ Company's security administrator to formulate a security policy that is appealing to both parties. Administration can be general or specific, dictating which users have access to which object methods.

Security Service Summary

In summary, the Security Service tackles the daunting task of security in a CORBA-distributed object system. The Security Service is designed in a way that provides consistent security policies between domains of objects residing in different ORBs and on different machines. It provides for access control at varying levels in your system and makes provisions for secure object communication across nonsecure networks. We have only scratched the surface of the Security Service in this section, but at least you have the information necessary to decide if this service is needed by your particular CORBA system.

Collection Service

Simply put, this is a great, long-needed service. As most of you probably know, a *collection* is a grouping of objects that supports operations for navigation and manipulation of the objects in the group. Some common collection types include lists, stacks, queues, and bags. Numerous flavors of collections exist, each providing types of behavior that can be leveraged based on your object collection needs. Some collections guarantee object uniqueness in the collection, while others support multiple instances of the same object. Some collections are ordered, while others are not. Regardless of the type of collection, it must be useable in multiple application architectures, so it must be able to hold and manipulate arbitrary types of objects.

You may be thinking "I already have a commercial collection package that works well. Why do I need the Collection Service?" The answer is important and it helps explain the power of the Collection Service. Your commercial collection package works fine in typical application architectures, but as soon as you move to distributed CORBA applications, a roadblock quickly arises. If you fill a list in a CORBA server, how do you pass it back to clients? Your list is not IDL-based, so it does not know how to archive and unarchive itself across the CORBA wire. Passing objects (your list) by value will be supported in CORBA 3.0, but for now it is not. Commercial extension packages could solve your problem, but they, too, limit your progress. If you build a C++ CORBA client and server, and use such a commercial package to pass your list, things may work. Unfortunately, as soon as you create a Java client, your architecture breaks, because your Java client does not know how to manipulate the list passed to it. The Collection Service is powerful because it defines a wide range of collections you can use. These collections know how to be passed across the CORBA wire and can be used by client and server on different platforms written in different languages. Thus, this service contains all the functionality you will find in a commercial collection package, but bundles it in a machine-independent, platform-independent manner.

Earlier, in the section titled "The Query Service," you learned this service can be used to extend the power of the Query Service, which already has defined a minimal amount of collection functionality. This is a great combination because you can now use the Query Service to provide results stored in a wide variety of collections that suit your development needs.

To explain this service further, we discuss the different interfaces available and describe the functionality associated with each. Note, a number of abstract interfaces provide the base operations for the collections you use. We do not include these in the interface descriptions. Instead, we highlight some of the more useful interfaces in three sections named concrete interfaces, restricted access interfaces, and, finally, iterator interfaces. Because so many interfaces are in these three groups, we restrict the discussion to a general description of each interface's behavior.

Concrete Collection Interfaces

These interfaces are called *concrete interfaces,* meaning they provide objects you can use. If you have worked with collection toolkits in the past, you will most probably recognize many of these interfaces.

- ◆ *Bag* and *SortedBag* are collections of objects with no key. They support multiple instances of the same object.

- ◆ *EqualitySequence* is an ordered collection of objects with no key. It keeps track of its first and last element, and provides next() and previous() operations. Objects in the collection can be tested for equality with similar object types.

- ◆ *Heap* is an unordered collection of objects without a key. It supports multiple instances of a given object.

- ◆ *KeyBag* and *SortedKeyBag* are collections of objects with one or more keys.

- ◆ *KeySet* and *KeySortedSet* are collections of objects with unique keys.

- ◆ *Map* and *SortedMap* are collections of objects with unique keys. Multiple keys can refer to the same object value.

- ◆ *Relation* and *SortedRelation* contain objects that may have one or more keys. Such collections provide the capability to test for equality across collections.

- ◆ *Set* and *SortedSet* are collections of objects without keys. The objects must support an equality operation to determine if a given object is contained in the set. Operations, such as union and intersection, can be invoked on these collections.

- ◆ *Sequence* is an ordered collection of objects not having keys, having a first and last element. Most objects have a next and previous link within the collection. There is no support for element equality, so multiple instances of an object can exist in this collection.

Restricted Access Collection Interfaces

Restricted Access collections constrain the manner in which you can add and retrieve objects. This is done to give each collection a specific behavior. All four of these interfaces are useful.

- ◆ *Deque* is a double-ended queue that is a restricted access Sequence. Deque only enables you to add or remove the first and last elements in the collection.

◆ *PriorityQueue* is a restricted access KeySortedBag. *PriorityQueue* is sorted based on object key, which represents the priority. You can only access the first member in the collection, which will be the one with the highest priority.

◆ *Queue* provides simple First In First Out (FIFO) capabilities. You can only add elements at the end of the queue, and must remove elements from the beginning of the queue.

◆ *Stack* is a restricted access Sequence. This collection exposes Last In Last Out (LIFO) capabilities because you can only add (push) elements at the end of the stack and remove (pop) elements from the same position.

Collection Iterator Interfaces

Iterators are objects you use to navigate a collection. Every collection has some factory facility for creating and returning an iterator. An iterator is tightly intertwined with its associated collection instance and can thus be used only for its associated collection instance. An iterator cannot exist outside the lifetime of its collection. Some iterators are used to traverse different collection types. Here is a list of the different iterators, and the collections with which they are used:

◆ Iterator is used by the Heap collection.

◆ KeyIterator is used by the KeyBag and KeySet collections.

◆ EqualityIterator is used by the Bag and Set collections.

◆ SequentialIterator is used by the Sequence collection.

◆ EqualityKeyIterator is used by the Map collection.

◆ KeySortedIterator is used by the KeySortedBag and the KeySortedSet collections.

◆ EqualitySortedIterator is used by the SortedBag and SortedSet collections.

◆ EqualitySequentialIterator is used by the EqualitySequence collection.

◆ EqualityKeySortedIterartor is used by the SortedMap and SortedRelation collections.

Collection Service Summary

In summary, the Collection Service provides a wide variety of powerful collections. These collections hold generic objects and can be passed between your distributed CORBA components in a language and machine-independent fashion.

Trading Service

This investigation of CORBA Services is almost finished – this is the final service description. This chapter began with a discussion of the Naming Service, which enables you to locate objects anywhere by name. The *Trading Service* has similar functionality, except it enables you to locate objects based on the services they perform. The Trading Service acts like a newspaper's classified ad section. Objects register (advertise) a service they provide with the Trading Service. This advertising process is called *exporting* because an object exports some capability it has and tells the Trading Service of the location of an interface providing that capability. Clients looking for a particular capability can then discover, or import, this particular service by asking the Trading Service to find an interface that provides the specific capability. The service also will store any properties you need to use when invoking the operation on the interface.

Let's look at a simple example of this process. Imagine you have created a Geometry object that provides different geometric operations, one being the computation of a polygon's area, called PolygonArea(). You would use the Trading Service to advertise this service and tell the service of the location of the interface providing the PolygonArea() operation. When a client needs such a service, it can ask the Trading Service if such a capability exists and, if so, the Trading Service provides the location of the interface supporting the PolygonArea() operation. Figure 4-16 illustrates this process.

The Trading Service can act on its own, or it can link to other traders in the same or different domains. When Trading Services link, they create a trading graph. This graph allows a client interacting with one Trader to have at its disposal all the services registered with all Trading Services in the graph. As a client, you can tell your Trading Service how you want to interact with the graph. You can indicate whether a request on your immediate Trader is passed on to others in the graph or you can indicate how many different Traders to which the request is forwarded. You control how your search takes place in the trading graph in three ways:

- ◆ *Policies* are name-value pair attributes used to describe the scope of a search. A policy enables you to set things such as *hop_count*, which indicates how many traders a search should visit.

- ◆ *Constraints* are limits on your search, specified by criteria contained in a well-formed constraint language passed to your Trading Service.

- ◆ *Preferences* enable you to dictate the ordering of services returned by a Trading Service search. A *min preference* returns services sorted in ascending order of value, while *max* returns the services in descending order. *Random* returns the services in random order and *first* returns the services in the order in which they are found.

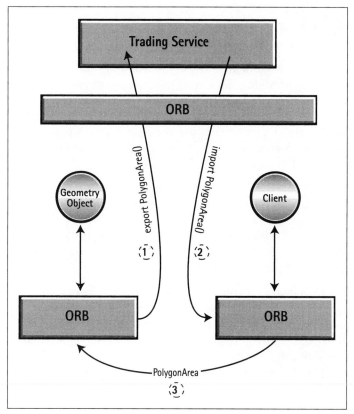

Figure 4-16: Using the Trading Service

To finish this section, we investigate some of the interfaces of the Trading Service. This will be done in two sections – Functional Interfaces and Admin Interfaces.

Functional Interfaces

These interfaces are used by clients when talking to Traders and by Traders when talking to other Traders.

- ◆ The *Lookup interface* defines a single operation named query(), to which you (the client) pass six parameters. These parameters are a service type, a constraint string, a preference string, a policies string, a set of desired properties to be returned, and a count of how many of these properties you have passed. The function returns an OfferIterator object. This is the operation used to find a service needed by your system.

- *OfferIterator* acts like other iterators, enabling you to traverse the set of objects returned by the query() operation mentioned above. This iterator has the traversal functions max_left(), and next_n().

- The *Register interface* is used to advertise object services with a Trading Service. The export() operation passes to a Trader an object reference, a service type, and a list of parameters to be used with the service. Withdraw() is used to remove the object service advertisement. Describe() returns information about a service registered with a Trader. Modify() can be used to change the description of a service already registered with a Trader. Finally, resolve() is used to find a Trader by name.

- The *Link interface* enables Traders to link and communicate with other Traders. The add_link() and remove_link() operations are used to create and remove links from one Trader to another. Modify_link() will change the properties associated with a given link, while describe_link() will return information about a specific link. You can use list_links() to obtain a list of all links owned by a given Trading Service.

- The *Proxy interface* enables run-time determination of the interfaces defined for a given service. This is used to provide more flexibility at runtime. A query mechanism is used to find a correct interface that corresponds to a client request. You use the export_proxy() operation to register a proxy with a Trader. This operation provides a target used to look up the actual interface when needed.

Admin Interfaces

These interfaces provide the capability for an administrator of a Trading Service to configure the properties of the Service.

The *Admin interface* provides list_offers() and list_proxies() operations that return lists of both of these types of registered services.

The *ServiceTypeRepository* enables you to create and register service types in a repository. The add_type() operation adds a new type to the repository. You invoke remove_type() to remove a named type from the type repository. List_types() provides a list of all types in the repository. Describe_type() and fully_describe_type() provide different levels of information on a particular service type stored in the repository.

Trading Service Summary

In summary, the Trading Service provides the capability to locate objects based on the services they provide. This service has a number of methods that enable you to control your search, as well as a number of ways you can search for a service.

The Current Status of CORBA Services

When talking about the status of CORBA Services, there is good news and bad news. Here's the bad news: Unfortunately, some of the CORBA Services are currently unavailable in the commercial market. If you need the functionality of one of the services not yet implemented, you may be forced to do it yourself. As mentioned earlier, we have been forced to do this wasteful process at times and it is not easy. If you are in this situation, first do you homework. Be sure an ORB vendor is not preparing the release of a version of a service you need. Do not reinvent the "Services wheel" unless no other options are available. That's all the bad news.

Now for the good news. ORB vendors did get a slow start toward the implementation of the different OMG Services. The good news is this slow start has received a jump start and new implementations of different services are popping up every day. This is a great time to be a CORBA programmer, especially one who needs functionality defined by one of the services. Here are some statistics about the current state of service implementations. These figures will most probably change for the better by the time you read this, but this is a good description of what is available.

- There are currently 16 ORB vendors with at least one service implemented.

- There are currently 8 ORB vendors with at least four services implemented.

- There are currently 2 ORB vendors with at least eight services implemented.

 For a great source of the currently available services, check out the Services Availability Matrix at this Web page: www/vex.net/~ben/ cosmatrix.html. This page is frequently updated, quite accurate, and looks at both commercial and free ORB vendors.

The current availability of services and the pace at which new ones are emerging is a great indication of the state of CORBA and CORBA Services. The OMG has done a fine job defining and designing the necessary services. ORB vendors are realizing vending services can be a lucrative business and they are rushing to get them to market as soon as possible. CORBA Services are here to stay – use them to your advantage whenever possible.

Summary

Try to use CORBA Services whenever possible. The services were designed to promote software reuse and created by determining the important, repetitive steps found in software development and then bundling them into individual middleware components that provide individual, powerful capabilities for your CORBA distributed applications. Because the services provide capabilities that most of our applications will need, you are bound to find a number of services that will plug into your application and immediately streamline your development cycle. Before you begin writing any code, refresh your memory with what each service is designed to do. If you find one that fits your needs, find a vendor that provides the service, and use it. The time and money you save will amaze you!

Chapter 5

Interface Definition Language: A Powerful Language

IN THIS CHAPTER

In this chapter, we present a description of the Interface Definition Language (IDL). IDL is a domain-specific programming language that is strong for its purpose. IDL is not designed to be used for general purpose, application-development work. In fact, trying to perform general programming tasks using IDL would be a waste of time. IDL lacks the proper programming constructs needed for a general-programming environment.

IDL is being used by most of the distributed-object frame work environments. Interface is a term that has become a popular way to express the implied contract between two individual entities. This contractual relationship is created for the mutual benefit of both entities.

- ◆ The reason to use IDL

- ◆ IDL syntax

- ◆ Exceptions

- ◆ Inheritance model

- ◆ IDL examples and descriptions

- ◆ Files generated by the compiler

The Reason to Use Interface Definition Language

IDL is a programming language that does exactly what its name suggests: it helps define interfaces. IDL is inherently object oriented in nature. To explain the previous statement, we want to take a slight diversion from this discussion and go toward object-oriented behaviors. The world of object-oriented systems and applications puts forward a hypothesis that every application program comprises a bunch of objects. These objects interact among themselves in a clean manner that qualifies the object. The hypothesis is well-supported by the knowledge that most applications written currently, whether they are new applications or conversions of the legacy systems, are written in an object-oriented approach. The developers of such systems have seen obvious benefits of using the object-oriented environment as the prime development platform. Furthermore, these application developers find it easy to explain the behavior of the system in an object-oriented manner. The ease of definition of such objects and capturing their behavior are some of the benefits of the system. Such benefits are more in terms of easy maintenance of the system and simplified manners of system expansion. They also tend to enable the developer to set some development rules and principles to follow. As we continue with this explanation, we discuss some of the details you must follow for the availability of object-oriented features.

The religion of defining rules and regulations does not always come out as bad as you are made to believe. If the restrictions are applied with foresight, then they serve a good purpose. At the speed with which the software industry is evolving, defining an application and keeping it static over the years is highly unprofessional and an unprofitable business strategy. It is bound to get obsolete in a year or two. Providing for the system to grow with ease over the years is an important design concern to the development process. An object-oriented system helps to a large extent in such development cycles. The system designer decides how much of the benefits he or she wants to derive from the development environment and at what cost. An object-oriented design strategy helps the system designer in many ways to keep his or her system fairly available for extensibility. It introduces the layering concepts, which helps modularizing the application in multiple levels. Modules interact among each other in a clean manner, keeping the dependencies well-documented and minimized.

Object-oriented applications interact with each other. The interactions exhibited by the objects are known as interfaces. An *interface* is a way for an object to expose its workings to the outside world restrictively, but sufficiently. The outside world communicates with the object via its interface. The interface defines the input parameters the object is working on and also defines the return value(s) from the objects. Every interface defined by an object has a certain goal to fulfill and the input parameters aid in the process. We have identified the interface is an important portion of the object-oriented application domain. Because of its importance, we must provide some specific ways and tools to capture the behavior of the object's interface. The approach of encapsulating the behavior of the objects should also result in isolating the inner workings of the object from the exposed interfaces. Using this strategy, you could expose the benefits of the object usage to the outside world and, at the same time, maintain the privacy of the object. IDL is provided with such functionality. IDL helps us describe the interface in a descriptive manner. The inputs to the interface and the outputs derived from them are specified in the interface definition file. The operational behavior of the system is well-hidden from the end user.

IDL is a strong declarative language that helps define an object's interface effectively. IDL provides all the language constructs required to define the object's interface. The language provides an easy way to define the most extraordinary interfaces required by any system. The strength of the language is in its simplicity. In the next few pages we discuss the language constructs and the keywords. The important question to resolve is the need for IDL. Is IDL truly needed ? Can the other programming languages be used to do the job of IDL and, if the answer is yes, do we need a special purpose language called IDL at all?

To begin with the justifications, the task of IDL can be done by the other general purpose programming languages. Even in the case of IDL, mappings are available from IDL to C++, IDL to C, IDL to Java, IDL to Smalltalk, and so forth. Even though mappings exist from IDL to many other programming languages, still IDL is used to write the interface definitions. In a distributed client and server programming environment, the client applications and the server applications could be written in two different languages. Such things are highly possible. If the interface were to be written in one specific language, then the developer must make a choice on the language in which to write the interfaces. Also, a way must exist to provide a mapping between the two languages. This is one of the important factors of deciding on a neutral language. The mappings currently exist from IDL to the other programming languages. It is a one-to-many map. And, because IDL is a new language designed for this purpose, it works out well to have such mappings. Having to pick up the existing general programming languages and overload them with the interface specific constructs would certainly be a challenging task. And having to provide the mappings from one existing language to another could result in overwhelming the existing language. Also, it is unclear whether the industry is ready to increase the weight of the programming language for specific domains. These are some of the serious concerns avoided by not selecting a particular general programming language.

The other factor is the portability issue. Interfaces written in IDL are highly portable from one environment to another. The same interface definition is used to generate the client and server stubs. These stubs could be in different languages and different operating systems altogether. Only the Object Request Broker must be supported in both the platforms for the applications to work. Another, ancillary issue important to consider is, with the advent of IDL, a new language is introduced in the industry. Hence, its design could be anything the designer wants. The other programming languages have been in the computer industry for a long time and if new changes are added to the programming languages, the industry would not accept the changes positively. The new changes will create tremendous confusion in the industry. Furthermore, the changes in the language must be weighed by the overhead, if any, incurred by the language itself. The addition may end up creating a significant decline in the performance of the language and also reduce its worthiness. The programmers may have to alter the way the program using this language and the compatibility factor would be of great concern. IDL helps to resolve all these concerns by simply introducing a new programming language for the interface definition. IDL helps avoid all the possible confusions. The language mapping capability helps in a smooth transition into the programming environment of the future. The benefits of IDL certainly outweigh the amount of extra effort it introduces in the application creation phase. In fact, calling the work extra effort is not completely justified, as it merely helps us modularize our work and builds a simplified component aware development environment.

Exceptions

In the common programming model, programmers often face situations viewed as unfavorable to the system. Such conditions must be met with utmost care. To such abnormal behavior in the environment into account, you need a proper mechanism built into the programming model. The conditions we discuss here may not necessarily end up being error cases, but many external concerns can create problems that must be resolved for the system to continue in its proper execution path. Such situations need fairly generic handling mechanisms. Error cases are specific, narrowed-down views of exceptions. Errors and cases specifically associated with them provide handling mechanisms that help the unfolding of the situation causing the errors. Take, for instance, a situation where a data file is being created to write down some data linked to the application and store it persistently. Such a task in programming would be handled in the following manner.

```
// Pseudo-Code snippet begins
// Try to create the data file
 FileHandle fh = _createFile( filename );
  if( fh == VALIDHANDLE )
 {
    int datawritten = _writeData( fh, datastream );
    if( datawritten == length of datastream )
      _closeFile( fh );
    else
      _ReportError( Write Error );
 }
 else
 {
    _ReportError( Create Error );
 }
// Pseudo-Code snippet ends
```

The previous snippet is pseudo code. All the member function names are fictitiously selected for the purpose of explaining a particular situation. In the previous pseudo code, a simple error-handling mechanism is displayed. The previous condition depicted only errors when the writing of data into the file is inaccurate and when the file creation fails. These are specific errors and the previous mechanism helps to identify them and report them to the system user. Most of the error-handling systems do not expect a recovery process.

Exceptions help the programmer report unusual behavior that may or may not have a direct impact on the program and its execution path. The intention of providing exception handling mechanisms is to help the user be aware of the situation and be prepared for an appropriate process to handle the situation. The exceptions could be reported from operating systems, runtime execution environments, applications executing in the user level, and so forth. Exception-handling systems provide detailed information about the exception. Some sort of structure filled with the exception information is passed on to the application, trapping the exception. The structure could give details about the state of the system, the reminiscent data structure that could provide hints of the corruption, and the possible solutions, the possible states of the other dependent modules, and so forth. All these are dependent on the type of exception generated and the way they are implemented by the system designer. Exceptions can be chained in a hierarchy. Many of the programming environments allow the system to generate exceptions and the applications have the control the trapping of the generated exception at different levels. Basically, if a particular layer does not process the exception, then it allows it to go upward, so the application at the higher layer would process it.

As an application programmer, you would expect as much information as possible to dissect the scenario. Many of the systems are designed in such a manner that the program could record the exceptions and generate dynamic handlers that could rectify the situation so further exceptions of this sort don't arise. These types of self-modifying programs are difficult to build and the basic principle in building such programs is dynamic diagnosing exceptions raised from the underlying system. The user of such systems is usually unaware of these conditions being handled underneath the covers. For instance, a network clustered system may have built-in exception handlers for load-balancing mechanisms. An overloaded node may generate exceptions, which could be trapped by the operating kernel and perform the needful, so the system does not go down during its operational hours.

These are some of the strong futuristic benefits in designing and working in an exception-aware environment. In a distributed environment, exception-handling mechanisms bring new challenges. The techniques of cascading exceptions from one machine to another due to the distributed nature create a huge impact on how to design the system. The involved issues are complex due to other variables playing an active role in the system. The network connections, different exceptions arising at different levels of the applications, and at different paths traveled by the data act as strong catalysts in such a system. They tend to restrict the levels of exception handling and the number of hops the exception can travel without complicating the issue further. Remember, one of the goals of providing exceptions handling is to simplify the error-handling system and help the error-recovery process. If the exception-handling system is designed in such a manner that it creates a cascading effect of exceptions themselves, then we are raising the stakes of operation and the chartered benefit could become a serious design bottleneck.

An IDL file can specify that a method in a server can raise an exception. This means the client routine must handle the exception. While several standard exceptions are built into the underlying ORB, you may specify custom exceptions in your IDL file. You can define custom exception data structures and user defined private exception handlers. The ORB supports a limited number of standard exceptions. The number of standard exceptions supported is limited to avoid the complication of the issues. The standard exceptions attempt to address all the major issues and error conditions without getting into the details. In case of exceptions, some process must generate exceptions for the handler to kick into action. The language construct for this is `raises`. So, in proper IDL, terminology exceptions must be raised. The standard exceptions do not have to be raised. They are raised internally by the system. The inner ORB structure will help in raising the standard exceptions if any violations occur in those regards. The user-defined exceptions and the custom exceptions must be raised. Because the system is unaware of the custom exceptions, the application must decide when to raise the custom exceptions; hence, it is impossible to raise the custom exceptions. Let's look at the standard exceptions. The following listed standard exception is defined in the OMG CORBA specifications.

```
#define ex_body {
    unsigned long minor;
    completion_status completed;
}
enum completion_status {
    COMPLETED_YES,
    COMPLETED_NO,
    COMPLETED_MAYBE
};
enum exception_type {
  NO_EXCEPTION,
  USER_EXCEPTION,
  SYSTEM_EXCEPTION
      };
exception    UNKNOWN ex_body;
exception    BAD_PARAM ex_body;
exception    NO_MEMORY ex_body;
exception    IMP_LIMIT ex_body;
exception    COMM_FAILURE ex_body;
exception    INV_OBJREF ex_body;
exception    NO_PERMISSION ex_body;
exception    INTERNAL ex_body;
exception    MARSHAL ex_body;
exception    INITIALIZE ex_body;
exception    NO_IMPLEMENT ex_body;
exception    BAD_TYPECODE ex_body;
exception    BAD_OPERATION ex_body;
exception    NO_RESOURCES ex_body;
exception    NO_RESPONSE ex_body;
exception    PERSIST_STORE ex_body;
```

```
exception   BAD_INV_ORDER ex_body;
exception   TRANSIENT ex_body;
exception   FREE_MEM ex_body;
exception   INV_IDENT ex_body;
exception   INV_FLAG ex_body;
exception   INTF_REPOS ex_body;
exception   BAD_CONTEXT ex_body;
exception   OBJ_ADAPTER ex_body;
exception   DATA_CONVERSION ex_body;
exception   OBJECT_NOT_EXIST ex_body;
```

The previous specification of the standard exceptions from the OMG has several enumerated types and a define associated with it. The first enumerated type is called completion_status. This can take in one of three possible values: COMPLETED_YES, COMPLETED_NO or COMPLETED_MAYBE. The COMPLETED_YES would imply the exception occurred after the specified task was completed. Exceptions occur while a particular task is being performed. If the job is performed by an object, then the exception could be defined at the object level or at a much finer level. Certain types of objects could be defined in such a manner that they contain varied methods. The methods could perform different types of processing for the object. In such a scenario, the different types of methods could give rise to different types of exceptions. In such objects, the exception, which is possible to be raised via a particular type of method, would be defined in that specific context. This would imply the different methods within the object have different exceptions defined within their visibility.

The COMPLETED_YES status would indicate the exception occurred after the specific method completed its task. The COMPLETED_NO status would indicate the exception occurred before the task was accomplished. In such an exception, this task is yet to be completed. The programmer could attempt to fix the exception-related problem and make another attempt to perform the specific task. This, again, is only possible if the exception is not critical enough. Only the programmer can decide on the criticality of the exception. Many times it is impossible to conclude whether the exception occurred before the task was accomplished. Various reasons could exist for such an abnormal scenario. The main task could have been done, but the ancillary housekeeping functions could have failed, in which case the exception could be raised. It becomes difficult for the system underneath to define the completeness of the core functionality; hence, the system may raise an exception, mentioning the status to be COMPLETED_MAYBE. For the system, the completeness of the task is defined by the bound of the entered method. If the method to which a particular exception is attached calls several other submethods, then they also fall into the bounds of the main method. If one of the submethod fails, the system counts it as the failure of the entire method and gives rise to the appropriate exception of the method. Getting a recovery procedure for such an exception could get tricky. The programmer typically would like to verify each subtask associated with the main method to verify the completion phase. The easiest and the most appropriate method to resolve such a situation is to run the process again. This would make sure the entire process is complete and the integrity of the systems is maintained. But doing this may not be easy. The subprocesses could be expensive in terms of resource and the time involved in the completion of the phases.

The second enumerated type, exception_type, is used to define and verify the type of exception. This also has three possible values: NO_EXCEPTION, USER_EXCEPTION and SYSTEM_EXCEPTION. The first value, NO_EXCEPTION, is simple to understand. It would indicate the exception is not valid enough to be called an exception. This could occur in many ordinary cases and is often redundant. It reduces the overhead caused to the application program in locating the data structure further ahead as it informs the invalidity of the data structure values. This helps save some redundant cycle time. The value USER_EXCEPTION indicates the exception is not a standard exception. This states the exception raised is a user-defined custom exception. User-defined exceptions would have their own specific exception handling data structure. The application would know about decoding the data as it is defined by the application itself. SYSTEM_EXCEPTION indicates the exception is a system-defined and standard exception.

Here's a simple exception-related example before we go further. This example will give us a first-hand sense of what an exception looks like and how it is defined and called. The code snippet provided in terms of an IDL script is provided for explanation and ignores many of the finer granularity associated with the real-life issues. The matter is simply defined and explained.

```
// The IDL file
interface FileIO {
  exception IOFail {
        string ioFail_Str;
        short  ioError_Code;
  }
  exception FileFail {
        string rwFail_Str;
  }
  int CreateFile( in string FileName ) raises( FileFail );
int ReadFile( in short FileHandle, out string FileData ) raises(
  IOFail );
int WriteFile( in short FileHandle, in string FileData ) raises(
  IOFail );
int CloseFile(in short FileHandle ) raises( FileFail );
boolean IsFilePresent( in string FileName );
};
```

Notice an interface is defined and called FileIO. The interface has five methods or operations defined. It also has two exceptions defined within the interface. The scope and the visibility of the exceptions are limited to the scope of the interface. The first exception defined is called IOFail. This exception has two data members defined inside it. The first is of type string and is called ioFail_Str and the second is of type short (short integer) and is called ioError_Code. Whenever an exception of type IOFail occurs, ioFail_Str is set to the error string that gives some indication of the error and the ioError_Code is set to the proper error code. The second exception is called FileFail and has just one data member. The lone data member is of type string and called rwFail_Str. In case of exceptions of type FileFail occurring, the rwFail_Str is set to the appropriate error string indicating the error. Notice the first exception defined has two data members and the second exception has only one data member.

Now let's look at the operations defined by the FileIO interface. The first operation is called CreateFile and it takes one parameter of type string. The parameter has the name of the data file; it is defined as the input parameter qualified by the in construct. This operation defines an exception with the help of the raises clause. The exception that could be generated with the help of this operation is called FileFail, which is articulated with the raises clause. Therefore, FileFail is the only user defined exception that could occur with the operation CreateFile apart from the standard exceptions. (Recall the standard exceptions are not defined with the raises clause.) The implementation of the method is not shown as it is irrelevant in this discussion.

The next operation is called ReadFile. This operation has two parameters: the first is FileHandle of type short; the second is FileData of type string. The first parameter is an input parameter; the second parameter is an output parameter. As an output parameter, the second parameter would imply that the client application would accept some valid data in it for the client application to be accessed. The valid data would be provided by the server side of the application. To speculate the functionality of the operation, the operation would request the server side of the application to read some data from the specified file on the server; the server would oblige the client by reading the data and returning it in the out bound parameter called FileData. The ReadFile operation has an IOFail exception defined within its vicinity. Later, when you code the server, you will create the ReadFile operation so it raises an IOFail exception in case of an error or any abnormal behavior exhibited. This is in addition to any standard exceptions that could be raised by the operation. The operation WriteFile also has a similar kind of structure with two parameters and an IOFail exception defined within its range. The only difference with WriteFile is the parameters are both of type input and the client would not be expecting any valid data back from the server side of the application. The CloseFile operation has one parameter and defines FileFail as an exception. This would imply the only user-defined exception CloseFile could raise is the FileFail exception.

The last operation defined within the interface is called IsFilePresent. This operation has one parameter. This operation is not defined with any custom exceptions (it has no raises clause), so this operation could only raise standard exceptions. The operation can generate no user-defined exception defined within the interface

Although this example doesn't show it, instances could occur where one operation may generate multiple exceptions. The previous example did not define any such operations, but this is possible in real life. In cases where multiple user-defined exceptions could be generated by one operation, they must be defined in similar manner.

```
// One operation having the capability of generating multiple user
  defined exceptions.
interface A {
…
…
boolean PerformTask( in short task_id, in string task_data ) raises(
  Exception1, Exception2, Exception3 );
};
```

The previous sample IDL code snippet describes a simple interface, which has one operation called PerFormTask. The operation defines three exceptions it could generate. The exceptions: Exceptions1, Exception2, Exception3 could be generated by the operation. All three are user-defined exceptions and must be defined within the vicinity of the interface, as was done in the previous example. Interfaces obey the standard inheritance principle, so the exceptions could be defined anywhere in the inheritance tree. In the following section, we'll look at the inheritance features within IDL. These three exceptions are in addition to the standard exceptions that could be generated by the operation.

Inheritance Model

We mentioned in the initial phases of the chapter that IDL is object-oriented. As you already know, object-oriented languages exhibit three features: inheritance, polymorphism, and encapsulation. This is not to say these are the only three deciding factors in characterizing a language as object-oriented but, nonetheless, these are the essential ones. Inheritance is a great asset for an object-oriented language. The inherited architecture assists in the reusability mechanisms and also avoids the redundancy in software design. Occasionally, in technical conferences arranged in the midst of technocrats, object-oriented people talk about the general design approach. These people always emphasize the design model, wherein, the specificity of the design must be stepped into from a generic start to a custom solution. They all have the same inheritance model in their minds, in one form or another. The inheritance model helps developers solve many problems. It helped us develop proper engineering etiquette. Inheritance allows for the acceptance of some behaviors from ancestors. Philosophically inheritance is true and it is not a new or unknown concept.

Figure 5-1 depicts a classical and simple business structure shown in terms of a block diagram. The structure has been recognized as the main module called *dept*. This is the root of our design. It has been observed in this business model that the finance department has its own operations, the engineering department has its operations, and the human resources department has its operations. Because all three departments belong to the same company, there do exist some commonalties. The commonalties must be obeyed by all the three departments, hence, they have been encapsulated into the main dept module. The fin_dept module inherits from the dept module, as does eng_dept and hr_dept. Because all three department modules inherit dept, they will receive all the data structures and operations associated with it. This allows the programs to make use of the data structures without the need of declaring their own. This is not to say specific departments wouldn't declare their own specific data structures and operations. But if they are common, then they need not be redefined at every level.

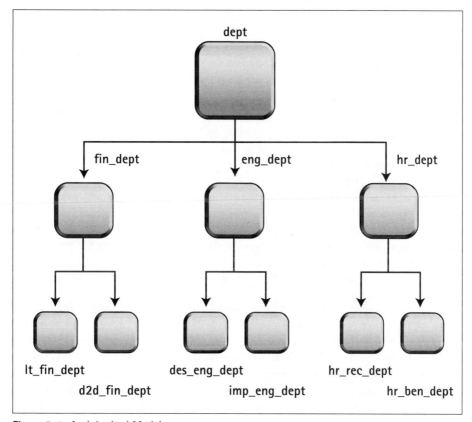

Figure 5-1: An Inherited Model

Further down in the design stream, we observe the finance department has two operational subdepartments, namely lt_fin_dept and d2d_fin_dept. The two finance subdepartments stand for the long-term financial planning division and the daily financial operations division. The engineering department has two subdepartments:

des_eng_dept and imp_eng_dept. These two engineering subdepartments are the design engineering division and the engineering implementation division. The human resources department has subdepartments hr_rec_dept and hr_ben_dept. The two human resources subdepartments are the human resources recruitment division and the human resources benefits division. The divisions in the department are done based on their functionalities. The inheritance model shows an is-a relationship. This implies lt_fin_dept is a fin_dept, which itself is a dept of some organization.

Two types of relationships are in the proper object-oriented world. The first is the inheritance model explained by the is-a relationship and the second one is the has-a relationship. The has-a relationship is more of a containment relationship. The most visible example of a has-a – or containment model – is the Component Object Model (COM) from Microsoft. A second look at our inheritance tree provides more information, which we must investigate to understand the applications of the principles. An instance of the interface dept would be a general entity. In fact, the existence of an instance of the interface of dept would be difficult to realize in the real world. Such an instance would immediately need to identify its existence by qualifying the type of department. This would require us to specify whether it is a finance department, an engineering department, or a human resources department. Furthermore, the department may be too big in itself and the interface may have to narrow down its services based on lt_fin_dept or d2d_fin_dept. Such precise interface specifications help to identify the operations that must be satisfied by the external entities. For example, the long-term investment strategies could be communicated with the interface for the lt_fin_dept and not with the interface for the d2d_fin_dept. Again, other types of operations must be interacted with the fin_dept only and not with its derivatives. For example, if the human department, hr_dept, must find out the hiring budget for the next fiscal year, then it would need to use the interface of the fin_dept. Because the hiring budget would include the possible expenses and the benefits for the employees the company can pay, fin_dept can only offer such operations.

We tried to study the inheritance model at a high level by taking into account some of the most common and possible scenarios. Other cases could certainly demand a different inheritance model, but those assumptions would also be different than the ones on which we've been working. The simplicity of inheritance is also maintained, as the goal here is to understand the issue of inheritance, rather than solving one specific problem. This example will help generate a good appreciation of the inheritance model. As you browse through the interface definitions, you will also have a good understanding of the role IDL plays in this arena. The IDL script for the following business model is shown in the following. Let's work through the script and understand in detail.

```
module Business_Model
{
typedef struct mon
{
```

```
    double   m_total;
    short    m_unit;
} MONEY;
interface dept
{
    exception Inv_Dept
    {
     string dept_error;
    };
    attribute short    dept_code;
    attribute string   dept_name;
    attribute string   emp_name;
    attribute short    emp_grade;
    attribute short    emp_id;
    attribute string   dept_head;
    void GetDeptCode( out short d_code )
      raises( Inv_Dept );
    void GetDeptName( out string d_name )
      raises( Inv_Dept );
    void GetEmpName( out string e_name );
    void GetEmpGrade( out short e_grade );
    void GetDeptHeadName( out string headname );
    void SetDeptCode( in short d_code );
    void SetDeptName( in string d_name );
    void SetEmpName( in string e_name );
    void SetEmpGrade( in short e_grade );
    void SetDeptHeadName( in string headname );
}; // interface dept scope ends
interface fin_dept : dept
{
    attribute short    tot_fin_emp;
    attribute MONEY    Company_Money;
    attribute MONEY    Company_Cash;
    void GetTotalMoney( out MONEY curr_money );
    void GetTotalCash( out MONEY curr_cash );
    void GetGenReport( out string short_rep );
    void GetTotFinEmp( out short fin_emp );
    void AlterTotalMoney( in MONEY curr_money );
    void AlterTotalCash( in MONEY curr_cash );
    void AlterTotFinEmp( in short fin_emp );
}; // interface fin_dept scope ends
interface eng_dept : dept
{
    attribute short   tot_eng_emp;
    attribute short   eng_prj;
    attribute short   sure_profit_prj;
    attribute short   prj_code;
    attribute short   unsure_profit_prj;
    attribute short   tot_rnd_phase;
    attribute short   tot_impl_phase;
    void GetEngEmp( out short emp );
    void GetTotalEngPrj( out short tot_eng_prj );
    void GetSureProfitPrj( out short sure );
```

```
  void GetUnsureProfitPrj( out short unsure );
  void GetRnDPrj( out short rnd );
  void GetImplPrj( out short impl );
  void GetEngReport( out string report );
  void AlterEngEmp( in short emp );
  void AlterTotalEngPrj( in short tot_eng_prj );
  void AlterSureProfitPrj( in short sure );
  void AlterUnsureProfitPrj( in short unsure );
  void AlterRnDPrj( in short rnd );
  void AlterImplPrj( in short impl );
}; // interface eng_dept scope ends
interface hr_dept : dept
{
  attribute short tot_hr_empl;
  void GetHrEmp( out short emp );
  void SetHrEmp( in short emp );
}; // interface hr_dept scope ends
interface lt_fin_dept : fin_dept
{
  attribute MONEY LT_Curr_Inv;
  attribute MONEY LT_Plan_Inv;
  void GetLTCurrInv( out MONEY tot_curr_lt );
  void GetLTPlanInv( out MONEY tot_plan_lt );
  void SetLTCurrInv( in MONEY tot_curr_lt );
  void SetLTPlanInv( in MONEY tot_plan_lt );
}; // interface lt_fin_dept scope ends
interface d2d_fin_dept : fin_dept
{
  attribute MONEY Oper_Cash;
  attribute short short_period;
  void GetOperCash( out MONEY c_cash );
  void GetStPeriod( out short st_period );
  void SetOperCash( in MONEY c_cash );
  void SetStPeriod( in short st_period );
}; // interface d2d_fin_dept scope ends
interface des_eng_dept : eng_dept
{
  attribute string curr_prj_code;
  attribute string curr_prj_desc;
  void GetCurrPrjCode( out string curr_code );
  void GetCurrDesc( out string desc );
  void SetCurrPrjCode( in string curr_code );
  void SetCurrDesc( in string desc );
}; // interface des_eng_dept scope ends
interface imp_eng_dept : eng_dept
{
  attribute int act_impl;
  void GetCurrImpl( out short impl_code );
  void GetCurrImplDesc( out string impl );
  void SetCurrImpl( in short impl_code );
  void SetCurrImplDesc( in string impl );
}; // interface imp_eng_dept scope ends
interface hr_rec_dept : hr_dept
```

```
{
  void GetEngReq( out short e_emp_req );
  void GetFinReq( out short f_emp_req );
  void GetEngReqDesc( out string e_desc );
  void GetFinReqDesc( out string f_desc );
}; // interface hr_rec_dept scope ends
interface hr_ben_dept : hr_dept
{
  attribute string benefits;
  void GetBenDesc( out string ben );
  void GetBudget( out MONEY mon );
  void SetBenDesc( in string ben );
}; // interface hr_ben_dept scope ends
}; // module Business_Model scope ends
```

The IDL script for the module Business_Model is shown in the previous example. The model is simple for the sake of explanation. At the same time, a complete model is necessary for the interface hierarchy and its explanation. The structure called MONEY is defined to use within the module definition and its scope is of the module Business_Model. All the interfaces defined within the scope of the module can use the structure. The exception Inv_Dept is defined within the interface dept. The design of the interfaces is such that all the interfaces are derived from the dept interface either directly or indirectly. Therefore, the content of the dept interface is available to every other interface. Even though the exception Inv_Dept is not defined globally within the module, it is available to all the interface definitions because of inheritance.

Scoping of identifier names and operation names is performed in a format much like C++. The scoping operator is ::. The scoping format is <scope>::<identifier>. The identifier must be directly present within the scope. The identifier can also be made available to the currently provided scope via inheritance. If the scope is an interface, then the declaration of the identifier must be present within interface definition or from the inherited interfaces.

In my example inheritance hierarchy model, the interface dept has an attribute called dept_code. We'll assume somewhere in our actual client code, the imp_eng_dept interface feels the need to perform an operation to retrieve the department code. It can easily make a call to GetDeptCode() operation. To resolve this call, the server object will check for existence of the operation by climbing the inheritance tree until it reaches the level where the actual code is present. It would then execute the code. The knowledge accumulated by the inheritance hierarchy is stored in the server code and used when required to perform such a job. The client could also make a call by using global scoping, which is done by having the :: in front of the identifier. Just having the :: in front of the identifier tells the system the scoping is at the file level. No walk of the inheritance tree is done in these cases.

When we discuss multiple inheritance, it is impossible not to talk about the situation of inheriting from two different parent interfaces, which themselves are derived from the same base.

In Figure 5-2, interface Interface_Two and Interface_Three are derived from interface Interface_One. Furthermore, interface Interface_Four is derived from both Interface_Two and Interface_Three. Such type of diamond-shape structure is perfectly legal in IDL. Some rules must be obeyed to make it perfectly legal and operable interface inheritance hierarchy. There could be ambiguities in resolving the right attribute and the right operations in the model and such ambiguities could be easily resolved by properly scoping the attributes and operations.

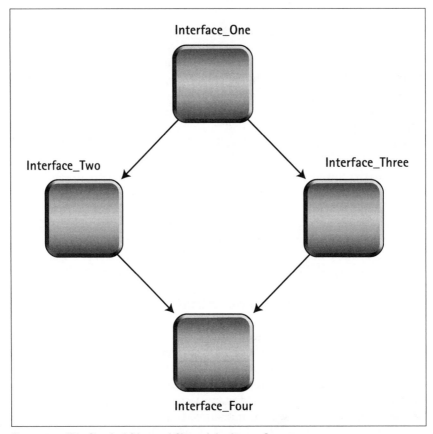

Figure 5-2: The Classical Diamond Shape Inheritance Structure

IDL Examples and Descriptions

We have seen in the preceding paragraphs that IDL is declarative in nature and is used to define the interface for an application. We can write our actual client portion and the server portion of the application in any programming language we desire. The only criterion is the target programming language should have a mapping provide from IDL. In essence, we must have a language mapping from IDL to our choice of programming language. This is no longer a limiting factor, as mappings are available from IDL to most programming languages like C, C++, Java, and so forth.

In this discussion, we assume the target programming language to be C++, hence, we use the IDL to C++ converting mechanisms. Most of the existing Object Request Broker vendors would provide an IDL to C++ conversion programming. Such tools would work on the specifications of the IDL to C++ language mappings provided by OMG.

Figure 5-3 shows the block level diagram of such a conversion process. We would write our interface scripts in a file with an extension of IDL. The conversion routine would read the IDL scripts from the source file and convert it into a C++ program.

Figure 5-3: From IDL to Target Language

Figure 5-4 shows the IDL to C++ compiler operates on the IDL source script and generates four output files. Among the generated output files are a pair of source files for the client side application and a pair of files for the server side application. The client-side files include a C++ source file and a corresponding header file and a similar construct for the server.

Here's an IDL example script. We'll compile the IDL file to generate the C++ target programs for the client and for the server side of the applications.

```
interface DBIface
{
  boolean LoginToDB( in string login, in string request );
  void GetData( in string query, out string result );
};
```

The previous example defines an interface DBIface. The interface provides two operations. The first operation returns a Boolean and is called LoginToDB. It takes in parameters: the first is an input parameter of type string and called login; the second is also an input parameter of type string called request. The second operation is called GetData and has no return value. GetData takes in two parameters: the first is an input parameter of type string called query; the second being an output parameter of type string called result.

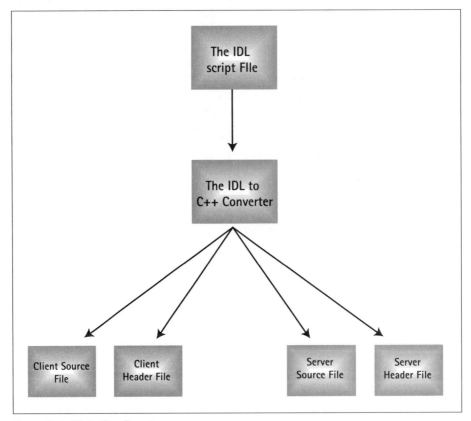

Figure 5-4: IDL to C++ Target

Files Generated by the Compiler

In the previous section, we defined an interface called DBIface. In this section, we browse through the output files generated by the compiler. For the purpose of our study, we work on the IDL to C++ compiler. The compiler would take an IDL script file as an input and generate the C++ and the equivalent header files for the client portion of the application and the server portion of the application. We will use the

Visigenics VisiBroker for my study. This is a trial version of the software that could be downloaded from the Visigenics Web page.

My example IDL file is called dbcon.idl. The IDL to C++ compiler module in VisiBroker is called idl2cpp. When we run idl2cpp on out input IDL file dbcon.idl, we get the output files as dbcon_c.hh, dbcon_c.cpp, dbcon_s.hh and dbcon_s.cpp. As the names suggest, dbcon_c.hh and dbcon_c.cpp are the client portion of the files. The files dbcon_s.hh and dbcon_s.cpp are the server counterpart. There would be many implementation details and differences in the source files as are revealed in the following discussion.

We begin by looking at the dbcon_c.hh file. The file listing is shown in the following. The header file has three classes defined: DBIface_var, DBIface_out, DBIface. The interface identifier DBIface maps to the class DBIface. Notice DBIface is derived publicly from CORBA_Object and the derivation is virtual, implying the multiple inheritance at a lower level would not cause a multiple data members to be defined within the object. The VISistream and VISostream are the VisiBroker input stream and output stream classes. They are needed for the system to be fully functional within the VisiBroker environment, so we could ignore their references for this discussion.

```
#ifndef _dbcon_c_hh
#define _dbcon_c_hh
/**

******************************************************************
******
*                                  *
*              - DO NOT MODIFY -             *
* This file is automatically generated by the VisiBroker IDL
compiler. *
* Generated code conforms to OMG's IDL-to-C++ 1.1 mapping as
specified *
* in OMG Document Number: 96-01-13                *
*                           *
* VisiBroker is copyrighted by Visigenic Software, Inc.       *
******************************************************************
******
*/
#include corba.h
#ifndef _DBIface_var_
#define _DBIface_var_
class DBIface;
typedef DBIface* DBIface_ptr;
typedef DBIface_ptr DBIfaceRef;
VISistream& operator>(VISistream&, DBIface_ptr&);
 VISostream& operator<<(VISostream&, const DBIface_ptr);
class DBIface_out;
class DBIface_var {
friend class DBIface_out;
private:
```

```
DBIface_ptr _ptr;
public:
void operator=(const DBIface_var&_v) {
if ( _ptr ) _release(_ptr);
if ( _v._ptr )
_ptr = _duplicate(_v._ptr);
else
_ptr = (DBIface_ptr)NULL;
}
static DBIface_ptr _duplicate(DBIface_ptr);
static void _release(DBIface_ptr);
DBIface_var();
DBIface_var(DBIface_ptr);
DBIface_var(const DBIface_var&);
~DBIface_var();
DBIface_var& operator=(DBIface_ptr);
operator DBIface_ptr() const { return _ptr; }
DBIface_ptr operator->() const { return _ptr; }
DBIface_ptr in() const { return _ptr; }
DBIface_ptr& inout() { return _ptr; }
DBIface_ptr& out();
DBIface_ptr _retn() {
DBIface_ptr _tmp_ptr;
_tmp_ptr = _ptr;
_ptr = (DBIface_ptr)NULL;
return _tmp_ptr;
}
friend VISistream& operator>(VISistream&, DBIface_var&);
friend VISostream& operator<<(VISostream&, const DBIface_var&);
friend istream& operator>(istream&, DBIface_var&);
friend ostream& operator<<(ostream&, const DBIface_var&);
friend VISostream& operator<<(VISostream&, const DBIface_var&);
};
class DBIface_out {
private:
DBIface *& _ptr;
static DBIface *_nil;
void operator=(const DBIface_out&);
void operator=(const DBIface_var&);
public:
DBIface_out(const DBIface_out& _o) : _ptr(_o._ptr) {}
DBIface_out(DBIface *& _p) : _ptr(_p) { _ptr = _nil; }
DBIface_out(DBIface_var& _v) : _ptr(_v._ptr) {
DBIface_var::_release(_ptr);
_ptr = _nil;
}
~DBIface_out() {}
DBIface_out& operator=(DBIface_ptr _p) {
_ptr = _p;
return *this;
}
operator DBIface_ptr& () { return _ptr; }
```

```
DBIface_ptr& ptr() { return _ptr; }
DBIface_ptr operator->() { return _ptr; }
};
#endif
class DBIface : public virtual CORBA_Object {
private:
static const CORBA::TypeInfo _class_info;
DBIface(const DBIface&) {}
void operator=(const DBIface&){}
public:
static const CORBA::TypeInfo *_desc();
virtual const CORBA::TypeInfo *_type_info() const;
virtual void *_safe_narrow(const CORBA::TypeInfo& ) const;
static CORBA::Object *_factory();
protected:
DBIface(const char *obj_name = NULL) : CORBA_Object(obj_name, 1) {}
virtual ~DBIface() {}
public:
static DBIface_ptr _duplicate(DBIface_ptr _obj) {
if ( _obj ) _obj->_ref();
return _obj;
}
static DBIface_ptr _nil() { return (DBIface_ptr)NULL; }
static DBIface_ptr _narrow(CORBA::Object *_obj);
static DBIface_ptr _clone(DBIface_ptr _obj) {
CORBA::Object_var _obj_var(__clone(_obj));
#if defined(_HPCC_BUG)
return _narrow(_obj_var.operator CORBA::Object_ptr());
#else
return _narrow(_obj_var);
#endif
}
static DBIface_ptr _bind(
const char *_object_name = NULL,
const char *_host_name = NULL,
const CORBA::BindOptions* _opt = NULL,
CORBA::ORB_ptr _orb = NULL);
virtual CORBA::Boolean LoginTODB( const char* _login,
const char* _passwd);
virtual void GetData( const char* _query,
char*& _result );
void GetData( const char* _query,
CORBA::String_out _result);
friend VISistream& operator>(VISistream& _strm, DBIface_ptr& _obj);
friend VISostream& operator<<(VISostream& _strm,
const DBIface_ptr _obj);
friend ostream& operator<<(ostream& _strm, const DBIface_ptr _obj) {
_strm << (CORBA::Object_ptr)_obj;
return _strm;
}
friend istream& operator>(istream& _strm, DBIface_ptr& _obj) {
VISistream _istrm(_strm);
_istrm > _obj;
```

```
return _strm;
}
};
#endif
```

The DBIface_ptr is a pointer to the DBIface object and so is DBIfaceRef. They are typedefs defined at the top of the header file. DBIface_var is a special class created for the DBIface object management purposes. It has a private data member defined called _ptr, which is of type DBIface_ptr. DBIface_var has overloaded the = operator to facilitate the copy method through the = operator. It also has methods call _duplicate, which will also allow to clone a DBIface, when passed as a pointer. The _release method would do the opposite of releasing the DBIface object referenced by the input pointer. There are many different ways of constructing the DBIface_var object are shown by the multiple constructors and many ways of accessing the DBIface object via its reference. Also observe the method in returns the pointer stored in the DBIface_var object and inout method returns a reference to the pointer. Later on in the code, you'll see the out method would release the DBIface object and return a NULL. We will discuss it later on when we look at the generated C++ source file for the client.

The DBIface_out class works on a reference to the DBIface pointer. The DBIface_var object declares the DBIface_out as a friend object to itself. This class would be used for the data operations on the DBIface object. These objects are never exposed to individually functional objects. Rather, their existence depends on the actual DBIface object and they are closely attached to it.

The DBIface object has type-related information about itself that could be used by many other floating objects and services. Many methods are defined in the DBIface object that have been added by the system. We look at the source code generated in the C++ file for the client application that would be helpful in explaining the functions of the methods.

The following listing is the client C++ source file generated by the compiler. We would have to link this file to our client application to use the ORB environment. The source listing may look complicated, but most of them are only requirements for the system to make optimal use of the VisiBroker environment.

```
/**
 ***********************************************************************
 *****
 *                                       *
 *            - DO NOT MODIFY -                   *
 * This file is automatically generated by the VisiBroker IDL
 compiler. *
 * Generated code conforms to OMG's IDL-to-C++ 1.1 mapping as
 specified *
 * in OMG Document Number: 96-01-13                   *
 *                              *
 * VisiBroker is copyrighted by Visigenic Software, Inc.          *
 ***********************************************************************
```

```
 */
#include dbcon_c.hh
DBIface_ptr DBIface_var:: _duplicate(DBIface_ptr _p) {
return DBIface::_duplicate(_p);
}
void DBIface_var::_release(DBIface_ptr _p) { CORBA::release(_p); }
DBIface_var::DBIface_var() : _ptr(DBIface::_nil()) {}
DBIface_var::DBIface_var(DBIface_ptr _p) : _ptr(_p) {}
DBIface_var::DBIface_var(const DBIface_var& _var) :
_ptr(DBIface::_duplicate((DBIface_ptr)_var)) {}
DBIface_var::~DBIface_var() { CORBA::release(_ptr); }
DBIface_var& DBIface_var::operator=(DBIface_ptr _p) {
CORBA::release(_ptr);
_ptr = _p;
return *this;
}
DBIface_ptr& DBIface_var::out() {
CORBA::release(_ptr);
_ptr = (DBIface_ptr)NULL;
return _ptr;
}
VISistream& operator>(VISistream& _strm, DBIface_var& _var) {
_strm > _var._ptr;
return _strm;
}
VISostream& operator<<(VISostream& _strm, const DBIface_var& _var) {
_strm << _var._ptr;
return _strm;
}
istream& operator>(istream& _strm, DBIface_var& _var) {
VISistream _istrm(_strm);
_istrm > _var._ptr;
return _strm;
}
ostream& operator<<(ostream& _strm, const DBIface_var& _var) {
_strm << (CORBA::Object_ptr)_var._ptr;
return _strm;
}
DBIface *DBIface_out::_nil = 0;
const CORBA::TypeInfo DBIface::_class_info(
DBIface,
IDL:DBIface:1.0,
&DBIface::_factory,
CORBA::Object::_desc(),
 0);
VISistream& operator>(VISistream& _strm, DBIface_ptr& _obj) {
CORBA::Object_var _var_obj(_obj);
_var_obj = CORBA::Object::_read(_strm, DBIface::_desc());
_obj = DBIface::_narrow(_var_obj);
return _strm;
}
VISostream& operator<<(VISostream& _strm, const DBIface_ptr _obj) {
 _strm << (CORBA_Object_ptr)_obj;
```

```
  return _strm;
}
const CORBA::TypeInfo *DBIface::_desc() { return &_class_info; }
const CORBA::TypeInfo *DBIface::_type_info() const { return
 &_class_info; }
void *DBIface::_safe_narrow(const CORBA::TypeInfo& _info) const {
if ( _info == _class_info)
return (void *)this;
return CORBA_Object::_safe_narrow(_info);
}
CORBA::Object *DBIface::_factory() {
return new DBIface;
}
DBIface *DBIface::_narrow(CORBA::Object *_obj) {
if ( _obj == CORBA::Object::_nil() )
   return DBIface::_nil();
else
   return DBIface::_duplicate((DBIface_ptr)_obj->
 safe_narrow(_class_info));
}
DBIface *DBIface::_bind( const char *_object_name, const char
 *_host_name,
const CORBA::BindOptions *_opt, CORBA::ORB_ptr _orb) {
CORBA::Object_var _obj= CORBA::Object::_bind_to_object(
 IDL:DBIface:1.0, _object_name, _host_name, _opt, _orb);
return DBIface::_narrow(_obj);
}
CORBA::Boolean DBIface::LoginTODB( const char* _login, const char*
 _passwd) {
CORBA::Boolean _ret = (CORBA::Boolean)0;
CORBA::MarshallOutBuffer_var _obuf(_create_request( LoginTODB, 1,
27350));
VISostream& _ostrm = *(VISostream *)(CORBA::MarshallOutBuffer*)_obuf;
_ostrm << _login;
_ostrm << _passwd;
CORBA_MarshallInBuffer_var _ibuf;
try {
_ibuf = _invoke(_obuf);
 }
catch (const CORBA::TRANSIENT& ) {
return LoginTODB( _login, _passwd);
 }
VISistream& _vistrm = *(CORBA::MarshallInBuffer *)_ibuf;
_vistrm > _ret;
return _ret;
}
void DBIface::GetData( const char* _query, char*& _result) {
CORBA::MarshallOutBuffer_var _obuf(_create_request( GetData, 1,
6413));
VISostream& _ostrm = *(VISostream *)(CORBA::MarshallOutBuffer*)_obuf;
_ostrm << _query;
CORBA_MarshallInBuffer_var _ibuf;
```

```
try {
_ibuf = _invoke(_obuf);
}
catch (const CORBA::TRANSIENT& ) {
GetData( _query, _result);
return;
}
VISistream& _vistrm = *(CORBA::MarshallInBuffer *)_ibuf;
_result = (char*)0;
_vistrm > _result;
}
void DBIface::GetData( const char* _query, CORBA::String_out
 _v__result) {
char* _result = (char*)NULL;
GetData( _query, _result);
_v__result = _result;
}
```

One of the important methods to discuss is the _bind method. The _bind method_ is a method introduced by the VisiBroker's IDL to C++ compiler. Because we are discussing an interface, having a bind method that would facilitate a bind to the ORB is essential. The _bind method calls the _bind_to_object on the global Object. This boils down to calling the method required to bind to the ORB. Because the interface registers with the system by providing its specifications, identifying the object within the dynamic registry-like repository maintained by VisiBroker is easy. The _bind also calls the _narrow, which is also generated by the compiler. The method helps in narrowing the object and pointing at the specific reference of its own type. If we cascade and look at the __narrow method, it does exactly the same. It first checks to see if the object reference is valid. If the object reference is found valid, then it tries to duplicate the object via its reference and the information of the object stored in the internal environment variable.

One of the interesting things to discuss is the LoginTODB method. If you remember from the IDL script, the LoginTODB method had two parameters and both were defined as input and of type string. The string data types end up being character pointers. Because the LoginTODB method is required to transfer data from the client to the server via the ORB frame work, you would expect some marshalling must be done. As expected, we do see some marshalling done using the MarshallOutBuffer data structure present within the global CORBA object. A request buffer that has the requested method embedded within the request buffer is created. Because it is an outbound request, we see the MarshallOutBuffer data structure being used and the request is being redirected to the output stream. VISostream creates the output stream and when data is entered into the output stream, it transfers it to the required destination. We also notice some C++ style exception handling being done with the help of the try and the catch block. The code generated has the exception-handling facility built for most of the standard errors.

The GetData method is one of the most interesting methods to study. The first question that should come to mind is: Why do we have two different GetData methods present in the C++ source file? The answer is simple if we follow through the code in a disciplined fashion. If we read the IDL script file, we notice the GetData method had two parameters, both being a string type. The first parameter is of input type and the second parameter is of output type. The definition of the method that maps to my definition in the IDL file is the following.

```
void DBIface::GetData( const char* _query, CORBA::String_out
 _v__result)
```

If we look at the source code associated with this particular method, we observe _result of type character pointer is defined and initialized to NULL. We will also see the second GetData method is called within our GetData. The second GetData or the GetData with more source code associated with it is generated by the VisiBroker's IDL to C++ compiler. Because GetData also must send data across to the server, we see some marshalling being done in them. The system generated GetData performs the same job of creating the specific request by embedding the method name that must be located at the server side. It creates an output stream and only writes the query in it. The second parameter is not written in the output stream, as it is of output type. Any output type parameter is never sent to the server. Instead, it is generated and the return values are transferred into them. This is exactly what happens. After the try and the catch block, we see an input stream is created. The result from the request is copied into the input stream and, later on, transferred to the output variable called _result. These methods explain the core of the client portion of the ORB application.

We have finished discussing the client portion of the generated files. Now let's discuss the server side. The compiler generates two files for the server side of the application. The header file is called dbcon_s.hh, and the C++ source file is called dbcon_s.cpp. We must link in the dbcon_s.cpp into our server side of the application to make our server side respond to the client requests.

```
#ifndef _dbcon_s_hh
#define _dbcon_s_hh
/**
*****************************************************************************
 *****
 *                                        *
 *              - DO NOT MODIFY -                *
 * This file is automatically generated by the VisiBroker IDL
 compiler. *
 * Generated code conforms to OMG's IDL-to-C++ 1.1 mapping as
 specified *
 * in OMG Document Number: 96-01-13                 *
 *                                     *
```

```
* VisiBroker is copyrighted by Visigenic Software, Inc.          *
*********************************************************************
*******
*/
#include dbcon_c.hh
class _sk_DBIface : public DBIface {
protected:
_sk_DBIface(const char *_obj_name = (const char *)NULL);
_sk_DBIface( const char *_service_name,
const CORBA::ReferenceData& _data);
virtual ~_sk_DBIface() {}
public:
static const CORBA::TypeInfo _skel_info;
// No op function to force base skeletons to be linked in
static void ___noop();
// The following operations need to be implemented
virtual CORBA::Boolean LoginTODB( const char* login,
const char* passwd) = 0;
virtual void GetData( const char* query,
char*& result) = 0;
// Skeleton Operations implemented automatically
static void _LoginTODB( void *_obj,
CORBA::MarshallInBuffer &_istrm,
CORBA::Principal_ptr _principal,
const char *_oper,
void *_priv_data);
static void _GetData( void *_obj,
CORBA::MarshallInBuffer &_istrm,
CORBA::Principal_ptr _principal,
const char *_oper,
 void *_priv_data);
};
template <class T>
class _tie_DBIface : public DBIface {
private:
CORBA::Boolean _rel_flag;
T& _ref;
public:
_tie_DBIface( T& _t,
const char *_obj_name=(char*)NULL,
CORBA::Boolean _r_f=0) :DBIface(_obj_name), _ref(_t) {
_rel_flag = _r_f;
_object_name(_obj_name);
}
_tie_DBIface( T& _t, const char *_serv_name,
const CORBA::ReferenceData& _id,
CORBA::Boolean _r_f=0) :_ref(_t) {
_rel_flag = _r_f;
_service(_serv_name, _id);
      }
~_tie_DBIface() { if (_rel_flag) delete &_ref; }
CORBA::Boolean rel_flag() { return _rel_flag; }
void rel_flag(CORBA::Boolean _r_f) { _rel_flag = _r_f; }
```

```
CORBA::Boolean LoginTODB( const char* login, const char* passwd) {
  return _ref.LoginTODB( login, passwd);
}
void GetData( const char* query, char*& result) {
_ref.GetData( query, result);
}
};
#endif
```

The server side of the header file has two classes defined. They are _sk_DBIface and _tie_DBIface. Both of these classes are derived from DBIface, which is present in the client header file. If you notice, the client header file is also included in the server header file. _sk_DBIface is generally called the skeleton class. The server side must be implemented by deriving an object from the _sk_DBIface class. The class _tie_DBIface is a template that could be used to define object instances of the class within the application.

Before we begin a detailed discussion of the source code generated by the compiler related to the server side header files, it's important to understand a few methods defined in the header file. Notice a LoginTODB method is generated that would map to the LoginTODB method declared by us in the IDL script file. Note, too, a _LoginTODB method is generated by the system. The same is true with the GetData method. It has a corresponding _GetData method generated by the system. The methods having the static void return types are the ones that would be activated by the Basic Object adapter when the respective request from the clients arrive. We will also see in the source code generated by the system that these methods generated by the system would internally invoke the actual methods that would actually perform the functions. Because these system-generated methods would be invoked by the Basic Object Adapter when the corresponding requests arrive, they would be in charge of marshalling the input request to generate the parameters for the local method. The methods would also marshall the return value to convert them back to the protocol specific data that could be transferred back to the client. Let's look at the listing of the server side of the source file to identify the functionality.

```
/**
*****************************************************************
******
*                                          *
*              — DO NOT MODIFY —               *
* This file is automatically generated by the VisiBroker IDL
compiler. *
* Generated code conforms to OMG's IDL-to-C++ 1.1 mapping as
specified *
* in OMG Document Number: 96-01-13                   *
*                              *
* VisiBroker is copyrighted by Visigenic Software, Inc.      *
*****************************************************************
*******
```

```
*/
#include dbcon_s.hh
static CORBA::MethodDescription __sk_DBIface_methods[] = {
{LoginTODB, &_sk_DBIface::_LoginTODB},
{GetData, &_sk_DBIface::_GetData}
};
const CORBA::TypeInfo _sk_DBIface::_skel_info( DBIface,
 (CORBA::ULong)2,
__sk_DBIface_methods);
_sk_DBIface::_sk_DBIface(const char *_obj_name) : DBIface(_obj_name)
 {
_object_name(_obj_name);
}
_sk_DBIface::_sk_DBIface( const char *_serv_name,
 const CORBA::ReferenceData& _id) {
_service(_serv_name, _id);
}
void _sk_DBIface::___noop() {}
void _sk_DBIface::_LoginTODB( void *_obj, CORBA::MarshallInBuffer
 &_istrm,
CORBA::Principal_ptr _principal, const char *_oper, void
 *_priv_data) {
VISistream& _vistrm = _istrm;
DBIface *_impl = (DBIface *)_obj;
CORBA::String_var login;
CORBA::String_var passwd;
_vistrm > login;
_vistrm > passwd;
CORBA::Boolean _ret = _impl->LoginTODB( login.in(), passwd.in());
VISostream& _ostrm = *(VISostream *)
(CORBA::MarshallOutBuffer*)_impl->_prepare_reply(_priv_data);
_ostrm << _ret;
}
void _sk_DBIface::_GetData( void *_obj, CORBA::MarshallInBuffer
 &_istrm,
CORBA::Principal_ptr _principal, const char *_oper, void
 *_priv_data) {
VISistream& _vistrm = _istrm;
DBIface *_impl = (DBIface *)_obj;
CORBA::String_var query;
CORBA::String_var result;
_vistrm > query;
_impl->GetData( query.in(), result.out());
VISostream& _ostrm = *(VISostream *)
(CORBA::MarshallOutBuffer*)_impl->_prepare_reply(_priv_data);
_ostrm << result;
}
```

The first thing to look at in the source file is the static array defined called
_sk_DBIface_methods. This array has the list of the possibly understood request by
the server side of the application. The system generated _LoginTODB method takes
in the data stream passed into it by the BOA. The input buffer is marshalled and the
parameters are generated. After the actual parameters are regenerated, the actual

implementation of LoginTODB method is invoked. The result from the LoginTODB method is then stored back into a newly generated marshaled output buffer. This is the return data to the client side of the application.

The system generated _GetData method is called by the BOA when the client requests a GetData. The input buffer is marshalled by the method and the input parameters are recreated. Then the actual GetData method on the server is invoked. The result obtained is marshalled back into the output stream, which would then be returned to the client side of the application.

The lingering question in our minds would be the amount of code generated by the system to perform a simple interface. It seems a bit too much for a small interface with only two operations defined, but the amount would not grow in a similar manner as the complexity level of the interface rises. In fact, most of the interfaces defined in the real-life projects would be rather complicated themselves. There probably would be multiple interfaces, each having many operations. In such systems, the code would not seem too much at all. It would all fall in place in a highly methodical order. With more experience in this environment, we would start expecting such methods being in the code and if someone must debug them, then we would know exactly know what to look for and where to look.

We have skipped discussions of some of the minor and not-so-materially important methods. Their understanding is not required to follow the working of the system. It has always been an unrealistic view for books to talk about a programming language and not have a complete programming example present in the chapter. We have remembered this issue in this chapter, so this section of the chapter has a complete example from the input scripts to the output of the scripts. A detailed explanation of the output helps us understand the programming matter in hand and provides valuable insights in helping us generate better code for our own projects.

Figure 5-5 shows the functional model of an IDL-based application. As shown in the figure, we have a client application that would have a linked section from the files generated by the IDL compiler. The linked section would have the marshalling and unmarshalling code linked into the client application. On the other side, we would have the server application linking on the server side of the code generated by the compiler. The server side would also have the marshalling and unmarshalling associated with it. The lines with the arrow heads show the flow of the data. The arrows merely show the directions and have no other significance in the figure. The lines also do not imply an explicit networked environment. The environment could be virtually anything: either a networked environment or a non-networked environment. For this explanation, we call it a virtual networked environment. The ORB and its linkages are not shown in the figure to reduce its complexity.

IDL Syntax

IDL has a set of syntax associated with it. The syntax is based on a grammar for the language. The OMG IDL grammar is a subset of ANSI C++ grammar. The OMG

IDL grammar has additional construct support for operation invocation mechanisms. The language supports the standard C++ like, constant declarations, the type system, and the operation declaration mechanisms. But it does not support complex data structures. The need to support such complex algorithmic data structures was not the purpose of IDL, as it was not to be a robust, general-purpose programming language. The OMG IDL grammar is expressed in EBNF (Extended Backus-Naur Format). The IDL source file has an extension of .idl. To start studying IDL we would begin with the reserved keywords. These are keywords recognized by the language environment and the language compiler.

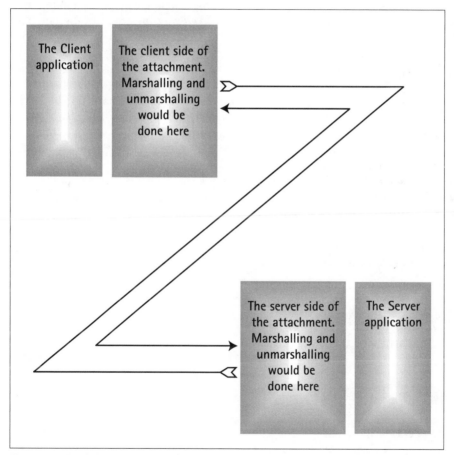

Figure 5-5: The IDL Functional Model

Keywords help the programming language and the user of the language to achieve a goal. They assist the programmer toward the target of generating an application using the programming language. The grammar of the language dictates the difficulty level. The language can be designed in such a manner that the grammar makes it inherently complex and slow or it could be designed to be optimum. The designer has the trade-off to make. If the language is designed to be simple, then it generally is difficult for such a language to be used in designing complex applications. An ordinarily designed language moves the maximum processing load on the application writer's shoulder. The programmer has to go through many iterations to get complex things worked out in the application. Because a simply designed language does not provide complex programming constructs and data structures within the language, the application programmer must build it on top of the system. IDL is one of those languages with a simple design and, hence, cannot be used to handle complex application designs. The generality is lost due to the lack of involved programming constructs. Making these arguments, however, does not in any way take away the credit of the language based on its prominent presence in the interface definition arena. Its strong presence is a result of the features it provides in designing the interfaces and the simplicity involved in such a situation. In the paragraphs to follow, we show the richness of the language and the strength in the specified domain.

IDL uses the same styles of comments as in C++. The characters /* start a comment and */ end it. They can spread over multiple lines. IDL also uses the characters // for single line comments. Comments started by /* can only be ended by */. But comments started by // end at the end of the line. The end of the line acts as the terminator for comments beginning with //. Comments in IDL cannot be nested. Within the these two styles of providing comments, neither one of them has precedence over the other. The precedence is actually generated from left to right.

In Figure 5-6, the comment begins on Line 1 with a /* and continues. The comment would end on Line 3 with a terminator of */. We notice a // character set is present in Line 1, but it does not have any significance as the comments cannot be nested and the precedence is generated from left to right.

Figure 5-6: The comment styles in IDL

Keywords

Figure 5-7 represents the keywords for OMG's IDL, which is case-sensitive. PAYMENT and payment are two different identifiers. Let's see what the different keywords mean. These keywords are discussed in detail to understand their needs and usage.

any This is a construct for type system. It is one of the data types declared in IDL. The any type specifies the value of any data type that could be accommodated. It could be a useful type at places where the specific type of data is not fixed. There are places where the expected data is unknown, but could be determined at the runtime by its value.

attribute This is an IDL keyword related logically to the interface definitions. The interfaces in IDL have attributes and operations. The operations are also called *methods. Attributes* are data members that qualify the interface object. Attributes have specific data types. The data types could be atomic or composite. Attributes can be set with particular values and these values can also be retrieved. You would assume each attribute would inherently be associated with at least two operations (or methods). In general, the operations would be a get operation and a set operation. The names of the operation would be specific to the implemented language and the terminology they follow.

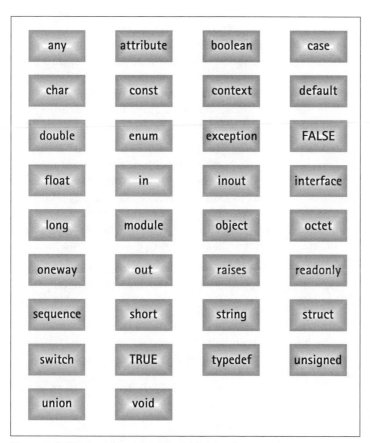

Figure 5-7: The Interface Language Definition Keyword Chart

boolean This is a data type declaration. This data type can hold values of either TRUE or FALSE. This is a binomial data type as the possible value set can contain just two results.

case This is an IDL keyword used in conjunction with the switch keyword. The case keyword is used to specify the possible values of the identifier in the switch clause. The values associated with the case statement must be of the same data type as the data type of the identifier in the switch clause.

char This is a data type in IDL. The char data type can hold values, which are 8 bits only. This represents a typical byte. The different language mappings may interpret them differently, but the basic meaning is the same.

const This is an IDL keyword enabling the programmer to define a constant variable. The variable is set to a constant value. The variable must be of any defined data type. The const keyword helps to set the value of the variable that cannot be altered programmatically.

context This is an IDL keyword used for maintaining and passing context-related information from the client to the server. The context keyword helps in defining the context to which an operation must be performed. The context information is like parameters that may effect the operation of the request, but are not directly linked to the request. The server is exposed to the context information from the client. The ORB makes sure the context information set for a request from the client is made available to the server. The server could query the context to retrieve the context values, which may alter the performance of the client request.

default This is an IDL keyword used in conjunction with the switch and the case clause. The switch clause has an identifier associated with it that maps to the possible values provided by the case clause. The default keyword is one of the possible values for the identifier from the switch clause. The default keyword would imply that if none of the values provided by the case clause map to the identifier, then the default would map. Only one default clause can be present. A switch statement may not have any default statement at all.

double This is an IDL data type declaration keyword used for floating point data. The keyword double helps in declaring a IEEE double precision floating point variable.

enum This is an IDL data type used for enumeration. It can hold a maximum of 232 values in the enumeration list. The order of the members of the enumeration list is dictated by their position in the list. Each member in the enumeration list must be a valid variable names.

exception   This is an IDL keyword used to define exception objects. This construct enables the programmer to define a user designed exception structure that would help to provide the specifications of the exception at runtime. Being a structure-like definition, it would enable the user to define the members, something that would satisfy the requirements.

FALSE   This is an internal define for the IDL used for variables of type Boolean. The Boolean variables can take two values and FALSE is one of them. This is more of a reserved word rather than a direct keyword.

float   This is an IDL data type declaration keyword used for floating point data. The keyword float helps in declaring an IEEE single-precision floating-point variable.

in   This is an IDL keyword used to qualify the parameters passed to a method. The keyword in implies the parameter is an input parameter and is passed in only one direction, from the client to the server. This is an important concept. If the server application modifies the parameter is declared as an in, then the client is unable to see the modifications directly, as the parameter is not directly returned back to the client application.

inout   This is an IDL keyword used to qualify the parameters passed to a method. The keyword inout would imply the parameter is an input as well as an output parameter. It is a bidirectional parameter. The parameter would be used for data to be passed from the client to the server and vice versa.

interface   This is an IDL keyword. The interface keyword helps in capturing the behavior of the object. The interface is an entity of its own with operations and attributes associated with it. It is a perfect way capturing similar kinds of acts of the object within one domain. An object could exhibit many interfaces. The interface would scope all the attributes and operations within it.

long   This is an IDL integer data type. It can store values up to four bytes. The long integer could be signed or unsigned. A signed long integer can store values from $-2@\text{sup}^{31}$ to $+2@\text{sup}^{31} - 1$. The unsigned long integer data type can store values ranging from 0 to $2@\text{sup}^{32} -1$.

module   This is an IDL keyword that formulates the operating module. A module contains interfaces and interfaces consists of attributes and operations. A *module* is an entity that encapsulates an object or a bunch of objects within an application. The module could contain many interfaces. The module scopes all the interfaces within it.

object   This is an IDL keyword, but it is more inherently used by the ORB. This is an interface implemented by the main module called CORBA. The object implementation has common operations and attributes that can be used by all the CORBA objects.

octet This is an IDL data type. It is an 8-bit data type that does not undergo any kind of alterations while passing through the communication channels. The value stored is guaranteed safety through the communication system.

oneway This is an IDL construct used to qualify methods. The keyword oneway implies the following method would be invoked in a unidirectional fashion. The client application could invoke the method on the server and would not be concerned about whether the request was received and performed by the server. Such methods do not have any return values.

out This is an IDL keyword used to qualify the parameters passed to a method. The keyword out would imply the parameter is an output parameter and is passed in just one direction, from the server to the client. This is an important concept. Ideally the client would provide space for the parameter, but conceptually the parameter value would be valid only after the call returns as the server application would pass in the relevant data in this parameter.

raises   This is an IDL keyword used for exceptions. The raises keyword is used to raise exceptions. IDL allows and understands exceptions and assists in exception handling. Some standard sets of exceptions exist and the user can define customized exceptions. The standard exceptions are raised even if they are not specified by the raises clause. If a particular method would like to invoke a user defined exception, then the raises clause should be used.

readonly   This is an IDL keyword that acts as a qualifier to the attributes. The keyword readonly would specify the attributes values can only be read. This would correspond to the language mappings that generate a get only operation for the attribute. The set operation would be absent.

sequence   The sequence is a one-dimensional array having two characteristics. The first characteristic is maximum size and the other characteristic is the length. This is more of a mathematical construct added to OMG IDL. Just as in mathematics, a sequence could be bounded or unbounded. If the length is specified explicitly, then the sequence is bounded or else it is unbounded. The length and the maximum size of the sequence must be defined in one way or another. If the length of the sequence is not defined, then the application program would not be in a position to retrieve the data in the sequence variable, as the data type size would be unknown. If the maximum size of the sequence is not provided, then the application program would not be in a position to decide how many more values are present in the sequence object.

short   This is an IDL integer data type. It can store values up to two bytes. The short integer could be signed or unsigned. A signed short integer can store values from $- 2@sup^{15}$ to $+2@sup^{15} -1$. The unsigned short data type can store values ranging from 0 to $2@sup^{16} -1$.

string   This is an IDL data type. A variable of type string will store in 8 bit data. A null is identified as the string terminator. The string can be viewed as a sequence of char. A string can be bounded or unbounded.

struct   This is an IDL keyword used to help create custom data types used in the application. The structure created by the struct keyword can consist of data members of various known types. The data types forming the members of the structure can be atomic of composite. This is identical to the C++ structure definition.

switch   This is an IDL keyword used to define a selection of a value among the provided option. The switch statement has an identifier whose value has to be mapped. The possible values are listed with the case clause.

TRUE   This is an internal define for the IDL, which is used for variables of type Boolean. The Boolean variables can take two values and TRUE is one of them. This is more of a reserved word rather than a direct keyword.

typedef   This is an IDL keyword used to create new data type definitions. The typedef keyword would take in an existing data type and an identifier. The identifier would become equivalent to the data type provided to typedef. It helps new versions of the existing data type, only the newer versions are identical to the existing formulated data types. It helps to create newer data types formed by the constructs like struct.

unsigned   This is an IDL keyword used to qualify the IDL data types. This is generally used in conjunction with the long or the short integer data types. This qualifies the integer data types by informing whether or not the signed bit is considered. The default for the long and short integer data types are signed, but the unsigned keyword can be used to override the default. The unsigned qualifier would allow the integer data types to contain positive values.

union   This is an IDL keyword, which is slightly different from the standard union definitions from C++ or C. The union definition is a mix of the union and the switch statements. The union construct comes along with the switch clause. The switch clause is, in turn, associated with the case statements, which are used to specific the possible cases for the identifier in the switch clause. The value of the union is the value of the identifier passed to the switch statement.

void   This is an IDL keyword. This is generally used to define the return value from a method. If a method has a return type of void, then it would imply the method returns nothing. No value should be expected back from the method.

The previous paragraphs explained the keywords of IDL. Our recommendation is, when you need to use a particular keyword, look it up to find its correct use. Learning these keywords and their use is important and, the more you study them, the easier using them will become.

Summary

In this chapter, we tried to impart a positive attitude toward, and a sense of requirement for, learning a new language. The way new concepts, such as a new programming language, enter my life intrigues me. The creativity is a key point of attraction in the high-technology industry. We have never regretted learning a new technology because it has always helped. In this chapter, we have, in small steps, shown why you would sense the need for IDL.

A serious concern in the software industry is how small projects become bigger and bigger. Ultimately, we see a huge, unmanageable monster. Then we see a negative phase; everything is discarded and a new sapling is born to replace it. The software development and management phase bears more headaches and spins more cycles toward maintaining the project than actually creating it. We must ask ourselves: Is all this worth it? If the answer is no, this would lead us to determine better ways and newer techniques in product-development methods to help achieve our goals.

The world has been constantly creating bigger problems for the software developers' community and we must constantly stand up to their needs. The continuous requirements generated by the world to solve bigger and more involved problems lead us to the path of creating bigger and more complex solutions. The solutions do solve the problems of the software consumer but, in turn, they create major problems for the developers. The developers and the development companies must manage the development and keep supporting the consumers. Our long quest to reduce the complexities has been answered by the word *modularity*. Modularization of the huge solution into small and manageable units has brought the charm back into software development. Component development has introduced an even higher level of operational independence into the modular world.

We introduced the important concerns of the IDL. The description of the language pertained to its creative approach of resolving complex issues in software design. The explanation of the most important factors of the language is provided in great levels of detail. Utmost care has been taken to see that the audience is not left in the dark as far as the explanation of the facts is concerned. The descriptive nature is spread throughout the chapter. An ample number of examples have been provided to help you understand the concepts. We realize IDL is not a general-purpose language, hence, the examples provided in the book are not generic in nature. The examples have been selected to bring out the strengths of the language. The attempt to create a sense of need is most important. Every possible discovery in the world was nurtured by the knowledge there existed a need for it. We tried to create a need in your minds: the reason for the existence of IDL. With this, we covered another new language in the computer science world and, with certainty, it has left us with more ways to reason and more available solutions to solve our daily computer-related jobs.

Part II

Client/Server
Application with CORBA

Chapter 6

Advanced CORBA Architecture

IN THIS CHAPTER

CORBA provides a strong, universal, powerful framework. The ORB is the middleware that establishes the client-server relationships between objects. Using an ORB, a client can transparently invoke a method on a server object, which can be on the same machine or across a network. The ORB intercepts the call and is responsible for finding an object that can implement the request, pass it the parameters, invoke its method, and return the results. The client needn't be aware of where the object is located, its programming language, its operating system, or any other system aspects that are not part of an object's interface. In so doing, the ORB provides interoperability between applications on different machines in heterogeneous distributed environments and seamlessly interconnects multiple object systems.

As a developer who wishes to use CORBA to its maximum potential, you need to understand exactly what CORBA is and why it exists. Now that you are familiar with the components of CORBA and their role in the architecture, we can delve more deeply into the architecture. This chapter describes the various components responsible for making all the actions of CORBA transparent to the end user. We discuss the Interface Repository, Implementation Repository, Dynamic Invocation Interface and Dynamic Skeleton Interface in this chapter. We also briefly discuss CORBA services, which is covered extensively in the next chapter.

- ◆ Interface Repository

- ◆ Dynamic Invocation Interface

- ◆ Dynamic Skeleton Interface

- ◆ CORBA Object Services

- ◆ Implementation Repository

Interface Repository

As described briefly in Chapter 2, the Interface Repository (IR) is a component of ORB that provides persistent storage of the interface definitions, acting as an online database and managing and providing access to a collection of object definitions specified in OMG IDL.

Using the ORB, the object definitions can be accessed either by using the object's publicly defined interfaces specified in OMG IDL or by using the IR. As the developer of the CORBA objects, you can decide which method you wish to use.

For the ORB to process requests correctly, the ORB must have access to the definitions of the objects it is handling. Object definitions can be made available to an ORB either by incorporating the information into the stub routines or as objects accessed through a dynamically accessible IR. The ORB uses the object definitions maintained to interpret and handle the values provided in the request. It uses these values to provide the type checking of request signatures, to assist in the checking of the correctness of interface inheritance graphs, and to assist in providing interoperability among different ORB implementations.

The Interface Repository provides for the storage, distribution, and management of collection of related object's interface definitions. As the information maintained by the IR is public, clients and services can also use the information. The repository can be used to manage the installation and distribution of the interface definitions, to provide interface information to the language bindings (like compilers), and to provide the components to the end-user environments. Before going into Implementation Repositories in depth, you should understand why the Implementation Repository is important.

Advantages of Having an Interface Repository

The ORB needs to understand and access the object definitions for its operations. The definitions provided by the repository are used in the following manner:

- The definitions help connect ORBs together. If our application works across ORBs, then it must use the same interface ID to describe these objects. These interfaces are defined in the IR.

- After an interface information is in the repository, the user can invoke the get_interface function and obtain information about any object dynamically. Another advantage of the IR is it enables the clients to create method invocations dynamically.

- The IR also helps in the type checking of the method signatures. The signatures define the method parameters and their types.

Scope of Interface Repositories

The IR is a set of objects that represents the information in it. These objects are accessible through a set of OMG IDL-specified interface definitions. As you know, an interface definition contains a description of the operation it supports, including the types and parameters, exceptions it may raise, and context information it may use. These operations operate on this object structure. There are also operations which help in extracting information in a bulk form, obtaining a block of information that describes a whole interface or a whole operation.

The IR defines the operation for retrieving information from the repository, as well as creating definitions within it. The definitions can be entered in the repository by compiling the OMG IDL definitions or copying objects from one repository to another. The repository uses modules as a way to group interfaces and navigate through those groups by name. Modules are comprised of constants, TypeDefs, exceptions, interface definitions, and other modules.

But not all interfaces will be visible in all repositories. This happens because the object implementations stored in the repository may be specific to an ORB. However, widely used interfaces will be available in most repositories.

One important use of an ORB is for connecting other ORBs together. When an object is passed in a request from one ORB to another, it may be necessary to create a new object in the receiving ORB to accommodate the received object. This may require locating the interface information in the IR of the receiving ORB. By getting the repository ID from the repository from the sending ORB, it is possible to look up the interface in a repository in the receiving ORB. To do this operation successfully, installing objects in both repositories with the same repository ID is necessary.

Interface Repository Interface – The Basics

To understand the concepts of the IR, it is important to understand what Names, Identifiers, Types, TypeCodes, and Interface Objects are.

NAMES AND IDENTIFIERS
Simple names are not necessarily unique within an IR. The names are always relative to explicit or implicit modules. In this context, the definitions are considered explicit modules. Scoped names uniquely identify modules, interfaces, constants, TypeDefs, exceptions, attributes, and operations within an IR.

Repository identifiers globally identify modules, interfaces, constants, TypeDefs, exceptions, attributes and operations. They can be used to synchronize definitions across multiple ORBs and Repositories.

TYPES AND TYPECODES
The IR stores the information about the types that are not interfaces in the data value called the *TypeCode*. From the TypeCode, determining the complete structure of a type is possible.

INTERFACE OBJECTS
Each interface managed in an IR is maintained as a collection of interface objects. These interface objects are:

   ◆ **Repository:** The top-level module for the repository name space. It can contain constants, TypeDefs, exceptions, interface definitions, and modules.

- ◆ **ModuleDef:** A logical grouping of interfaces. It can contain constants, TypeDefs, exceptions, interface definitions, and other modules.

- ◆ **InterfaceDef:** An interface definition. It can contain constants, types, exceptions, operations, and attributes.

- ◆ **AttributeDef:** The definition of attributes of the interface.

- ◆ **OperationDef:** The definition of an operation on the interface. It contains the lists of parameters and exceptions raised by this operation.

- ◆ **TypeDef:** The base interface for definitions of named types that are not interfaces.

- ◆ **ConstantDef:** The definition of named constants.

- ◆ **ExceptionDef:** The definition of an exception that can be raised by an operation.

The CORBA specification defines a minimal set of operations for interface objects. The possible additional operations, which the IR could provide, could include the versioning of interfaces. The interface specification for each interface object lists the attributes maintained by that object. Many of these attributes correspond directly to the OMG IDL statements.

There are three ways to locate an interface in the IR:

1. **By obtaining an <InterfaceDef> object directly from the ORB.**

   This method is useful when an object is encountered whose type is unknown at compile time. By using the get_interface() operation on the object reference, it is possible to retrieve the IR information about the object. Using the information, the client could perform operations on the object.

2. **By navigating through the module name space using a sequence of names.**

   This method is useful when the information about a particular interface is desired. Starting from the root module of the repository, it is possible to obtain entries by name.

3. **By locating the <InterfaceDef> object that corresponds to a particular repository identifier.**

   This is useful when working across ORBs. A repository entry must be globally unique. Thus, we can obtain the interface identifier from one repository and the details about the interface from another that is closer.

The CORBA specification defines a minimal set of operations for interface objects. The possible additional operations, which the IR could provide, could include the versioning of interfaces. The interface specification for each interface object lists the attributes maintained by that object. Many of these attributes correspond directly to the OMG IDL statements. Figure 6-1 shows how the IR is arranged.

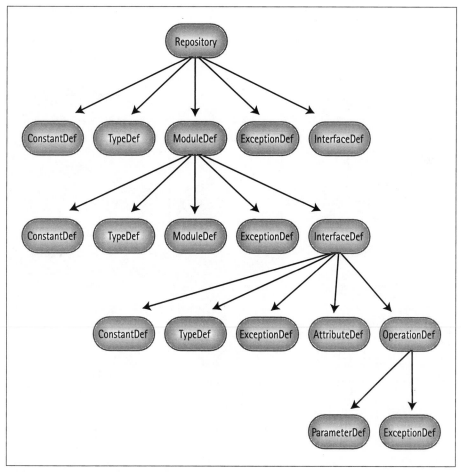

Figure 6-1: Interface Repository Containment Hierarchy

The Interface Repository Class Hierarchy

Several abstract interfaces are used as base interface for other objects used in navigating the IR. Three abstract superclasses cannot be inherited: IRObject, Container, and the Contained. All IR objects are inherited from the IRObject. Objects that are containers inherit navigation operations from the Container interface. Objects that are contained inherit their navigation from the Contained interface. These classes are not instantiable. The IR classes provide operations that enable you to read, write, and destroy the metadata stored in the repository. Figure 6-2 illustrates the Interface Repository class hierachy.

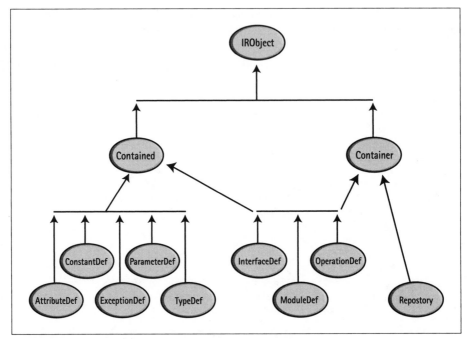

Figure 6-2: Interface Repository Class Hierarchy

IROBJECT

```
module CORBA{
        interface IRObject{
        // read interface
        readonly attribute DefinitionKind def_kind;

        // write interface
        void destroy();
        };
};
```

As mentioned, the IRObject interface represents the most generic form from which all other Interface Repository interfaces are defined. The def_kind attributes identifies the type of definition. The destroy object causes the object to cease to exist. If the object is a container, then the destroy is applied to all its contents. If the object is contained in some way, then the object is removed.

CONTAINED

The Contained interface is inherited by all the IR interfaces contained by other IR objects. All objects within the IR, except the root object (Repository) and definitions of anonymous (ArrayDef, StringDef and SequenceDef), and primitive types are contained by other objects.

CONTAINER

The Container interface is used to form the containment hierarchy in the Interface Repository. A Container can contain any number of objects derived from the Contained interface. All Containers, except the Repository are derived from the Contained.

Managing Interface Repositories

IRs help the programs to determine and manipulate the type information at run time. Objects, programs, and stubs depend on the information installed in the repository. Thus, updates to the repository must be done with care to avoid disrupting the environment. Different techniques are available that assist in this operation.

A Coherent Repository is one whose contents can be expressed as a valid collection of OMG IDL definitions. Validity is represented by the no-name collisions, parameters having known types, no duplicate operation names, and valid interfaces. As information is added to the repository, it is possible the repository may pass through incoherent states. The IR itself cannot make all repositories have coherent information. The repository will report errors it detects, but it may not report all the errors that happen. Despite this limitation, the expectation is a combination of conventions, administrative controls, and tools that add information to the repository will work to create a coherent view of the repository information.

Replication increases the availability and performance of a shared database. Under this approach, interface information is stored in multiple repositories. Using repository IDs, the repositories can establish the identity of the interfaces and other information across the repositories.

Multiple repositories may also be used to insulate production environments from development activities. Developers may be enabled to make arbitrary updates to their repositories, but an administrator may control updates to widely used repositories. Some repository implementations might enable sharing of information and some would enable copying of common information to maintain consistency, but the end result should be of a repository facility that creates the impression of single coherent repository. Some repositories may use Object Services (described later in this chapter), which include the transaction control and concurrency control when updating the repository. These services are designed so they can be used without changing the operations that update the repository.

The IR provides version control, allowing new versions to be created and allowing the old versions to continue to be valid. The newer versions have distinct repository IDs and are completely different as far as repository and ORB are concerned. The IR provides storage of versions for named types, but does not specify any additional versioning mechanism or semantics.

Dynamic Invocation Interface

The ORB's Dynamic Invocation Interface (DII), as the name suggests, enables a client to create and invoke operations dynamically. The request to an object using this interface obtains the same semantics as a client using the operation's stubs as generated from the type specification. A request generated using the DII consists of the Object Reference, an operation, and a list of parameters. The ORB in its part encapsulates this procedure from the client.

Parameters in a request are supplied as elements in a list; each element is of type NamedValue. The actual parameters supplied are each placed in its native data format in these elements. The parameters passed are checked for their types at run time. The parameters must be passed in the same order as the parameters defined in the operation in the IR.

The NamedValue structure is as follows:

```
typedef unsigned long Flags;
struct NamedValue{
    Identifier  name;       // argument name
    any         argument;   // argument
    long        len;        // length of the argument
                            // value
    Flags       arg_modes;  // argument mode flags
};
CORBA_NamedValue *CORBA_NVList;
```

The NamedValue structure as previously defined is a well-defined data type in OMG-IDL and is used either as a parameter type directly or as a mechanism for describing the arguments to a request. It contains an argument name, argument value (the actual value for the parameter; notice the type is any), length of the argument, and a set of argument mode flags.

The argument name is the argument identifiers specified in the OMG IDL for a specific operation. The argument value (any) consists of a TypeCode and a pointer to the data value. *len* is the actual number of bytes the value occupies. The behavior of NamedValue is undefined if the len value is inconsistent with the TypeCode. The arg_modes field defines the behavior by specifying if the associated value in the argument is an input-only argument, output-only argument or allows both input and output. (We discuss these in detail in Chapter 7.)

The NVList is a pseudo object useful for constructing the parameter lists. The NamedValue and Flag are both defined in the CORBA module. The NamedValue and NVList structures are used in the request operations to describe arguments and return values. They are also used in the context object routines to pass lists of property names and values. The NVList structure is partially opaque and can only be created using the ORB create_list operation.

Memory Usage

The values for output argument data that are unbounded strings or unbounded sequences are returned as pointers to dynamically allocated memory. The request routines provide a mechanism, which keeps track of out-arg memory, required when that memory must be released. If the out-arg memory is associated with the argument list, then it will automatically be freed when the list is deleted. If the out-arg memory is not associated with an argument list, then the programmer is responsible for freeing each parameter.

Return Status

Many routines in the DII return a Status result. The result is indicated as a status code. It is defined in the CORBA modules as

```
typedef unsigned long Status;
```

Confirming CORBA implementations are not required to return this status code. Instead the definition

```
typedef void Status;
```

is a confirming implementation. In this case, no status code result is returned, except the usual inout Environment argument. Implementations are required to specify which Status is implemented.

Request Operations

```
module CORBA{
interface Request{              //PIDL
    Status add_arg(
      InIdentifier  name,       //argument name
      InTypeCode    arg_type,   //argument datatype
      invoid        *value,     //argument value to
                                //be added
      inlong        len,        //length/count of
                                //argument value
      inFlags       arg_flags   //argument flags
    );
    Status invoke(
      inFlags  invoke_flags;    //invocation flags
    );
    Status delete();
    Status send(
      inFlags  invoke_flags;    //invocation flags
    );
```

```
        Status get_response(
          inFlags  invoke_flags;    //invocation flags
        );
}
}
```

The request operations are defined in the terms of Request pseudo object. And as it creates a pseudo object, create_request operation is performed on the object to be invoked. The create_request function creates an ORB request. The actual invocation occurs by calling the invoke or by using the send/get_response calls.

add_arg: Incrementally adds arguments to the request.

invoke: The operation calls the ORB, which performs the method resolution and invokes an appropriate method. If the method returns successfully, then the result is placed in the result argument specified on create_request. Control does not return to the caller until the operation is complete.

delete: This operation deletes the request.

send: Initiates an operation according to the information in the request. Unlike invoke, send returns control to the caller without waiting for the operation to finish. To find out when the operation is done the caller must use the get_response or get_next_response operations. The out parameters and the return value must not be used until the operation is done.

Another function – send_multiple_requests – also acts like the send command, except it initiates more than one request in parallel. Like send, this function returns to the caller without waiting for the operation to finish.

get_response: Determines if the request has completed. If the get_response operation is done, the out parameter and the return values defined in the request are valid. Similar to get_response, the get_next_response returns the next request that completes. The order in which the requests are returned is not necessarily related to the order in which they finish.

Dynamic Skeleton Interface

The Dynamic Skeleton Interface (DSI) is a way to deliver requests from an ORB to an Object Implementation, which does not have a compile-time knowledge of the object it is implementing. Figure 6-3 demonstrates the Dynamic Skeleton Interface.

The DSI is to the server-side what the DII is to the client-side. Just as the object implementation cannot distinguish if the client is using type-specific stubs or DII, the client that invokes the object cannot determine if the implementation is using a type specific skeleton or the DSI to connect the implementation to the ORB.

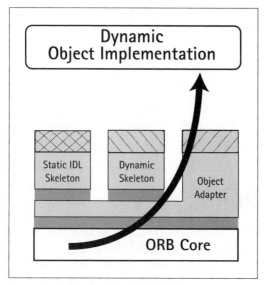

Figure 6-3: Dynamic Skeleton Interface

The DSI implements all requests on a particular object by having the ORB invoke the same upcall routine, the Dynamic Implementation Routine (DIR). As the language binding for all DIRs has the same signature, a single DIR can be used as the implementation for many objects, with different interfaces. To invoke an operation for an object, the DIR is passed with the all-explicit operation parameters, which include the indication of the object invoked and the operation requested. All this information is encoded in the request parameters. The DIR can use the invoked object, its object adapter, and the IR to learn more about the particular object and invocation.

ServerRequest Pseudo-Object

Analogous to the Request pseudo-object in the DII, the ServerRequest object captures the explicit state of the request for the DSI.

```
Module CORBA {
    Pseudo interface ServerRequest{
        Identifier    op_name();
        Context       ctx();
        void          params(inout NVList params);
        Any           result();
    };
}
```

op_name: Used for returning the name of the operation being invoked. According to OMG IDL's rules, these names must be unique among all operations supported by this object's most-derived interface.

ctx: If the operation is not an attribute access, ctx returns the context information defined in OMG IDL for operation. Otherwise, this context is empty.

params: Used to retrieve the operation parameters. They appear in the NVList in the order in which they appear in the OMG IDL specification (left to right).

result: Is used to find out where to store any return value for the call.

Implementation Repository

Not to be confused with the Interface Repository, the *Implementation Repository* contains information that allows the ORB to locate and activate the various implementations of objects. Although most of the information in the Implementation Repository is specific to an ORB or operating environment, the Implementation Repository is the conventional place for recording such information. Ordinarily, installation of implementations and control of policies related to the activation and execution of object implementations is done through operations on the Implementation Repository. Figure 6-4 illustrates an Implementation Repository.

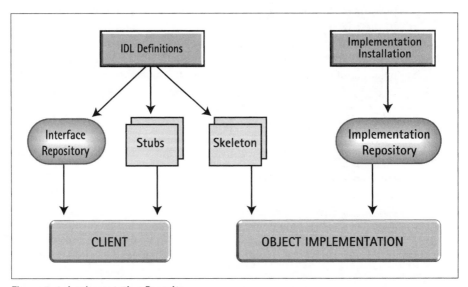

Figure 6-4: Implementation Repository

In addition to its role in the functioning of the ORB, the Implementation Repository is a common place to store additional information associated with implementations of ORB objects. For example, debugging information, administrative control, resource allocation, and security might be associated with the Implementation Repository. Usually activating an object requires a symbol table or other database that has the specified path to the object or server and other necessary information. Such information could be the last time the object or server was accessed. If another CORBA object issues a request to a nonrunning CORBA object, the Implementation Repository allows the activation of the requested object and the passing of the original request. At run time, this activity is invisible to the developer.

The Implementation Repository is the place where information about an object implementation (also known as server) is stored. The CORBA 2 specification gives you only an idea of what the implementation repository is for, but does not specify the interface to it; it's up to the vendors of the Implementation Repository to create the interface. The Implementation Repository contains methods for creating, destroying and finding entries. An implementation repository entry is defined by interface ImplementationDef. There is also an entry for each server that contains the Server Name, Activation Mode, Shell command or loadable module path and a list of repository IDs for the sever. The name uniquely identifies the server. The activation mode tells the BOA whether the server should be activated once (shared server), once for each object instance (unshared server), once for each method invocation (per method server), or not at all (persistent server). The BOA executes the shell command whenever the server has to be started. The activation mode library is used for loading servers into the same process as the client during runtime. Instead of a shell command you have to specify the path of the loadable server module for library activation mode. Finally there is a repository ID for each IDL interface implemented by the server.

The Basic Object Adapter expects information describing the implementations to be stored in an Implementation Repository. The Implementation Repository ordinarily is updated at program installation time, but may be set up incrementally or otherwise. ImplementationDef contains objects with an OMG IDL interface, which capture this information. The Implementation Repository is logically distinct from the IR, although they may in fact be implemented together.

Summary

CORBA provides a flexible framework for distributed heterogeneous object-oriented computing environments. Software design becomes easier with frameworks. CORBA is a single step on the road to object-oriented standardization and interoperability. With CORBA, users gain access to information transparently, without having to know what software or hardware platform it resides on or where it is located on an enterprises' network. In this chapter we discussed the few main components that make this framework work. In the later chapters we will use the information gained in this chapter which will help in better understanding and deployment of CORBA systems.

Chapter 7

Building Dynamic Invocation Interface Client Applications

IN THIS CHAPTER

In previous chapters, the CORBA examples were based on the Static Invocation Interface. The Static Invocation Interface is provided by the IDL Compiler in the form of client stubs that are linked into your application. This approach works fine for interfaces which rarely change and for which you have access to the IDL during client development. An entire class of client applications exists, however, that do not meet these criteria. Consider an application requirement for a client that can adapt to a changing server interface. Can this be done in CORBA? The answer is Yes! This is not for the faint of heart, though. A lot of the power provided by the IDL Compiler is not accessible on the client side.

The Dynamic Invocation Interface (DII) gives the programmer the ability to discover a server's IDL interface at run time and dynamically construct and invoke requests on a CORBA server. This is accomplished without any prior knowledge of the details of the server interface as defined in the servers IDL source file. However, clients and the client developers must have reasonable knowledge of the server interface. Simply put, the client must have an understanding of what the interface does and what sort of attributes and operations can be expected from the interface.

The DII relies heavily on the IR. As you have seen, the Interface Repository (IR is a server that enables clients to retrieve information about a particular object's IDL interface. The IR IDL is specified by OMG in the CORBA specification. All clients who use the DII must have access to an IR server on which the target server has registered its IDL.

- ◆ The Interface Repository

- ◆ How to run and populate the Interface Repository

- ◆ The Interface Repository class and instance hierarchy

- ◆ Interrogating and traversing the Interface Repository

- ◆ The four steps to making a Dynamic Invocation Interface request

- ◆ Type checking using CORBA::Any and CORBA::TypeCode

The Interface Repository

This section provides an in-depth discussion of the Interface Repository (IR). It explains the need for the IR in Dynamic Invocation Interface applications and that the IR is a standard defined by the OMG in the CORBA specification. Specifically, we provide the following information in this section.

◆ Definition of the capabilities and utility of the IR

◆ Procedures for running and populating the IR

◆ Procedures for interrogating and traversing the IR

◆ Hierarchy of classes and instances in the IR

◆ Considerations specific to VisiBroker

What Is the Interface Repository?

The IR is a standardized server that enables clients to retrieve information about any CORBA::Object's IDL interface. The IR IDL is specified by OMG in the CORBA specification. All clients who use the DII must have access to an IR server on which the target server has registered its IDL.

You can think of the IR as a library of interfaces (see Figure 7-1) that can be retrieved programmatically. The IR stores the definition of the interfaces. Clients may retrieve and examine this information to decide which server to activate, which operation to invoke, or which attribute to request. The IR maintains a complete definition of all data that can be declared in an IDL description. The following list details the abstract concepts contained in the IR.

◆ Repositories

◆ Modules

◆ Interfaces

◆ Attributes

◆ Operations

◆ Constants

◆ Exceptions

◆ Structures

◆ Unions

◆ Enumerations

- ◆ Type Defines
- ◆ Strings
- ◆ Sequences
- ◆ Arrays
- ◆ Primitives

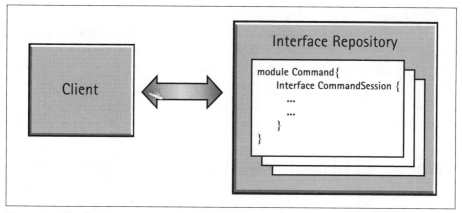

Figure 7-1: The IR

The IR is necessary for run-time determination of what the interface of a target CORBA server looks like. Without a programmatic way to access and interpret the interface of a server, you can not write clients that can create and issue requests on the fly; our only recourse would be prior knowledge of the server IDL via a client stub.

Remember we are talking about a dynamic invocation not a static invocation. We will learn more about how to construct the client-side dynamic invocation later in this chapter.

Generally speaking, the IR consists of the IR server executable, the IDL file describing the IR, and the convenience functions provided by the CORBA::ORB and CORBA::Object classes. The IR executable provides direct access via CORBA to the information contained in the repository. Remember, the IR is in itself accessible as a CORBA object. Therefore, as you learned in the last chapter, to bind and access the IR server you need a client stub that can be accessed by running the IR IDL through the IDL compiler. Remember, this IDL is specified by OMG, so it will not vary from vendor to vendor. The convenience functions are activated in most vendors' ORBs by means of compiler defines. If you use the convenience functions you must have the proper compiler defines. This chapter also describes how to set the VisiBroker defines in the section about compiling a client.

Although the IR is a CORBA standard, this does not mean that you will get one when you purchase an ORB. IRMost ORB vendors do provide all of the IR pieces with the basic CORBA development package. However, some vendors charge extra for the IR or don't provide one. Caveat Emptor! Make sure you define your system requirements before you purchase an ORB development environment. Also make sure you read and understand any license agreements and run-time fees associated with the ORB daemon and IR server.

Running and Populating the Interface Repository

For a client application to use the IR, an IR server must be running somewhere on the network and it must be populated with the interface definition that the client wishes to retrieve. There are several executables provided in the VisiBroker package related to the IR.

◆ irep The IR server. This is the server that implements the IR IDL. It can be run on the command line as a console application or as an NT service. In the console application mode it provides a command prompt for listing and saving the contents on the IR.

◆ idl2ir A command-line utility that uses the Java run-time environment to populate the IR from an IDL file. This utility binds to a running IR server and adds the contents of the IDL file to the IR.

The first step is to make sure osagent is running, and then to start up the IR server, irep Make sure that osagent is running before you run irep. In a command- prompt window, change directories to the ex0701 directory and type the following command:

```
start irep -console MyRep CommandSession.idl
```

The command start is a convenient command when running and debugging clients and servers from the command line. If used with a command-line program, start tells Windows to run the command in a separate DOS window started from the current working directory. This can be helpful if you are starting three or four commands from the same directory. The examples in this chapter start osagent, irep the server, and the client all from the same directory. It saves starting up four DOS windows and doing a separate cd in each window.

This command starts the irep executable. The -console option tells the program it will be running as a console application as opposed to an NT service and provides the irep command prompt. MyRep is the name given to the repository created with this invocation of the server. Multiple may be running at any given time. Recall that CORBA objects each have names that can be used in the call to bind(). This is the name of the CORBA object that is an IR and may be used in the call to bind() when a client wishes to connect to a particular IR. Lastly, CommandSession.idl gives irep an IDL file to use to initially populate the IR.

A new command-prompt window appears and a new irep process is running in it. The first thing you notice is a large number followed by a prompt. Typing '?' and return at the prompt gives a listing of available commands from the irep command shell. The output should look similar to the following:

```
IOR:000000000000002649444c3a7669736967656e69632e636f6d2f697274782f52
65706f7369746f72793a312e300000000000000200000000000005a000100000000
000e3230352e3136302e31352e38340004190000003e00504d43000000000000026
49444c3a7669736967656e69632e636f6d2f697274782f5265706f7369746f72793a
312e30000000000000064d79526570700000000000000001000000240000000000000001
0000000100000014000000000000000000000001010900000000
-> ?
Commands:  l<idl-name>      [l]ookup
           s                [s]ave
           a<file-name>     save [a]s
           r<file-name>     read from
           q                [q]uit
->
```

The large number is the output of the CORBA::ORB::object_to_string () function call. We talk more about this when we talk about generic object references. There is functionality to read and write IDL files representing the interfaces in the IR, and a lookup command to print a particular interface definition to the console window. Using the lookup command without any arguments prints the entire contents of the IR to the console window. For the IDL file we used to initialize the IR the output is the following:

```
-> l
Looking up: ""
module Command {
  interface CommandSession;
  exception InvalidArguments {
  };
  interface CommandSession {
  readonly attribute string username;
    string ls(
      in string dir
    )
    raises(
      ::Command::InvalidArguments
    );
    string cd(
      in string dir
    )
    raises(
      ::Command::InvalidArguments
    );
    string pwd(
    );
    long echoLong(
      in long val
    );
    string echoString(
      in string str
    );
  };
};
->
```

For a client to find the interface definition in the IR, the interface must be registered with the IR. You have just seen one method of populating the IR with an interface definition. However, specifying the interface on the command line may not be convenient in your environment. It may require intervention by a system administrator who has access to the file read by the IR on start up. A second method uses the utility program **idl2ir** to read an IDL file and add the definition to the IR. The following commands start the IR and populate it with the server interface definition.

```
start irep -console MyRep
idl2ir CommandSession.idl
```

The output from the IR console application is identical to the above output. For a full list of the options available on the **idl2ir** utility refer to the VisiBroker users manual.

Administration of the IR should be a major consideration in a deployed system. Ensuring that the IR is populated is an administrative task that must be addressed in your system's fielding plan. For a deployed interface you must ensure that **idl2ir** is called when the system starts the IR. Most ORB implementations do not have security controls on the IR. OMG does not specify administrative or management techniques for the IR, although the subject is mentioned in the CORBA specification.

> The IR is not protected by access or security controls. Clients have full read and write access to the IR. Mischievous clients can both corrupt the IR and get sensitive information from IRit.

The Interface Repository Classes

The CORBA specification as published by OMG defines a standard IDL for the IR. Most ORB vendors compile the IDL for you and supply the C++ class declarations in their header files. However, you have to find the IDL file in the vendor's distribution and compile it yourself. VisiBroker supplies a single header file named ir_c.hh. This is the client stub for the IR. My discussion of the IR focuses on its definition from the IDL perspective.

In this section we discuss the basic types defined by the IR IDL, the pseudo-abstract interfaces, and the specific definition interfaces that describe concrete concepts in the IR. "IR Types" discusses the basic and some of the derived types providing the foundation of the IR class hierarchy "Class Hierarchy" describes the terminal classes most commonly used by clients. "Instance Hierarchy" covers the example server, IDL, and how it is represented in the IR. If you are eager to get to the coding examples, skip ahead to "Interrogating and Traversing the IR" and use the following sections for reference.

IR TYPES

The IR consists of a set of objects that fully describe interfaces. Several base classes never get instantiated directly: IRObject, Container, and Contained. IDL does not support abstract interfaces in the same way that C++ supports abstract classes. It is left to the servers implementing the interfaces never to instantiate an object of this type. In addition, the TypeCode interface provides a mechanism to determine the unique type for attributes, parameters, etc. Using TypeCodes is discussed later in this section. Table 7-1 illustrates the base object types used in the definition of the IR interface.

TABLE 7-1   IR BASIC OBJECT TYPES

Object Type	Base Type	Attributes	Description
IRObject	None	DefinitionKind def_kind	This object is the root interface of the IR object hierarchy. It has one attribute that defines the object type. This allows a form of run-time type information (RTTI) for IR interface types.
Container	IRObject	None	Container objects contain other IRObjects. The Container interface supplies a method to look up a particular object or retrieve a list of Contained objects.
Contained	IRObject	RepositoryId id Identifier name VersionSpec version Container defined_in ScopedName absolute_name Repository containing_repository	Contained objects provide attributes to allow applications to upwardly traverse the instance hierarchy and to gain various scoped and non-scoped names to identify the interface component.
TypeDef	IDLType Contained	None	TypeDef is a base interface used for defining enumerations and aliases (TypeDef).
IDLType	IRObject	TypeCode type	IDLType provides the mechanisms to perform RTTI for primitive, derived, and interface types.

Continued

TABLE 7-1   **IR BASIC OBJECT TYPES** *(Continued)*

Object Type	Base Type	Attributes	Description
TypeCode	None	None	TypeCode objects provide a mechanism to uniquely type primitives and derived types. The method TypeCode::kind() returns a value of type TCKind. TCKind is an enumeration that has values predefined for the IDL primitive types.

The IR has several built-in types of run-time type checking, which may be confusing at first. Several enumerations, the IDLType object, and the TypeCode object illustrate this as described in the following:

CORBA::DefinitionKind This is an attribute on the CORBA::IRObject interface. It is used to identify the different objects used in the IR. Because the IR has the generic concept of container and contained, a mechanism is needed to determine the type of container or contained.

CORBA::Container objects have an operation called contents() that returns a sequence of CORBA::Contained objects. Using the CORBA::IRObject::def_kind attribute we can determine whether this is a ModuleDef, InterfaceDef, and so forth.

CORBA::TypeCode This object allows creation of run-time type checking information.

CORBA::PrimitiveKind This is used to determine the type of CORBA::PrimitiveDef objects. Enumeration values exist for all primitive type keywords defined by the IDL language. The CORBA::PrimitiveDef object is defined in Table 7-2.

So far you have seen the basic types used by the IR. These classes are never instantiated directly. TypeCode is the one exception.

TABLE 7-2   **TERMINAL OBJECT TYPES**

Object Type	Attributes	Contained Types	IDL Keyword	Description
Repository	None	ConstantDef TypeDef ExceptionDef ModuleDef InterfaceDef	None	Repository defines an instance of an IR. It contains definitions for all registered IDL files.

Continued

TABLE 7-2   **TERMINAL OBJECT TYPES** (Continued)

Object Type	Attributes	Contained Types	IDL Keyword	Description
ModuleDef	None	ConstantDef TypeDef ExceptionDef ModuleDef InterfaceDef	module	ModuleDef defines a module declaration. It contains definitions for all constants, TypeDef exceptions, modules, and interfaces defined within its scope.
InterfaceDef	InterfaceDefSeq base_interfaces	ConstantDef TypeDef ExceptionDef AttributeDef OperationDef	interface	InterfaceDef defines an interface declaration. It contains definitions for all constants, TypeDef, exceptions, attributes, and operations defined within its scope.
AttributeDef	TypeCode type IDLType type_def AttributeMode mode	Not a Container	attribute	AttributeDef defines an attribute of an IDL interface. The AttributeMode parameter may have values of ATTR_NORMAL or ATTR_READONLY.
OperationDef	TypeCode result IDLType result_def ParDescriptionSeq params OperationMode mode ContextIdSeq contexts ExceptionDefSeq exceptions	Not a Container	()	OperationDef defines an operation on an interface. It contains a TypeCode and IDLType. The OperationMode attribute may be one of OP_NORMAL or OP_ONEWAY. The last four attributes represent the result: a sequence of ParameterDescription structures describing the operation's parameters, a sequence of ContextIdentifiers that can be passed into a request, and a sequence of ExceptionDef interfaces describing the exceptions this operation can raise.
ConstantDef	TypeCode type IDLType type_def any value	Not a Container	const	ConstantDef defines a constant that is scoped to the repository, module, or interface in which it is contained.

Continued

TABLE 7-2   TERMINAL OBJECT TYPES *(Continued)*

Object Type	Attributes	Contained Types	IDL Keyword	Description
ExceptionDef	TypeCode type StructMemberSeq members	None	exception	ExceptionDef defines a user-defined exception. Its attribute is a sequence of StructMember structures defining each structure member. Remember within IDL grammar, exceptions look like structures.
StructDef	StructMemberSeq members	None	struct	StructDef defines a user-defined structure. Its attribute is a sequence of StructMember structures, which describe each member of the structure.
UnionDef	TypeCode discriminator_type IDLType discriminator_type_def UnionMemberSeq members	None	union	UnionDef defines a user-defined union. Its attributes are TypeCode and IDLType for the union discriminator and a sequence of UnionMember structures describing each member of the union.
EnumDef	EnumMemberSeq members	Not a Container	enum	EnumDef defines a user-defined enumeration. Its attribute is a sequence of EnumMember structures describing each enumeration value.
AliasDef	IDLType original_type_def	Not a Container	TypeDef	AliasDef defines a TypeDef in an IDL file. Its attribute is the IDLType of the original type.
StringDef	unsigned long bound	Not a Container	string	StringDef defines a string. The bound attribute defines the maximum length of the string.

Continued

TABLE 7-2   **TERMINAL OBJECT TYPES** *(Continued)*

Object Type	Attributes	Contained Types	IDL Keyword	Description
SequenceDef	unsigned long bound TypeCode element_type IDLType element_type_def	Not a Container	sequence	SequenceDef defines a sequence defined within an IDL file. Its attributes are the maximum length of the sequence and the TypeCode and IDLType of the elements contained in the sequence.
ArrayDef	unsigned long bound TypeCode element_type IDLType element_type_def	Not a Container	none	ArrayDef defines a user-defined array type. Like the SequenceDef, its attributes are the maximum length of the sequence, the TypeCode and IDLType of the elements contained in the array.
PrimitiveDef	PrimitiveKind kind	Not a Container	none	PrimitiveDef defines the IDL language's primitive types. Its attribute is type PrimitiveKind. PrimitiveKind is an enumeration of values representing the IDL language primitive types (that is, float, int, long and so forth).

CLASS HIERARCHY

The IR class hierarchy is depicted in Figure 7-2. The leaf nodes of the class hierarchy are the objects that we deal with from a programmatic perspective. The non-terminal classes are not directly instantiated by the IR. If you are going to be interrogating and traversing the IR, this picture should be helpful in understanding the relationships between classes defined by the IR IDL.

Note that certain classes are marked with an asterisk. These classes can utilize the operation CORBA::Contained::describe(). This operation provides a structure definition of each type of contained object. Each interface derived from CORBA::Contained defines a structure description of itself. The operation describe() returns this description structure. In addition, InterfaceDef defines a structure FullInterfaceDescription and the operation describe_interface(). We will use describe_interface() to traverse an interface in the section, "Interrogating and Traversing the IR."

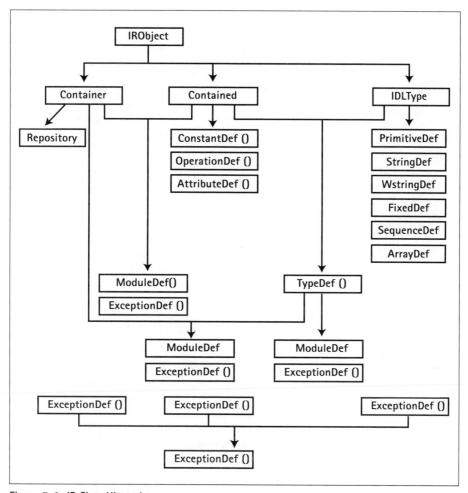

Figure 7-2: IR Class Hierarchy

 There is no ParameterDef interface. Parameters are described in the OperationDef interface.

HIERARCHY OF INSTANCES

We have shown the object types and class hierarchy defined by the IR. In this section we look at an example of the hierarchy of instances in a running IR. Let's refer to the example IDL file we have been using. Listing 7-1 is the contents of the IDL file.

Listing 7–1 CommandSession IDL

```
module Command
{
  exception InvalidArguments {};

  interface CommandSession
  {
      readonly string username;
      string ls(in string dir)
                            raises(InvalidArguments);
      string cd(in string dir)
                            raises(InvalidArguments);
      string pwd();
      long echoLong(in long val);
      string echoString(in string str);
  };
};
```

This IDL defines a single module named Command (Incidentally, for such a short example defining a module is probably not necessary, although it is good programming style. As interfaces grow, there is more of a chance for name space collision. It is better to deal with scoping issues earlier than later.) Within the module Command a single user-defined exception InvalidArguments and a single interface Command::CommandSession are defined. The Command::CommandSession interface provides five operations and a single attribute. Figure 7-3 illustrates the hierarchy of object instances contained by the Interface Repository.

The ParameterDescription and ExceptionDescription objects are the description interface supported by CORBA::Contained contained objects. Remember that OperationDef is derived from Contained only. It is not derived from Container and therefore it cannot contain other Def type objects. The only way to get parameter and exception information is through the description structures.

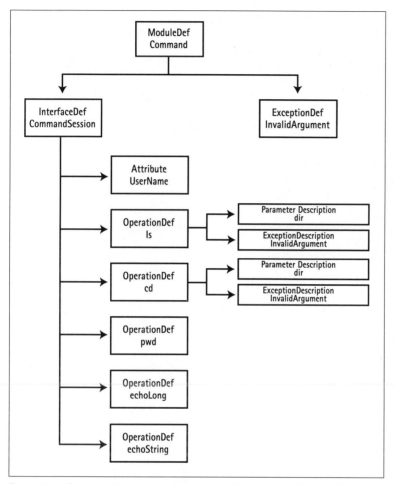

Figure 7-3: CommandSession Interface Description contained by the IR

Interrogating and Traversing the Interface Repository

Now that you have a good background on the IR, let's look at some code written to retrieve information stored there. This first example is part of the DII client we build later in this chapter and prints the information to the screen using the description facilities provided by the InterfaceDef interface.Two methods can be used to retrieve the InterfaceDef object for a given CORBA::Object. First, you can bind directly to the IR and use the operation CORBA::Repository::lookup_id().This method assumes that you have or can construct the Repository ID for the interface about which you wish to inquire. Second, the CORBA::Object class provides a convenience function, CORBA::Object::get_interface() to access the IR to retrieve the InterfaceDef object. Most vendor implementations of this function assume that the

IR server is available. If the IR is not available, CORBA::InterfaceDef::_nil() is returned. As we discuss in the next section, the IR can be bound to and accessed just like any other CORBA server using the object activation daemon.

First we look at the client's main loop that calls an internal function to print information retrieved from the IR. The client main loop is shown in listing 7-2. The complete source file for this example is located on the companion CD.

Listing 7-2 Client main loop using the decode_interface() function

```
#include <stdio.h>
//
// define _VIS_INCLUDE_IR before including any server/client
// headers.
//
// NOTE: Most CORBA implementations require some special
// compiler defines and libraries to use the Implementation
// Repository. This extends to the CORBA::Object methods
// which return IR objects (e.g. CORBA::Object::_get_interface()).
// VisiBroker requires compiler defines but does not use
// special libraries.
// Make sure you read and understand the directions for
// using the IR supplied with your
// CORBA implementation
//
#define _VIS_INCLUDE_IR
#include "CommandServer_c.hh"
//
// Globals
//
CORBA::ORB_var orb;

int main(int argc, char** argv)
{
  orb = CORBA::ORB_init(argc, argv);
  .
  .
  CORBA::Object_ptr session;
  session = login(ProgramOptions.hostname,
                          ProgramOptions.connectMethod);
  //
  // The main command loop where we will accept user
  // commands and send them on to the server
  //
  while (1)
  {
      char cmdline_buffer[1024];
      char *cmdline = cmdline_buffer;
      cout << ProgramOptions.hostname << "> ";
      cin.getline(cmdline_buffer, 1024, '\n');
      //
      // Handle special cases
      //
```

```
        if ( ! strcmp("q", cmdline) )
        {
            session->_release();
            exit(0);
        }
        else if ( ! strcmp("?", cmdline) )
        {
            //
            // decode_interface() is where we will
            // talk about the IR
            // objects and what they buy us
            decode_interface(session);
            continue;
         else if ( cmdline[0] == '\0' )
        {
            continue;
        }
        .
        .
    }
  return 1;
}
```

This client should look similar to clients you have seen in earlier chapters. One important note is at the top of this listing. Most CORBA implementations require you to explicitly indicate your desire to use the IR. For VisiBroker, this is defining the preprocessor variable _VIS_INCLUDE_IRI have defined this variable at the top of this source file. If you do this in VisiBroker, remember it must be done before CORBA.h is included. We have also defined this variable in the Makefile. this is a more accepted way. However, we wanted to make the source file case clear. Unlike other vendors, VisiBroker does not require linking to any special libraries to use the IR.

Taking a look at the logic of the client main loop, you see the client's first order of business is to initialize the ORB. Next, a pointer to a CORBA::Object is obtained via the login() function. The client's login() function will be discussed later in this chapter. For now, suffice it to say that we are getting an object reference to a Command::CommandSession object defined in the CommandSession.idl file. Next, the client enters a **while** loop to accept user-command input. The command *q* causes the client to exit. The command *?* causes the client to call the decode_interface() function. The function decode_interface() accepts as an argument a **CORBA::Object_ptr.** It prints information retrieved from the IR to the screen.IR. Listing 7-3 shows the decode_interface() function.

Listing 7–3 IR Interrogation and Traversal

```
void
decode_interface(CORBA::Object_ptr obj)
{
  //
```

```
// Start to decode the interface
//
CORBA::InterfaceDef_ptr pInterface;
try
{
  pInterface = obj->_get_interface();

  if (pInterface == CORBA::InterfaceDef::_nil())
  {
    cout << "_get_interface() failed" << endl;
    cout << "Is your InterfaceRepository running?"
<< endl;
    cout << "Is the " << obj->_repository_id()
            << " interface registered?" << endl;
    return;
  }
  CORBA::InterfaceDef::FullInterfaceDescription_var fid;
  fid = pInterface->describe_interface();
  unsigned int i, j;
  cout << "Attributes: " << endl;
  for ( i = 0; i < fid->attributes.length(); i++ )
    cout << "     " << fid->attributes[i].name << endl;
    cout << "Operations: " << endl;
    for ( i = 0; i < fid->operations.length(); i++ )
    {
      cout << "    " << fid->operations[i].name;
      for ( j = 0;
j < fid->operations[i].parameters.length();
j++ )
      {
        cout << " ";
        cout << fid->operations[i].parameters[j].name;
      }
      cout << endl;
      for ( j = 0;
j < fid->operations[i].parameters.length(); j++ )
      {
        cout << "        ";
        cout << fid->operations[i].parameters[j].name;
        cout << " = "
        cout << // non-standard
         fid->operations[i].parameters[j].type->kind();
        cout << endl;
      }
  }
  catch (const CORBA::Exception& excep) {
      cout << "Unable to decode Interface" << endl;
      cout << excep << endl;
      exit(1);
  }
}
```

The decode_interface() function is a generic function that takes a CORBA::Object_ptr and prints information retrieved from the InterfaceDef object. It uses the CORBA::Object convenience function CORBA::Object::get_interface() to retrieve the InterfaceDef object from the IR. The operation CORBA::InterfaceDef::describe_interface() is called to obtain a CORBA::InterfaceDef::FullInterfaceDescription structure. The FullInterfaceDescription structure contains a series of lists of the description structures mentioned earlier. These description structures describe the other Def type objects such as AttributeDef and OperationDef.

The first loop prints all of the attributes. The attributes member of the FullInterfaceDescription object is a sequence of AttributeDescription structures. The sequence length can be determined by the length() method. The [] operator has been overridden to provide the i'th member of the structure. Each AttributeDescription structure is dereferenced in turn and the name structure member is printed.

OperationDescription sequence is used similarly for operations. However, for each operation we also print the parameter name. Each OperationDescription has a sequence of ParameterDescription structures. Initially we print the parameter name and then on a separate line we process each parameter separately and provide its type. The type member of the ParameterDescription structure is a CORBA::TypeCode object. The operation CORBA::TypeCode::kind() provides the TCKind enumeration value. VisiBroker has overridden the streaming operators to print a string representation of the base TCKinds. This non-standard extension can be useful in coding and debugging.

The output of the decode_interface() function is shown below where the CORBA::Object in question is our Command::CommandSession object. This is a fairly complete definition of the interface defined in CommandSession.idl

```
Connected to CommandServer Unknown
 through interface CommandServer
 with repository id IDL:CommandServer:1.0
login: joe_user
localhost> ?
Attributes:
    username
Operations:
    ls dir
      dir = CORBA::TCKind:tk_string
    cd dir
      dir = CORBA::TCKind:tk_string
    pwd
    echoLong val
      val = CORBA::TCKind:tk_long
    echoString str
      str = CORBA::TCKind:tk_string
localhost>
```

There is one subtle point in this example. We said this example will not run without the IR running. If you try to run this example without i rep running, the program prints the following lines:

```
Connected to CommandServer Unknown
 through interface CommandServer
 with repository id IDL:CommandServer:1.0
login: joe_user
localhost> ?
_get_interface() failed
Is your InterfaceRepository running?
Is the IDL:Command/CommandSession:1.0 interface registered?
localhost>
```

By examining the decode_interface() function, you see that the return result is checked immediately after the call to CORBA::Object::get_interface(). This function does not throw an exception, it returns a CORBA::InterfaceDef::_nil() result. So how does this function actually work? Figure 7-4 should clarify matters. The function CORBA::Object::get_interface() binds to an IR server and tries to retrieve the CORBA::InterfaceDef object for the Repository Id associated with this CORBA::Object If it fails, it returns a **nil** value because it is trying to act as a local function.

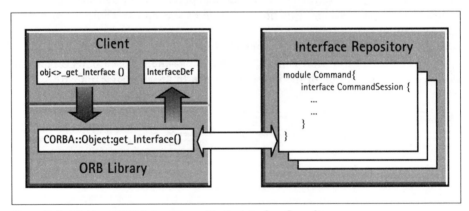

Figure 7-4: Client and ORB interaction with the Interface Repository

Considerations Specific to Visigenics

We have shown how to run i rep in the preceding sections. One last consideration is automatically activating the IR. The following discussion touches on the issue of system administration of the IR.

ACTIVATING THE IREP

Remember, irep is just another CORBA server. It implements the OMG standard IR IDL. Just like any other server, it may be activated by object activation facilities. In the case of VisiBroker, this is the oad application discussed in the last chapter. As stated earlier, it is a system management function to insure that irep is loaded with correct interface definitions when started.

You can use irep in console mode to load all the interfaces you wish, and then use the "save as" command to save them all to a single file. This file can then be specified as one of the command-line arguments to oadutil. The following session shows an example of this.

```
start irep -console MyRep
idl2ir CommandSession.idl
idl2ir CommandServer.idl
```

In the irep command window issue the lookup and save as commands:

```
IOR:000000000000002649444c3a7669736967656e69632e636f6d2f697274782f52
65706f7369746f72793a312e3000000000000000020000000000000005a000000000
000e3230352e3136302e31352e38340004b30000003e00504d430000000000000026
49444c3a7669736967656e69632e636f6d2f697274782f5265706f7369746f72793a
312e30000000000000064d79526576700000000000000010000002400000000000001
00000001000001400000000000000000000000001010900000000
-> 1
Looking up: ""
module Command {
  interface CommandSession;
  exception InvalidArguments {
  };
  interface CommandSession {
    readonly attribute string username;
    string ls(
      in string dir
    )
    raises(
      ::Command::InvalidArguments
    );
    string cd(
      in string dir
    )
    raises(
      ::Command::InvalidArguments
    );
    string pwd();
    long echoLong(
      in long val
    );
    string echoString(
      in string str
    );
```

```
  };
};
interface CommandServer {
  string login_string(
    in string username,
    in string password
  );
  any login_any(
    in string username,
    in string password
  );
};
-> a MyRep.idl
Saving to:  MyRep.idl
The IR was saved to:  MyRep.idl
-> q
Quitting...
```

Both IDL files are now resident in the IR. The following command registers the IR with the object activation daemon supplying the appropriate command-line arguments. This example assumes you have VisiBroker installed in the default location (`C:\Visigenic\vbroker`).

```
oadutil reg -i Repository -o MyRep -cpp
 C:\Visigenic\vbroker\bin\irep.bat -a MyRep.idl
Completed registration of repository_id    =    IDL:Repository:1.0
object_name       =    MyRep
reference data    =
path_name         =    C:\Visigenic\vbroker\bin\irep.bat
activation_policy =    SHARED_SERVER
args              =    (length=1)[MyRep.idl; ]
env               =    NONE
for OAD on host 1.1.1.1
```

You must make sure the file MyRep.idl is in the directory where irep is spawned. The irep application must be able to locate this file, or you can specify an absolute pathname.

Dynamic Invocation Interface

So far in this chapter, we have discussed the IR. Working with the IR is a necessary prerequisite to using the Dynamic Invocation Interface (DII). This part of the chapter leads you through a definition of the Dynamic Invocation Interface, providing a basis for understanding which applications may be candidates for the DII. It also discusses the four steps in using the DII and provides an example of a client that uses the DII to create and invoke requests on a CORBA server.

What Is the Dynamic Invocation Interface?

The Dynamic Invocation Interface (DII) is a client-side application-programming interface used for accessing the low-level CORBA objects and methods, which are in turn used in communication requests to a CORBA server. The IDL compiler generates for you a client stub that wraps all of the low level calls in a convenient object-oriented interface on a per-server basis. The client stub mechanism is referred to as the Static Invocation Interface. The limitation with the Static Invocation Interface occurs when dealing with evolving servers or servers that try to provide additional functionality over their development life cycle.

Consider our `Command::CommandSession` interface from the previous sections (refer to Listing 7-1). You can see that this interface provides basic functionality for listing directory structures. While this is a nice interface for our example, suppose that you wish to add new functionality to "cat" a file to the client window. In the Static Invocation Interface you would need to add an IDL function, for example:

```
string cat(in string filename);
```

You would then implement this function in your server implementation. This is the file `CommandSession.cpp` in our example. The candidate function implementation might look like the following:

```
char * CommandSession_i::cat(const char * filename)
{
  cout << "cat " << filename << endl;
  // We are not passing cmd across CORBA
  // It is only used internally. So using
  // malloc here is ok.
  char *cmd = (char *)malloc(4 + strlen(filename) + 1);
  strcpy(cmd, "cat ");
  strcat(cmd, filename);
  char *out = command(cmd);
  cout << out << endl;
  free(cmd);
  return out;
}
```

After rebuilding your server you are ready to go. But what about the client? Using the Static Invocation Interface, you must add functionality to the client to call session → cat()to recompile the client because the IDL file has changed. Now think of all the deployed clients you may have. You must distribute the new client executable to all those sites or you will have many angry users.

In the Dynamic Invocation Interface, it is the client that discovers what methods are available on a given server. The client manages creation and invocation of the requests sent to the server. If we add the cat functionality to the server from my example, the client would not need to be changed at all. The client does not even need to be recompiled! In fact, during development of this server example we added the **echoLong** and **echoString** functions to the server and did not recompile the client. You are free to extend this interface to add whatever commands you deem necessary in your environment, and you should not have to expand the client at all.

Client Considerations

Which applications are good candidates for using the Dynamic Invocation Interface? Generally there are two considerations. The client and the client developer must have the following knowledge.

◆ Reasonable knowledge of the server functionality.

◆ Reasonable knowledge of the server interface convention.

What do we mean by reasonable knowledge? You need to know what the server is supposed to do and how the high level functionality of the server will be provided. Consider a DII client written to connect to a banking server. Obviously, you would not expect this client to work when connected to a server that serves HTML pages. Knowledge of the server interface convention is more detailed and concrete, perhaps supplied as a draft of the IDL specification. Most of this information should be readily available once design of the server has been completed.

The user can also supply reasonable knowledge of the server functionality, whether this is a person, or another application that is a client of our DII client. The amount of information needed will vary on a server by server basis.

In this example, reasonable knowledge of the target server consists of the following points of information:You can get a Command::CommandSession object from the CommandServer interface (see Listing 7-4).

◆ The CommandSession server supports command-line oriented functionality.

◆ Each command represents a separate operation in the CommandSession interface.

◆ Return values are appropriate to operating system commands; for example, return values are printable and no CORBA objects are used as return values.

These are fairly straightforward statements. In addition, draft **Command:: CommandSession** and **ComandServer** servers were created. The **Command:: CommandSession** server provided the cd and pwd functionality only. With this knowledge, we created the DII client for the **Command::CommandSession** interface.

A few more comments on the **CommandServer** interface are necessary at this point. We discuss more about why the **CommandServer** exists later in this chapter. First, the **CommandServer** is intended to provide the central debarkation point for creating and administering **Command::CommandSession** objects. You can see that **CommandServer** provides the login functionality. This is where user authentication should be provided, as well as other system administrative functions relating to providing remote operating system access. For example, it is useful to have an operation on the **CommandServer** that displays all the users who have active **Command::CommandSession** objects.

Listing 7-4 CommandServer IDL

```
interface CommandServer
{
// Returns a string object reference to a
// CommandSession
    string    login_string(in string username,
                                in string password);
// Returns a CORBA::Any object reference to a
// CommandSession

    any       login_any(in string username,
in string password);
};
```

The **CommandServer** does not actually provide any password protection. You are free to add whatever support you deem necessary. A clean object destruction mechanism was not implemented either. Objects left from previous clients may be available for mischievous clients to bind to directly without logging in.

The Four Steps to Making a Dynamic Invocation Interface

In this section, we discuss the four steps needed to write clients that use the Dynamic Invocation Interface. When performed in order, these steps enable a client to invoke an operation on a remote server without the client stub support.

- ◆ Obtain a CORBA::Object reference
- ◆ Create and populate a CORBA::Request object
- ◆ Invoke the CORBA::Request operation
- ◆ Get the results of the request

Each of these steps is described in detail in the next four sections. For now, let us look at the process from a high level perspective. There are several CORBA-compliant ways to accomplish each of these steps. The following diagram, Figure 7-5, illustrates the overall process in relation to the example application.

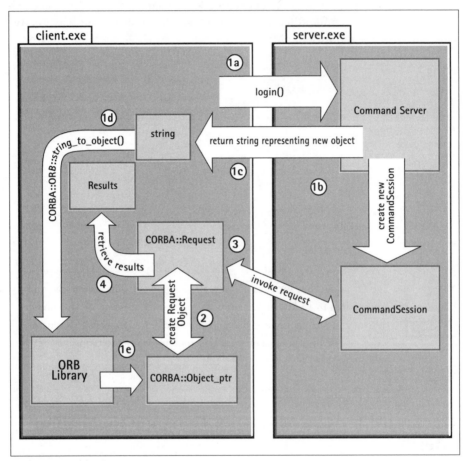

Figure 7-5: High –Level View of the DII Process

You see from this diagram that step one involves invoking the login_string() operation on the CommandServer. The CommandServer instantiates a new Command::CommandSession object and invokes the ORB function object_to_string(). The CommandServer passes back this stringified object reference. The client then invokes the ORB to convert this string reference to an actual CORBA::Object_ptr. Once we have a CORBA::Object_ptr, we can create a CORBA::Request object and populate it. Calling one of the invoke methods of the CORBA::Request object sends the remote invocation to the Command::CommandSession object. When the invocation has returned, you can interrogate the CORBA::Request object to obtain the results.

Before we examine these steps in detail, let us revisit our client main loop, shown in Listing 7-5. Again, the full source listing may be found on the companion CD. The special cases examined earlier have been omitted. You can see the structure of the main loop follows the four-step method. We use four functions: login(), create_request(), invoke_request(), and process_results() to illustrate the four steps. We have made every effort to make this application robust enough to handle a variety of errors. At every step we check the return value to ensure that we can continue. We expect the return value from login() to produce a valid CORBA::Object. If it does not we simply exit as there is nothing more that can be done. We expect create_request() to return a non-nil CORBA::Request object. We use CORBA::Request::_nil() as a return value to indicate an error condition. If we do get a CORBA::Request::_nil() return value, we punt the current request and wait for new user input. Lastly, invoke_request() returns the return value of the CORBA::Request object. This is a CORBA::Any object. If this value is CORBA::Any::_nil(), we assume an error occurred and do not process the return results. Each of these four functions will print error messages to stdout indicating the cause of the error. In the following sections, pay special attention to all of the error checking. Developers of Distributed Object Systems must provide a lot of error checking to provide robust clients to their user community.

Listing 7-5 Client Main Loop

```
int main(int argc, char** argv)
{
  orb = CORBA::ORB_init(argc, argv);
  parse_command_line(argc, argv);
  //
  // login() is where we will talk about
  // step 1 - obtaining a generic object reference
  //
  CORBA::Object_ptr session;
  session = login(ProgramOptions.hostname,
                         ProgramOptions.connectMethod);
  //
  // The main command loop where we will accept user
  // commands and send them on to the server
  //
  while (1)
  {
    .
    .
    //
    // create_request() is where we will talk about
    // step 3 - creating and populating a CORBA::Request
    //
    CORBA::Request_ptr request;
    request = create_request(session, cmdline,
```

```
ProgramOptions.createMethod);
    if ( request == CORBA::Request::_nil() )
    {
       continue;
    }
    //
    // invoke_request() is where we will talk about
    // step 4 - invoking the request
    //
    CORBA::Any_ptr response;
    response = invoke_request(session, request);
    if ( response == CORBA::Any::_nil() )
    {
       continue;
    }
    //
    // process_response() is where we will talk about
    // step 5 - receiving the response
    process_response(session, request);
  }
  return 1;
}
```

The following sections describe several methods for doing the different steps. You can control the behavior of the client with command-line options. The -? option will print the usage message. Refer to the following output for details on the command-line switches.

```
C:\>client -?
client [options] [hostname]
-s - resolve using string_to_object()
-o - create list using create_operation_list()
-l - create list using own NVList()
-i - request using invoke()
-d - request using send_deferred()
-v - verbose output
```

STEP ONE — OBTAIN AN OBJECT REFERENCE

In the last chapter you saw two ways to get a CORBA::Object reference. Both involved knowing the exact type of the object and having the client stub. In this section we need to obtain an object reference which is essentially untyped. What we are after is an object of type CORBA::Object. There are essentially two ways to do this. The first is to pass back a stringified object reference and use the function CORBA::ORB::string_to_object() to convert the string to an object reference on the client side. The second is to return an object of type CORBA::Any. Now, let's look at the login functions supplied by the **CommandServer** implementation.

Listing 7-6 Server side login functions

```
char *
CommandServer_i::login_string(const char * username,
const char * password)
{
   printf("Received login request for user = %s\n", username);
   CommandSession_i* session = new CommandSession_i(username);
   CommandSession_i::_duplicate(session);
   _boa()->obj_is_ready(session);
   return CORBA::ORB_init()->object_to_string(session);
}
CORBA::Any_ptr
CommandServer_i::login_any(const char * username, const char *
 password)
{
   printf("Received login request for user = %s\n", username);
   CommandSession_i* session = new CommandSession_i(username);
   CommandSession_i::_duplicate(session);
   _boa()->obj_is_ready(session);
   //
   // Convert to a generic object reference
   //
   CORBA::ORB_var orb = CORBA::ORB_init();
   CORBA::Object_ptr pObj =
      orb->string_to_object(orb->object_to_string(session));
   CORBA::Object::_duplicate(pObj);
   CORBA::Any_ptr any = new CORBA::Any();
   any->replace(CORBA::_tc_Object, pObj);
   return any;
}
```

The first function login_string() uses the CORBA::ORB::string_to_object()
method to convert the **Command::CommandSession** implementation object
instance to a string representation. The second function uses string_to_object() and
object_to_string() to convert the **Command::CommandSession** implementation to
a reference to CORBA::Object. The reference is then duplicated and passed back to
the client. The client side login() function is shown in Listing 7-6.

Listing 7-6 Client side login functions

```
CORBA::Object_ptr
login(const char *hostname, ConnectionMethod connectMethod)
{
  //
  // Bind to a server on the requested host
  //
  CommandServer_ptr server;
  try
  {
      server = CommandServer::_bind();
  }
```

```cpp
    catch (const CORBA::Exception& excep) {
        cout << "Unable to bind to server on host "
<< hostname << endl;
        cout << excep << endl;
        exit(1);
    }
    //
    // Let the user know we connected
    //
    const char *object_name = server->_object_name();
    const char *interface_name = server->_interface_name();
    const char *repository_id = server->_repository_id();
    object_name = object_name ? object_name : "Unknown";
    interface_name = interface_name ? interface_name : "Unknown";
    repository_id = repository_id ? repository_id : "Unknown";
    cout << "Connected to CommandServer " << object_name << endl
        << " through interface " << interface_name << endl
        << " with repository id " << repository_id
        << endl << endl;
    //
    // Start the login sequence
    //
    char username[255];
    char password[255];
    cout << "login: ";
    cin.getline(username, 255, '\n');
    sprintf(password, "*");
    CORBA::Object_ptr session;
    switch (connectMethod)
    {
      case StringToObjectMethod:
      {
        if (ProgramOptions.verbose)
          cout << "Connecting with" "StringToObjectMethod" << endl;
        char *sessionString;
        try
        {
          sessionString = server->login_string((const char *)username,
                          (const char *)password);
        }
        catch (const CORBA::Exception& excep)
        {
          cout << "Unable to login to server" << endl;
          cout << excep << endl;
          exit(1);
        }
        //
        // Convert the string to an object reference
        //
        session = orb->string_to_object(sessionString);
        //
        // Check to see we have a valid session
        //
```

```
      if (CORBA::is_nil(session))
      {
        cout << "Server returned bad session" << endl;
        exit(1);
      }
    }
    break;
    case TypeAnyMethod:
    {
      if (ProgramOptions.verbose)
        cout << "Connecting with TypeAnyMethod" << endl;
      CORBA::Any_ptr any;
      try
      {
        any = server->login_any((const char *)username,
                                (const char *)password);
      }
      catch (const CORBA::Exception& excep)
      {
        cout << "Unable to login to server" << endl;
        cout << excep << endl;
        exit(1);
      }
      session = *(CORBA::Object_ptr *)any->value();
    }
    break;
    default:
    cout << "Unsupported connection method" << endl;
          exit(1);
  }
  server->_release();
  return session;
}
```

Notice the error checking which is performed in this function. Try-catch blocks bracket all calls to the remote server. As you saw in the last section, almost anything can go wrong in a call to a remote server. In addition, the CORBA to C++ mapping makes heavy use of the try-catch-throw mechanism. We also check that the return value from CORBA::ORB::string_to_object() is not CORBA::Object::_nil(). This method does not throw exceptions, but instead uses a _nil() return value. Another method of obtaining a generic object reference is to use the function CORBA::ORB::resolve_initial_references(). This function takes an interface name as a string value and returns a CORBA::Object reference to a server of this type. This would not be appropriate in this example because we wish to control the creation and distribution of **Command::CommandSession** objects.

Many dissimilarities have been noticed in ORB vendors' support for obtaining generic object references. We were unable to verify the CORBA::Any return method would work on all ORBs.

In addition to the two methods cited above, VisiBroker provides a nonstandard extension to the CORBA::ORB class to obtain a generic object reference. VisiBroker defines a method called CORBA::ORB :: bind() which may be used to bind to an object by the string definition of its interface. This should not be confused with the return value of CORBA::ORB::object_to_string(). CORBA::ORB::object_to_string() returns a string which represents a particular instance of an object. However, this methodology would not be suitable for this example. You don't want clients to bind directly to **CommandSession** objects without going through the **CommandServer** interface.You have seen how to obtain a generic object reference in this section. The next section shows how to create and populate a dynamic request.

STEP TWO – CREATING AND POPULATING A REQUEST
The next step to creating a dynamic request is to create and populate a CORBA::Request object. Creating and populating the CORBA::Request object actually involves two objects that are intricately related. The first is a CORBA::NVList, which represents the parameters passed to the operation. The second is the CORBA::Request object itself.

A CORBA::NVList is a list of CORBA::NamedValue objects. A CORBA::NamedValue object, as its name implies, consists of a string name and a CORBA::Any object as the value. CORBA::Any objects represent values of any type. They have a discriminator to determine the type of the value, and member functions to retrieve the value, which the programmer must then cast to the appropriate type.

Two different ways exist to create the CORBA::NVList object.

- Use CORBA::ORB::create_list() to create a CORBA::NVList. Use the CORBA::NVList::add(), CORBA::NVList::add_value() or CORBA::NVList::add_item() methods to add NamedValue objects to the list.

- Use CORBA::ORB::create_operations_list() to create a presized, pretyped CORBA::NVList. Retrieve the CORBA::Any objects which represent the values and use CORBA::Any::replace() to change the value.

We look at both of these methods for creating a suitable CORBA::NVList. In this example, you can specify the method the client will use to create the CORBA::NVList by specifying either the -1 or -o options on the client command line.

To create the CORBA::Request object we use CORBA::Object::create_request() operation. Alternately you can use the CORBA::ORB::create_request() operation. CORBA deliberately does not define constructors for the CORBA::Request class. The CORBA specification dictates that a client must use one of these two methods to create a request object. The reason for this lies in the underlying implementation of the CORBA::Request class and its tie to the CORBA::Object class.

Creating and populating the request is by far the most code intensive part of the Dynamic Invocation Interface. Listing 7-7 shows the first method of creating the CORBA::NVList object. The first order of business when creating a request is to get the definition of the target operation. Consult the IR to find the OperationDef object for the target operation. The following list covers the steps involved in this task.

1. Get the InterfaceDef object via a call to CORBA::Object::get_interface().I discussed this before when traversing the IR.

2. Use the CORBA::Container::lookup_name() operation to retrieve a sequence of CORBA::Contained objects which match the method name the user typed on the command line. Note that you can limit which CORBA::Contained objects are returned from this function by specifying the enumeration value CORBA::dk_Operation. Other enumeration values exist to limit the search to other types.

3. Check to see that you got one and only one OperationDef returned in the sequence and that the OperationDef is not nil.

Now that you have an OperationDef object you can pass it to the ORB. The function CORBA::ORB::create_operation_list() will return an appropriately sized CORBA::NVList object. Each of the CORBA::NamedValue objects in the list has its name member set and its CORBA::Any object member value appropriately typed. The last step in this method is to set the values in the CORBA::NVList object. The assign_value() function takes the string argument specified on the command line, converts it to the type specified by the CORBA::Any object, and assigns the value to the CORBA::Any object. We discuss more about typing CORBA::Any objects later in the section "Type Checking in a Dynamic Invocation Interface Application."

Listing 7-7 create_request() using create_operation_list()

```
CORBA::Request_ptr
create_request(CORBA::Object_ptr obj, char *command_line,
CreateMethod req_method)
{
  CORBA::Request_var request;
  CORBA::Request_ptr pRequest;
  char *p, *q, *op;
  op = p = q = command_line;
  q = next_arg(p);
  //
```

```
// In any case we really need the OperationDef to type check
// the arguments
//
CORBA::InterfaceDef_var pInterface = obj->_get_interface();
if ( pInterface == CORBA::InterfaceDef::_nil() )
{
    cout << "_get_interface() failed" << endl;
    cout << "Is your InterfaceRepository running?" << endl;
    cout << "Is the " << obj->_repository_id()
<< " interface registered?" << endl;
    return CORBA::Request::_nil();
}
CORBA::ContainedSeq_var pContained
  = pInterface->lookup_name(p, 1,
(CORBA_DefinitionKind)CORBA::dk_Operation,
FALSE);
if ( pContained->length() == 0 )
{
    cout << "CORBA::InterfaceDef::lookup_name()"
<< " returned zero Contained objects" << endl;
    return CORBA::Request::_nil();
}
if ( pContained->length() > 1 )
{
    cout << "CORBA::InterfaceDef::lookup_name()"
<< " returned more than one item" << endl;
    return CORBA::Request::_nil();
}
CORBA::OperationDef_var pOperation
= CORBA::OperationDef::_narrow(pContained[(CORBA::ULong )0]);
if ( pOperation == CORBA::OperationDef::_nil() )
{
    cout << "CORBA::InterfaceDef::lookup_name()"
<< " did not find an OperationDef for " << p << endl;
    return CORBA::Request::_nil();
}
//
// Now create an NVList to add to the Request
//
CORBA::NVList_ptr pList;
switch (req_method)
{
  case CreateOperationList:
  {
    if (ProgramOptions.verbose)
      cout << "Creating List with CreateOperationList" << endl;
    CORBA::NVList_var operation_list;
    orb->create_operation_list(pOperation, operation_list.out());
    pList = CORBA::NVList::_duplicate(operation_list);
    for ( int i = 0; i < operation_list->count(); i++ )
    {
      CORBA::Any_ptr value;
      value = operation_list->item(i)->value();
```

```
        p = q;
        if ( p == NULL )
        {
          cout << "Not enough args passed on command line" << endl;
          return CORBA::Request::_nil();
        }
        q = next_arg(p);
        //
        // assign_value is where we will talk about the CORBA::Any
        // object and client side type checking
        //
        if ( ! assign_value(value, p) )
        {
          return CORBA::Request::_nil();
        }
      }
    }
    break;
    case CreateList:
    {
    .
    code omitted
    .
    }
    break;
  }

  //
  // Initialize the return type
  //
  CORBA::NamedValue_var result;
  orb->create_named_value(result.out());
  CORBA::NamedValue_ptr pResult
          = CORBA::NamedValue::_duplicate(result);
  CORBA::TypeCode_ptr    pTypeCode = pOperation->result();
  CORBA::Any_ptr         pResultValue = pResult->value();
  pResultValue->replace( pTypeCode, pResultValue );
  obj->_create_request(CORBA::Context::_nil(),
                       op,
                       pList,
                       result,
                       request.out(),
                       0);
  pRequest = CORBA::Request::_duplicate(request);
  return pRequest;
}
```

Once you have completed building the CORBA::NVList object, you have one more thing to do before creating the request object. You must initialize the return value. You tell the request and the server what type of return value you expect. Again, you get this information from the OperationDef object. If the return value is incorrectly initialized, the subsequent invocation of the request causes the ORB to throw an exception. Use the operation CORBA::ORB::create_named_value() to create a CORBA::NamedValue object. The name member of the NamedValue object is not used by the return mechanism in the ORB and may be left uninitialized. However, the type of the CORBA::Any must be set. Use the CORBA::Any::replace() to set the type.

In the example, both methods of creating the CORBA::NVList object ultimately use the same operation to create the CORBA::Request object. The operation CORBA::Object::create_request() takes the string name of the operation, the parameter list, and the result to create the request object. At this point you are done creating our CORBA::Request object.

Listing 7-8 shows the second method for creating the CORBA::Request object. Using this method go back to the CORBA::InterfaceDef::FullInterfaceDescription structure to get the information for building the parameter list. Traverse the list just as shown in decode_interface() to find the **OperationDescription** structure for the target operation. If you find it, call CORBA::ORB::create_list to create an empty CORBA::NVList. By traversing each of the parameters you can construct CORBA::Any objects to represent each of the parameters for the operation. First set the type using CORBA::Any::replace() (remember we will talk more about CORBA::Any objects later). Again use the assign_value() function to set the value. Next, you translate the enumeration value of type CORBA:: ParameterMode to a constant value defined in the CORBA name space. Finally, you may add the value to the list by specifying its name, value, and mode. The rest of the function is identical to the previous method.

Listing 7-8 create_request using create_list()

```
CORBA::Request_ptr
create_request(CORBA::Object_ptr obj, char *command_line,
CreateMethod req_method)
{
  .
  .
  .
  switch (req_method)
  {
  .
  .
  .
  case CreateList:
  {
    if (ProgramOptions.verbose)
    cout << "Creating List with CreateList" << endl;
    CORBA::InterfaceDef::FullInterfaceDescription_var fid;
    fid = pInterface->describe_interface();
    unsigned int i, j, opIndex = -1;
    for ( i = 0; i < fid->operations.length(); i++ )
    {
      if ( !strcmp(fid->operations[i].name, op) )
        opIndex = i;
    }
```

```
      if ( opIndex == -1 )
      {
        cout << "Unable to find operation in FullInterfaceDescription"
<< endl;
        return CORBA::Request::_nil();
      }
      CORBA::NVList_ptr list;
      orb->create_list(0, list);
      pList = list;
      for ( j = 0;
            j < fid->operations[opIndex].parameters.length(); j++ )
      {
        CORBA::Any_ptr any = new CORBA::Any();
        any->replace(fid->operations[opIndex].parameters[j].type,
                      any);
        p = q;
        if ( p == NULL )
        {
          cout << "Not enough args passed on command line" << endl;
          return CORBA::Request::_nil();
        }
        q = next_arg(p);
        //
        // assign_value is where we will talk about the CORBA::Any
        // object and client side type checking
        //
        if ( ! assign_value(any, p) )
        {
          return CORBA::Request::_nil();
        }
        CORBA::Long mode = CORBA::ARG_IN;;
        switch (fid->operations[opIndex].parameters[j].mode)
        {
          // CORBA::PARAM_IN etc. are defined in
          // CORBA::InterfaceDef::FullInterfaceDescription
          //           ::ParameterDef::ParameterMode.
          case CORBA::PARAM_IN:
            mode = CORBA::ARG_IN;
            break;
          case CORBA::PARAM_OUT:
            mode = CORBA::ARG_OUT;
            break;
          case CORBA::PARAM_INOUT:
            mode = CORBA::ARG_INOUT;
            break;
        }
        list->add_value(fid->operations[opIndex].parameters[j].name,
                                          *any, mode);
      }
      pList = list;
    }
  break;
```

```
    .
    .
    .
}
    .
    .
    .
}
```

STEP THREE – INVOKING THE REQUEST

The last section showed how to create a dynamic request. Now we will show how to invoke this request on the server. It should come as no surprise to find that there are multiple ways of invoking the request. We will discuss all of the methods and show two of the most common. The invocation methods can be divided into two categories, synchronous and deferred synchronous. Synchronous requests block the caller until the server returns. Deferred synchronous requests do not block the caller, but provide both blocking and non-blocking functions to check on the return status.

The singular synchronous invocation is supplied by the CORBA::Request object. This method is CORBA::Request::invoke(). Here the caller blocks until the server is finished processing the request and passes back the return value. The client is free to examine the results at this point and delete the request.

Three deferred synchronous requests are supplied by CORBA.

♦ CORBA::Request::send_oneway()This method instructs the ORB to send the request and return immediately. The operation should not be using any out or inout parameters.

♦ CORBA::ORB::send_deferred()This method tells the ORB to send the request and return immediately. The server will process the requests and send the result back to the ORB where it may be picked up later. The request object provides functions to facilitate the retrieval of the results.

♦ CORBA::ORB::send_multiple_requests_deferred() This method instructs the ORB to send multiple request objects to the server at once. The function returns immediately. The client may use the same functions mentioned previously to check on the status and get the return values of the invocation.

The next section discusses the operations to retrieve deferred synchronous results in depth.

Listing 7-9 shows two methods for performing invocations. The first method is the CORBA::Request::invoke() operation. This operation blocks until the server finishes processing the request. When this method returns, the result parameter has been populated with the return value. The synchronous method requires checking the request object for exceptions before proceeding. The second method calls CORBA::ORB::send_deferred() which takes as a parameter the CORBA::Request object. Because the request has not yet fully been serviced, checking the exception member is superfluous.

Listing 7-9 invoke_method() function

```
CORBA::Any_ptr
invoke_request(CORBA::Object_ptr obj, CORBA::Request_ptr request)
{
  try
  {
    switch (ProgramOptions.requestMethod)
    {
      case Invoke:
        if (ProgramOptions.verbose)
          cout << "Invoking request with invoke()" << endl;
        request->invoke();
        break;
      case SendDefered:
        if (ProgramOptions.verbose)
          cout << "Invoking request with send_deferred()" << endl;

          request->send_deferred();
        break;
    }
  }
  catch (const CORBA::Exception& excep)
  {
    cout << "Error invoking request" << endl;
    cout << excep << endl;
    return CORBA::Any::_nil();
  }
  CORBA::Environment_ptr pEnv = request->env();
  if ( pEnv->exception() )
  {
    cout << "Exception in request" << endl;
    cout << *(pEnv->exception()) << endl;
    return CORBA::Any::_nil();
  }
  return request->result()->value();
}
```

Use the result value as a signal to the main loop to determine if you should continue processing this request. If there was an exception on the synchronous invocation, the value should be nil. Because the return result was initialized to a non-nil value in the deferred case, it should still be intact.

STEP FOUR – GETTING A RESPONSE
So far you have created a request and sent the invocation to the server. In the synchronous case the return value is already set. In the deferred synchronous case you

must still retrieve the result. There are two functions for checking the status of a deferred invocation.

◆ **CORBA::Request::poll_response()** This function asks the request object if the server has returned yet. It returns true if it has and false otherwise.

◆ **CORBA::Request::get_response()** This function blocks until the server does return. A client can use this function when it has finished doing parallel tasks and wants to wait to get the result from a remote invocation.

In addition, when the function CORBA::ORB::send_multiple_requests_deferred() is used, the functions CORBA::ORB::poll_next_response() and CORBA::ORB::get_next_response() provide the equivalent functionality as poll_response and get_response respectively. Even if the client used the send_multiple_requests_deferred() function it can still call poll_response() and get_next_response() on the individual request objects in the list.

The example calls CORBA::Request::get_response() so the process blocks until the server returns. Obviously, no parallel task must be performed. the results from the deferred invocation are returned, the process can continue to handle the result.

Listing 7-9 process_response()

```
void
process_response(CORBA::Object_ptr obj, CORBA::Request_ptr request)
{
  try
  {
    switch (ProgramOptions.requestMethod)
    {
      case Invoke:
        break;
      case SendDefered:
        //
        // Use get_response() so we block until we
        // get an answer. Use poll_response()
        // to check without blocking.
        //
        request->get_response();
        break;
    }
  }
  catch (const CORBA::Exception& excep)
  {
    cout << "Error invoking request" << endl;
    cout << excep << endl;
    return;
  }
  CORBA::Environment_ptr pEnv = request->env();
```

```
if ( pEnv->exception() )
{
  cout << "Exception in request" << endl;
  cout << *(pEnv->exception()) << endl;
  return;
}
//
// Everything looks good lets try to print.
// Here is a preview of the CORBA::Any class.
//
CORBA::Any_ptr value = request->result()->value();
switch (value->type()->kind())
{
case CORBA::tk_string:
  {
    char *returnVal = *(char **)value->value();
    cout << returnVal << endl;
  }
  break;
case CORBA::tk_long:
  {
    CORBA::Long returnVal = *(CORBA::Long *)value->value();
    cout << returnVal << endl;
    break;
  }
default:
  cout << "This client cannot receive args of type "
<< value->type()->kind() << endl;
  }
  return;
}
```

The final task deals with printing the results. We start discussing   the CORBA::Any object here and finish in the next section, "Type Checking in a DII Application." First, retrieve the CORBA::Any object, which represents the value of the result using the statement:

```
CORBA::Any_ptr value = request->result()->value();
```

The function CORBA::Request::result() returns the CORBA::NamedValue object that was previously initialized. This object has been populated by the ORB with the return value of the remote invocation. The function CORBA::NamedValue::value() returns the CORBA::Any object which represents the value of the NamedValue. The example does not handle all possible return values, although the switch statement could easily be extended to handle all types – even references to CORBA::Objects.

Once you have the value, use the following statement to determine the type of the returned result.

```
switch (value->type()->kind())
```

Based on this type convert the value appropriately and print it to the terminal. The next section continues the discussion of the CORBA::Any and CORBA::TypeCode objects.

Type Checking in a Dynamic Invocation Interface Application

The previous section briefly introduced type checking as it related to retrieving return values. In this section, we continue discussion of the type checking facilities provided by CORBA in the CORBA::Any and CORBA::TypeCode objects. The CORBA::Any object is a wrapper around a single value. It contains, as an attribute, a CORBA::TypeCode object that defines the type of the enclosed value. This total package provides an easy and type-safe mechanism to pass parameters and return values.

Previously, we mentioned the client's assign_value() function. This function is detailed in Listing 7-10. This function accepts as arguments a pointer to a CORBA::Any object and a string value to assign to the CORBA::Any. Before invoking this function, the caller must ensure that the CORBA::TypeCode object is properly set.. In creating the request, the type is set based on information stored in the OperationDef object, or by using the type that was set by the call to CORBA::ORB::create_operation_list(). To set the type manually we used the following line of code:

```
any->replace(fid->operations[opIndex].parameters[j].type, any);
```

With the type code properly set, you can then invoke the assign_value() function with one of the arguments supplied on the command line.

Listing 7-10 Using the CORBA::Any object in the assign_value function

```
CORBA::Boolean
assign_value(CORBA::Any_ptr any, const char *arg)
{
   switch (any->type()->kind())
   {
   case CORBA::tk_string:
        *any <<= arg;
        break;
   case CORBA::tk_long:
        {
            CORBA::Long i = atoi(arg);
            *any <<= i;
            break;
        }
   default:
        cout << "This client cannot send args of type "
<< any->type()->kind() << endl;
```

```
        return FALSE;
    }
    return TRUE;
}
```

The switch statement accesses the **CORBA::TypeCode** object and invokes the CORBA::TypeCode::kind() operation. The return type of the CORBA::TypeCode::kind() function call is **CORBA::TCKind**. **CORBA::TCKind** is an enumeration where each of the IDL primitive types including references to **CORBA::Objects** are defined. Refer to the documentation or the header files supplied with your ORB to obtain a complete list of enumeration values. Becoming familiar with all the possible types now can save headaches later.

By providing a case statement for each of these types, we are able to supply code to convert from the command-line string representation to an appropriate type defined by CORBA. Notice that we have also included the default case. It would be poor programming etiquette if you did not inform the user that you could not convert values to the target type. As you saw in the return value example of the last section, it is an easy task to write additional case statements to handle all types defined by CORBA.

Summary

This chapter has described the mechanisms to create and invoke a dynamic request on a remote server without having the client-side stub. The example could be even more robust by providing all type checking cases on both the sending and receiving sides. By providing this functionality you could conceivably write a DII client to drive any interface from the command line. Of course, the login code would need to be modified to bind to any object type.

This chapter gives you a solid foundation for developing your own DII clients. In designing and developing DII client applications you should remember several points.

- ◆ DII client applications are clients of the IR, although you may not bind directly to the IR.

- ◆ DII clients must be able to get a generic reference to a CORBA::Object.

- ◆ The target interface must be registered with an IR.

- ◆ The developer of a DII client must have reasonable knowledge of the target server.

Armed with this knowledge, you can write robust client applications that take advantage of servers whose interfaces are enhanced over time.

Chapter 8

Multithreaded CORBA Servers

IN THIS CHAPTER

This chapter discusses the different types of threading models that may be used to create multithreaded CORBA servers, beginning with an overview of multithreaded programming and focusing on the threading package provided by the Windows95/NT operating system. However, most operating systems will provide similar support. We discuss the creation, destruction, and management of threads. Once we have shown how to multithread an application, we show a shared counter example that illustrates one of the pitfalls of multithreaded programming: competition for resources. Next, we discuss the basic objects and functions used to synchronize thread execution. In this section, we update the shared counter example to allow multiple threads to use the counter safely without interfering with one another.

- ◆ Multithreading overview

- ◆ Thread management

- ◆ Thread synchronization

- ◆ Multithreaded CORBA counter

- ◆ Server threading models

- ◆ Connection management

- ◆ Multithreaded example

THE NEXT MAJOR SECTION of this chapter shows the shared counter as a CORBA object. We present the server and show the build options needed to build multithreaded CORBA servers. From this example, we discuss five threading models commonly used to build CORBA servers. In our last major topic, we discuss connection management.

We conclude this chapter by applying the principles discussed to a more programmatically complex example. We look at a functionally rudimentary document control server, discuss how to apply multithreading strategies to the design, and give our reasoning for choosing a particular multithreading model. We also discuss connection management policies and other multithreading considerations as applied to this example.

Multithreading Overview

In this section, we give an overview of multithreading programming techniques. We begin with a definition of multithreading, followed by a discussion of the Windows95/NT threading package. We discuss the creation, destruction, and management of threads. We conclude this section with a discussion of thread synchronization.

If you have never written a multithreaded application, this chapter provides you with all the tools you need to begin writing solid multithreaded applications. If you are already familiar with multithreaded programming, you can skim the next few sections as a refresher, before moving on to the section entitled "Multithreaded CORBA Counter."

What Is Multithreading?

A few years ago, multitasking was all the buzz. An operating system that could perform more than one task at a time was a novel concept. A multitasking operating system enables you to use your spreadsheet application while your word processor is printing your document in the background. The operating system takes care of scheduling the application's use of the CPU, so every application gets a few milliseconds at a time to do its work. Humans are inherently multitasking. We are constantly doing more than one thing at once. We drive our cars to work in the morning while listening to the radio and thinking about all the work that must be done during the day. Our brains take care of managing the resources necessary to carry out these tasks.

Multithreading is nothing more than multitasking within a single application. The programmer needn't worry about scheduling the threads for execution, however. The operating system takes care of the scheduling for you.

A *process* is an instance of a running executable consisting of a private virtual address space, code, data (that is, global variables, and stack frames), and system resources (that is, files handles, pipes, and windows). A *thread* is a path of execution through the process's code segment. Most programmers are already familiar with single-threaded programs. A *single-threaded program* consists of a single path of execution through the code. The program executes from start to finish following a particular logical path. A *multithreaded program* consists of multiple concurrent paths of execution through a process's code segment. The single process performs multiple tasks simultaneously. These tasks may be different instances of the same task or a mixture of different tasks. Note, the thread is the smallest unit used by the operating system to schedule CPU time.

A thread is often described as a lightweight process. Threads within a process share the address space, code, data, and system resources. This sharing of data and resources allows the threads to communicate and synchronize their actions. We will discuss synchronization in the section "Multithreading Synchronization." Some operating systems, including Windows 95/NT, provide a mechanism to maintain a set of data local to a thread, which may be retrieved using a thread identifier or some other such index. Typically, there is one heap all threads share and there are multiple stacks, one per thread. For example, let's look at a typical Figure 8-1 shows an example of what may occur in a typical word processor at any given time. We can see a thread accepts user input from the keyboard. These events are translated into modifications of the data, which represents the document. A request is generated for a different thread to paint the screen as a result of these modifications. In the background, another thread is preparing to print the document and spooling the request to the print queue.

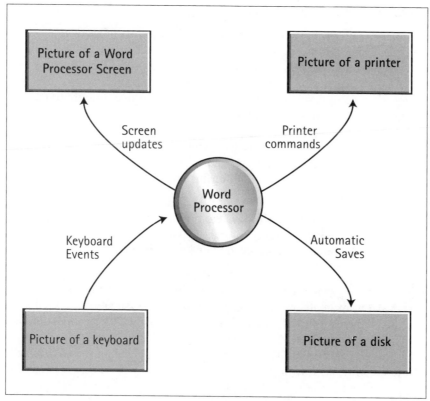

Figure 8-1: Multithreading in a Word Processor

Depending on the application, multithreading may have different benefits. The following are a few of the potential benefits that may be gained by multithreading your application.

♦ **Concurrency.** Applications providing services that block during execution, while waiting on system resources or system functions can achieve greater throughput by allowing other tasks to execute while the system wait occurs.

♦ **Parallelism.** Applications that perform multiple, independent tasks can achieve a better response time when thread priorities are managed properly. Consider an application that receives input (for example, a keyboard, mouse, or event channel), provides feedback (for example, paint a window or send events to a device), and performs some processing (for example, process an event received on the input channel). This application could benefit from multithreading by allowing each of these tasks to be performed in a separate thread.

♦ **Enhanced Control.** Applications that may become overloaded with requests can use thread management functions to suspend low-priority tasks and boost the priority of threads executing urgent tasks.

Multithreading can provide the previous benefits when one or more of the following conditions occur in an application.

♦ There are lengthy tasks that are independent of one another. For example, consider a task that computes an amortization schedule based on some input arguments. Each invocation of this task can be carried out in a separate thread.

♦ There are tasks that use a slow system resource, for example, a task that sends data to remote server for storage. Each invocation of this task can be carried out in a separate thread allowing other threads to use the CPU without getting blocked.

♦ There are few shared resources between threads that must be exclusively locked. For example, applications that use a slow system device, such as a printer, where all threads using this resource must wait for completion of the printing task. Note, the application can be restructured so only one thread needs access to this slow resource. This application would then fall into the previous category.

♦ The application can be structured to provide cooperating independent services. Windowing applications are the major example of this class. Usually event-driven, these applications are typically characterized by threads that manage user input, manage screen refresh, and provide background processing for printing and other lengthy tasks.

For multiple threads – each executing concurrent tasks – to achieve a higher level goal, a mechanism is needed to provide synchronization. Most threading packages also contain several classes or data structures that provide synchronization functionality. We discuss synchronization in depth later in this chapter. For now, a way will exist for a thread to claim ownership of a resource (for example, file handle, pipe, global variable, or heap variable). Once granted ownership of this resource, the thread can use or modify the resource while no others can. When the thread is finished, it will signal it is finished by releasing the lock on the resource so other threads may use it in the same manner.

Many different packages are available for managing threads. Usually the base operating system provides the lowest level access to thread management. Software vendors have supplied many higher level packages designed for specific application classes. For example, Microsoft Foundation Classes (MFC) provides a threading package that is tailored for use and integrated with the MFC programming model. Also, RogueWave provides a high level generic threading package called Threads.h++. Others are available. Surfing the Web will show you how predominate multithreaded programming has become based on the number and types of threading packages available.

 In most cases, mixing threading packages in an executable does not cause any problems. While programming, however, you should choose one threading package and stick with it throughout your code.

The Windows 95/NT Threading Package

The Windows operating system provides a robust set of functions to manage processes and threads. In this section, we discuss the basics of thread creation, destruction, and management. Refer to the Win32 SDK documentation supplied with the Visual C++ compiler for more information on using processes and threads. We begin with a general description of the thread functions and then we show an example of a multithreaded counter in the next section.

CREATING THREADS

The Windows95/NT threading package provides one function to create a thread. The idea behind the CreateThread function is, you supply it with the address of a function. This function is then executed in a separate thread and runs simultaneously. Your call to CreateThread, therefore, normally returns immediately as the new thread gets launched and begins running.

The CreateThread() function shown in the following creates a thread and returns a handle to the thread object via the return value and an identifier return through the lpThreadIdentifier parameter.

```
HANDLE CreateThread(
    LPSECURITY_ATTRIBUTES        lpThreadSecurityAttributes,
    DWORD                        dwInitialStackSize,
    LPTHREAD_START_ROUTINE       lpThreadControllingFunction,
    LPVOID                       lpThreadParameter,
    DWORD                        dwThreadCreationFlags,
    LPDWORD                      lpThreadIdentifier
);
```

This function takes the following as arguments: A pointer to security attributes, an initial stack size for the thread, a pointer to the controlling function of the thread (that is, the function to be executed in the new thread), a pointer to a parameter to pass to the thread controlling function, and an additional creation parameter, which defines the state of the thread upon creation. See the Visual C++ documentation for a description of thread security attributes. The stack size specified is only the initial stack size. The stack size will grow as needed to accommodate necessary stack frames as function calls are made.

The thread-controlling function is the function the thread executes upon start up. A single parameter of type LPVOID is passed to the thread function. This is how you communicate initial startup data to the thread. We use this parameter in our counter example to pass a pointer to a structure that contains among other things the shared counter.

Finally, the thread can be started in different states, depending on the value of the dwThreadCreationFlags parameter. The thread can be started in a suspended state if the CREATE_SUSPENDED flag is passed as the value of the dwThreadCreationFlags parameter. A call to ResumeThread() is needed to start the thread in this case. If a value of zero is passed, the thread will execute immediately upon creation.

STOPPING THREAD EXECUTION

Two methods stop a thread permanently. The owner of the thread may stop it with a call to TerminateThread(), the thread itself may stop itself with a call to ExitThread(), or return from the controlling function. Using the ExitThread() function is better style. The operating system will call ExitThread() when the thread returns, however, if it has not yet been called.

The function ExitThread() is shown in the following. It takes a single argument that is the exit code of the thread. The operating system uses the return value of the thread function as the exit code if return is used instead of ExitThread(). This exit code may be obtained by the main thread by calling GetExitCodeThread().

```
VOID ExitThread(
    DWORD        dwThreadExitCode
);
```

The TerminateThread() function shown in the following takes a handle to a thread and an exit code to apply to the termination of the thread. The handle is the one returned from the call to CreateThread(). The exit code is stored with the thread object so subsequent calls to GetExitCodeThread() return this value.

```
BOOL TerminateThread(
    HANDLE       hThread,
    DWORD        dwThreadExitCode
);
```

 Terminating or exiting a thread does not free all resources associated with a thread. You must call CloseHandle() on the handle returned from the call to CreateThread() to properly clean up after a thread. If you do not call CloseHandle(), your application will leak system resources in the kernel libraries. Our example application calls CloseHandle() at the end of the main function as a clean-up step. For more information on CloseHandle(), see the Win32 SDK reference manual in the Visual C++ documentation.

SUSPENDING AND RESUMING THREADS

You can temporarily pause a thread's execution by calling SuspendThread(). To restart a suspended thread, use the ResumeThread() function. These two function provide a powerful mechanism for an application to control the amount of resources it consumes. When a thread is in a suspended state, the scheduler do not allocate any CPU time to the thread. These two functions are shown in the following. The hThread parameter is the handle returned by the CreateThread() function.

```
DWORD SuspendThread(
    HANDLE       hThread
);

DWORD ResumeThread(
    HANDLE       hThread
);
```

Windows95/NT threads have a suspend count. Successive calls to SuspendThread() increment the suspend count. ResumeThread() decrements the suspend count. When the suspend count is zero, the thread is available to be executed. The scheduler will schedule the thread as normal when its suspend count is zero.

MANAGING THREADS

Several functions enable you to manage execution of threads effectively within your application. Several of these are discussed in this section. Generally, operating systems supply several functions that allow for thread control, which are operating-system specific. We note the operating system-specific functions as we discuss them and we explain the reasons for their existence. Two attributes can be set that effect a thread's execution. These attributes are a thread priority and a thread affinity mask. You can adjust the amount of CPU time an individual thread gets by adjusting its *thread priority*. The function SetThreadPriority() gives access to this attribute. The *thread affinity mask* is a bit vector that represents the processors on which a thread can execute. This attribute is specific to WindowsNT. A similar attribute is only found on operating systems that support multiple processors. You can set the thread affinity mask using the function SetThreadAffinityMask().

An executing thread may need access to its handle or identifier. These may be retrieved by the thread using the functions GetCurrentThread() and GetCurrentThreadId(), respectively. We use the GetCurrentThreadId() function in our counter examples to show which thread is incrementing the counter at any given time.

Most operating systems that provide process-level security also provide thread-level security. WindowsNT supports thread-level security. It maintains the concept of thread ownership and provides various levels of access to thread attributes. Security flags are specified at thread creation time. A thread must have access to the attribute it wishes to modify or the operating system will generate an error. See the Visual C++ documentation for a complete discussion of the thread security attributes provided by the operating system.

Multithreading Counter Application

Now that you know how to create and execute threads, we'll look at the Hello World example of multithreaded programming, the shared counter. This application is probably the simplest application you can imagine to use for a multithreaded programming. The application consists of a single counter shared by multiple threads. Each thread increments the counter a specified number of times. In our example, the value of the counter is printed both before and after the increment to determine proper operation.

As you have probably guessed, this example isn't going to work well. We have talked about thread creation and management, but have not yet talked about thread synchronization. The ulterior motive of this example is to show how badly things can go wrong if you ignore thread synchronization.

First, let's look at our example code in Listing 8-1. The source code for this example is located in directory ex0801. At the top of the file, you will see a TypeDef for a structure we will pass to threads as they are created. This structure contains all the information the thread function needs to operate properly. It contains a pointer to an integer, which contains its thread ID, a pointer to the counter, and the number of times to increment the counter. The next section of code is the thread-controlling function. This is a function that takes a single parameter of type LPDWORD and returns a value of type DWORD.

Within the body of the function is a single for-loop, which increments the counter counterMax times. Both before and after the increment, we print the thread ID and the value of the counter. When we are done, we call ExitThread() to indicate this thread has finished its task. The call to Sleep() in the middle of the for-loop simulates some processing that may occur based on the value of the counter. It also ensures the thread will be descheduled. The problem we are about to see occurs whether we make the call to Sleep(). The call to Sleep() simply insures it will occur almost every time.

TIP If you are having problems localizing a resource competition problem, put in some calls to the Sleep() function around the problem area. Sleep() gives up the thread execution time slice and causes other threads to be scheduled. If you don't see the problem appear, move the calls to Sleep() around. Sometimes this can be a powerful tool for locating resource conflicts.

Listing 8-1: Unsynchronized counter.cpp

```cpp
#include <stdio.h>
#include <iostream.h>
#include <windows.h>
TypeDef struct _ThreadParams
{
    LPDWORD pThreadId;
    int *pCounter;
    int counterMax;
} ThreadParams;
DWORD
ThreadFunc(LPDWORD lpdwParam)
{
    ThreadParams *pThreadParams = (ThreadParams *)lpdwParam;
    char buffer[80];
    for ( int i = 0; i < pThreadParams->counterMax; i++ )
    {
```

```
        //
        // Print out the value before the increment
        //
        sprintf(buffer, "Thread = %04d: Preincrement  = %05d\n",
                        *pThreadParams->pThreadId,
                        *(pThreadParams->pCounter));
        fprintf(stdout, buffer);
        fflush(stdout);
        //
        // Simulate going off and doing something else.
        // Sleep will also insure that this thread give up its
        // time slice as well.
        Sleep(10);
        //
        // Now try to increment the counter
        //
        *(pThreadParams->pCounter) += 1;

        //
        // Print out the result after the increment
        //
        sprintf(buffer, "Thread = %04d: Postincrement = %05d\n",
                        *pThreadParams->pThreadId,
                        *(pThreadParams->pCounter));
        fprintf(stdout, buffer);
        fflush(stdout);
    }
    ExitThread(0);
    return 1;
}
int
main(int argc, char **argv)
{
    if ( argc < 2 )
    {
        cout << "usage: " << argv[1] << " counter_max" << endl;
        exit(1);
    }
    int counterMax = atoi(argv[1]);
    if ( counterMax < 1 )
    {
        cout << "counter must be positive value" << endl;
        exit(1);
    }
    //
    // Set up the counter and ids used by the individual threads
    //
    int counter = 0;
    DWORD dwThreadId1, dwThreadId2;
    ThreadParams ThreadParam1, ThreadParam2;
    //
    // Set up the parameter structures to pass to the threads
    //
```

```
    ThreadParam1.pCounter = &counter;
    ThreadParam1.pThreadId = &dwThreadId1;
    ThreadParam1.counterMax = counterMax;
    ThreadParam2.pCounter = &counter;
    ThreadParam2.pThreadId = &dwThreadId2;
    ThreadParam2.counterMax = counterMax;
    //
    // Create the threads
    //
    HANDLE hThread1, hThread2;
    hThread1 = CreateThread(
        NULL,                         // security attributes
        0,                            // stack size
        (LPTHREAD_START_ROUTINE) ThreadFunc, // thread function
        &ThreadParam1,                    // argument to thread function
        0,                            // creation flags
        &dwThreadId1);                    // returns the thread id
    // Check the return value for success.
     if (hThread1 == NULL)
    {
        cout << "Unable to create thread 1" << endl;
        exit(1);
    }

    hThread2 = CreateThread(
        NULL,                         // security attributes
        0,                            // stack size
        (LPTHREAD_START_ROUTINE) ThreadFunc, // thread function
        &ThreadParam2,                    // argument to thread function
        0,                            // creation flags
        &dwThreadId2);                    // returns the thread id
     // Check the return value for success.
     if (hThread2 == NULL)
    {
        cout << "Unable to create thread 2" << endl;
        exit(1);
    }
    //
    // Hang out for awhile
    //
    Sleep(10000);
    // Clean up and go home
    TerminateThread(hThread1, 1);
    TerminateThread(hThread2, 1);
    CloseHandle(hThread1);
    CloseHandle(hThread2);
    return 0;
}
```

The main function starts with some general bookkeeping. Next, the structures to be passed to the two threads are created and initialized. We use a single local variable as the counter. Once the structures are initialized, we call CreateThread() twice to create two threads, passing in the two structures.

In our calls to CreateThread(), we pass a NULL as the security attributes. This value tells the thread package we want to use the default values. Similarly, the initial thread stack size is set to 0, which causes the stack size to be set to a default value. The creation flags are set to 0, meaning the threads start as soon as they are created.

Remember, the pointer to the counter we passed to the threads is a local variable to the main function. Therefore, this variable sits in the stack frame of the main function. We use a call to Sleep() to keep the main function alive for ten seconds. This gives the threads a chance to run. (The operating system provides functions whereby you can wait for a thread to finish but, because this is a basic example, we're not using those here.) Also, note, when the main function of this program exits, it will terminate the threads regardless of whether we call TerminateThread().

As our last step, we clean up. If the threads haven't finished yet, the call to TerminateThread() will stop them. We then call CloseHandle() to deallocate any operating system resources consumed by the thread-creation process. The output of this example is shown in Listing 8-2. Take a minute and study the first four lines.

Listing 8-2: Output of unsynchronized counter example

```
Thread = 0164: Preincrement  = 00000
Thread = 0059: Preincrement  = 00000
Thread = 0164: Postincrement = 00001
Thread = 0059: Postincrement = 00002
Thread = 0164: Preincrement  = 00002
Thread = 0059: Preincrement  = 00002
Thread = 0164: Postincrement = 00003
Thread = 0164: Preincrement  = 00003
Thread = 0059: Postincrement = 00004
Thread = 0059: Preincrement  = 00004
Thread = 0164: Postincrement = 00005
Thread = 0164: Preincrement  = 00005
Thread = 0059: Postincrement = 00006
Thread = 0059: Preincrement  = 00006
Thread = 0164: Postincrement = 00007
Thread = 0059: Postincrement = 00008
Thread = 0164: Preincrement  = 00008
Thread = 0059: Preincrement  = 00008
Thread = 0164: Postincrement = 00009
Thread = 0059: Postincrement = 00010
```

Both threads grab the counter at the same time. They both look at the counter and see it is zero and print this. Thread 0164 then is the first to increment the counter and prints the result it sees: one. Thread 0059 gets rescheduled and goes on its merry way to increment the counter. After it has incremented the counter, it prints the result: two. Because neither thread has a way to claim ownership of the counter while inside the for-loop, both threads access the counter during the print-increment-print cycle.

This is a simple example of a counter – a single integer – whose only operation is increment. Nothing gets hurt if the counter doesn't contain the expected value. The output may look like a mesh, but abnormal program faults would not occur. You can imagine the damage that would be done if this were a linked list or other data structure. Think of two threads trying to insert a node in a linked list at the same spot. The list would probably be corrupted beyond repair and the next thread to try to traverse the list would probably crash the program. In a similar example, imagine trying to traverse the list while some other thread was inserting a new node.

This example is to familiarize you with one of the biggest pitfalls of multi-threaded programming: competition for resources. We look at other pitfalls in the section "Synchronization Strategies." In the next section, we discuss synchronization and show several different ways to fix our shared counter example.

Multithreading Synchronization

Synchronization allows multiple threads to use resources cooperatively without interfering with one another. Generally, set of objects or data structures represent different types of locks. A set of functions are also supplied that allow a thread to check the status of a lock or block waiting to acquire the lock. We begin this section with a discussion of the wait functions, followed by a discussion of each of the standard types of synchronization objects.

SYNCHRONIZATION FUNCTIONS

Two main functions are used to wait on synchronization objects: WaitForSingleObject(), and WaitForMultipleObjects(). A synchronization object can be in one of two states, signaled or nonsignaled. In the *signaled state,* the object is available for use. In the *nonsignaled state,* the object is presently locked or executing. These wait functions do not return until either the synchronization object enters a signaled state or a user-specified timeout occurs. When waiting for either one of these conditions to occur, these functions enter an efficient wait state, which consumes little system resources.

The WaitForSingleObject() function prototype is shown in the following:

```
DWORD WaitForSingleObject(
    HANDLE   hHandle,
    DWORD    dwTimeoutInMilliseconds
);
```

The *hHandle parameter* is a handle to the object on which to wait. The *hHandle* parameter is the handle returned by the appropriate create function. The *dwTimeoutInMilliseconds* is the maximum number of milliseconds to wait for the object specified by the handle parameter.

The WaitForMultipleObjects() function prototype is show in the following:

```
DWORD WaitForMultipleObjects(
    DWORD          nHandleCount,
    CONST HANDLE *lpHandles,
    BOOL           bWaitAll,
    DWORD          dwTimeoutInMilliseconds
);
```

The *nHandleCount* parameter specifies the number of handles in the lpHandles array. The *bWaitAll* flag instructs the function when to return. If the value of bWaitFlag is TRUE, the function returns when all objects in the lpHandles array have signaled. If value of bWaitFlag is FALSE, the function returns when any one object signals. In the latter case, the return value of WaitForMultipleObjects() indicates which object in the array signaled. The *dwTimeoutInMilliseconds* is the maximum number of milliseconds to wait for the object specified by the handle parameter.

You will be using these two functions in the samples in the next section, "Synchronization Objects."

SYNCHRONIZATION OBJECTS

Synchronization objects are different types of locks that allow an application to control how many threads have access to a resource. In this section, we discuss the following three types of synchronization objects:

◆ Critical Section

◆ Mutex

◆ Semaphore

Using these three types of objects, we can control how many threads have access to the counter at any given time.

The critical section

The *critical section object type* is used to grant exclusive access to a section of code. Typically, a critical section is used to group a section of code that must be executed sequentially without interruption. Each section of code to be locked needs a separate critical section object allocated for it. You can think of the critical section object as a traffic cop and the code as the road. The critical section object allows one – and only one – thread exclusive access to that segment of code. Just as you would not want a single traffic cop watching multiple intersections, you would not want a single critical section object guarding multiple code segments. Exceptions exist to this rule, however.

When using a critical section object, an application must take the following steps:

- ◆ Allocate a critical section object

- ◆ Call the function InitializeCriticalSection()

- ◆ Repeatedly call EnterCriticalSection() and LeaveCriticalSection() to gain and relinquish access to the guarded section of code

- ◆ Call DeleteCriticalSection() to return system resources

The following paragraphs describe these functions in detail.

Critical Section objects are allocated locally or in the heap. Once the critical section is allocated, it is initialized with the function InitializeCriticalSection(). You must call InitializeCriticalSection() before attempting to use the critical section. The prototype for this function is shown in the following:

```
VOID InitializeCriticalSection(
    LPCRITICAL_SECTION lpCriticalSection
);
```

The single parameter to the function InitializeCriticalSection() is a pointer to the critical section object to be initialized.

The function EnterCriticalSection() returns when access to the code segment is granted to the caller. The prototype for this function is shown in the following:

```
VOID EnterCriticalSection(
    LPCRITICAL_SECTION lpCriticalSection
);
```

The single parameter to the function EnterCriticalSection() is a pointer to the requested critical section object.

The function LeaveCriticalSection() is used to signal the current owner has finished with the critical section. The prototype for this function is shown in the following:

```
VOID LeaveCriticalSection(
    LPCRITICAL_SECTION lpCriticalSection
);
```

The single parameter to the function LeaveCriticalSection() is a pointer to the critical section object to which the thread has ownership.

The function DeleteCriticalSection() is used to deallocate the resources associated with the critical section object. If an application does not call DeleteCriticalSection(), the application leaks system resources in the kernel libraries. The prototype for this function is shown in the following:

```
VOID DeleteCriticalSection(
    LPCRITICAL_SECTION lpCriticalSection
);
```

The single parameter to the function DeleteCriticalSection() is a pointer to the critical section object that is to be deallocated.

Now we use a critical section to fix our counter example. This method works for our example because only one section of code uses the shared counter. Listing 8-3 shows how we modified the previous example to use a critical section. The source code for this example is located in the directory ex0802.

 A mutex is a conceptually better choice for locking the counter than a critical section. See the next section titled "The mutex" for a discussion on using a mutex.

In the main function, we added a line that allocates the critical section on the stack. Following this, we make a call to have the critical section initialized. We pass a pointer to the critical section in the ThreadParams structure. The thread function uses this pointer in calls to EnterCriticalSection() and LeaveCriticalSection(). Last, we call DeleteCriticalSection() as we clean up before exiting from the main function.

Also, note how we have replaced the call to Sleep() in the main function with two calls to WaitForSingleObject(). In the Windows95/NT thread package, thread handles can be used in the wait calls. Just as synchronization objects have signaled and nonsignaled state, so do threads. A thread is signaled when it has returned from its thread-controlling function or called ExitThread(). Otherwise, the thread is in a nonsignaled state.

Listing 8-3: Synchronization using a critical section

```
#include <stdio.h>
#include <iostream.h>
#include <windows.h>
[code ommitted]
DWORD
ThreadFunc(LPDWORD lpdwParam)
{
    ThreadParams *pThreadParams = (ThreadParams *)lpdwParam;
    char buffer[80];
    for ( int i = 0; i < pThreadParams->counterMax; i++ )
    {
        //
        // Lock this section of code so no other thread
        // can use it. This will work here because we know
        // that this section of code is the only one which
```

```
        // accesses the counter. Another approach would be
        // to use a Mutex in conjunction with using
        // the counter.
        //
        EnterCriticalSection(
                pThreadParams->lpCriticalSection);
        //
        // Print out the value before the increment
        //
        [code omitted]
        //
        // Tell the OS we are done with this section
        // of code.
        //
        LeaveCriticalSection(
                pThreadParams->lpCriticalSection);
    }
    ExitThread(0);
    return 1;
}

int
main(int argc, char **argv)
{
    //
    // Allocate a critical section object to
    // synchronize the threads
    //
    CRITICAL_SECTION criticalSection;
    InitializeCriticalSection(&criticalSection);
    [code omitted]
    //
    // Hang out for awhile
    //
    WaitForSingleObject(hThread1, INFINITE);
    WaitForSingleObject(hThread2, INFINITE);
    //
    // Clean up and go home
    //
    DeleteCriticalSection(&criticalSection);
    CloseHandle(hThread1);
    CloseHandle(hThread2);
    return 0;
}
```

The output of the synchronized counter application is shown in Listing 8-4. Notice each thread has access to the code segment exclusively for the print-increment-print cycle. In this example the counter increments in an orderly fashion. Next, we look at how to achieve this same effect using a mutex.

Listing 8-4: Output of synchronized counter example

```
Thread = 0176: Preincrement   = 00000
Thread = 0176: Postincrement  = 00001
Thread = 0166: Preincrement   = 00001
Thread = 0166: Postincrement  = 00002
Thread = 0176: Preincrement   = 00002
Thread = 0176: Postincrement  = 00003
Thread = 0166: Preincrement   = 00003
Thread = 0166: Postincrement  = 00004
Thread = 0176: Preincrement   = 00004
Thread = 0176: Postincrement  = 00005
Thread = 0166: Preincrement   = 00005
Thread = 0166: Postincrement  = 00006
Thread = 0176: Preincrement   = 00006
Thread = 0176: Postincrement  = 00007
Thread = 0166: Preincrement   = 00007
Thread = 0166: Postincrement  = 00008
Thread = 0176: Preincrement   = 00008
Thread = 0176: Postincrement  = 00009
Thread = 0166: Preincrement   = 00009
Thread = 0166: Postincrement  = 00010
```

The mutex

The *mutex object* represents a mutually exclusive lock. A *mutex* is used to grant exclusive access to a resource. Only one thread can lock the mutex at any given time. You can think of the mutex as an occupied flag on a resource. When the resource is occupied, no other thread may use the resource. A rule of thumb for mutex utilization is a one-to-one correspondence should be between mutexes and shared resources which can be used by a single thread at a time. In our counter example, a mutex is a conceptually better choice for a locking mechanism because the actual resource we are trying to lock is the shared counter (a single integer). If we were to add a decrement function, the critical section solution would fail to work. Because both the increment and decrement function would be critical sections guarded by separate critical section objects, we would have a situation where one thread could be trying to increment the counter, while another thread could be trying to decrement the counter. This would cause the exact type of race conditions seen earlier. The solution in such a case is to use a mutex. (As you can see, then, the advantage to using a mutex is it can be used in several different sections of code, while a critical section only guards one section of code.)

Mutex objects are created by calling the CreateMutex() function. The CreateMutex() function returns a HANDLE, which is later used to reference the mutex. The prototype for this function is shown in the following:

```
HANDLE CreateMutex(
    LPSECURITY_ATTRIBUTES  lpMutexAttributes,
    BOOL                   bInitialOwner,
    LPCTSTR                lpMutexName
);
```

This function takes as parameters a pointer to a security attributes structure, a flag indicating whether the caller wishes to be the initial owner, and – optionally – a string representing a name for the mutex. See the Visual C++ documentation for a description of synchronization object security attributes. The *bInitialOwner* flag specifies whether the calling thread wishes to be the owner on creation of the mutex. If this flag is set to TRUE, the mutex will be created in the nonsignaled state. The last parameter is an optional name for the mutex. If a name is specified at creation time, this name may then be specified in a call to OpenMutex(). This allows programs to adopt a naming convention for mutex objects and allows the operating system to manage passing out handles to the mutexes. Remember, the handle created by a call to CreateMutex() must be closed with a call to CloseHandle() to free the operating system resources associated with the mutex.

Once a named mutex has been created using the CreateMutex() function call, a handle to the mutex can be subsequently retrieved with a call to OpenMutex(). This handle can then be used as a parameter to one of the wait functions. The prototype for this function is shown in the following:

```
HANDLE OpenMutex(
    DWORD               dwDesiredAccess,
    BOOL                bInheritHandle,
    LPCTSTR             lpMutexName
);
```

This function takes as parameters a DWORD representing the desired access to the mutex object, a flag indicating whether the object handle is inheritable, and the name of the mutex to be opened. We discuss access to objects later in this chapter. The bInheritHandle parameter indicates whether the handle can be passed to another process created with the function CreateProcess(). Just as threads can share synchronization objects, so can processes share synchronization objects. This sharing is possible because the actual synchronization objects reside in the operating system. Applications simply have handles to these system resources. The last parameter is the name of the mutex to be retrieved. The lpMutexName parameter is case-sensitive.

Once a thread has acquired ownership of the mutex via a call to one of the wait functions, the thread should call ReleaseMutex() when it is finished with the resource the mutex guards. The return value indicates a success status. A value of TRUE indicates the release succeeded. The prototype for this function is shown below.

```
BOOL ReleaseMutex(
    HANDLE              hMutexHandle
);
```

This function takes a single parameter, which is the mutex to release. When the mutex is released, the object reverts from a nonsignaled state to a signaled state. The signaled state indicates it is available for use.

Now we use a mutex to fix our counter example. The source code for this example is located in the directory ex0803. In the main function, we added a line that creates a mutex with a call to CreateMutex(). We pass the handle to the mutex in the ThreadParams structure. The thread function uses this handle in calls to WaitForSingleObject() and ReleaseMutex(). Last, we call CloseHandle() on the mutex handle as we clean up before exiting from the main function. Listing 8-5 shows how to use a mutex.

Listing 8-5: Using a mutex

```
#include <stdio.h>
#include <iostream.h>
#include <windows.h>
TypeDef struct _ThreadParams
{
    LPDWORD pThreadId;
    int *pCounter;
    int counterMax;
    HANDLE hMutex;
} ThreadParams;
DWORD
ThreadFunc(LPDWORD lpdwParam)
{
    ThreadParams *pThreadParams = (ThreadParams *)lpdwParam;
    char buffer[80];
    for ( int i = 0; i < pThreadParams->counterMax; i++ )
    {
        //
        // Try to lock the mutex to gain access to the
        // resource. Wait forever for the mutex by
        // passing INFINITE.
        //
        WaitForSingleObject(pThreadParams->hMutex, INFINITE);
        //
        // Print out the value before the increment
        //
        [code omitted]
        //
        // Tell the OS we are done with this section of code.
        //
        ReleaseMutex(pThreadParams->hMutex);
    }
    return 0;
}
int
main(int argc, char **argv)
{
    [code omitted]
```

```
    //
    // Allocate a mutex object to synchronize the threads
    //
    HANDLE hMutex = CreateMutex(NULL, FALSE, NULL);
    //
    // Set up the parameter structures to pass to the threads
    //
    ThreadParam1.pCounter = &counter;
    ThreadParam1.pThreadId = &dwThreadId1;
    ThreadParam1.counterMax = counterMax;
    ThreadParam1.hMutex = hMutex;
    ThreadParam2.pCounter = &counter;
    ThreadParam2.pThreadId = &dwThreadId2;
    ThreadParam2.counterMax = counterMax;
    ThreadParam2.hMutex = hMutex;
    [code omitted]
    //
    // Clean up and go home
    //
    CloseHandle(hMutex);
    [code omitted]
    return 0;
}
```

The output of the mutex counter application is identical to that shown in Listing 8-4 for the critical section object. Again, each thread has access to the code segment exclusively for the print-increment-print cycle. In this example, the counter increments in an orderly fashion. Next, we show how to use a semaphore to achieve the same effect.

The semaphore

The *semaphore object* represents a finite access lock. A mutex is used to grant a limited number of threads simultaneous access to a resource. The semaphore is initialized with the total number of threads that have simultaneous access. This total number of threads can then lock the semaphore. You can think of the semaphore as the chairs in a game of musical chairs. As each thread locks the semaphore, they are sitting down in chairs. When all the chairs are occupied, any subsequent calls to lock the semaphore wait until one thread gets up from a chair (releases the semaphore). When the chairs are full, no other thread may use the resource. A rule of thumb for semaphore utilization is there should be a one-to-one correspondence between semaphores and shared resources, which can be used by a finite number of threads at a time.

As you have probably deduced by now, the mutex is only a degenerate semaphore. The mutex is a semaphore whose maximum count has been set to one. We now use a semaphore with a maximum count of one to fix our counter example.

Semaphore objects are created by calling the CreateSemaphore() function. The CreateSemaphore() function returns a HANDLE which is later used to reference the semaphore. The prototype for this function is shown in the following:

```
HANDLE CreateSemaphore(
    LPSECURITY_ATTRIBUTES lpSemaphoreAttributes,
    LONG                  lInitialCount,
    LONG                  lMaximumCount,
    LPCTSTR               lpName
);
```

This function takes as parameters a pointer to a security-attributes structure, an initial count, a maximum count, and – optionally – a string representing a name for the semaphore. See the Visual C++ documentation for a description of synchronization object security attributes. This value must be greater than or equal to zero and less than or equal to lMaximumCount. If the value of lInitialCount is zero the semaphore is created in the nonsignaled state. The last parameter is an optional name for the semaphore. If a name is specified at creation time, this name may then be specified in a call to OpenSemaphore(). This allows programs to adopt a naming convention for semaphore objects and allows the operating system to manage passing out handles to the semaphores. Remember, the handle created by a call to CreateSemaphore() must be closed with a call to CloseHandle() to free the operating system resources associated with the semaphore.

Once a named semaphore has been created using the CreateSemaphore() function call, a handle to the semaphore can be subsequently retrieved with a call to OpenSemaphorex(). This handle can then be used as a parameter to one of the wait functions. The prototype for this function is shown in the following:

```
HANDLE OpenSemaphore(
    DWORD   dwDesiredAccess,
    BOOL    bInheritHandle,
    LPCTSTR lpSemaphoreName
);
```

This function takes as parameters a DWORD representing the desired access to the mutex object, a flag indicating whether the object handle is inheritable, and the name of the semaphore to be opened. We discuss access to objects later in this chapter. The *bInheritHandle* parameter indicates whether the handle can be passed to another process created with the function CreateProcess(). Just as threads can share synchronization objects, so can processes share synchronization objects. This sharing is possible because the actual synchronization objects reside in the operating system. Applications simply have handles to these system resources. The last parameter is the name of the semaphore to be retrieved. The lpSemaphoreName parameter is case-sensitive.

Once a thread has acquired ownership of the semaphore via a call to one of the wait functions, the thread should call ReleaseSemaphore() when it is finished with the resource the semaphore guards. The return value indicates a success status. A value of TRUE indicates the release succeeded. The prototype for this function is shown in the following:

```
BOOL ReleaseSemaphore(
    HANDLE      hSemaphore,
    LONG        lReleaseCount,
    LPLONG      lpPreviousCount
);
```

This function takes as parameters a handle to the semaphore to release, a LONG to add to the semaphore counter, and a pointer to a LONG to accept the previous value of the semaphore count. When the semaphores count is greater than zero, the object reverts from a nonsignaled state to a signaled state. The signaled state indicates it is available for use.

Now we use a semaphore to fix our counter example. The source code for this example is located in the directory ex0804. In the main function, we added a line that creates a semaphore with a call to CreateSemaphore(). We pass the semaphore handle in the ThreadParams structure. The thread function uses this handle in calls to WaitForSingleObject() and ReleaseSemaphore(). Finally, we call CloseHandle() on the semaphore handle as we clean up before exiting from the main function. Listing 8-6 shows how to use a semaphore.

Listing 8-6: Using a semaphore

```
#include <stdio.h>
#include <iostream.h>
#include <windows.h>
TypeDef struct _ThreadParams
{
    LPDWORD pThreadId;
    int *pCounter;
    int counterMax;
    HANDLE hSemaphore;
} ThreadParams;
DWORD
ThreadFunc(LPDWORD lpdwParam)
{
    ThreadParams *pThreadParams = (ThreadParams *)lpdwParam;
    char buffer[80];
    for ( int i = 0; i < pThreadParams->counterMax; i++ )
    {
        //
        // Try to decrement the semaphore to gain access to the
        // resource. Wait forever for the semaphore by
        // passing INFINITE.
        //
        WaitForSingleObject(pThreadParams->hSemaphore, INFINITE);
        //
        // Print out the value before the increment
        //
        [code omitted]
        //
        // Tell the OS we are done with this section of code.
        //
```

```
        LONG prevCount;
        ReleaseSemaphore(pThreadParams->hSemaphore, 1, &prevCount);
    }
    return 0;
}
int
main(int argc, char **argv)
{
    [code omitted]
    //
    // Allocate a semaphore object to synchronize the threads
    //
    HANDLE hSemaphore = CreateSemaphore(NULL, 1, 1, NULL);
    //
    // Set up the parameter structures to pass to the threads
    //
    ThreadParam1.pCounter = &counter;
    ThreadParam1.pThreadId = &dwThreadId1;
    ThreadParam1.counterMax = counterMax;
    ThreadParam1.hSemaphore = hSemaphore;
    ThreadParam2.pCounter = &counter;
    ThreadParam2.pThreadId = &dwThreadId2;
    ThreadParam2.counterMax = counterMax;
    ThreadParam2.hSemaphore = hSemaphore;
     [code omitted]
    //
    // Clean up and go home
    //
    CloseHandle(hSemaphore);
    [code omitted]
    return 0;
}
```

The output of the semaphore counter application is identical to that shown in Listing 8-4 for the critical section object. Again, each thread has access to the code segment exclusively for the print-increment-print cycle. In this example, the counter increments in an orderly fashion.

SYNCHRONIZATION STRATEGIES
Six basic rules of thumb exist for multithreaded programming:

◆ Use a critical section to lock sections of code that must be executed sequentially and without interruption.

◆ A one-to-one relationship should exist between locks — either mutexes or semaphores — and the resources multiple threads share.

◆ Use the synchronization object to lock the resource immediately before modifying and release the object immediately after modifying the resource.

◆ Use the synchronization object when reading the resource if modification of the resource may effect the application's ability to read the resource (linked lists).

◆ Use a mutex when only one thread at a time may access a resource.

◆ Use a semaphore when a limited number of threads at a time (*n* threads) may access a resource.

Finally, when using synchronization objects, be careful of deadlock situations. A deadlock usually occurs when two threads are each trying to lock two resources in the opposite order. For example, Thread1 and Thread2 both need to lock mutexA and mutexB. Thread1 locks mutexA first. Likewise, Thread2 locks mutexB first. Then Thread1 waits infinitely on mutexB while Thread2 waits infinitely on mutexA. Neither thread will ever be able to obtain its needed lock. This is a *deadlock*. With careful planning, deadlocks can be avoided. This example can be easily fixed by reversing the order of locking in either thread.

If you are trying to write portable code for a multithreading application, stick to the basic functions listed in the following. Generally, any threading package supports these functions at a minimum. The function names and signatures will differ, however. You need to supply #ifdef alternatives for the different threading packages.

◆ CreateThread

◆ TerminateThread

◆ SuspendThreadResumeThread

◆ GetCurrentThreadId

◆ Semaphore

◆ Mutex

◆ CriticalSection

Another approach is to use a third-party threads package, such as RogueWaves's Threads.h++. This will enable you to write generic multi-threading code and to leave the integration to the underlying threads package to a software vendor.

Multithreaded CORBA counter

Now that we've shown a solid background in multithreaded programming techniques, we are ready to try our first multithreaded CORBA example. If you are unfamiliar with multithreaded programming techniques, please review the previous section. If you are already familiar with multithreaded programming techniques – including thread creation and synchronization – then you have jumped to the right place.

We start this section with some considerations for creating multithreaded CORBA servers. In the following three sections, we present a multithreaded CORBA counter object and discuss the implications multithreading has on this example. The next section deals with building multithreaded CORBA servers in the VisiBroker/Windows development environment. The last section shows how to run this example and discusses the results.

Multithreaded CORBA Basics

Most ORB vendors provide a reentrant version of the ORB libraries. Neither the CORBA specification nor the ORB vendors, however, provide any safeguards for the implementation objects written by the application programmers. The programmer's responsibility is to ensure the implementation of the applications objects are multithread safe. This means the objects and methods you write must be reentrant and any resources you use must be properly synchronized. Resources include but are not limited to global variables, member variables, and system resources.

 It is your responsibility to write safe code for the implementation of any multithreaded CORBA objects you define. You must provide proper synchronization for the use of any member variables and resources.

The reentrant versions of the ORB libraries provide proper synchronization for the ORB, BOA, and other classes provided for in the CORBA specification. This means multiple threads may safely call any of the underlying CORBA methods without worrying about synchronization issues. Some ORB vendors provide prebuilt threading models to assist you in managing the number of threads created in your server. We discuss server threading models in detail in the next section. VisiBroker chooses a default model that is adequate for our purpose in this example.

The Interface Definition Language

In this example, we show a simple CORBA counter object. One potential application for this CORBA object is as a hit counter for HTML pages. You can access the CORBA object via a Java client. You learn more about CORBA/Java integration in Part III of this book, "Web Applications with CORBA." We use this example to show how to internally synchronize a CORBA object that expects to be accessed by multiple CORBA invocations simultaneously. In this example, we show when and where synchronization is necessary. In addition, this example shows when synchronization can be safely ignored if the consequences are acceptable.

The Interface Definition Language (IDL) for the CORBA counter is shown in the following. You can see a readonly attribute representing the value and a single operation increment(). Clients may retrieve the current value of the counter via the attribute value and may increment the value using the operation increment().

```
interface counter
{
    readonly attribute long value;

    long increment();
};
```

In the IDL, we make no allusion regarding the multithreading capability of this CORBA object. The client does not care or even need to know if the server that hosts this CORBA object is multithreaded. From the client's point of view, all CORBA objects are the same. Method calls are made on the object blindly with the expectation they will either be successful or raise an exception.

In fact, it is the server that is in complete control of the multithreaded status of the executable. The CORBA objects contained therein do not have any knowledge of the threading model the server is employing. Therefore, you should always be cautious when serving an implementation of a CORBA object in your multithreaded server. As a multithreaded CORBA server programmer, you must know whether the implementation of the object you are going to serve is multithread safe. If you did not write it and it does not claim to be multithread safe, it probably is not multithread safe. A quick glance at the source code will tell you immediately. For this example, we unequivocally know whether our object is multithread safe. We will write it ourselves!

The Server

Now let's look at the source code for the implementation of the CORBA counter object. Note, we are providing the synchronization internal to the object's source code. This internal synchronization is necessary due to the multithreaded nature of the CORBA server in which this CORBA counter object resides.

We could possibly use the CORBA Concurrency Service to achieve this synchronization. However, this places the responsibility of the synchronization of the object on the client. The Concurrency Service should be used to synchronize access to resources that are retrieved from a server, manipulated on the client side, and then updated within the original server. The Concurrency Service is used to synchronize resources that are shared across processes. Multithread synchronization should be used for resources that cannot be updated external to the object that manages the resource. In other words, multithread synchronization is used to synchronize resources that are internal to a process. In our example, the attribute representing the counter is internal to the object implementation. If the value attribute were read-write, the Concurrency Service would be necessary to allow synchronization between clients. These two situations are shown in Figure 8-2. Although we could use the Concurrency Service in our counter example, it would limit the use of our counter object to systems that have the Concurrency Service available. For such a basic object type as a counter, this would be overkill and unduly limit the usefulness of our object, as well as place an undue burden on the client.

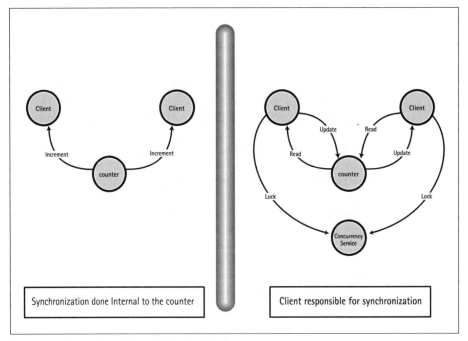

Figure 8-2: Internal vs. External Synchronization

Our previous examples of counters have been based on a procedural programming model. The main function allocated the synchronization object and passed it to the thread function as a parameter. In the object-oriented model — the synchronization object — in this case a mutex, is maintained as a member variable. The header file for the counter object implementation is shown in Listing 8-7. You can see it has two member variables: a handle to a mutex and a long integer representing the value. Both attributes are defined as private members. Next you can see four methods: a constructor, a destructor, the accessor for the value, and the increment method.

Listing 8-7: Counter.h

```
#ifndef _Counter_h
#define _Counter_h
#include <windows.h>
#include "counter_s.hh"
class Counter : public _sk_counter
{
    HANDLE m_hMutex;
    CORBA::Long m_counter;
public:
    Counter(const char *name);
    ~Counter();
    CORBA::Long value();
    CORBA::Long increment();
};
#endif
```

The source file for the counter implementation is shown in Listing 8-8. The first method is the constructor. The *constructor* starts by printing the object name to the console. After this status message, the constructor creates a mutex with the function CreateMutex(), and initializes the counter to zero. In the *destructor,* the only action to be performed is to close the handle associated with the mutex, which frees the system resources associated with the mutex.

Listing 8-8: Counter.cpp

```
#include "Counter.h"

Counter::Counter(const char *name)
                    : _sk_counter(name)
{
    cout << "Constructing new counter named "
            << name << endl;
    m_hMutex = CreateMutex(NULL, FALSE, name);
    m_counter = 0;
}
Counter::~Counter()
{
    CloseHandle(m_hMutex);
}
CORBA::Long
Counter::increment()
{
        char buffer[512];
        //
        // Lock the mutex
```

```
        //
        WaitForSingleObject(m_hMutex, INFINITE);
        //
        // Print out the value before the increment
        //
        sprintf(buffer,
                "Thread = %04d: Preincrement  = %05d\n",
                GetCurrentThreadId(),
                m_counter);
        fprintf(stdout, buffer);
        fflush(stdout);
        //
        // Simulate going off and doing something else.
        // Sleep will also ensure that this thread give up
        // its time slice as well.
        Sleep(10);
        //
        // Now try to increment the counter
        //
        m_counter += 1;
        //
        // Print out the result after the increment
        //
        sprintf(buffer,
                "Thread = %04d: Postincrement = %05d\n",
                GetCurrentThreadId(),
                m_counter);
        fprintf(stdout, buffer);
        fflush(stdout);
        //
        // Tell the OS we are done
        //
        ReleaseMutex(m_hMutex);
        return m_counter;
}
CORBA::Long
Counter::value()
{
    //
    // Since we are not modifying the value
    // only polling the present value
    // it is OK not to lock the counter resource.
    // If the operations performed on the resource
    // cause it to be in an unstable state during
    // update we would have to lock the resource
    // before polling for it's value.
    return m_counter;
}
```

The method Counter::increment() is the heart of the synchronization example. Notice we lock the mutex before we enter the print-increment-print cycle. This ensures only one thread is accessing the increment function at a time. If we did not lock access to the private member variable using the mutex, we would have seen results similar to those shown in Listing 8-2.

In the method Counter::value(), we simply return the present value of the counter. Notice we did not lock the mutex before retrieving the value from m_counter. The consequence of not locking the mutex is the counter could be in the process of being incremented as we are returning the value. Because we are only returning the value, we believe this behavior is acceptable. We should note this to clients of this counter through the counter object's documentation, however. If it is unacceptable for multiple threads accessing the counter as the value is returned, we could implement the Counter::value() function as shown in the following. This function ensures the counter is not being incremented when the return value is collected.

```
CORBA::Long
Counter::value()
{
    CORBA::Long return_value;
    WaitForSingleObject(hMutex, INFINITE);
    return_value = m_counter;
    ReleaseMutex(hMutex);
    return return_value;
}
```

The Client

Now that we have seen how the counter is implemented, we'll look at the client. The client we have chosen to implement binds to a named counter and increments the counter a user-specified number of times. The source for the client is shown in Listing 8-9.

Listing 8-9: Client_Main.cpp

```
#include "counter_c.hh"
int
main(int argc, char **argv)
{
    CORBA::ORB_var orb = CORBA::ORB_init(argc, argv);
    counter_ptr counter = counter::_bind(argv[1]);
    int count = atoi(argv[2]);
    for ( int i = 0; i < count; i++ )
    {
        cout << counter->increment() << endl;
    }
    return 0;
}
```

You should notice the client has no knowledge of the multithreaded nature of the server. The call to increment assumes the object implementation will do the right thing. In the following sections, we build and run the client and server.

Build Options for Multithreading

Most compilers require certain switches be set to generate reentrant code. The Visual C++ compiler is no exception. In the makefile, you see we have set the /MT compiler switch. This instructs the compiler to generate reentrant functions. See the Visual C++ documentation or the documentation for your compiler for a complete discussion of the necessary switches.

In addition to compiler switches, you must link your client and server using the reentrant version of the ORB libraries. VisiBroker provides the reentrant version of the ORB library in the file liborb_r.lib. If you're using something other than VisiBroker, consult the documentation for your ORB to determine the correct library to use.

Testing the CORBA Counter

To test the server, we would like to run several clients against this server simultaneously. The major problem is starting all the clients before any one of them finishes. We will use a neat trick in Windows to accomplish this feat. First, start the server using the following command:

```
start server MyCounter
```

Change focus to the server window and type **CTRL-S**. This suspends all output to the console window. It also has the neat side effect of causing the application to suspend as soon as it tries to write to the console window. Next, start several clients by repetitively executing the following command:

```
start client MyCounter 5
```

This command tells the client to bind to a specific instance of a counter object. The second parameter tells the client to make five calls to the increment operation of this counter object. Finally, change focus back to the server window and type CTRL-Q. The server resumes printing to the console. Depending on how many clients you started, your output should look similar to that shown in Listing 8-11. The default-threading model chosen by VisiBroker is the thread per session model. We discuss this and other models in the next section. Congratulations! You have created your first multithreaded CORBA server and implemented your first multithread safe CORBA object.

Server Threading Models

Now that you have created your first multithreaded CORBA server and implemented your first multithread safe CORBA object, we need to discuss how to manage the threads created by the ORB for servicing client request. You can imagine what will happen when hundreds, or even thousands, of clients connect to your server simultaneously and start invoking operations on your CORBA object. Hundreds or even thousands of threads may potentially be created to service these requests. This is where server-threading models can help.

A *server-threading model* defines a policy for creation and management of threads within a server. We will discuss five server-threading models in this section. These models will provide you with the broad range of strategies to manage thread allocation in your CORBA servers. This list is not exhaustive, however. These are only five commonly used threading models. You are free to create and implement your own model provided your ORB allows access to its internal event dispatching mechanisms. Some ORBs allow this low-level access, while others do not. If the standard threading models do not meet your needs, be sure to choose an ORB for your application that allows you this low-level access.

VisiBroker provides several out-of-the-box threading models that require minimal configuration and even enable you to change the model at runtime. However, VisiBroker does not allow access to the low-level event dispatching mechanism necessary to create your own threading model. In the middle of the spectrum is another commercial ORB named PowerBroker, which provides both prebuilt threading models and access to the low-level event dispatching mechanism. Orbix falls on the other end of the spectrum because it provides no prebuilt threading models. You have ultimate control over the event dispatching mechanism, however. IONA currently provides sample code to implement a wide variety of server-threading models at its Web site. Note, event dispatching is not part of the CORBA specification. Different vendors have implemented event dispatching differently. Therefore, you should be cautious if you plan to migrate from one ORB vendor to another during multithread development.

In this section, we use the CORBA counter example to show the behavioral differences between the different server-threading models. One of the powerful features VisiBroker provides is the capability to configure the server-threading model at runtime. Visigenics has chosen to implement the different threading models via the Basic Object Adapter (BOA). The threading model you use is based on the BOA you select. The configuration can even be done on the command line.

Before we begin, you may want to build the counter applications in the ex0805 directory on the enclosed CD-ROM. The makefile in this directory will build a client and two versions of the server. One version of the server is single threaded, single.exe, and the other is multithreaded, server.exe.

The Single-Threaded Model

The single-threaded model is the simplest of all models. In the *single-threaded model,* a server has one thread for processing client requests. Each request is processed in turn. When a server is processing requests, all other clients block until their turn. While this model ensures the server will not have a problem with thread management, it limits the usefulness of the server for servicing a large volume of client requests. Figure 8-3 illustrates the single-threaded model.

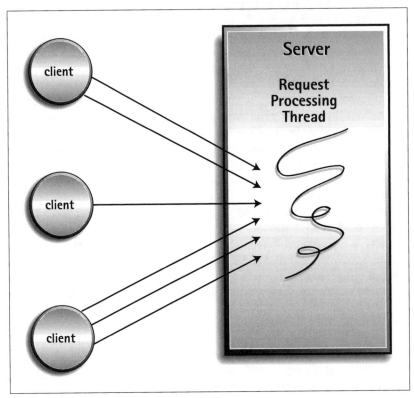

Figure 8-3: The Single-Threaded Model

Now let's look at the output for our single-threaded counter example. The section "Testing the CORBA Counter" describes how to run multiple clients against the counter server. We use the same methodology here, except for the command that starts the counter server. Replacing the server invocation with the following command starts the single threaded example.

```
start single MyCounter
```

The output from this scenario is shown in Listing 8-10. Notice only one thread ID is in this listing. The server only has one thread to process client requests. Therefore, this is the only ID that appears in the output. All clients share this same thread for request processing.

Listing 8-10: Single-threaded counter output using four clients

```
Server Initializing ...
        ThreadMax     = 0
        ConnectionMax = 5
Constructing new counter named MyCounter
Thread = 0202: Preincrement  = 00000
Thread = 0202: Postincrement = 00001
Thread = 0202: Preincrement  = 00001
Thread = 0202: Postincrement = 00002
Thread = 0202: Preincrement  = 00002
Thread = 0202: Postincrement = 00003
Thread = 0202: Preincrement  = 00003
Thread = 0202: Postincrement = 00004
Thread = 0202: Preincrement  = 00004
Thread = 0202: Postincrement = 00005
Thread = 0202: Preincrement  = 00005
Thread = 0202: Postincrement = 00006
Thread = 0202: Preincrement  = 00006
Thread = 0202: Postincrement = 00007
Thread = 0202: Preincrement  = 00007
Thread = 0202: Postincrement = 00008
Thread = 0202: Preincrement  = 00008
. . .
```

The Thread-per-Session Model

In the *thread-per-session model,* a new thread is allocated for each connection to the server. Therefore, each client may have its own thread in the server. This model allows each client to carry out processing in the server without blocking for other clients, provided no competition exists for an internal resource. The clients are still subject to blocking in the case where a method is called that uses an internal synchronization object to synchronize thread access to an internal resource. For example, a client of our counter will never block when calling the value() method. The value() method does not use the mutex for synchronization. A client may block when calling the increment() method, however, if another client is currently using the increment() method.

The thread per session model is shown in Figure 8-4. We see the act of binding by each client causes a new thread to be created in the server. This threading model may have grave impact on servers that expect to have a large number of clients. However, it is a good choice for servers who expect a small number of clients and wish to give the client programmer maximum flexibility in how requests are serviced. We discuss selecting the appropriate model in the section titled "Multithreaded CORBA Design Example."

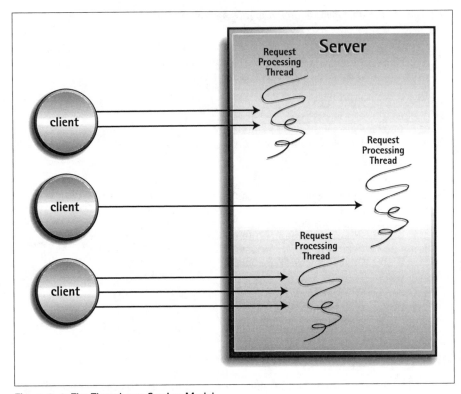

Figure 8-4: The Thread-per-Session Model

Now let's look at the output for our thread-per-session counter example. As we mentioned before, VisiBroker enables us to select the threading model and set the model parameters on the command line. The section "Testing the CORBA Counter" describes how to run multiple clients against the counter server. We use the same methodology here except for the command that starts the counter server. Replacing the server invocation with the following command starts the thread-per-session example. The -OAid command line switch tells VisiBroker which BOA to select. In this case, the TSession parameter tells VisiBroker to select the thread per session BOA.

```
start server MyCounter -OAid Tsession
```

The output from this scenario is shown in Listing 8-11. The first thing to note is the ThreadMax value that is set to 1024. Even though we allow each client to receive its own thread for processing, the BOA still limits the amount of threads to 1024. You cannot change this value. We will discuss the ConnectionMax value in the section entitled "Connection Management in VisiBroker." Note, four thread IDs are in this listing. We have used four clients. Each is assigned a thread to service their requests. Every new request made by the same client reuses the same thread. The thread is destroyed when the connection to the object is closed. The connection is closed by the client upon releasing the object.

Listing 8-11: Thread-per-session counter output using four clients

```
Server Initializing ...
        ThreadMax     = 1024
        ConnectionMax = 5
Constructing new counter named MyCount
Thread = 0194: Preincrement  = 00000
Thread = 0194: Postincrement = 00001
Thread = 0126: Preincrement  = 00001
Thread = 0126: Postincrement = 00002
Thread = 0205: Preincrement  = 00002
Thread = 0205: Postincrement = 00003
Thread = 0188: Preincrement  = 00003
Thread = 0188: Postincrement = 00004
Thread = 0194: Preincrement  = 00004
Thread = 0194: Postincrement = 00005
Thread = 0126: Preincrement  = 00005
Thread = 0126: Postincrement = 00006
Thread = 0205: Preincrement  = 00006
Thread = 0205: Postincrement = 00007
Thread = 0188: Preincrement  = 00007
Thread = 0188: Postincrement = 00008
Thread = 0194: Preincrement  = 00008
. . .
```

The Thread Pool Model

The *thread pool model* creates a finite number of threads to service client requests. Each request made to the server is assigned a thread. The request is carried out in the context of the thread. When processing is finished, the thread is placed back in the pool of available threads to await a new request. Clients blocks in two cases. First, the client will block if no threads are available. The client stays in a blocked state until a thread is available. Second, the client blocks when a method is called that uses an internal synchronization object to synchronize thread access to an internal resource. This is as noted previously for the thread-per-session model.

The thread pool model is shown in Figure 8-5. We see each request processed through the event dispatching mechanism in the server is allocated to a thread in the thread pool. Requests made after all threads have been allocated must wait until a thread is finished processing and returned to the thread pool. This threading model may have a grave impact on servers that are expected to have a high degree of availability. Requests may be waiting for a long time or may even timeout if the request processing is of long duration. This is a good choice for servers who expect a large number of clients and whose method invocations are of long duration, however. In this situation, the thread-per-session model would cause an explosion of threads in the server. This model gives the server programmer the capabilityto limit the number of threads created in the server. We discuss more about selecting the appropriate model in the section titled "Multithreaded CORBA Design Example."

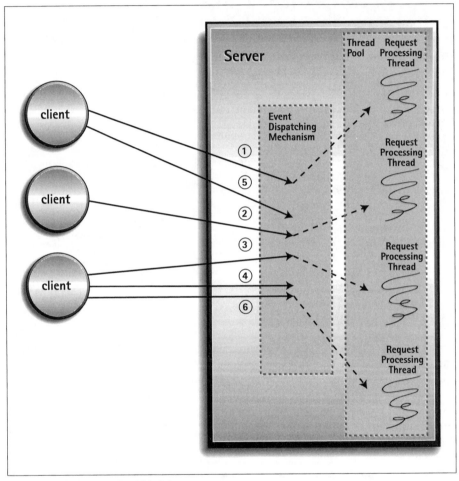

Figure 8-5: The Thread Pool Model

Now look at the output for our thread pool counter example. As we mentioned before, VisiBroker enables us to select the threading model and set the model parameters on the command line. The section "Testing the CORBA Counter" describes how to run multiple clients against the counter server. We use the same methodology here, except for the command that starts the counter server. Replacing the server invocation with the following command starts the thread pool example. The -OAid command line switch tells VisiBroker which BOA to select. In this case, the TPool parameter tells VisiBroker to select the thread pool BOA. The -OAthreadMax parameter sets the maximum number of threads in the pool. We have chosen two for our example:

```
start server MyCounter -OAid TPool -OAthreadMax 2
```

The output from this scenario is shown in Listing 8-12. The first thing to note is the ThreadMax value that is set to 2. This is the value to which we have set threadMax on the command line. By default, no limit is set on the number of threads in the thread pool. You must set a value via the command line or programmatically if you do not wish to swamp your system with threads. We discuss the ConnectionMax value in the section entitled "Connection Management in VisiBroker." Notice two thread IDs in this listing. We have used four clients. Each request is assigned one of the threads in the thread pool to service the request. The thread is recycled into the thread pool when servicing of a request is completed.

Listing 8-12: Thread pool counter output using four clients

```
Server Initializing ...
        ThreadMax    = 2
        ConnectionMax = 5
Constructing new counter named MyCounter
Thread = 0182: Preincrement  = 00000
Thread = 0182: Postincrement = 00001
Thread = 0181: Preincrement  = 00001
Thread = 0181: Postincrement = 00002
Thread = 0182: Preincrement  = 00002
Thread = 0182: Postincrement = 00003
Thread = 0181: Preincrement  = 00003
Thread = 0181: Postincrement = 00004
Thread = 0182: Preincrement  = 00004
Thread = 0182: Postincrement = 00005
Thread = 0181: Preincrement  = 00005
Thread = 0181: Postincrement = 00006
Thread = 0182: Preincrement  = 00006
Thread = 0182: Postincrement = 00007
Thread = 0181: Preincrement  = 00007
Thread = 0181: Postincrement = 00008
Thread = 0182: Preincrement  = 00008
. . .
```

The Thread-per-Object Model

The thread-per-object model is a more specific form of thread pool. In the *thread-per-object model,* each object instance allocated by the server receives a thread to carry out client requests. All clients of this object share the same thread for that object. This model gives the server programmer the flexibility to create servicing threads for objects that may have long-lived operations, while allowing objects with short-lived operations to be serviced without interference. This model may be thought of as single threading on a per-object basis. Figure 8-6 shows an illustration of the thread-per-object model. This model is not supported by VisiBroker.

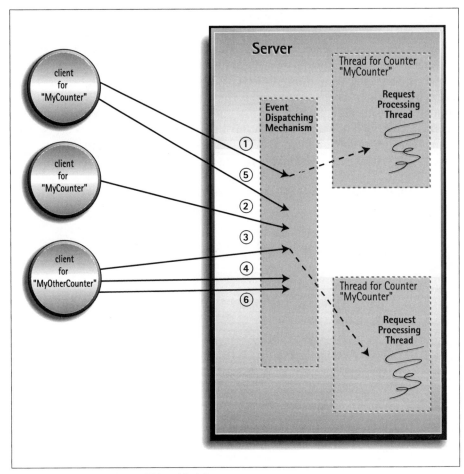

Figure 8-6: The Thread-per-Object Model

The Thread-per-Operation Model

The thread-per-operation model is analogous to the thread-per-object model. The difference is threads are allocated on an operation basis. Therefore, all invocations of a specific method of an object instance will use the same thread. The *thread-per-operation model* may be thought of as single threading on a per-operation basis.

Other Models

The previous descriptions may have given you ideas for other models. For instance, what about a thread-pooling model on a per-object basis? Perhaps we could call this The "thread pool-per-object model." Under this model, we may be enabled to assign a set number of threads to each object for servicing of its requests. High-priority objects may get more threads than low-priority objects. What if you just can't design your system properly without this threading model? Well, the good news is you can write your own. The bad news is you must find an ORB vendor that allows access to the event-dispatching mechanism. And the rest of the bad news is the threading model code you write will assuredly be tied to that ORB.

Connection Management in VisiBroker

In this section, we discuss how to manage the number of TCP/IP connections that are used for client-server communications. We look at the connection management facilities and discuss the details clients and servers may employ. This discussion is specific to VisiBroker. Your ORB may provide similar functionality, however. Refer to your ORB's documentation to determine what, if any, support for connection management is available. Connection management plays an important role in the performance of your CORBA server.

What is Connection Management?

Simply put, *connection management* is the methodology to manage the number of TCP/IP connections between clients and servers. Connection management is discussed in general terms in the CORBA specification. The information presented in the CORBA specification is targeted at ORB vendors implementing the General Inter-ORB Protocol (GIOP) and the Internet Inter-ORB Protocol (IIOP). The specification provides general behavior for opening and closing of TCP/IP connections between clients and servers. It is up to the ORB vendor to ensure their implementation complies with the specified behavior. The specification does not state an implementation of an ORB should provide any programmatic interface for connection management.

Some ORB vendors, VisiBroker included, have chosen to expose some of the connection management configuration variables to the application programmer. Other ORB vendors describe their connection management policy in the ORB documentation. Understanding how a vendor has implemented connection management enables the application programmer to influence the number of TCP/IP connections between clients and servers through the design of the system. This does not provide definitive control over the number of connections, however.

Figure 8-7 shows a typical situation involved in client-server communications. A TCP/IP connection is used to send the GIOP or IIOP messages that represent the invocation of a method on a remote CORBA object. The process of binding finds an appropriate TCP/IP connection or sets up a new TCP/IP connection if an appropriate connection cannot be found. Clients can influence the number of connections between the client and server. Servers can limit the total number of connections they will accept.

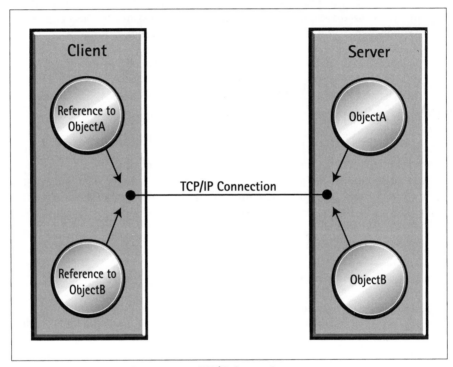

Figure 8-7: Multiplexing Requests on a TCP/IP Connection

The payoff of connection management is in performance. By managing the number of connections made between client and server, the client achieves a performance increase by reusing an existing connection. The server achieves a benefit in limiting the number of system resources created and destroyed.

Server-Side Connection Management

The server has two functions that allow it to manage the number of active connections. These functions are available as methods of the BOA object. The first is CORBA::BOA::connection_count(). This method returns the current number of open connections. The second is CORBA::BOA::connection_max(). This method allows the server to set the maximum number of connections it will accept.

In addition to these two methods, a maximum idle time can be specified on the command line. When the idle time on a connection exceeds this value, the connection may be automatically closed by VisiBroker. VisiBroker automatically closes this connection only if a request is made to set up a new connection and the maximum number of connections has been reached. This parameter is specified on the command line using the -OAconnectionMaxIdle command line switch. The following example illustrates its use:

```
start server MyCounter -OAconnectionMaxIdle 30
```

This command starts our example server and sets the connection maximum idle time to 30 seconds.

Client Side Connection Management

VisiBroker provides the connection management on the client side with the goal of keeping the minimum number of connections between a particular client and a particular server. All requests between a particular client-server pair are multiplexed across the same connection. This increases performance because the client does not have to incur the overhead of creating a new connection for each object or method it accesses in the remote server. This type of connection management is the default behavior of the bind() method.

While the server is largely interested in limiting the number of connections made to it, the client's concern is establishing enough connections to optimize request queuing to the server. Because all requests are multiplexed across the same connection, different threads must wait in line to have their requests sent to the server. If you have an object whose requests are high priority, you may wish to make a new connection dedicated to the owner of this object reference. You may make a new connection to the server via a call to _clone(). The _clone() method duplicates an object reference and establishes a new TCP/IP connection to the server. Again, remember the _clone() function is VisiBroker specific. Figure 8-8 illustrates the difference between _bind() and _clone().

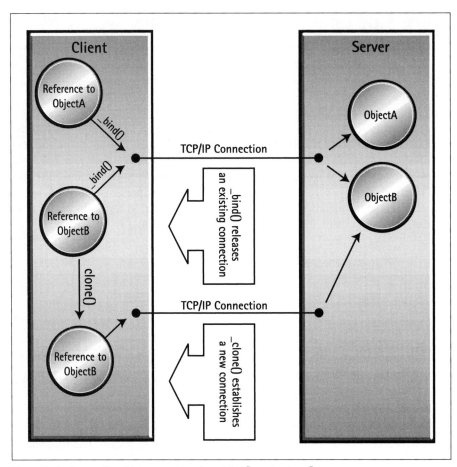

Figure 8-8: Connection Management using _bind() and _clone()

Multithreaded CORBA Design Example

In this section, we consider two examples of multithreaded CORBA systems. We discuss some design considerations for each and propose a reason for selecting a threading model and a connection management policy for each. First, we look at a source code control system and then a fractal-image generation system. We hope to show you how to tie together the concepts presented in this chapter to design a solid scaleable CORBA system.

Document Control System

As our first example, consider a rudimentary document control system. As a first pass, we might propose for this server the IDL definition shown in Listing 8-13.

Listing 8-13: Proposed document control IDL

```
interface Project;
interface File;
TypeDef sequence<Project> ProjectList;
TypeDef sequence<File> FileList;
interface Project {
    readonly attribute string projectName;
    readonly attribute ProjectList subprojects;
    readonly attribute FileList;
    ...
    [Project Methods]
    ...
};
interface File {
    readonly attribute string filename;
    attribute string description;
    ...
    [Other File Attributes]
    ...
    boolean lock();
    boolean unlock();
    OctetSequence checkout();
    boolean checkin(in OctetSequence file_contents)
        raises(NotLocker);
    ...
    [Other File Methods]
    ...
};
interface DC_Session : Project {
    readonly attribute string projectName;
    ...
    [DC_Session Attributes and Operations]
    ...
};
interface DocumentControl_Server {
    DC_Session login(in string projectName, in string username,
                      in string password)
        raises(InvalidLogin);
};
```

The server provides objects that represent a user session, projects, subprojects, and files. The system has a user-control capability facilitated through the DC_Session object. The *DC_Session* is a subclass of the Project interface. The DC_Session object then represents the root project. This project object may contain subprojects or files. The file object enables the user to lock a file for editing, check in a modified file, check out a file modified by another user, and unlock the file. In addition, the system will meet the following requirements:

- ◆ The server shall accept requests from multiple clients.

- ◆ The server shall be able to support up to 30 simultaneous clients.

- ◆ Each client shall be serviced in an equal manner, regardless of the type of request.

Last, we impose one design constraint on the system. The client invocations on the server will be sequentially ordered, except in cases of abnormal termination of the client. The implication is each client will have only one outstanding request except if it must perform an emergency logout. The emergency logout will be in the case of a program fault in the client.

Given these requirements and design criteria, we ask ourselves the following questions: What type of threading model should we use? What type of connection management policy, if any, should we use? What other multithreaded considerations apply to this system?

We would select a thread-per-session model for this example. Because we know we will have multiple clients and they must be served simultaneously, we know our system must be multithreaded. Because each client must be treated in an equal manner, regardless of the type of request, this leads us to believe each client should have a separate thread dedicated to servicing that individual client. This is further supported by the design constraint that each client would have sequential operations. Thus, as the clients queue their requests to the thread allocated for them, each request would be serviced in turn. If a client requested the check-in of a large file, the client would have to wait until the file was finished before any other of its requests were serviced. However, while the long check-in was occurring, another client may perform several traversals of the project hierarchy without being impeded.

Our requirement for 30 simultaneous users effectively dictates our connection management policy. Setting the number of connections on the server to 30 would achieve this requirement and allow us to budget systems resources for a finite number of threads. This would also ensure we would provide an acceptable level of performance for each client.

The rule of thumb for multithreaded programming still applies to this example. However, we may be confronted with synchronization issues beyond the multithreaded variety. Synchronization of the description attribute from the File interface may become important. Because clients may retrieve this value, subsequently modify it, and return it to the File object, it may be necessary to use the CORBA Concurrency Service to ensure two users are not attempting to modify this attribute at once.

Although stripped down, this example has been used to illustrate some basic concepts involved in multithreaded CORBA server design and some implementation considerations. The requirements and design constraints are certainly not complete. They were chosen to be those that would have the most impact on the choices set forth. Other requirements and constraints may well have an impact, however.

Fractal Image Generation

Finally, let's look at a fractal image generator. *Fractal images* are pretty pictures generated from a mathematical equation. By varying the constants in the equation, we can generate an infinite number of nice images. You can think of this as a mathematical SpiroGraph. However, generation of these images can be CPU-intensive, depending on the complexity of the equation you choose. We would like to provide an object we could populate with the equations constant values and have it be able to generate one of these images. The image generation is a long-lived method that is CPU-intensive. We wouldn't wish to have many of these threads running at once. A Thread Pool Model would greatly benefit our server. We can limit the number of threads, thereby limiting the stress on the CPU. At the same time, we could select a large number for the maximum number of connections. This would enable a large number of clients to connect and wait until a thread is available to create their fractal image.

Summary

In this chapter, we have shown all the ingredients necessary to create robust multithreaded CORBA servers: Good multithreaded programming techniques, different threading models, and connection management. We have shown how to apply these principles when designing multithreaded CORBA systems. We touched on the CORBA Concurrency Service and showed how it relates to multithreaded programming. Our design example showed how the Concurrency Service might be applied in conjunction with a multithreaded server. The next section of this book will expand on this concept and move you toward distributed CORBA across the Web.

Part III

Web Application with CORBA

Chapter 9

CORBA and Java

IN THIS CHAPTER

In this chapter, we explore on the evolving relationship between CORBA and Java, focusing on the following topics:

◆ How CORBA and Java interrelate

◆ What CORBA and IIOP contribute to the Web and enterprise applications

◆ How to implement a CORBA server in Java

◆ How client classes and server implementation classes relate to the Java classes and interfaces generated by a Java IDL compiler

◆ How to implement a CORBA client in Java

◆ How to use CORBA advanced features in client applets

◆ How to deploy an applet-based CORBA client

◆ How corporate firewalls and the Java security model impact a CORBA system architecture

◆ What initiatives are underway to improve the integration of CORBA and Java

WHEN WE BEGAN DEVELOPING CORBA-based applications using the earliest ORB implementations, we were pleased with the relative simplicity introduced by CORBA's object-oriented abstraction of network APIs. We saw CORBA as an important step in the long-term progression toward more intuitive and adaptable software technologies. CORBA's goal of a platform-independent, language-neutral, object-oriented, and distributed-system infrastructure was a watershed for enterprise applications. Interestingly, as CORBA-compliant ORBs were becoming available, the Web was also beginning its period of exponential growth. At about the same time, Sun began publicizing and preparing Java for general release as a tool for developing platform-independent and network-centric applications— or *applets*.

As the first versions of the Java Developer's Kit became available, we began developing client-side applications in Java was pleased with the productivity improvements from the automated memory management, pure object orientation,

345

and platform independence. As with CORBA, Java simplified the development and management of network-centric enterprise applications.

With such parallel natures and goals, CORBA and Java make a natural partnership. Together they have dramatically raised the functionality and adaptability of enterprise-wide applications. Developers of Internet browsers, relational and object-oriented databases, transaction processing monitors, operating systems, and enterprise applications are re-engineering their products to use these two enabling technologies.

The CORBA community moved quickly to define the Interface Definition Language (IDL) to Java language mapping. As shown in Figure 9-1, these two technologies have several common core aspects. Both CORBA and Java are:

◆ object-oriented

◆ syntactically aware of the distinction between interface specification and implementation

◆ designed for platform independence

◆ designed to support object location independence

◆ fundamentally network-centric

◆ standards with multivendor participation and support

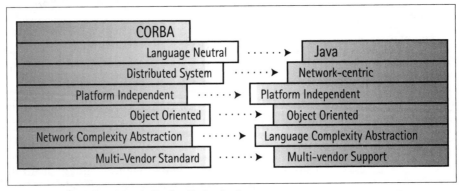

Figure 9-1: CORBA and Java's Similar Underpinnings

Furthermore, Java's native support for threads, garbage collection, exceptions, and built-in complex data types, as well as its pure object orientation made the definition of CORBA's Java language mappings a relatively painless process.

The definition of CORBA's Java mapping testifies to the CORBA vision. The majority of the CORBA specification occurred in the early 1990s – roughly three years prior to the release and general awareness of the Java language. Despite this timing, the OMG responded quickly to the industry's zealous acceptance of Java by incorporating it into the CORBA architecture. The result: a farther-reaching CORBA infrastructure and a more robust Java. The OMG's participatory organizational structure and CORBA's focus on specification rather than implementation were designed specifically for this type of adaptability. If the incorporation of Java is any indication, the innate adaptability of the OMG and CORBA provides a strong argument for its long-term viability as a solution for mission-critical application interoperability.

What Does CORBA Contribute to the Web?

How does CORBA add value to Web protocols already supporting client/server interactions? As with other applications, CORBA brings order, robustness, adaptability, and an intuitive software model to distributed Web-based applications. Although CGI has been an important technology and is appropriate in many circumstances, it can be cumbersome and counterintuitive for moderately to highly complex distributed applications. Furthermore, the CGI and Fast CGI protocols lack CORBA's scaleability for applications and applets with interactive user interfaces. While adaptable to many information retrieval and display applications, the retransmittal and regeneration of much of the user interface for each client/server invocation in CGI does not meet the responsiveness requirements of most interactive user interfaces.

From an adaptability perspective, the implementation of a CGI script series to support a Web-based GUI to an enterprise server is a poor solution – a less obvious but important fact for enterprise applications. While CGI may be a common solution for data distribution to a Web browser, it is not a preferable middleware solution for interserver communication. In contrast, as Figure 9-2 suggests, creating a CORBA-based API to an enterprise server results in Web-based GUI and other enterprise application accessibility for servers. Figure 9-2 illustrates the architectural flexibility and utility of a CORBA-based middleware solution by depicting a downloaded applet communicating with an enterprise server while that server interacts with a second non-Web based enterprise application. In general, CORBA is an adaptable inter-process communication infrastructure appropriate for most distributed systems – including the Web – while CGI is a protocol appropriate for less responsive and complex subsets of client/server interactions.

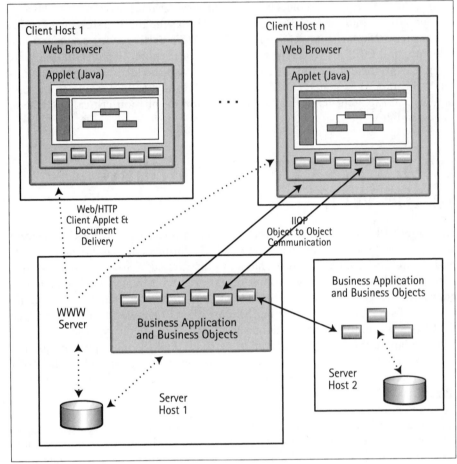

Figure 9-2: A Simple CORBA- and Java–Based Architecture

What Does CORBA Contribute to Java?

Because the Web functions without Java, and Java exists without the Web, CORBA's contribution to Java can be separated from its contribution to the Web.

Java was originally envisioned as an enhancement to static Web pages; it has evolved, however, into an excellent option for enterprise applications (particularly on the client-side). As a result of this evolution, Java applications need to interoperate with back-end legacy systems in a scaleable, heterogeneous, and robust manner. While the stated shortcomings of CGI and the language homogeneity of Java's Remote Method Invocation (RMI) argue against use of these protocols, the robustness, platform and language neutrality, and flexibility of CORBA can bind Java into the enterprise.

How to Use CORBA with Java

Figure 9-2 illustrated the architecture of a simple application built on CORBA and Java using a Web browser to provide the client-side Java virtual machine. As with any Java-enabled Web page, when the client browser parses the Web page's APPLET tag, the lazy Java class loader downloads the minimum applet class files necessary to support the executing Java applet. Java class files (providing client-side ORB runtime functionality) may be included in this download sequence. Under other circumstances, the client-side ORB classes may have been installed on the client host as part of the Web browser installation, thereby eliminating a dynamic download of these classes. However, no prior need exists for ORB modules or executables to reside on the client's computer and enable the applet's CORBA-based communication back to the server. All necessary Java classes can be dynamically downloaded.

Once the applet is initialized and executing on the client machine, it establishes an ORB-based connection to one or more ORB-enabled servers residing on the same host as the Web server that served up the applet. The default behavior of the Java security manager necessitates this colocation of the Web server and the target ORB servers within the illustrated architecture. Under its default configuration, the Java security model prevents a dynamically downloaded applet from establishing a socket connection to a host from which it was not downloaded. (The mechanisms to overcome this restriction are discussed later in the chapter.)

With the applet executing and connected to the server, Java objects in the applet may begin invoking functions on any ORB-enabled objects in the server applications.

Several appealing aspects of this client/server interaction paradigm, both from the user's and the developer's prospective, follow:

◆ Developers need only develop the client application once to execute on a multitude of platforms.

◆ Servers with IDL interfaces are accessible to any other enterprise applications in addition to the Web-based client.

◆ Intuitive, scaleable, and object-oriented implementation of the client to server communication.

◆ Minimal (or even zero) administration of the client host to support use of the client applet.

◆ A more intuitive programming model adds user functionality in a timely manner.

Using CORBA in combination with Java results in dynamic, adaptable, user-friendly, and developer-friendly software systems.

Developing the Application

The next few sections illustrate the programming steps in the development of a CORBA-enabled Java client and server. As an example, we use a small system that provides video and audio titles to a user on-demand. The design of our application, illustrated in Figure 9-3, is similar to the generic design illustrated in Figure 9-2.

The code samples from our media-on-demand client and server use CORBA's Java language mapping and are ORB-independent wherever possible. However, because ORB vendors provide interesting proprietary extensions to their ORBs, some code is specific to a particular ORB product. In these cases, wherever possible, we illustrate the implementation using both VisiBroker for Java and Iona's OrbixWeb (the most common CORBA compliant Java-enabled ORBs). Download evaluation copies of VisiBroker for Java from `http://www.visigenic.com` and Iona's OrbixWeb from `http://www.iona.com`.

Our media access server provides controlled access to and creation of user accounts, data about each available audio and video title, and play initialization of media titles. The server also interacts with the legacy billing system, which tabulates billing and payment data and issues billing statements.

On the client-side, the applet pictured in Figure 9-4 peruses and selects audio and video titles and allows access to online billing statements. Streaming video and audio players play the multimedia files on the client computer.

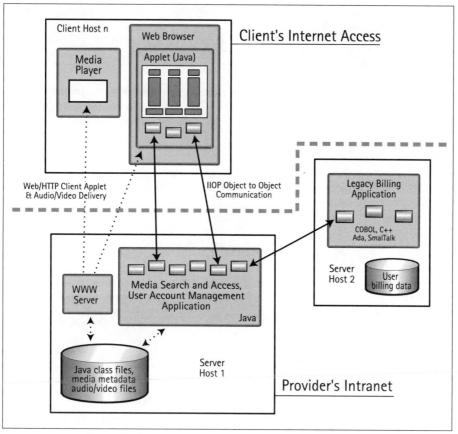

Figure 9-3: Our Sample CORBA and Java Application

Implementing a CORBA Server in Java

If scalability is not a large concern, implementing a CORBA-enabled server is a relatively straightforward process. Implementation involves the following activities:

1. Design and definition of the server's IDL interface.

2. Generation of the stub and skeleton classes and interfaces using the ORB's IDL compiler.

3. Design and implementation of the server's Java classes that implement the functionality defined by the server's IDL interface.

4. Design and implementation of any other functionality necessary but not visible to the client applets and applications.

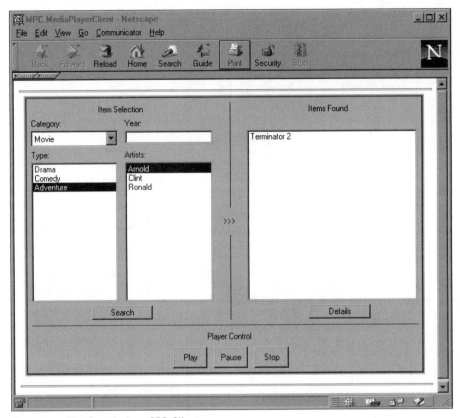

Figure 9-4: The Sample Java ORB Client

Defining and Compiling an Interface Definition Language Interface

In general, implementing a server in Java does not create special implications for the server's IDL interface. While interface design is a critical development step, IDL's language neutrality prohibits any underlying implementation language idiosyncrasies from bleeding through to the server's IDL interface.

In light of CORBA's enterprise stature, IDL's language neutrality is vitally important; it can be a slight negative in some circumstances, however. CORBA's current lack of support for object pass-by-value represents one disadvantage. Unlike Java's RMI, which does support pass-by-value, a client application cannot send or receive an entire object from the server. RMI's problem space is more narrow than CORBA's problem space, however. RMI only functions in an all-Java environment and is not language-neutral. A Java client cannot use RMI to make invocations on a server written in Smalltalk, for example, thereby greatly minimizes the pass-by-value problem. In the meantime, the OMG is developing a pass-by-value capability for inclusion in the CORBA architecture. This capability will be an important advancement of the CORBA standard.

Listing 9-1 provides the IDL interface for our sample application.

Listing 9-1: IDL interface for our multimedia access server

```
//————————————————————
//   Type Definitions and Declarations
//————————————————————
// Forward Declarations
interface MediaItemI;
//Exception Declarations
exception NoSuchMediaType {};
exception NoSuchAccount {};
exception NoSuchGenre {};
exception UserAccountNameNotAvailable {};
//Type Definitions
sequence<string> StringListType;
struct BasicItemInfoType {
    string name;
    MediaItemI itemRef;
};
struct DetailedItemInfoType {
    BasicItemInfoType basicInfo;
    string artists;
    string year;
    string review;
    string synopsys;
    string bannerPageURL;
    string country;
    float costPerMinute;
    float duration;
};
//————————————————————
//     Interface Definitions
//————————————————————
interface MediaManagerI {
StringListType getMediaTypes();
StringListType getAllGenresOfType(in string mediaType)
    raises(NoSuchMediaType);
StringListType getAllArtistsOfType(in string mediaType)
    raises(NoSuchMediaType);
BasicItemInfoListType getItemsMatchingCriteria(
    in string mediaType,
```

```
        in string genre,
        in string artist,
        in string year);
};
interface MediaItemI {
DetailedItemInfoType getDetailedInfo();
BasicItemInfoType getBasicInfo();
oneway void play(in UserAccountI customer);
void playComplete(in UserAccountI customer);
};
interface UserAccountManagerI {
short createAccount(in string userAccountName,
        in string password,
        in string phoneNumber)
        raises(UserAccountNameNotAvailable);
short deleteAccount(in unsigned long
        accountNumberToDelete)
        raises(NoSuchAccount);
UserAccountI startSession(in string userAccountName)
        raises(NoSuchAccount);
};
interface UserAccountI {
StatementType getStatement();
        short makePayment(in string creditCardNumber,
        in string expirationDate);
};
```

The server's IDL interface provides access to the singleton MediaManager and UserAccountManager objects, MediaItem, and UserAccount objects. The MediaManager object manages and provides high-level access to MediaItem objects. By using the MediaManagerI interface to select a specific MediaItem, the client achieves direct access to the MediaItem object through the MediaItemI interface. The UserAccountManagerI and UserAccountI interfaces function in a similar fashion, supporting management, perusal, and updates to user account information such as name, address, preferences, and billing status.

Compiling the IDL interface generates several Java source files compliant with CORBA's Java language mapping. These files provide the implementation of client stub classes and server skeleton classes. (In later sections we discuss Java stubs and skeletons in great detail.) Client-side *stub* classes, often called proxies, perform the actual CORBA-compliant distributed communication with the server, marshall function parameters, and return values to and from Internet Inter-ORB Protocol (IIOP). Server-side skeletons play a similar role for the server. The server-side classes also forward incoming client invocations to the underlying implementation objects, however.

Naming Your Classes

Some ORB products suggest the following naming convention that derives the name of a class that implements an IDL interface: suffix the interface name with an abbreviation of the word "implementation" (such as `MediaManagerImpl`). While this convention may seem appropriate or harmless on the surface, it can cause difficult naming problems in real-world systems. Due to its inflexibility and ORB-centricity, we do not recommend this convention.

Most implementation classes possess purpose and functionality regardless of whether an ORB is used to make this functionality available to remote clients. Furthermore, CORBA separates interface definition from functional implementation by design. As a result, it is not uncommon to shift the roles of implementation classes without altering the corresponding IDL interface. Additionally, as a development effort progresses, IDL interfaces will probably be created for classes not originally predicted as visible to ORB clients. This process is the natural evolution of the design and implementation process. Plus, if you base your class naming convention on the preceding ORB-centric approach, any of these eventualities will necessitate renaming one or more classes and (probably) its containing file.

We recommend adding a suffix to the name of each IDL interface — not the implementation classes — with an abbreviation of the word "interface" (such as, `MediaManagerI`). This convention enables developers to use the interface's core name (`MediaManager`) as an implementation class name, if appropriate, and avoids locking implementation classes into the IDL interface layer as with ORB-related suffixes like "impl."

CORBA's Java language mapping is more extensive and detailed than the mappings for other programming languages. Strict mapping areas include the signatures of many ORB runtime components and the signatures of stub and skeleton classes. For a Java-enabled ORB to claim CORBA compliance, it must have runtime components with conformant function signatures and produce stub and skeleton classes with conformant signatures. Imagine the benefits from this greater capability to plug-and-play ORB components from different Java ORB products, especially when viewed in concert with the mobility of Java class files. An applet can be downloaded to a client machine in which a set of runtime class files already reside. These class files can then be used by the client applet and, in turn, interact with the applet's stub classes regardless of the providing ORB vendor.

Implementing an Interface Definition Language Interface in Java

The additional implementation complexity from CORBA-enabling a server application resides two places: the server's initialization code; and the intersection of the server's implementation classes and the skeleton classes produced by the IDL compiler. This intersection must accomplish the mapping between IDL functions and data structures and the server's implementation of the corresponding functions and data structures. The process can be straightforward for simple functions and data types; for complex, user-defined data types, however, the process can possess meaningful complexity. Java's built-in complex data types provide some help.

Listing 9-2 contains the `main()` function of my media access server. As with any Java application, this function is automatically called when the server is launched. Our main function establishes the connection with the ORB object itself by calling its `ORB.init()` function. The ORB class provided with CORBA-compliant Java ORBs assists with server activation, client/server connection establishment, and other ORB management functions. `org.omg.CORBA.ORB.init()` is a static function on the ORB class that initializes and informs the ORB the server is running and ready to receive client invocations. Its return value is a reference to an ORB object. Internally, this function typically initiates a thread for which to listen and handle client connections.

The Java language mapping defines three overloaded `ORB.init functions`:

1. `public static ORB init(String[] args, java.util.Properties);`

2. `public static ORB init(java.applet.Applet app, java.util.Properties);`

3. `public static ORB init();`

The first initializes the ORB for a Java application while the second initializes the ORB for a Java applet. The third is provided as a convenience: it simply allows an application to access an ORB object to use its facilities (such as Typecode creation support).

After initializing the ORB object, the `main()` function creates my server's singleton objects, `MediaManager` and `UserAccountManager`. After constructing these objects, pass their references to the `ORB.connect()` function, which places the reference of the passed object into the ORB's object table. The object table is a data structure internal to the ORB management classes and is used by those classes to locate target implementation objects when invocations arrive at the server. Each ORB-enabled object should be passed to `ORB.connect()` when it is ready to receive incoming function calls.

Listing 9-2: Server's main() function

```
public class MediaOnDemandServer
{
public static org.omg.CORBA.ORB orb;
public static void main(String[] args)
{
orb = org.omg.CORBA.ORB.init(args,null);
MediaManager mediaMgr = null;
UserAccountManager userMgr = null;
mediaMgr = new MediaManager();
orb.connect(mediaMgr);
userMgr = new UserAccountManager();
orb.connect(userMgr);
}
}
```

Listing 9-3 contains the constructor of the MediaManager class. This function instantiates my MediaItem objects, passing a reference to the ORB.connect() function.

Listing 9-3: MediaManager constructor

```
public MediaManager()
{
items[0] = new MediaItem("Action Movie 1", (float)3.0,
  "http://www.somedomain.com/movies/am1Review.html",
  "http://www.somedomain.com/movies/am1.mov");
MediaPlayerServer.orb.connect(items[0]);
items[1] = new MediaItem("Action Movie 2", (float)3.5,
  "http://www.somedomain.com/movies/am2Review.html",
  "http://www.somedomain.com/movies/am2.mov");
MediaPlayerServer.orb.connect(items[1]);
items[2] = new MediaItem("Music Album 1", (float).25,
  "http://www.somedomain.com/movies/ma1Review.html",
  "http://www.somedomain.com/movies/ma1.avi");
MediaPlayerServer.orb.connect(items[2]);
items[3] = new MediaItem("Music Album 2", (float).25,
  "http://www.somedomain.com/movies/ma1Review.html",
  "http://www.somedomain.com/movies/ma1.avi");
MediaPlayerServer.orb.connect(items[3]);
}
```

Listings 9-2 and 9-3 illustrate our server's initialization sequence. Once the server's initialization process concludes, clients may begin making ORB calls to the server's objects.

Now that we have addressed the server's initialization code, we need to provide implementations for the functions declared in the IDL interface. The IDL compiler generated skeleton classes for each interface (we discuss Java skeleton classes at length in later sections). To ORB-enable my server's implementation classes, a linkage between these classes and the skeleton classes must be established. Most

ORB products support two methods of creating this linkage. Based on the difference between inheritance and delegation, the distinction between these two methods is extremely important when Java is the server's implementation language. Figure 9-5 illustrates the two approaches and the disadvantage of using the inheritance-based approach when implementing your server in Java.

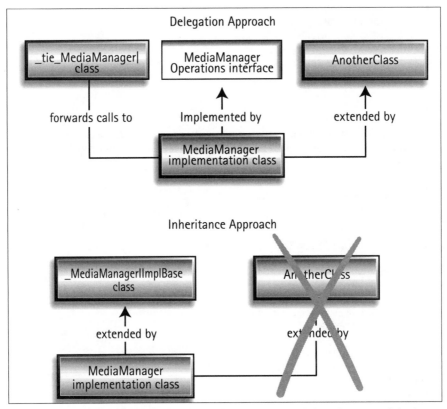

Figure 9-5: Connecting Implementation and Skeleton Classes, Delegation versus Inheritance

The inheritance-based approach requires that the class implementing an IDL interface *extend* (inherit the interface and implementation of) a base class generated by the IDL compiler. This base class allows the ORB to forward incoming calls to the implementation object, provides some convenience functions, and (either directly or through inheritance) provides some marshalling and unmarshalling convenience functions.

In contrast, the delegation-based approach eliminates the need for the implementation class to extend an ORB-generated class and allows it to *implement* (inherit the interface of) a Java interface generated by the IDL compiler. This approach is often called the *tie* method because an implementation object is tied to a skeleton object at runtime by passing its reference to the tie object's constructor. Passing an implementation object to its tie object is necessary so the ORB can, via the tie object, forward incoming calls to the implementation object. A tie object delegates the handling of incoming function calls to its implementation object.

When implementing a server in Java, the proper approach is more important than in most programming languages, due to Java's lack of support for multiple inheritance. As illustrated in Figure 9-5, selecting the inheritance method to connect your implementation to the ORB skeleton forfeits the opportunity to have your implementation class inherit from another class.

The declaration of our MediaManager implementation class using the inheritance-based approach is:

```
public class MediaManager extends _MediaManagerIImplBase { }
```

The implementation class extends the IDL-generated base class. The IDL compiler generates the skeleton code such that it calls functions on the base class (MediaManagerIImplBase), but by virtue of inheritance and late binding, the runtime function calls will be invoked on the extending implementation class, MediaManager. Using the delegation-based approach, the implementation class implements a Java interface generated by the IDL compiler.

```
public class MediaManager implements _MediaManagerIOperations { }
```

The generated Java interface, MediaManagerIOperations, provides an inheritance base for implementation classes and, as a result, enforces Java's CORBA language mappings for the implemented IDL interface. is Listing 9-4 provides the Java interface generated for the MediaManagerI IDL interface.

Listing 9-4: Java interface _MediaManagerIOperations, generated by IDL compiler

```
public interface _MediaManagerIOperations
{
public String[] getMediaTypes() ;
public String[] getAllGenresOfType(String mediaType)
throws MPS.or.NoSuchMediaType;
public String[] getAllArtistsOfType(String mediaType)
throws MPS.or.NoSuchMediaType;
public MPS.or.BasicItemInfoType[] getItemsMatchingCriteria(String
 mediaType,
    String genre,
    String artist,
    String year) ;
}
```

The MediaManager implementation class must implement and adhere to this interface specification provided by _MediaManagerIOperations.

Listing 9-5 illustrates an additional coding step required by the delegation approach. Rather than constructing the implementation object and letting the construction of its skeleton base class establish the link with the ORB skeleton (the inheritance approach), we must construct the implementation object and its tie object, passing the implementation object to the tie object's constructor. Then, as the server receives function calls from clients, the tie object receives and forwards (delegates) them to its implementation object.

Listing 9-5: Server's main() function using the tie approach

```
public class MediaOnDemandServer
{
public static org.omg.CORBA.ORB orb;
public static void main(String[] args)
{
orb = org.omg.CORBA.ORB.init(args,null);
MediaManager mediaMgr = null;
UserAccountManager userMgr = null;
MediaManagerI mediaMgrI = null;
UserAccountManagerI userMgrI = null;
//Create the implementation object
mediaMgr = new MediaManager();
//Create the tie object
mediaMgrI = new _tie_MediaManagerI(mediaMgr);
orb.connect(mediaMgrI);
//Create the implementation object
userMgr = new UserAccountManager();
//Create the tie object
userMgrI = new _tie_UserAccountManagerI(userMgr);
orb.connect(userMgrI);
}
}
```

The second aspect of adapting your implementation class to its corresponding IDL interface consists of working with the incoming and outgoing data types, as specified in the IDL to Java mapping. The Java interface definition in Listing 9-4 shows the Java data types that map to the IDL data types used in my MediaManagerI IDL interface, found in Listing 9-1. As discussed earlier, several characteristics of the Java language simplify its integration with CORBA. This aspect can be illustrated by examining how IDL data types are mapped onto Java.

For example, when implementing a CORBA server in C++, an IDL sequence of strings is mapped to a specially generated C++ class built to handle a list of strings. Because Java has a built-in array type, a sequence of items can be mapped to a Java array, further simplifying the use of CORBA in a Java environment. Listing 9-6 implements the MediaManager.getMediaTypes() function. The example creates and populates the array of media type names and returns it to the calling skeleton. The calling skeleton class and the ORB marshall the array's content and returns it to the calling client, allowing Java's garbage collection to free the array's memory.

Listing 9-6: Implementation of `GetMediaTypes()`

```
public String[] getMediaTypes()
{
String types[] = new String[6];
types[0] = new String("Movie");
types[1] = new String("Music Album");
types[2] = new String("Song");
types[3] = new String("Television Show");
types[4] = new String("Athletic Event");
types[5] = new String("Speech/Narration");
return types;
}
```

Due to CORBA's lack of support for standardized pass-by-value, IDL structs are often used to set and obtain an object's state. Listing 9-7 implements the `MediaManager.getItemsMatchingCriteria()` function that returns an array of IDL structs.

Listing 9-7: Implementation of `getItemsMatchingCriteria()`

```
public BasicItemInfoType[] getItemsMatchingCriteria(
    String mediaType, String genre,
    String artist, String year)
{
  BasicItemInfoType matches[] = new BasicItemInfoType[2];
  matches[0] = new BasicItemInfoType(
    "Action Movie 1", items[0]);
  matches[1] = new BasicItemInfoType(
    "Action Movie 2", items[1]);
  return matches;
}
```

CORBA's Java language mapping calls for any user-defined IDL struct to be mapped to a corresponding Java class. The `getItemsMatchingCriteria()` function, therefore, returns an array of references to `BasicItemInfoType` objects. The IDL compiler generates the `BasicItemInfoType` class in response to my definition of the `BasicItemInfoType` IDL struct. As the code suggests, a CORBA-compliant Java class generated for an IDL struct declares a constructor that takes as a parameter each value comprising the struct. The implementation uses this constructor to create the `BasicItemInfoType` objects requested by the client and returns them to the calling skeleton. The skeleton and the ORB then silently marshall the objects into IIOP for transmission to the client.

Multithreading Your CORBA–Based Server

Multithreading helps achieve responsive and scaleable CORBA systems. The need for multithreading arises when many clients demand concurrent access to one or more objects. Servers often handle clients more efficiently by spawning one or more concurrent threads to handle concurrent client demands, especially when the server interacts with other servers while handling client requests. Examine the inefficiency in this example: a client's attempt to access the media access server is blocked as the server waits for a response from the legacy billing application necessitated by the handling of another client's request.

The multithreading-based solution to poor responsiveness spawns one or more threads to handle a client request. These threads respond to a client request without blocking other incoming requests. Java's innate threading support helps implement this solution.

To illustrate the use of Java threads in handling incoming CORBA requests, we have extended the media access server. Using OrbixWeb, a simple implementation of multithreaded request handling in the media access server requires the addition of two classes. Listing 9-8 contains their implementation.

Listing 9-8: Thread-based request filter and request dispatcher classes

```
public class MediaThreadFilter extends ThreadFilter
{
  public MediaThreadFilter()
  { super(); }

  public boolean inRequestPreMarshal(Request rqst)
  {
    Thread rqstThread = new MediaRqstDispatcher(rqst);
    rqstThread.start();
    return false;
  }
}
class MediaRqstDispatcher extends Thread
{
  private Request rqst;
  public MediaRqstDispatcher(Request newRqst)
  { rqst = newRqst; }
  public void run()
  {
    try{_CORBA.Orbix.continueThreadDispatch(rqst);}
    catch(Exception exc)
    {
      System.out.println(
        "Exception at thread dispatch." +
        exc.toString());
      return;
    }
  }
}
```

OrbixWeb provides the `ThreadFilter` abstract base class to give developers access to incoming ORB requests at various points during the marshalling process. The ORB's marshalling sequence that processes each incoming request invokes the empty functions of the base ThreadFilter class, passing the incoming request object as the functions' parameters. The MediaThreadFilter class inherits from ThreadFilter and overrides its inRequestPreMarshal function, thus providing an appropriate function implementation for the server.

As illustrated in Figure 9-6, overriding the inRequestPreMarshall function of the ThreadFilter class enables us to intercept an incoming request prior to the unmarshalling process and spawn a thread to handle the request without blocking other incoming client calls. We spawn a thread by constructing an instance of the MediaRqstDispatcher thread class, sending it the request object, and calling its start function.

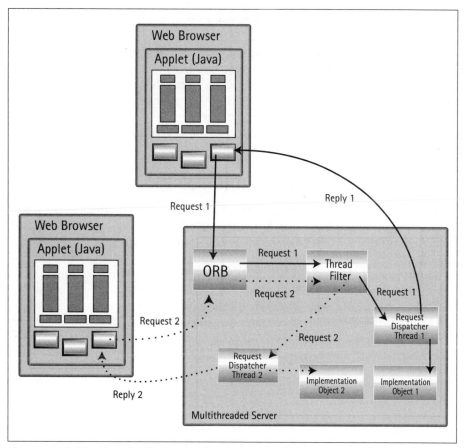

Figure 9-6: A Multithreaded Server Handling Concurrent Client Invocations

As with any Java Thread object, the start function in turn calls the run function. The overloaded run function simply instructs OrbixWeb to continue handling the incoming request within the current, but newly created, thread. The ORB request handling sequence then proceeds to unmarshall the request and make the targeted function call on the targeted implementation object, passing in the unmarshalled input parameters. Finally, when the function returns from the implementation object, the return value and any out or in/out values are marshalled and sent in reply to the client's request – all within the thread spawned for this request.

The solid lines of Figure 9-6 represent the function calls made in support of the remote invocation from client one, while the dotted lines represent the function calls made for the invocation from client two. Without multithreading, client two would have been blocked while the server handled the request from client one, but multithreading allows the server to handle and reply to both client requests concurrently. To safely reap the benefits of this approach, however, your implementation objects must also be implemented in a thread-safe manner.

The preceding multithreading code samples are specific to OrbixWeb. This application gives the developer full control and responsibility to implement a server's threading policies relating to ORB request handling. This responsibility enables (or forces, depending on your point of view) a developer to implement any necessary threading policy to support the required server responsiveness. VisiBroker for Java, on the other hand, offers two precanned threading policies to the developer. To use a VisiBroker threading policy, simply set a configuration parameter: this capability produces a certain amount of simplicity, but the developer maintains less control over a server's threading policy.

What Does a Java IDL Compiler Produce?

Before we illustrate how to design and implement a CORBA client in Java, let's demystify some of the ORB's capabilities by taking a closer look at the Java classes and interfaces that a CORBA-compliant Java IDL compiler produces for a given IDL interface.

As discussed in the previous section, most ORBs support a delegation and an inheritance-based mechanism to create the linkage between a developer's implementation class and a generated skeleton class. To provide these two mechanisms, several Java classes and interfaces must be generated by the IDL compiler for each IDL interface. Figure 9-7 uses the UML notation to illustrate the classes and interfaces that support the delegation-based approach for the MediaManagerI IDL interface.

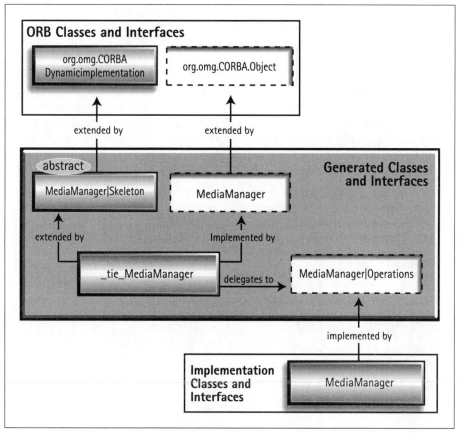

Figure 9-7: Java Constructs Generated by an IDL to Java Compiler, Delegation Approach

The generated classes and interfaces in the center box of Figure 9-7 fulfill the following responsibilities:

_MediaManagerISkeleton is an abstract base class that inherits from org.omg.CORBA.DynamicImplementation to provide the functionality required by CORBA's Dynamic Skeleton Interface (DSI). DSI is the server-side analog to the client's Dynamic Invocation Interface (DII) and eliminates the requirement that the ORB have compile-time knowledge of an implementation class's function signatures to perform an upcall to the targeted function. *Upcall* refers to the function call coming from the ORB to the targeted function in the implementation object (or in the tie object if the tie approach is used). In Figure 9-8, the ORB, when using the DSI to make an upcall, dynamically creates a DSI ServerRequest object and passes it to a DSI compliant _invoke function implemented in the skeleton class. In the example, the _MediaManagerISkeleton class provides the appropriate implementation of _invoke() for the specific functions defined in the MediaManagerI IDL interface. _invoke() interrogates the passed ServerRequest object to evaluate the

name of the target function; in this example, getMediaTypes(). _invoke() then
extracts the input parameters from the ServerRequest object and invokes the target function. To support the _invoke() function, the _MediaManagerISkeleton
class also houses a requisite set of subbed-out abstract functions: one for each target function. These functions are necessary because _invoke() can call a target
function as if it were in the same scope (the same class or interface). The inheriting
tie class then provides an implementation of these abstract functions, as required
by the abstract designation of the base class. As we've previously discussed, the tie
object's implementation of these functions simply makes the corresponding call,
getMediaTypes(), on its implementation object.

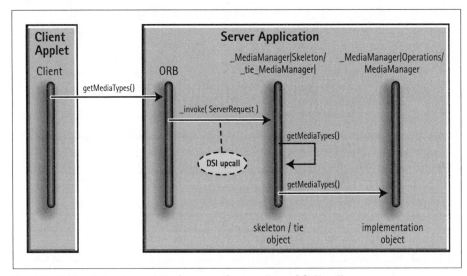

Figure 9-8: The Object Interaction Sequence Surrounding a DSI Upcall

MediaManagerI is a Java interface definition that extends the org.omg.
CORBA.Object interface and contains the function declarations compliant with
CORBA's Java language mapping. derived from the IDL function declarations in the
MediaManagerI IDL interface, these declarations define the functions that must be
implemented by the implementation class or the ties class when using the delegation approach. org.omg.CORBA.Object, from which MediaManagerI inherits, is a
base interface required by CORBA for all implementation and tie classes.

_tie_MediaManagerI is often referred to as the tie class. It extends
_MediaManagerISkeleton and implements MediaManagerI. In the delegation-
based approach, this important class creates the linkage between the implementation class, MediaManager, and the ORB classes. At runtime, a reference to the
implementation object passes into its tie object's constructor. The tie object receives
upcalls from the ORB and uses this reference to forward (delegate) incoming

function calls to the implementation object. As such, the tie object's implementation of each function declared in the MediaManagerI interface simply calls the corresponding target function in its implementation object.

MediaManagerIOperations is a Java interface that only provides an inheritance base for an implementation class. When the implementation object reference is passed to the tie object, it is stored as a reference of type MediaManagerIOperations.

The preceding class and interface hierarchy may seem overly complex, but in keeping with good object-oriented principles, each class and interface has a distinct and separate role. For example, note _MediaManagerISkeleton and MediaManagerI are inherited by the tie class from separate lines of inheritance. Why not have them inherit through the same line of inheritance? Why not just combine them into a single class? The answer is primarily based on the object-oriented principle of separation of concerns. The _MediaManagerISkeleton class focuses on the requirements imposed by the dynamic skeleton interface while MediaManagerI focuses on the more basic requirements of the org.omg. CORBA.Object interface and the static skeleton interface (SSI). These areas of functionality have different concerns and are separated by design.

Figure 9-9 illustrates the classes and interfaces that support the inheritance-based approach for establishing the link between the MediaManager implementation class and the generated ORB classes.

The MediaManagerISkeleton and MediaManagerI in Figure 9-9 fulfill the same responsibilities described in Figure 9-7. The tie class is no longer necessary and is replaced by the _MediaManagerImplBase abstract base class, however. In the inheritance-based approach, _MediaManagerImplBase simply provides a set of constructors and forms the inheritance base for the implementation class. Notice the MediaManagerIOperations Java interface is not necessary using this approach. The implementation class inherits the function signatures required by the MediaManagerI IDL interface and the Java language mapping from the MediaManagerI Java interface now within its upstream inheritance tree. But also notice the implementation class has used up its single inheritance token to become ORB-enabled; this is the disadvantage of the inheritance-based approach when Java is the server's implementation language.

Figure 9-10 illustrates Java classes and interfaces generated by the IDL compiler in support of the client-side ORB functionality.

When the MediaManagerI Java interface resides on the server, it contains the Java function declarations derived (in compliance with CORBA's Java language mapping) from the corresponding IDL functions in the MediaManagerI IDL interface. But rather than imposing this interface contract on the server-side implementation or tie classes, here MediaManagerI Java imposes the interface contract on the client-side stub class. The stub class's interface implementation performs the CORBA-compliant remote method invocations on the server when one of its functions is invoked by a client object.

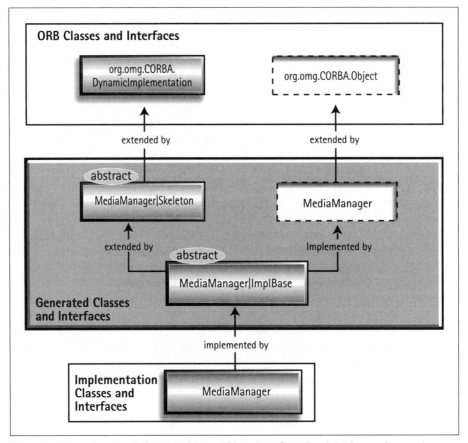

Figure 9-9: Java Constructs Generated by an IDL to Java Compiler, Inheritance Approach

Note _MediaManagerIStub's inheritance from org.omg.CORBA.portable.
ObjectImpl in Figure 9-10. This ObjectImpl class is a key aspect of the Java language mapping. It enforces the standardized interface to client stubs. CORBA's Java language mapping is more extensive than its other language mappings, which helps CORBA and Java systems take maximum advantage of the Java class file mobility. With a complete standardization of ORB runtime components, stubs, and skeletons, there is less need to dynamically download vendor-specific ORB components. This standardization can potentially allow, for example, an applet developed using OrbixWeb to download to a Netscape client where it interacts with and uses the embedded VisiBroker ORB runtime classes.

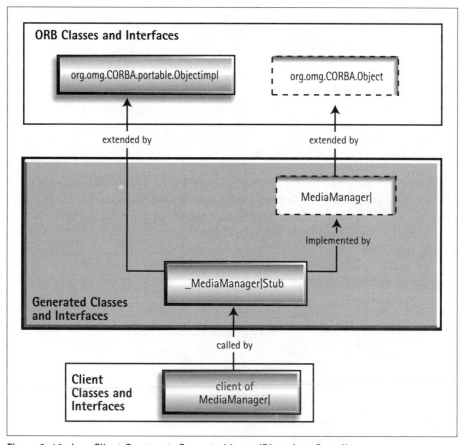

Figure 9-10: Java Client Constructs Generated by an IDL to Java Compiler

Some additional support classes generated by the IDL compiler are not represented in the preceding figures. For each user-defined interface, data type, and exception defined in an IDL file, a helper and a holder class is generated. *Holder classes* are used when an object reference or value is passed as an out or inout parameter. For example, if one of the StringListType data types (an IDL sequence of strings) is passed as an inout parameter, an instance of StringListTypeHolder is created to help marshall and unmarshall the list of strings into a Java string array and hold the resulting string array while the target function is called on the implementation object. The declaration of the StringListTypeHolder class follows in Listing 9-9. The _read and _write functions assist with the unmarshalling and marshalling of parameters whose type is StringListType while the _type function returns the CORBA type code for the StringListType. Type codes enhance type safety when working with incoming and outgoing parameters.

Listing 9-9: Signature of a generated Holder class

```
public final class StringListTypeHolder
    implements org.omg.CORBA.portable.Streamable
{
public String[] value;
public StringListTypeHolder();
public StringListTypeHolder(String[] value);
public void _read (org.omg.CORBA.portable.InputStream _stream);
public void _write (org.omg.CORBA.portable.OutputStream _stream);
public org.omg.CORBA.TypeCode _type ();
}
```

While holder classes hold function parameters, *helper* classes contain static functions to assist with marshalling and unmarshalling parameters of the given type. Helper classes also help to interrogate CORBA Any objects that house values of the given type. Listing 9-10 provides the declaration of the StringList TypeHelper class.

Listing 9-10: Signature of a generated Helper class

```
public class StringListTypeHelper
{
public static void insert (org.omg.CORBA.Any any,
                    String[] value);
public static String[] extract (org.omg.CORBA.Any any);
public static org.omg.CORBA.TypeCode type();
public static String ID ();
public static String[] read (org.omg.CORBA.portable.InputStream
  _stream);
public static void write (org.omg.CORBA.portable.OutputStream
  _stream,
                    String[] value);
}
```

The insert and extract functions set and get, respectively, the string array — an IDL sequence of strings maps to a Java String array — value housed by an Any. The type and ID functions return, respectively, the CORBA type code and type ID for the StringListType data type. Finally, the read and write functions assist with the unmarshalling and marshalling of StringListType-type parameters.

Implementing a CORBA Client in Java

Generally, implementing a CORBA-based client is much easier than implementing a CORBA-based server. Clients typically need not worry about handling incoming ORB events from multiple sources, loading objects, implementing IDL interfaces, supporting persistent objects, and so forth. In some circumstances, however, the complexity of the CORBA aspects of a client applet rivals a server. We address some of these more complex issues in subsequent sections; in this section, we describe how to achieve the basic client/server interaction.

The Java applet is a client to the media access server discussed earlier and Listing 9-1 defines the IDL interface with which we must interact. The server contains two high-level, ORB-visible objects created when the server initializes. These objects are instances of `MediaAccessManagerI` and `UserAccountManagerI`. To establish connectivity with one of these objects, the client applet must initialize itself with the client-side ORB runtime by calling `ORB.init()` and acquire a remote object reference. A reference to a remote object is actually a local proxy object — also called a stub. This object makes CORBA-based distributed object invocations intuitive to the client developer by encapsulating and isolating the calling object from the complexity of distributed, heterogeneous communication.

A few mechanisms allow a client applet to create or get access to its first remote object reference. Once the applet has created its first remote reference, it can create others in the same manner or begin making calls to the server, thereby receiving other remote object references as function return values. Some of the mechanisms available for acquiring the first remote reference include:

◆ Accessing a CORBA naming service for an object with a given name.

◆ Querying a CORBA trader service for one or more objects with a given set of characteristics.

◆ Using a mechanism such as "bind," supported by some ORB products, that allows clients to describe location and identification properties of a remote object.

◆ Invoking the CORBA-compliant ORB function `string_to_object()`, which takes a stringified IOR and constructs a corresponding proxy object.

This last mechanism is suited to Java applet-based clients. The stringified IOR may be embedded as a parameter in the `APPLET` tag of the referencing HTML page and accessed at applet initialization. The applet's `APPLET` tag follows:

```
<APPLET  code=MPC.MediaPlayerClient  width=590  height=400>
<param name=mediaMgrIORString value="** IOR string goes here **">
<param name=userMgrIORString value="** IOR string goes here **">
</APPLET>
```

Notice the last two APPLET tag parameters are IOR string placeholders. These placeholders are normally long and largely unintelligible stringified IORs. But, for readability, we've replaced them here with imaginary placeholders. The two stringified IORs are created by the server using CORBA's `object_to_string` function. As part of the server's initialization process, the function writes these two strings to a file. We then embed them in the `APPLET` tag as part of the applet deployment process.

Note these two strings do not change at each start of the server. For simplicity, the server creates the two strings at every launch. The strings only need to change if the server is moved to another computer with a different IP address or if the server is reconfigured to listen for remote connections on a different socket. In subsequent sections of this chapter, we address a solution to this problem using CORBA's naming service. Listing 9-11 illustrates the client applet establishing connectivity with the media access server using stringified IOR's embedded in its APPLET tag.

Listing 9-11: Connecting to server objects using IORs in the APPLET tag

```
public boolean initializeServerConnection()
{
//Retrieve the stringified object references from the APPLET
 parameters
String mediaMgrIORString = getParameter("mediaMgrIORString");
String accountMgrIORString = getParameter("userMgrIORString");
// Initialize the client ORB runtime
ORB.init(this, null);
// Use the stringified object references
// to create and initialize proxy objects
try {
  theMediaMgr = ORB.string_to_object(mediaMgrIORString);
  theUserAccountMgr = ORB.string_to_object(accountMgrIORString);
}
catch(SystemException exc) {
  displayMsg ("Connection failed.\n" +
           "Unexpected System exception:\n" +
           exc.toString ());
   return false;
}
// Construct the proxy wrapper objects,
// a design convention
theMediaMgrWrapper =
         new MediaMgrProxyWrap(theMediaMgr);
theUserAccountMgrWrapper =
         new UserAccountMgrProxyWrap(theUserAccountMgr);
return true;
}
```

The initialization code in Listing 9-11 handles the CORBA standard exceptions. Exceptions are yet another area where a standard facility of Java simplifies its coexistence with CORBA. Due to the comparatively higher failure potential, exceptions play an important role in distributed systems and, as such, the CORBA standard. However, all programming languages and compilers do not support exceptions to the same extent or in the same manner. Because IDL compilers generate source code and must often support multiple source code compilers for a given language, uneven exception support creates inconsistency and complexity in ORB products targeted at those languages and compilers. In contrast, the Java language and the JDK compiler have innate and consistent support for exception handling, which results in more robust and streamlined Java ORB implementations.

A final note about the code in Listing 9-11: after initializing the client-side proxies using `object_to_string`, we pass the proxy object references to proxy wrapper class constructors. CORBA does not require the use and creation of proxy wrapper objects, but these objects can be a useful design convention when developing a CORBA client of meaningful complexity. In this design, illustrated in Figure 9-11, a proxy wrapper invokes the requested function on the actual proxy object, handles generated exceptions as appropriate for the applet (which may entail displaying a message dialog or generating an applet-specific, higher-level exception), and deals with complex IDL data types.

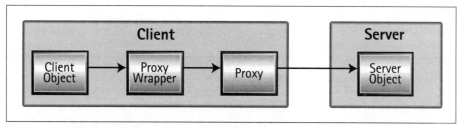

Figure 9-11: Remote Object Invocation using a Proxy Wrapper

Under the right circumstances, this design pattern results in a more modular and maintainable client application. Listing 9-12 illustrates the `getMediaTypes()` function implementation of the client's `MediaManagerProxyWrap` class.

Listing 9-12: `getMediaTypes()` function of the proxy wrapper class

```
void getMediaTypes(Choice mediaTypeContainer)
{
String[] mediaTypes;
//Invoke the corresponding call
//on the server object
try {
  mediaTypes = theMediaMgr.getMediaTypes();
}
catch(System Exception exc) {
  //Handle any exception appropriately
  MediaPlayerClient.showMessageDialog(
   "The Media Access Service could not be contacted. Please try
  again later.");
  return;
}
//Traverse and use the returned data structure appropriately
for(int i = 0; i < mediaTypes.length(); i++)
{
```

```
mediaTypeContainer.addItem(mediaTypes[i]);
}
}
```

The getMediaTypes function implementation in the MediaManager proxy wrapper class uses its reference to the MediaManagerI ORB proxy object to make the corresponding remote invocation and handle resulting exceptions. The exception handler displays a user-friendly error message in a modal dialog box. If the remote call succeeds, as it typically does, the function uses the resulting string array to populate the java.awt.Choice widget passed to it. The function that called the wrapper function need not concern itself with any aspect of CORBA-based communication, exception handling, or data structures. This strategy provides developers with a good division for task allocation in the client development effort as well as a more manageable client design.

Smart Proxies

Some ORB products provide a proprietary extension called smart or intelligent proxies. *Smart proxies* are proxies with additional application-specific intelligence. These proxies are typically implemented by inheriting from (extending) the base proxy classes generated by the IDL compiler. The proxy wrapper example uses a delegation-based approach to implement a smart proxy. The proxy wrapper performs some application-specific functionality, but delegates handling of the ORB call to the real proxy object.

You can also implement a proxy wrapper using the inheritance-based approach employed by most smart proxy facilities. This alternative approach is considered more elegant by some developers, but it also relies on a proprietary ORB extension (which is not necessarily a bad situation if your application needs the proprietary extension).

Using this approach, the proxy wrapper class inherits — rather than delegates — from the actual proxy class. Consult your ORB's documentation on smart proxies if this alternative appeals to you.

Using the Naming Service to Connect

The previous section used stringified object references embedded in an APPLET tag to create remote object references. A downside exists to this approach, however. CORBA's stringified object references contain the necessary data to allow a client to connect to a remote object. This data typically includes the host identifier on which the object resides and the TCP/IP port on which the object accepts connections. This approach presents a problem if the object's server is moved to another host or if the server is reconfigured to listen on a different TCP/IP port. As a result, avoid distributing a large number of stringified object references in APPLET tags — or by any other means.

Instead, distribute the necessary few configuration values for a client to connect to an application-independent naming service, which can obtain one or more remote references to application-specific objects. It's much easier to ensure and manage the permanent locatability of a single, application-independent naming service object than to ensure and manage the permanent locatability of many application-specific objects.

Assuming the name server contains the named object references and naming contexts represented in Figure 9-12, here is the new APPLET tag for the client using the naming service to connect to the server objects:

```
<APPLET  code=MPC.MediaPlayerClient  width=590  height=400>
<param name=namingServiceName value="NameService">
<param name=mediaServerContextName value="MediaServerContext">
<param name=mediaMgrServerObjectName value="MediaManager">
<param name=userMgrServerObjectName value="UserManager">
</APPLET>
```

The preceding tag has location-independent object names and naming contexts rather than stringified object references in the APPLET tag. We use the following values:

- The name of the naming service, in concert with configuration values that specify the host and TCP/IP port for the remote naming service, obtains a reference to the naming service's root-naming context. We address how to configure the remote host and port values later.

- The name of the media access server's naming context scopes the object names to the media access server's naming context.

- The media manager and user manager object names, in conjunction with the media access server's context name, create the unique names of these specific objects.

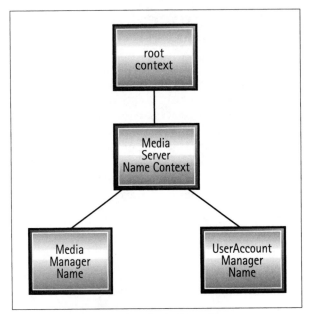

Figure 9-12: Named Objects in the Name Server

Listing 9-13 is the new applet initialization code. It uses the preceding parameters to connect to the naming service and ask for remote references to the MediaManager and UserAccountManager objects.

Listing 9-13: Connecting to server objects using the naming service

```
public boolean initializeServerConnection()
{
org.omg.CORBA.Object genericRootContext;
NamingContext rootNamingContext;
//————————————
//Initialize the naming service, naming context
//and object names
//————————————
//Retrieve parameters from the APPLET tag
String namingServiceName =
getParameter("namingServiceName");
String mediaServerContextName =
getParameter("mediaServerContextName");
String mediaMgrServerObjectName =
getParameter("mediaMgrServerObjectName");
String userMgrServerObjectName =
getParameter("userMgrServerObjectName");
//————————————
//Initialize the local ORB object and connect
//to the remote naming service
```

```
//————————————————
//Initialize the client ORB runtime
ORB.init(this, null);
//Use the naming service name to connect to the naming service
try {
  genericRootContext =
    ORB.init().
    resolve_initial_references(namingServiceName);
  rootNamingContext = NamingContextHelper.
    narrow(genericRootContext);
}
catch( SystemException sysExc ) {
  displayMsg ("Connection failed.\n" +
    "Unexpected System exception:\n" +
      sysExc.toString() );
  return false;
}
catch(org.omg.CORBA.ORBPackage.InvalidName invName) {
  display.print("Connection failed.\n" +
      "Unexpected System exception:\n" +
            invName.toString() );
  return false;
}
//————————————————
//Resolve and initialize the MediaManagerI
//object reference
//————————————————
//Create the MediaManager name using the name
//of the media server context and the MediaManager
//object name within that context
NameComponent[] mediaManagerName = new NameComponent[2] ;
mediaManagerName[0] = new NameComponent(mediaServerContextName,
                                   mediaServerContextName);
mediaManagerName[1] = new NameComponent(mediaMgrServerObjectName,
                                   mediaMgrServerObjectName);
//Get the media manager object reference from
//the naming service and narrow it to the
//MediaManagerI object type
theMediaMgr =
   MediaManagerIHelper.narrow(
     theNamingService.resolve(mediaManagerName));
//Construct the proxy wrapper object
//(a design convention)
theMediaMgrWrapper = new MediaMgrProxyWrap(theMediaMgr);
//————————————————
//Resolve and initialize the UserAccountManagerI
//object reference
//————————————————
...
```

Repeat the preceding code for the user account manager object.

```
...
return true;
}
```

Although the naming service code is more complex in comparison to the stringified object reference code, the naming service approach is a superior method.

In the first section of the `initializeORBConnection` function in Listing 9-13, we simply initialize the local variables based on the contents of the APPLET tag parameters. The next section initializes the local ORB object by calling its `init()` function and calls `resolve_initial_references()` on the local ORB object. This section is the CORBA-compliant mechanism to obtain a reference to the root-naming context in a name server. The chosen ORB product implements this function, but, in general, uses the name of the naming server passed to it, in concert with other configuration values containing the remote host and TCP/IP port on which the naming server can be contacted.

Once connected to the name server's root naming context, we can start requesting named object references. An object's name is housed in a `NameComponent` and composed of the object name and its context name. To construct the `MediaManagerI` `NameComponent`, we use the `mediaServiceContextName` and the `mediaMgrServerObjectName`. We then ask the naming service root context to *resolve* the `NameComponent` — to give us the remote object reference associated with the media manager object name. The application-independent naming service is not aware of the application-specific interface types, however. Before using the resolved reference, we should narrow it to the appropriate type, `MediaManagerI`. As discussed in preceding chapters, narrowing an object reference is the CORBA equivalent of a type cast.

While a bit more involved than stringified IORs, use of the naming service results in a more manageable system, particularly in an environment where client applets are installed on client computers. If we embed stringified IORs for many of the server objects in APPLET tags (or worse yet, in the client code), we will likely have a significant administration problem when we move a server or a server-side object.

Using the Trader Service to Connect

Some high-level decision makers in the Internet product market suggest IIOP will eventually replace HTTP for a large portion of Internet traffic. This reasonable prediction spotlights the possible applications of the CORBA Trader Service on the World Wide Web. As Figure 9-13 illustrates, a clear analogy can be drawn between the Trader Service and a Web search engine. A Web search engine enables a Web site developer to register a URL, which is then parsed (or crawled, in Webspeak) and indexed by the search engine. Subsequent queries to the search engine display the URL as a potential match if the query keywords match the URL keywords.

Similarly, the CORBA Trader Service defines the IDL interfaces necessary to allow registration and searching of objects based on descriptions and service properties. For example, assume you are writing an applet to provide a new RSA-based digital signature in response to a user request. The applet could connect to a trader service – a "Web object search engine" – and make an ORB call requesting a list of references to objects that provide digital signature generation services using RSA. If a match is found, the applet uses the returned object reference to make an ORB call to that object's implementation of a well-defined IDL interface for this service.

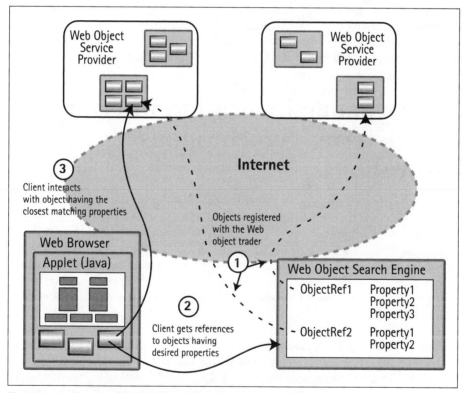

Figure 9-13: How the CORBA Trader Service Fits into the Web

The media access client applet could be improved using this Web object search engine. Rather than limit the user to the movies and songs from one server, you could modify the applet to enable the user to request a search for media access objects providing songs written by a specific author during a specific decade, for example. The applet then calls the Web object search engine with the user query and a returned reference interacts with the new multimedia object server.

Multithreading a Client's Invocations

Given Java's capability to operate in a thin client environment, many CORBA-client applications written in Java have GUIs and need responsiveness when dealing with GUI events. However, the potential latency associated with remote server invocations often undermines relations with interactive GUIs.

An applet's GUI may not provide appropriate responsiveness if it fails to respond to user events while making one or more remote object invocations in response to a previous event. While the typical CORBA-based client/server interactivity is responsive, sometimes heavy server load results in a perceptible delay in responsiveness.

One solution: use threads when making remote server invocations. With this strategy, you create one or more background `Thread` objects to invoke and handle one or more calls to the server. As the background thread waits for responses to its remote invocations, the rest of the applet can respond to additional GUI events.

The Dynamic Invocation Interface and Deferred Synchronous Invocations

A less appealing alternative to threads when making remote object calls uses CORBA's Dynamic Invocation Interface (DII) and its support for deferred synchronous request invocations.

The DII is an alternative to the SII (static invocation interface). The *SII* is the normal mechanism used by the developer to make a remote invocation. Its interface is embodied in the stubs generated by the IDL compiler in conformance with a server's IDL interface. The DII, on the other hand, does not rely on the existence of statically compiled stubs and their requisite function signatures. Instead, it provides a set of generic classes and functions that allow the client application to dynamically construct and invoke a remote request. This request can be invoked in a synchronous (blocking) or deferred synchronous (nonblocking) mode. Deferred synchronous invocations enable the client to continue processing immediately after invoking a normally synchronous remote request. The request can be polled later to check for a response.

Listing 9-14 contains the implementation of the `getArtists()` function using this approach.

Listing 9-14: Invoking the synchronous `getArtists()` function asynchronously

```
void getArtists(String selectedType, List artistsContainer)
{
Request mTypesRequest;
```

```
try {
//Create the request object
mTypesRequest = theMediaMgr._request("getArtists ");
}
catch (SystemException ex) {
//Handle any exception appropriately
MediaPlayerClient.showMessageDialog(
  "The Media Access client software you are using is out of date.");
return;
}
try {
//Insert the request's arguments
mTypesRequest.add_in_arg().insert_string(selectedType);
mTypesRequest.set_return_type(
  StringListTypeHelper.type());
}
catch (SystemException ex) {
//Handle any exception appropriately
MediaPlayerClient.showMessageDialog(
  "The Media Access client software you are using is out of date.");
return;
}
try {
//Invoke the request asynchronously, deferring the
//return value
mTypesRequest.send_deferred();
}
catch (SystemException ex) {
//Handle any exception appropriately
MediaPlayerClient.showMessageDialog(
"The Media Access client software you are using is out of date.");
return;
}
//Add the request to a local list so that it
//may be periodically polled for a response.
addRequestToList(mTypesRequest);
}
```

The last line of the `getArtists()` function simply adds the request object to a list of requests. You should maintain the list of requests invoked using `send_deferred` to periodically poll for and handle request responses. The following `pollRequests` function in Listing 9-15 performs this task by looping through the list of requests and calling the `poll_response` function on each request. If the return value of this function is true, the request's target operation is assessed and the appropriate return value and out parameters are extracted and passed to a response handler function.

Listing 9-15: Polling request objects for a response

```
void pollRequests()
{
```

```
//Loop through the deferred request objects
for(int i = 0; i < 100; i=i+1)
{
//If the function has returned
if(deferredSynchronousRequests[i].poll_response())
{
    //If the function target was "getArtists"
    if(deferredSynchronousRequests[i].
    operation.equals("getArtists")
    {
      //Extract the value from the request's return value
      String[] artists = deferredSynchronousRequests[i].
        result().value();
      //Use the return value
      handleGetArtistsResponse(artists);
    }
    else if(...)
    {
      //Handle other target functions
      ...
    }
}
}
}
```

Using the DII is an complicated approach; the preceding listings do not completely address the DII's complexity. However, its capabilities are useful when a client application does not and cannot have compile-time knowledge of a server's interface. For example, an applet designed to debug and test server interfaces would parse the server's interface repository at runtime and dynamically build and invoke calls on those interfaces. In a following section, we develop this applet, discuss CORBA's Interface Repository (IR) in detail, and revisit the utility of the DII in relation to IR.

Distributing a Client Applet

After implementation of the client applet, we need to deploy its class files to support the chosen applet distribution scheme. While often overlooked, the efficient movement of necessary Java class files (for the applet as well as the ORB) to the user's computer is a vital and intricate issue. The potential need to download the ORB support classes exacerbates the download delay problem. The following factors underscore the distribution problem and potential solutions:

◆ Java's lazy class loader

◆ Web browser caching

◆ Client-side administration

◆ Java Archive (JAR) files

◆ Automated, channel-based distribution

The obvious deployment goal is to minimize the time delay and frequency of applet downloads, but you also need to manage the occasional odd behavior resulting from dependence on Java's lazy class loader. The class loader does not download a class file until necessary to support the functioning applet (as when a class function is invoked or an instance of the class is created). However, a user may be surprised when a seemingly minor interaction with the applet's GUI results in a delayed response as the class loader silently downloads one or more class files from the server. You can eliminate these delays by forcing the download of all classes at initialization: call a null static function on each class from within a low priority background thread or by embedding all the class files in a JAR file.

Building your applet's many class files into a single JAR file significantly lessens its total download time. Although a separate HTTP connection must be created for each downloaded file, a JAR file contains all class files and only needs to create one connection. If you have a large number of class files, the time savings can be substantial, though the entire download must occur in a single chunk at applet initialization.

TIP You need to identify the classes required by your applet to create the smallest JAR file. To identify this minimum set of Java class files, try using the class profiling capability of Netscape's Java console. Before loading the HTML page referencing your applet, start the Java console and maximize its applet profiling by pressing the 9 key on your keyboard. Then load the Web page that references your applet. The Java console outputs the name of each class file loaded by Java's loader to support the executing applet. Be sure to exercise some of your applet's capabilities to ensure Java's lazy loader loads all the classes your applet needs.

The capability of browsers to cache Java class files on the client host is improving. Users manually clear their cache, however, and the browser frequently deletes cached files to make room for new files. For these reasons, do not rely heavily on the user's client-side cache to eliminate download delays. A promising new innovation, automated applet distribution using channels, addresses this problem. Marimba Channels, for example, is an automated distribution product bundled with the Netscape client. Using Marimba, applet class files can be associated with specific distribution channels from which they are automatically updated on the client computer only when necessary. Once downloaded, they are separately managed from the browser's cache and safe from its nonconfigurable and simplistic cache management policies.

Although establishing and managing distribution channels requires some client- and server-side administration, the management of automated distribution channels in large enterprise systems is worth the effort.

Although installing applet class files on client hosts maintains the other benefits of Java, it sacrifices the zero-client-administration benefit of Java applets. Client users are periodically required to download and install the new class files. This disadvantage may be mitigated by large applets used in an enterprise's intranet environment in which the client update process can be effectively managed.

The Firewall Problem

When a distributed system is deployed behind a corporate firewall on an intranet, the firewall provides security against potential eavesdroppers. When your distributed application must venture outside a corporate firewall to participate in an extranet or the Internet, however, firewall navigation can pose a difficult problem.

Most corporations protect their internal networks from outside influences by establishing one or more firewall proxy hosts (also called bastion hosts). A *bastion host* is a computer through which incoming and outgoing network connections are routed, monitored, and potentially denied. The software application that resides on a bastion host and performs the monitoring of network connection requests is called a *firewall proxy*. Firewall proxies can be configured to disallow or permit external connections to and from specific groups of IP addresses for specific transmission protocols. For example, to enable employee access to Web resources, many firewall proxies allow HTTP connections to most external IP addresses.

CORBA's over-the-wire protocol, IIOP, is not immune to the firewall problem. The comparative youth of network protocols undermines IIOP on this issue. A network protocol must gain a level of ubiquity before most firewall proxy vendors support it in their mission-critical products. IIOP-enabled firewall proxies are a critical component in the acceptance of Java and CORBA-based applications on extranets and the Internet.

Figure 9-14 represents the architecture of the multimedia-on-demand system modified to acknowledge the likely existence of a provider's (server-side) firewall. Note the following architecture changes: the addition of a bastion host, insertion of an IIOP-capable firewall proxy, and relocation of the Web server and its content (Java class files, HTML pages, and multimedia files) to the bastion host. This architecture provides the necessary client-side functionality with full protection for the legacy billing application and other critical or private corporate data.

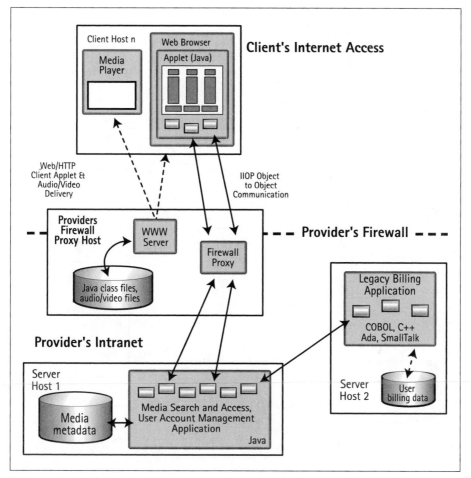

Figure 9-14: The Sample Application with a Server-side Firewall

The critical enabling technology in this architecture is the IIOP-aware firewall proxy. This proxy forwards IIOP invocations to a specified set of objects residing within the media search and access server while guarding against external invocations on the legacy billing application. For this architecture to function properly, however, the IIOP invocations emanating from the client applet must contain the IOR of their ultimate target. The interoperable object reference of the target object in the media search and access server must be embedded in the IIOP packet set to the bastion host. The firewall proxy recognizes the incoming IIOP packet, extracts the target IOR, and forwards the invocation to the target object.

Although the architecture in Figure 9-14 is more realistic than originally suggested in Figure 9-3, it still may not fully acknowledge the firewall problem. Figure 9-15 builds further on the architecture to address the likely existence of a client-side firewall.

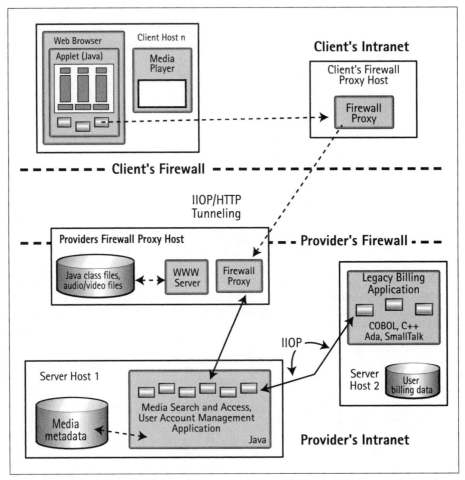

Figure 9-15: The Sample Application with a Server-side and Client-side Firewall

With a client-side firewall proxy, the server application provider (in this case, the provider of the media access server) may have no control over its configuration. Therefore, you cannot count on its capability to allow IIOP connections from its protected client computers to an external server or even recognize the IIOP protocol. Some ORB vendors employ protocol tunneling to solve this problem. Using this solution, the applet running in the client's browser dynamically detects the failure of its IIOP connection attempt to the server due to a client-side firewall intervention. After making this assessment, the client applet embeds (tunnels) the IIOP request into an HTTP request and sends it to the provider's firewall proxy – taking advantage of most firewall proxies' acceptance of outgoing HTTP requests. The provider's proxy then extracts the IIOP packet from the HTTP request and forwards it to the target object.

OrbixWeb and VisiBroker for Java both have built-in support for firewall navigation and server-side IIOP request forwarding. OrbixWeb uses HTTP tunneling to traverse client-side firewalls and works in concert with WonderWall, IONA's IIOP-aware firewall proxy. Similarly, VisiBroker for Java works with its server-side IIOP proxy, Gatekeeper.

CORBA and the Java Security Model

Java's security model and additional security restrictions often imposed by Internet browsers have important implications for applets that must connect (open a socket) back to one or more servers. By default, Java only allows an applet to open a socket connection to a computer from which the applet was downloaded. This restriction prevents a malicious applet from interacting with computers inside a corporate firewall once downloaded to the client's computer. Java overcomes this restriction by installing the applet on the client's computer and then loading it into the browser from the local hard drive. However, Web browsers now eliminate the privileged socket connection status of locally-loaded applets. As a result, applet signatures provide the best liberal server connectivity policy for applets.

The capability of a CORBA-enabled applet to connect to more than one server on more than one host is attractive to enterprise system developers. We recommend enterprise developers use the capabilities of the JDK and their chosen Web browser to create digitally signed applets under these circumstances. Digital signatures, however, produce some limited client-side administration. Although the user's Web browser informs the user the downloaded applet requests special privileges and requires user acknowledgment, this notification is mitigated by the benefits of a CORBA- and Web-based enterprise system.

An Applet Using CORBA's Interface Repository

CORBA's IR enables a client application to dynamically ask a remote object about its interface characteristics. Using the IR, a remote CORBA object can be dynamically interrogated to reveal every aspect of its interface. Before we write a Java applet with the IR, let's review some of its design traits and functionality.

Because every aspect of an object or server's interface can be examined, the interface of the Interface Repository is intricate. Figure 9-16 uses the UML notation to create an object-oriented representation of a portion of the IR's interface inheritance hierarchy.

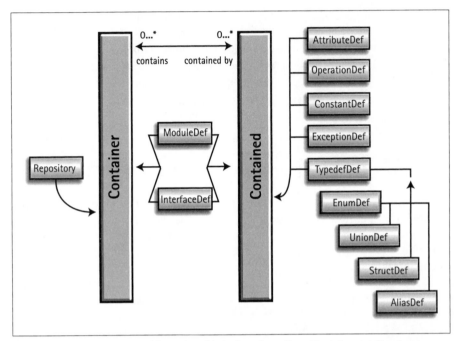

Figure 9-16: The Inheritance Hierarchy of Interface Repository Containment Constructs

Interface objects can be classified on whether they are containers for other inter-face objects, contained by other interface objects, or both options. Repository objects, for example, can contain interface objects like `ModuleDefs` and `InterfaceDefs` but cannot be contained by them. `ModuleDefs` and `InterfaceDefs`, on the other hand, can be contained by other interface objects and may also be containers for interface objects like `AttributesDefs` and `OperationDefs`. `AttributeDef` and `OperationDef` objects may be contained in other interface objects but cannot be containers for other interface objects. Any container object can be asked to provide its contents by invoking the function in Listing 9-16:

Listing 9-16: The `contents()` function in the `Container` interface

```
interface Container :IRObject {
...
ContainedSeq contents(in DefinitionKind limit_type,
      in boolean exclude_inherited);
...
};
```

The function returns a `ContainedSeq`, a typedef representing a sequence of references to contained objects. Once we have a reference to a contained object, we interrogate its characteristics by calling its `describe` function in Listing 9-17:

Listing 9-17: The `describe` function in the `Contained` interface

```
Interface Contained:IRObject {
...
  Description describe();
...
};
```

This function returns a `Description` name/value pair, in which the string name indicates the nature of the contained item (`InterfaceDescription`, `OperationDescription`, and so forth) and the value is a structure containing its componential description. As illustrated in Listing 9-18, the value of an `InterfaceDescription` contained item, for example, is housed in a data structure defined in the CORBA standard.

Listing 9-18: Definition of the `FullInterfaceDescription` data structure

```
struct FullInterfaceDescription{
  Identifier name;              //Interface name
  RepositoryID id;              //Unique ID
  RepositoryID defined_in;      //Container ID
  VersionSpec version;          //Interface version
  OpDescriptionSeq operations;  //Operation descriptions
  AttrDescriptionSeq attributes;//Attribute descriptions
  RepositoryIdSeq baseInterfaces;//Inherited interfaces
  TypeCode type;                //Interface typecode
}
```

The operations field of the preceding data structure is of type `OpDescriptionSeq`, a sequence of `OperationDescriptions`. Listing 9-19 illustrates an `OperationDescription` data structure defined in the CORBA standard.

Listing 9-19: Definition of the `OperationDescription` data structure

```
struct OperationDescription{
  Identifier name;    //Operation name
  RepositoryID id;    //Unique ID
  RepositoryID defined_in; //Container ID
  TypeCode result;  //Return value type
  OperationDef::OperationMode mode; //oneway or normal
  sequence<OperationDef::ContextIdentifier> contexts;
    //Context identifiers
  sequence<ParameterDescription> parameters;
    //Function parameters
  sequence<ExceptionDescription> exceptions;
    //Function exceptions
}
```

After reviewing the IR design, the result of the following function should be clear:

```
InterfaceDef CORBA.Object._get_interface();
```

All CORBA-compliant ORB objects inherit from CORBA::Object. Given a reference to an ORB object, we obtain a reference to its interface definition object by calling _get_interface(). Recall from Figure 9-16 the returned type, InterfaceDef, inherits from Contained. As a result, we can call its describe() function to obtain its FullInterfaceDescription. Alternatively, the InterfaceDef IDL interface provides describe_interface(), which also returns a FullInterfaceDescription.

We use these IR facilities to implement an object interrogation applet. The applet can, given any CORBA object reference, examine the object's interface and present its operations characteristics to the user. The applet may then test the object's functions (using the capabilities of the DII) to dynamically build and invoke functions (requests) on the remote object.

Figure 9-17 illustrates the development time and runtime components to provide the available functionality from the IR and DII. The diagram also suggests five primary steps or events to use these components:

1. Compile the IDL interface using the IDL compiler switch necessary to force its population of the interface repository. The IDL compiler also produces stub and skeleton classes.

2. Compile the application and skeleton classes to produce the server application.

3. Once the server has been launched and the client applet is running, it calls _get_interface() on the target object. This function is defined in the org.omg.CORBA.Object base interface and returns a reference to the object's InterfaceDef.

4. Invoke describe_interface() on the InterfaceDef object acquired in step 3. This call returns the full description of the attributes and operations housed within the object's interface, and implemented by the target object.

5. After the client has constructed a Request object using the operation definitions acquired in step 4, it uses the DII to send the Request object to the target object by calling invoke() on the Request object.

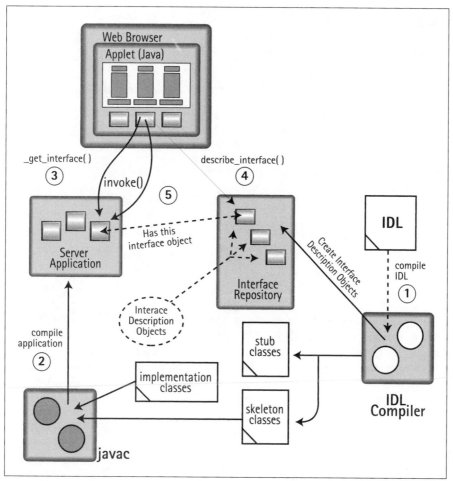

Figure 9-17: The Components and Steps Required to Use CORBA Interface Repository

The class InterfaceTester in Listing 9-20 houses the object interrogation applet core. As illustrated in steps 3 – 5 of Figure 9-17, the class obtains an object's interface description, presents it to the user, and invokes methods on the object's interface using the DII.

Listing 9-20: Acquiring a reference to the target object's interface definition

```
class InterfaceTester
{
private Repository theRepository;
private Contained containedItem;
private InterfaceDef anInterface;
private InterfaceDef.FullInterfaceDescription
 anInterfaceDescription;
```

```
private orb.omg.CORBA.Object remoteObject;
  void interrogateObject()
{
remoteObject = getObjectToInterrogate();
try{ anInterface = remoteObject._get_interface();}
catch(…) { …handle exceptions … }
try{ anInterfaceDescription = anInterface.describe_interface(); }
catch( … ) { …handle exceptions …}
for(int i = 0; i < anInterfaceDescription.operations.length(); i++)
{
displayOperation(anInterfaceDescription.operations[i]);
}
for(int j = 0; j < anInterfaceDescription.attributes.length(); j++)
{
displayAttribute(anInterfaceDescription.attributes[j]);
}
}
```

The interrogateObject() function obtains a remote object reference by calling getObjectToInterrogate() and acquires a reference to the object's interface definition by calling its _get_interface() function (provided by the base class CORBA.Object). With a reference to the object's interface definition object, we obtain the complete definition of the interface by simply calling its describe_interface() function. This function returns a FullInterfaceDescription object as illustrated in Listing 9-20. We use the contents of this object to display the interface's operations and attributes to the user. The FullInterfaceDescription object houses an array of OperationDescriptions and an array of AttributeDescriptions. We loop through the content of the operations and attributes arrays and display the content of each array.

The displayOperation and addParamToDisplay() functions in Listing 9-21 interrogate the parameters and low-level characteristics of an operation description and populate the corresponding applet display widgets. addParamToDisplay() illustrates some of the detailed information available from the IR. This function evaluates the mode and type of the parameter and concatenates them with the parameter name for display purposes. CORBA defines an enumerated value indicating the parameter's mode – in, out, inout – and a set of type code kind constants to support the evaluations of type codes. We compare the kind constants associated with each operation parameter to the kind constants associated with the string and short types and populate the type display string appropriately. For simplicity, the applet only knows how to interact with shorts and strings. However, the constructs used with these data types also apply to the other IDL-supported data types.

Listing 9-21: Parsing and displaying the acquired interface definition

```
public void displayOperation(OperationDescription op)
{
operationList.insert(op.identifier);
for(int i = 0; i < op.parameters.length(); i++)
```

```
{
addParamToDisplay(op.parameters[i], i);
}
{
public void addParamToDisplay(ParameterDescription param, int index)
{
  String mode;
  String type;
  if(param.mode == PARAM_IN)
    mode = " in ";
  else if(param.mode == PARAM_OUT)
    mode = " out ";
  else if(param.mode == PARAM_INOUT)
    mode = " inout ";
  else
    mode = " unknown ";
  if(param.type.kind.value == TCKind._tk_short)
    type = " short ";
  if(param.type.kind.value == TCKind._tk_string)
    type = " string ";
  operationsList.insert(mode + type + param.name)
}
```

The following functions in Listing 9-22 provide the object-testing capabilities of the interrogation applet. They use the operation descriptions retrieved from the IR for a given object to build and invoke a request object using the DII. Importantly, the applet can invoke functions on any CORBA object with an interface defined in an accessible interface repository. We do not need to compile in stubs specific to the objects we want to test.

The testObject() function in Listing 9-22 simply loops through each of the object's operation descriptions acquired from the IR and invokes the testOperation function on each description.

Listing 9-22: Implementation of testObject()

```
public void testObject()
{
for(int i = 0; i < anInterfaceDescription.operations.length(); i++)
{
  testOperation(anInterfaceDescription.operations[i]);
}
}
```

To build and invoke a Request object with the DII, the testOperation() function in Listing 9-23 first creates a request by calling the static function _request, a function supported by all CORBA-compliant objects. We then loop through the operation's parameter descriptions and pass each description to addParamToRqst().

Listing 9-23: Testing each function in the target object using the DII

```
public void testOperation(OperationDescription opDescr)
{
Request rqst;
NamedValue result;
try {
  //Set the name of the function to be invoked
  // by the request
  rqst = theMediaMgr._request(opDescr.identifier);
}
catch (…) { … handle exceptions … }
for(int i = 0; i < opDescr.parameters.length(); i++)
{
  addParamToRqst(rqst, opDescr.parameters[i], i);
}
try{ rqst.invoke(); }
catch(…) { … handle exceptions … }
try{ result = rqst.result(); }
catch( … ) { … handle exceptions … }
displayOperationTestResult(result);
}
```

Somewhat similar to the `addParamToDisplay()` function, `addParamToRqst()` in Listing 9-24 evaluates the mode and type of the parameter and obtains the GUI widget input value as completed by the user. This value is fed into the request's parameter list using `add_in_arg()`.

Listing 9-24: Adding a parameter to a DII `Request` object

```
public void addParamToRqst(Request rqst, ParameterDescription param,
  int index)
{
  //Is it an in parameter
  if(param.mode == PARAM_IN)
  {
    //Is the constant representing the
    //parameter's type equal
    //to the constant representing the short type
    if(param.type.kind.value == TCKind._tk_short)
    {
    //Get the input value from the GUI list
    //widget and parse it into a short
    short paramVal =
      Short.parseShort(inputValues.getItem[index]);
    //Insert the parameter into the
    //request parameter list
    rqst.add_in_arg().insert_short(paramVal);
    }
    else if(param.type.kind.value == TCKind._tk_string)
    {
      //Get the input value and insert it
      //into the request parameter list
```

```
      rqst.add_in_arg().insert_string(
         inputValues.getItem[index]);
   }
 }
 else if(param.mode == PARAM_OUT)
 { ... handle out parameters ... }
 else if(param.mode == PARAM_INOUT)
 { ... handle inout parameters ... }
}
```

Finally, the `displayOperationTestResult` function in Listing 9-25 evaluates the type of the operation's return value and displays the result to the user. The return value of an invoked Request is housed in the value field of a `NamedValue` object. The value field is of type *Any*, a CORBA data type that can hold a value of any type. The type field indicates the type of the value held by an `Any`. Listing 9-25 evaluates the `Any`'s type field, compares it to `TCKind` constants for the short and string basic types, and displays the resulting value.

Listing 9-25: Acquire and display the result from an invoked DII request

```
public void displayOperationTestResult(
   NamedValue result, int index)
{
if(result.value.type().kind.value == TCKind._tk_short)
{
   short resultValue;
   //Extract the short return value
   try{resultValue = result.value.extract_short();}
   catch(...) { ...handle exceptions ... }
   //Display the return value in the GUI list widget
   resultValues.addItem(Short.toString(resultValue), index);
}
else if(result.value.type().kind.value ==
   TCKind._tk_string)
{
   String resultValue;
   //Extract the string return value
   try{ resultValue = result.value.extract_string(); }
   catch(...) { ...handle exceptions ... }
   //Display the return value in the GUI list widget
   resultValues.addItem(resultValue , index);
}
}
}
```

With most ORB products, interface repository use requires additional software configuration steps. At development time, you typically need to instruct the IDL compiler to populate an interface repository with the interface definitions as it compiles the IDL. Often, the interface repository itself is a separate executable that needs to be launched and/or registered with the ORB activation service. Also, a client's interaction with the IR requires a client have access to its supporting, client-side class files. With an applet, this access may require a dynamically download of the files, thereby adding to the download delay. To streamline this process, examine the section on applet distribution for some mechanisms in this chapter.

The Callback Pattern

The callback pattern frequently occurs in CORBA systems with applet-based thin clients. In this pattern, the client connects to the server and passes it a reference to a client-side callback object. The server then uses this reference to invoke functions on the client. Using the media access server and client as an example, Listings 9-26 and 9-27 illustrate the callback pattern.

The IDL in Listing 9-26 is the MediaItemI interface with a modified play() function that takes a reference to a MediaClientCallbackI object. The MediaClientCallbackI interface is implemented by the client applet and called by the server — if the server's status changes while a media item streams to the client computer.

Listing 9-26: Modified IDL interface to support client callbacks

```
interface MediaItemI
{
DetailedItemInfoType getDetailedInfo();
BasicItemInfoType getBasicInfo();
oneway void play(in UserAccountI customer,
  in MediaClientCallbackI client);
void playComplete(in UserAccountI customer);
};
  interface MediaClientCallbackI
{
  oneway void displayServerStatusMessage(
    in string statusMessage);
};
```

The play() and displayServerStatusMessage() functions in the IDL interfaces are declared oneway. Declaring a oneway play function enables the server to invoke the client callback function from within the play function without creating a deadlock situation. The displayServerStatusMessage function, however, is oneway to optimize the server's performance; We do not want the server to be blocked while it waits for a returning invocation on the client's callback object.

Listing 9-27 contains the implementation of the pertinent callback-related functions. The client provides the reference to its callback object to the server as a parameter to the play() function. At a later time, the server calls its own sendMessageToCurrentViewers() function that uses the callback object references to invoke the displayServerStatusMessage function on each client's MediaClientCallback object.

Listing 9-27: Implementation of the server's callback-related functions

```
class MediaItem
{
  void play(UserAccountI customer,
  MediaClientCallbackI client)
  {
    //Add the customer and its callback
    //reference to the list of current viewers
    addCustomerViewer(customer, client);
  }
  void sendMessageToCurrentViewers(String message)
  {
    for(int i = 0; i < numberOfCurrentUsers; i++)
    {
      //Use the callback reference to call
      //the remote client object
      try
      {
      currentCustomerViewers[i].client.
        displayServerStatusMessage(message);
      }
      catch(...) { ...handle exceptions ... }
    }
  }
}
class MediaClientCallback
{
  MediaClientCallback
  { }
  void displayServerStatusMessage(
    String statusMessage)
  {
    MediaPlayerClient.showMessageDialog(statusMessage);
  }
}
```

A Better Coexistence for CORBA and Java

Due to the comfortable marriage of Java and CORBA, several movements propose to extend and improve their interoperability even further. Some of the realistic and short-term initiatives focus on the following aspects of CORBA and Java:

◆ Extending CORBA's Interface Repository standard to support the needs of a network-centric, heterogeneous component model like JavaBeans.

◆ Allowing RMI to use JRMP and IIOP as its over-the-wire protocol.

◆ Defining a bidirectional language mapping between IDL and Java.

◆ Extending the notion of CORBA object names to support the object naming requirements of the Java Web environment.

The following sections discuss the technical aspects of these initiatives.

CORBA's Interface Repository and the JavaBeans Component Model

Since its earliest incarnations, the CORBA standard has included an API (IR) that allows a client to investigate the interface definition of server objects at runtime. The Java Developer's Kit (JDK) also includes a somewhat similar API that allows one Java object to examine the interface characteristics of another Java object. Java refers to this process as reflection and introspection, which are supported by the its `java.lang.reflect` and `java.beans` packages.

The fundamental difference between the CORBA and Java APIs is Java's introspection is designed to support the requirements of the JavaBeans component model. A basic characteristic of component models (and JavaBeans in particular) is the characteristics of compliant components can be interrogated, manipulated, and interlinked at a granular level through a standardized interface. In JavaBeans terminology, this characteristic means a component's method signatures can be interrogated, properties can be obtained and set, and generatable events can be examined and subscribed to at development time through the introspection-related classes.

While CORBA's IR API and Java's reflect package support full standardized interrogation of an object's IDL interface, the CORBA IR does not provide the additional semantic standardization, featured in Java's introspection, necessary to distinguish between events, properties, and methods. In this area, CORBA's interface repository specification is likely to be extended (with Java's introspection approach as the model) to support the introspective requirements imposed by a component model. The result: a language- and platform-independent component model whose components may reside on the local or remote host.

RMI over-the-Wire Using Internet Inter-ORB Protocol

Java's RMI API supports location transparency for object-to-object interactions. It is restricted, however, to all Java environments in which both the client and the server applications are implemented in Java. This all-Java requirement is too onerous for most enterprise-distributed systems, where interoperability with special purpose, non-Java legacy applications is the rule rather than the exception. However, RMI and its wire protocol, Java Remote Method Protocol (JRMP), provide capabilities not available in CORBA and IIOP. Object pass-by-value is a most visible example: using RMI, Java objects can be passed by value to remote Java objects. CORBA does not support a standardized pass-by-value mechanism. But while CORBA does not offer every RMI capability, RMI does not provide the language independence and robust distributed-system infrastructure of CORBA.

As a result, CORBA and IIOP will be extended to provide pass-by-value and other RMI-like capabilities while RMI will be extended to support IIOP as its wire protocol (to the extent that IIOP can support RMI's functionality). JRMP will remain as an alternative to RMI wire protocol until CORBA and IIOP evolve to support all of RMI's capabilities. RMI's expected support for both protocols, therefore, is likely to result in situations illustrated in Figure 9-18. In this case, the interoperability of RMI and CORBA results in a hybrid system; JRMP is used when the full functionality of RMI is needed in an all-Java environment and IIOP is used when CORBA strengths are necessary or when the system must interact with a non-Java application.

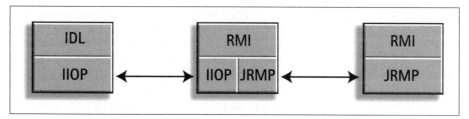

Figure 9-18: RMI on IIOP and JRMP

A Bidirectional Mapping Between Java and IDL

CORBA's IDL language mappings standardize the language-specific source code generated for a given IDL interface. Because the IDL syntax has a limited scope, using IDL as the starting point simplifies the standardization process. The utilitarian simplicity of IDL, a declarative interface specification language, contrasts with the richness and corresponding complexity of most object-oriented programming languages. As a result, the standardization of a reverse mapping – how IDL would be generated from a set of C++ class header files, for example – is a complex task.

Under some circumstances, however, the definition of a reverse (or bidirectional) mapping eliminates separate definitions of IDL interfaces for classes. A bidirectional IDL compiler could automatically generate the necessary IDL interfaces. This approach would be appropriate if CORBA and IDL were adopted as the standard interface language for a distributed-system component model (like future versions of JavaBeans). Components would then be implemented in Java, run through a Java-to-IDL compiler, and packaged as enterprise-capable components.

Based on this logic, Java-to-IDL compilers are available but still unstandardized. If you were to write a Java class and run it through two such compilers, the result may be two different IDL interface definitions – a bad situation if a standardized IDL-based component model is your goal. To rectify this problem, the OMG will very likely standardize the bidirectional mapping for Java and IDL.

Generating IDL interfaces from core application class definitions is not an appropriate course of action under many circumstances, however. Many good distributed systems make special allowances for the negative impact of distributing an application on performance, robustness, and manageability. Many of these allowances are embodied in the IDL interfaces of the cooperating subsystems. Distributed system architectures can go awry if developers simply create a fine-grained IDL interface for any class whose functionality must be accessible to client applications. The process of defining an IDL interface and developing the underlying implementation classes for complex applications correctly results in an adaptation layer that sits on top of the application's core functionality and below the ORB skeleton classes.

Naming Objects in CORBA and on the Web

Items referenced on the Web are named and then referenced using URLs. Most aspects of the Web infrastructure are tightly integrated with the URL naming scheme `protocol://hostID:portNumber/directory/path/of/referenced/item`. In the CORBA environment, on the other hand, objects are named using a hierarchical naming scheme, `rootNamingContext/domainSpecificNaming-Contect/applicationSpecificNamingContext/nameOfSpecificObject`. Objects are then referenced with an interoperable object reference (IOR) that may have been acquired from a naming service using the object name or from another source. The IOR houses the information necessary to locate the object.

In at least one way, CORBA's approach to object naming and locating betters the Web's URL-based approach. CORBA creates a clear distinction between an object's name and its location. This name can always be used to obtain the object's reference, regardless of the object's location. If a Web page or CGI is moved, however, its URL must change. Any applications holding the URL can no longer access the Web page without the new URL. This inflexibility results from the URL's dual role as the object's name and its location.

Despite this inflexibility, the Web's wild success gives its underlying protocols – especially HTTP's URL protocol – a great deal of momentum. Therefore, CORBA has to coexist with this protocol in appropriate situations, and as a result, tools and standards are rapidly evolving to supplement CORBA's conventional object naming and referencing scheme. One of the technological advancements providing support for new Web-oriented object naming schemes is the inclusion of object request brokers in Web server products. This integration of ORBs and Web servers blurs the line between these two technologies to capitalize on both approaches. Integration of ORBs and Web servers allows, for example, the Web server to interpret appropriately formatted URLs as CORBA object invocations or as requests to resolve the URL into a CORBA object reference (similar to CORBA's Naming Service). Imagine calling a function on a remote CORBA object using the following lines embedded in a Web page:

```
remoteRef =
object_from_URL(
  iiop://hostID:portNumber/hierarchical/object/name);
remoteRef->functionName(parameter1,parameter2);
```

This marriage of IIOP and HTTP addresses one of the nagging problems with some CORBA-based systems: the transmission of large text and binary data files. Long sequences of IDL octets can be forced to house a long stream of data, but this solution does not adhere to CORBA's mission to make distributed systems more intuitive. A better solution capitalizes on the standard Web technologies designed to correctly and efficiently handle large and small data files based on their MIME type.

The OMG is standardizing the transfer of streaming multimedia bulk data over TCP/IP. The initiative, the Audio Visual Streams standard, is an important advancement for CORBA and the first Domain Task Force standard approved by OMG. For more information on how the Audio Visual Streams standard impacts the CORBA's integration with Web protocols, visit the OMG Web site at http://www.omg.org.

Figure 9-19 illustrates the future direction of the IIOP and HTTP marriage by suggesting scaleable and responsive multimedia applications will be easier to develop, manage, and maintain. Web servers will become CORBA-compliant Web object brokers supporting granular object-to-object interactions and efficient multimedia bulk data and applet distribution.

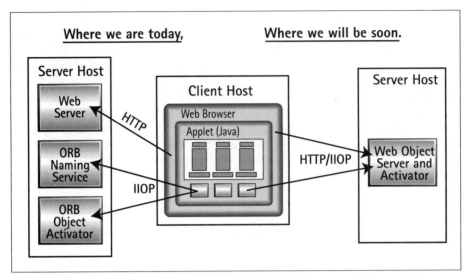

Figure 9-19: ORBs, Web servers, and the Complementary Coexistence of IIOP and HTTP

The merger of HTTP with IIOP has compelling possibilities, combining the scalability, robustness, and intuitive nature of CORBA interoperability with the ubiquity and flexibility of HTTP. We look forward to building new systems enabled by the marriage of these two protocols.

Summary

Automated memory management, built-in thread support, and applet mobility make Java an ideal choice to implement CORBA client and servers. We anticipate the combined use of Java and CORBA will become commonplace in enterprise systems. Because of wide support for IIOP in firewall proxies, availability of free or low cost ORB implementations, and built-in support for IIOP in server-side Web applications such as data blades and Web servers, however, IIOP may not become the standard Internet protocol. But based on recognition of CORBA's strengths and wide industry acceptance, we look forward to a growing number of adaptable and robust systems built on CORBA and Java.

Chapter 10

CORBA and Object–Oriented Databases

IN THIS CHAPTER
The coexistence of CORBA and object-oriented databases is becoming an increasingly common requirement for object-oriented systems. And the CORBA community uses the term *object database adapter* (ODA) to refer to an application layer or module that allows a CORBA-based server to offer the services of its Object-Oriented Database (OODB) resident persistent objects to its CORBA clients. In other words, an ODA adapts a server's persistent objects to CORBA-based client-server interaction. This chapter illustrates the design patterns applicable to the development of ODAs.

- ◆ Why OODBs are attractive additions to CORBA and Web-based applications.

- ◆ How the strengths of an ORB and the strengths of an OODB relate, and when they should be combined with an ODA to support a distributed, object-oriented system.

- ◆ Patterns that can be applied to designing an ODA to CORBA-enable your OODB-based server.

- ◆ How scalability is impacted by the use of CORBA to provide client access to an OODB-based server.

- ◆ How CORBA's Portable Object Adapter (POA) enhances the ability to integrate an ORB middleware solution effectively with an OODB-based server.

Why an Object-Oriented Database?

JUSTIFYING THE SELECTION of a particular technology or tool is an important issue for software developers. The following paragraphs provide a brief introduction to object-oriented databases and describe the motivations or reasons behind their growing acceptance in CORBA- and Web-based systems.

Object-oriented databases (OODBs) are becoming increasingly prevalent in enterprise applications. Their acceptance is even greater in CORBA and Web-based systems. The acceptance of OODBs on the Web is due to their innate support for infinitely complex datatypes, their natural fit with the object-oriented nature of Java, and the freedom often enjoyed by Web-based application developers to select the best technology for the job, regardless of its comparative youth.

In many ways the Web is an unconventional application space. Applications are delivered just-in-time, contain complex combinations of graphics, text, and scripts, and applets are assembled and delivered on demand. Complex scalability issues are the rule rather than the exception.

The flexibility provided by an OODB is a good solution to some of these unconventional demands. Developers are free to design, implement, and use complex object-oriented datatypes to support the needs of their Web application without concern for whether persistence of these complex structures is problematic.

Given Java's pure object-orientation, OODBs are a natural fit. Java's database capabilities (JDBC) provides a lowest common denominator API for accessing relational databases. But for Java applications that need not use a legacy relational database, an OODB is a very natural choice. Subsequent sections illustrate how the use of an OODB with any object-oriented language, such as Java, can significantly streamline the development process.

Another interesting force behind the acceptance of OODBs on the Web is the fact that many Web-based application developers are not forced to build on legacy decisions or to use legacy technologies. As a result, there can be a greater willingness to select the best methodology, tool, or technology for the job, even if it is comparatively new. And, not surprisingly, often an object-oriented technology is determined as the best approach. Applications having an object-oriented design also benefit because there are supporting tools specifically designed to operate in an object-oriented system. Selecting an object-oriented persistence mechanism and object-oriented middleware, for example, allows developers to apply design concepts decisions to multiple layers of the application architecture. It is this line of reasoning that often contributes to the selection of an OODB as the persistence mechanism in Web-based applications unfettered by legacy relational databases.

While object-oriented data bases are fairly common in Web-based systems they are even more common in CORBA-based systems. Developers of CORBA-based systems often recognize that using object-oriented middleware in concert with an object-oriented persistence mechanism can result in a streamlined design and development process. This is because OODB persistence of application objects is not at odds with the use of those objects. The well-documented "impedance mismatch" that exists when using a relational database to provide persistence for an object-oriented application does not exist when using an OODB. Using an OODB, persistent objects neither must be manually mapped out of persistent storage to use them, nor must they be mapped into the database to store them. Rather, persistent objects are used and can interact with one another while they are still in persistent storage.

For at least one class of application an OODB can provide significantly better performance than a relational database. It is widely accepted that relational databases excel at handling large quantities of simple data, but are less adept at handling a large number of complex interobject relationships. In stark contrast, OODBs excel at such tasks. This is primarily because these object relationships are themselves persistent and do not need to be recreated for any given relationship traversal.

As an example, we used OODBs to provide object persistence for complex product model applications on more than one occasion. A fundamental characteristic of product models is they are comprised of complex webs of product decomposition hierarchies. Furthermore, the usage patterns of these applications revealed a heavy emphasis on the need to examine a product's parts decomposition and a de-emphasis on the need to query the innate properties of a long list of products. In other words, it was far more important to provide fast response for inter-object relationship traversals than it was to provide fast object attribute queries. This class of application experiences better performance using an object-oriented database.

How Object-Oriented Database Management Systems Work

As illustrated in Figure 10-1, most object-oriented database (OODB) management systems are designed to automatically and silently transfer one or more persistent objects into the memory space of the client application. In OODB terminology this automated transfer of persistent objects is called object swapping and the client application's memory segment into which persistent objects are swapped is called the client object cache. Persistent object swapping occurs automatically when the client application dereferences a pointer to a persistent object, making interaction with persistent objects intuitive. Persistent objects that are swapped into the client object cache remain known to and, to a certain extent, managed by the ODBMS. This supports the requirements of the OODB's transaction facility and its optimized management of the client object cache.

Figure 10-1 illustrates the fundamental characteristic of OODBs that makes their use so intuitive. In this scenario, object A interacts with persistent object B by simply invoking a function on it, which implicitly necessitates dereferencing a pointer to that persistent object. The OODB client library (compiled into the client) detects that a new persistent object has been dereferenced and swaps it from the OODB's object server and into the client object cache. Most OODB systems also provide complex cache optimizations that swap groups of related or collocated objects into and out of the client object cache. In fact, some OODBs will, by default, transfer all objects residing on a given page to the client application. Such OODBs are often called *page servers*. Other OODBs, however, transfer only the dereferenced object by default, and are often called *object servers*.

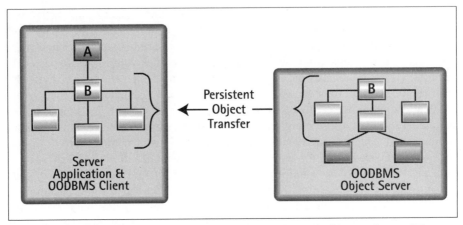

Figure 10-1: Persistent Objects are Automatically Swapped into the Memory Space of the Client Application.

In the previous paragraphs we used the term client to refer to an application that uses an OODB to access or store persistent objects. An OODB client application is one with an OODB client object cache. Client makes sense here because, in fact, applications having a persistent object cache are clients of the OODB's object or page server. While we refer to OODB applications as database clients they should not be confused with CORBA clients. In this chapter the OODB client applications are CORBA-based servers, offering the services of their Persistent Objects to their CORBA clients.

Using CORBA with an Object-Oriented Database

This chapter presents several approaches appropriate for ODA design and implementation. First let's take a closer look at the problem that an ODA is intended to address. Figure 10-2 generically illustrates where an application-specific ODA resides in relation to other architectural components. It illustrates that an ODA is designed to take an incoming ORB call and ensure that it, and its parameters, are ultimately routed to the appropriate persistent object-handling database transactions, persistent object discovery, and parameter datatype conversions along the way. Given this functional goal, an ODA is either collocated with (and possibly part of) the ORB's skeleton objects, or resides between the skeleton objects and the persistent objects. Because the primary focus of this chapter is application-specific ODAs it focuses on ODAs that reside between the ORB's built-in functionality and the server's persistent objects. In contrast, generic, commercially available ODAs exist that are more tightly integrated with either the ORB's or the OODB's built-in functionality. But even these ODAs use aspects of the patterns suggested here to accomplish their goals.

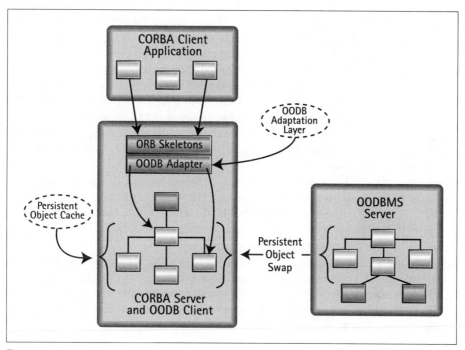

Figure 10-2: How an ODA Relates to Other Architectural Components

It would be difficult and probably inappropriate to implement an OODB adapter that recreates the highly scaleable and intelligent object-distribution mechanisms that are built into most object-oriented database management systems. Why pay the money for an OODB and then turn around and rebuild it? As discussed above, most OODBs are designed to swap persistent objects into the object cache of client applications. OODB system developers have invested expertise, time, and money in building and optimizing these persistent object distribution schemes. Attempting to home grow a CORBA-based object distribution scheme with similar scalability, concurrency, and reliability requirements is probably an unrealistic goal. So why implement an ODA to CORBA-enable your server? Why not just make all of your CORBA clients be direct clients of the ODBMS server? The answer lies in the fact that CORBA and ODAs fill a gap not addressed by the persistent object distribution schemes built into most OODBs. The object distribution schemes of most OODBs do not have the same strengths or focus as CORBA's distributed object interaction scheme. Notice the careful distinction here between an *object distribution mechanism* (OODB client object caching) and a *distributed object interaction* mechanism

(CORBA). This is the fundamental distinction between classic OODB client-server interaction and classic CORBA client-server interaction.

CORBA is a distributed system infrastructure based on object location independence. It is primarily focused on providing the means to interact with an object, regardless of its location (or its implementation language or the underlying operating system). This is in contrast to the main goals of most OODBs. OODBs are primarily focused on providing the means to interact with a large number of persistent objects in an intuitive, scaleable, and reliable manner. Location independence is not a primary goal of most OODBs. Most OODBs swap persistent objects into the local client object cache for most object-to-object interactions. As a result, OODBs are not intended to operate in an environment where the OODB client applications are distributed over a geographically dispersed wide area network (WAN). The resulting network overhead would be too limiting. In contrast, CORBA's location-independent object-to-object interaction is intended for geographically dispersed WANs. In many cases, combining the strengths of an OODB's persistent object cache with the strengths of CORBA's remote object communication makes sense.

Identifying the situations where CORBA's distributed object interaction scheme is appropriate and necessary to allow remote clients to interact with objects resident in an OODB-based server application can be challenging. Avoid using CORBA when the object distribution capabilities of the OODB alone suffice. Once you determine that CORBA is necessary, you need to adapt your server's persistent objects to CORBA's location-independent object interaction model. The complexity of your server application and its scalability requirements determine the size of this job. Aspects to consider include:

- Adaptation of the server's persistent implementation classes to the server's IDL interfaces
- Adaptation of the input and output parameters declared within the functions of the persistent classes to their corresponding IDL datatypes declared in the IDL interface functions
- Scalability to a large number of persistent objects
- Scalability to a large number of concurrent CORBA clients
- Concurrent client access to server objects
- Distributed transaction handling

Design Patterns for Object Database Adapters

This part of the chapter presents several methods for adapting a CORBA-based server to underlying, persistent OODB objects. The adaptation methods are presented in the form of design patterns, structured to help you digest the appropriateness, design, and strengths of each approach. The following structure is used:

◆ **Pattern Name** – The name of the pattern. Although we were early adopters of the combination of CORBA and OODBs and have used most of the patterns presented here, in practice our intent is not to suggest the pattern names chosen are the most appropriate.

◆ **Rationale** – This is the generic problem addressed by the pattern.

◆ **Design** – An illustration and description of the architectural considerations, class design, and responsibilities of the classes participating in the pattern. Because the patterns suggested here are design patterns rather than implementation patterns this section is the core of each pattern's description

◆ **Implementation** – Explanation and samples of the source code implementing the pattern's critical components. In most cases there is more than one approach to implementing the pattern's Design. The code samples are intended to illuminate the responsibilities of each class presented in the Design section, but, are not intended to dictate the implementation approach

◆ **Synopsis** – A review of the pattern's scalability, strengths, weaknesses, and core characteristics.

Some of the patterns illustrated in the subsequent sections take very different approaches to designing an ODA. One of the patterns, Interface Object, is not in keeping with the direct object-to-object interaction suggested by so many prototypical CORBA-based applications and instructional material. This is because many prototypical CORBA applications do not deal with the heavy scalability requirements and stringent deadlines that exist in real-world systems where a server may house millions of persistent objectsAs you consider these patterns, keep in mind that zealous application of object-oriented principles is not necessarily the best approach for all circumstances. The following is a synopsis of each pattern:

◆ **Interface Object** – A scaleable Adapter pattern with a straightforward design and implementation. To achieve this combination of simplicity and scalability some object-oriented aspects of CORBA client-server interaction paradigms are sacrificed

◆ **Object Service** – A more complex pattern that creates the illusion that clients are interacting directly with individual persistent server objects. In fact, scalability is maintained by allowing a few transient server objects, called Object Service instances, to front for a large number of persistent objects

♦ **Threaded Object Service** – The multithreaded version of the Object Service pattern. Multithreading this pattern enhances its responsiveness and scalability to multiple concurrent clients

♦ **Pinned Object** – This pattern maximizes responsiveness to client requests by locking each persistent object into the server's memory. Because of this, it is inappropriate for servers that must scale to a large number of persistent objects. This shortcoming can be mitigated by using an Evictor object designed to flush objects from the server based on object usage and dormancy

Before we jump into the design patterns, let's look at the application used to illustrate the utility, strengths, and weaknesses of these patterns.

Listing 10-1 contains the IDL interface of an employee administration server designed to support some aspects of an employee administration system. This application and its IDL interface is a bit more complex than those you might typically encounter in CORBA instructional material. Using a more complex and realistic IDL interface will more adequately convey the strengths and weaknesses of the ODA design patterns.

The server's IDL interface definition is comprised of two interfaces, EmployeeAdministratorIF and EmployeeIF. The EmployeeAdministratorIF provides the management and factory services for the set of employees, while the EmployeeIF interface provides the employee services. Not surprisingly, these interfaces reflect the design of the server's underlying application, which has a singleton persistent EmployeeAdministrator instance, which manages the set of persistent Employee instances. Notice that using the interface naming convention suggested in Chapter 9 avoids any potential name clash between our implementation classes and the generated ORB skeletons. The IDL interface names are suffixed with "IF". This avoids name clashes without requiring lengthy changes. to the names. As explained in Chapter 9, altering the name of implementation classes in deference to the names of IDL interfaces creates problems. This is because the application's implementation classes and IDL interfaces evolve through the development and maintenance process.

Listing 10-1: IDL interface for our employee administration server

```
//Forward Declarations—————————
interface EmployeeIF;
interface EmployeeAdministratorIF;
//Data Types——————————
struct EmployeeInfoStruct{string name;
            string ssn;
            string title;
            string hireDate;
            string iD;};
typedef sequence<EmployeeInfoStruct> EmployeeInfoList;
struct EmployeeDetailsStruct{float salary;
```

```
                string photoURL;
                string resumeURL;
                string iD;};
//Interface Definitions————————————
interface EmployeeAdministratorIF
{
 EmployeeIF createEmployee(in string newName,
                in string newSSN,
                in string newTitle,
                in float newSalary,
                in string hireDate);
 short deleteEmployee(in string employeeID);
 EmployeeInfoList getEmployees();
 EmployeeIF getEmployee(in string iD);
};
interface EmployeeIF
{
 EmployeeDetailsStruct getDetails();
 void setDetails(in EmployeeDetailsStruct newDetails);
 void increaseSalary(in float percentIncrease);
 void decreaseSalary(in float percentDecrease);
 void addSubordinate(in string newSubordinateID);
 void removeSubordinate(in string subordinateID);
 EmployeeInfoList getSubordinates();
};
```

The IDL interface includes the definition of two structs. While the use of structs is less prevalent in non-distributed object-oriented applications it is common in CORBA-based distributed systems. This results from two factors: First, the network overhead associated with distributed object interaction does not afford the luxury of making a series of individual function calls, each tasked to get a single object property. Second, there has not been a standard CORBA mechanism to support passing objects by value. One of the roles of an ODA layer is to map the server's internal data structures to and from the complex structs and sequences defined in the server's IDL interface.

Listing 10-2 contains the mainline routine that is common to some of the patterns. It is straight forward because we have abstracted the design and implementation idiosyncrasies of each pattern to a level lower than the initialization code called from within the main function. So Listing 10-2 uses only those design properties common to most of the patterns; the use of an ORB, an OODB, and a singleton instance of the Adapter class.

The code samples used to illustrate the design patterns use Object Store PSE Pro as their OODB and Orbix or OrbixWeb as their object request broker. PSE Pro is a low cost object-oriented persistent storage engine available from Object Design Inc. (ODI). It can be downloaded from ODI's Web site at www.odi.com. Similarly, an evaluation copy of Orbix or OrbixWeb is available from IONA at www.iona.com.

So let's take a closer look at what's happening in the main function. The first task is to initialize the OODB's memory fault handler using the macro provided by Object Store PSE, OS_PSE_ESTABLISH_FAULT_HANDLER. Most OODBs automatically page persistent objects into the persistent object cache of the application when a persistent object pointer is dereferenced. In Windows, PSE discovers that a pointer to an unswapped, persistent object has been dereferenced by capturing the memory fault generated by the operating system, thus, the need to initialize PSE's memory fault handler prior to interaction with the OODB. Next, the main function indirectly forces construction of a singleton Adapter object by calling its static instance()function. Very little is done in the Adapter's constructor. It is the Adapter's initializeDB() and initialize() functions where most of the interesting initialization occurs. But the implementation of these functions differs for each pattern, so we defer discussion about their details. In general, however, initializeDB() establishes the server's connection to its database, while initialize() creates the objects comprising the Adapter's design.

Now that the server's ORB, ODA, and application layers are initialized notify the ORB that the server is ready to accept client ORB requests by calling impl_is_ready, passing in the server name. And finally, when the server exists, terminate PSE's memory fault handler.

Listing 10-2: The Mainline Routine of the Employee Administration Server

```
#include "idl\EmployeeAdminServer.hh" //ORB Skeletons
#include <os_pse/ostore.hh>      //OODB include file
#include "Adapter.h"       //Adapter declaration
#include <iostream.h>
int main(int argc, char** argv)
{
  //Initialize the OODB memory fault handler
  OS_PSE_ESTABLISH_FAULT_HANDLER
  //Force construction of the Adapter and its components
  Adapter:instance();
  //Instruct the adapter to initialize the OODB client
  //and open the EmployeeAdminServer database
  Adapter:instance()->initializeDB();
  //Instruct the adapter to perform any additional
  //initialization that may be necessary
```

```
       Adapter:instance()->initialize();
       //Notify the ORB that the server is accepting requests
       CORBA:Environment env;
       try{CORBA:Orbix.impl_is_ready("EmployeeAdminServer",
                   CORBA:Orbix.INFINITE_TIMEOUT,
                   env); }
       catch(CORBA:SystemException& sysExc)
        {cerr << "System Exception:" << endl;
         cerr << &sysExc << endl;
         exit(1);}
       catch(...)
        {cerr << "Exception at server initialization." << endl;
         exit(1);}
       //Close the EmployeeAdmin DB
       Adapter:instance()->getDB()->close();
       //Terminate the OODB memory fault handler
       OS_PSE_END_FAULT_HANDLER
       return 0;
}
```

Interface Object Pattern

The Interface Object pattern is appropriate for a quick, simple CORBA-OODB Adapter.

RATIONALE

The primary advantages of this pattern are its simplicity and its ability to scale to a large number of persistent objects and concurrent database clients (not to be confused with CORBA clients). But if you want to capitalize on and maximize the object-oriented nature of CORBA, skip this pattern and go on. This pattern's simplicity and scalability are achieved at the expense of CORBA's object-oriented client-server interaction.

DESIGN

As illustrated in Figure 10-3 this pattern allows CORBA clients to interact with the server's persistent objects indirectly. The Adapter's Interface Objects receive all up calls from the ORB skeletons, filling the role of implementation objects from the point of view of the ORB. The core aspects of this pattern's design are that a single Interface Object provides client access to all persistent objects of a given class, and that the client indicates the target persistent object by explicitly passing the persistent object's ID to the server with each remote function call. The Interface Objects then use this ID to locate and acquire a reference to the target persistent object.

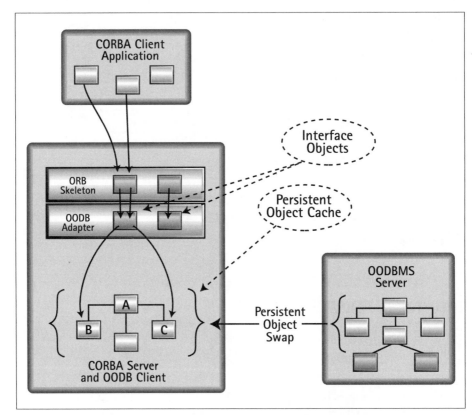

Figure 10-3: Client-Server Interaction Using the Interface Object Pattern

Figure 10-4 shows the Interface Object pattern. The design includes the Adapter, EmployeeIFObject, EmployeeAdminIFObject, and the skeleton "tie" classes generated by the IDL compiler. When the server application is launched, the singleton Adapter object is constructed. It then creates the singleton instances of EmployeeIFObject and EmployeeAdminIFObject, the Interface Objects for the employee administration server. The Adapter then constructs the ORB tie object associated with each Interface Object.

Most of the patterns presented use the "tie" approach to establish the ORB-to-implementation linkage, so each Interface Object is passed to the constructor of its corresponding tie object. As a result, each incoming ORB request is delegated to an Interface Object which fronts for many persistent objects. The multiplicity indicator on the relationship between the EmployeeIFObject class and the persistent Employee class in Figure 10-4 indicates a single Interface Object instance is associated with multiple persistent objects. This fundamental aspect of this pattern enhances its scalability by reducing the ratio of in-memory ORB objects to persistent objects.

An Interface Object has three primary responsibilities:

◆ managing database transactions

◆ locating the target persistent objects using the object ID passed with each
client request

◆ handling datatype conversions as function parameters are passed from the
ORB middleware to the server's persistent objects

These three tasks must be performed by any ODA. Interaction with persistent
objects requires transaction management. This pattern uses "per call" transactions.
Before interacting with a persistent object, the Interface Object starts a transaction
and after completion, the Interface Object commits or aborts the transaction.

Per-call transactions are used here for simplicity. The patterns presented in this
chapter are not dependent on starting and committing transactions each client
request rather than across multiple requests.

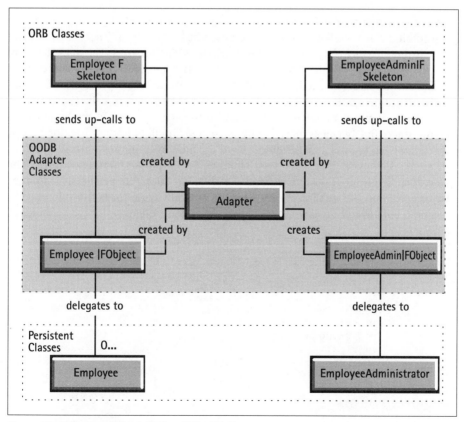

Figure 10-4: Design of the Interface Object Pattern

To maximize scalability, this pattern requires a single Interface Object to provide access to many persistent objects. This limits the number of ORB objects consuming the server's memory and the number of ORB objects requiring a slot in the ORB's object table. It requires the acquisition of a reference to the target persistent object for each client request. This second role of Interface Objects is done by building a database query keyed on the requested target object ID, or by passing the target object ID to a function housing our own implementation of an object search algorithm.

Finally, the Interface Objects map the incoming and outgoing IDL function parameters and parameter datatypes to those required by the function signatures enforced by the persistent classes. In many cases this is not a complex process, but when the IDL function definition consumes or produces a complex datatype (such as a sequence of structs), or if the persistent class consumes or produces a complex datatype (such as a persistent dictionary of persistent object references), it can necessitate a complex code segment.

IMPLEMENTATION

The Interface Object pattern sacrifices some object-oriented character of CORBA's inter-process communication to achieve simplicity and scalability. The result is the need to alter our nice IDL interface presented in Listing 10-1. The less appealing result is the interface definition provided below, in Listing 10-3. The data structure definitions have not changed from Listing 10-1. The interface changes address this pattern's requirement that clients explicitly indicate the target persistent object by passing the object's ID as the final parameter to each function call. Therefore, an additional parameter, targetObjectID, is added to each function in the EmployeeIF IDL interface. But because there is one persistent EmployeeAdministrator object, there is no need to pass a target object ID to the EmployeeAdministratorIF interface functions. However, there are two changes to EmployeeAdministratorIF. The createEmployee function now returns a string, the ID of the persistent employee just created, and the getEmployee function now always returns the reference to the single EmployeeIF instance rather than a different reference for each employee ID passed to it.

Listing 10-3: Modified IDL interface to meet the requirements of the Interface Object Pattern

```
interface EmployeeAdministratorIF
{
  string createEmployee(in string newName,
            in string newSSN,
            in string newTitle,
            in float newSalary,
            in string hireDate);
  short deleteEmployee(in string employeeID);
  EmployeeInfoList getEmployees();
  EmployeeIF getEmployee();
};
```

```
interface EmployeeIF
{
 EmployeeDetailsStruct getDetails(in string targetObject);
 void setDetails(in EmployeeDetailsStruct newDetails,
                 in string targetObject);
 void increaseSalary(in float percentIncrease,
                 in string targetObject);
 void decreaseSalary(in float percentDecrease,
                 in string targetObject);
 void addSubordinate(in string newSubordinateID,
                 in string targetObject);
 void removeSubordinate(in string subordinateID,
                     in string targetObject);
 EmployeeInfoList getSubordinates(in string targetObject);
};
```

THE ADAPTER CLASS   Listing 10-4 is the declaration of the Adapter class for this pattern. The Adapter is instantiated and initialized when the server is launched (see Listing 10-2). Its role is to initialize the objects comprising the ODA layer and the server's database, and to instantiate the ORB layer's tie objects. Let's look more closely at some of its functions.

Listing 10–4: Declaration of the Adapter Class

```
#include <os_pse\ostore.hh> //OODB include file
#include <CORBA.h>
#include "idl\EmployeeAdminServer.hh" //Generated skeletons
#define ADMINISTRATOR_ROOT "Administrator_DB_Root"
#define EMP_ADMIN_IF_NAME "EmployeeAdministratorIF"
#define EMP_IF_NAME "EmployeeIF"
class Adapter
{
public:
  static Adapter* instance();
  ~Adapter();
  CORBA:Object* getIFObject(const char* serviceName);
  void initializeDB();
  void initialize();
  os_database* getDB();
protected:
  Adapter();
private:
  static Adapter* theAdapter;
  EmployeeIF* employeeService;
  EmployeeAdministratorIF* employeeAdminService;
  os_database* theDB;
};
```

If you are familiar with design pattern literature you may have noticed from Listing 10-4 that the Adapter class uses the singleton pattern described by Gamma and others. The singleton pattern ensures that one Adapter object is created that is then easily accessible to other objects. The Adapter constructor is protected and the static `instance()` function creates or returns the reference to the Adapter instance Listing 10-5 shows the Adapter constructor and its static `instance()` function.

Listing 10-5: The Adapter class's use of the singleton pattern

```
Adapter* Adapter:theAdapter = 0;
Adapter:Adapter()
{
  theDB = 0;
  cout << "The adapter has been constructed" << endl;
}
Adapter* Adapter:instance()
{
  if(!theAdapter)
    theAdapter = new Adapter();
  return theAdapter;
}
```

The `main()`function in Listing 10-2 showed that once the Adapter instance is created, access to the server's database is established by invoking `Adapter:initializeDB()`, which is shown in Listing 10-6. We suggest you peruse PSE's API documentation on the ODI Web site if you want to know more. But even if you are unfamiliar with PSA's API, Listing 10-6 should be readable. It initializes the PSE at run time and creates or opens the server's database stored in the file `EmployeeAdminServer.db`. Once the database is open a transaction is started and an attempt is made to locate the persistent EmployeeAdministrator object using a named database root. If the EmployeeAdministrator is not found it is created and associated with a named data base root. Finally, the database transaction is committed.

Listing 10-6: The Adapter's database initialization function

```
void Adapter:initializeDB()
{
  os_database_root* adminRoot;
  EmployeeAdministrator* theAdmin;
  //Initialize the OODB client runtime
  objectstore:initialize();
  //Initialize the OODB's transaction manager
  os_transaction:initialize();
  //Open the database, create it if it does not exist
  theDB = os_database:open("EmployeeAdminServer.db",
            0,
            0666);
  os_transaction:begin();
  {
    //Try to get DB root pointing to EmployeeAdministrator
```

```
  adminRoot = theDB->find_root(ADMINISTRATOR_ROOT);
  //If the root does not exist create it
  if(!adminRoot)
  {
    adminRoot = theDB->create_root(ADMINISTRATOR_ROOT);
    //Create singleton EmployeeAdministrator
    theAdmin = EmployeeAdministrator:instance();
    //Associate the emp admin instance with new root
    adminRoot->set_value(theAdmin);
  }
  }
  os_transaction:commit();
  cout << "The database has been initialized."<< endl;
}
```

After the database is initialized the ODA initialization is completed by calling `Adapter:initialize()`, found in Listing 10-7. This indirectly forces creation of the singleton employee interface object and the singleton employee administrator interface object by calling their static `instance()`functions. Like the Adapter class, the EmployeeIFObject and EmployeeAdminIFObject classes use the singleton pattern to ensure one instance is created and accessible at run time. Then the corresponding skeleton or "tie" objects are constructed, passing in the new interface object instances as the delegate implementation objects.

Listing 10-7: The Adapter initialization of its supporting objects

```
void Adapter:initialize()
{
  //Create the employee interface object
  EmployeeIFObject:instance();
  //Create the employee interface object ORB/tie object
  //passing in the employee interface object to it
   employeeService =
   new TIE_EmployeeIF(EmployeeIFObject)
    (EmployeeIFObject:instance());
  //Create the employee admin object service
  EmployeeAdminIFObject:instance();
  //Create the employee admin object service ORB/tie
  //object, passing in the employee admin object service
   employeeAdminService =
   new TIE_EmployeeAdministratorIF(EmployeeAdminIFObject)
    (EmployeeAdminIFObject:instance());
}
```

Once Adapter:initialize()has completed, each of the Adapter's design components illustrated in Figure 10-4, has been created and initialized. The only remaining Adapter function of any significance is getIFObject, provided in Listing 10-8. getIFObject is used for easy access to the EmployeeIF and EmployeeAdministratorIF tie objects.

Listing 10-8: The Adapter provides access to the server's tie object

```
CORBA:Object* Adapter:getIFObject(
  const char* serviceName)
{
  if(strcmp(serviceName,EMP_IF_NAME)==0)
    return employeeService;
  else if(strcmp(serviceName,EMP_ADMIN_IF_NAME)==0)
   return employeeAdminService;
  else
    return 0;
}
```

THE EMPLOYEEADMINIFOBJECT AND EMPLOYEEIFOBJECT INTERFACE OBJECT CLASS This pattern's Interface Objects create a buffer between the idiosyncrasies of the ORB and the OODB server. They (1) manage database transactions, (2) locate the target persistent object, and (3) handle any necessary datatype conversions as function parameters are passed from the ORB middleware to the server's persistent objects. Let's look more closely at each of these responsibilities.

The definition of EmployeeAdminIFObject, the Interface Object class fronting for the EmployeeAdministrator persistent class, is provided in Listing 10-9. In the next few paragraphs illustrate the role of this class by examining the implementation of its functions.

Listing 10-9: Declaration of the Interface Object class servicing the EmployeeAdministratorIF IDL interface

```
#include "idl\EmployeeAdminServer.hh"
#define EMPLOYEE_ADMINISTRATOR_DB_ROOT_NAME
  "Administrator"
class EmployeeAdministrator;
class EmployeeAdminIFObject
{
public:
  virtual ~EmployeeAdminIFObject();
  static EmployeeAdminIFObject* instance();
  //Begin implementation of IDL functions
  char* createEmployee(const char* newName,
          const char* newSSN,
          const char* newTitle,
          float newSalary,
          const char* hireDate,
          CORBA:Environment& );
  short deleteEmployee(const char* employeeID,
          CORBA:Environment& );
  EmployeeInfoList_var getEmployees(CORBA:Environment& );
  EmployeeIF_var getEmployee(CORBA:Environment& );
  //End implementation of IDL functions
protected:
  EmployeeAdminIFObject();
private:
```

```
    static EmployeeAdminIFObject* theEmployeeAdminIFObject;
    EmployeeAdministrator* findTargetObject();
};
```

Interface Object Classes Handle Database Transactions

Transaction management is a core issue creating a clear division between the typical ORB middleware object and a server's Persistent Object. It is an OODB's transaction management that allows several OODB clients to safely make concurrent reads and writes to Persistent Objects. As a result, any ODA must manage database transactions. Tthis is one of the responsibilities of the Interface Objects. Prior to interaction with persistent objects, an Interface Object starts a transaction, After updates to persistent objects, it commits or aborts the current transaction. The getEmployees function in Listing 10-10 illustrates this transaction handling. A transaction is started by calling PSE's os_transaction:begin() prior to interacting with the persistent EmployeeAdministrator object. When the transaction is complete, call os_transaction:commit(), or os_transaction:abort().

Listing 10-10: An Interface Object handling transactions and datatype conversions

```
EmployeeInfoList_var
EmployeeAdminIFObject:getEmployees(CORBA:Environment& env)
{
 EmployeeInfoList_var employeeInfoList;
 CORBA:ULong i = 0;
 os_transaction:begin();
 {
  Employee* employees[MAX_EMPLOYEES];
  EmployeeAdministrator* target;
  target = findTargetObject();
  if(target)
  {
   employeeInfoList = new EmployeeInfoList(MAX_EMPLOYEES);
   target->getEmployees(employees);
   while(employees[i])
   {
    employeeInfoList[i].name =
     CORBA:string_dup(employees[i]->getName());
    employeeInfoList[i].ssn =
     CORBA:string_dup(employees[i]->getSSN());
    employeeInfoList[i].title =
     CORBA:string_dup(employees[i]->getTitle());
    employeeInfoList[i].hireDate =
     CORBA:string_dup(employees[i]->getHireDate());
    employeeInfoList[i].iD =
     CORBA:string_dup(employees[i]->getID());
    i++;
   }
  }
 }
}
```

```
os_transaction:commit();
employeeInfoList->length(i);
return employeeInfoList;
}
```

Interface Object Classes Handle Datatype Conversions

Listing 10-10 also illustrates the second responsibility of Interface Objects – performing datatype conversions as function parameters and return values are sent between the server's ORB layer and its persistent object layer. For simple datatypes this is not a significant issue, but for complex datatypes it can be quite involved. For example, the EmployeeAdministratorIF IDL interface declares that getEmployees returns a sequence of EmployeeInfoStructs. However, the corresponding function in the persistent EmployeeAdministrator class, as you might expect, returns a list of references to persistent Employee objects. So the implementation of `EmployeeAdminIFObject:getEmployees()` must transform the result of its call to the persistent `EmployeeAdministrator:getEmployees` to the sequence of EmployeeInfoStructs required by the ORB layer. Listing 10-10 illustrates this code.

Interface Object Classes Handle Persistent Object Discovery

In Listing 10-10, getEmployees() calls `findTargetObject()` to acquire a reference to the persistent EmployeeAdministrator object. This is the third and final responsibility of Interface Objects. The Interface Object pattern suggests that each Interface Object class has a `findTargetObject` function. Listing 10-11 shows EmployeeAdminIFObject's `findTargetObject()`. It depends on the fact that the server's employee database houses a single persistent instance of EmployeeAdministrator accessible using a named database root. The database root is located and the EmployeeAdministrator object is retrieved and returned to the caller.

Listing 10-11: An Interface Object handling Persistent Object Discovery

```
EmployeeAdministrator* EmployeeAdminIFObject:findTargetObject()
{
  //Assumes that a transaction is already active
  EmployeeAdministrator* empAdmin = 0;
  os_database_root* empAdminDBRoot;
  os_database* employeeDB;
  employeeDB = Adapter:instance()->getDB();
  empAdminDBRoot =
   employeeDB->find_root(
     EMPLOYEE_ADMINISTRATOR_DB_ROOT_NAME);
  if(empAdminDBRoot)
  {
```

```
    empAdmin =
    (EmployeeAdministrator*)(empAdminDBRoot->get_value());
  }
  return empAdmin;
}
```

To end the discussion of the EmployeeAdminIFObject class, let's briefly look at its ()function in Listing 10-12. This function provides an easy way for clients to acquire an ORB reference to the singleton EmployeeIFObject, or more accurately, a reference to its EmployeeIF tie object. Because getEmployee does not interact with the database a transaction is unnecessary. It acquires the EmployeeIF reference from the Adapter object, casts it to its proper type using the EmployeeIF:_narrow function, and returns it to the client. The client may then use it and the ID of a persistent Employee object to invoke a function in the EmployeeIF IDL interface.

Listing 10-12: A function called to acquire the ORB reference to the EmployeeIF tie object

```
EmployeeIF_var
EmployeeAdminIFObject:getEmployee(CORBA:Environment& )
{
 EmployeeIF_var employee;
 employee =
  EmployeeIF:_narrow(Adapter:instance()->getIFObject(
    EMP_IF_NAME));
 //Ensure that the ORB does not delete the employee tie
 //object during its reply marshalling
 EmployeeIF:_duplicate(employee);
 return employee;
}
```

To enhance scalability, this pattern intentionally avoids having too many of the server's persistent objects in memory at any given time. So it is necessary to locate and swap persistent objects into the server's persistent object cache when handling a client request. In the employee application the employee object ID passed into each function defined in the EmployeeIF interface locates the target persistent object.. Listing 10-13 shows that the targetObjecID parameter passed into getDetails()is then passed to EmployeeIFObject:findTargetObject(), where it is used as the key to locate and acquire a reference to the target persistent employee object. The employee reference is used to interrogate the employee object as we build the EmployeeDetailsStruct requested by the client.

Listing 10-13: The getDetails function in the Interface Object servicing the EmployeeIF IDL interface

```
EmployeeDetailsStruct_var
EmployeeIFObject:getDetails(const char* targetObjectID,
              CORBA:Environment& env)
{
```

```
EmployeeDetailsStruct_var employeeDetails;
os_transaction:begin();
{
 Employee* target;
 target = findTargetObject(targetObjectID);
 if(target)
 {
   employeeDetails = new EmployeeDetailsStruct;
   employeeDetails->salary = target->getSalary();
   employeeDetails->photoURL =
    CORBA:string_dup(target->getPhotoURL());
   employeeDetails->resumeURL =
    CORBA:string_dup(target->getResumeURL());
   employeeDetails->iD =
    CORBA:string_dup(target->getID());
 }
}
 os_transaction:commit();
 return employeeDetails;
}
```

SYNOPSIS

Figure 10-5 summarizes the scalability of the Interface Object pattern. This pattern maximizes scalability in terms of the number of persistent objects that can be made available to CORBA clients from a single CORBA-based server. This scalability results from the fact that individual Interface Objects provide access to a large number of persistent objects.

A positive side effect of this is that persistent objects are not pinned in memory across several client requests. They are located, used, and let go for each client request. The OODB cache manager is free to flush the persistent objects from the client cache when necessary. As a result, this pattern also scales well to a system architecture that has multiple clients of the OODB server. When persistent objects are pinned into the client object cache of a given application there is a much greater likelihood that other clients of the OODB object server are forced to wait until they are given write access to those objects. Because the Interface Object pattern does not pin persistent objects in memory across several client invocations, delays resulting from object contention are much less likely.

It is worth pointing out, however, the optimized cache management of some OODBs does not always flush unreferenced persistent objects out of the client's cache. If there are no other applications contending for a cached object and if the client does not explicitly request that its cache be flushed, then the unreferenced objects remain in the client cache until the space they occupy is needed. This can significantly enhance the performance of some applications because previously requested target objects may already be in the local cache.

Advantages	Shortcomings
• Supports a very large number of persistent objects with minimal server side memory consumption.	• Request handling is slower than patterns allowing persistent objects to remain in the server's memory for many client invocations.
• Ensures very fast traversal of the ORB's active object table.	
• Accelerates object loading by taking advantage of the optimized query capabilities of the underlying OODB.	
• Maximizes concurrent access to the underlying database server since persistent objects are not locked into CORBA server memory.	

Figure 10-5: Scalability of the Interface Object Pattern

Object Service Pattern

The Object Service pattern is appropriate for creating an ODA for an OODB server that must support object-oriented client interaction with a large number of persistent objects.

RATIONALE

This pattern may be more appealing than the Interface Object pattern discussed in the previous section because it affords client applications the object-oriented interaction paradigm that makes CORBA so appealing. However, this pattern may be less appealing to some because it introduces additional complexity and some additional overhead. The additional complexity is necessary to achieve object-oriented client interaction while maintaining scalability. This pattern minimizes the ORB's object table traversal, persistent object locking, and server memory consumption by requiring a single object-service instance to front for many persistent objects.

DESIGN

As illustrated in Figure 10-6, the Object Service pattern requires client applications to interact with a server side persistent object by way of an ObjectService instance, which fronts for all (or many) instances of a particular persistent class. Object Service instances reside in the Adapter layer and are tied to the ORB skeletons, or tie objects, when the server is initialized. As client requests arrive at the server, the adapter's object loader intercepts them and directs them to the appropriate Object Service instance. It is a key aspect of this pattern that, from the ORB's perspective, the Object Service instance fills the role of the implementation object. In other words, it is the Object Service instance that is passed to the tie object's constructor and, therefore, receives all up calls delegated by the tie object. This is why Figure 10-6 shows multiple client objects interacting with a single skeleton (tie object) and a single object service instance in the Adapter layer, but multiple persistent objects in the application layer. For a given IDL interface, the adapter loader always loads the same Object Service instance, which then locates and invokes the targeted function on the targeted persistent object.

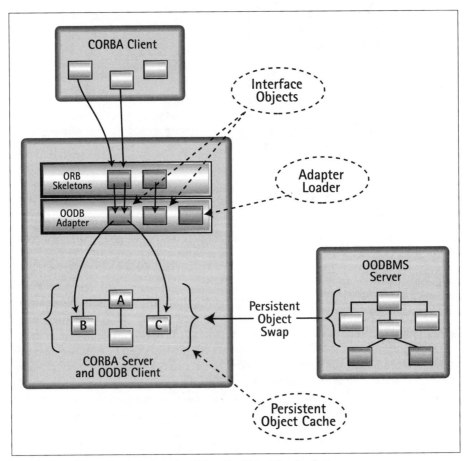

Figure 10-6: Client-Server Interaction Using the Object Service Pattern

An important advantage of this pattern is that client applications need not be aware of any aspect of the internal workings of the pattern. When a client asks for an ORB reference to a persistent employee object, the server constructs the reference (a tie object in this case), and passes the ID of the persistent employee object to the reference's constructor. So, unbeknown to the client, whenever it uses this reference to invoke a function on the remote object, the target persistent employee ID is passed to the server as part of the ORB request packet. And as up calls arrive at the Object Service instance it locates and acquires a reference to the target persistent object using the embedded ID.

Figure 10-7 provides a closer look at the classes comprising the Object Service pattern. The Adapter layer houses the Adapter class, the AdapterLoader class, and the EmployeeObjectService and EmployeeAdminObjectService Object Service classes. While the ORB layer simply houses the tie classes generated by the IDL compiler and the default loader class.

The load function of the default loader is automatically invoked by the ORB each time the target of an incoming request is not in the ORB's object table. The default load function takes no action, so for the Object Service pattern we extend the default loader class for my special needs. We discuss specialized implementation of the load function in the AdapterLoader class in more detail later. It funnels the incoming ORB requests to the Object Service instances by way of their tie objects. It is this cooperation of the loader, Object Service instances, and tie objects that affords the client applications the illusion that they are directly interacting with the server's persistent objects. In fact, each client request is intercepted by an Object Service instance, which then locates the target persistent object and forwards the request to it.

Notice Figure 10-7 indicates a one-to-many relationship between the EmployeeObjectService class and the Employee class. A fundamental aspect of this pattern, which greatly enhances its scalability, is that a single EmployeeObjectService instance is associated with multiple (zero or more) persistent Employee objects. This pattern's Object Service classes, EmployeeAminObjectService, and Employee ObjectService provide the services to locate and interact with persistent objects. The pattern derives its name from this provision of persistent Object Services.

IMPLEMENTATION
Let's consider the various facets of implementation.

THE ADAPTER CLASS   This pattern's Adapter class sets up and provides access to the other components of the Adapter. Listing 10-14 declares the Adapter class. It provides functions for initialization of and access to other Adapter components.

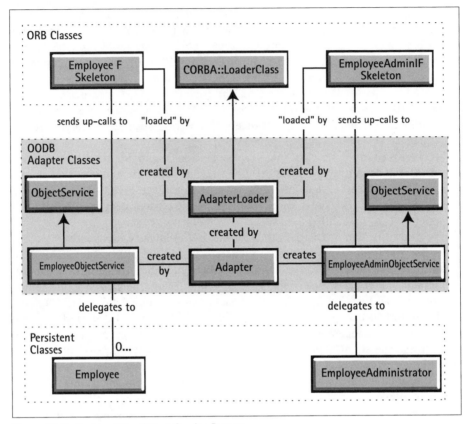

Figure 10-7: Design of the Object Service Pattern

Listing 10-14: The Object Service pattern's adapter class declaration

```
#include <os_pse\ostore.hh> //OODB include file
#include <CORBA.h>
#include "idl\EmployeeAdminServer.hh"
#define ADMINISTRATOR_ROOT "Administrator_DB_Root"
class ObjectService;
class EmployeeObjectService;
class AdapterLoader;
class Adapter
{
public:
  static Adapter* instance();
  ~Adapter();
  CORBA:Object* getObjectService(const char*
              serviceName);
  ObjectService* getObjectServiceImpl(const char*
                serviceName);
  void initializeDB();
```

```
    void initialize();
    os_database* getDB();
protected:
    Adapter();
private:
    static Adapter* theAdapter;
    AdapterLoader* theLoader;
    EmployeeIF* employeeService;
    EmployeeAdministratorIF* employeeAdminService;
    os_database* theDB;
};
```

As in the Adapter class designed for the Interface Object pattern, we use Gamma's singleton pattern to ensure one Adapter object is created and is then easily accessible to other objects. In keeping with this pattern, the Adapter constructor is protected and the `static Adapter:instance()`function, shown in Listing 10-15, creates or returns the reference to the Adapter instance.

Listing 10-15: The Adapter class uses the singleton pattern

```
#include "Adapter.h"
#include "AdapterLoader.h"
#include "EmployeeObjectService.h"
#include "EmployeeAdministratorObjectService.h"
#include "EmployeeAdministrator.h"
#include <string.h>
#include <iostream.h>
Adapter* Adapter:theAdapter = 0;
Adapter:Adapter()
{
    theLoader = 0;
    theDB = 0;
    cout << "The adapter has been constructed" << endl;
}
Adapter* Adapter:instance()
{
    if(!theAdapter)
        theAdapter = new Adapter();
    return theAdapter;
}
```

The Adapter object initializes the server and the objects comprising the Adapter and ORB layers using its `initializeDB()` and `initialize()` functions. These functions are called when the server is launched, as was shown in Listing 10-1. The `initialize()` function in Listing 10-16 indirectly forces creation of the singleton employee object service and employee administrator object service instances by calling their `instance()` functions. Once this is done it creates the corresponding skeleton or tie objects, passing in the Object Service instances as the delegate implementation objects. The `initializeDB()` function is identical to the one discussed for the Interface Object pattern.

Listing 10-16: Implementation of adapter initialization functions

```
void Adapter:initialize()
{
  //Create the employee object service
  EmployeeObjectService:instance();
  //Create the employee object service ORB/tie object
  //passing in the employee object service
   employeeService =
   new TIE_EmployeeIF(EmployeeObjectService)
     (EmployeeObjectService:instance());
  //Create the employee admin object service
  EmployeeAdminObjectService:instance();
  //Create the employee admin object service ORB/tie
  //object, passing in the employee admin object service
   employeeAdminService = new
   IE_EmployeeAdministratorIF(EmployeeAdminObjectService)
   (EmployeeAdminObjectService:instance());
  theLoader = new AdapterLoader();
}
void Adapter:initializeDB()
{
  os_database_root* adminRoot;
  EmployeeAdministrator* theAdmin;
    //Initialize the OODB client runtime
  objectstore:initialize();
  //Initialize the OODB's transaction manager
  os_transaction:initialize();
  //Open the database, create it if it does not exist
  theDB = os_database:open("EmployeeAdminServer.db",
             0,
             0666);
  os_transaction:begin();
  {
   //Try to get DB root pointing to EmployeeAdministrator
   adminRoot = theDB->find_root(ADMINISTRATOR_ROOT);
   //If the root does not exist create it
   if(!adminRoot)
   {
     adminRoot = theDB->create_root(ADMINISTRATOR_ROOT);
     //Create singleton EmployeeAdministrator
     theAdmin = EmployeeAdministrator:instance();
     //Associate the emp admin instance with new root
     adminRoot->set_value(theAdmin);
   }
  }
  os_transaction:commit();
  cout << "The database has been initialized."<< endl;
}
```

The remaining Adapter functions, getObjectService and getObjectServiceImpl, are provided in Listing 10-17. The AdapterLoader uses getObjectService to acquire references to Object Service instances in response to object faults generated by incoming ORB requests. Object faults are generated by the ORB when it discovers that the object targeted by an incoming request is not in the ORB's object table. The ORB gives the loader the opportunity to load the targeted object. In keeping with this pattern's scalability goals, the loader always returns the appropriate Object Service tie object by passing an Object Service name to getObjectService().Finally, getObjectServiceImpl() is used by the loader to acquire references to the Object Service implementation objects to pass on the ID of the target persistent object.

Listing 10-17: Implementation of Adapter:getObjectService function()

```
CORBA:Object* Adapter:getObjectService(const char*
                    serviceName)
{
  if(strcmp(serviceName,"Employee")==0)
    return employeeService;
  else if(strcmp(serviceName,"EmployeeAdmin")==0)
   return employeeAdminService;
  else
    return 0;
}
ObjectService* Adapter:getObjectServiceImpl(const char*
                    serviceName)
{
  if(strcmp(serviceName,"Employee")==0)
   return (EmployeeObjectService:instance());
  else if(strcmp(serviceName,"EmployeeAdmin")==0)
   return (EmployeeAdminObjectService:instance());
  else
    return 0;
}
```

THE ADAPTERLOADER CLASS   This pattern's strength is its ability to allocate the incoming client requests to the appropriate Object Service instance and then to the appropriate Persistent Object. The AdapterLoader class in Listing 10-18 assists with this process. It inherits from the ORB's base class CORBA:LoaderClass and over-rides its virtual load() function. By default, the ORB calls the loader's load() function whenever the requested target object is not in the ORB's object table. The load() function loads or locates the object needed to handle the incoming request. To do this, the load function uses the targetInterface parameter passed from the ORB that contains the name of the targeted IDL interface. This is passed to Adapter:getObjectService()to get a reference to the Object Service instance servicing that IDL interface. In the employee administration server this is either the EmployeeAdminObjectService, or the EmployeeObjectService tie object. The reference is then returned to the ORB as the request's target object. Prior to returning the tie object, the load function also provides the request's target object ID to the

Object Service implementation object using its setTargetObject function. The ID is embedded in the marker portion of the client reques,t and is available to the load function in the marker parameter.

Listing 10-18: The AdapterLoader class implementation

```
#include "AdapterLoader.h"
#include "ObjectService.h"
#include "Adapter.h"
#include <iostream.h>
#include <CORBA.h>
AdapterLoader:AdapterLoader() : CORBA:LoaderClass(1)
{cout << "The loader has been constructed" << endl;}
AdapterLoader:~AdapterLoader()
{;}
CORBA:Object_ptr AdapterLoader:load(const char*
                    targetInterface,
                    const char* marker,
                    CORBA:Boolean isBind,
                    CORBA:Environment& env)
{
  CORBA:Object_ptr objectService;
  ObjectService* objectServiceImpl;
 //Get a reference to the object service
  objectService =
   Adapter:instance()->getObjectService(targetInterface);
 //Get a reference to the object service implementation
  objectServiceImpl =
   Adapter:instance()->getObjectServiceImpl(
               targetInterface);
  //If the object service is valid
  if(objectService && objectServiceImpl)
   {
   //Set the ID of the target persistent object
    objectServiceImpl->setTargetObjectID(marker);
   //Return the "loaded" object service
    return objectService;
   }
   else
    return 0;
}
```

THE OBJECTSERVICE BASE CLASS   All Object Service classes inherit from the ObjectService base class. This simple class is shown in Listing 10-19. It provides a mechanism to set and get the ID of the current targeted Persistent Object. The target object ID is used as the key to search for Persistent Objects targeted by a given client request.

Listing 10-19: Implementation of the ObjectService base class

```
class ObjectService
{
public:
ObjectService(const char* newServiceName)
{
  serviceName = new char[strlen(newServiceName)+1];
  strcpy(serviceName, newServiceName);
  currentTargetID = 0;
}
virtual ~ObjectService()
{
  if(currentTargetID)
  delete [] currentTargetID;
  if(serviceName)
  delete [] serviceName;
}
void setTargetObjectID(const char* iD)
{
  if(currentTargetID)
   delete [] currentTargetID;
  currentTargetID = new char[strlen(iD)+1];
  strcpy(currentTargetID, iD);
}
char* getCurrentTargetID()
{ return currentTargetID; }
char* getServiceName()
{ return serviceName; }
 private:
   currentTargetID;
  char* serviceName;

};
```

**THE EMPLOYEEOBJECTSERVICE AND EMPLOYEEADMINOBJECTSERVICE
CLASSES** Object Service instances, the singleton instances of EmployeeObject-
Service and EmpAdminObjectService, effectively create a buffer between the idio-
syncrasies of the ORB and the OODB server. They (1) manage database transactions,
(2) locate target Persistent Objects, and (3) handle any necessary datatype conver-
sions as function parameters are passed from the ORB middleware to the server's
Persistent Objects. Since the jObject Service instances are a key component of the
Object Service pattern let's look at each of these responsibilities.

Listing 10-20 provides the definition of the EmployeeObjectService class. The
next few paragraphs illustrate the responsibilities of this class by looking more
closely at the implementation of its functions.

Listing 10-20: Declaration of the EmployeeObjectService object service class

```
#include "ObjectService.h"
#include "idl\EmployeeAdminServer.hh"
class Employee;
class EmployeeObjectService : public ObjectService
{
public:
 virtual ~EmployeeObjectService();
 static EmployeeObjectService* instance();
 //Implementation of IDL interface
 void increaseSalary(float percentIncrease,
         CORBA:Environment&);
 void decreaseSalary(float percentDecrease,
         CORBA:Environment&);
 short addSubordinate(const char* newSubordinateID,
          CORBA:Environment&);
 short removeSubordinate(const char* subordinateID,
         CORBA:Environment&);
 EmployeeInfoList_var getSubordinates(CORBA:Environment&);
 void updateInfo(const char* newName, const char* newSSN,
        const char* newTitle, const char* newHireDate,
        CORBA:Environment&);
 void setPhotoURL(const char* newURL, CORBA:Environment&);
 void setResumeURL(const char* newURL, CORBA:Environment&);
 EmployeeDetailsStruct_var getDetails(CORBA:Environment&);
 void setDetails(EmployeeDetailsStruct newDetails,
        CORBA:Environment& );
 //End of IDL implementation
protected:
 EmployeeObjectService();
private:
 Employee* findTargetObject();
 static EmployeeObjectService* theEmployeeObjectService;
};
DEF_TIE_EmployeeIF(EmployeeObjectService);
```

Object Service Classes Handle Database Transactions

Transaction management is a core issue creating a clear line of separation between the typical ORB middleware object and a server's Persistent Object. It is an OODB's transaction management that allows several OODB clients to safely make concurrent reads and writes to Persistent Objects. As a result, any ODA must manage database transactions. Handling OODB transactions is one responsibility of the Object Service instances. Prior to interaction with Persistent Objects, the Object Service instance starts a transaction. After updates to Persistent Objects are complete, the Object Service instance commits or aborts the current transaction. Listing 10-21 illustrates this transaction handling in the increaseSalary()function. Before interacting with Persistent Objects we start a transaction by calling PSE's os_transaction:begin().When we are done interacting with Persistent Objects, we call os_transaction:commit().

Object Service Classes Handle Persistent Object Discovery

To enhance scalability, this pattern intentionally avoids having many Persistent Objects in the server's memory at any given time. As a result, it is necessary to locate and swap Persistent Object's into the server's Persistent Object cache when handling a client request. The employee application locates the target persistent Employee object using the employee's ID, which is embedded in every EmployeeIF ORB reference sent to a client. When an incoming client request is finally delegated to the EmployeeObjectService instance, the employee ID has been extracted by the AdapterLoader from the client request and passed to the Object Service instance. Listing 10-21 shows how the ID is used as the key to a database query or as the parameter to the findTargetObject function housing my own employee search routine. Listing 10-21 shows this function returning a persistent Employee reference that is used to invoke `increaseSalary()` on the persistent Employee object.

Listing 10-21: How Object Service Instances handle transactions and Persistent Object Discovery

```
void EmployeeObjectService:increaseSalary(float percent,
                    CORBA:Environment& env)
{
 os_transaction:begin();
 {
  Employee* target;
  target = findTargetObject();
  if(target)
    target->increaseSalary(percet);
 }
 os_transaction:commit();
}
```

Listing 10-22 is a simple algorithm for locating the target Persistent Object using the object's ID. It delegates the Employee ID search to the persistent EmployeeAdministrator object, which simply loops through all of its Employee objects looking for a match. We're certain you can imagine more advanced search techniques to expedite this search.

Listing 10-22: Implementation of EmployeeObjectService:findTargetObject()

```
Employee* EmployeeObjectService:findTargetObject()
{
 //Assumes that a transaction is already active
 Employee* target;
 target = EmployeeAdministrator:instance()->getEmployee(
   getCurrentTargetID());
 return target;
}
```

Object Service Classes Handle Datatype Conversions

The third responsibility of an Object Service instance is to perform datatype conversions as function parameters and return values are sent between the server's ORB layer and its Persistent Object layer. For simple datatypes this is not a significant issue, but for complex datatypes, it can be quite involved. For example, the Employee IDL interface defines a getSubordinates()function which returns a sequence of EmployeeInfoStructs. However, as you might expect, the corresponding function in the persistent Employee class returns a list of references to persistent Employee objects. In this implementation of EmployeeObject-Service:getSubordinates, we must create an EmployeeInfoStruct for each returned Employee reference, placing each struct in a sequence, which it then returns to the client.

Listing 10-23 illustrates the parameter type mapping required by getSubordinates(). The function starts a transaction and finds the target Persistent Object. It then calls getSubordinates on the target Persistent Object, acquiring an array of references to persistent Employee objects. Obviously this array can't be sent back over the wire to the client. Neither the ORB, nor the client understands what to do with the local array of references to persistent Employee objects. So we create the sequence of EmployeeInfoStructs required by the IDL interface and populate a struct for each subordinate Employee. After interacting with the Persistent Objects we end the transaction and return the EmployeeInfoList.

Listing 10-23: How Object Service instances handle datatype conversions

```
EmployeeInfoList_var EmployeeObjectService:getSubordinates(
  CORBA:Environment& env)
{
 EmployeeInfoList_var employeeInfoList;
 CORBA:ULong i = 0;
 os_transaction:begin();
 {
  Employee* employees[MAX_EMPLOYEES];
  Employee* target;
  target = findTargetObject();
  if(target)
  {
   employeeInfoList = new EmployeeInfoList(MAX_EMPLOYEES);
   target->getSubordinates(employees);
   while(employees[i])
   {
    employeeInfoList[i].name =
     CORBA:string_dup(employees[i]->getName());
    employeeInfoList[i].ssn =
     CORBA:string_dup(employees[i]->getSSN());
    employeeInfoList[i].title =
     CORBA:string_dup(employees[i]->getTitle());
    employeeInfoList[i].hireDate =
     CORBA:string_dup(employees[i]->getHireDate());
```

```
  employeeInfoList[i].iD =
   CORBA:string_dup(employees[i]->getID());
   i++;
  }
 }
}
os_transaction:commit();
employeeInfoList->length(i);
return employeeInfoList;
}
```

A final important aspect of the Object Service pattern is housed in the getEmployee function in Listing 10-24. In preceding paragraphs we referred to the fact that Persistent Object IDs are embedded in the EmployeeIF references sent to clients. Close examination of the EmployeeAdministratorIF IDL interface reveals that the only way to acquire an EmployeeIF reference representative of a pre-existing persistent Employee is by calling getEmployee, and passing an employee ID. An employee ID may have been acquired by browsing the results of getEmployees. In other words, the data structures returned by calling getEmployees do not contain EmployeeIF references, just employee properties and the employee's ID. This approach avoids the onerous task of building an EmployeeIF tie object for each employee returned by getEmployees on the slim chance that the client needs further interaction with each employee object. Rather, the client must get the specific employee it needs by calling EmployeeAdministrator:getEmployee(const char* employeeID) The getEmployee function creates an EmployeeIF tie object, passing the singleton EmployeeObjectService as its delegate, and the target employee ID received from the client as its marker. We discussed earlier that the content of the marker is the key to locating the ultimate persistent target object of a given EmployeeIF invocation.

Listing 10-24: Implementation of EmployeeAdminObjectService:getEmployee

```
EmployeeIF_var EmployeeAdminObjectService:getEmployee(
  const char* employeeID, CORBA:Environment& )
{
  EmployeeIF_var employee;
  employee = new TIE_EmployeeIF(EmployeeObjectService)
   (EmployeeObjectService:instance(), employeeID);
  return employee;
}
```

A vital, yet subtle aspect of the getEmployee function in Listing 10-24 is that using the var reference type results in the ORB's deletion of the EmployeeIF tie object as part of its reply marshalling process. The reply marshalling performed by the ORB requires that it release memory referenced by a _var type. This is desireable in this case because this pattern's scalability goals require that neither server's object table nor its memory space be consumed by tie objects referencing specific persistent Employee instances, which may number into the tens of thousands.

Object Interaction Diagrams

With several objects cooperating within the Object Service pattern, the sequence of events triggered by a client's request is fairly intricate. Using Employee Administrator:getEmployees and Employee:increaseSalary(), the object interaction diagrams in Figures 10-8 and 10-9 illustrate the role of each server object.

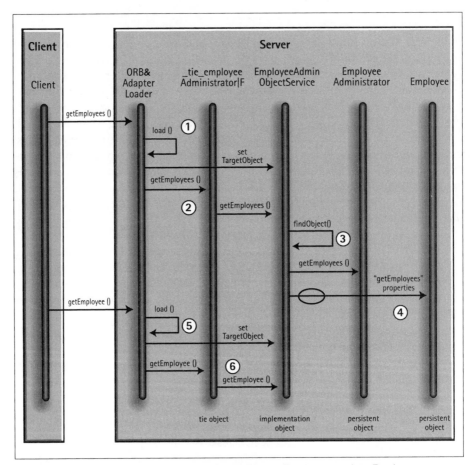

Figure 10-8: Object Interaction Sequence Supporting getEmployees and getEmployee

When the server is launched, a singleton EmployeeAdminObjectService instance is constructed, as is the AdapterLoader. All subsequent incoming invocations on the EmployeeAdministratorIF interface are funneled, by the AdapterLoader, to the EmployeeAdminObjectService instance. Figure 10-8 illustrates the object interaction sequence triggered by a client's request to browse the persistent employees by calling `getEmployees()` and then connecting to a specific employee object using getEmployee. Each numbered interaction is further described as follows:

1. When the getEmployees request arrives at the server there is no object corresponding to the employee administrator object reference in the server's ORB object table. As a result, the ORB generates an object fault and gives the AdapterLoader the opportunity to provide the object by calling its `load()` function. Its load function discovers that the call was targeted at the EmployeeAdministratorIF interface and returns the EmployeeAdministratorIF tie object. Prior to returning, the load function extracts the ID of the target Persistent Object from the marker value embedded in the client request packet and calls `EmployeeAdminObjectService:setTargetObjectID()`.

2. The ORB then resumes its normal call processing by passing the getEmployees request to the EmployeeAdministrator tie object returned by `AdapterLoader:load()`in Step 1. As usual, the tie object unmarshalls the request and delegates handling of the call to its implementation object, the singleton EmployeeAdminObjectService.

3. In keeping with the role of Object Service instances the EmployeeAdminObjectService starts a database transaction and calls findTargetObject. `findTargetObject()`uses the ID of the target Persistent Object provided in Step 1 to locate and provide a reference to the target Persistent Object. The returned reference points to the persistent EmployeeAdministrator which, because the client called getEmployees, is asked to provide the list of persistent Employee objects.

4. Each persistent employee in the array acquired in Step 3 is then used to build and add an EmployeeInfoStruct to the EmployeeInfoList returned to the client.

5. After browsing the employee properties returned in Step 4, the client connects to a specific employee object by calling getEmployee on the EmployeeAdministrator object, passing that employee's ID.

6. getEmployee simply constructs an EmployeeIF ORB reference, a tie object, using the persistent Employee ID passed by the client as the tie object's marker and the EmployeeObjectService instance as the object's delegate. Note that this newly created tie object is then released by the ORB when the request's reply marshalling is complete. This enhances scalability by preventing the ORB's object table from becoming swamped with employee tie objects. The client may then use the returned EmployeeIF object reference to make requests on the persistent employee object.

Figure 10-9 represents a sequence of object interactions that may follow those illustrated in Figure 10-8. It illustrates the client using the employee reference acquired from calling getEmployee to invoke increaseSalary()on a persistent Employee instance.

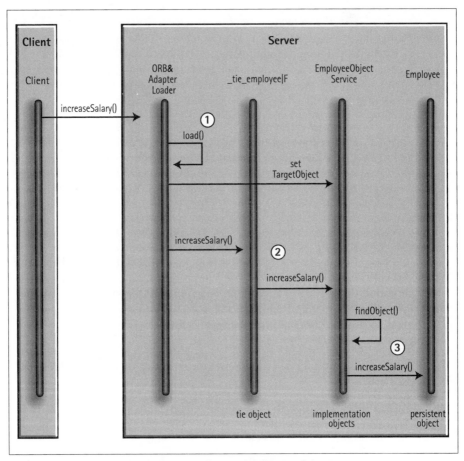

Figure 10-9: Object Interaction Sequence Supporting increaseSalary

Each numbered interaction depicted in Figure 10-9 is described as follows:

1. The client uses an EmployeeIF ORB object reference to invoke increaseSalary()on an employee object. As expected, the tie object referenced by the ORB object reference is not in the ORB's object table. It was released after being returned to the client at the end of Step 6 in Figure 10-8. As a result, the ORB gives the AdapterLoader the opportunity to load the referenced object. In response, the load function extracts the

ID of the target Persistent Object from the "marker" value embedded in the client request packet, calls `EmployeeObjectService:setTargetObject-ID()`passing in the object ID, and, finally, returns the EmployeeIF tie object.

2. As usual the ORB then delivers the request to the EmployeeIF tie object which unmarshalls the request and delegates it to its implementation object, the singleton EmployeeObjectService.

3. In keeping with the role of Object Service instances the EmployeeObjectService starts a database transaction and calls findTargetObject, which uses the ID of the target Persistent Object provided in Step 1. The returned reference should point to the targeted persistent Employee. If the object was found the corresponding increaseSalary function is invoked on it. Finally, the transaction is committed.

SYNOPSIS

Figure 10-10 summarizes the scalability of the Object Service pattern. In general this pattern maximizes scalability for the number of Persistent Objects that can be made available to CORBA clients from a single CORBA-based server. This scalability results from the fact that a single ORB visible object, the Object Service instance's tie object, provides access to a large number of Persistent Objects and because Persistent Objects are not pinned in memory across several client requests. Requiring that a single Object Service instance front for a large number of Persistent Objects greatly reduces the ratio of ORB objects to Persistent Objects and, therefore, allows the server to scale to a larger number of Persistent Objects.

Because this pattern does not pin Persistent Objects in the local object cache the OODB is free to flush them from the client cache, if necessary, to make room for others to be paged in. This pattern can also scale well to a system architecture that has multiple clients of the OODB server. When Persistent Objects are pinned into the client cache of a given application there is a greater likelihood that other applications are forced to wait until they are given write access to those objects. But because this pattern does not pin persistent objects in memory across client invocations, delays resulting from object contention are less likely.

However, as Figure 10-10 shows, this pattern's scalability advantages are not achieved without a performance cost. Because Persistent Objects are not pinned in memory across several client requests, they must be frequently reacquired. Each time an incoming ORB request necessitates interaction with a Persistent Object a reference to it must be acquired using a query based on the target object ID. However, because this is a query performed by the OODB on Persistent Objects, as opposed to being performed by the ORB on its active object table, we reap the optimization benefits of the OODB's query facility.

Advantages

- Supports a very large number of persistent objects with minimal server side memory consumption.

- Ensures very fast traversal of the ORB's active object table.

- Accelerates object loading by taking advantage of the optimized query capabilities of the underlying OODB.

- Maximizes concurrent access to the underlying database server since persistent objects are not locked into the server's persistent object cache.

Shortcomings

- Request handling is slower than patterns allowing persistent objects to remain in the server's memory for many client invocations.

- Request handling is slower than the Interface Object pattern as a result of frequent creation and deletion of ORB objects.

Figure10-10: Scalability of the Object Service Pattern

Threaded Object Service Pattern

RATIONALE

The Threaded Object Service pattern is a variation of the single-threaded Object Service pattern discussed previously. Client responsiveness and scalability are enhanced by allowing each Object Service instance to operate in its own thread, creating the opportunity for multiple clients to have concurrent interaction with the server.

DESIGN

Figure 10-11 illustrates the architectural implications of this pattern. It is comprised of the Object Service instances described in the single threaded version of this pattern, an object loader, thread filter, and an ObjectServiceThread instance for each Object Service instance. As with the single threaded version, this combination of objects affords the client applications the appearance that they are directly interacting with the server's Persistent Objects. In fact, each client request is intercepted by an Object Service instance that locates the target persistent object and forwards the client request to it.

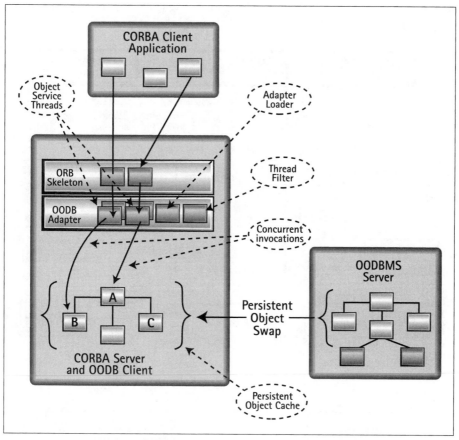

Figure 10-11: Client-Server Interaction Using the Threaded Object Service Pattern

Figures 10-12 and 10-13 offer a closer look at the design of this pattern. The distinguishing characteristic of this multithreaded pattern is the existence of an AdapterThreadFilter and the ObjectServiceThread instances. When the Adapter object is initialized it creates the AdapterThreadFilter and an ObjectServiceThread for each ObjectServiceInstance. As client requests arrive at the server it is the AdapterThreadFilter that intercepts and funnels them to the appropriate ObjectServiceThread, where they are queued. And as an ObjectServiceInstance finishes handling one request its corresponding ObjectServiceThread dispatches the next queued request. The improvement over the single-threaded version arises from the server's ability to be more responsive to client requests. One ObjectService instance may be handling one request in its own thread while another ObjectService instance concurrently handles a different request in its thread.

The remaining aspects of the design in Figure 10-12 are similar to the single-threaded version. You can refer back to that design discussion for further details.

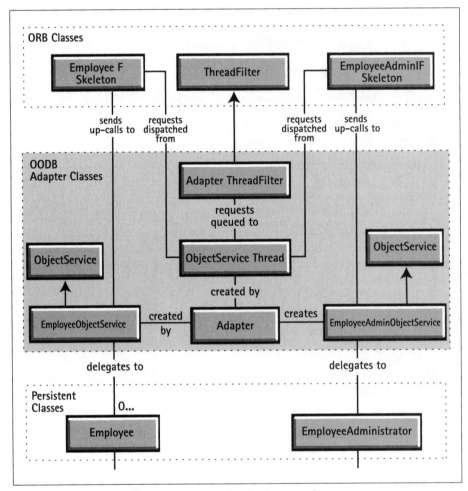

Figure 10-12: Design of the Threaded Object Service Pattern — Part 1

Figure 10-13 illustrates the remainder of this pattern's design. In addition to the classes in Figure 10-12 the Threaded Object Service pattern depends on the AdapterLoader class. It inherits from and overrides the load() function in the ORB's base loader class, CORBA:LoaderClass. Similar to the single-threaded version the loader's load() function is called by the ORB when its unmarshalling sequence generates an object fault. Object faults are generated when the target ORB object reference contained in the client's request packet is not in the ORB's object table. Given this pattern's design, object faults are generated frequently. So, we override the base class's load() function, which takes no action, with my own implementation that loads and returns a skeleton object reference representing the appropriate Object Service instance.

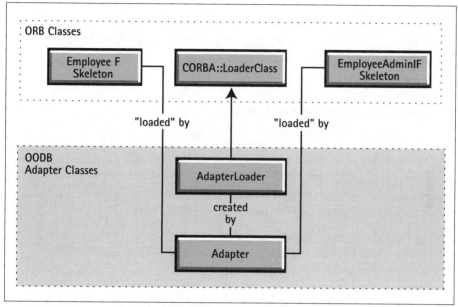

Figure 10-13: Design of the Threaded Object Service Pattern — Part 2

IMPLEMENTATION

The core differences between this pattern and its single-threaded counterpart are the AdapterThreadFilter and the ObjectServiceThread classes. The code samples provided focus on these classes.

The AdapterThreadFilter shown in Listing 10-25 inherits from the base ThreadFilter class provided with the ORB and overrides its `inRequestPreMarshall`function. When the server is launched, the singleton Adapter instance is constructed and initialized, as in the single-threaded version. But for the multithreaded version the `Adapter:initialize()` function creates a single instance of AdapterThreadFilter and an ObjectServiceThread instance for each IDL interface. And as each ObjectServiceThread is constructed it adds itself to a hash table managed by the AdapterThreadFilter, using the name of the IDL interface it services as the hash value.

The design in Figure 10-12 shows that the AdapterThreadFilter inherits from the base ThreadFilter class provided with the ORB. At run time the ORB is designed to call the inRequestPreMarshall function on the base ThreadFilter object, giving it the opportunity to dispatch the request to an existing thread, or create a new one. But our AdapterThreadFilter class overrides the base class's inRequestPreMarshall()method, which takes no action. The implementation of `AdapterThreadFilter:inRequestPreMarshall()`shown in Listing 10-25 gets the ObjectServiceThread instance that should handle the request using the request's target IDL interface as the key into the ObjectServiceThread hash table described above. Once the proper ObjectServiceInstance is acquired it is instructed to queue the client's request by calling its queueRequest function.

While the other patterns' code samples are implemented in C++, these code samples are implemented in Java. Java's built-in support for threads makes it an appropriate choice here.

Listing 10-25: The AdapterThreadFilter Java class

```
public class AdapterThreadFilter extends ThreadFilter
{
 static Hashtable objServiceThreadList = new Hashtable();
 private String mostRecentTargetD;
 public AdapterThreadFilter()
 { super(); }
 public boolean inRequestPreMarshall(Request req)
 {
  ObjectServiceThread objectServiceThread;
  org.omg.CORBA.Object target;
  String targetInterface;
  target = req.target();
   targetInterface =
     _OrbixWeb.Object(target)._interfaceMarker();
  objectServiceThread =
   (ObjectServiceThread)objServiceThreadList.get(
                   targetInterface);
  if(objectServiceThread!=null)
  {
   objectServiceThread.queueRequest(req,
                   mostRecentTargetD);
   return false;
  }
  return true;
 }
 void setCurrentPersistentTarget(String newTargetObjectID)
 { mostRecentTargetD = new String(newTargetObjectID); }
}
```

Listing 10-26 shows the constructor for ObjectServiceThread. When the employee administration server is launched the `Adapter:initialize()` function creates two instances of ObjectServiceThread, one for the EmployeeObjectService instance and another for the EmployeeAdminObjectService instance. And as you see from Listing 10-26 the ObjectServiceThread constructor requires a reference to the AdapterThreadFilter object, a reference to its associated Object Service instance, and a reference to the corresponding Object Service ORB object (because we use the tie approach for ORB implementation linkage. But the most important point about the constructor is the object adds itself to the thread filter's ObjectServiceThread hash table, using the name of the IDL interface that it services as its hash value. After constructing the ObjectServiceThreads the `Adapter:initialize()` method calls their `start()` methods. As with typical Java threads the `start()` method invokes the thread's `run()` method.

Listing 10-26: Implementation of the constructor for AdapterObjectThread

```
class ObjectServiceThread extends Thread
{
 private Vector queuedRequests = new Vector();
 private AdapterThreadFilter theThreadFilter;
 private ObjectService objectServiceImpl;
 private org.omg.CORBA.Object objectService;
 public ObjectServiceThread(
      AdapterThreadFilter threadFilter,
      ObjectService newObjectServiceImpl,
           org.omg.CORBA.Object newObjectService)
 {
  theThreadFilter = threadFilter;
   objectServiceImpl = newObjectServiceImpl;
  objectService = newObjectService;

  theThreadFilter.objServiceThreadList.put(
    objectServiceImpl.getServiceName(), this);
 }
```

As the AdapterThreadFilter receives incoming requests it identifies which ObjectServiceThread should handle the request and calls its queueRequest() method, included in Listing 10-27. queueRequest()adds the request to its ObjectServiceThread's request queue and calls notifyAll() to notify the thread to wakeup and handle the request. When the thread returns from its wait() statement in getNextResponse(), also in Listing 10-27, it determines whether or not there is a request in its queue. If there is, it returns it to the caller. In our case the caller is the thread's run() function that loops for the life of the thread, calling getNextResponse() in each cycle.

Listing 10-27: Implementation of ObjectServiceThread's queueRequest and getNextRequest

```
public synchronized void queueRequest(Request req,
                     String targetObjectID)
 {
  int last;
   QueuedRequest qReq;
   qReq = new QueuedRequest(req, targetObjectID);
  last = queuedRequests.size();
  queuedRequests.insertElementAt(qReq, last);
  notifyAll();
 }
 public synchronized QueuedRequest getNextRequest()
 {
  QueuedRequest qReq;
  int numRequests;
  numRequests = queuedRequests.size();
  while(numRequests <=0)
  {
   try{ wait(); }
   catch(Exception waitExc) { }
   numRequests = queuedRequests.size();
  }
```

```
  qReq = (QueuedRequest)queuedRequests.firstElement();
  queuedRequests.removeElementAt(0);
  return qReq;
}
```

As is typical of a Java thread, the `ObjectServiceThread:run()` method, shown in Listing 10-28, was invoked at server initialization. It immediately enters its loop and cycles for the life of the thread. Upon entering the loop, the first function it calls is its own `getNextResponse()` function described above. Once `getNextResponse()` returns with a client request to be handled by the Object Service instance, it uses the returned marker (the ID of the target persistent object), to set the ID of the target persistent object. Using the marker as the ID of the target persistent object should be familiar to you from the single-threaded version of this pattern. Now that the Object Service instance has been properly notified of the request's target persistent object, OrbixWeb is told to dispatch the request in the current thread. In other words, the client request is dispatched to the tie object where it is unmarshalled and delegated to the Object Service instance.

Listing 10-28: The run() Function for the ObjectServiceThread class

```
public void run()
{
 QueuedRequest qReq;
 while(true)
 {
  qReq = getNextRequest();
  if(qReq != null)
  {
   objectServiceImpl.setTargetObjectID(
                qReq.targetObjectID);
   _OrbixWeb.Object(objectService)._marker(
                qReq.targetObjectID);
   try{_CORBA.Orbix.continueThreadDispatch(qReq.request);}
   catch(Exception exc)
       {System.err.println("Error - " + exc); return ; } }
  }
 }
}
```

SYNOPSIS

Figure 10-14 summarizes the scalability of the Threaded Object Service pattern. Similar to the single-threaded Object Service pattern, this pattern maximizes scalability of the number of persistent objects that can be made available to CORBA clients from a single CORBA-based server and in terms of multiapplication contention for Persistent Objects. As in the single-threaded version, request handling performance is sacrificed somewhat to do this. The performance hit is counterbalanced here by using multiple threads to service client requests. Responsiveness to multiple client requests is improved because each Object Service instance is operating in its own thread, allowing concurrent handling.

Advantages	Shortcomings
• Improves the server's responsiveness by handling multiple concurrent requests in parallel.	• Request handling is slower than patterns allowing persistent objects to remain in the server's memory for many client invocations.
• Supports a very large number of persistent objects with minimal server side memory consumption.	• The design and implementation are more complex.
• Ensures very fast traversal of the ORB's active object table.	
• Accelerates object loading by taking advantage of the optimized query capabilities of the underlying OODB.	
• Maximizes concurrent access to the underlying database server since persistent objects are not locked into the server's persistent object cache.	

Figure 10-14: Scalability of the Threaded Object Service Pattern

Pinned Object Pattern

For some OODB applications supporting a large number of Persistent Objects in the server is not a major factor. If your server is not likely to interact with more than a few thousand objects, does not and will not have more than one OODB client contending for the same Persistent Objects, but must be very responsive to client requests, then the Pinned Object Pattern may be an appropriate choice.

RATIONALE

The core characteristic of this pattern is that an ORB-enabled Instance Adapter object exists for each Persistent Object accessible to the server's clients. This eliminates the need to dynamically create ORB objects and adapter objects, and to dynamically locate the targeted Persistent Object for each client request. Each request is sent to the Instance Adapter indicated by the request's ORB reference and then directly to the Persistent Object associated with that Instance Adapter. Each Persistent Object is pinned in the server's Persistent Object cache (in local memory) because the Adapter holds the database open and each Instance Adapter hold a reference to a Persistent Object.

DESIGN

As indicated in Figure 10-15 this pattern results in a transient Instance Adapter object for each Persistent Object with which clients may wish to interact. The Instance dapters are created and associated with their persistent counterparts when the server process is initialized and destroyed when the server process dies.

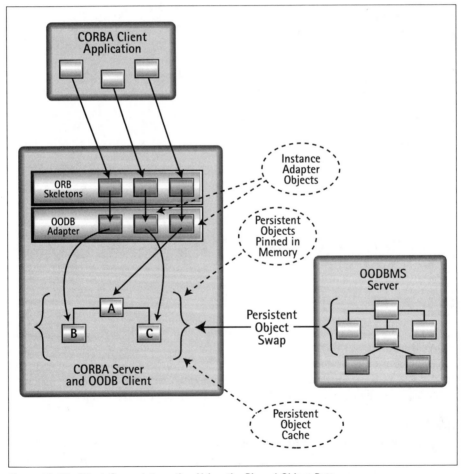

Figure 10-15: Client–Server Interaction Using the Pinned Object Pattern

As you can see from Figure 10-16, an advantage of the Pinned Object pattern is its simplicity. It is comprised of the Adapter class, the Instance Adapter classes, EmpAdminInstAdapter and EmployeeInstAdapter. The Adapter is responsible for initializing the server, the server's database, and the Instance Adapters at process initialization. An Instance Adapter class exists for each IDL interface and manages database transactions and performs datatype conversions when function parameters are passed from the ORB middleware to a Persistent Object. Transaction management and datatype conversions have been discussed previously so we will not rehash them here. Notice that the Instance Adapters don't need to locate target Persistent Objects for each client request as was necessary in the Object Service and Interface Object patterns. This is because each Instance Adapter object is given a reference to a single Persistent Object at construction. All invocations arriving at that Instance Adapter are then delegated to that persistent instance. Hence, the pattern's name, Instance Adapter.

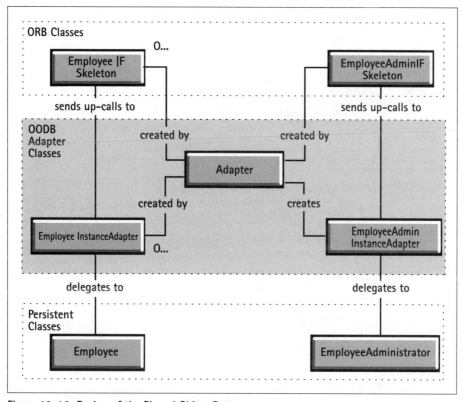

Figure 10-16: Design of the Pinned Object Pattern

IMPLEMENTATION

A side effect created by this pattern's design is the freedom to make the server's IDL interface fully object-oriented. The Object Service pattern failed to return an EmployeeIF reference in the EmployeeInfoStructs returned by getEmployees. It was too time consuming to build a reference for each employee object. In the Pinned Object Pattern, the EmployeeIF objects already exist. They can be efficiently added to the EmployeeInfoStructs populated by getEmployees. This eliminates the ODA's dependence on Employee object IDs. A client always uses an EmployeeIF reference to pass an employee as a parameter or to interact with an employee. The IDL interface in Listing 10-29 is the new and improved IDL interface that maximizes the use of CORBA's distributed object interaction model. Notice that the EmployeeInfoStruct now includes an employee reference, and that several functions now accept or return employee references, rather than employee IDs.

Listing 10-29 : New and improved IDL interface afforded by the design of the Pinned Object pattern

```
//Forward Declarations———————————
interface EmployeeIF;
interface EmployeeAdministratorIF;
//Data Types————————————
struct EmployeeInfoStruct{string name;
                string ssn;
                string title;
                string hireDate;
                string iD;
                                EmployeeIF employee;};
typedef sequence<EmployeeInfoStruct> EmployeeInfoList;

struct EmployeeDetailsStruct{float salary;
                string photoURL;
                string resumeURL;
                string iD;};
//Interface Definitions———————————
interface EmployeeAdministratorIF
{
  EmployeeIF createEmployee(in string newName,
                in string newSSN,
                in string newTitle,
                in float newSalary,
                in string hireDate);
  short deleteEmployee(in EmployeeIF employeeID);
  EmployeeInfoList getEmployees();
};
interface EmployeeIF
{
  EmployeeDetailsStruct getDetails();
  void setDetails(in EmployeeDetailsStruct newDetails);
  void increaseSalary(in float percentIncrease);
  void decreaseSalary(in float percentDecrease);
```

```
void addSubordinate(in EmployeeIF newSubordinate);
void removeSubordinate(in EmployeeIF subordinate);
EmployeeInfoList getSubordinates();
};
```

Listing 10-30 shows the declaration of the Adapter class for this pattern. As with the preceding patterns, the Adapter class is responsible for initializing the ODA and establishing connectivity with the server's database. It still uses the singleton pattern to ensure that one instance of itself is constructed and easily accessible. Because this pattern's design is less complex, so is the implementation of the Adapter's initialize() method. So let's take a closer look at the implementation of this method.

Listing 10-30: Declaration of the Adapter class for the Pinned Object pattern

```
#include <os_pse\ostore.hh> //OODB include file
#include <CORBA.h>
#include "idl\EmployeeAdminServer.hh"
#define ADMINISTRATOR_ROOT "Administrator_DB_Root"
class Adapter
{
public:
  static Adapter* instance();
  ~Adapter();
  void initializeDB();
  void initialize();
  os_database* getDB();
protected:
  Adapter();
private:
  static Adapter* theAdapter;
  EmployeeAdministratorIF* employeeAdminIF;
  os_database* theDB;
};
```

The distinguishing characteristic of the initialization process required by the Pinned Object Pattern is the need to construct a tie object and an Instance Adapter object for each and every Persistent Object with which a client may wish to interact. The Adapter:initialize() method, shown in Listing 10-31, begins this process by constructing the EmployeeAdministratorIF tie object and its implementation object, an instance of EmpAdminInstAdapter (and in fact, the only instance of this class as there is only one persistent EmployeeAdministrator). The method concludes by calling the EmpAdminInstAdapter:initialize(), which is provided in Listing 10-33.

Listing 10-31: Implementation of Adapter:initialize()

```
void Adapter:initialize()
{
```

```
os_database_root* adminRoot;
EmployeeAdministrator* employeeAdministrator;
EmpAdminInstAdapter* empAdminInstAdapter;
os_transaction:begin();
{
 //Get DB root pointing to EmployeeAdministrator
 adminRoot = theDB->find_root(ADMINISTRATOR_ROOT);
 //Get the EmployeeAdministrator pointer from the root
 employeeAdministrator =
   (EmployeeAdministrator*)adminRoot->get_value();
 //For the persistent employee administrator create its
 //Instance Adapter.
 empAdminInstAdapter =
   new EmpAdminInstAdapter(employeeAdministrator);
 //For the persistent employee administrator create its
 //tie object and its Instance Adapter.
 employeeAdminIF =
   new TIE_EmployeeAdministratorIF(EmpAdminInstAdapter)
     ( empAdminInstAdapter );
 //Initialize the Instance Adapter
 empAdminInstAdapter->initialize();
 }
 os_transaction:commit();
}
```

Listing 10-32 shows the declaration of the Instance Adapter class that adapts instances of the persistent EmployeeAdministrator class to the EmployeeAdministratorIF IDL interface. Similar to Interface Objects in the Interface Object pattern and Object Service instances in the Object Service pattern, Instance Adapters are responsible for handling database transactions (using per-call transactions) and performing datatype conversions necessary to create and interpret complex IDL datatypes defined in the IDL interface. However, in this pattern it is unnecessary for Instance Adapters to handle Persistent Object discovery. Each Instance Adapter object already holds a reference to a single Persistent Object with which it interacts to service the client's request. This simplifies the Instance Adapter's code because there is no need to search for the target Persistent Object. More importantly, it significantly accelerates the handling of any given client request, because the overhead of an object search is gone.

Each Instance Adapter is handed the reference to its corresponding Persistent Object, the one it adapts to the ORB layer, as a parameter to its constructor. In Listing 10-31 you saw the Adapter object constructing the EmpAdminInstAdapter and passing a pointer to the singleton persistent EmployeeAdministrator.

Listing 10-32: Declaration of the EmployeeAdministrator Instance Adapter class

```
#include "idl\EmployeeAdminServer.hh"
#include "EmployeeAdministrator.h"
#define EMPLOYEE_ADMINISTRATOR_DB_ROOT_NAME
  "Administrator"
```

```
class EmpAdminInstAdapter
{
public:
  EmpAdminInstAdapter(EmployeeAdministrator* persistentObj);
  virtual ~EmpAdminInstAdapter();
  short initialize();
  //Begin implementation of IDL functions
  EmployeeIF_var createEmployee(const char* newName,
                 const char* newSSN,
                 const char* newTitle,
                 float newSalary,
                 const char* hireDate,
                 CORBA:Environment& );
  short deleteEmployee(EmployeeIF* employee,
          CORBA:Environment& );
  EmployeeInfoList_var getEmployees(CORBA:Environment& );
  //End implementation of IDL functions
private:
  EmployeeAdministrator* persistentObject;
  EmployeeIF* employeeIFs[MAX_EMPLOYEES];
  CORBA:ULong numEmployees;
};
DEF_TIE_EmployeeAdministratorIF(EmpAdminInstAdapter);
```

The `Adapter:initialize()` method in Listing 10-31 concluded by calling `EmpAdminInstAdapter:initialize()`, shown in Listing 10-33. This method completes initialization of the ODA by constructing a tie object and an Instance Adapter (an instance of EmployeeInstAdapter) for each persistent Employee. The TIE_EmployeeIF objects are the ORB objects placed in the ORB's object table, while the EmployeeInstAdapter objects double as the implementation object and the Persistent Object's Instance Adapter. In other words, when a TIE_EmployeeIF receives an up-call from the ORB, it delegates it to its EmployeeInstAdapter implementation object, which then interacts with its associated persistent Employee object to service the client's request.

Listing 10-33: Initialization of the Instance Adapter objects

```
short EmpAdminInstAdapter:initialize()
{
  Employee* employees[MAX_EMPLOYEES];
  long i = 0;
  //Get the list of persistent employees
  persistentObject->getEmployees(employees);
  //For each persistent employee create its tie object
  //and its Instance Adapter.
  while(employees[i])
  {
   employeeIFs[i] =
     new TIE_EmployeeIF(EmployeeInstAdapter)
      ( new EmployeeInstAdapter(employees[i]) );
   i++;
```

```
    }
    numEmployees = i;
    cout << "The employee administrator instance adapter ";
    cout << "has been constructed." << endl;
    return 1;
}
```

Because this pattern requires a tie object and Instance Adapter to be in memory for each Persistent Object visible to the client, a few lines of code must be added to any function that creates or deletes a Persistent Object having a corresponding Instance Adapter. The createEmployee method in Listing 10-34 illustrates this point. A tie object and an Instance Adapter object are constructed any time a persistent Employee is constructed. This maintains the principle behind this pattern — Each persistent object directly interacting with a CORBA client is directly accessible using an ORB object reference.

Listing 10-34: How to handle Persistent Object creation when using the Pinned Object pattern

```
EmployeeIF_var EmpAdminInstAdapter:createEmployee(
                const char* newName,
                const char* newSSN,
                const char* newTitle,
                float newSalary,
                const char* hireDate,
                CORBA:Environment& env)
{
  Employee* employees[MAX_EMPLOYEES];
  os_transaction:begin();
  {
   Employee* emp;
   emp = persistentObject->createEmployee(newName, newSSN,
                  newTitle, newSalary,
                  hireDate);
   employeeIFs[numEmployees] =
     new TIE_EmployeeIF(EmployeeInstAdapter)
      (new EmployeeInstAdapter(emp));
  }
  os_transaction:commit();
  EmployeeIF:_duplicate(employeeIFs[numEmployees]);
  numEmployees++;
  return employeeIFs[numEmployees-1];
}
```

Listing 10-34 illustrates an additional step needed when creating an ORB visible Persistent Object, and Listing 10-35 illustrates the additional steps required when deleting an ORB visible Persistent Object. Whenever an ORB visible Persistent Object is deleted, its corresponding tie and Instance Adapter objects must also be deleted. When the client requests deletion of an EmployeeIF reference, deleteEmployee()acquires a reference to the associated implementation object

(an employee Instance Adapter). With Orbix, this is done by invoking the DEREF
macro on the EmployeeIF reference and casting the result to the appropriate type.
You then ask the implementation object for its associated Persistent Object (the
persistent Employee being deleted). So, the EmployeeAdministrator is told to delete
the Employee, and the EmployeeIF tie object is released (its reference count is
decremented to zero which results in its deletion).

Listing 10-35: How to handle Persistent Object deletion when using the Pinned Object Pattern

```
short EmpAdminInstAdapter:deleteEmployee(
                EmployeeIF* emp,
                CORBA:Environment& env)
{
  short result = 0;
  os_transaction:begin();
  {
   Employee* persistentEmp;
   EmployeeInstAdapter* empInstAdapter;
   //Get the ORB object's implementation object
   //which is the employee's Instance Adapter
   empInstAdapter = (EmployeeInstAdapter*)DEREF(emp);
   //Get the Instance Adapter's persistent employee
   persistentEmp = empInstAdapter->getPersistentObject();
   //Instruct the employee administrator to delete the
   //persistent employee
   persistentObject->deleteEmployee(persistentEmp);
   //Find the ORB object's slot in our local list
   //end release it from memory
   for(unsigned long i=0; i < numEmployees; i++)
   {
     if(employeeIFs[i] == emp)
     {
      CORBA:release(emp);
      employeeIFs[i] = 0;
      result = 1;
      break;
     }
   }
  }
  os_transaction:commit();
  return result;
}
```

Listing 10-36 shows the last code segment included for this pattern. It is
included to illustrate its simplicity. Compare it to the corresponding function in the
Interface Object and Object Service patterns. You find that they are more complex
and less efficient because they are forced to locate the target Persistent Object
dynamically for each incoming invocation. In this version this is unnecessary. Each
EmployeeInstAdapter holds a reference to its Persistent Object, which is pinned in
memory for the life of the server process. The result is a more efficient and more

succinct ODA. In fact, aspects of this pattern's Instance Adapters are so succinct and simple that implementing a tool to generate Instance Adapter classes may be a realistic and worthwhile undertaking.

Listing 10-36: A Simple Instance Adapter function illustrating the simplification of the ODA layer when using the Pinned Object pattern

```
void EmployeeInstAdapter:increaseSalary(
                float percentIncrease,
                CORBA:Environment& env)
{
 os_transaction:begin();
 {
   persistentObject->increaseSalary(percentIncrease);
 }
 os_transaction:commit();
}
```

SYNOPSIS

In contrast to the Object Service pattern, the Pinned Object pattern focuses on optimizing the speed of the server's request handling at the expense of the server's ability to support a large number of persistent objects. It also sacrifices the pattern's ability to support an architecture allowing multiple OODB clients to interact with the same Persistent Objects. Because the Persistent Objects are pinned into the server's memory they cannot be directly updated by any other OODB client. However, other applications could interact with the Persistent Objects indirectly, through the server application's IDL interface. Figure 10-17 summarizes the scalability of the Pinned Object Pattern.

Summary

When combined, CORBA and object-oriented databases can result in a system design that more readily capitalizes on the benefits of object-oriented design. While the real-world issues involved with combining an OODB server application with a CORBA-based middleware solution, can be intricate and somewhat complex, the alternative combinations are far less appealing. Furthermore, the fact that there is not a conceptual mismatch between CORBA's goals and the principles underlying most OODBs bodes well for the confluence of these two technologies. As CORBA evolves to adopt the Portable Object Adapter (POA) – which is more friendly to scaleable data base adaptation than is the BOA – and as the new and improved Persistent Object Service builds on the POA, standardized and commercialized integration of ORBs and OODBs will become commonplace.

Advantages	Shortcomings
• Request handling can be faster than patterns allowing persistent objects to be flushed from the server's memory between client invocations.	• The server may become memory bound if a large number of persistent objects are pinned in memory. So this pattern may not scale well to server's providing client access to a very large number of persistent objects. However, this can be mitigated by adding an Evictor object that flushes objects from the server's memory based on object usage and dormancy.
• The design and implementation is less complex.	
• Can be enhanced by adding an Evictor object that flushes objects from the server's memory based on object usage and dormancy.	• Traversal of the ORB's active object table will be slow as the number of active objects grows.
	• Limits concurrent access to the underlying database server since persistent objects are pinned into the CORBA server's memory.

Figure 10-17: Scalability of the Pinned Object Pattern

Part IV

What's Next?

CHAPTER 11:

Looking Ahead with CORBA

Looking Ahead with CORBA

IN THIS CHAPTER
In this chapter we describe the new technologies the OMG has been proposing to add to CORBA. We cover conceptual factors relating to CORBA-specific technologies, focusing on the following topics:

- Multiple interfaces and composition facilities
- Object pass-by-value
- Messaging Service
- CORBA Component Model
- Persistent State Services
- More portable servers
- CORBA scripting

How the OMG Consortium Functions

THE STANDARDS BODY functions in the following manner: When the consortium creates a set of requirements for a new service, they introduce a Request For Proposals (RFC), which is kept open for a predetermined, specified amount of time. The members of the consortium are then free to submit proposals for the standard. The RFC documents the requirements these proposals must satisfy.

The participants of the consortium submit their proposals in the form of a RFP. In their RFPs, they try to provide a specification for the service that spans all the requirements listed in the original RFC. After detailed discussions on the proposal the consortium creates a substantiation. This process is both rigorous and time-consuming. This is generally accomplished by appointing a task group to work on an implementation based on the proposal.

This is the way to generate and accept standards. It is an open consortium, which will debate any kind of issues related to the submitted proposals Any group or organization can respond to an RFC. The acceptance of the proposal is based on many factors, including: How is the proposal attempting to solve the requirements?

Are the solutions foolproof? How well can the solution handle boundary conditions? How extensible is the approach? Does it lead to any kind of constriction in the near future?

Recently, a whole gamut of new object services and extensions have been proposed by the OMG consortium. The proposals were made by the participants who feel the CORBA object model, overall, lacks the extensibility features generally needed by the universally accepted object model. The goal of the consortium is to make the CORBA object model and the services provided by the model globally accepted as the industry standard for developing distributed applications. To support this cause, they have been looking into all the possibilities of covering all major arenas that will be affected by this work. Members of the consortium cannot simply suggest ways to enhance CORBA, however; they must develop and implement the solution, remembering it would have diverse implications as far as its usage is concerned. The solution cannot narrow down any solution technique. It must lead to newer features and provide integration with other closely related services. It can, in no way, be a half-cooked design. Because of this, you may observe the consortium does not only consist of people providing a base, highly hypothetical, object model. Rather, the consortium is equally, if not more, occupied by thinkers of a particular vertical solution sector.

The participants have their own charters to accomplish in the vertical business sector. They are solving problems for various industries such as the healthcare sector, the financial sector, the insurance sector, and the manufacturing sector. The working groups have their heads deep in the real world trying to accept the standards and to provide a solution to the business world. This is one of the true strengths of the consortium, which is interested in solving the problems in a well-disciplined manner. The consortium is not here to provide us with yet another superior technology that would suffocate in the real world due to its lack of capabilities of solving the real-life problems, which we know have numerous operating constraints. The solutions provided by the concentrated effort are highly scaleable in nature and have an extensive reach.

The new object services and extensions are based on the design principles of CORBA. They are simple, flexible, lightweight, interoperable, and extensible. These are a few of the guiding principles of the new services: The services must be generic in nature to move the solution into other domains easily or with the least number of changes. The generic nature of a solution must be tested under extremely diverse conditions. The generality of the services should be complimented by their simplicity. Simple solutions do not necessarily end up being ordinary solutions. The services, therefore, should have a simple interface. The possibilities of the services being used in different business sectors are great, hence, the developer of the service must take proper care to see they do not frighten away new customers. The services working together should be in a position to resolve any complex problem within its domain. The complexity of the problem should be explained to the implementor with ease so natural intelligence of the implementor also plays an active role. My opinion is artificial intelligence combined with natural intelligence can solve all of the world's existing problems and we should be working toward this goal. The services should be well-designed to perform optimally within their application area. None of the services are chartered to be one solution for all problems. The services are well-distinguished and tend to work on specific concerns extremely well.

The developers create the service to be transparent in nature and have systematic dependencies. Furthermore, they keep the dependencies as minimal as possible to keep the system lightweight. A distributed service operating over a highly distributed and integral system needs to migrate its execution levels. This would be benefited by the fact that the service is as lightweight as possible. The developers must minimize the baggage. Further, it must be able to associate itself dynamically with the environment. To do this, the service must be able to detect its current status, query for its dependencies within the provided environment, and attach itself to the other available services, and so on. The dynamic attachment attribute makes the distributed service self-adaptable and provides an easy working environment to the end user.

COBRA is a highly distributed object model and tends to make the network and the transport below it transparent to the applications using it. Hence, it needs to provide some good ways to manage the Quality of Service (QOS) provided by the environment, so services working on it may tend to provide the same quality of service to the end users. The end users would rely on the services, hence, the quality must be managed by the service providers and must be within the acceptable range for the end users.

QOS is an important consideration in such environments. It is based on the performance, the reliability, and many aspects related to it. The application developers using the service must be aware of these factors so they can leverage it and make the applications robust within the operating environment. Predictability is a major concern in such a service-based environment. Once these concerns are properly prioritized, then implementation of these services should become manageable. Although this does not reduce the difficulty levels, they are modularized. The solution becomes purely a matter of implementation with the right kind of approach. The service designs must be open-ended, so they can be easily integrated with the future object services.

The consortium is also thinking of newer services at this point: The replication services, the complete transaction services for state integrity, error logging and operations logging services, internationalization, storage and retrieval services, and so on. All these are services that would make the CORBA development environment a complete system. All the possible requirements envisioned within a development environment would be satisfied by the CORBA services.

In the next few pages of this chapter, we discuss various CORBA Facilities. These facilities are interfaces directed toward horizontal end users. CORBA defines the CORBA Services, which are general services required for the development of

CORBA-based applications. They are also used as building blocks for bigger interoperable components. The services are targeted toward the essential features required for the development of CORBA-aware applications. The CORBA Facilities, on the other hand, are horizontal in nature. The facilities work in coordination with the existing operating environments. The facilities aid in defining the transition phases into rather specific systems. They help bridge the gaps between other environments, including distributed object frameworks and flat structured development environments. They help reduce the impedance mismatch between concepts from diverse worlds.

In the following pages, we also discuss some of the new standards currently in the proposal status. (They may even be accepted as standards by the time you read this.) Many participants have started working on the proposals. As we described earlier, any proposal must have an implementation to back it up. This provides valid proof of the system and the assumptions made in it. Past experiences have shown some proposals issued and accepted proved impractical in the industry. Further, experience shows having at least a few implementations from different vendors to validate the proposals is a good idea. One vendor's implementation may end up being in conflict with the others, especially when the consortium also consists of vertical market participants who are more interested in solving their own specific problems. When this happens, it helps the consortium detect ways the RFC can be misinterpreted.

Multiple Interfaces and Composition Facilities

As you know, CORBA objects support interfaces. Ideally, the number of interfaces an object can support is limitless. Physical constraints exist, of course, but the CORBA specification itself does not set any limits. The OMG has suggested the interfaces supported by the objects should be more or less within the same logical domain. Further, in the real world, many instances have occurred where the same object reference required interfaces from multiple domains. As a result, the OMG decided to create a standard for the composition of interfaces on a single object. The plan is to allow the creation of a Composition Facility that would assist in creating objects that consists of logically distinct services by the usage of multiple interface definitions.

The Request for a Proposal for multiple interfaces and composition facilities included some distinct requirements. Any submission in response to the proposal, therefore, must clearly provide satisfactory solutions to these requirements to be considered for acceptance as a solution. For this particular RFP, the requirements are:

- ◆ **Multiple service:** Allow an object to support different interfaces, where the interfaces represent logically distinct services.

- ◆ **Versioning:** Allow a composite object to support different versions of the same interface definitions.

- ◆ **Sessions:** Support a means for an object to maintain per-client context by the use of multiple instances of a service within an object implementation.

- ◆ **Fully qualified operation names:** Allow a composite object to support different interface definitions with the same operation names.

- ◆ **Flexible subtyping:** Allow an explicit interface to become a sufficient, but unnecessary condition for subtyping.

- ◆ **COM support:** Allow better support for the COM object model.

- ◆ **Interface visibility:** Allow the developer to control visibility and/or access to an object's functions based on interface definitions, lists of operations, or other criteria.

In the next few paragraphs, we discuss the effect of several of these. A well-understood fact is, because of the new stipulations in the proposal, the underlying assumptions have to be altered. The suggested changes must be descriptive and documented. Furthermore, they must be for the good of the system, meaning no changes would be acceptable that would render the older version of the software unusable. Any changes made to the system must be backward-compatible, so the older versions of the software can still work with the new underlying system. Also, the new suggested solution should make a valid attempt to describe a migration path for developers of the older version of the system to move easily to the new technique.

Multiple Services and Versioning

Previously, CORBA objects had no documented way to support multiple versions of a particular interface. An interface of a CORBA object is required to perform a service. Under a multiple interface situation, an instance of an interface could also be called a service. An interface is a high-level abstraction of a service. Therefore, objects exhibiting multiple interfaces could also be used to exhibit multiple services.

The classification of a service is a whole new ball game. The classification is based on the nature of the service. In the existing approach, the developer of an interface could gather logically related functionalities and group them under one interface. The proposal for multiple interface and composition facility demands a new way of formulating object services. It also requires a compositional strategy that could encompass logically different services to be hosted under one object domain. This would give rise to a composite structure that would be in a position to host such interfaces which are not only distinct in nature, but that also have the capabilities of multiple versions instantiated by the client. Ideally, it could be the same client that could request different versions of the same interface to be active at the same time. Also, these multiple instances would be exhibited by the same object.

This situation could overload the underlying system, however. The base structure now needs to allow concurrent access to the object within the same client context. This would require multiple instances of the object to be present to protect its internal data from being overwritten by multiple accesses. The composition must be in a position to exhibit similar characteristics as those of the base objects. Furthermore, for the older versions of the software to function properly, the transparencies must be maintained. The composition formed must not create extra object management overheads. Computer theorists have classically observed that new features suggested to an existing system orthogonally overloads the base system. The new features come with an overhead that far outweighs the benefits gained. Some extra work may be needed for the system to be functional, but some deciding criteria must work in line with the overall existing system performance.

The multiple interface support could also be seen in two different ways. It could be a fairly persistent approach, wherein the composition is decided at the system initialization phase. Hence, it could occur as a straight map of the persistent format. This is a static view. Many applications working on the system with this approach can rely on the consistency of the underlying system. The other approach could be fairly dynamic in nature. The dynamic nature of the composition could be decided based on the need. This approach would require the system provide an encapsulated design. The compositional encapsulation provided by the system would require the run-time execution model to fill up the void positions. The system would, in essence, fill up the dynamic positions with the right interface on demand. No tight binding is provided within the environment. This is a complex solution but, nonetheless, is effective. The implementation would be complicated as the persistent system and the run-time map are different, but the object must manage a different view with respect to its background functionalities. The flexibility offered by such systems is tremendous and could be used in varied development environments. The usage of the system increases greatly as the self-adaptive nature is portrayed with vigor. It helps propagate a well-adaptive and common development platform used for multiple domains. This is not the exact requirement, but it would certainly be needed in the near future as flexibility becomes the most important driving factor.

The implementation will satisfy the current proposal if it provides a way to have a persistent approach of managing the interfaces within its compositional bounds. Also, the implementation should provide, in a simple fashion, the functionality needed by the multiple object accesses, rather than requiring the client to maintain the multiple version context. The need for such a facility is basic in nature. The client application must perform such tasks every now and then, and the awareness for such a feature is versatile. The resultant compositional strategy is also present in the client application domain for a number of years. It was never viewed by the OMG world for a long time. Many server-type applications have been providing such a feature to its related clients for data access. The revolution is in making this approach accepted as an industry standard and also making the facility generic in nature, so it could be accepted by the majority of the application within the domain without going through the specific overheads themselves.

Figure 11-1 shows a pictorial representation of the CORBA object having multiple interfaces. The figure consists of two sections. The first section, Section 1, shows the CORBA object and the interface objects separately. As shown, the interface objects are also self-contained entities. Although they are specialized objects, they are each individual objects, in that they have data and allow for construction, destruction, and so on. The second section, Section 2, shows the compound CORBA object. The CORBA object is compounded with the interfaces. This compound object is an entity of its own. It does not have separate, uniquely identifiable objects of its own.

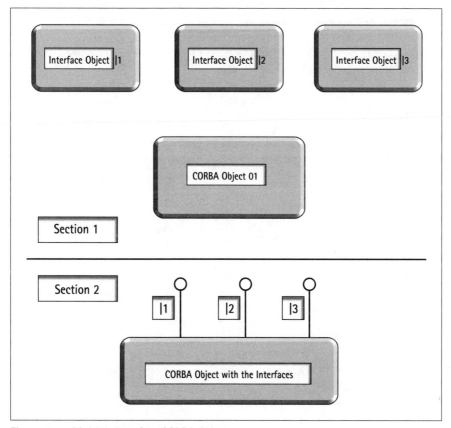

Figure 11-1: Multiple Interface CORBA Object

The object composition could make use of inheritance, as well as aggregation logic. A pure inheritance model may not satisfy the requirements. In the case of inheritance, one would create a new object that inherits from the base object definition. This implies two different objects exist. This may not be a good approach, as we may not need the base object at all. The composition could just accumulate the partial required interfaces of some existing objects to formulate the new composite object. Here we are also talking about having them extract only the required portion of an object. The developer must study the implications of such a behavior to reason the results of these operations on an object. In a loose sense, the object is fragmented into more units. It does not actually fragment the base object, but the views portrayed are much so. While the concept could, indeed, be looked upon as antiobject-oriented, that is not the point here. The concern is to simplify the usage and the strong beliefs of object-oriented approach are not legally violated. Furthermore, because the object still exists in its indivisible base form, no cause for alarm exists.

Figure 11-2 shows an example of an inheritance hierarchy of the interface. The interface objects obey the same inheritance principles and rules as any other CORBA object. For all intents and purposes, the client program can view them as CORBA objects, but cannot use them each independently. The inheritance hierarchy shows interface I3 being derived from interface I1 and I2. Further down, interface I5is derived from interface I4 and interface I3.

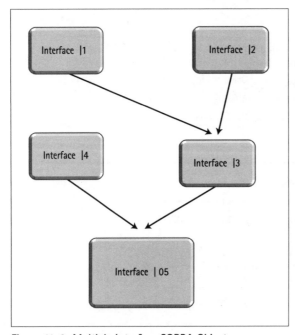

Figure 11-2: Multiple Interface CORBA Object

The new system must provide a well-documented way of versioning interfaces. This is a difficult problem to solve. The developer must predetermine many issues to observe the versions of an interface. The integrity of an interface is maintained by its data members and operations. The structure of any interface would represent a particular recognizable unit of an interface. Any change to the structure could ideally represent another interface or a different version of the same interface.

The first question to answer is: "When does one interface become a totally different interface and when does it become a different version of the same interface?" There must be a strong demarcation between a different interface and a new version of the same interface. The addition of operations to an interface within the same functional domain does not pose a difficult problem. Making decisions in such cases becomes relatively simple. The problem arises when new operations are added to the existing interfaces that belong to a completely different domain and when interfaces are removed from the interface. These are not clean solution-providing situations. We will not provide solutions to these problems in this chapter. Our intent is to make you aware of the problems and the related issues with the new specifications. This is not to say the new specifications would cause problematic situations. The new proposal will certainly benefit the users of the technology. These requirements are the product of tremendous hours of brain-storming. The consortium has certainly felt a lack of a standard specification in the area. The system developers have encountered these problems in generating their CORBA-based systems and provided their own solutions. Because the problem keeps appearing, a strong reason exists for a standard solution. Any new additions to an existing product must be thought about deeply before the addition is made to the existing product. We are sure all the developers would agree with us.

To consider the problems and possibilities in the versioning of interfaces, a dedicated set of minds is needed. While this may seem like a simple issue on the surface, it has grave implications, and all the scenarios must be dealt with in detail. That is the reason OMG has a new RFC altogether for the versioning of interfaces. The OMG would certainly like to integrate the techniques in the RFC into the versioning of the interfaces in case of multiple interfaces and compositional facility. One of the most difficult issues about versioning of interfaces is this: As we all know by now, interfaces are made of operations or methods. Ideally speaking, if any operation changes its form in any manner, then we ought to version it. If an operation is a version, would that imply the interface also gets a new version? If this is true, then any small change in the interface in its form, structurally or functionally, would result in a new version. Is this an acceptable solution? The problem is we are making the versioning principle too fine in granularity. If this is not an acceptable answer, then what constitutes a version? The integrity of the interface is greatly challenged. We know this is a difficult question. Frankly speaking, we are not attempting to answer the question. We leave the versioning concern at this point for the reader to ponder.

Sessions

When a server-like application such as a database server or a network server allows multiple connections, then the server application must provide a means to manage sessions of connection from the client. We are sure many readers have experienced this. We have all seen database servers requiring us to log into the database with a login and a password. Once we authenticate ourselves with the database server, we can perform operations within our levels. Different users have different privileges associated with them that determine the type of operations that can be performed. The server then starts a session with the client. Once the session is started, it remains active until a disconnect operation is initiated by the client itself or is due to some problem created by external factors, such as a broken connection transport.

The sessions are managed by the server application, which provides all the client's access through the session. A CORBA-compliant server application, hosting CORBA objects, should similarly be in a position to manage its operations through sessions. Therefore, the server objects providing multiple interfaces should not result in any conflicts. The multiple interfaces, which may also be a version, need to allocate proper resources based on the sessions they are actively maintaining. The critical sections must be provided accordingly so data is not overwritten due to concurrent accesses. This will help maintain session integrity, which is vital. This requires extra management overheads the interface should inherently provide. The implementations must provide extra intelligence and, accordingly, provide that the applications can make use of. These intelligent hooks would help the applications properly manage the resources associated with the object interfaces. Multiple versions of interfaces – active at the same time within the same sessions – is the most tricky situation to handle. After all, we would want our server objects to be as much concurrent as possible.

Concurrency comes with a tremendous amount of management overhead. We needn't stress how important this matter is for multiple versions of the same interface. The concept of multiple versions of the same interface being active at the same time opens a big can of worms. Many conditions must be dealt with that would never occur in case of a single version of the interface. We have already experienced the concurrency threat in a multithreaded programming situations. Multiple interfaces may contain shared code and data, which needs to be protected from concurrent access. The re-entrancy of the common code and data zone will also be a concern in this issue. The code has to be re-entrant. Some solutions to the problems exist, but the applicability of the solution depends on the system architecture and its implementation design. Because it may not be a one-to-one programming paradigm match, it could offer some resistance. Some of the available solutions may need to be re-thought for the multiple interface situation. Hence, it would involve a lot of work to make solutions based on these operating criteria.

Fully Qualified Operation Names

Namespaces have been the topic of discussion in most of the programming models. Programming languages, data-oriented driver application domains, resource management in networked environment, and similar applications frequently are faced with the pending question of resolving namespaces. Namespace, in general, refers to a proper channel by which a resource is identified. For instance, a data member within an object can be fully identified not only by itself, but by its fully qualified name. In this instance, the fully qualified name would be comprised of the object name followed by the data member. Using fully qualified names helps resolve name clashes within the operating domain. Every resource, when referred to by its fully qualified name, would uniquely identify the resource and would avoid resources being misrepresented and misused. Namespaces help generate hypothetical channels that build guided paths to the resource names.

Composite objects are formed by different interfaces locked into one reference point. This essentially means different operations and associated resources from different interfaces should be uniquely identified. Hence, the system should provide a fully qualified name resolution mechanism. It becomes absolutely important, considering different individuals may be developing the interfaces and there are no built-in naming conventions that would avoid having resource name clashes. Fully qualified names precariously resolve the issue. No resources are lost in the multiple interfaced composite object, as a well-defined path can reach every leaf within the hierarchy. Fully qualified operation name resolutions remove any implied naming convention the interface designer would have to follow. A fairly noble belief is to name operations in a manner that would give the user an idea of its behavior. But, because this is not a strict rule, no immediate violations would occur if the programmer did not follow them. Thanks to the qualified naming mechanism, no need exists for such a restrictive model.

COM Support

The Component Object Model (COM) provides a mechanism for objects to support multiple interfaces and aggregation features. Based on the aggregated design, the object must provide some means for its users to browse through all the interfaces provided by the object. Hence, they provide the querying model, according to which the user could query the object to help it locate the required interface.

The CORBA model supports the navigation of multiple interfaces through the CORBA:Composite interface type. The *CORBA:Composite interface type* provides a mechanism that allows interfaces to be related when an inheritance relationship does not exist and there may be multiple versions of the interface floating around. So the system must be in a position to return the right version of the interface to be requested by the client. This is where the CORBA:Composite interface comes in. The capability to satisfy the client based on the correct version of the interface is a rather new concept, which has not been practiced in most of the existing distributed object models. A proper persistent view of this model would be a great success to the multiple interface and composition feature. We believe a good persistent model of the multiple interface and multiple versions of the interface could only come into existence from an efficient design of the model and would have a tremendous impact on the performance of the system.

The multiple interface and composition feature must be able to support the COM model. The interoperability between the two models should not expose any impedance mismatch. The integration should be done rather smoothly, as both the models aim to solve the same problem. The navigational model supported by COM should be supported in one form or another. The client applications written for a specific COM infrastructure would have the navigation code, and for the CORBA infrastructure to interoperate with it, the same client code should be respected. This would be an important enough reason for the navigation feature to be supported by the CORBA model. The COM system allows the client application to query for one interface at a time. Because of this, many requests are going from the client to the server and, in a similar fashion, many requests are returned from the server application to the client application. This should be taken care of in the navigational approach adopted by the CORBA model. This could be viewed as a tremendous performance hog. Such improvements would be considered good compliments to the CORBA system.

Multiple interfaces and their compositions must have proper mechanisms for accessibility and control. The accesses to the multiple interfaces are complicated further because of the multiple versions of an interface. The visibility must be well-defined for multiple versions of the interfaces. Furthermore, the access mechanism has to span over the operations specifying the interfaces. With the advent of composite objects, the developer of the interface is faced with a difficult question of bounds of access. With interfaces, the designer could define alternative interfaces for different users based on the authentication levels. The rights of the user can be verified during connection time and, accordingly, interfaces provided to it. Now, with the composite nature, this demarcation becomes difficult. The granularity of the decision making process becomes rather finer in nature. Various instances could exist wherein the process actually exposes the operations from a composite interface and checks for the user's rights. The system would need a much more disciplined approach for such operations. The openness of the system must be properly guarded to avoid intrusion into the application servers. This, although it falls under the security domain, also can offer solutions from this particular angle. The solutions can be sweetly merged with the rather strict security checks. This would lead to a highly open-ended interpretable design that could adapt to the available situation. Application server security is an important concern and must be dealt with utmost precautions. The new proposed architecture can in no way make the work of the security system more complex than it already is. Furthermore, because the propositions would be subjected to a consortium of companies, the propositions would be faced with rather strong criticism if the proposal suggested any overheads on the existing solutions.

Object Pass-by-Value

Application development works around data. Data is the key to all the programming tasks undertaken. We develop applications that, given a particular type or set of data, do some analysis on them and return the data to the viewer in some acceptable format. The data is shown to the end user in some order and/or format understood by them and appreciated. This is why and how applications sell in the market. In a programming project, the data is passed around from one module to another. It is massaged, altered, and worked so it can be passed from one module to another and from one application to another. The transferring of data is done in two modes: a static mode and an active mode.

For example, consider a real-time data acquisition system that collects data through one of the communication ports. The application or underlying communications software reads the data in and passes it through some filters to verify the importance of the data to the application. Some of the data collected by the underlying system may be data intended for other applications; this data would be filtered out in this process. The relevant data might be stored by this real-time application in some specific format as a data file. Another application within the real-time application suite might read the data and draw graphs for the user to do his or her analysis. This data could also be read by some database software to do some data reporting. Because the data is persistently stored on a medium, it could be shared by many applications. This sort of sharing is rather static in nature. The persistent format is important, but it could end up being a bottleneck for the system's interoperability. The most important issue is exposing the file format to all the possible future accessors of the data. The benefit is apparent when the data is kept alive beyond the execution life of the program.

The second type of data sharing is active in its behavior. This kind of data sharing is done when the applications are in their execution phase. The active data sharing is done both within an application and between more than one application. The basic school of thought here is that data is passed from one module boundary to another in the format of a package, which is understood by both the sender and the receiver. Narrowing this thought more would lead us to discuss the actual data-passing methods used by the operations and methods. With object-oriented design patterns, data is always encapsulated within the object. The relevance of the data is associated with the operations and is tied down to the object. So, in the following discussion we speak in terms of objects, which, in actuality, are a superset of data.

Objects can be passed either by value or by reference. Passing of objects by *value* involves making a copy of the data. In essence, we are dealing with two copies of the data. The calling routine has the original copy and the receiving routine uses a copy that lives in its local space. The other method of passing data is by reference. When data is passed by *reference,* the calling routine actually passes a reference to the data to the receiving routine. The receiver then directly accesses the actual data passed to it via the reference. There is only one copy of the data in this style. This style works out well for some types of applications, but also creates problems for other types of applications. It boils down to the specific requirements of the system.

In the next few paragraphs, we discuss an object's pass-by-value requirement from the OMG. CORBA supports passing of objects via reference only. But many CORBA programmers have found a great need for pass-by-value. The following are the requirements mentioned in the request for a proposal. We address most of the requirements and argue the need for the requirements.

Here are some of the questions we answer:

◆ What is the relationship between the identity of the object in the sending context and the object itself in the receiving context (including any security implications)?

◆ What is the relationship between the implementation in the sending context and the implementation in the receiving context? Must this relationship be identical? If not, how do you establish the equivalency for the purposes of passing by value?

◆ What happens when no appropriate implementation is available in the receiving context?

◆ What is the relationship between the primary (or most-derived) interface of an object being passed in the sending context, the interface type of the parameter declaration, and the primary (or most-derived) interface of the object in the receiving context? Can any object supporting the declared parameter interface type be passed by value? If an object being passed in the sending context supports interfaces that are more derived than the parameter interface, will the resulting object in the receiving context also support those more-derived interfaces ?

When objects are passed, there exists a sender and a receiver. The sender initiates the data transfer and the receiver responds by accepting the data passed to it. Because two active entities exist, two contexts would be associated with them. The sender has a context and the receiver has a context. For all intents and purposes, these contexts are independent of each other and different from one another. When an object is instantiated within a defined space, the object's identity is linked to the operational space. The CORBA system guarantees the uniqueness of the object within that particular space. Because the operational space has a discontinuous bound, it is impossible for the object to be uniquely identifiable at some other operational space. When objects are passed from one operational space to another, if the passing is done by reference (the case with CORBA currently), then no negative implications exist. The objects stay where they were actually created. The accessor is pointing to it from another section of the application, hence, none of the objects' referential integrity is violated. Some implications exist to this process, but they tend not to be a problem. When the objects are passed by value, however, then the objects are copied into another operational space, which is different from the existing one and the object may no longer be unique.

The original creation of the instance of the object is exposed to the sender's context. If the object is associated with different kinds of resources, these resources may be unavailable to the receiver's context. Hence, the passing of the object by value from the sender to the receiver must be in a position to address the incompatibility. Certainly it is insufficient for someone to point at the incompatible scenarios, but the proposal should resolve the issue if and when it arises. This becomes a difficult solution to offer because the problem is dynamic in nature. One solution cannot be proposed to this problem because of the diverse nature of the problem. It can arise for a variety of reasons. The developers implementing the specification must analyze all the error-generating conditions and provide a remedy accordingly. If other objects must be created before the object being passed, then that requirement must be passed to the receiver. The receiver must create the proper environment for the creation of the passed object within its own space. For instance, the actual object passed may need 2K of space on the operational stack, but the other dependencies may require the allocation of another 10K of stack space. Such extraordinary conditions make this a difficult problem. The complexity of the matter is increased many times when the sender is a client process space and the receiver is a server application in another process space. And with CORBA in the picture, the client application and the server application could be executing on two different machines. The object, therefore, must be streamed from the client space to the server space.

The other major issue with this philosophy is the security measures that must be taken to arrange a proper object flow. The security rights of the object may be different in different working spaces and must be respected. Security brings in a new perspective to the problem. The generic rules are suddenly not operational anymore. The receiving system must scrutinize the entire context of the sender for it to work properly. The ideal condition is when both the sending context and receiving context are identical in nature. Under this scenario, all the data that exists in the sender's context also exists within the receiver's context and there is no difference in security rights. But in most of the practical scenarios, this is not the case. During these situations, there must be a proposed mapping present that the system would follow to formulate an equivalence relationship between the two contexts. Because it is not realistically possible to have unique solutions for each condition, the equivalence relationship should for the most part be orthogonal. A possibility does exist for the developers of the system, however, to group the problems based on certain criteria and then provide solutions for them. Such a grouping of the problems is a difficult task. Some loss is likely for certain cases. The developers creating the policies describing such cases must provide a backtracking mechanism for the situation.

No one wants to accept a compromise without knowing the actual implications. Compromises are made to make the majority happy. This is a good approach, but it has a downside to it. Some people do not benefit from the policies of the compromises. A proper software engineering effort would be to identify the negative effect felt by the group that opposes compromises and minimize these effects. Also, it would be good for the team to work around those scenarios. In the case of the issue we have been discussing, the object created within the sender's context has an implementation attached. The creation of the object and the implementation attached to it are not separable. Because of the existence of the implementation, the object is created. When an application transfers the object to another application space, the object may not have an implementation attached. Because the object was not created within the receiver's context, the receiver may not store the implementation of the object in its local space. What happens during this situation? The solutions involve having the implementation available within the receiver's operational space. Whether the implementation is also migrated with the object or the implementation is generated with the help of some hints is an important deciding factor. Even if the developers of the system choose to migrate the implementation, they must decide whether the entire implementation is migrated or some subset is migrated. The subsequent fact of deciding the important subset of the implementation that could be migrated is an overwhelming decision for the developers to make.

If part or all of the implementation is to be regenerated, the policy should have a basic technique that would provide hints the receiving end would follow to regenerate the implementation. An alternative is for the developers of the policy to look at the implementation of the object. If it is possible, we should develop code that would break up the implementation to incorporate a strategy that would allow building blocks of the implementation. Such a possibility leads to a simplified path to complex problem domain. We may view the system from a microscopic point and would end up seeing the intrinsic design flaws. If we use simpler building blocks, this will open up the system for newer design perspective and interoperable environment. Imagine a scenario wherein the implementation of the objects within the domain can be expressed as sequential blocks inheriting a functional hierarchy. This would be the simplest form of exhibiting object behavior and functionality. The building block, which we are suggesting, would be at a secondary level. One level would have the object implementation done in a particular programming language. After the developers have finished the implementation, they might consider a tool that could capture the operations of the object.

To understand it in a more basic term, imagine the implementation of the object, from start to finish, cast into a die. Once the entire implementation is complete or the die is prepared, the entire implementation can be broken up into smaller blocks that could be put together to get back the original implementation. The sender breaks up the implementation by taking the big block and producing smaller units of them. This is a secondary level operation and it does not have to have any prior knowledge of the primary implementation. The only benefit of the secondary level transformation is to reduce the overhead in passing the data locks around. Once this is achieved and no data is lost, the process consists of breaking up the implementation from a higher level and then regenerating the implementation back by collecting the chunks. You could try to write code that would regenerate the original implementation without requiring the entire set. We are not proposing a complete solution to this process. That is not the goal of this chapter. Many refinements must be made to the process.

The requirements go further to describe a proposed path to the accepted solution. To consider the object and its implementation compatibility, the developer must determine the basic operational data structures. Discovering how much the implementation is derived from the basic data structures is important. If the derivations are somewhat shallow, then the solution could be a bit simpler. But, if the derivations take many twists and turns, and the interfaces have a large derivation hierarchy, then the solution could be onerous. The developer, in creating the solution, must identify the possibilities of passing the declared data structures as parameters, either directly or indirectly. The software using the indirect method could assume intelligent hints while passing data structures around the distributed system.

Now we discuss the importance of passing objects by value and why this should be added to the CORBA specification. First, we formulate some requirements. When a program passes objects by value, it makes a copy of the object and passes this copy from the sender to the receiver. In CORBA, the clients and server are generally executing in two different machines. When the object is passed by reference, if the receiver intends to access any data or operation within the object, it can do so using the reference passed to it. But every such access would end up in wire traffic because the object is still within the sender's domain. This can be slow. Furthermore, simply having a reference in the receiver's space does not guarantee the object still exists in the sender's domain. The sender and receiver, along with the system underneath, must work together to sustain the objects within the sender's domain.

Passing an object by value would solve these issues. The receiver works on the object in its own operational space. The object is created locally within the receiving processes address space and the life of the object could be controlled by the server application. Also, accessing the object is much simpler and faster. No network traffic is involved. After the receiver is finished with the object, it returns the object to the original calling routine. If the alterations done to the object must be returned to the caller routine, then a similar object transfer method would take place. The synchronization of the object would be managed by the caller routine.

These are some of the pressing concerns of passing an object by value. The OMG expects most of the changes made by the new proposals will be clarified by the respondents of the proposals. The changes and additions to the Interface Definition Language, if any are proposed, will be submitted to the consortium by the OMG for careful observation. In general, the OMG has not proposed any changes to the existing IDL, but some members of the consortium have suggested additions.

Messaging Service

Typical client-server applications have always relied on *messaging* as a core part of the infrastructure. Messaging has been a key component in any distributed application framework. Objects in multiple domains coordinate with each other using messaging techniques. Many different messaging architectures have existed. Each messaging structure was based on the type of operational model on which it was designed to work. CORBA makes use of messaging to coordinate between services and the client and objects within services. The messaging service in CORBA, because of its usage, is different from other forms of messaging. The architecture is versatile for the type of usage requested in the Object Request Broker. Under previous messaging systems in CORBA, the messaging module would be distributed among all the consumers of the service. So every module within an application, which used messaging, had some pieces of messaging built into the module. Hence, many applications distributed the messaging routines and most of the basic message passing was repeatedly found in all the different kinds of modules existing within the application.

The need for messaging is felt over the entire distributed application environment. It a fairly intrinsic part of the infrastructure. The messaging system needs to be well-integrated with the underlying system. The exposure of the inner workings of such a low-level service and the distribution of the messaging modules throughout the system is not a good design decision. The messaging system must be a self-contained service with well-defined interfaces for other services and applications. The OMG has proposed a different picture for message passing systems. Under this proposal, messaging would be a service of its own. It would be a dedicated service that has its own processing kernel. The messaging service could lend its service to any other service desiring it.

OMG issued a request for a proposal for the messaging service. The goal of this request for a proposal is to update the existing messaging service with the new usage requirements. As is the case of the other proposal requests, OMG has provided certain requirements that must be satisfied for the proposal to be accepted as a standard. Let's look at the requirements to acquire a better understanding of the needs in a proposal.

First, the proposal specifies interfaces must be present in the service that enable clients to make requests on an object without blocking the client execution thread. Further, interfaces must exist that enable clients to make requests that may not complete during the lifetime of the client execution environment, (that is, the client process may terminate before the response arrives) and that enable clients to establish a mechanism that will receive the response and process it appropriately. Interfaces must exist that enable client and servers to specify the quality of service employed when making or responding to a request. Finally, interfaces must exist that allow object servers to control the order in which incoming requests are processed.

CORBA exhibits a client-server programming model. Typically in this model, clients and servers execute at different address spaces and most of the practical execution is at different machines altogether. The requests issued by a client are directed toward a server application. This request is issued as a message. The message consists of the request encoded in the specified format and the proper address of the server. The request is transferred to the server via the network. Because client applications and the server applications communicate over a network, they must undergo the network latency. The response time to a request made by a client application made to the server application would be determined by the network traffic along with the path it travels. Some network routes may be slow due to the difference in the routing speeds and some may have bottlenecks in the network mesh designs. But the bottom line is the client and servers cannot assume specific time intervals for the requests and responses. A good system would have some way to inform the client the request was transferred to the server. Theoretically, this response time could be any positive time interval. It could be fast, as expected in most of the cases, or it could be a slow process. Obviously, the response time is not expected to be slow and the industry would not accept a very slow-performing server.

Figure 11-3 depicts an ordinary message-based client-server application-execution model. The client and the server work at the opposite ends of the network. In an ordinary message based environment, you generally have a client side of the message library and the server side of the message library. The client side of the message library is linked to the client application. It provides the client application the right interfaces needed for making the application message aware. The same things are made available to the server side of the application by the server-side message library. The messages are queued by the messaging libraries at either end. In such an environment multiple, such messaging executables are actively available due to its tight linkages to the application making use of it. The message queues maintained by these libraries as the queues are dedicated.

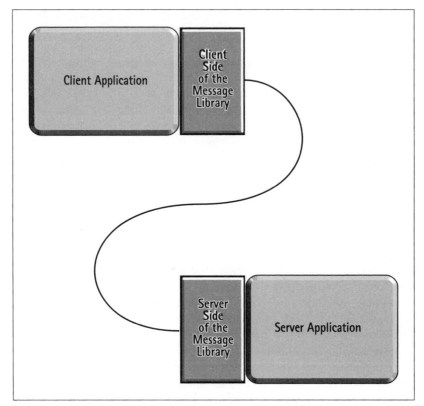

Figure 11-3: A Normal Message-Based Client-Server Framework

It would be ideal for the model to provide a way for the client application to continue on with its job after sending the request. Once the server application completes performing the request, it sends the response back to the client application, accompanying any additional data obtained as a result of the performed operation. The standard messaging mechanisms do not provide a defined answer to the blocking issue with the client. When the client sends a request, it waits till the request returns, and then continues with its remaining tasks. Such a blocking technique offered by the messaging is a bottleneck for high performing application domains. One of the requirements is to specify a standard way of performing asynchronous calls from the clients.

We have devised many ways to work around client blocking while the request is being performed by the server. First, we have thread-based implementations. According to thread-based implementations, we can fork of a thread to do the job. Within the application, when the time comes to send a message to the server, we generally create a *thread*. The thread is then forked. The thread, within its body, prepares the message and sends it to the server application. The thread then waits for the message to complete and loops around till it receives a response from the client. Meanwhile, the main thread of operation continues on with its further commitments. The code is arranged in such a manner that, as soon as the message managing thread terminates, it informs that main thread of operation. The main thread can then work on the return value from the server. Most of the existing messaging applications work in this manner. This is a well-known method and has been in use for a long time. The work-around is effective in most cases. In fact, most of the synchronous environments are made to give a asynchronous look and feel in this manner. This works well with operating environments that support threads. This would not work in operating environments that do not support thread-based functionalities.

Another work-around that also has been used for some time is *the callback mechanism*. The clients can register callbacks with the server routine. When the server is done with satisfying the requests, it calls the callback method. The callback method is in the client's address space, which can then transfer the data to the client and allow the client to continue with its processing. The callback is registered as a pointer to the method. The callback method is equally effective.

You may argue that CORBA offers a way to defer the response from the synchronous connection. This, indeed, is true and we are not arguing against it. The deferred synchronous request is offered in the Dynamic Interface Invocation mechanism. This feature is not available in all messaging formats. For instance, Static Interface Invocation does not allow calls to be deferred synchronous. Hence, the requirement for the new proposal is to specify a standard way of making calls asynchronous. There are some guidelines to observe in generating the new mechanism. The new solution should in no way require any changes to the operating model of the client and server applications. Messaging is an important part of the Object Request Broker, but it has been served as a separate service and it must work on the assumptions of the base kernel. It cannot require the existing base engine to change. Also, the new changes suggested must be backward-compatible. So any new application, designed with the specifications, should work on the existing CORBA-base engine. The backward-compatibility issue is taken care of. The new specifications may end up rendering more optimal solutions to the other services interacting with it. The newer design ideas and better implementation techniques could be well-suggested, but no assumptions can be made on them. The proposal further lead to the other services suggesting newer proposals for better working designs. It obviously must justify the changes proposed but no such restrictions exist.

The next set of requirements is geared toward the reliability and safe execution modes. The client and the server applications are connected to each other via the network. In cases where the client application and the server application are executing within the same machine, the network is not present. Because CORBA comprises many components, some of them executing on other machines, it would be safe to say the network is practically unavoidable. It may be possible that the server application is unavailable to the client because the network connection is broken or the network server, on which the server application is executing, is down or for another reason. In such cases, it would be the system's responsibility to manage the messages and send requests to the server. They should not be lost. The requests are termed as persistent requests. So the requests would live until they are obtained by the intended receiver. This would bring in fault tolerance to the system.

Let's look at the same issue from another angle. The response from server applications to the client application may come to the client after the client has already terminated. This is again caused by network delays. The client needs to process the response and the system needs to specify some solution. The request for proposal suggests a new set of system interface called the *Response Management Interface.* The response management interface should be able to take care of response persistent issues. The request for a proposal goes one step further in defining an abstract entity called the Response Manager. The *Response Manager* is an architectural entity whose sole purpose is to manage the request-response mechanisms. The Response Manager would be an active skeletal module that would be loaded and active at every client site. The manager would be registering the client application and all the requests sent by it to the server application. The Response Management Interface would coordinate with the Response Manager module so none of the requests or responses go unnoticed.

Furthermore, the Response Manager module would have to gather enough information from the client application so that if the client has terminated and a persistent response arrives, then it could wake the client to process it. The amount of work involved in waking the client application may be reduced. The client must be able to restore the status wherein the response data would make sense to the client. Of course, these would mean major modifications to the client application working technique. The response manager should be able to expose enough interfaces so the client could register its relevant data with the manager. It would be even better if the response manager could accumulate this information without too many alterations done to the client applications. The Response Manager would have to provide efficient management of the response and request relations based on the client. The client may issue many requests to the server. The response manager should not exhibit visible time delays during the correlation phase.

Most of the service specifications demanded by the OMG have not been strict about the quality of service requirements. This does not mean OMG is uninterested in the quality of the service. The expectations probably were more in regard topossible implementations of the services. Once the service was accepted by the standard body, improvements would be the next step in the development phase. Getting the entire industry to accept a standard is a difficult task. If it were to be complicated by adding too many refinements, then the task could be impossible. Hence, the effort from the OMG is effectively channelized.

Figure 11-4 shows a new distributed messaging architecture. The new messaging framework expected with the proposal should be on similar nature. The overall design idea is the same with some minor design optimizations. The actual implementation design would be shown the respondents of the proposals. The main idea behind this work is to have a distributed messaging service that is CORBA-aware.

In this kind of the model, instead of the client applications linking in the client side of the messaging library, the client would connect to the messaging service offered by the client side of the ORB. This is depicted in the diagram by the two clients, namely Client 1 and Client 2, connecting to the client side of the ORB. The client side of the ORB would maintain its own queue. It has only one message queue attached to each client ORB. The queue would store messages for every client attached to it.

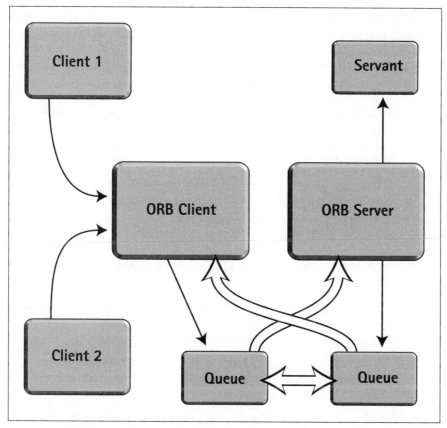

Figure 11-4: The Distributed Messaging Architecture Framework

The server side of the ORB has an attachment to the servant (or the server application). Multiple servants could be registered with one server-side ORB. The server-side ORB also maintains one message queue. Such a type of architecture reduces the amount of identical messaging code actively present within the environment. Code is reused by multiple modules.

The request for a proposal for the messaging service requires some interfaces that could be used by CORBA to monitor the quality of service. Quality of service is expressed in terms of reliability of the service, the capability to express some faith on the completion of the service, and some criteria to determine the time factor involved. Quality of service could have many factors and is best expressed regarding the kind of service on which it must be observed. Quality of service is important in a messaging service. The reliability factor must be high. The system should provide some parameters based on which a time prediction could be made about the service. The performance of the service can be gauged by it. The quality of the system is also determined by the amount of predictability of its performance and external variables that drive the show. The effects of those external variables must also be taken into account. Although the proposal does not emphasize the quality of service specification enough, it is an essential factor and must be given more importance. Some of the specific measures of quality of service are as follows:

Acknowledgment level When a request is delivered to a receiver, some level of acknowledgment must be received by the sender. This would be one way for the client to be assured of the delivery of the message. The acknowledgment could be offered at various levels.

Time-to-live When the request is to be issued by the client to the receiver and the request is not received by the receiving module because of some extraordinary problem, then the request must be kept alive for a specific period. The request cannot be alive for an unlimited period of time. If the request is not delivered during the specified time, then the sender must be notified so it can work around the problem or rollback on its tasks. This time would be an essential measure of the quality of service.

Priority Different messages would have different levels of priority and importance associated with them. The messaging service should be able to provide sufficient priority levels and also enable the end users to deduce their own priority levels.

Cost The maximum amount of resources the user is ready to dedicate for the message to be delivered and/or received would determine the cost commitment offered by the application. This is a secondary measure of the quality of service.

Delivery reliability The delivery reliability is closely associated with the cost associated with the message. The interface should be able to provide the reliability factor of the messaging service. This would help the client applications to determine the type of messaging service during run time.

Routing The routing information of the message would provide the users more descriptive information of the message-transfer process. It could be beneficial to users in certain types of applications.

Ordering The service should enable the sender and receiver of the messages to order the requests; receipt of certain types of messages before others would be useful. The same could apply to the sender.

The previous mentioned some of the criteria that help determine the quality of service. These quality-of-service factors become the deciding matter by the user in owning a service. The end users would only like to use the service, especially services related to a message-delivery system that offers performance satisfaction. The service is graded by its reliability, fault-tolerant behavior, execution performance, and ease of use. Service attributes like fault tolerance and reliability are the most important. A service that did not focus on either of these matters would most likely not be accepted as a standard. Hence, OMG gives special emphasis to the service-delivery guarantee mechanisms.

CORBA Component Model

An application can be built in various ways. If the desired application is known to be large, then the system could be designed to be one large block. This would be the most primitive way to build an application but, nevertheless, it is in practice in many system-developing shops. This method was tried and tested under many circumstances. Developers have faith in this system-building technique and put it to use whenever desired. The reason we call this a primitive approach is this particular type of model does not make use of the most advanced technology available within the programming domain. Such types of application are generally not extensible. Technology scalability, which would mean expunging the older mechanisms of doing things and introducing newer techniques of performing the same task, is not well-supported in this type of model.

The reason for this is that most of the working parts are closely tied to each other. Modules are not easily separable. To remove a working module and replace it with another would be a nearly impossible task. The dependencies exhibited by the individual modules are strong. Software engineering is not only about developing a good product, it also takes into consideration the management aspects, the maintainability, and improvements in the existing system. Often, the development shops are faced with the dilemma of what to do with the older version of the system. There is a constant search for refining the process of reusing the existing functionalities for the new version. No one has yet found a perfect solution, but the search continues. The ideal situation would be for the developer to take the existing application, in any form, and add the newer functionalities to it. No changes to the older form are required. We have all tried to attain that state and we have not come close to that kind of system. We do not live in an ideal world and cannot expect such a type of model to be realized, but we can certainly get as close as possible.

Component models were introduced to assist application developers to rewrite their application for the most new releases. It would facilitate them in providing newer functionalities to the existing system without going through the process of redeveloping the entire application. The developers could easily generate the newer modules and deploy it to the client so the clients can make use of them without needing to uninstall the old version and reinstalling the newer version. Partial updates can be well-done without the upsetting the consumers of the products. In the real world, we do not always rewrite every new version of our application program, but we frequently find our old design was incapable of handling the newly generated requirements and we redesign. We move some amount of working application code into the new design. Due to the changes suggested by the new design, the older assumptions may not stay relevant. Reuse can be done in two ways: We can either reuse code or reuse design. During a small fraction of time, we may be in the position of reusing both code and design. But, is there a norm by which we can always reuse code and design? We are sure the answer from the majority of you would be *no*. Reuse is a strong attribute that, perhaps, we haven't been able to exploit much. Furthermore – given the changing technology trends – we should attempt to attain a reusable design more rather than reusing code.

Reusability of code within the same application suite or same application version is a good characteristic. If you are a part of a project with more than one executing module, then writing code that could be reused by some other module is a perfectly good way of reusing code. This is exactly what reusing code is all about. But when the code is for a totally different type of application then, maybe, forcing ourselves to write reusable code could be too much of a strain. Possibly, writing new code would be a much better alternative, because we could do more in terms of satisfying the requirements with the new code. Reusing the old code may end up limiting our abilities. We would never want a new technique applied to our programming principles to be our bottleneck. Hence, whenever someone talks about reuse, we must think hard to see what we gain by doing it. One thing is for certain – there is no gospel in programming. Most of the preachers say things they have applied or have seen applied at many situations. It is not to imply it will solve all our problems. Most of the solving techniques are available for us and we must pick and choose the best solution.

Now let's discuss the component model. The *Component Model* is a new way of looking at developing huge applications. The main idea behind the Component Model is reducing the size of the working modules, so the sum of these working modules make up the application. The components become the building blocks for the application. The blocks are put together in some specified sequence to build the application. The sequence to be observed to build the application depends on the type of the application to be built. This would unload the individual modules from maintaining the relationship between them. The problem faced in having the individual modules store the interdependencies among themselves is it makes the system unportable. The portability is lost as the system is loaded with these intrinsic relationships. The behavior cannot be altered as it would imply the modules must be broken down. The breaking of modules and reworking on the code are not what component technology preaches. According to component technology, modules must be built in such a manner that they could be used off the shelf to build the application. The integration between the modules should be fairly generic and run time-oriented. No tight binding is preferred.

Dynamic binding of the modules is favorable as it helps in easy accumulation of the modules and also helps the portability factor. Furthermore, along with reusing the source code, we also have to reuse the design. The components are designed in such a manner that they can mold themselves into any form desired. Such a system is freely available to render its service to any kind of environment. It makes the development work much more useful as working modules can be easily reused. The proposition of such an environment would be difficult to obtain because it would introduce many new concepts that may not be accepted by the existing minds. More objections would be noticed because of the familiarity of the system and existence of properly aged and successful applications in the industry. Recently, however, we have seen some of these component models spreading their wings. These are some of the initial entries in the market and many models would be introduced in the near future. Many of the existing models in the industry are not well-developed, but they are making a statement of the new revolution.

CORBA has noticed the wave of component technology is catching up. Whenever we talk of a distributed framework, the component technology becomes fairly intrinsic to discuss. It took the world a little time to understand and to explain the relationship in some form. The description is not strong enough to be understood by the majority of people, but the work done by the researchers in this area will make it easy to understand. The best way to explain a concept to the developers' world is to have a functional framework. The framework may not be fully functional and it need not exhibit all the characteristics. It could be a gradual incremental process. In fact, having a gradually developing framework with an extensible design is the best way to form this structure. The growing system would incorporate a new design philosophy. Components designed in this manner can depart from the system when completed. The designed components are complete and are ready to be tried and tested.

Figure 11-5 shows a pictorial representation of the CORBA component working within a CORBA environment. The diagram shows a CORBA object, which is interacting with five other CORBA-aware components. The components are a handy way to provide additional features to the existing products and also to provide improvements to the system without any update overheads. The updated version of the system can work with the latest version of the available component. Also, some applications can be written to work with specific versions of the component that offered certain desired functionalities. Component-aware development environments are an excellent way of offering solutions in the dynamic problem zone. Many real-life applications in the past need these features. CORBA makes such system available for development within some constraints. The constraints may not be limitations necessarily, but bounds within which the system would react optimally. Further work in this area may also reduce any available limitations.

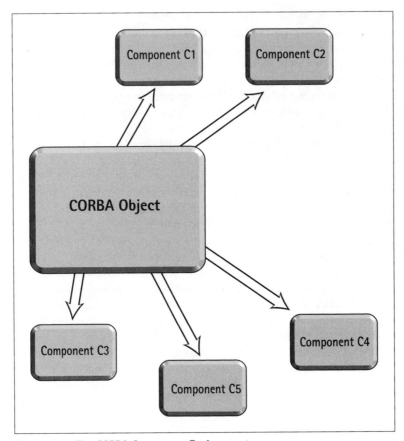

Figure 11-5: The CORBA Component Environment

Components follow a standard framework convention. Hence, one component can initiate communication with other components of the same framework. The components query each other's attributes, capabilities in terms if services, and so forth. It would bring in standardization in the diverse development area. Components extend reusability of design along with the code. The reusable design serves a much stronger cause. The encapsulation of the implementation by the components makes them movable from one development environment to another without any overheads. The dependencies are well-documented. None of them causes any performance bottlenecks. Because the components are not closely tied to any particular application, they could be used by multiple servers at the same time. If properly designed, they could be servicing requests from different applications at the same time. This is truly taking reuse to the extreme end.

Components, indeed, bring in a different perspective to application development. They do not come with all glories. Components introduce a certain amount of delay during the initiation process. Consider an instance wherein an application is written as a number of components. The components are all executing within the environment. Componentizing a system makes the application a smaller entity statically. When the application starts executing, it must obtain the components, which could satisfy its queries to complete its task. The application must look for the components at a well-defined point of reference. Once the components are located, it would have to initiate communication with the components. A certain amount of time would be spent in performing the initiation process. Such a time delay would not be observed for a noncomponent application, but the gains are tremendous with the component technology and it has been recognized by the OMG consortium.

Requirements specified by the OMG for the request for proposal for the component model for CORBA are listed in the following sections.

Component Model Elements

Responses shall clearly define the concept of component type and the structure for a component typing system, and shall specify mechanisms for establishing and expressing component type identity.

Responses shall define a concrete concept of component instance identity and a reliable means to determine whether two interface references belong to the same component instance.

Responses shall describe the life cycle of a component and specify interfaces and mechanisms for managing its life cycle.

Responses shall describe the association between a component and its interfaces and their relative life cycles. These descriptions shall be consistent with responses to the Multiple Interface RFP.

Responses shall specify interfaces to expose and manage component properties. Properties are an externally accessible view of a component's abstract state that can be used for design-time customizing of the component and that support mechanisms for notification (event generation) and validation when a property's value changes. Responses shall define the relationship between component properties and IDL interface attributes, if any.

Responses shall specify interfaces and mechanisms for generating component-events and for installing arbitrary component-event handlers (listeners) for specific component-events generated by components. The component-event mechanism shall be coordinated with the property mechanisms to support component-event generation when property values are modified. The relationship between this component model's event mechanism and the existing CORBA Event Service shall be clearly defined. If a response does not make use of the existing Event Service, it shall provide a rationale for this decision.

Component Description Facility

Responses shall specify an information model that describes components. In conjunction with the information model, responses shall specify a set of interfaces for a programmatic representation of this information model and a textual representation (that is, a descriptive language) for the information model. The language may be any extension to IDL or a complementary adjunct to IDL. Responses shall provide a rationale for their decision regarding the form of the language and its relationship to IDL. The information model shall capture all the salient features of components.

Responses shall specify how component descriptions are stored in a repository. The relationship between this repository and existing CORBA repositories, including the Interface Repository, Implementation Repository, and the forthcoming Meta Object Facility shall be clearly defined. The information models supported by the description language and the repository shall be completely isomorphic. The mapping between the description language and the repository contents shall be reflexive.

Programming Model

Responses shall describe a mapping from the component description information to a concrete programming model and define how that programming model is expressed in programming languages that support IDL mappings.

The mapping shall automate the generation of as many programming details as reasonably possible. For example, if the information in the component description contains a complete description of the component's state, the response shall describe how methods for serializing that state will be generated from the description.

Responses shall specify interfaces and mechanisms to maximize the portability of component implementation code between compliant implementations of the specification. To this end, responses shall clearly define the relationship between elements of the component model and the interfaces specified in the Enhanced ORB Portability specification, particularly the POA and its related interfaces. Responses shall specify how the behaviors and policies supported by the POA interfaces apply to components and describe the relationships between servants and component implementations. If possible, responses shall define how implementations of objects required by the POA – such as servant managers – may be automatically generated from component description.

Responses shall specify how components can be passed as value parameters in CORBA requests. This specification shall be aligned with responses to the Objects by Value RFP.

Mapping to JavaBeans

Responses shall specify a mapping from the proposed component model to the JavaBeans component model. Responses shall define and address the mapping between the intersection of the two component models (that is, it is not a requirement that the two models be isomorphic).

The mapping shall permit a CORBA component to present itself as a JavaBean to Java programs and application-building tools based on JavaBeans.

The mapping shall support both run-time and design-time needs. Responses shall describe how component descriptions are mapped to BeanInfo structures, so visual application building tools that rely on BeanInfo can be used to configure and assemble CORBA components and JavaBeans interchangeably.

The mapping shall maximize interoperability between features of the CORBA component model and the JavaBeans model.

The version of the Java Beans specification that shall be used is JavaBeans 1.0 Revision A, unless it is superseded by a revised specification issued before the submission due date. The specification is available at `<http://splash.javasoft .com/beans/beans.100A.pdf>`.

The JavaBeans specification is still under development and significant new features are being considered. Submitters should track these developments. Information about new draft specifications is available on the JavaBeans Web page at `<http://splash.javasoft.com/beans>`.

Classifying Components

Components can be classified by their type and behavior. The typing system must be versatile and scaleable. Extensive coverage of the typing system would benefit in the ubiquitous nature of the system. The specification requires a complete documented approach of the typing system. Even better would be a system that could lead the subtyping facilities within the environment. The subtyping facility is a much better solution because the type system needn't be overloaded for all applications. Specific applications and their domain, if required, could benefit from the subtyped component ware environment. The type system must also be able to provide sufficient information for the application to arrange itself accordingly. In fact, providing extensive public information must be the first prerequisite of such a system. The component identity must be maintained uniquely within the provided environment. Furthermore, if multiple environments are activated within the same instance, then any identity clashes must be harmoniously resolved. The end user application must not be exposed to any system identity crises. The components should be allowed to execute multiple instances. The environment must support multiple working copies of the same component and also provide well-defined methods to transfer data, as well as execute methods from each other's work space. Interaction among the instances of the same component is important. This would be precluded by a proper authentication mechanism.

The application should be allowed to check the environment at any time during the execution. Run-time type-checking features should be built into the system. The components would have a specific lifetime. The execution time of the component is generally defined by the component itself and, sometimes, the external system variables affect them. Along with this, the component-aware environment must be able to provide proper management interfaces for controlling the life of the component. Using the interfaces, the component can expose its execution path (at a very high level) and execution life to the environment. The environment could use this information to perform intelligent management of the entire system. It could expose this information to other components that exhibit appropriate rights to acquire this information. It could also perform resource scheduling based on the information provided to it and make the environment more efficient. Also, providing this information may lead to the environment's controlling the life of the component object, when required. Life cycle management of the executing components makes the environment the controller and many of the problems created by the badly behaving application could be eliminated.

The new interfaces defined for the component management by the environment should take into consideration the new specifications. Multiple interface specifications should be undertaken by the system. It should share and coordinate with the other new interfaces provided for making the system compliant with the newer specifications. This is important as the differences could be difficult to reconcile once the standards are introduced. The components' external state should be exposed to the environment. Any changes made to them must be informed to all the interested parties. An event notification system should be in place. The notification would help the other components and the environment to update its view. Also, the update procedure should be streamlined with utmost care. This should be mostly a background process, as it has nothing to do with the actual task of the components. The side effects like these should not become bottlenecks for system performance.

The persistent state of objects has been one of the hottest topics of discussion in the distributed technology world. Applications would like to provide consistent views of themselves. Consistency increases reliability. Other communicating applications can rely on the state of the object and do not have to perform extraordinary tasks to maintain a consistent view of the other end. The component-aware environment should provide serialization of the object's state. The persistent view can be maintained with the serialization of the object. The serialization of the object to a specific device could also be ultimately used in replicating live objects across communicating channels. The serialization should be provided with transacting support to provide a consistent state. This would, in turn, require the environment to manage transactions at a low level. The need for transactions at this level would not be extensive but, nonetheless, would be effective.

We specifically like the idea of the OMG asking for the proposal to provide externalization of the state-over-communication channels. Generally, when objects must be moved around from one environment to another, they cannot be active. Hence, such objects must be deactivated and then transferred. This introduces latency and also such a static state of objects cannot validate its status. Once the object is copied to the other environment, it must be loaded by them. Meanwhile, the object's semantic state within the parent environment could be modified and it would be unable to let the other environment know about it. Streaming of live objects over communication channels reduces the latency. Also, if required, the object can store the knowledge of its clones so it can itself replicate when material changes have been made to it. Policies can also be used to manage these types of behavior. Interoperating the serialization techniques with other services is also a beneficial plan. Integration with services like messaging services can make the system much more intelligent.

The proposal should also specify event generation and default event-handling mechanisms. The event-handling mechanisms could further be customized by the user. The default listeners implemented should coordinate with the property mechanisms so any changes to the property would generate events. This is particularly worth mentioning because most of the components developed have to do these things. Hence, instead of letting every application write these things over and over again, they could be easily generated by the environment and hooks could be provided to the component applications. Because the generic event-handling code is identical, it could be easily shared by multiple application. CORBA has a well-defined Event Service. It is not clear enough whether this event generation mechanism should coordinate with the CORBA Event Services. But future needs may generate such a kind of requirement and it would be good to have a path of coordination defined at this stage. All events could end up being channeled through the CORBA Event Services in the near future. No study has been done to see whether this could be a feasible solution. It may well end up being a bad approach for the generic system, but some applications may need to make use of this feature to expose its events to all the available components and services. Furthermore, providing a path for integration would never harm the existing model.

The component model must be descriptive. It should have a representation model that could be expressed in textual format, using some type of descriptive language. The programmatic representation of this model would have descriptions of the interfaces supported by the components, the attributes, and the classification of the components. In doing so, the suggestion could propose any extensions to the IDL language. We are dissatisfied with this feature. The IDL is getting too overloaded with newer extensions. If this continues, one day we may have IDL as a general-purpose programming language. The information model should have the capabilities of ranking the important features of the components. This could be semantic in nature and a new language could be a better choice than IDL extensions. The new language serves the purpose of not overloading the IDL. The drawback is we are exposed to another language. The new language would bring in new constructs and we have to learn it to make use of the features.

The component description must be stored within the available repositories. The component should also support the Meta Object Facility. This could become huge when the free from object structure is realized. The meta objects could be used to generate the components and express the component behavior. The components could also be classified with the help of the meta objects. The classification becomes much easier as no semantics are involved in the frame. The description of the component object model must be mapped to other programming languages. This mapping should be done with as little loss of data as possible. Some loss of data is apparent, but minimizing the loss is important. The portability issue of the component objects has to be paid special attention. The responses should specify its relationship with the new Portable Object Adapter (POA). *POA* was introduced to extend the portability within the object adapters. POA talks about the servant and the object user. The specification for the component model should thoroughly explain the POA interfaces and the coordination of the component model with the servant. Because POA would be the standard adapter for the next generation CORBA model, the component model must be able to perform a first-hand interaction with it. OMG has requested a proposal on object-pass-by-value. The component model must be able to adhere to the object-pass-by-value standards. It would have a big implication if it cannot work optimally with it.

The component model to be adapted by the OMG would become the standard CORBA component model. To make it a standard, it must interact with existing component object models in the industry. This would make the system extensible and increase its use. One of the popular component object models today in the industry is JavaBeans. Hence, the specification of the component model for CORBA must address the JavaBean integration. The CORBA component model needs to use the JavaBean features to make the CORBA components interoperate with the JavaBean environment without any changes to the code base. CORBA component objects should be viewed as a Bean to any Java program or JavaBean environment. All the Bean attributes must be made available to the CORBA component. Any overlap in design must be reviewed and worked on with utmost care. Impedance mismatch, if any, must be addressed. Ideally the impedance mismatch must be completely removed. The CORBA model must emulate the JavaBean model. It is possible for the two models to differ in their thought process for the inner workings, but the difference should be resolved internally by the CORBA component model. A good system always provides an interoperability path to the existing models. The introspection feature available in Beans must be supported by the CORBA component model.

Persistent State Service

Computing is all about data. We write applications that work around data. The applications, based on the programming principles applied and exposed to the operational contexts, modify the data. The validation of data makes the system usable by the end user. Consider a financial accounting system for instance: the system takes the financial data as input and stores it in some specified format. From the data stored, various kinds of reports are generated, which help the users understand the financial status of the organization. The data stored in the system could be dumb in its truest form. The application working on the data makes it readable and understandable for the user and, thus, the end user is pleased to see the reports and charts from the data. The data is streamed into different types of secondary devices. The storage of data and its retrieval are fairly important facts that must be addressed with utmost precision. Loss of data could be crucial for the business that relies on it. The business could end up losing millions of dollars if the data is not stored accurately. In a distributed-development environment, the same data is being used and shared by multiple applications. Many systems base their existence on the data stored. So it becomes even more important for a good system in place that takes care of the data. The OMG needs to emphasize it and have a dedicated service for the persistence of data. The current request for a proposal is for the Persistent State Service Version 2.0. CORBA deals extensively with data and the proposal must be well-specified and extensible for all-purpose use.

Data is stored on a device in a particular format. Only when it is read in that particular format will it make any sense. For instance, consider the word *Sukanta*. This may seem like a simple collection of English letters. When put in a column that expect names of persons, it would be interpreted as the name of a human being. The word *Sukanta* has an implied attribute that can be made visible when placed at the right place. Data always has semantics attached for the user to make sense of it. Raw data is difficult to interpret by any application that does not know its format. It is garbage unless well-interpreted. The semantics attached to the data informs the application where the data would make sense and where it should be applied. Some data store in a secondary format level within itself. The application has to know the primary format and the application would interpret it and generate the implied meaning.

Applications take input from the users. These input are worked on with the implied logic within the program. The data is fully prepared by the application. Now the application must store the data for it to retrieve it later. That data must be stored in some format at its current level so other applications can make good use of it. Persistent State Service in part assists us in doing so. There is more to it than the mere storage of data in some format and we will understand in greater detail as we progress. The request for a proposal solicits the management of persistence of CORBA objects. The OMG had a previous version of Persistent Object Service. Applications based on Persistent Object Services were developed, but it was found Persistent Object Services were unscalable. It was extremely difficult for vendors to develop under Persistent Object Services specifications. Persistent Object Services were not universally accepted because of the limitations in the design. The interoperability was negligible. Because of these reasons, the OMG decided to put an end to Persistent Object Services. Persistence State Services came into existence to do the job Persistent Object Service was designed to do. Only, Persistence State Services was made more scaleable and usable. Development issues were taken into consideration and the life of the vendors was made much easier.

Persistence State Service needs to provide persistence to the CORBA object independent of the lifetime of the client applications that access the object. As far the client applications are concerned, the CORBA object will stay at a particular location independent of the external circumstances. The applications are aware of proper methods of accessing the object. Whenever they need to access the object, they make use of the known mechanism to access it and they are guaranteed access to it. The inner workings of the actual storage is encapsulated within the storage subsystem. The client application as well as the hosting server are unaware of it. The process reduces the amount of knowledge to be carried around by multiple working entities. The knowledge of the object's serialization within a storage device is placed at the right section and multiple beliefs from different working entities are avoided.

The requirements for the proposal by OMG are listed in the accompanying sidebar.

A Persistent State is a CORBA object that uses the Persistent State Services to make its state persistent. Implementors of Persistent States require some way to specify the description of the object's state. The description of the object could be fairly diverse and cover many aspects. The state needs to store not only the actual objects, but also many other ancillary attributes. For example, consider an object A that is active within an environment. We assume the object communicates with four other objects within the same environment. The communication between the objects could be a lengthy transaction expected to persist for a long time (lengthy transactions are generally active for a very long time). If the system – due to some unavoidable circumstances – needs to shut down itself, then the objects must be stored within the storage subsystem. The objects were loaded and modified during the process, so the modification must be stored. This event occurred when object A was in the middle of its transactions with the other objects. A good behavior would be to shut down the system and store all the object's current states. Later, when the system comes up, all the objects that were active could be loaded and the execution could continue. Such a type of system would need to store the current state of the entire application, which in our case consists of many objects communicating with each other. If the current states of all the objects are not stored, then the application does not retain its execution context. When the application becomes active the next time, it would not know from where to start. It would imply that the application may have to start its operations all over again, which is a waste of time and resources.

OMG Proposal Requirements

Interfaces for implementing Persistent States (PSs). A *PS* is simply a CORBA object whose state is preserved by the PSs.

A means — compatible with IDL — for defining persistent state and interfaces (sometimes called *schema*).

Interfaces supporting one or more datastores. A datastore will be considered as the following or an equivalent technology: Flat Files.

These interfaces must allow object implementations to achieve and maintain their persistence without regard to the implementation choice of the datastore: System; Object Database Management System; Relational Database Management System; or Hierarchical Database Management System.

Support for efficient access, via CORBA, to the states of a large number of possibly fine-grained objects.

The Persistent State Services must be capable of providing interfaces that would facilitate such behavior. This makes the environment reliable and restorable. The fault-tolerant behavior is also closely linked. The Persistent State Services could provide a robust basis for fault tolerance. The OMG requirements do not talk about fault tolerance with the Persistent State Services. This is a logical extension, though. Little difference exists in the basis of fault tolerance and Persistent States. Fault tolerance goes to a greater extent in providing availability around the clock, seven days a week, and it is much more involved. A good fault-tolerances mechanism could start from this point. Persistent State Services also lay the foundation of consistency within the application environment. Clients of the Persistent State Services would expect to use the CORBA objects in a normal fashion. The Persistent State Services would manage the objects and the client is relieved of any extraordinary work related to managing the objects. Automatic persistence should be provided and the behavior should be kept transparent from the clients. The implementors of the storage subsystem need to provide this kind of feature in it. If the system needs resources to perform the automatic persistence, which would be the case all the time, the clients should not be exposed to it. The management must be done under the covers and the host server or the client should not be penalized for it. Background processing would be the perfect answer to it and the granularity of the operations would be dependent on the implementors environment. Performance of the service would play a key role in this service definition and implementation.

The Persistent State of the object must be defined statically. The definition informs the subsystem of the object's structure. The physical form of the object is needed to use for persistence. The definition must be provided in some IDL-compatible form. Because of the extensive usage of IDL for the object's structure definitions and its allowable behaviors, IDL compatibility for most of the descriptions provided by the CORBA services is a must. These definitions of the objects are also termed as schema by the OMG. We prefer to view what the OMG terms *schemas* as a meta definition of the object, rather than overloading the term. The word *schema* limits the structural view of the object. All objects of a particular inheritance would look alike according to a schema. For example, consider a database definition and that one of the classes within the database schema is called user-identity. Instances of *user-identity* would have the same schema. The definition of the object to be persisted should be more like the meta information of the object and would like to provide some more information about the object's state. For instance in the example of user-identity, one instance of user-identity probably needs to store the current activities of the object and the persistent definition would need some way to express it.

The persistent information about the objects must be stored some place. Databases are the most logical choice for such storage. In fact, databases are a much wider concept than how the industry generally views them. Databases come in various forms, shapes, and sizes. These are all different views of databases. We have relational databases, hierarchical databases, object databases, and object-relation databases. Any documented storage format could be viewed as a storage subsystem. A well-documented flat file could also be viewed as a storage subsystem. This would not be the best choice for most of the practical cases, but it would work. Object databases have gained popularity in today's world and they deserve it. Many of the large relational database vendors have started moving into the object database business because of the industry demand. A consortium exists, mostly comprised of object database vendors, called the Object Database Management Group (ODMG). The goal of the ODMG is to standardize object database interfaces. A standard must be adopted within the object database world because, otherwise, each object database vendor would push its own interface into the market. We have all noticed they are all doing this currently. This native interface introduced by the vendors divides the industry and brings in a hoard of incompatibilities in the market. Applications written in one particular object database cannot be moved onto another object database because of its native interface infliction. Not only can it not move, but it would also make interoperability of the application with other object databases using the application nearly impossible. The application developers must build multiple bridges and numerous conversion processes for moving around data.

The Persistent State Services must provide interfaces to a storage subsystem that could be implemented by any type of storage implementor. The implementation could be done using a flat file, an object database, or a relational database. Their Persistent State Services should not offer any such limitation. Although having support for as many individual database products as possible is nice, this may not be practical. So industry standards like the ODMG must be supported extensively. Compliance to such standards makes one standard unification process relatively simpler. Also, in the practical world, releasing a product in the proper time frame so the industry can actually use it and not have the product become obsolete before release is possible.

The Persistent State Services must provide efficient access to the state objects. The *state instances* of the object could be defined as one large object or multiple fine-grained objects. The Persistent State Services' interfaces are responsible for managing either of the situations. Efficiency mechanisms must be independent of the matter. The service would be shared by many clients and many would use it in different ways. The Persistent State Services should be able to handle such diversified usage. The service is expected to introduce new interfaces that should work in conjunction with other OMG services, like object-pass-by-value, multiple interfaces, and so forth. So the proposal should be well-rounded in its design approach. No default assumptions should be made in the submission. Any assumptions made on other services must be properly justified. The submitted proposals should talk about the transactions built within the Persistent State Services. Whether they are exposed or not would be purely up to the designer of the service. But a good discussion of the transactions – taking place beneath the covers – would provide the service consumers valuable insights and help them make better use of the service.

More Portable Servers

CORBA Version 1.0 had Basic Object Adapter specification defined. This was the first object adapter and was, indeed, basic in nature. The object adapter has an important role in the Object Request Broker environment. When a client needs to coordinate with a server object, the initial conversation is started with the object adapter. The object adapter is responsible for accepting the request, locating the servant, activating the servant, and creating an object instance. Once the initiation is done, the client object and server can continue with the communication, thus, the object adapter is in the heart of the operation. The original Basic Object Adapter specification was too narrow in design and had many drawbacks, so the implementors had to make many assumptions. Because the assumptions differed from one implementation to another, portability was questionable. As we have seen, the object adapter starts the client and servant communication process. If the initialization process is not portable, then the entire system starts working on those assumptions. After receiving many complaints from the ORB vendors, the OMG decided to kill the specification. No more work would be done on the Basic Object Adapter anymore. The new adapter specification is called the *Portable Object Adapter (POA)*. POA is portable, has taken into consideration all the design constraints BOA had, and has made them solvable. POA is far more scaleable and portable. With POA, clients written to an ORB from one vendor can easily work with another ORB written by a totally different vendor. All the vendor-specific assumptions have been properly addressed by POA. Hence, they have become a recognizable industry standard.

POA supports much richer functionalities. POA supports objects with persistent identities. It enables the developer to build objects whose existence can be guaranteed beyond the life of the creator or activator. POA provides an object a means to survive multiple-server life span. The most important feature POA introduced was a transparent object-activation model. To understand this transparent activation model, let's walk through the state transition of the system. Consider an example of a client who wants to issue a request to the server to be serviced. The client is unaware of the exact location of the servant. The client only knows the servant is available within this domain andissues the request to the ORB core. The ORB core immediately activates the object adapter, which locates the servant through the implementation repository. Once the servant is located, object adapter activates an instance of the servant. The client is unaware of any of these processes. The servant comes up and lets the adapter know it is up and running. The adapter hands over the client's reference along with the request. From then on, the adapter does not come between the client and server communication. The client does not have a hint this interaction is going on underneath the covers. The POA acts transparently. All this time, the client is given the view of the server object constantly being active. This transparency helps the portability factor. The guts of the actual operation are not revealed to the client application. Each ORB vendor practices its own activation mechanism. Also, the client application is highly portable. The implementation repository and the interface repository could be built using any kind of data store. Object databases are used widely now, but you could use relational databases or any traditional structured flat-file formats.

Before we go further, let's get familiar with some of the vocabulary used with the object adapter environment:

Client A *client* is a computational context that makes requests on an object through one of its references. The client could be an application running on one terminal communicating with an ORB. Considering a client as an application is a generalization. A client could be a particular module of an application, so we could have an application with multiple modules. Each module could act as a client to one server. The computational context reduces the scope of the client. Within one application, multiple clients could actually be making requests.

Server A *server* is a computational context in which the implementation of an object exists. Generally, a server corresponds to a process. Note, clients and servers are roles programs play with respect to a given object. A program that is a client to one object may be a server to another object. The same process may be a client as well as the server. To simplify the issue, a client is generally an entity that requires services to be rendered by some other entities. The server is an entity that serves a request.

For instance, if you go to a bank to deposit a check, the individual going to the bank becomes a client of the bank as a whole. The individual needs a service and becomes the client. The teller on the window serves the individual by accepting the check and depositing it in to the person's account. The teller serves a request and is a server. Assume there arises a complexity in the process and the teller cannot perform the task. In this case, the teller would go to his or her manager and request assistance. In this scenario, the teller becomes a client and the manager becomes the server. So the teller could be a client, as well as a server, at the same time. Only the point of reference decides the role. A server is again a generalization.

Object An *object* is used to refer to a CORBA object that has an identity, has an interface and has an implementation. The object's identity is known by the object itself and the server environment in which it is active. The client is not aware of the object's identity. It does not make sense for the client to have the object's identity as the identity does not completely identify the object. There is other context information that — combined with the object's identity — forms the object reference. The client identifies the object by its reference. The object reference is type aware.

Servant A *servant* is a programming language object or entity that implements requests on one or more objects. A servant generally exists within the context of the server. The server is like an entire process. Many active entities could live within the server. These entities are the servants. The servants operate within the bounds of the server. When a client makes a request on an object reference, the request goes through the ORB. The ORB works on the request and transforms it into a servant invocation. The location of the servant and activation is done via the ORB. This is analogous to having a thread pool within a multithreaded environment. Any request coming to the system picks up an available thread for operation and starts performing the task. Multiple servants could be used to serve an object. Consequently, the request from the client may end up using multiple servants for its completion.

Object ID An *Object ID* is used by POA and the user supplied implementation to identify a particular abstract CORBA object. Object ID values may be assigned and managed by POA or they may be assigned and managed by the implementation. The Object ID values are hidden from the client and encapsulated in the object reference. Object IDs have no standard form; they are managed by the POA as uninterpreted octet sequences. The Object ID, although it does not have any specific meaning, is used by the underlying system to help locate in the secondary device for storage and retrieval. When the object is alive the Object ID needs more semantics to be interpretable. Then it becomes a totally different type called the *object reference*.

Object Reference The *object reference* is an entity used to identify the object uniquely from any location or point-of-view. The object reference guarantees the holder a valid end point. The holder will never be penalized for accepting and using the object reference. If the object is no longer reachable, then the system underneath would provide an exception that could be processed by the caller. No abrupt termination would result.

A POA has the capability of generating Object IDs, so a POA can locate objects uniquely. This would imply that a POA can support namespaces. Also, a POA can have other POAs nested with itself, so a hierarchy of namespaces can be contained by a POA. This is a strong attribute of POA because the objects and their hierarchy can be respected within a POA. In the general programming world, we encounter object hierarchy most of the time and the POA has a perfect model to associate the object hierarchy with itself. The nested POA model encourages multiple POAs to be present within a single server. Each POA could be used to work on an object from different domains. Objects from different storage systems could be used by one server. The individual dedicated POA would help to locate and activate them. Even then, the client would not know about any of this.

With the POA model, one servant could be used to support multiple object instances. The multiplexing can be done by the servant and the POA. This means the servant can disassociate itself from the object to some extent. The separation is rather sparse. The object location is maintained transparent by POA. If not explicitly mentioned, all objects implemented by POA will be transparent to the clients.

The activation models supported by POA are rather interesting. Activation of the object generally has two parts: the first part is the request or is an entity that needs the object activated. It generates the activation request. Then, there is the actual object being activated and this is the CORBA object. The CORBA object is the one that serve the request from the client, so it is the second part of the activation. The BOA activation model concentrated on the activation of the server. The individual entity within the server, which would actually perform the task, was not provided with enough credit. The server activation process is a much heavier operation. This model carries extra overheads that are not actually required. The activation model supported by POA is much finer in operational granularity.

The explicit activation model takes into account the individual servants. Any servant that must be explicitly activated must be registered within the POA. The POA namespace and hierarchy facilitate the registration process. The developer would make POA calls to register his or her servants. POA also supports an implicit activation feature. Whenever an object identity is queried, the implicit activation would occur. If, at any time, an attempt is made to convert a servant into an object reference, an implicit activation may occur. The implicit activation depends on the defined policy. The on-demand activation mechanism allows objects to be activated when demand for the object arises. In this type of model, an indirection is provided. The objects that could be activated are listed in the indirect set in some shape or form. Whenever the object listed within this indirect set is needed, it is activated. This reduces the direct object pointing overhead by the system.

The BOA specification had no mention of threading models. The implementor needs to decide on what kind of threading model, if any, must be used. The POA goes an extra step in addressing the threading policy. the threading model is not discussed in detail by POA, however. POA supports two types of threading model: ORB-controlled threaded and single-threaded behavior. The requirement in no way limits the execution of a POA-compliant ORB to a multithreaded environment only. Most of the execution environments existing today support threads, so having some kind of policy associated with it is essential. Also, a threaded environment will help developers build portable servers that have good performance. The specification of POA does not mention any particular thread package, so no strings are attached.

In case of a single-threaded environment, all requests of the POA to the servants are serialized. The implementor could either process all the request in one thread — making it a single thread — or they could also synchronize among multiple threads, one at a time. Because in a single-threaded environment only one thread could be active, the synchronization would let only one thread execute at any instance. The ORB-controlled threads are used in environments in which the ORB actually controls the execution of threads. The number of threads executing within a POA can be determined and used. Although we generally intend the ORB-controlled model to have multiple threads, it is not specifically mentioned in the POA specification. What is definite is the ORB should have the controlling power. The developer has the power of making those decisions. Because the POA does not discuss in detail about the specifics of threading policy, this specification is somewhat limited. The object developer must be ready to handle any synchronization and critical section handling within the object implementation for a multiple-threaded environment.

POA is an acceptable specification because of some of the clarity put forward within the specification. BOA was practically unusable because of the ambiguities. The complications of BOA were due to the amount of assumptions made by the developers. The BOA architecture was unclear, which led different developers to have different designs of essential components. The object implementation was allowed maximum control of the object's behavior and it could define the attributes of the object. The object's states and its transitions from one state to another could be defined by the implementation. The object's relationship with other entities within the system could be defined and fully managed by its implementation. The object's storage and its retrieval can be completely manipulated by the object implementation. It is possible to have objects behave differently to different external variables. These behaviors can be controlled via policies. The POA allows the objects to exhibit policy-based behavior. This makes the system far more extensible than the BOA. Overall, the POA has many more features than the BOA. It is actually possible to have a decent implementation of POA by an ORB vendor and not have the client applications unportable. But POA is also limited. Many issues must be cleared by the POA specifications, which we assume some proposal will do. In any case, we should have much clearer POA specifications issued in the future.

CORBA Scripting

CORBA has been working relentlessly for the standards to come together. The standards are used to simplify the developers' lives and to assist the developers in building applications. One positive step identified from OMG is the effort to introduce the component object model. Developing applications become simple within a distributed component environment. No one likes to develop an application that first must build an environment on which it would work and, later on, actually develop the application. So the resistance to develop applications has been strong. The OMG realizes this and understand that to make this a popular industry technology, they must simplify the entire system so ordinary programmers can make use of them. We have seen the flow toward this kind of model.

The industry is flooded with rapid programming development tools. They are called Rapid Application Development environment (RAD). These RADs have strong, well-developed class libraries with most of the involved functionalities for development purposes provided by the vendors. Any programmer who wants to use it simply must make such calls. We are a strong proponent of such RAD development environments, and were involved in one such effort early in 1993 and 1994. Such tools come with an embedded programming language and virtual machine with an active run time available. One of the most popular development environments supporting the virtual machine and execution strategy, which is a household name for all intents and purposes, began with this basic concept.

Generally, the scripting language is not strong. By providing a good class library with facilities of linking in executable code written in much stronger programming languages, this becomes the best possible solution. The majority of the population is not an exceptionally strong programming force and to address the needs of these users, we must provide a simpler programming environment to make them feel comfortable. The simple code generators help do these things. These environments do not require programs to be compiled. The scripts are generated automatically by taking some input from the developers. The inputs demanded from the user provide enough guidance to the system to generate relevant scripts. Because these environments have a functional p-machine underneath, the code starts interpreting by the command from the user. The run-time interpretation is called *p-code execution*. From the users point-of-view it is simple.

Here are the specified requirements from the RFP. The requirements are simple in nature. They try to address all the attributes of such environments. Fortunately, we have the benefit of having many such environments used in the industry. These have been in use for a while and they have been stress-tested by the users. Much feedback and many remarks are available, so generating the requirements for the OMG was not difficult.

Mandatory Requirements

Responses shall specify a scripting language that fits naturally into the CORBA object and proposed component models and shall take account of experiences with other successful scripting languages.

Responses shall define the elements of a scripting language and concrete expressions of these elements in terms of CORBA technology.

Responses shall build upon existing specifications and be aligned with other simultaneously emerging specifications.

Scripting Language Elements

Responses shall clearly define the concept of object-oriented scripting.

Responses shall describe the relationship between scripts and the CORBA-proposed component model. In particular, responses shall describe how scripts interact with and control the proposed components.

Responses shall describe how scripts can invoke operations on CORBA objects.

Responses shall specify interfaces and mechanisms for controlling component-events and for installing arbitrary component-event handlers (listeners) for specific component-events generated by the proposed components. The language shall be aligned with the proposed CORBA-component event mechanism. The relationship between the proposed CORBA-component model's event mechanism and the scripting language shall be clearly defined.

Responses shall specify how the scripting language exposes and manages proposed component properties.

Requirements for Programming Model

The response shall support both run-time and design-time needs. Responses shall describe how the scripting language can be used to configure and assemble proposed CORBA components.

The scripting language shall be designed for use in a visual run-time environment (desktop, browser, and so forth) as well as a nonvisual run-time environment (middle-tier application server).

Considerations in Generating a Programming Environment

Whenever a programming environment is generated, a few important steps must be taken into consideration. The requirements specified by the OMG articulate them well. In a programming environment, we must first consider the base operating environment upon which it would be working. This could be comprised of the host operating system or any shell on which the execution is supposed to take place. For instance, a programming language designed for a particular operating system should not have a heavy design focus on multithreaded features when it is known the operating system would never support multithreaded execution strategies. This would be a waste of time, effort, and valuable resources for a case that would never take place. Of course, it may help developers solve the programming aspects, but is a final zero-sum gain.

The CORBA scripting service would operate on a CORBA-compliant ORB. The CORBA scripting service should try to attempt a one-to-one match between the execution model and the scripting language supported by it. This should not pose too many difficulties in the case of CORBA because the base environment is extensive and any aid needed from the environment would be possibly satisfied in a compliant manner. There should not be any impedance mismatch, or realistically speaking, very little impedance mismatch. A proper scripting language cannot be built optimally without the inclusion of a good programming model. The programming model would guide the scripting language constructs. The programming model is well-known and has been tested in a number of ways by the industry. A proper scripting effort was not directly mounted, but much less quantified work has been done. The goals of these other scripting needs have been slightly different as they were targeted to specific services, rather than for the CORBA environment as a whole. Nonetheless, they are certainly a positive learning experience.

The programming models are not considered important for developing today's scripting language and good reasons exist for doing it. Companies have been inventing faster execution processors on a regular basis, which is both good and bad for the computing community. The bad part is companies must allocate more dollars for upgrading hardware regularly. This could be a lot of money for huge corporations. The good part is, because hardware vendors provide increasingly faster processors, the software side can cut a slack in the optimally matching program models. This does not in any way stand as a justification for bad programming habits or bad design practices. These are facts observed in the industry. Also, because the rapid scripting models do code interpretation, they can provide various kinds of optimization techniques. The source is not compiled into any machine code, hence, no tight bindings with the hardware architecture is present in the executable code. The run-time interpretation engine can perform intelligent context-related look-aheads to provide excellent optimizations. Dead code can easily be identified and isolated during the execution phase.

Every single execution of the scripts is interpreted by the run-time interpretor, so the scripts are highly portable. The scripts can be generated in one operating environment and, without any modification, easily executed in another environment. Java is a big example of this. The Java model has run times or Java virtual machines available in most of the existing operating systems. If the virtual machine is available, then Java applications can execute without any changes made to the source code.

CORBA scripting must exhibit a similar kind of behavioral model. CORBA scripting must generate object-oriented scripts. CORBA is an object-oriented distributed environment. Hence, the scripting language would naturally have to be object oriented and provide distributive constructs. It could be an incremental step toward the next version of CORBA scripts. We believe if they do not support distributive language constructs, then it could be a total failure in the near future. The model would not match well. The proposal must show a well-defined relationship between the CORBA script and the CORBA component model. The component model should be a big driving factor in this proposal, as well. CORBA scripting must provide native component model support. Also, it must make available smart integration facilities to most of the newer specifications. The responses need to have a CORBA object-operation invocation feature. The invocation mechanisms must be well-documented and a clear execution path must be shown by the proposal. Component event-handling mechanisms and default event listeners must be supported by the CORBA scripting model. The CORBA scripting language should provide intrinsic hooking mechanisms. These hooks could be plugged into the system so the events generated by the internal system can call these hooks when required. The basic nature of this operation demands an extensive integration with the CORBA framework. It requires close coordination with the working environment and can be only attained by the method hookup mechanisms.

Different ORB vendors would have their own proprietary implementation techniques. The specifications are introduced by the standard body to facilitate standard interaction among the ORB and third-party client applications. This also facilitates interoperability among ORBs from different vendors. The scripting language features to be specified must properly document every aspect, which would effect external entities in a clear fashion. This tells us that although the language hookup calls with the environment could be implemented by the vendors in a vendor-specific manner, the operational approach should be generalized. It could go to the extent of defining the interfaces of which the scripting language should make use, to provide close interaction with the operating environment. The current specification does not require these features but we are certain they would be important. We speak from a practical implementor's point-of-view and it seems clear this would be needed. Perhaps it is currently considered internal, but it certainly will announce its presence when multiple implementations in the industry come up.

The CORBA scripting facility should provide an extensive policy-based enhancement system. The policies should be dynamically configurable, as well as alterable when desired. The policies could be introduced for the compilation techniques, the resource usage techniques, and system management techniques. In general, interpretive systems are slow. The execution of the CORBA scripting should be acceptable. They should use the advanced compilation techniques of altering all the newly added code when optimizing them for execution. These are all implementation specifics we are discussing, but we think they are important enough to mention. The scripting engine should enable users to modify the run-time code without having to rerun the entire system. This particular technique is a judgment call and is based on the specific situation. Sometimes the changes made during the execution phase by the developers have so many diverse implications, they could not be optimized during the same execution phase. In such cases, the system must start its execution all over again. Most of the time while executing, however, minor changes are made by the developers, which do not have vast implication over the program, so this model would usually be followed.

The CORBA scripting should have a visual run-time environment as well as a nonvisual run-time environment. This would imply the scripting system should enable the users active interaction during execution. This is a request-based process. The client's requests drive the system's execution and often guides it through the proper paths. In a nondedicated system, we may also need to have the CORBA scripting execution model. These types of system would expect the scripting environment to allow intelligent drivers to drive the execution. The run-time configurations would assist in this process. Also the execution model should be able to concur on its own, based on some policies. In a multitier application development environment such factors are essential as they allow the multilevels to execute without interference.

If possible, the CORBA scripting service could provide mappings from other rapid development environments. Mappings to the popular RAD systems would encourage end users of those systems to make use of the benefits and availability of CORBA-based environment. They can use the many services in different vertical markets offered by CORBA without making too many changes to their applications. These other RAD tools have been in the industry for some time and many companies have committed serious resources to them in terms of development hours and money. With the new distributed system, we can do two things: ignore the market's value and try to start a new wave or try, to some extent, to be compatible with them we prefer the latter approach, because there is a strong business sense to it. Once the existing developers are exposed to the benefits of the distributed architecture, they would never go back to other ways of doing things. This would also offer the industry a proper migration path from one environment to another by converting the past resource to a fruitful system of the future. Respecting each other's effort is a good software design and development attitude, which will pay off handsomely in the future.

Summary

In this chapter, we tried to sum up the entire CORBA effort. CORBA is a vast topic to cover. Most of the CORBA-specific technologies we discussed are in their infancy. Most are in their initial-proposal mode. It is difficult to say which of them will survive rugged scrutiny. We feel all the previous extended services are needed for CORBA, as a successful environment, to move to the next level. The extended services cover the major aspects that would make the technology versatile and universally acceptable for all problem domains.

This chapter provides you with the basis of understanding the advanced concepts presented. Our recommendation is when studying the material, read this rather intense chapter to start and try to get as much of the topic as possible. By doing this, you will have absorbed around 80 percent of the material. Once you have a good basis, do some light reading elsewhere to cover the aesthetics of the topic. Many magazine articles and other books are available that cover these topics from different perspectives. After reading this book, other books will be easy for you to understand.

This chapter focused more on the conceptual factors. We took utmost care to maintain a standard of explaining the concepts to the reader. We began subsections with an overview of the topic leading the reader into the right frame to understand the concepts. In most of the subsections, we expressed our own views and provided a proper justification. This method is helpful in explaining the concepts. The discussion is arranged around the requirements of the specification. Because most of the requirements do not yet have any initial submissions, we did not want to introduce any bias into the topic. Evaluating the requirements from the point-of-view of a practical user has been our approach. Overloading the chapter with too much information has a disadvantage and we tried to avoid that method. Most the extra information does not directly effect the situation; some that do have indirect impact may convolute the reader's thought process

CORBA is a sound technology and it continues to mature with time. Many big development shops have begun to invest considerable sums of money on ORB-based development. The work gives the standards body a greater boost in getting more services involved in this standards process. The OMG consortium has picked up the difficult task of bringing in a standard approach to develop distributed applications. A good thing about this effort is vendors who are actually committing to versions of ORBs in the industry are participating in the consortium. Their participation is rather active. They are actually involved in proposing standards in different supported services. After a thorough investigation of the service specification, it is accepted as a standard, so chances of narrowly designed specification becoming a standard are impossible. But there have been instances when such a thing occurred. The OMG has been reactive to fixing such problems. The decision-making process in the OMG is slower than a normal organization and this is properly justified by indulgence in the validation process.

Appendixes

Appendix A

About the CD-ROM

The CD-ROM that accompanies this book contains all the code examples from the book, as well as some useful third-party software.

System Requirements

- ◆ Windows 95 or NT
- ◆ Pentium 100 or better
- ◆ 100MB space (minimum)
- ◆ 32 RAM (minimum)
- ◆ C++ Compiler installed
- ◆ Vigibroker ORB installed

Trial Demo Software

Several pieces of trial demo software on this CD-ROM are included, which you should find useful. For further help with the installation, turn to the last page of this book.

IBM Visual Age for Java

This software enables you to create Java and JavaBeans applications without much effort. The software comes with MindQ's interactive Java tutorial, which teaches you how to work with Java in a visually enriched environment. More information about Visual Age can be found at `http://www.software.ibm.com/ad/vajava/` and more information about MindQ's interactive Java Tutorial can be found at `http://www.mindq.com`.

To install, copy the entire contents of the IBM VAJ\SETUP directory to an empty temporary directory on your hard drive and run the SETUP.EXE program found in this temporary directory.

IBM Web Runner

VisualAge WebRunner Toolkit works with Visual Age for Java software and helps you create JavaBeans and Servlets. More information can be found at `http://www.software.ibm.com/ad/webrunner/`.

To install Web Runner, refer to the ReadMe.html file found on the CD-ROM in the D:\IBM Web Runner directory.

IONA's OrbixWeb

OrbixWeb from IONA Technologies helps Java developers create flexible and scalable CORBA applications. Find more information at `http://www.iona.com`.

To use this demo, you need to obtain a license from IONA's Web site.

To install OrbixWeb on Windows, execute the OW30PROF.EXE program found in the D:\orbixweb\WIN32 directory on the CD-ROM. To install on Solaris, follow the standard Solaris installation for the OW30PROF.TAR file found in the \orbixweb\SOLARIS directory on the CD-ROM.

IONA's Orbix 2

Also from IONA, Orbix 2 helps you create CORBA applications for distributed environments. More information can be found at `http://www.iona.com/products/orbix/orbix/index.html`.

As with OrbixWeb, to use this demo, you need to obtain a license from IONA's Web site.

To install Orbix2 on Windows, execute the SETUP.EXE file found in the \orbix 2\ORBIX directory on the CD-ROM.

Sun's JDK 1.1.5

This development environment helps you run all your Java/JavaBeans applets and applications. More information on the JDK itself can be obtained from `http://www.javasoft.com/products/jdk/1.1/`. The JDK enables you to:

 ◆ Develop applets that run in browsers supporting Java 1.1, such as HotJava Version 1.0 and future versions of Netscape Navigator and Microsoft Internet Explorer.

 ◆ Develop Java applications.

To install on Windows, execute the jpp115-win32.exe file found in the \JDK directory on the CD-ROM. If you wish to install the JDK on a Solaris computer, you need to obtain it from the Sun Web site, as shown in the previous section.

Appendix B

Noted Web Sites

The following are Web sites developers you should visit regularly.

OMG Web Site	`http://www.omg.org`
Distributed Object Computing Group	`http://info.gte.com/ftp/doc/doc.html`
OpenDoc's Web Site	`http://opendoc.apple.com/`
IONA Technologies	`http://www.iona.com`
Vesigenic Web Site	`http://www.vesigenic.com`
Useful CORBA Resource Site	`http://www.acl.lanl.gov/CORBA/`
Object Database Management Group	`http://www.odmg.org/`
Earthlink's Developer's Site	`http://www.developer.com`
Microsoft's Developer's Site	`http://www.microsoft.com/msdn/`
Netscape's Developer's Site	`http://developer.netscape.com`
JavaWorld Online Magazine	`http://www.javaword.com`
Web Week Online Magazine	`http://www.webweek.com`
JavaSoft's Web Site	`http://www.javasoft.com`
Java Report Online	`http://www.javareport.com`

Appendix C

CORBA Services at a Glance

TABLE C-1. A QUICK SERVICE DESCRIPTION.

Service	Description
Naming	Allows a system to create, delete, and find object names dynamically using a powerful, logical naming convention.
Event	Allows your system to create and handle events. This service supports different event models, such as the push-and-pull model, as well as both generic and typed events.
Persistent Object	Provides a generic storage facility for objects, using a number of different datastores. This service will work with RDBMs, OODBMSs, or any other datastore that fits the requirements of your system.
Transaction	Enables you to create and manage simple or nested transactions, which adds a greater level of control, error detection, and reliability to your CORBA system.
Concurrency Control	Provides management of concurrent client access to shared resources, which can be objects, files, or any other entity in your system that needs protection.
Relationship	Enables you to create dynamic relationships between objects or groups of objects, with no required change to the objects being included in a relationship.
Life Cycle	Takes care of problems associated with copying, moving, and deleting groups of objects related by an object graph.
Externalization	Describes an approach for saving an object's state in memory, disk, or elsewhere, and restoring it at a later time. This service can be used to pass objects by value across CORBA.
Query	Provides generic query capability, enabling you to query for objects using a wide variety of datastores.

(Continued)

TABLE C-1. A QUICK SERVICE DESCRIPTION. *(Continued)*

Service	Description
Licensing	Tackles distributed object licensing concerns. Highly configurable, this service enables you to build licensing approaches that fit your application and the consumers who will use it.
Property	With this service, you can dynamically create attributes, which can be used to extend commercial, shrink-wrapped objects.
Time	Provides a universal source for time across your distributed CORBA components. Also facilitates timed-events in your system.
Security	Allows secure communication between objects, while providing user authorization and security auditing.
Collection	Provides a powerful set of collection objects, such as stacks, queues, and bags.
Trading	Finds objects based on the services, or operations, they provide for clients.

TABLE C-2. SERVICE DEPENDENCIES.

Service	Other Service Dependencies
Naming	Does not rely on other services.
Event	Does not rely on other services.
Persistent Object	Uses the Externalization Service to provide one protocol for storing and transferring objects. Depends on the Life Cycle service for doing complex object operations.
Transaction	Can depend on the Concurrency Control service to provide locking capabilities during transactions.
Concurrency Control	Does not rely on other services.
Relationship	Does not rely on other services.
Life Cycle	Depends on the Naming Service. Complex uses of this service will also depend on the Relationship Service.

(Continued)

TABLE C-2. SERVICE DEPENDENCIES. *(Continued)*

Service	Other Service Dependencies
Externalization	Uses the Life Cycle Service when externalizing both simple and complex objects. This service may also use the Relationship Service to avoid circular references when streaming complex objects.
Query	Does not rely on other services, but can use functionality found in the Life Cycle, Persistent Object, Relationship, Concurrency Control, Transaction, Property, and Collection Services.
Licensing	Depends on the Event Service and the Security Service. It may use the Relationship Service to provide some functionality (based on service implementation).
Property	Does not rely on other services.
Time	Relies on interfaces provided with the Event Service for use with timed events.
Security	Does not rely on other services.
Collection	Does not rely on other services.
Trading	Does not rely on other services.

Quick Reference

The IDL/C++ Language Specification Mapping

Mapping Module Names

First, and perhaps most important, is how to deal with name space. In all cases, an IDL module is mapped to a C++ namespace of the same name. To clarify, if an IDL module looked like:

```
module MyModule {
  … // Some definitions
};
```

The corresponding C++ code would be the following:

```
namespace MyModule {
  … // Some definitions
}
```

MAPPING INTERFACES

IDL interfaces are mapped to C++ classes. Each class encapsulates type definitions, constants, operations, and any exceptions defined by the interface. There are two important details about CORBA-compliant C++ programs:

- ◆ A C++ program cannot create or hold an instance of an interface class
- ◆ Use a pointer to reference an interface class

By abstracting away interfaces from the program's functionality, the underlying implementation of interfaces is left open to different mechanisms. One example implementation that would be impossible if interfaces could be directly instantiated is having an abstract base class for the interface. The IDL syntax for declaring an interface is:

```
interface MyInterface {
  struct myStruct {
short myShort;
  };
};
```

C++ code that uses the IDL interface (after being translated into C++ code) would look like:

```
MyInterface::myStruct struct;        // Defines a variable of type
  myStruct
struct.myShort = 3;                  // Uses the structure's only field
```

Three ways that *do not* conform to the standard include:

```
MyInterface myInterface;                     // Cannot declare an
  instance of MyInterface
MyInterface *myInterface;            // Cannot declare a pointer to
  the interface
void someMethod( MyInterface &param )        // Cannot declare a
  reference to the interface
```

OBJECT REFERENCES

Having interfaces you cannot use defeats the purpose of having any interfaces at all. Two ways exist to reference an object in C++, using the code translated from IDL. Given an interface, MyInterface, the two constructs are MyInterface_var, and MyInterface_ptr. A MyInterfaceRef also exists and remains for historic reasons. Avoid the interface MyInterfaceRef. The difference between a _var and _ptr is a _var instance variable releases any memory allocated to it when the number of references to it becomes zero or it gets assigned to another variable. The _ptr allows for more straightforward pointer manipulations to which C++ programmers are accustomed.

OBJECT REFERENCE OPERATIONS

CORBA's base class, Object, has three basic operations. These include duplicate, release, and is_nil. Remember, the operations are performed on an object reference and not on the object implementation itself. The methods release and is_nil are tied directly to the Object class. The implication here is they can then be used within CORBA's namespace, as shown here:

```
void release( Object_ptr obj );
Boolean is_nil( Object_ptr obj );
```

The release function indicates the caller will not make any further references to the object passed in as the given parameter. In turn, this allows the resources allocated to the given object to be released if there are no other references to it. In addition, any calls to release on an object that has already been set to nil are ignored. No exceptions are thrown by release or is_nil.

Finally, the duplicate function yields a new object reference with the same static type as the reference provided. The IDL code looks like the following:

```
interface MyInterface {
  ...
  };
```

The resulting C++ code for the previous IDL source is:

```
class MyInterface {
 public:
      static MyInterface_ptr _duplicate( MyInterface_ptr obj );
      ...
};
```

In the previous syntax, if the object reference passed in to the _duplicate method is nil, the returned object reference will also be nil.

MAPPING BASIC TYPES

The next important part of IDL consists of how C++'s basic types are mapped to the interface definition language. Table 1-1 illustrates the IDL type and its corresponding C++ type.

TABLE 1-1. BASIC TYPE MAPPING FROM IDL TO C++.

IDL Type	C++ Type
boolean	CORBA::Boolean
char	CORBA:::Char
double	CORBA::Double
float	CORBA::Float
long	CORBA::Long
long double	CORBA::LongDouble
long long	CORBA:LongLong
octet	CORBA::Octet
short	CORBA::Short
unsigned long	CORBA::ULong
unsigned long long	CORBA:ULongLong
unsigned short	CORBA::UShort
wchar	CORBA::WChar

The previous mapping assumes the family of Longs (long, long double, long long, and so forth) generate equivalent numeric C++ types. This implies the native C++ types must support IDL semantics and can be manipulated by the corresponding built-in C++ operations. If this is not the case, then an alternate mapping to C++ classes (whose behavior matches that expected by IDL) must be used instead.

MAPPING NIL

Each interface defines a static member method named _nil. It is responsible for returning a nil object reference of that particular type of interface. The following C++ code illustrates how to check for nil:

```
Boolean result = is_nil( A::_nil() );
```

Note, you may not use the C++ == operator to compare the instance A's _nil result, but must pass that result into the is_nil function. Because nil, as defined by CORBA, is equivalent to C++'s NULL, programmers may not invoke methods on a nil (read: NULL) interface.

MAPPING BOOLEANS

Unless the C++ compiler being used supports the type bool, it is recommended that programmers use 0 to represent FALSE and 1 to represent TRUE. No behavior is defined for values outside of 1 or 0.

MAPPING CONSTANTS

In IDL, declared constants are mapped to a C++ definition that, optionally, defines storage, depending on the declaration scope. This implies, in certain circumstances, a constant's value must be used instead of its name. Consider the following IDL code:

```
const string aString = "a string";

interface MyInterface {
 const float magic_number = 42;
 typedef long vectors[ magic_number ];
};
```

The resulting code generated in C++ would look like:

```
static const char *const aString = "a string";

class MyInterface {
 public:
      static const Float magic_number;
      typedef long vectors[ 42 ];
};
```

WIDE CHARACTER AND WIDE STRING CONSTANTS
Wide characters and wide strings in IDL are mapped directly to literal characters in C++. The only difference is an L precedes the literal. Examine the following IDL code:

```
wchar wc = 'X';
wstring ws = "abc123";
```

The corresponding C++ code would look like:

```
static const CORBA::WChar const wc = L'X';
static const CORBA::WChar *const ws = L"abc 123";
```

INTEGERS AND FLOATS
The conversions for the remaining data types are shown in Table 1-1.

CONSTANTS
There are two cases for declarations of constants; they vary depending on their scope. Constants declared within an IDL interface map onto public final static variables for the corresponding C++ interface.

Constants not declared within an IDL interface map onto a public interface. Internal to that public interface is a variable named "value," whose value happens to be that of the declared IDL constant. The name of the C++-based public interface becomes the name of the declared IDL constant. Handling constant declarations this way is fine because the extra classes are only required at compile time. Intelligent compilers should be able to inline the classes during runtime execution.

To ensure clarity, take the following IDL constant definition:

```
module MyExample {
  const long myLongConst = -456;
};
```
The generated C++ code would look like:
```
package MyExample;

public interface myLongConst {
  public final static int value = (int)(-456L);
}
```

ENUMERATIONS
Enumerated types in IDL map exactly the same way as their C++ counterpart. That is, the IDL code shown here is written the same in C++:

```
enum EnumType { first, second, third, fourth };
```

STRINGS

The IDL string is mapped to the C++'s null-terminated character pointer. The CORBA module, however, declares a String_var that is essentially a wrapper object for a character pointer. CORBA-compliant software must allocate strings using the following global CORBA functions:

```
namespace CORBA {
  char *string_alloc( ULong len );
  char *string_dup( const char * );
  void string_free( char * );
};
```

WIDE STRINGS

Wide string types map directly to C++'s CORBA::WChar* type. To allocate memory dynamically and to release memory, for these types, the following global CORBA functions must be used:

```
namespace CORBA {
  WChar *wstring_alloc( ULong len );
  void wstring_free( WChar * );
};
```

No exceptions are thrown. If there is not enough memory remaining for the allocation, a null pointer is returned.

STRUCTURES

Like the enumeration type, the IDL struct type maps directly to the C++ struct. This means all field variables can be directly manipulated. The resulting C++ structs are not supposed to have user-defined constructors. A simple IDL and C++ struct would look as follows:

```
struct MyStruct {
  long myLong;
};
```

UNIONS

The name of an IDL union maps directly to the name of a corresponding C++ class. The class's constructor does not attempt to initialize the union. Consider the following IDL code for a union:

```
typedef long Age;

struct Person {
  short height;
};

union MyUnion switch( long ) {
```

```
case 1: string name;
case 2: Age age;
case 3:
case 4: Person person;
default: long height;
};
```

The resulting C++ code would be:

```
typedef Long Age;

struct Person {
 Short height;
};

class MyUnion {
 public:
      MyUnion();
      MyUnion( const MyUnion& );
      ~MyUnion();

      void _d( Long );                 // Discriminator
      Long _d() const;

      void name( const char * );       // Frees the old storage,
 and copies parameter
      void name( const String_var& );  // Frees the old storage,
 and copies parameter
      void name( char * );         // Frees the old storage, no
 copy made
      const char *name() const;        // Regular accessor

      void age( Long );
      Long age() const;

      void person( const Person& );    // Performs a deep-copy
 of the structure
      const Person &person() const;    // Read-only structure
 access
      Person &person();                // Read-write structure access
};
```

The accessor methods for the types struct, union, sequence, and any are special cases whereby a read-write object is returned. Looking deeper into the union syntax, the array type generates different C++ code than that previously shown. The following IDL code illustrates:

```
union MyUnion switch( long ) {
 default: long anArray[ 4 ][ 5 ];
};
```

The generated C++ code looks as shown here:

```
class MyUnion {
 public:
        void anArray( long arg[ 4 ][ 5 ] );
        typedef long _anArray_slice[ 5 ];
        _anArray_slice * array();
};
```

This particular syntax is explained further in the section on Arrays.

SEQUENCES

A C++ class having a minimum-length attribute and a maximum-length attribute is mapped from an IDL sequence. Bounded sequences do not give the software developer the ability to alter the maximum length, as defined by the IDL specification. Reasonably, for unbounded sequences, the programmer may adjust the maximum length of the sequence at any point. Suppose the following IDL specification is given:

```
typedef sequence<long> MyUnboundedSequence;
typedef sequence<MyUnboundedSequence, 10> MyBoundedSequence;
```

The resulting C++ code generated would be:

```
class MyUnboundedSequence {
 public:
        MyUnboundedSequence();
        MyUnboundedSequence( ULong max );   // Sets the maximum limit
        MyUnboundedSequence( ULong max,
                        ULong length,
                        Long *value,
                        Boolean release = FALSE );
        MyUnboundedSequence( const MyUnboundedSequence& );
        ~MyUnboundedSequence();
};

class MyBoundedSequence {
 public:
        MyBoundedSequence();
        MyBoundedSequence(   ULong length,
                        Long *value,
                        Boolean release = FALSE );
        MyBoundedSequence(   const MyBoundedSequence& );
        ~MyBoundedSequence();
};
```

ARRAYS

The mapping of arrays from IDL to C++ goes directly to the familiar C++ array declaration. Using array elements of type string, or object, generates type code as used in structure members. In other words, the old memory associated with the array element is released if a new assignment to that element is performed. The mapping is complicated when slice types are taken into consideration. The following IDL code:

```
typedef long MyLongArray[ 9 ][ 10 ];
```

Translates to the following C++ code:

```
typedef Long MyLongArray[ 9 ][ 10 ];
typedef Long MyLongArray_slice[ 10 ];
```

Because regular C++ arrays are used for the mapping from IDL arrays, a problem creeps in when using the type-safe "any" type. To solve this problem, a compliant-CORBA implementation must include a C++ type whose name begins with the array name, and ends in _forany (read: for any). Its C++ code definition looks like:

```
class Array_forany {
  public:
        Array_forany( Array_slice *, Boolean nocopy = FALSE );

        ... // Other member methods are defined for specific array
  types
};
```

TYPEDEFS

An alias is used to map IDL's typedefs into C++. Consider the IDL following syntax:
```
typedef long MyLong;

interface MyInterface;
typedef MyInterface AnInterface;
```

This maps to the following C++ code:

```
typedef Long MyLong;

// ... Skipping the interface definition for MyInterface

typedef MyInterface AnInterface;
typedef MyInterface_ptr AnInterface_ptr;
typedef MyInterface_var AnInterface_var;
typedef MyInterfaceRef AnInterfaceRef;      // Should not be used, as
  it remains for historical purposes
```

ANY TYPE

IDL's any type has two objectives: Type-safety and the ability to handle type values unknown at implementation compile time. To help isolate the problems associated with creating an any type that does not match a particular TypeCode, function overloading is used within the IDL's corresponding C++ code. To accomplish this task, all C++ types generated from IDL code must be unique. Three exceptions exist to this rule:

- ◆ Boolean, char, octet, and wchar are not required to map to any specific C++ type.

- ◆ Unbounded and bounded strings always map to char *. The any type, if set to a string, therefore requires the string be bounded.

- ◆ Arrays of different sizes cannot be differentiated, which means a special way to create, or set, an any type when using an array must be dealt with separately.

So a value can be set in an any type (while insuring type-safety), the following overloaded operator must be implemented, in C++, for each data type, DT:

```
void operator <<= ( Any&, DT );
```

The previous function definition is fine for types passed by value. These include:

- ◆ Double, Float, Long, LongDouble, LongLong, Short, ULong, ULongLong, Ushort Enumeration types

- ◆ Unbounded string types

- ◆ Object references (variables ending with _ptr)

The C++ syntax for using the previous assignment operator would look as follows:

```
Long myLong = 15;
Any myAny;
myAny <<= myLong;
```

Similar syntax is used for arrays, and unbounded character strings. To extract information from the any type, the following function is defined:

```
Boolean operator >= ( const Any&, DT& );
```

The result of the operation is the data type is extracted into DT. If the Any variable does not contain at least one instance of the given data type (DT), then the operation returns FALSE. Otherwise, it returns TRUE and the value in DT may be used as normal.

BOUNDED STRINGS, BOOLEANS, CHARS, OCTETS, AND WCHAR

As mentioned in the Any type section, the IDL type of Boolean, char, octet, wchar, and bounded string do not have to map to distinct C++ types. A way must exist to distinguish between them, however, so the any type (which is type-safe) can use them. This is true for bounded and unbounded strings because they both map to char *. The solution comes from adding helper structures, and helper functions, to the Any class.

These structures, and overloaded functions, are as follows:

```
class Any {
struct from_boolean {
 from_boolean( Boolean b ) : val( b ) {}
 Boolean val;
};

struct from_octet {
 from_octet ( Octet o ) : val( o ) {}
 Octet val;
};

struct from_char {
 from_char( Char c ) : val( c ) {}
 Char val;
};

struct from_string {
        from_string( char *s, ULong b, Boolean nocopy = FALSE ) :
        val( s ), bound( b ) {}
 char *val;
 ULong bound;
};

struct to_boolean {
 to_boolean( Boolean &b ) : ref( b ) {}
 Boolean &ref;
};

struct to_octet {
 to_octet( Octet &o ) : ref( o ) {}
 Octet &ref;
};

struct to_string {
 to_string( char *&s, ULong b ) : val( c ), bound( b ) {}
 char *&val;
 ULong bound;
};

void operator <<= (from_boolean);
void operator <<= (from_char);
void operator <<= (from_octet);
void operator <<= (from_string);

Boolean operator >= (to_boolean) const;
Boolean operator >= (to_char) const;
```

```
Boolean operator >= (to_octet) const;
Boolean operator >= (to_string) const;
};
```

There are, of course, other methods to the Any class. However, the previously ones listed directly relate to how Booleans, chars, octets, and are differentiated from one another. To use an octet with an instance of Any, the basic syntax looks as follows:

```
Octect myOctet = 042;
Any myAny;
myAny <<= Any::from_octet( myOctet );
```

UNSAFE ANY

Three operations are not type-safe, as defined by the Any class. Their definitions are shown here:

```
void replace( TypeCode_ptr, void *value, Boolean release );
TypeCode_ptr type() const;
const void *value() const;
```

The first function, replace(...), is for types that (for whatever reason) are not possible to insert via the type-safe interface. The second function returns a pseudo-object reference to the TypeCode associated with the any instance. The third function returns a generic pointer to the information contained within the any instance. If no information is available, the value function returns null. Note, value's return value may only be type-casted to types the ORB recognizes. This means the usage of the value function will reduce the portability of the code.

EXCEPTIONS

The CORBA::UserException class is the base class for all IDL-mapped C++ exceptions. The UserException class, in turn, has CORBA::Exception as its parent class. For any given piece of code, all CORBA exceptions may be caught as follows:

```
try {
 // ... code that possibly generates an error goes here
}
catch( const UserException &ue ) {
 // ... code to handle user exception goes here
}
catch( const SystemException &ue ) {
 // ... code to handle system exceptions goes here
}
```

Of course, it is possible to catch a specific exception, leaving the rest to propagate up the call-stack hierarchy.

OPERATIONS AND ATTRIBUTES

IDL operations generate C++ methods given the name of the operation. For all attributes that may be read and changed, two methods of the same name as the attribute are generated. One for reading the contents of the attribute, the other for setting its contents. For attributes defined as read-only, only the method for reading the attribute is generated.

The following IDL code represents a simple IDL definition:

```
interface MyInterface {
  void someFunction();
  oneway void oneWayFunction();
  attribute long myLong;
};
```

The resulting C++ code to use an instance of MyInterface would look like:

```
MyInterface_var myInterface;
myInterface->someFunction();
myInterface->oneWayFunction();
Long result = myInterface->myLong();
myInterface->myLong( result * 2 );
```

PARAMETER PASSING

The mapping for passing parameters is meant to be quick and easy. The type *P* is used to represent primitive types, enumerations, and object references. For a given interface, MyInterface, the parameter is specified as MyInterface_ptr.

For read-only parameters, that is IN parameters, memory can be allocated in one of two ways. When given a variable-length type, the callee is responsible for allocating some — if not all — of the memory. When given a fixed-length type, like a structure, the caller should allocate memory. To avoid confusion, IDL maps the fixed-length data type, DT, to DT&. The variable-length data type, DT, becomes DT*&.

The out and inout arguments force the mapped function to release memory for memory used previously in variable-length data when a _var type is given. To help illustrate these concepts, examine the following IDL code:

```
struct MyStruct {
  string myString;
  float myFloat;
};

void someFunction( out MyStruct p );
```

Simple C++ code that makes use of the above definitions would look like:

```
MyStruct_var myStruct;
someFunction( myStruct );
// ... The myStruct variable is then free to have its members
 (myString and myFloat) used.

// ... The previous values stored in myStruct are freed, and new
 memory allocated to the structure
// members.
someFunction( myStruct );

MyStruct *structurePointer;
someFunction( structurePointer );
// ... The structurePointer variable is then free to have its
 members used.

// Since we're now using a pointer, the members are not necessarily
 freed. We must free it
// manually.
delete structurePointer;
someFunction( structurePointer );
```

As previously mentioned, all variable-length data must be explicitly released before it is reassigned or rewritten. This applies equally well to both out and inout argument types. One simple way to assure this happens is given in the two code snippets presented here. First the IDL code:

```
interface MyInterface;
void someFunction( inout string aString, intout MyInterface anObject
 );
```

The C++ code that ensures the arguments are properly handled would look like this:

```
void MyInterfaceimpl::someFunction( char *&aString, MyInterface_ptr
 &anObject ) {
 String_var tempString = aString;
 MyInterface_var tempObject = anObject;
 aString = // New data is allocated, and assigned, here
 anObject = // New reference is assigned here
}
```

The responsibilities for storage related to out and inout parameters are complex, but well-defined. The following numbered rules are made reference to in Table 1-2. Caller represents the code that calls upon a member method that has an out and/or inout parameter. Callee represents the code that is called upon.

1. Caller allocates all memory. The only exception is for the memory that is encapsulated and handled within the calling parameter. For inout parameters, the caller is responsible for giving an initial value. For out parameters, the caller allocates memory but it is up to the callee to set the memory to valid values.

2. Caller allocates memory for the object reference. The inout parameters must have an initial value, set by the caller. To change the initial value, the callee must use CORBA::release on the given value. If the caller wishes to continue to use the inout parameter value after the function call, the variable must first be duplicated. The caller must handle the release of memory allocated to the out parameters and object references. Any memory allocated internally by the object references must be released by the object itself.

3. Caller allocates a pointer, then passes the out parameter by reference to the callee. The callee points to a valid instance of the parameter's type. The callee returns a pointer similar to the one given. The caller is responsible for releasing the memory allocated to the returned pointer. The return value may not be null.

4. Caller must allocate the pointer and the memory the pointer points to in the case of inout string parameters (includes both char * and wchar * types). Caller must allocate memory for the strings using string_alloc(), or wstring_alloc(), respective to the type of the inout parameter. The caller must release the allocated memory with string_free() or wstring_free(). Callee may not return null for its arguments.

5. Assignment or modification of a sequence parameter or a parameter of type any, may result in the memory being freed before reallocation is requested. The behavior depends on the Boolean release parameter used in the creation of the types in question.

6. Caller must create a pointer to an array slice, with the same dimensions as the original array save for the first index declaration. Thus, the array slice is passed by reference to the callee. The callee is responsible for returning a pointer to either the same array, or one of similar type. The callee may not return a null pointer. The caller is responsible for releasing the memory used by the returned pointer. After the call has completed, the caller must first make a copy of the memory used by the returned pointer into a new location before the caller may modify the memory.

Table 1-2 lists, for each type of parameter, the rule that governs the behavior when it is an out, inout, or return value.

TABLE 1-2. MEMORY MANIPULATION RULES FOR CALLER AND CALLEE.

Argument Type	Inout Parameter	Out Parameter	Return Value
any	5	3	3
array, fixed	1	1	6
array, variable	1	6	6
boolean	1	1	1
char	1	1	1
double	1	1	1
enum	1	1	1
fixed	1	1	1
float	1	1	1
long	1	1	1
long double	1	1	1
long long	1	1	1
object reference pointer	2	2	2
octet	1	1	1
sequence	5	3	3
short	1	1	1
string	4	3	3
struct, fixed	1	1	1
struct, variable	1	3	3
union, fixed	1	1	1
union, variable	1	3	3
unsigned long	1	1	1
unsigned long long	1	1	1
unsigned short	1	1	1
wchar	1	1	1
wstring	4	3	3

PSEUDO OBJECTS

The interface definition for pseudo-objects is the same as that of regular objects, except for two details. First, their name has the prefix "pseudo." Second, because they are not classified as true IDL objects, they may reference other serverless objects normally forbidden by IDL. A serverless object does not inherit from CORBA::Object, does not get registered with an ORB, and does not necessarily have the same IDL rules for managing memory, as shown in Table 1-2.

The prefix "pseudo" does not mean the object is definitely serverless. The object in question has the freedom to be implemented as a regular CORBA object, in addition to being implemented serverless. In other words, the object will either adhere to the IDL previous rules defined or will conform to the rules that follow.

Serverless Mapping

In general, pseudo interfaces become implemented like regular interfaces. This section covers the specific cases where the implementations may differ.

The first thing to note is, because serverless objects do not inherit from CORBA::Object, the Object::create_request method may not be available. Within the CORBA namespace, two functions have been overloaded for serverless objects:

```
void release( ServerlessObject_ptr );
Boolean is_nil( ServerlessObject_ptr );
```

The memory management rules may not abide by the rules stated above due to some serverless objects merely being containers for other serverless objects. Thus, it would not be intuitive for the callers to be forced into freeing the memory that is returned by access methods of such container types. Other scenarios are possible.

Another general rule that governs the behavior of pseudo-objects is that for a given serverless object, ServerlessObject_ptr, its definition may be a simple one to one mapping of ServerlessObject *. Included in each C++ class that represents a pseudo-object is the following two static member methods:

```
static ServerlessObject_ptr _duplicate( ServerlessObject_ptr p );
static ServerlessObject_ptr _nil();
```

ENVIRONMENT

Exception information can be made available by request operations to the Environment. The Environment class is made available for handling exceptions when real exceptions are not possible or must be avoided. The Environment has two main member methods used to set and get information about the current exception.

Via the get operator, a pointer to the current exception is returned. It is up to the Environment to free memory associated with that pointer. The exception is cleared by a call to the Environment's clear() method. This is the same as calling the

Environment's set method with a null exception parameter. The IDL syntax for the Environment is shown here:

```
pseudo interface Environment {
 attribute exception exception;
 void clear();
};
```

Because the attribute is not read-only, the resulting C++ code has overloaded methods for getting and setting the exception's value. The generated code would be similar to the following:

```
class Environment {
 public:
       void exception( Exception * );
       Exception *exception() const;
       void clear();
};
```

The memory passed into the exception(Exception *) is maintained by the Environment. The return value of the Exception *exception() method is kept secure by the Environment; the caller should make no attempt to release it.

NAMEDVALUE PAIR
The NamedValue class encapsulates a name with its associated value. It is used to detail method parameters and return values. The class includes a name, a value, and a flag. The flag may have values of ARG_IN, ARG_OUT, and ARG_INOUT. Consider the following interface specification:

```
pseudo interface NamedValue {
 readonly attribute Identifier name;
 readonly attribute any value;
 readonly attribute Flags flags;
};
```

The corresponding C++ code would look similar to:

```
class NamedValue {
 public:
 const char *name() const;
       Any *value() const;
Flags flags() const;
};
```

The memory associated with the name() and value() methods belongs to the NamedValue instance; the caller should not try to release the memory.

NAMEDVALUE LIST
This class encapsulates a list of NamedValue classes. Its IDL definition is as follows:

```
pseudo interface NVList {
  readonly attribute unsigned long count;

  NamedValue add( in Flags flags );
  NamedValue add_item( in Identifier item_name, in Flags flags );
  NamedValue add_value(      in Identifier item_name,
                        in any value,
                        in Flags flags );
  NamedValue item( in unsigned long index ) raises (Bounds);
  void remove( in unsigned long index ) raises (Bounds);
};
```

In C++, the generated code would look like:

```
class NVList {
  public:
        ULong count() const;
        NamedValue_ptr add( Flags );
        NamedValue_ptr add_item( const char *, Flags );
        NamedValue_ptr add_item(    const char *,
const Any&,
Flags );
        NamedValue_ptr item( ULong );
        NamedValue_ptr add_item_consume( char *, Flags );
        NamedValue_ptr add_value_consume( char *, Any *, Flags );
        Status remove( ULong );
};
```

The rules for handling memory with the NVList are given here:

◆ The return value from the add_XYZ methods is kept alive by the NVList; the caller should not attempt to free the associated memory.

◆ The char * and Any * parameters are no longer valid after calling either add_item_consume, or add_value_consume. To change the value attribute of a NamedValue, the caller should use the corresponding value method.

◆ The remove method uses CORBA::release on the NamedValue that gets removed.

CONTEXTS
Contexts give additional, but optional, information about a method invocation. The IDL syntax for a Context is given in the following:

```
pseudo interface Context {
  readonly attribute Identifier context_name;
```

```
readonly attribute context parent;

Status create_child( in Identifier child_ctx_name, out Context
child_ctx );

Status set_one_value( in Identifier propname, in any propvalue );
Status set_values( in NVList values );
Status delete_values( in Identifier propname );
Status get_values(  in Identifier start_scope,
in Flags op_flags,
in Identifier pattern,
out NVList values );
};
```

Once translated, the C++ code for the previous IDL syntax becomes:

```
class Context {
 public:
      const char *context_name() const;
      Context_ptr parent() const;

      Status create_child( const char *, Context_ptr& );
      Status set_one_value( const char *, const Any& );
      Status set_values( NVList_ptr );
      Status delete_values( const char * );
      Status get_values( const char *, Flags, const char *,
 NVList_ptr& );
};
```

The memory returned by calls to context_name() and parent() are controlled by the Context instance; callers should not attempt to release their memory.

REQUEST

The support for DII is given chiefly by the Request object. To perform a new request on a given object, the request may be created using the simple "request creation" method, as defined by the Object class:

```
Request_ptr Object::_request( Identifier operation );
```

The contexts, and their parameters, can be put in after creation by using the accessor methods for the corresponding attributes. Consider the following sample C++ code:

```
Request_ptr request = someObject->_request( "someFunction" );
*(request->arguments()->add( ARG_IN )->value()) <<= someArgument;

// ... code before invocation

request->invoke();
```

```
// Verify that no exception was thrown.
if( request->env()->exception() == NULL )
 *(request->return_value()) >= someResult;
```

It is easier, however to use the predefined helper methods. The previous syntax may be rewritten as:

```
Request_ptr request = someObject->_request( "someFunction" );
reqest->add_in_arg() <<= someArgument;

// ... code before invocation

request->invoke();

// Verify that no exception was thrown.
if( request->env()->exception() == NULL )
 *(request->return_value()) >= someResult;
```

Finally, another way exists that requests can be created. A request can be constructed by using either of the _create_request methods found in CORBA's Object class. The following C++ code gives its prototype:

```
Status Object::_create_request(    Context_ptr ctx,
                   const char *operation,
                   NVList_ptr arg_list,
                   NamedValue_ptr result,
                   Request_ptr &request,
                   Flags req_flags );

Status Object::_create_request(    Context_ptr ctx,
                   const char *operation,
                   NVList_ptr arg_list,
                   NamedValue_ptr result,
                   ExceptionList_ptr,
                   ContextList_ptr,
                   Request_ptr &request,
                   Flags req_flags );
```

The C++ definitions of Request, ContextList, and ExceptionList are as follows:

```
class ExceptionList {
 public:
      ULong count();
      void add( TypeCode_ptr tc );
      void add_consume( TypeCode_ptr tc );
      TypeCode_ptr item( ULong index );
      Status remove( ULong index );
};

class ContextList {
 public:
```

```
        ULong count();
        void add( const char *ctxt );
        void add_consume( char *ctxt );
        const char *item( ULong index );
        Status remove( ULong index );
};

class Request {
 public:
        Object_ptr target() const;
        const char *operation() const;
        NVList_ptr arguments();
        NamedValue_ptr result();
        Environment_ptr env();
        ExceptionList_ptr exceptions();
        ContextList_ptr contexts();

        void ctx( Context_ptr );
        Context_ptr ctx() const;

        Any &add_in_arg();
        Any &add_in_arg( const char * );
        Any &add_inout_arg();
        Any &add_inout_arg( const char * );
        Any &add_out_arg();
        Any &add_out_arg( const char * );
        void set_return_type( TypeCode_ptr tc );
        Any &return_value();

        Status invoke();
        Status send_oneway();
        Status send_deferred();
        Status get_response();
        Boolean poll_response();
};
```

The way memory is managed for each of the previous classes is listed here:

◆ Request: Return values from target, operation, arguments, result, env, exceptions, contexts, and ctx are controlled by the particular instance of Request; callers should not release the associated memory.

◆ ExceptionList: Callers should not use the TypeCode_ptr after a call to add_consume. The memory returned from a call to the item method should not be released by the caller.

◆ ContextList: Callers should not use the char * parameter after a call to add_consume. The memory returned from a call to the item method should not be released by the caller.

Special Considerations:

This section describes parts of the specification that do not directly deal with syntactical structure of either IDL or C++, but should be taken into consideration on their own merit.

VALUE ADDED EXTENSIONS

The specification for the C++ stubs and skeletons as they relate to ORB interfaces, is not cast in stone. Vendors are free to add their own extensions to the specification presented here. It is then up to the software developers to weigh the pros and cons of using the proprietary extensions, or stay "pure" (*pure* meaning you only develop code that relies on the standards set by the OMG),

NAME COLLISIONS

Naming conflicts between C++ and IDL are handled simply. Generally put, IDL names and identifiers are generated directly into C++ source code. If the code generated has a naming collision, that name will have an underscore (_) placed as a prefix.

The IDL/Java Language Specification Mapping

MAPPING MODULE NAMES

First, and perhaps most important, is how to deal with name space. In all cases, an IDL module is given the same name of the corresponding Java package.

MAPPING BASIC TYPES

The next important part of IDL consists of how Java's basic types are mapped to the interface definition language. Table 1-3 illustrates the IDL type and its corresponding Java type.

TABLE 1–3. BASIC TYPE MAPPING FROM IDL TO JAVA.

IDL Type	Java Type	Exceptions
boolean	boolean	
char	char	CORBA:DATA_CONVERSION
double	double	

(Continued)

TABLE 1–3. BASIC TYPE MAPPING FROM IDL TO JAVA. *(Continued)*

IDL Type	Java Type	Exceptions
float	float	
long	int	
long long	long	
octet	byte	
short	short	
string	java.lang.String	CORBA::DATA_CONVERSION
		CORBA::MARSHALL
unsigned long	int	
unsigned long long	long	
unsigned short	short	
wchar	char	
wstring	java.lang.String	CORBA::MARSHALL

As you can see, the mappings are quite straightforward, but note two important points: First, because Java's Strings aren't a basic type, but rather true Objects, be aware they must be marshalled. Inherently, this means instances of java.lang.String are prone to potential error conditions that true basic types are not susceptible to (upon receiving any such potential error, a CORBA::MARSHALL exception will be thrown). Second, because IDL chars are 16-bit, compared to Java's 32-bit characters, if a character being marshalled happens to be out of range for a given character set, the CORBA::DATA_CONVERSION exception will be thrown. Consequently, because a String in Java consists of chars, it follows that a DATA_CONVERSION exception applies equally well to Java's Strings as it does Java's basic character type.

TABLE 1–4. FUTURE TYPE MAPPINGS FOR IDL TO JAVA.

IDL Type	Java Type	Exceptions
fixed	java.math.BigDecimal	CORBA::DATA_CONVERSION
long double	undefined	

Although not supported in Java's 1.0.2 specification, the long double and fixed IDL types may make a showing in future versions of Java. For all practical purposes, they remain unsupported.

NULL
The null keyword represents objects that do not reference any active portion of memory. Arrays and Strings in IDL should have their Java-based counterpart zeroed out, to indicate they are no longer valid. For an Array, this means setting all of its elements to null; for a String, it means assigning it to the empty string (""). Do not set the reference to an Array to null, if it is to be marshalled across the network.

BOOLEANS
In IDL, a one to one correlation exists between TRUE and Java's true keyword. Similarly, IDL has FALSE equivalent to Java's false.

CHARACTERS
As mentioned, Java has 16-bit characters to conform to the Unicode standard. When you use a Java-based CORBA implementation, you should assume CORBA will perform range checking and throw an exception (CORBA::DATA_CONVERSION) if the character is not within a valid character set.

To void the overhead of range checking, IDL has wchar. You can think of wchar as a one-to-one mapping on Java's char. No range checking is performed.

OCTETS
An octet in IDL is an 8-bit member, directly corresponding to Java's basic type of byte.

STRINGS
A string in IDL, as the previous table shows, maps onto Java's java.lang.String object. Both range checking and bounds checking are done on the string as the string is marshalled. If a character of the string is not within the proper range, then a CORBA::DATA_CONVERSION exception is thrown. If the bounds of the string have been violated, then a CORBA::MARSHAL exception is thrown.

The main difference between a string in IDL and a wstring in IDL is when a java.lang.String becomes a wstring, there is no range checking required. Thus, the only exception you should be ready to catch is the CORBA::MARSHAL exception.

INTEGERS AND FLOATS
The conversions for the remaining data types are shown in Table 1-1.

FUTURE TYPE MAPPINGS
Table 1-2 shows two IDL types that have yet to be cast in stone. Although no definition for the long double type exists, a corresponding type may be added to Java

in one of three ways. The first is as a basic type. The second is as a new package in the java.math.* hierarchy. The third is java.math.BigFloat. As the IDL specification stands to date, the fixed point type maps onto Java's java.math.BigDecimal. At press time, you probably should not consider using this type, if you have other options to choose.

CONSTANTS

Two cases exist for declarations of constants; they vary depending on their scope. Constants declared within an IDL interface map onto public final static variables for the corresponding Java interface.

Constants not declared within an IDL interface map onto a public interface. Internal to that public interface is a variable named "value," whose value happens to be that of the declared IDL constant. The name of the Java-based public interface becomes the name of the declared IDL constant. Handling constant declarations this way is fine because the extra classes are only required at compile time. Intelligent compilers should be able to inline the classes during runtime execution.

To ensure clarity, take the following IDL constant definition:

```
module MyExample {
  const long myLongConst = -456;
};
```

The generated Java code would look like:

```
package MyExample;
public interface myLongConst {
  public final static int value = (int)(-456L);
}
```

ENUMERATIONS

The enum type in IDL is transformed into a Java final class, which is then given the same name as the enum's declared name. That Java class contains public final static integer variables ranging from the start of the enumeration to the end of the enumeration. Additionally, the Java class contains public final static variables declared as the class type itself. These variables are then instantiated using the values of the aforementioned integer variables as parameters. This slight obscurity allows for strong type checking, as well as providing an easy facility for using Java-based enumerations in switch statements.

To help clarify, if the IDL enumeration type definition looked like:

```
enum MyEnum { y, z };
```

Then the corresponding Java class would look similar to:

```
public final class MyEnum {
  public final static int _y = 0;
  public final static MyEnum y = new MyEnum( _y );
```

```
public final static int _z = 1;
public final static MyEnum z = new MyEnum( _z );

public int value() { ... }
public static MyEnum from_int( int value ) { ... }

private MyEnum( int value ) { ... }
}
```

STRUCTURES

An IDL structure maps to a Java class whose member variables are named correspondingly. That Java class is created with two constructors. The first is an empty constructor to allow the values of the members variables to be assigned after creating the structure. The second constructor allows for all fields of the class to be assigned upon creation. The lack of accessor methods in the generated Java code is to help reduce code size, code complexity, while increasing runtime execution speed.

To help clarify, if the IDL structure type definition looked like:

```
struct MyStruct {
 long myLong;
 string myString;
};
```

Then the corresponding Java class would look similar to:

```
public final class MyStruct {
 public int myLong;
 public String myString;

 public MyStruct() { }
 public MyStruct( int aLong1, String aString1 ) { ... }
}
```

UNIONS

Like enumerations and structures, the name of an IDL union maps directly to the name of a corresponding Java class. Another way to perform unions would have been to use an abstract superclass whose subclasses represent the separate cases. This model was abandoned due to the number of typecasts and, consequently, the number of individual classes that would have to be generated. Because Java has no concept of unions, it was decided to emulate unions with Java classes that have the following properties:

- ◆ A default constructor
- ◆ Accessor method for the discriminator, appropriately named **discriminator()**

- ◆ One accessor method for each branch
- ◆ One modifier method for branch
- ◆ One modifier method for every branch that has two case labels, or more
- ◆ One default modifier, if needed

The additional complexities of unions are resolved in Java by the rules that follow:

1. If there happens to be a naming conflict, the same rule of prefixing the conflicting name with an underscore is applied.

2. If the expected branch has not been set, the exception CORBA::BAD_OPERATION will be thrown by a call to any of the accessor methods.

3. If a branch has more than one case label, the modifier for that branch that is simpler sets the discriminate to the value of the first-case label. Also, another modifier method for that branch is created. This extra modifier takes an explicit discriminator parameter to help differentiate.

4. If the branch happens to be the default case label, the modifier method sets the discriminate to a value that is unique among all the other case labels.

5. If the set of case labels includes all possible values for the discriminate, it is up to the IDL to Java compiler to issue an error message and not produce erroneous Java code.

6. Finally, **default()** (or **_default()** in the event of a name clash) is the name of the default modifier when a default case label is unspecified and all possible discriminate values are not used.

To help clarify, if the IDL union type definition looked like:

```
union MyUnion switch( MyEnum ) {
  case first: long winner;
  case second: short placement;
  case third:
  case fourth: octet showing;
  default: boolean finished;
};
```

Then the corresponding Java class would look similar to:

```
public final class MyUnion {
  public MyUnion() { ... }

  public <switch-type> discriminator() { ... }
```

```
public int winner() { ... }
public void winner( int value ) { ... }

public short placement() { ... }
public void placement( short value ) { ... }

public byte showing() { ... }
public void showing( byte value ) { ... }
public void showing( int discriminator, byte value ) { ... }

public boolean finished() { ... }
public void finished( boolean value ) { ... }
}
```

SEQUENCES

An IDL sequence is mapped to a Java array of the same name. In each place the type of the sequence is needed (like an array of integers), an array of the mapped type is used. A bounds check is not performed until the bounded sequence is marshalled. If the array bounds have been exceeded, a CORBA::MARSHAL exception is thrown.

ARRAYS

The mapping for IDL arrays into Java happen in the same fashion as the IDL bounded sequence. Like sequences, the array bounds access is checked at the time of marshalling. It should come as no surprise that a CORBA::MARSHAL exception is thrown if the array bounds have been breached. The array's length is visible to Java by using an IDL constant. That constant is then mapped according to the rules for generating Java constants from IDL.

To help clarify, if the IDL array type definition was:

```
const long myArrayBound = 42;
typedef long MyArray[ myArrayBound ];
```

Then the corresponding Java class would look similar to:

```
public final class MyArrayHolder implements
 org.omg.CORBA.portable.Streamable {
public int[] value;

public MyArrayHolder() { ... }
public MyArrayHolder( int[] initial ) { ... }

public void _read( org.omg.CORBA.portable.InputStream i ) { ... }
public void _write( org.omg.CORBA.portable.OutputStream o ) { ... }
public void org.omg.CORBA.TypeCode _type() { ... }
}
```

INTERFACES

Unsurprisingly, a Java interface is given the same name as its IDL counter-part. A helper class is created as well. Its name is derived from the name of the interface plus the suffix "Helper."

The Java interface extends the org.omg.CORBA.Object interface. Inside the Java interface is contained the signatures of each operation. All the methods, then, can be invoked on any object that is a reference to the aforementioned Java interface.

The Helper class has a single goal in life: To hold a static narrow method. The static narrow method permits an org.omg.CORBA.Object to narrow its object reference to a more specific type (be it a class, or interface). If a more specific type cannot be found (that is, the org.omg.CORBA.Object instance cannot be narrowed via the Helper class), then a CORBA::BAD_PARAM exception is thrown.

Attributes (that is, instance variables) are get mapped to a pair of accessor and modifier methods. Following classic C++ and Smalltalk conventions, the name of the accessor and modifier methods overload the name of the instance variable they represent. The typical Java convention is to prefix instance variable accessors and modifiers with get and set, respectively. However, this would usually lead into "ugly" looking method names, due to indeterminable capitalization. Finally, it should be noted that read-only attributes have no associated modifier method.

The syntax of an IDL interface might look as follows:

```
module InterfaceModule {
  interface MyInterface {
      attribute long myValue;
      readonly attribute long myReadOnlyValue;
      long interfaceMethod( in long value ) raises( anException );
  };
};
```

Assumeing such an IDL interface was used, the generated Java code would look like:

```
package InterfaceModule;
public interface MyInterface extends org.omg.CORBA.Object {
  int myValue();
  void myValue( int i );
  int myReadOnlyValue();
  int interfaceMethod( int value ) throws
  InterfaceModule.anException;
}

public class MyInterfaceHelper {
  ... // Other interface-related code

  public static MyInterface narrow( org.omg.CORBA.Object obj ) { ...
  }
}
```

PARAMETER PASSING

IDL defines three ways to pass parameters. The first, as previously hinted, are IN parameters. The second are OUT parameters. The third are INOUT parameters. IN parameters, being the simplest, are directly equivalent to Java's call-by-value parameters. That is, after returning from the method call, IN parameters are guaranteed to have the value they had before the method call. OUT parameters are call-by-result parameters. INOUT parameters are call-by-result parameters.

The IDL syntax is shown as follows:

```
module MyModule {
  interface MyInterface {
      long myMethod(in long inValue,
out long outValue,
inout long inoutValue )
  };
};
```

The resulting Java code would look like:

```
package MyModule;
public interface MyInterface {
  int myMethod(      int inValue,
IntHolder outValue,
IntHolder inoutValue );
}
```

For the OUT and INOUT parameters, proper holder classes must be created. This is because Java can only pass parameters by value (even if a parameter is an object reference, the reference's value does not change for the duration of the method call).

EXCEPTIONS

Exceptions in IDL are mapped like structures. In effect, they map to a class that has instance variables and constructors that stem from Java's exception classes. For example, the CORBA system exceptions (such as CORBA::MARSHALL) inherit, for all intents and purposes, from java.lang.RuntimeException. Similarly, user-defined exceptions inherit (indirectly) from java.lang.Exception.

SYSTEM EXCEPTIONS

The exception org.omg.CORBA.SystemException is the base from which all CORBA System Exceptions are derived. It should be noted that each derived exception is declared as a final class. Furthermore, the base class has no public constructor, thereby prohibiting it from being instantiated. Table 1-5 lists the standard IDL exceptions, as well as their Java-based counter-parts.

TABLE 1-5. SYSTEM EXCEPTION MAPPINGS.

IDL Exception	Java Class
CORBA::BAD_CONTEXT	org.omg.CORBA.BAD_CONTEXT
CORBA::BAD_INV_ORDER	org.omg.CORBA.BAD_INV_ORDER
CORBA::BAD_OPERATION	org.omg.CORBA.BAD_OPERATION
CORBA::BAD_PARAM	org.omg.CORBA.BAD_PARAM
CORBA::BAD_TYPECODE	org.omg.CORBA.BAD_TYPECODE
CORBA::COMM_FAILURE	org.omg.CORBA.COMM_FAILURE
CORBA::DATA_CONVERSION	org.omg.CORBA.DATA_CONVERSION
CORBA::FREE_MEM	org.omg.CORBA.FREE_MEM
CORBA::IMP_LIMIT	org.omg.CORBA.IMP_LIMIT
CORBA::INITIALIZE	org.omg.CORBA.INITIALIZE
CORBA::INTERNAL	org.omg.CORBA.INTERNAL
CORBA::INTF_REPOS	org.omg.CORBA.INTF_REPOS
CORBA::INVALIDTRANSACTION	org.omg.CORBA.INVALIDTRANSACTION
CORBA::INV_IDENT	org.omg.CORBA.INV_IDENT
CORBA::INV_FLAG	org.omg.CORBA.INV_FLAG
CORBA::INV_OBJREF	org.omg.CORBA.INV_OBJREF
CORBA::MARSHALL	org.omg.CORBA.MARSHALL
CORBA::NO_IMPLEMENT	org.omg.CORBA.NO_IMPLEMENT
CORBA::NO_MEMORY	org.omg.CORBA.NO_MEMORY
CORBA::NO_PERMISSION	org.omg.CORBA.NO_PERMISSION
CORBA::NO_RESOURCES	org.omg.CORBA.NO_RESOURCES
CORBA::NO_RESPONSE	org.omg.CORBA.NO_RESPONSE
CORBA::OBJ_ADAPTER	org.omg.CORBA.OBJ_ADAPTER
CORBA::OBJECT_DOES_NOT_EXIST	org.omg.CORBA.OBJECT_DOES_NOT_EXIST
CORBA::PERSIST_STORE	org.omg.CORBA.PERSIST_STORE

(Continued)

TABLE 1-5. SYSTEM EXCEPTION MAPPINGS. *(Continued)*

IDL Exception	Java Class
CORBA::TRANSACTIONREQUIRED	org.omg.CORBA.TRANSACTIONREQUIRED
CORBA::TRANSACTIONROLLEDBACK	org.omg.CORBA.TRANSACTIONROLLEDBACK
CORBA::TRANSIENT	org.omg.CORBA.TRANSIENT
CORBA::UNKNOWN	org.omg.CORBA.UNKNOWN

Each exception includes at least three components. A literal string, a minor code, and a completion code. The default constructor for the exceptions sets the minor code to zero, has the completion code set to COMPLETE_NO, and uses the empty string. A second constructor allows the exception to be created using three arguments to set the three components. Last, a third constructor makes it possible to create one of the exceptions with a string to represent the reason for the exception being thrown.

ANY TYPE

A CORBA class org.omg.CORBA.Any is used to map to the Any type as defined by IDL. The Any class has the capability to insert and extract instances of predefined types. A CORBA::BAD_OPERATION is thrown if the extract operations contain a mismatched type. To clarify, examine the following class definition:

```
package org.omg.CORBA;
public abstract class Any {
  public abstract org.omg.CORBA.TypeCode type();
  public abstract void type( org.omg.CORBA.TypeCode t );

  public abstract short extract_short() throws
  org.omg.CORBA.BAD_OPERATION;
  public abstract void insert_short( short s );

  public abstract int extract_long() throws
  org.omg.CORBA.BAD_OPERATION;
  public abstract void insert_long( int i );

  public abstract long extract_longlong() throws
  org.omg.CORBA.BAD_OPERATION;
  public abstract void insert_longlong ( long l );

  public abstract short extract_ushort() throws
  org.omg.CORBA.BAD_OPERATION;
  public abstract void insert_ushort( short s );
```

```
public abstract int extract_ulong() throws
org.omg.CORBA.BAD_OPERATION;
public abstract void insert_ulong( int i );

public abstract long extract_ulonglong() throws
org.omg.CORBA.BAD_OPERATION;
public abstract void insert_ ulonglong ( long l );

public abstract float extract_float() throws
org.omg.CORBA.BAD_OPERATION;
public abstract void insert_float( float f );

public abstract double extract_double() throws
org.omg.CORBA.BAD_OPERATION;
public abstract void insert_double( double d );

public abstract boolean extract_boolean() throws
org.omg.CORBA.BAD_OPERATION;
public abstract void insert_boolean( boolean b );

public abstract char extract_char() throws
org.omg.CORBA.BAD_OPERATION;
public abstract void insert_char( char c ) throws
org.omg.CORBA.DATA_CONVERSION;

public abstract char extract_wchar() throws
org.omg.CORBA.BAD_OPERATION;
public abstract void insert_wchar( char c );

public abstract byte extract_octet() throws
org.omg.CORBA.BAD_OPERATION;
public abstract void insert_octet( byte b );

public abstract org.omg.CORBA.Any extract_any()
throws org.omg.CORBA.BAD_OPERATION;
public abstract void insert_any( org.omg.CORBA.Any a );

public abstract org.omg.CORBA.Object extract_Object()
throws org.omg.CORBA.BAD_OPERATION;
public abstract void insert_Object( org.omg.CORBA.Object o );

// Throws the marshal exception when the typecode is inconsistent
with the value
public abstract void insert_Object(
org.omg.CORBA.Object o,
org.omg.CORBA.TypeCode t ) throws org.omg.CORBA.MARSHALL;

public abstract String extract_string() throws
org.omg.CORBA.BAD_OPERATION;
public abstract void insert_string( String s )
throws org.omg.CORBA.DATA_CONVERSION, org.omg.CORBA.MARSHALL;
```

```
public abstract String extract_wstring() throws
org.omg.CORBA.BAD_OPERATION;
public abstract void insert_wstring( String s ) throws
org.omg.CORBA.MARSHALL;
}
```

Although not shown, the previous class also has methods for obtaining equality, as well as ways to stream arbitrary data. This class is important because there are predefined types that simply do not map to any classes already present in the Java language. The streaming methods (not shown) are not meant for programmers that will be using CORBA in Java. Instead, they are present to support portable interfaces for Stub and Skeleton ORBs.

NESTED TYPES

In IDL, type declarations can be made within interfaces. Java, however, does not permit classes to be defined within interfaces (although classes, called Inner classes, can be declared within other classes). The basic reason behind types embedded within interfaces is scope. A type, or class, declared within an interface is visible only to that interface. Thus, a work-around to this problem is done by having the word *Package* appended to the name of the IDL type.

If the IDL code looked like:

```
module MyExample {
  interface MyInterface {
       exception myException { };
  };
};
```

The resulting Java code would look like:

```
package MyExample.MyInterfacePackage;
public final class myException extends org.omg.CORBA.UserException {
  ... }
```

TYPEDEFS

Java lacks a construct for issuing arbitrary type definitions. In IDL, two kinds of types exist: simple types and complex types. Those IDL types that directly correspond to any of Java's basic types (such as char, int, long, byte, and so forth) are mapped into those types. This means any typedefs that are merely type declarations for simple types are translated to the corresponding basic type, for all occurrences of that particular TypeDef. Complex TypeDefs are broken down until a simple type, or a user-defined type, is found.

Pseudo Objects

Pseudo objects usually take the form of processes, or threads, on the client and/or the server. Standard IDL pseudo-objects either map to a given Java language construct or become defined as a pseudo-interface. The use of a pseudo-interface typically results with a Java construct adhering to the following rules:

- The construct is not a CORBA object

- The construct has no Helper classes

- The construct has no Holder classes

- The construct maps to a public abstract class, that does not inherit any other class or interface

- The construct has no representation in the Interface Repository

You should note that a particular definition for a given section of the Pseudo-Interface Definition Language (PIDL) might override the aforementioned rules. All pseudo-interfaces, then, are mapped to the org.omg.CORBA package.

PIDL EXCEPTIONS

A few standard CORBA PIDL exceptions exist. These exceptions include BadKind, Bounds, and InvalidName. As previously noted, they do not have Helper or Holder classes and they are not included in the Interface Repository. Programmers can use them as regular user exceptions because they inherit from org.omg.CORBA.-UserException.

ENVIRONMENT

Exception information can be made available by request operations to the Environment. Its class definition looks as follows:

```
package org.omg.CORBA;
public abstract class Environment {
  void exception( java.lang.Exception except );
  java.lang.Exception exception();
  void clear();
}
```

NAMEDVALUE PAIR

The NamedValue class encapsulates a name with its associated value. It is used to detail method parameters and return values. The class includes a name, a value, and a flag. These are defined in the following IDL code:

```
typedef unsigned long Flags;
typedef string Identifier;
const Flags ARG_IN = 1;
const Flags ARG_OUT = 2;
const Flags ARG_INOUT = 3;
const Flags CTX_RESTRICT_SCOPE = 15;
```

```
pseudo interface NamedValue {
  readonly attribute Identifier name;
  readonly attribute any value;
  readonly attribute Flags flags;
};
```

The corresponding Java code would look similar to:

```
package org.omg.CORBA;
public interface ARG_IN {
  public final static int value = 1;
}

public interface ARG_OUT {
  public final static int value = 2;
}

public interface ARG_INOUT {
  public final static int value = 3;
}

public interface CTX_RESTRICT_SCOPE {
  public final static int value = 15;
}

public abstract class NamedValue {
  public abstract String name();
  public abstract org.omg.CORBA.Any value();
  public abstract int flags();
}
```

NAMEDVALUE LIST

This class encapsulates a list of NamedValue classes. Its IDL definition is as follows:

```
pseudo interface NVList {
  readonly attribute unsigned long count;

  NamedValue add( in Flags flags );
  NamedValue add_item( in Identifier item_name, in Flags flags );
  NamedValue add_value(      in Identifier item_name,
                      in any value,
                      in Flags flags );
  NamedValue item( in unsigned long index ) raises (CORBA::Bounds);
  void remove( in unsigned long index ) raises (CORBA::Bounds);
};
```

Obtaining an item, using the item(...) method, will cause a Bounds exception to be thrown if the given index is less than 0 or greater than the number of items in the NVList. The remove(...) method also throws a Bounds exception if the index is invalid. The other methods add a NamedValue instance to the list, given certain pieces of information (as identified by the parameters). In Java, the generated code would look like:

```
package org.omg.CORBA;
public abstract class NVList {
  public abstract int count();
  public abstract NamedValue add( int flags );
  public abstract NamedValue add_item( String item_name, int flags );
  public abstract NamedValue add_item(     String item_name,
org.omg.CORBA.Any value,
int flags );
  public abstract NamedValue item( int index ) throws
  org.omg.CORBA.Bounds;
  public abstract void remove( int index ) throws
  org.omg.CORBA.Bounds;
}
```

You should note the typedef *Identifier* has been broken down into its primary *String* component.

EXCEPTION LISTS

These abstract classes are used to encapsulate the possible exceptions that can be thrown by IDL operations. In essence, they keep a current list of IDL TypeCodes:

```
pseudo interface ExceptionList {
  readonly attribute unsigned long count;
  void add( in TypeCode exc );
  TypeCode item( in unsigned long index ) raises (CORBA::Bounds);
  void remove( in unsigned long index ) raises (CORBA:Bounds);
};
```

The Java code produced from the previous IDL code would look like:

```
package org.omg.CORBA;
public abstract class ExceptionList {
  public abstract int count();
  public abstract void add( TypeCode exc );
  public abstract TypeCode item( int index ) throws
  org.omg.CORBA.Bounds;
  public abstract void remove( int index ) throws
  org.omg.CORBA.Bounds;
}
```

CONTEXTS

Contexts are used to specify how context strings must be resolved before they are transmitted with the request invocation. The IDL syntax for a Context is given in the following:

```
pseudo interface Context {
  readonly attribute Identifier context_name;
```

```
readonly attribute Context parent;
Context create_child( in Identifier child_ctx_name );
void set_one_value( in Identifier propname, in any propvalue );
void set_values( in NVList values );
void delete_values( in Identifier propname );
NVList get_values( in Identifier scope_type, in Flags op_flags, in
Identifier pattern );
};
```

Once translated, the Java code for the previous IDL syntax becomes:

```
package org.omg.CORBA;

public abstract class Context {
  public abstract String context_name();
  public abstract Context parent();
  public abstract Context create_child( String child_ctx_name );
  public abstract void set_one_value( String propname,
  org.omg.CORBA.Any propvalue );
  public abstract void set_values( NVList values );
  public abstract void delete_values( String propname );
  public abstract NVList get_values( String scope_type, int op_flags,
  String pattern );
}
```

CONTEXT LISTS

Context lists are analogous to NamedValue lists. That is, they contain an arbitrary number of Contexts. The IDL code for context lists is similar to that for NamedValue lists:

```
pseudo interface ContextList {
  readonly attribute unsigned long count;
  void add( in string context );
  string item( in unsigned long index ) raises (CORBA::Bounds);
  void remove( in unsigned long index ) raises (CORBA::Bounds);
};
```

The Java code for the previous pseudo interface is translated as:

```
package org.omg.CORBA;

public abstract class ContextList {
  public abstract int count();
  public abstract void add( String context );
  public abstract String item( int index ) throws
  org.omg.CORBA.Bounds;
  public abstract void remove( int index ) throws
  org.omg.CORBA.Bounds;
}
```

Special Considerations:

This section describes parts of the specification that do not directly deal with syntactical structure of either IDL or Java, but should be taken into consideration on their own merit.

JAVA VERSION

The mapping described in this reference is based on the JDK 1.0.2 specification. In the future, the OMG may wish to flesh out the mapping further to provide developers with a richer IDL implementation.

VALUE ADDED EXTENSIONS

The specification for the Java stubs and skeletons as they relate to ORB interfaces are not cast in stone. Vendors are free to add their own extensions to the specification presented here. It is then up to the software developers to weigh the pros and cons of using the proprietary extensions, or stay "pure" (*pure* meaning you only develop code that relies on the standards set by the OMG).

NAME COLLISIONS

Naming conflicts between Java and IDL are handled simply. Generally put, IDL names and identifiers are generated directly into Java source code. If the code generated has a naming collision, that name will have an underscore (_) placed as a prefix.

RESERVED NAMES

The actual mapping from IDL to Java requires the reservation of certain names, used by CORBA's internal purposes. These cover:

*type*Helper, where *type* is a user-defined type in IDL

*type*Holder, where *type* is a predefined type in IDL

*basicJavaType*Holder, where *basicJavaType* is one of Java's primitive types

*interface*Package, where *interface* is a name of an interface in IDL

Java's keywords, including:

abstract	default	private	throw
if	boolean	implements	throws
transient	public	double	void
protected	do	break	import
byte	instanceof	return	try
else	case	extends	int
short	catch	interface	volatile

long	static	super	while
final	char	finally	switch
synchronized	float	class	native
this	const	new	for
package	continue	goto	

Using any of the mentioned names for a user-defined IDL type, or IDL interface, will cause the mapped Java name to have an underscore prefix. This assumes the IDL type, or interface, is a legal IDL name.

DEFINING TRANSIENT OBJECTS

There are two portions to a transient object. The first is called the Servant Base Class. Its role is to map all the IDL interfaces into their basic implementations within Java. Thus, given an IDL interface called *interfaceName*, the resulting base class, in Java, would look like:

```
public class _interfaceNameImplBase implements interfaceName {
   ...
}
```

Once a Servant Base Class is written, the programmer must also write a Servant Class. A given Instance of a Servant Class is required to implement an ORB object. It should be obvious that the Servant Class extends the *_interfaceName*ImplBase class. In doing so, the Servant Class must implement the public methods, as defined in *_interfaceName*ImplBase, as well as those defined in *interfaceName*, and any public methods that may be defined by interfaces that *interfaceName* may extend.

CREATING A TRANSIENT OBJECT

Creating a Transient object is quite straightforward: the Servant Class is instantiated.

CONNECTING A TRANSIENT OBJECT

Given an instance of an ORB, connecting a transient object to that ORB is done by calling the ORB's connect(. . .) method, using an instance of the transient object you wish to connect. Any calls to the connect(. . .) method after a successful connection are disregarded. Remember, a connection may happen automatically if the transient object is passed as a parameter to an object that is not a local (that is, Java-based) object. ORB vendors have the liberty to connect transient objects at any time, but are required to perform the connection on a hard-coded call to the connect(. . .) method.

DISCONNECTING A TRANSIENT OBJECT

Given an instance of an ORB, connecting a transient object to that ORB is done by calling the ORB's disconnect(...) method, using an instance of the transient object you wish to disconnect. Any calls to the disconnect(...) method after a successful disconnection are disregarded. After the disconnection, any further requests to the transient object will cause a CORBA::OBJECT_DOES_NOT_EXIST exception to be raised. Requests to the transient object that are not done through the ORB will be successful.

Organization Detail:

This section presents some of the more important classes, and goals, behind CORBA.

HOLDER CLASSES

Because Holder classes are used extremely often in Java code that has been generated from IDL code, we've moved them into their own section to simplify matters. This means Unions, Structures, Enumerated types, and every place where a new class is generated from an IDL file, there are really two classes created. The exception to this rule is with the Array. The only responsibility the Holder class has is to allow its particular type of generated class to be written to, or read from, an output stream, or input stream, respectively. Holder classes, in general, have the following syntactical definition:

```
public final class Holder implements
  org.omg.CORBA.portable.Serializable {
  ... // Additional member variables
  ... // Additional member methods

  public void _read( org.omg.CORBA.portable.InputStream i ) { ... }
  public void _write( org.omg.CORBA.portable.OutputStream o ) { ... }
  public org.omg.CORBA.TypeCode _type() { ... }
}
```

Included in the member variables is an instance of the type of Holder that is being wrapped. For example, an IntHolder would have an int as a member variable. That int would represent the value being held.

STREAMING APIS

A simple way to read and write objects over a network is to convert the object into a stream and perform regular stream operations on the object's series of bytes. CORBA's streaming APIs are responsible for performing that task. They go one step further and enable the reading and writing of Java's basic types via streams. The Java classes look as follows:

```
package org.omg.CORBA.portable;

public abstract class InputStream {
  public abstract boolean read_boolean();
  public abstract char read_char();
  public abstract char read_wchar();
  public abstract byte read_octet();
  public abstract short read_short();
```

```
public abstract short read_ushort();
public abstract int read_long();
public abstract int read_ulong();
public abstract long read_longlong();
public abstract long read_ulonglong();
public abstract float read_float();
public abstract double read_double();
public abstract String read_string();
public abstract String read_wstring();

public abstract void read_boolean_array( boolean[] value, int
offset, int length );
public abstract void read_char_array( char[] value, int offset, int
length );
public abstract void read_wchar_array( char[] value, int offset,
int length );
public abstract void read_octet_array( byte[] value, int offset,
int length );
public abstract void read_short_array( short[] value, int offset,
int length );
public abstract void read_ushort_array( short[] value, int offset,
int length );
public abstract void read_long_array( int[] value, int offset, int
length );
public abstract void read_ulong_array( int[] value, int offset, int
length );
public abstract void read_longlong_array( long[] value, int offset,
int length );
public abstract void read_ulonglong_array( long[] value, int
offset, int length );
public abstract void read_float_array( float[] value, int offset,
int length );
public abstract void read_double_array( double[] value, int offset,
int length );

public abstract org.omg.CORBA.Object read_Object();
public abstract org.omg.CORBA.TypeCode read_TypeCode();
public abstract org.omg.CORBA.Any read_any();
public abstract org.omg.CORBA.Principal read_Principal();
}
```

Note, the only way to create a CORBA input stream is from an instance of a CORBA output stream. To create a CORBA output stream, you must ask the ORB, via its create_output_stream() method. Thus, we have a CORBA output stream API that looks as follows:

```
package org.omg.CORBA.portable;

public abstract class OutputStream {
  public abstract org.omg.CORBA.portable.InputStream
  create_input_stream();
```

```
public abstract write_boolean( boolean value );
public abstract write_char( char value );
public abstract write_wchar( char value );
public abstract write_octet( byte value );
public abstract write_short( short value );
public abstract write_ushort( short value );
public abstract write_long( int value );
public abstract write_ulong( int value );
public abstract write_longlong( long value );
public abstract write_ulonglong( long value );
public abstract write_float( float value );
public abstract write_double( double value );
public abstract write_string( String value );
public abstract write_wstring( String value );

public abstract void write_boolean_array( boolean[] value, int
offset, int length );
public abstract void write_char_array( char[] value, int offset,
int length );
public abstract void write_wchar_array( char[] value, int offset,
int length );
public abstract void write_octet_array( byte[] value, int offset,
int length );
public abstract void write_short_array( short[] value, int offset,
int length );
public abstract void write_ushort_array( short[] value, int offset,
int length );
public abstract void write_long_array( int[] value, int offset, int
length );
public abstract void write_ulong_array( int[] value, int offset,
int length );
public abstract void write_longlong_array( long[] value, int
offset, int length );
public abstract void write_ulonglong_array( long[] value, int
offset, int length );
public abstract void write_float_array( float[] value, int offset,
int length );
public abstract void write_double_array( double[] value, int
offset, int length );

public abstract void write_Object( org.omg.CORBA.Object value );
public abstract void write_TypeCode( org.omg.CORBA.TypeCode value
);
public abstract void write_any( org.omg.CORBA.Any value );
public abstract void write_Principal( org.omg.CORBA.Principal value
);
}
```

DESIGN GOALS

From the start, the ORB Portability Interfaces were designed with three goals in mind:

◆ Size

Because the browser environment is one of the predominant environments in which Java bytecode is executed, the amount of code that must be sent from the server to the client must be minimal. One direct result of having a minimal amount of code downloaded to the client is that memory requirements are kept as low as possible.

◆ Performance

When the IDL code is translated into Java stub code, that code must execute reasonably quickly. This means avoiding the creation of unnecessary objects, as there is an implied two-fold deficiency. The first is creating objects is an expensive operation; the second is the garbage collector must collect the objects when they are no longer being used, which takes away execution time.

◆ Reverse Mapability

This design is advantageous because it precludes the addition of extra methods to user-defined types, like structures and exceptions, to insure upward compatibility with future versions of CORBA. In effect, it enables vendors, if they so choose, to add proprietary interfaces, so long as they also support all of CORBA's APIs.

Glossary

Aggregation Model

The aggregation model allows the application to form composite objects. The basic job of a composite object is to combine interfaces from different objects into a single interface.

any

This is a construct for type system. It is one of the data types declared in IDL. The "any" type specifies the value of any data type that could be accommodated.

Application Objects

Application Objects constitute the uppermost layer of the reference model. They are built by independent vendors who control the interfaces of the objects.

attribute

This is an IDL keyword related logically to the interface definitions.

bind

The act of establishing a CORBA communication link between a client and a CORBA object.

BOA

The Basic Object Adapter, which is an adapter designed for use in most applications that do not have unusual data and communication requirements. CORBA specifications require a BOA adapter be available in every ORB.

Boolean

This is a data type declaration. Values associated with Boolean could take in only two values: a TRUE and a FALSE.

callback pattern

The callback pattern is a frequent occurrence in CORBA systems with applet-based thin clients. In this pattern, the client connects to the server and passes it a reference to a client-side callback object. The server then uses this reference to invoke functions on the client.

case

This is an IDL keyword used in conjunction with the "switch" keyword. The "case" keyword is used to specify the possible values of the identifier in the "switch" clause.

char

This is a data type in IDL. The "char" data type can hold values that are 8 bits only. This represents a typical byte. The different language mappings may interpret them differently, but the basic meaning is the same.

client stub

Created through compilation of IDL, this piece of software provides a communication layer between clients and the ORB.

client stubs

The stubs present access to the OMG IDL-defined operations on an object in a way that is easy for programmers to predict, once they are familiar with the OMG IDL and the language mapping for the particular programming language.

Collection Service

Provides a powerful set of collection objects, such as stacks, queues, and bags.

common facilities

Commercially also known as CORBAfacilities, common facilities provide a set of generic application functions that can be configured to the specific requirements of a particular configuration. These are facilities – printing, document management, database, and electronic mail facilities – that sit closer to the user.

concurrency control

A mechanism to control clients and their interaction with shared resources.

Concurrency Control Service

Provides management of concurrent client access to shared resources, which can be objects, files, or any other entity in your system that needs protection.

Concurrent License

A license that allows a company to purchase a set number of licenses that could be used at one time from anywhere on a network.

Connection Management

The methodology to manage the number of TCP/IP connections between clients and servers.

const

This is an IDL keyword enabling the programmer to define a constant variable. The variable is set to a constant value. The variable must be of any defined data type. The "const" keyword helps to set the value of the variable that cannot be altered programmatically.

Consumer

A term used in the Event Service that refers to a party interested in a specific event.

containment and delegation

Containment and delegation take a step further in the aggregation model. In aggregation, the composite object exposes the interface of the other objects it aggregates within itself. These other objects and their interfaces are also available to the client objects to access directly, without going through the composite object. The containment and delegation model is built especially for the outer object to contain the inner objects completely.

context

This is an IDL keyword used to maintain and pass context-related information from the client to the server. The "context" keyword helps to define the context to which an operation must be performed. The context information is similar to parameters that may effect the operation of the request, but are not directly linked to the request.

CORBA

The Common Object Request Broker Architecture (CORBA) as a specification allows applications to communicate with one another no matter where they are located or who designed them. CORBA 1.1 was introduced in 1991 by Object Management Group and defined the Interface Definition Language (IDL) and the Application Programming Interfaces (API) that enable client/server object interaction within a specific implementation of an Object Request Broker (ORB). CORBA 2.0, adopted in December of 1994, defines true interoperability by specifying how ORBs from different vendors can interoperate.

CORBA Services

Individual software components designed to promote a greater amount of software reuse.

COS

An acronym for Common Object Services, COS is a prefix on many of the services' modules.

cout

The standard output stream used by C++ programs.

Critical Section

The Critical Section object type is used to grant exclusive access to a section of code. Typically, a critical section is used to group a section of code that must be executed sequentially without interruption. Each section of code to be locked needs a separate critical section object allocated for it.

daemon

A background process that does work for your system.

datastore

The actual implementation that stores and retrieves an object's data.

DCOM

DCOM (Distributed Component Object Model) is a distributed object frame architecture designed by Microsoft. Microsoft initially came out with a component object model (COM) and, later on, enhanced the architecture to be used in a distributed environment.

default

This is an IDL keyword used in conjunction with the "switch" and the "case" clause. The "switch" clause has an identifier associated with it that maps to the possible values provided by the "case" clause. The "default" keyword is one of the possible values for the identifier from the "switch" clause.

Deferred Synchronous Request

A request that does not block the caller until the request is satisfied but, instead, provides blocking and nonblocking calls to check on the status of the request.

DII

An acronym for Dynamic Invocation Interface, which gives a programmer the capability to discover a server's IDL interface at run time and to construct and invoke requests dynamically on a CORBA server. To use DII, the client must compose a request (in a way common to all ORBs) including the object reference, the operation, and a list of parameters.

distributed objects

A distributed computing system can be defined as a system of multiple autonomous processors that do not share the primary memory, but that cooperate by sending messages over a communication network. This definition captures the behavior of physically separated components and logically autonomous modules communicating via messages. Or, a distributed system can be defined as a system whose components have encapsulation boundaries that are opaque in both directions. That is, both client access to component resources and component access to client resources are inaccessible except through messages mediated by component interface. These components are called *distributed objects*.

DLL

An acronym for Dynamic Link Library, DLLs are loaded by the client application and cannot exist on their own. DLLs need a process to load them.

Domain Interfaces

Domain Interfaces represent vertical areas that provide functionality of direct interest to end users, particularly application domains. Domain interfaces may combine some common facilities and object services, but they are designed to perform particular tasks for users within a certain vertical market or industry.

double

This is an IDL data type declaration keyword used for floating point data. The keyword "double" helps declare a IEEE double-precision floating-point variable.

DSI

A server side analogue to DII is the Dynamic Skeleton Interface (DSI). With the use of this interface the operation is no longer accessed through an operation-specific skeleton, generated from an IDL-interface specification.

enum

This is an IDL data type used for enumeration. It can hold a maximum of 232 values in the enumeration list. The order of the members of the enumeration list is dictated by their position in the list. Each member in the enumeration list must be a valid variable name.

ESIOP

Environment-Specific Inter-ORB Protocol. ESIOP is specific to certain environments. CORBA specifies DCE as the first of many optional ESIOPs (pronounced *E-SOPs*).

Event Service

Allows your system to create and handle events. This service supports different event models, such as the push and pull model, as well as both generic and typed events.

exception

A programming mechanism that provides efficient and easy error-handling in your application.

exception

This is an IDL keyword used to define exception objects. This construct enables the programmer to define a user-designed exception structure to help provide the specifications of the exception at run time. Being a structure-like definition, it would enable the user to define the members, something that would satisfy the requirements.

Externalization Service

Describes an approach for saving an object's state in memory, disk, or elsewhere, and restoring it at a later time. This service can be used to pass objects by value across CORBA.

FALSE

This is an internal define for the IDL used for variables of type "Boolean." The "Boolean" variables can take two values and "FALSE" is one of them. This is more of a reserved word rather than a direct keyword.

Flat Transaction

A single transaction bracketing a small number of events.

float

This is an IDL data type declaration keyword used for floating point data. The keyword "float" helps in declaring an IEEE single-precision floating point variable.

frame works

Frame works are established working sets for a programming environment. Frame works help developers save considerable time in project development work.

Generic Event

A type of event that does not understand what type of data it is passing, but simply takes a single input parameter of type *any* (a generic object).

GIOP

General Inter-ORB Protocol. GIOP defines a set of message formats and common data representations for communications between ORBs. The whole idea behind GIOP was the ORB-to-ORB transactions.

GUID

Globally Unique Identifier. Every object class registered within a registry is uniquely identified by a 128-bit GUID. The composition of the 128-bit identifier keeps this identifier unique for every class definition.

IDL

Interface Definition Language is a programming language that does exactly what its name suggests: helps define interfaces. IDL is inherently object-oriented in nature.

IIOP

Internet Inter-ORB Protocol. IIOP has become synonymous with CORBA and is heard of more commonly on the Internet in reference to CORBA. This protocol specifies how GIOP messages are exchanged over a TCP/IP network.

implementation repository

The implementation repository contains information that allows the ORB to locate and activate implementations of objects. It provides a run-time repository of information about the classes the server supports: the objects that are instantiated and their IDs.

in

This is an IDL keyword used to qualify the parameters passed to a method. The keyword "in" implies the parameter is an input parameter and is passed in only one direction: from the client to the server.

In parameter

A type of parameter passed to a CORBA object function used by the function in a read-only mode.

inout

This is an IDL keyword used to qualify the parameters passed to a method. The keyword "inout" implies the parameter is an input, as well as an output parameter. It is a bidirectional parameter. The parameter would be used for data to be passed from the client to the server and vice versa.

InOut parameter

A type of parameter passed to a CORBA object function that can be changed during the life of the function.

interface

This is an IDL keyword. The "interface" keyword helps in capturing the behavior of the object. The interface is an entity of its own with associated operations and attributes. It is a perfect way to capture similar kinds of acts of the object within one domain. An object could exhibit many interfaces. The "interface" would scope all the attributes and operations within it.

interface repository

A server that enables clients to retrieve information about a particular object's IDL interface. Using this information, a client can access an object at run time without knowing the object's interface at compile time.

IOR

Interoperable Object References, or IORs, associate a collection of tagged profiles with object references, which help to provide information about how to contact the object using the mechanism of a particular ORB.

IUnknown

The "IUnknown" interface is the gateway to all object servers. Using the "IUnknown" interface pointer, the client could walk through all the interfaces supported by the client. The "IUnknown" interface helps the client locate the right kind of interface needed for the job.

Java

Java is a platform-independent programming language created by Sun Microsystems. Java, like COM, provides a mechanism for components to discover one another's interfaces at run time, but they can also run on different platforms by virtue of the Java Virtual Machine.

Java applets

Created by Sun Microsystems, Java applets are Web components that were platform independent and written in Java.

JavaBeans

An extension of applets, which can run as applets outside any container application. Java Class Loaders can download any libraries a component needs along with the component. JavaBeans needn't be registered the way ActiveX components are, which makes them suitable for building highly dynamic systems. JavaBeans can interact with application builder tools.

Library Object Adapters

Library Object Adapters are primarily used for objects that have library implementations. Library Object Adapters access persistent storage in files and do not support activation or deactivation, as the objects are assumed to be in the client's program.

Licensing Service

Tackles distributed object-licensing concerns. Highly configurable, this service enables you to build licensing approaches that fit your application and the consumers who will use it.

Life Cycle Service

Takes care of problems associated with copying, moving, and deleting groups of objects related by an object graph.

long

This is an IDL-integer data type. It can store values up to four bytes. The "long" integer could be signed or unsigned. A signed long integer can store values from -2^{31} to $+2^{31} - 1$. The unsigned long integer data type can store values ranging from 0 to $2^{32} -1$.

marshalling

The first half of marshalling is the act of breaking an object down into a sequence of bytes and then sending that stream of bytes to an awaiting computer. The second half of marshalling consists of taking that same stream and creating a usable object on the waiting computer. When you see the words *marshall an object*, this means to send that object from one computer to another.

MFC

The acronym for Microsoft Foundation Classes, which is a base set of classes used by Windows programmers.

module

This is an IDL keyword that formulates the operating module. A "module" contains interfaces and interfaces consist of attributes and operations. A "module" is an entity that encapsulates an object or a bunch of objects within an application. The "module" could contain many interfaces. The "module" scopes all the interfaces within it.

msdev

Shorthand for Microsoft Developer Studio, an integrated development environment that supports a number of Microsoft compilers.

multithreading

Multitasking within a single application, where the operating system schedules the different tasks for execution. A multithreaded program consists of multiple concurrent paths of execution through a process's code segment.

mutex

The mutex object represents a mutually exclusive lock used to grant exclusive access to a resource. Only one thread can lock the mutex at any given time.

Naming Service

Allows a system to create, delete, and find object names dynamically, using a powerful, logical-naming convention.

nested transaction

This type of transaction has smaller sibling subtransactions, which are embedded within a larger, encompassing parent transaction.

nmake

A compiler program bundled with Microsoft's Visual C++.

Node Locked License

A license that grants permission for a piece of software to be used on a single computer.

Nonsignaled State

The state of a synchronization object that is currently locked and unavailable for use.

NVList

A list of CORBA NamedValue objects. This list type can be used to pass generic objects between your CORBA objects.

OAD

Visigenic's Object Activation Daemon, which is used to assist in automatic activation of CORBA objects when they are required by clients.

object

An abstract entity that understands and executes a well-defined set of commands.

Object Adapter

The primary way an object implementation accesses services provided by the ORB is through an Object Adapter. The Object Adapter sits on top of the ORB's core communication services and accepts requests on behalf of the server's objects. It provides the run-time environment for instantiating server objects; passing requests to them and assigning them Object IDs.

Object ID

An Object ID is used by POA and the user is supplied implementation to identify a particular abstract CORBA object.

Object Implementation

Defines operations that implement a CORBA IDL interface. Object Implementations can be written using languages like C, C++, Java, Smalltalk, and Ada. An Object Implementation can be structured in a variety of ways. It defines the methods for operations of the objects and procedures for activating and deactivating objects. An Object Implementation also defines methods to object states and ways to control access and to implement methods.

Object Persistence

An object's capability to maintain its state outside the scope of the client or object that originally created it.

Object Reference

An entity used to identify the object uniquely from any location or point-of-view. The object reference guarantees the holder a valid end point.

Object-Oriented Database Adapter

Uses a connection to the object-oriented database to provide access to the objects stored in it.

octet

This is an IDL-data type. An octet is an 8-bit data type that does not undergo any kind of alterations while passing through the communication channels. The value stored is guaranteed safety through the communication system.

OMG

The acronym for the Object Management Group, which oversees the design of CORBA and all its related components. OMG was founded in 1989 to standardize object-oriented software and to create and promote component-based software implementations and standard interfaces for Distributed Object Computing.

oneway

This is an IDL construct used to qualify methods. The keyword "oneway" implies the following method would be invoked in a unidirectional fashion. The client application could invoke the method on the server and would not be concerned about whether the request was received and performed by the server. Such methods have no return values.

ORB

The acronym for Object Request Broker. ORB is used in one of two ways: It can refer to the ORB library, which is a library of communication functionality used by both client and server. It can also refer to the ORB Daemon, which assists servers in the registration of objects and then helps clients find these objects.

ORB Interface

ORB Interface provides various functions, such as converting object references to strings and vice versa, and creating the argument list for requests made through the Dynamic Invocation Interface.

ORPC

Object-Oriented Remote Procedure Call. The ORPC model deals with objects as an addressable entity rather than just methods.

OSAGENT

Visigenic's ORB Daemon, which is used to establish communication links between clients and desired CORBA objects.

Out

This is an IDL keyword used to qualify the parameters passed to a method. The keyword "out" would imply that the parameter is an output parameter and is passed in only one direction: from the server to the client.

Out parameter

A type of parameter created and returned by a call to a CORBA object function.

Persistent Object Service

Provides a generic storage facility for objects, using a number of different datastores. This service will work with RDBMs, OODBMSs, or any other datastore that fits the requirements of your system.

POA

This is the acronym for Portable Object Adapter. POA was introduced to extend the portability within the object adapters. POA talks about the servant and the object user.

Principal

A Principal is a human user or system entity registered in and authentic to the system. Initiating principals are the ones that initiate activities. An initiating principal may be authenticated in a number of ways, the most common of which for human users is a password.

process

A instance of a running executable consisting of a private virtual address space, code, data (global variables, stack frames, and so forth) and system resources (file handles, pipes, windows, and so forth).

Property Service

With this service, you can dynamically create attributes, which can be used to extend commercial, shrink-wrapped objects.

Proxy

This is an object that sits in place of another object. A Proxy ensures message traffic to and from its associated object occurs correctly.

Pure Virtual Function

A parent class function that must be implemented by child classes to avoid a compile-time or run-time error.

Query Service

Provides generic query capability, enabling you to query for objects using a wide variety of datastores.

RAD

Rapid programming development tools, known as Rapid Application Development environment. RADs have strong, well-developed class libraries, which have most of the involved functionalities for development purposes provided by the vendors.

raises

This is an IDL keyword used for exceptions. The "raises" keyword is used to raise exceptions. IDL allows and understands exceptions and assists in exception handling. Some standard sets of exceptions exist and the user can define customized exceptions.

readonly

This is an IDL keyword that acts as a qualifier to the attributes. The keyword "readonly" would specify the attributes values can only be read. This would correspond to the language mappings that generate a get-only operation for the attribute. The set operation would be absent.

reentrant

Usually refers to code that can be used in multithreaded programs.

Reference Counting

A memory management approach that keeps track of the number of references to a given object. This approach allows the same object to be shared by many different objects, while using a fairly simple bookkeeping mechanism.

Relationship Service

Enables you to create dynamic relationships between objects or groups of objects, with no required change to the objects being included in a relationship.

RMI

Remote Method Invocation is another distributed object technology, which is part of the Java 1.1 Development Kit and is a solution for building distributed Java-only applications.

RollBack

The process of recovering from an error that occurs during a transaction.

RPC

Remote Procedure Call was introduced by the Open Software Foundation (OSF), a consortium of companies defining and accepting standards. RPC is a part of the Distributed Computing Environment (DCE) propagated by the consortium.

Security Service

Allows secure communication between objects, while providing user authorization and security auditing.

semaphore

The semaphore object represents a finite access lock initialized with the total number of threads that have simultaneous access to it.

sequence

The "sequence" is a one-dimensional array with two characteristics: the first characteristic is maximum size; the second characteristic is the length. This is more of a mathematical construct added to OMG IDL.

servant

A programming language object or entity that implements requests on one or more objects. A servant generally exists within the context of the server. The server is like an entire process.

server skeleton

Created through compilation of IDL, this piece of software provides a communication layer between servers and the ORB.

short

This is an IDL-integer data type. It can store values up to two bytes. The "short" integer could be signed or unsigned. A signed short integer can store values from -2^{15} to $+2^{15}-1$. The unsigned short data type can store values ranging from 0 to $2^{16}-1$.

Signaled State

The state of a synchronization object that is available for use.

Single-Threaded Model

This is the simplest of all CORBA programming models. In this model, a server has one thread for processing client requests.

Site License

A license that allows a company to pay a fixed price for unlimited use of a software product on its network.

start

A command that tells DOS to run a given command in a separate window started from the current working directory.

string

This is an IDL data type. A variable of type "string" will store in 8 bit data. A null is identified as the string terminator. The string can be viewed as a "sequence" of "char." A "string" can be bounded or unbounded.

struct

This is an IDL keyword used to help create custom data types used in the application. The structure created by the "struct" keyword can consist of data members of various known types. The data types forming the members of the structure can be atomic of composite. This is identical to the C++ structure definition.

Supplier

A term used in the Event Service that refers to the originator of an event.

switch

This IDL keyword is used to define a selection of a value among the provided option. The "switch" statement has an identifier whose value has to be mapped. The possible values are listed with the "case" clause.

Synchronous Request

A request that blocks the caller until the request is satisfied.

System Exception

A type of exception defined by CORBA that is readily available in your program.

thread

A path of execution through the process's code segment. A thread is often described as a lightweight process. Threads within a process share the address space, code, data, and system resources.

Thread-per-Session Model

Another type of CORBA threading model, in which a new thread is allocated for each connection to the server. Therefore, each client may have its own thread in the server. This model allows each client to carry out processing in the server without blocking for other clients, provided no competition exists for an internal resource.

Thread-Pool Model

A CORBA-threading model that creates a finite number of threads to service client requests. Each request made to the server is assigned a thread. The request is carried out in the context of the thread. When processing is finished, the thread is placed back in the pool of available threads to await a new request.

Thread Synchronization

Allows multiple threads to use resources cooperatively without interfering with one another.

TIE

A CORBA-architecture approach that enables you to associate an existing C++ object with a new skeleton CORBA object, thus saving you large amounts of rewriting time.

Time Service

Provides a universal source for time across your distributed CORBA components. Also facilitates timed-events in your system.

Trading Service

Finds objects based on the services, or operations, they provide for clients.

transaction

A small event that monitors some work done by your application.

Transaction Service

Enables you to create and manage simple or nested transactions, which adds a greater level of control, error detection, and reliability to your CORBA system.

transient

Objects that may move from computer to computer, across network boundaries, are labeled as transient.

TRUE

This is an internal define for the IDL that is used for variables of type "Boolean." The "Boolean" variables can take two values and "TRUE" is one of them. This is more of a reserved word rather than a direct keyword.

Typed Event

An event propagation approach that allows applications to define an interface using IDL that is well-understood by both suppliers and consumers.

TypeDef

This is an IDL keyword used to create new data type definitions. The "TypeDef" keyword would take in an existing data type and an identifier. The identifier would become equivalent to the data type provided to "TypeDef."

union

An IDL keyword, this is slightly different from the standard "union" definitions from C++ or C. The "union" definition is a mix of the "union" and the "switch" statements.

unsigned

This IDL keyword is used to qualify the IDL data types. This is generally used in conjunction with the "long" or the "short" integer data types. This qualifies the integer data types by informing whether the signed bit is considered.

User Exception

A type of exception defined by you, which is specific to your CORBA object implementation.

UTC

The Universal Time Coordinated standard — a measurement of time represented in 100 nanosecond increments since October 15, 1582 — the beginning of the Gregorian calendar.

void

An IDL keyword that generally is used to define the return value from a method. If a method has a return type of "void," then it would imply the method returns nothing. No value should be expected back from the method.

INDEX

A

access identity, 30

access locks
  mutex objects as, 312
  semaphore objects as, 315

activating
  BOA, 77–78, 88
  the irep in VisiBroker, 270–272

Active Desktop, 11–12

ActiveX
  distributed objects and, 11–12
  Java applets and, 8

Adapter:initialize() method, 453–454

Adapter class
  declaring, 417–418
    for Object Service Pattern, 428–429
    for Pinned Object Pattern, 453
  implementing, 427–431
    Adapter:getObjectService function(), 431
    adapter initialization functions, 430
  initializing
    database function for, 418–419
    supporting objects, 419
  providing access to server's tie object, 420
  singleton pattern with, 418, 429

AdapterLoader class, 431–432

AdapterObjectThread constructor, 447

adapters
  BOA, 68–69
  Library Object, 68
  OODB, 69

AdapterThreadFilter Java class, 445–446

Admin interfaces, 194

aerospace/defense CORBA applications, 17

APPLET tag
  connecting client to server objects, 375
  connecting server objects to, 371–372

applets
  ActiveX and, 8
  distributing client, 382–384
  implementing CORBA client in Java, 370–374
  using CORBA IR, 387–396
    adding parameters to DII Request object, 394–395
    contents() function in Container interface, 388
    data structures, 389
    describe function in Contained interface, 389
    with DII request results, 395
    implementing test()Object function, 393
    parsing and displaying acquired definition of interfaces, 392–393
    referencing definition of target interfaces, 390–392

Application Objects OMA components, 54, 55

applications. *See also* DII client applications; future CORBA developments; VisiBroker 3.0; Windows 95/NT Threading package; writing CORBA applications
  basic CORBA development, 78–81
  (continued)

589

(continued)

NOTES

NOTES

Java™ Development Kit Version 1.1.5 Binary Code License

This binary code license ("License") contains rights and restrictions associated with use of the accompanying software and documentation ("Software"). Read the License carefully before installing the Software. By installing the Software you agree to the terms and conditions of this License.

1. **Limited License Grant.** Sun grants to you ("Licensee") a non-exclusive, non-transferable limited license to use the Software without fee for evaluation of the Software and for development of Java compatible applets and applications. Licensee may make one archival copy of the Software and may re-distribute complete, unmodified copies of the Software to software developers within Licensee's organization to avoid unnecessary download time, provided that this License conspicuously appear with all copies of the Software. Except for the foregoing, Licensee may not re-distribute the Software in whole or in part, either separately or included with a product. Refer to the Java Runtime Environment Version 1.1.5 binary code license (`http://java.sun.com/products/jdk/1.1/index.html`) for the availability of runtime code which may be distributed with Java compatible applets and applications.

2. **Java Platform Interface.** Licensee may not modify the Java Platform Interface ("JPI", identified as classes contained within the "java" package or any subpackages of the "java" package), by creating additional classes within the JPI or otherwise causing the addition to or modification of the classes in the JPI. In the event that Licensee creates any Java-related API and distributes such API to others for applet or application development, Licensee must promptly publish an accurate specification for such API for free use by all developers of Java-based software.

3. **Restrictions.** Software is confidential copyrighted information of Sun and title to all copies is retained by Sun and/or its licensors. Licensee shall not modify, decompile, disassemble, decrypt, extract, or otherwise reverse engineer Software. Software may not be leased, assigned, or sublicensed, in whole or in part. Software is not designed or intended for use in on-line control of aircraft, air traffic, aircraft navigation or aircraft communications; or in the design, construction, operation or maintenance of any nuclear facility. Licensee warrants that it will not use or redistribute the Software for such purposes.

4. **Trademarks and Logos.** This License does not authorize Licensee to use any Sun name, trademark or logo. Licensee acknowledges that Sun owns the Java trademark and all Java-related trademarks, logos and icons including the Coffee Cup and Duke ("Java Marks") and agrees to: (i) to comply with the Java Trademark Guidelines at `http://java.sun.com/trademarks.html`; (ii) not do anything harmful to or inconsistent with Sun's rights in the Java Marks; and (iii) assist Sun in protecting those rights, including assigning to Sun any rights acquired by Licensee in any Java Mark.

5. **Disclaimer of Warranty.** Software is provided "AS IS," without a warranty of any kind. ALL EXPRESS OR IMPLIED REPRESENTATIONS AND WARRANTIES, INCLUDING ANY IMPLIED WARRANTY OF MERCHANTABILITY, FITNESS FOR A PARTICULAR PURPOSE OR NON-INFRINGEMENT, ARE HEREBY EXCLUDED.

6. **Limitation of Liability.** SUN AND ITS LICENSORS SHALL NOT BE LIABLE FOR ANY DAMAGES SUFFERED BY LICENSEE OR ANY THIRD PARTY AS A RESULT OF USING OR DISTRIBUTING SOFTWARE. IN NO EVENT WILL SUN OR ITS LICENSORS BE LIABLE FOR ANY LOST REVENUE, PROFIT OR DATA, OR FOR DIRECT, INDIRECT, SPECIAL, CONSEQUENTIAL, INCIDENTAL OR PUNITIVE DAMAGES, HOWEVER CAUSED AND REGARDLESS OF THE THEORY OF LIABILITY, ARISING OUT OF THE USE OF OR INABILITY TO USE SOFTWARE, EVEN IF SUN HAS BEEN ADVISED OF THE POSSIBILITY OF SUCH DAMAGES.

7. **Termination.** Licensee may terminate this License at any time by destroying all copies of Software. This License will terminate immediately without notice from Sun if Licensee fails to comply with any provision of this License. Upon such termination, Licensee must destroy all copies of Software.

8. **Export Regulations.** Software, including technical data, is subject to U.S. export control laws, including the U.S. Export Administration Act and its associated regulations, and may be subject to export or import regulations in other countries. Licensee agrees to comply strictly with all such regulations and acknowledges that it has the responsibility to obtain licenses to export, re-export, or import Software. Software may not be downloaded, or otherwise exported or re-exported (i) into, or to a national or resident of, Cuba, Iraq, Iran, North Korea, Libya, Sudan, Syria or any country to which the U.S. has embargoed goods; or (ii) to anyone on the U.S. Treasury Department's list of Specially Designated Nations or the U.S. Commerce Department's Table of Denial Orders.

9. **Restricted Rights.** Use, duplication or disclosure by the United States government is subject to the restrictions as set forth in the Rights in Technical Data and Computer Software Clauses in DFARS 252.227-7013(c) (1) (ii) and FAR 52.227-19(c) (2) as applicable.

10. **Governing Law.** Any action related to this License will be governed by California law and controlling U.S. federal law. No choice of law rules of any jurisdiction will apply.

11. **Severability.** If any of the above provisions are held to be in violation of applicable law, void, or unenforceable in any jurisdiction, then such provisions are herewith waived to the extent necessary for the License to be otherwise enforceable in such jurisdiction. However, if in Sun's opinion deletion of any provisions of the License by operation of this paragraph unreasonably compromises the rights or increase the liabilities of Sun or its licensors, Sun reserves the right to terminate the License and refund the fee paid by Licensee, if any, as Licensee's sole and exclusive remedy.

IDG BOOKS WORLDWIDE, INC.
END-USER LICENSE AGREEMENT

<u>READ THIS</u>. You should carefully read these terms and conditions before opening the software packet(s) included with this book ("Book"). This is a license agreement ("Agreement") between you and IDG Books Worldwide, Inc. ("IDGB"). By opening the accompanying software packet(s), you acknowledge that you have read and accept the following terms and conditions. If you do not agree and do not want to be bound by such terms and conditions, promptly return the Book and the unopened software packet(s) to the place you obtained them for a full refund.

1. <u>License Grant</u>. IDGB grants to you (either an individual or entity) a nonexclusive license to use one copy of the enclosed software program(s) (collectively, the "Software") solely for your own personal or business purposes on a single computer (whether a standard computer or a work-station component of a multiuser network). The Software is in use on a computer when it is loaded into temporary memory (RAM) or installed into permanent memory (hard disk, CD-ROM, or other storage device). IDGB reserves all rights not expressly granted herein.

2. <u>Ownership</u>. IDGB is the owner of all right, title, and interest, including copyright, in and to the compilation of the Software recorded on the disk(s) or CD-ROM ("Software Media"). Copyright to the individual programs recorded on the Software Media is owned by the author or other authorized copyright owner of each program. Ownership of the Software and all proprietary rights relating thereto remain with IDGB and its licensers.

3. <u>Restrictions On Use and Transfer</u>.

   (a) You may only (i) make one copy of the Software for backup or archival purposes, or (ii) transfer the Software to a single hard disk, provided that you keep the original for backup or archival purposes. You may not (i) rent or lease the Software, (ii) copy or reproduce the Software through a LAN or other network system or through any computer subscriber system or bulletin-board system, or (iii) modify, adapt, or create derivative works based on the Software.

   (b) You may not reverse engineer, decompile, or disassemble the Software. You may transfer the Software and user documentation on a permanent basis, provided that the transferee agrees to accept the terms and conditions of this Agreement and you retain no copies. If the Software is an update or has been updated, any transfer must include the most recent update and all prior versions.

4. <u>Restrictions On Use of Individual Programs</u>. You must follow the individual requirements and restrictions detailed for each individual program in the "What's on the CD-ROM?" section of this Book. These limitations are also contained in the individual license agreements

recorded on the Software Media. These limitations may include a requirement that after using the program for a specified period of time, the user must pay a registration fee or discontinue use. By opening the Software packet(s), you will be agreeing to abide by the licenses and restrictions for these individual programs that are detailed in the "What's on the CD-ROM?" section and on the Software Media. None of the material on this Software Media or listed in this Book may ever be redistributed, in original or modified form, for commercial purposes.

5. <u>Limited Warranty</u>.

   (a) IDGB warrants that the Software and Software Media are free from defects in materials and workmanship under normal use for a period of sixty (60) days from the date of purchase of this Book. If IDGB receives notification within the warranty period of defects in materials or workmanship, IDGB will replace the defective Software Media.

   (b) IDGB AND THE AUTHORS OF THE BOOK DISCLAIM ALL OTHER WARRANTIES, EXPRESS OR IMPLIED, INCLUDING WITHOUT LIMITATION IMPLIED WARRANTIES OF MERCHANTABILITY AND FITNESS FOR A PARTICULAR PURPOSE, WITH RESPECT TO THE SOFTWARE, THE PROGRAMS, THE SOURCE CODE CONTAINED THEREIN, AND/OR THE TECHNIQUES DESCRIBED IN THIS BOOK. IDGB DOES NOT WARRANT THAT THE FUNCTIONS CONTAINED IN THE SOFTWARE WILL MEET YOUR REQUIREMENTS OR THAT THE OPERATION OF THE SOFTWARE WILL BE ERROR FREE.

   (c) This limited warranty gives you specific legal rights, and you may have other rights that vary from jurisdiction to jurisdiction.

6. <u>Remedies</u>.

   (a) IDGB's entire liability and your exclusive remedy for defects in materials and workmanship shall be limited to replacement of the Software Media, which may be returned to IDGB with a copy of your receipt at the following address: Software Media Fulfillment Department, Attn.: *CORBA 3 Developer's Guide*, IDG Books Worldwide, Inc., 7260 Shadeland Station, Ste. 100, Indianapolis, IN 46256, or call 1-800-762-2974. Please allow three to four weeks for delivery. This Limited Warranty is void if failure of the Software Media has resulted from accident, abuse, or misapplication. Any replacement Software Media will be warranted for the remainder of the original warranty period or thirty (30) days, whichever is longer.

   (b) In no event shall IDGB or the authors be liable for any damages whatsoever (including without limitation damages for loss of business profits, business interruption, loss of business information, or any other pecuniary loss) arising from the use of or inability to use the Book or the Software, even if IDGB has been advised of the possibility of such damages.

(c) Because some jurisdictions do not allow the exclusion or limitation of liability for consequential or incidental damages, the above limitation or exclusion may not apply to you.

7. <u>**U.S. Government Restricted Rights**</u>. Use, duplication, or disclosure of the Software by the U.S. Government is subject to restrictions stated in paragraph (c)(1)(ii) of the Rights in Technical Data and Computer Software clause of DFARS 252.227-7013, and in subparagraphs (a) through (d) of the Commercial Computer – Restricted Rights clause at FAR 52.227-19, and in similar clauses in the NASA FAR supplement, when applicable.

8. <u>**General**</u>. This Agreement constitutes the entire understanding of the parties and revokes and supersedes all prior agreements, oral or written, between them and may not be modified or amended except in a writing signed by both parties hereto that specifically refers to this Agreement. This Agreement shall take precedence over any other documents that may be in conflict herewith. If any one or more provisions contained in this Agreement are held by any court or tribunal to be invalid, illegal, or otherwise unenforceable, each and every other provision shall remain in full force and effect.

my2cents.idgbooks.com

Register This Book — And Win!

Visit **http://my2cents.idgbooks.com** to register this book and we'll automatically enter you in our fantastic monthly prize giveaway. It's also your opportunity to give us feedback: let us know what you thought of this book and how you would like to see other topics covered.

Discover IDG Books Online!

The IDG Books Online Web site is your online resource for tackling technology — at home and at the office. Frequently updated, the IDG Books Online Web site features exclusive software, insider information, online books, and live events!

10 Productive & Career-Enhancing Things You Can Do at www.idgbooks.com

- Nab source code for your own programming projects.
- Download software.
- Read Web exclusives: special articles and book excerpts by IDG Books Worldwide authors.
- Take advantage of resources to help you advance your career as a Novell or Microsoft professional.
- Buy IDG Books Worldwide titles or find a convenient bookstore that carries them.
- Register your book and win a prize.
- Chat live online with authors.
- Sign up for regular e-mail updates about our latest books.
- Suggest a book you'd like to read or write.
- Give us your 2¢ about our books and about our Web site.

You say you're not on the Web yet? It's easy to get started with IDG Books' *Discover the Internet*, available at local retailers everywhere.

CD-ROM Installation Instructions

THE **CD-ROM** THAT accompanies this book contains not only the examples from the chapters, but also assorted third-party software.

Place the disc in the CD-ROM drive on your computer and open the readme file for important installation and content information.

Then, to take advantage of the CD, all you must do is go to the different folders, which takes you to the right software.

For example, if you want to find the examples from Chapter 2, go to the directory called "Book_Ex" and then the directory called "chapter2."

Likewise for the third-party software. If you want to install IBM Visual Age for Java, go to the "IBM VAJ" directory and look for the **setup.exe** file.

That's all there is to it!

For a listing and description of the software on the CD-ROM, see Appendix A, "About the CD-ROM."